BIOLOGICALLY INSPIRED COGNITIVE ARCHITECTURES 2011

Frontiers in Artificial Intelligence and Applications

FAIA covers all aspects of theoretical and applied artificial intelligence research in the form of monographs, doctoral dissertations, textbooks, handbooks and proceedings volumes. The FAIA series contains several sub-series, including "Information Modelling and Knowledge Bases" and "Knowledge-Based Intelligent Engineering Systems". It also includes the biennial ECAI, the European Conference on Artificial Intelligence, proceedings volumes, and other ECCAI – the European Coordinating Committee on Artificial Intelligence – sponsored publications. An editorial panel of internationally well-known scholars is appointed to provide a high quality selection.

Series Editors:
J. Breuker, N. Guarino, J.N. Kok, J. Liu, R. López de Mántaras,
R. Mizoguchi, M. Musen, S.K. Pal and N. Zhong

Volume 233

Recently published in this series

ISSN 0922-6389 (print)
ISSN 1879-8314 (online)

Biologically Inspired Cognitive Architectures 2011

Proceedings of the Second Annual Meeting of the BICA Society

Edited by

Alexei V. Samsonovich

George Mason University, USA

and

Kamilla R. Jóhannsdóttir

University of Akureyri and Reykjavik University, Iceland

IOS
Press

Amsterdam • Berlin • Tokyo • Washington, DC

ISBN 978-1-60750-958-5 (print)
ISBN 978-1-60750-959-2 (online)
Library of Congress Control Number: 2011939631

Publisher
IOS Press BV
Nieuwe Hemweg 6B
1013 BG Amsterdam
Netherlands
fax: +31 20 687 0019
e-mail: order@iospress.nl

Distributor in the USA and Canada
IOS Press, Inc.
4502 Rachael Manor Drive
Fairfax, VA 22032
USA
fax: +1 703 323 3668
e-mail: iosbooks@iospress.com

LEGAL NOTICE

The publisher is not responsible for the use which might be made of the following information.

PRINTED IN THE NETHERLANDS

Biologically Inspired Cognitive Architectures 2011
A.V. Samsonovich and K.R. Jóhannsdóttir (Eds.)
IOS Press, 2011

v

Preface

This volume documents the proceedings of the Annual International Conference on Biologically Inspired Cognitive Architectures BICA 2011, which is the Second Annual Meeting of the BICA Society, and the fourth annual BICA meeting. Like in the previous years, the main body of the present volume contains a wide variety of ideas and approaches documented in research papers, position papers and abstracts presented at the conference that are all sorted alphabetically by the last name of the first author, with the exception of the first introductory chapter (intended as a guide to the Reader). The main body is followed by two supplementary parts. All papers and abstracts included in this volume were carefully peer-refereed by the Program Committee members and external reviewers (the acceptance rate was 83%).

Throughout this book, the acronym "BICA" stands for Biologically Inspired Cognitive Architectures: computational models that incorporate formal mechanisms of human and animal cognition, drawn from cognitive science and neuroscience into artificial intelligence (for a definition, please see the first and the last chapters). The series of BICA conferences was initiated in 2008 under the umbrella of AAAI Fall Symposia Series, as a follow-up on the abruptly terminated DARPA BICA program. Over the last 4 years, BICA conference developed into a mid-size international conference organized and sponsored by the BICA Society. The conference focuses on emergent hot topics in computer and brain sciences unified by the challenge of replicating the human mind in a computer.

Given the size of the volume, even a brief overview of its content cannot be given in a short preface. Therefore, for an introduction, we refer the reader to the first chapter (by K.R. Jóhannsdóttir and A.V. Samsonovich) that provides a brief overview of this volume, placing it in the broader context of recent emergent developments in the field of BICA. This introductory chapter also serves as a read-me-first document and a guide to the book. Papers reflected in it are grouped by topics and are connected to each other. *Anybody who wants to start learning about the field of BICA by reading this book is encouraged to start with the introductory chapter.*

We would like to thank all members of the Organizing and Program Committees for their help with the organization of this conference, selection and review of the materials. In particular, we are very grateful to Drs. Antonio Chella, Brandon Rohrer, and Christian Lebiere for their active service on the Core Organizing Committee. We also wish to thank all those who helped us with local organization and arrangements, including Mr. Michael Galvin, Ms. Grace Radfar, Ms. Nicole Charles, and many others. The last, but not the least, is our great thanks to Chris Poulin for his generous financial support of the discussion panel on the Roadmap to Human-Level AI, made possible via a donation to the BICA Society from Patterns and Predictions.

Alexei V. Samsonovich and Kamilla R. Jóhannsdóttir, Editors

BICA 2011 Conference Committees

Chairs

Alexei V. Samsonovich
George Mason University, USA

Kamilla R. Jóhannsdóttir
University of Akureyri and Reykjavik University, Iceland

Organizing Committee

Core Organizing Committee Members

Antonio Chella (University of Palermo, Italy)
Christian Lebiere (Carnegie Mellon University, USA)
Andrea Stocco (University of Washington, Seattle, USA)
Brandon Rohrer (Sandia National Laboratories, USA)

Extended Organizing Committee Members

Stan Franklin (University of Memphis, USA)
Stephen Grossberg (Boston University, USA)
Alexander A. Letichevsky (Glushkov Institute of Cybernetics, Ukraine)
Vladimir G. Red'ko (Scientific Research Institute for System Analysis RAS, Russia)
Vadim L. Ushakov (National Research Nuclear University MEPHI, Russia)
Michael Sellers (Online Alchemy, USA)
David C. Noelle (University of California Merced, USA)
Terry Stewart (University of Waterloo, Canada)
Rodrigo Ventura (Instituto Superior Tecnico, Portugal)

Program Committee

Members

Myriam Abramson (US Naval Research Laboratory, USA)
Tsvi Achler (University of Illinois at Urbana Champaign, USA)
Sam Adams (IBM Research, USA)

John Irvine (Draper Laboratory, USA)
David Israel (Artificial Intelligence Center, SRI International, USA)
Magnus Johnsson (Lund University Cognitive Science, Sweden)
Benjamin Johnston (University of Technology, Sydney, Australia)
William Kennedy (George Mason University, USA)
Paul Kogut (Lockheed Martin Inform. Systems & Global Services, USA)
Jeff Krichmar (University of California, Irvine, USA)
James Kroger (New Mexico State University, USA)
András Lőrincz (Eotvos Lorand University, Budapest, Hungary)
Richard Lau (Telcordia, USA)
Christian Lebiere (Psychology Department, Carnegie Mellon University, USA)
Emmanuel Lesser (Nuance Communications, Antwerp, Belgium)
Simon Levy (Washington & Lee University, USA)
Igor Linkov (US Army Engineer Research and Development Center, USA)
Giuseppe Lo Re (University of Palermo, Italy)
Bradley Love (University of Texas at Austin, USA)
Thomas Lu (NASA Jet Propulsion Laboratory, USA)
Rose Luckin (University of Sussex, UK)
Evguenia Malaia (Purdue University, USA)
Maria Malfaz (Univeristy Carlos III, Madrid, Spain)
Riccardo Manzotti (IULM University, Milan, Italy)
Christophe Menant (IBM, France)
Elena Messina (National Institute of Standards, USA)
Steve Morphet (SRC Inc., USA)
Hector Munoz-Avila (Lehigh University, USA)
Catherine Myers (Rutgers University, USA)
Waseem Naqvi (Raytheon, USA)
Danielle Nardi (DIS, "Sapienza" Università di Roma, Italy)
Guenter Neumann (DFKI, Germany)
Tatsuya Nomura (Ryukoku University, Japan)
Rony Novianto (University of Technology, Sydney, Australia)
Andrew Nuxoll (University of Portland, USA)
Andrea Omicini (Università di Bologna, Italy)
Charles Peck (IBM Research, USA)
Carlo Penco (University of Genoa, Italy)
Giovanni Pezzulo (ILC-CNR, Italy)
Robinson Pino (AFRL/RITC, Neuromorphic Computing, USA)
Roberto Pirrone (University of Palermo, Italy)
Roberto Poli (University of Trento, Italy)
Michal Ptaszynski (Hokkaido University, Japan)
James Reggia (University of Maryland, USA)
Pablo Roman (University of Chile, Santiago, Chile)
Derek Rose (University of Tennessee, USA)
Paul Rosenbloom (University of Southern California, USA)
Pier-Giuseppe Rossi (University of Macerata, Italy)
Christopher Rouff (Lockheed Martin ATL, USA)

External Reviewers

Sponsors

BICA Society (http://bicasociety.org): sponsor of BICA 2011

Patterns and Predictions (http://www.patternsandpredictions.com/): sponsor of the discussion panel "Roadmap to Human-Level AI", a part of BICA 2011

BICA 2011 conference was held Friday, Saturday and Sunday, November 4–6, 2011, in Arlington, Virginia, USA.

Contents

Conference Papers and Extended Abstracts

Biologically Inspired Cognitive Architectures 2011
A.V. Samsonovich and K.R. Jóhannsdóttir (Eds.)
IOS Press, 2011
doi:10.3233/978-1-60750-959-2-3

Biologically Inspired Cognitive Architectures: One More Step Forward

Kamilla R. JÓHANNSDÓTTIR [a,1] and Alexei V. SAMSONOVICH [b]

[a] *University of Akureyri and Reykjavik University, Iceland*
[b] *George Mason University, Fairfax, Virginia, USA*
kamillarj@gmail.com, asamsono@gmu.edu

Abstract. This chapter provides a brief overview of the volume of BICA 2011 Proceedings, viewed in the broader context of recent emergent developments in the field of BICA. The present conference is the fourth event in the BICA conference series, and the Second Annual Meeting of the BICA Society. In addition to being a guide to the book, this chapter provides a general overview of the field of BICA, and is recommended to anybody who wants to learn about the field by reading this book.

Keywords. BICA; cognitive architectures; roadmap to human-level AI

Introduction

This volume documents the second International Conference on Biologically Inspired Cognitive Architecture (BICA). BICA has in recent years emerged as a powerful new approach that integrates traditional brain and mind research with AI in the search for the computational equivalence to the human mind. What distinguishes BICA from previous approaches is the emphasis on understanding the foundation of biological systems as a whole. In particular, BICA aims to create a self-sustainable human-level learner, capable of adapting to any environmental challenges, even ultimately blending in with humans. Such a goal requires the cooperation of researchers from various disciplines where the challenge of creating a human level learner is addressed and researched at various levels of abstraction. The present volume demonstrates well the richness and variety of BICA research with the unified focus of creating an artificial mind equivalent to its biological counterpart. Topics addressed here include, mechanisms of perception, cognition and action, memory, learning, metacognition, self-regulation and emotion, and constrained by biological inspirations and adapted for computational implementations.

This introductory chapter is primarily intended as a guide to the volume of BICA 2011 Proceedings and a general overview of the scientific field of BICA. The chapter provides a brief overview of the volume and the conference, placing the presented papers and abstracts, which are sorted alphabetically, in a broader context of recent emergent developments in the field. Therefore, *anybody who wants to start learning about the field of BICA by reading this book is encouraged to start with this introductory chapter.*

---

[1] Corresponding Author.

1. Historical Context and Ideology of the BICA Conference Series

A cognitive architecture is a computational framework for the design of intelligent agents. A BICA is a cognitive architecture that incorporates human and animal cognition, drawn from cognitive science and neuroscience into artificial intelligence. Currently, biological systems provide the only physical examples of the level of robustness, flexibility, and scalability that we want to achieve in artificial intelligence. Therefore, learning from biological systems and using biological constraints is critical for achieving the goal of human equivalent cognitive architecture. This idea is the essential motivation for the BICA Conference Series.

The series of BICA conferences was initiated in 2008 under the umbrella of AAAI Fall Symposia Series, as a follow-up on the DARPA[2] BICA program that coined the term "BICA" in 2005, but unfortunately was abruptly terminated in 2006. Over the last 4 years (2008-2011), BICA conference developed from a AAAI Symposium into a mid-size international conference organized and sponsored by the BICA Society (http://bicasociety.org/meetings/events/). The conference focuses on emergent hot topics in computer and brain sciences unified by the challenge of replicating the human mind in a computer.

Today there are many conferences, each of which partially covers the intersection of biology, artificial intelligence and cognitive science. The BICA conference is one of them. Other examples listed below include conferences at various scales: from about 100 to about 35,000 participants.

- AAAI: Conference on Artificial Intelligence, plus AAAI Spring/Fall Symposia (http://www.aaai.org/Conferences/AAAI/aaai.php);
- ICCM: International Conference on Cognitive Modeling (http://iccm2010.cs.drexel.edu/);
- CogSci: Annual Conference of the Cognitive Science Society (http://cognitivesciencesociety.org/conference_overview.html);
- ICDL: International Conference on Development and Learning, recently unified with EpiRob: Epigenetic Robotics (http://www.icdl-epirob.org/);
- AGI: Artificial General Intelligence conference (http://agi-conf.org/);
- IJCNN: International Joint Conference on Neural Networks (http://www.ijcnn2011.org/);
- SfN = Society for Neuroscience Annual Meeting (http://www.sfn.org/);
- EUCogII = European Network for the Advancement of Artificial Cognitive Systems, Interaction and Robotics – Members Conference (http://www.eucognition.org/index.php?page=fifth-conference-general-info);
- BICS: Brain Inspired Cognitive Systems (http://www.bicsconference.org/).

The BICA conference is in a sense a unique representative of this kind. On the one hand, its scope is extremely broad and extends beyond the scope of any of the above examples. It includes, yet is not limited to, neuroscience, computer science, and cognitive science. On the other hand, the focus and the mission of the BICA conference are extremely narrow: this conference addresses the challenge of creating a real-life computational equivalent of the human mind (or the BICA challenge: please see the manifesto by Chella et al. at the end of the volume, for a definition). This

---

[2] Defence Advanced Research Projects Agency (http://www.darpa.mil/)

challenge requires that we better understand at a computational level how natural intelligent systems develop their cognitive, metacognitive, and learning functions. BICA provide a powerful new approach toward gaining this kind of understanding. Still, despite impressive successes and growing interest in BICA, wide gaps separate different approaches from each other and from solutions found in biology. Disjoined scientific schools and research communities often speak different languages and are reluctant to integrate their efforts. At the same time, the growing community of researchers unified by the BICA challenge need their own forum and own venues. As a confirmation of this statement, we see growing success and growing interest in BICA conference during the last four years (the numbers of conference talks are, in 2008: 47; in 2009: 51; in 2010, including the pre-conference workshop: 58; in 2011, expected based on this volume: 79).

The spirit of the BICA conference is one of excitement and opportunity. It is a place for people to come together with ideas and have an informal discussion. The conference represents a good mix of short research-in-progress or position statements and longer discussion panels. Longer talks are used to set the stage for discussions. We see the main value of this conference in providing a forum for productive discussions that generate new ideas and new collaborations.

2. General Topics of the Volume

The extremely multidisciplinary nature of the BICA challenge explains the width of the spectrum of topics covered by this conference. We start with a brief summary given as a list, in which the predominant topics are sorted alphabetically. For each listed topic, papers and abstracts included in this volume that primarily address this topic are cited in parentheses. A more detailed overview of selected topics follows in the next section.

- B in BICA and vital biological constraints (Uscinski et al.; Howard et al.; Ritter et al.; Sylverster et al.; Treur; Szumowski et al.; Holland et al. ; Rutledge-Taylor et al.; Dunin-Barkowski; Noelle)
- BICA in learning technologies and education (Minnery; Boicu; Herd et al.)
- BICA models of neurological disorders (Aziz & Klein; Naze & Treur; Levy et al.)
- BICA models of robust learning mechanisms (Rohrer; Coward & Gedeon; Vityaev & Demin; Connolly et al.)
- Bootstrapped and meta-learning (Gaglio et al.)
- Bridging the gap between artificial and natural intelligence (Rothganger et al.; Fahlman; Sylvester et al.; Chen et al.; Herd et al.; Finlayson & Winston)
- Cognitive Decathlon and a Grand Challenge for BICA (Minnery)
- Cognitive mechanisms informed by neuroscience (Uscinski et al.; Rothganger et al.; Stewart & Eliasmith; Vineyard et al.; Diamond et al.; Howard et al.; Juvina et al.; Minnery; Krichmar & Wagatsuma; Sylverster et al.; Downing; Kogut et al.; Levy et al.; Connolly et al.)
- Comparison of forms of learning in BICA (Pennington et al.; Herd et al.; Noelle)
- Critical mass of a universal human-level learner (Samsonovich)
- Environments, tests and metrics for BCIA (Minnery; Pope et al.; Veksler)

- Episodic memory in BICA (Goertzel et al.; Vineyard et al.; Diamond et al.; Howard et al.; Snaider & Franklin; Walker et al.)
- Fundamental theoretical questions in BICA research (Holland et al.; Samsonovich; Sierra)
- Funding opportunities for BICA research (Minnery)
- Higher-order emotional and metacognitive BICA (Waser; Rutledge-Taylor et al.; Gaglio et al.; Peck & Kozloski; Sanz & Sanchez)
- Imagery and dreaming in BICA (Rosenbloom; Rutledge-Taylor et al.; Treur)
- Implementations in ACT-R and Soar (Freiman & Ball; Ritter et al.; Rutledge-Taylor et al.; Juvina et al.; Kennedy; Chen et al.; Rosenbloom)
- Language acquisition and symbol grounding in BICA (Herd et al.; Finlayson & Winston; Sierra; Perlovsky; Harrington)
- Language capabilities and social compatibility of BICA (Balistreri et al.; Freiman & Ball; Finlayson & Winston; Sierra)
- Learning by reasoning and analogy (Minnery; Kogut et al.; Szumowski et al.)
- Learning from experience and observation (Karnowski et al.; Chelian et al.; Red'ko & Koval; Rohrer; Kushiro & Takeno; Robertson & Laddaga; Krichmar & Wagatsuma; Tarifi et al.)
- Life-long learning, cognitive development and evolution of BICA (Red'ko & Koval; Pennington et al.; Vernon)
- Metacognition and metalearning (Balistreri et al.; Gaglio et al; Rosenbloom)
- Minimal substrate for machine consciousness (Takeno; Katayama & Takeno; Chella & Manzotti; Manzotti et al.; Krichmar & Wagatsuma)
- Models of emotions and emotionally intelligent BICA (Novianto & Williams; Chella, Sorbello et al.; Katayama & Takeno; Kushiro & Takeno; Snaider & Franklin; Horswill & Lisetti; Naze & Treur; Treur; Ritter et al.; Gaglio et al.; Levy et al.; Peck & Kozloski; Sanz & Sanchez)
- Neuromorphism and scalability of BICA (Achler & Bettencourt; Uscinski et al.; McBride; Rothganger et al.; Krichmar & Wagatsuma; Reimers; Downing; Peterson; Klein; Dunin-Barkowski; Noelle)
- Perception, cognition and action in BICA (Diamond et al.; Chelian et al.; Surowitz; Chen et al.; Szumowski et al.)
- Physically or virtually embodied BICA (Goertzel et al.; Diamond et al.; Rohrer; Rosenbloom; Krichmar & Wagatsuma)
- Psycho-linguistic inspirations (Freiman & Ball; Monner & Reggia; Finlayson & Winston; Harrington)
- Psychological constraints for BICA (Stracuzzi; Kennedy; Rothganger et al.; Diamond et al.; Horswill & Lisetti; Reimers; Kitajima & Toyota; Vernon)
- Reinforcement learning in BICA (Rohrer; Vityaev & Demin; Pennington et al.; Noelle)
- Roadmap to human-level general AI (Balistreri et al.; Minnery; Vernon)
- Self-regulation and self-regulated learning in BICA (Rossi & Carletti; Herd et al.)
- Semantic memory and knowledge representation in BICA (Jung et al.; Goertzel et al.; Kogut et al.)
- Social compatibility and ethical values in BICA (Balistreri et al.; Waser; Horswill & Lisetti)

- Supervised vs. unsupervised learning in BICA (Karnowski et al.)
- The Self, self-model and personality in BICA (Diamond et al.; Waser; Chella, Sorbello et al.; Takeno; Peck & Kozloski)
- Toward a complete human-equivalent BICA (Dunin-Barkowski)

3. The BICA challenge: Detailed Selected Topics Overview

Solving the BICA challenge of creating a human-level intelligent machine (defined by Chella, Lebiere, Noelle and Samsonovich in this volume) requires multidisciplinary research carried out at various levels of cognitive and brain functioning. As can be seen by the research topics of papers and abstracts presented in this volume, a broad range of issues are being addressed. Together these studies will bring us closer to the multifaceted problem of creating the computational equivalence to the human mind. In this section we will address in more detail three topics central to solving the BICA challenge, and in particular where we are and where we need to go in the future.

3.1. Cognitive mechanisms informed by neuroscience

Central to the goal of BICA is the aim to move away from top-down, manual programming in order to simulate biological systems towards the modeling of systems capable of self-organization and learning based on some yet to be identified critical mass. Therefore, the very foundation of the BICA challenge rests on a better understanding of biological systems at the level of neurons as well as neural circuits. Several papers in this volume address this topic. The studies presented in this volume help shed light on various issues such as how neurons encode information, even at the more abstract level of neural circuit. Various work has for example been done in simulating the hippocampus, a mechanism critical for spatial cognition and recording memories. Matching the principles of the brain to AI algorithms is now done under more guidance from neuroscience research by considering neurophysiological constraints. A better understanding of how biological systems naturally develop their cognitive and learning functions may help us bridge the gap between simulating the workings of neural circuit and higher level cognitive architecture.

3.2. Self-regulation and consciousness

A system capable of self-regulation and learning must necessarily have a model of self that allows it to better adapt to its surroundings. A relatively rich body of evidence emerging from neuroscience, developmental psychology, and philosophy suggests that some form of self-knowledge is the key component underlying flexibility, adaptation and learning in biological systems [1,2]. Awareness of self is also central to cognitive functions such as metacognition and reasoning that make human-level intelligence possible. Several papers in this volume address the topic of self-regulation, self-modeling and a related concept of machine consciousness. The concept is for example explored in relation with the ability to predict future states in the environment. The ability to anticipate action and consequences has already been explored in cognitive science research [3] and might prove important for further progress in simulating self-regulation and learning in artifacts. The point is also made that creating a reliable self-model may be more critical for AI than the measured intelligence of an architecture. This is an important point given that the concept of self is not well-defined in AI research.

A somewhat novel approach to the study of consciousness is taken in this volume where machine consciousness is examined within the externalist approach through for example, agent-environment relationship. The question being asked here is whether it is possible to apply externalist architecture in the fields of robotics. The concept of consciousness is also explored in the context of dreaming states and in the relation to a model of self. Future work should aim to better understand and define the various aspects of the concept of self and consciousness as well as how these two concepts relate. Better definition would help clarify the minimum requirements for achieving self and/or consciousness in cognitive architectures.

3.3. Emotion and metacognitive ability

The main body of human cognitive abilities is acquired through learning and meta-learning (i.e., acquisition of learning skills, bootstrapped learning, cognitive growth), which thus are the key to development of adult human-level intelligence. When studying meta cognitive abilities and higher order cognition one has to examine emotion. It is widely accepted in cognitive science today that emotion affects most aspects of cognition including thinking and reasoning. In fact studies in neuroscience have shown that without emotions reasoning becomes virtually impossible. The papers presented here address metacognitive abilities both by examining language acquisition and use and also by looking the requirements for rational thought. The issue of emotion reaction triggering for different events is also addressed.

4. Concluding Remarks: The roadmap to solving the BICA challenge

The papers and abstracts presented in this volume demonstrate the richness in the field of BICA inspired research and the tremendous progress that has been made in understanding biological learning and intelligence. Each year the BICA series brings us a step closer to the ultimate goal of creating a computational equivalence to the human mind. The strength of BICA is first and foremost represented in its multidisciplinary approach taken to solve this challenge as BICA brings together researchers from otherwise disjointed disciplines such as AI, neuroscience, cognitive science and psychology. Further progress requires a clear roadmap to solve the BICA challenge. One question is whether the meaning of the "BI" in BICA should be broadened to match the needs of the challenge. A new perspective on this issue is proposed by Chella, Lebiere, Noelle and Samsonovich in their manifesto.

References

[1] J. LeDoux, The self: clues from the brain, *Annals of the New York Academy of Sciences*, **1001** (2003), 295-304.
[2] M. Lewis, The emergence of consciousness and its role in human development, *Annals of the New York Academy of Sciences*, **1001** (2003), 104-133.
[3] C. D. Frith, S. J. Blakemore, D. M. Wolpert, Abnormalities in the awareness and control of action, *Philosophical Transactions: Biological Sciences*, **355** (2003), 1771-1788.

Biologically Inspired Cognitive Architectures 2011
A.V. Samsonovich and K.R. Jóhannsdóttir (Eds.)
IOS Press, 2011
doi:10.3233/978-1-60750-959-2-9

Evaluating the Contribution of Top-Down Feedback and Post-Learning Reconstruction

Tsvi Achler [a,1] and Luís M. A. Bettencourt [a]

[a] *Los Alamos National Labs, Synthetic Visual Cognition Group*

Abstract. Deep generative models and their associated top-down architecture are gaining popularity in neuroscience and computer vision. In this paper we link our previous work with regulatory feedback networks to generative models. We show that generative model's and regulatory feedback model's equations can share the same fixed points. Thus, phenomena observed using regulatory feedback can also apply to generative models. This suggests that generative models can also be developed to identify mixtures of patterns, address problems associated with binding, and display the ability to estimate numerosity.

Keywords. Top-Down Feedback, Generative Models, Regulatory Feedback.

Introduction

Arguably in both neural modeling and machine learning, feedforward methods of signal classification are simpler and more common, for example: traditional Neural Networks, Perceptrons, and Support Vector Machines[1-3]. Using these methods, the relation of $\mathbf{Y}=\mathbf{WX}$ or $\mathbf{Y}=f(\mathbf{W},\mathbf{X})$ are solved. $\mathbf{W}$ represents learned feedforward transformation through weights. $\mathbf{Y}$ represents the activity of a vector of labeled nodes or outputs $\mathbf{Y}=(Y_1, Y_2, Y_3,\dots Y_L)^{\mathrm{T}}$. $\mathbf{X}$ represents signal to be recognized, which can be decomposed in terms of individual features $\mathbf{X}=(X_1, X_2, X_3,\dots X_J)^{\mathrm{T}}$. $\mathbf{W}$ is typically optimized to reveal differences between labeled data, thus mapping sets of input to output classes. Learning $\mathbf{W}$ may require a comparison of inputs to outputs using feedback and varies in specifics between algorithms, but once $\mathbf{W}$ is defined recognition is a feedforward process.

Despite the simplicity and success of these procedures for single object classification, matching human-like recognition capacity continues to be a bottleneck limiting performance in human-level tasks and modeling. Limitations arise, especially with mixtures of patterns. Compared to these recognition algorithms, the brain is more adept at processing mixtures of patterns. This can be observed in many recognition paradigms: natural scenes, sounds, speech, and odorant mixtures, where several individual patterns can be

---

[1] Corresponding Author.

inextricably intermixed.

Mixtures are problematic if algorithms are not able to infer states of co-occurrence as such, after learning single patterns. If a network can recognize n=*5,000* single patterns then there are about *12 million* two pattern combinations *k=2*, and *21 billion* three pattern *k=3* combinations possible. If a network can recognize n=*100,000* patterns, there are *5 billion k=2* and *167 trillion k=3* combinations and so on.

Because of the potential difficulties stemming from combinatorial explosions, learning mixtures as individual classes is not scalable, thus not practical. If networks do not have a mechanism to infer mixtures they may require training for all possible combinations in an environment.

The brain must process pattern mixtures more efficiently because it only has a limited – if large – number of neurons and synapses. It cannot train or designate these many neurons (neither for smell, sound, or vision) for each possible combination. There are not enough resources let alone the time needed for such preparation.

1.1. Top-Down Contribution

Sensory processing regions of the brain such as thalamus, olfactory bulb, sensory cortex have a massive amount of output-to-input feedback pathways that exceed feedforward pathways[4-8].

Despite this evidence, top-down influences are more difficult to incorporate into models and solve as the mathematics often leads to a nonlinear, and often non-convex, optimization problem. Thus many existing top-down models incorporate feedback for spatial attention filtering and in general do not contain as much feedback connections as feedforward e.g.[9,10]. Can mixture processing be improved with massive top down feedback?

2. Generative Models

A class of models called generative models, which has a foundation in Bayesian Statistical Inference, is gaining increasing attention and popularity in many aspects of science and medicine[11]. They are also gaining popularity in logic and neuroscience[12,13]. Most generative models are based on a 1:1 ratio of number of feedforward to feedback connections; furthermore, in most models the feedback connection weights are fully reciprocal, i.e. identical in both directions[14,15]. These types of algorithms are associated with Probabilistic Reasoning, Independent Component Analysis, Blind Source Separation e.g.[13,16,17], and have been used to learn efficient representations[18-20], including those typical of mammalian primary visual and auditory cortex.

Our focus here is not on learning through generative models or other methods. We assume reasonable connections are previously learned. Instead, we focus on how the "reasoning/inference" aspect of generative models aids in mixture processing by connecting them to our previous findings. We assume **W** is previously learned and fixed and ask what reasoning/inference aspects extend previous findings to arbitrary mixes of patterns?

2.1. Inference of Generative Models

The key mechanism of generative models that we focus on here is the use of top down feedback to "Explain Away" causes and effects[13]. For example, if two causes explain an observation, and one cause is known with some certainty, then the known cause will explain the observation and the other is deemed unlikely.

More specifically, suppose a house may be moved due to an earthquake or a tornado (assume both events are approximately equally rare). Now if the house has been moved and there was a tornado, this actually reduces the chance that an earthquake has occurred. Tornado "explains away" earthquake. This is a top down manipulation because the facts that house moved and tornado was present do not comprise a new observation about an earthquake. However the significance of their co-interaction correctly offers a more likely explanation than earthquake.

3. Regulatory Feedback and Generative Models

Our previous work on Regulatory Feedback Networks showed that they can solve mixture problems associated with binding[21], pattern mixtures[22,23], and numerocity[24]. Regulatory Feedback shares many features of generative models. The ratio of feedforward to feedback connections is 1:1 and feedforward weights are similar to feedback weights. However the equations are in a different form.

In this paper we show that solutions to our algorithm are identical to typical generative model solutions. Thus what holds true in our algorithm holds true in generative models, under certain general conditions. Thus generative models are expected to give mixture processing benefits. We limit our discussion to positive values of **X**, **Y**, without loss of generality.

3.1. Generative Model Fixed Points

The principle of a generative model is that it generates a reconstruction to match an original image so that the energy $E=\|X - W^{-1}Y\|^2$ is minimized, usually subject to sparseness constraints. This energy is the log-likelihood of the probability of **Y**, given **X** and **W**, and the solution of the minimization is the maximum likelihood value of **Y**. For simplicity we rewrite this equation with $M=W^{-1}$, assuming the inverse exists.

We can use the pseudoinverse to calculate $\mathbf{M}=\mathbf{W}^{-1}$ based on $\mathbf{W}$. Thus generative models and regulatory feedback can be used as a method to take feedforward weights learned in a discriminative manner and apply them in a generative manner. Differentiating E relative to Y, gives

$$X - MY = 0 \qquad (1)$$

Equation (1) is commonly taken as the gradient of Y, leading to effective dynamics, with a fixed point given by (1). Suppose $\mathbf{X}$ an image from the environment, $\mathbf{MY}$ is the internal reconstruction of that image, which we shall label $\tilde{X}$.

$$\tilde{X} = MY \quad \text{or} \quad \tilde{X}_k = \sum_{l=1}^{L} M_{kl} Y_l \qquad (2)$$

If the reconstruction matches the input then $\mathbf{X}= \tilde{X}$. From equation 1 this is a fixed point: $\mathbf{X}- \tilde{X} = 0$, and the minimization of E can be found to be well defined as it is an explicitly bounded from below function. Some complications and subtleties arise when sparseness terms, which regularize the number and intensity of the states Y that can be used to reconstruct the input, are introduced, but are beyond the aim of the this paper. Functions that find the same fixed-points (though matched reconstructions) are equivalent from the point of view of their asymptotic states.

3.2. Regulatory Feedback

In this section we show that regulatory feedback equations[21-25] have the same fixed points. In those papers, for simplicity, we limited $\mathbf{M} \in \{0,1\}$. Here we allow $\mathbf{M}$ to have positive real values. We build up the regulatory feedback equations by starting with internal reconstruction. Similar to the generative model, the reconstruction term in this model is given in equation 2.

Instead of comparing reconstruction with the input using subtraction, in regulatory feedback it is achieved using division or what we occasionally refer to as "shunting". Based on division we define a "dynamic salience" term S_k corresponding to every input element X_k to evaluate the accuracy of recognition.

$$S_k = \frac{X_k}{\tilde{X}_k} \qquad (3)$$

S_k measures the how well the information is accounted for by reconstruction

(reconstruction error) and this information is used to modify the state of the network. The state of the network is determined by an update rule, which can be also referred to as an equation of motion:

$$Y_i(t+1) = \frac{Y_i(t)}{\left(\sum_{j=1}^{J} M_{ji}\right)} \sum_{k=1}^{J} M_{ki} S_k \tag{4}$$

It can be appreciated that whenever an input feature is correctly reconstructed $X_k = \tilde{x}_k$ and that $S_k=1$. Assuming that whole the image is correctly reconstructed then all $\sum S_k=1$. In that case the equation becomes:

$$Y_i(t+1) = Y_i(t) \frac{\sum_{k=1}^{J} M_{ki} 1}{\left(\sum_{j=1}^{J} M_{ji}\right)} \tag{5}$$

and

$$Y_i(t+1) = Y_i(t) \tag{6}$$

The values of Y_i do not change over time and this is a fixed point. This is identical to the generative model where fixed points arise when the reconstruction matches the inputs.

The complete equation can be written as:

$$Y_i(t+1) = \frac{Y_i(t)}{\left(\sum_{j=1}^{J} M_{ji}\right)} \sum_{k=1}^{J} M_{ki} \left(\frac{X_k}{\sum_{l=1}^{L} M_{kl} Y_l(t)}\right) \tag{7}$$

or alternatively:

$$Y_{t+1} = \frac{Y_t}{V} M^T \frac{X}{MY_t} \tag{8}$$

$$\text{where} \quad V = \sum_{j=1}^{J} M_{ji} \qquad\qquad (9)$$

The important findings for this work is that when the reconstruction matches the input ($\mathbf{X} = \tilde{X}$) identical fixed points can be found in generative models and regulatory feedback. Though this equivalence was obtained in the absence of explicit sparness inducing terms, their introduction can be made as well in such a way that both types of dynamics remain equivalent in terms of their asymptotics. In this way the fixed-point solutions are the same whether generative methods (e.g. based on least squares) or the regulatory feedback optimizations are used.

4. Summary and Conclusions

We have shown that, using the same connectivity structure, regulatory feedback and generative models have identical fixed points and the same asymptotic solutions.   Moreover, standard optimization methods have been shown to converge to the fixed points[16]. Regulatory feedback has also been shown to converge to the same fixed points[21-23].

Regulatory feedback has been demonstrated to be better able to process mixtures compared to feedforward models. This is demonstrated whether the mixtures are summed together[23] in intensity or combined as a union [22]. The mixtures can contain multiple additions of the same pattern (repeats) and the networks are able to determine the pattern mixture's numerocity[24]. They are also able to resolve certain binding scenarios: i.e. to determine whether subcomponent parts belong together[21].

Rerunning numerical simulations on the tests above using a least-squares method to solve the generative equation (1) we obtain the same results except for the union cases and some instances of the binding cases. The instances of binding and unions that did not settle on the same solutions had input patterns outside the fixed points or linear combinations of the fixed points. In those cases both models converged, however differing results can be expected in different methods solving the generative model as no guarantees are made outside of the fixed points. The significance of the differences between methods is beyond the scope of this paper and will be discussed in future work.

In summary, we have shown is that generative methods can generalize to mixtures of patterns not seen before and subsequently do not suffer from a combinatorial explosion. This can be preserved even if an optimization method is nonlinear (such as regulatory feedback). Such properties may underlie the key to human-like mixture processing and the role of top-down feedback found throughout the brain.

Acknowledgements

We would like to thank Peter Loxley for his input and granting agencies that have helped support this work namely: IC Posdoc program and the LANL LDRD Synthetic Cognition project 2009006DR.

References

[1] Rosenblatt, F. 1958. "The perceptron: a probabilistic model for information storage and organization in the brain." Psychological Review 65 (6) (November): 386-408.

[2] Rumelhart D.E. and J.L. McClelland, Parallel distributed processing : explorations in the microstructure of cognition. Computational models of cognition and perception. 1986, Cambridge, Mass.: MIT Press.

[3] Vapnik V.N., The nature of statistical learning theory. 1995, New York: Springer. xv, 188 p.

[4] Famiglietti, E. V., Jr. and A. Peters. "The synaptic glomerulus and the intrinsic neuron in the dorsal lateral geniculate nucleus of the cat." J Comp Neurol 144(3): 285-334 (1972).

[5] Felleman, D. J. and D. C. Van Essen., "Distributed hierarchical processing in the primate cerebral cortex." Cereb Cortex 1(1): 1-47 (1991).

[6] LaBerge, D. "Attention, awareness, and the triangular circuit." Conscious Cogn 6(2-3): 149-81 (1997).

[7] Chen, W. R., W. Xiong, et al. "Analysis of relations between NMDA receptors and GABA release at olfactory bulb reciprocal synapses." Neuron 25(3): 625-33 (2000).

[8] Douglas, R. J. and K. A. Martin. "Neuronal circuits of the neocortex." Annu Rev Neurosci 27: 419-51 (2004).

[9] Mozer, M. C. (1991). The perception of multiple objects: a connectionist approach. Cambridge, Mass., MIT Press.

[10] Itti, L. and C. Koch (2001). "Computational modelling of visual attention." Nat Rev Neurosci 2(3): 194-203.

[11] Malakoff D, "Statistics: Bayes Offers a 'New' Way to Make Sense of Numbers" Science (1999): v286 p5444.1460

[12] Olshausen, B. A., Field, D. J., Sparse coding with an overcomplete basis set: A strategy employed by V1? Vision Research 37:3311-3325, 1997.

[13] Judea Pearl, Probabilistic reasoning in intelligent systems: networks of plausible inference, Morgan Kaufmann Publishers Inc., San Francisco, CA, 1988

[14] G.F. Harpur and R.W. Prager. Development of low-entropy coding in a recurrent network. Network, 7:277–284, 1996.

[15] Friston K (2005) A theory of cortical responses. Philos Trans R Soc Lond B Biol Sci 360(1456):815–836

[16] Hyvärinen A, J Karhunen, E. Oja (2001) Independent Component Analysis, New York: Wiley, ISBN 978-0-471-40540-5

[17] Comon P. (1994): Independent Component Analysis: a new concept?, Signal Processing, Elsevier, 36(3):287–314

[18] Foldiak, P., Forming sparse representations by local anti-Hebbian learning, Biol. Cybern., 64:165- 170, 1990

[19] Zeiler M, D Krishnan, G Taylor, R Fergus, Deconvolutional Networks for Feature Learning, CVPR 2010

[20] Hinton, G. E. and R. R. Salakhutdinov. "Reducing the dimensionality of data with neural networks." Science 313(5786): 504-7 (2006).

[21] Achler, T., Amir, E., Input Feedback Networks: Classification and Inference Based on Network Structure, Artificial General Intelligence Proceedings V1: 15-26, 2008

[22] Achler, T., C. Omar, E. Amir. "Shedding Weights: More With Less." Proceedings of the 2008 IEEE International Joint Conference on Neural Networks (2008)

[23] Achler, T. "Using Non-Oscillatory Dynamics to Disambiguate Simultaneous Patterns." Proc of the 2009 IEEE International Joint Conference on Neural Networks (2009)

[24] Achler, T., Vural D., Amir, E., Counting Objects with Biologically Inspired Regulatory-Feedback Networks, International Joint Conference on Neural Networks Proceedings, 2009

[25] Achler, T. (2007). "Object classification with recurrent feedback neural networks." Proc. SPIE Evolutionary and Bio-inspired Computation: Theory and Applications 6563.

16

Biologically Inspired Cognitive Architectures 2011
A.V. Samsonovich and K.R. Jóhannsdóttir (Eds.)
IOS Press, 2011
© 2011 The authors and IOS Press. All rights reserved.
doi:10.3233/978-1-60750-959-2-16

Computational Modeling of Therapies related to Cognitive Vulnerability and Coping

Azizi Ab Aziz[a], Michel C.A. Klein[b]

[a,b]Agent Systems Research Group, Department of Artificial Intelligence
Vrije Universiteit Amsterdam, De Boelelaan 1081a,
1081 HV Amsterdam, The Netherlands
{mraaziz,michel.klein}@few.vu.nl

Abstract. Due to recent research, the neurobiological elements behind mental disorders such as depression become more and more clear. This paper presents an integrated computational model based on neurobiological insights and psychological theories. The model is used to analyse the effect of existing psychological treatments. The simulation experiments give an insight in the interaction between different cognitive components in mental disorders and illustrates why different treatments can have different effects for people with different genetic dispositions.

Keywords., Computational Modeling in Therapy, Cognitive Models in Cognitive Vulnerability and Coping, Simulation.

1. Introduction

Cognitive vulnerability and coping are important elements of the explanation of mental disorders, such as depression [4]. More and more, the neurobiological elements behind these disorders become clear. With the increased understanding of these mechanisms, also the possibilities increase to create adequate computational models of mental diseases. Such models can contribute to a better understanding of the mechanism, form a basis for e-mental health applications and can be used for the analysis of the effect of (combinations of) therapies.

In this paper, an integrated computational model is described that uses knowledge about cognitive vulnerability and coping. The model is a combination of two previously developed models and describes the dynamics of the cognitive states over time. A more detailed discussion for both domain models can be found in [1][2]. The integrated model is extended with a sub-model that describes two specific psychological treatments, i.e. Acceptance and Commitment Therapy (ACT), and Rational Emotive Behavioural Therapy (RBET). The combined model is used to analyse the effect of these treatments by performing simulation experiments.

The remainder of the paper is organized as follows. In Section 2, some recent insights about the neurobiological background of mental disorders are reviewed. Based on this, the subsequent section presents the integrated dynamic model of cognitive states related to mental disorders. In Section 4, a sub-model is introduced that describes the treatments. Both are used as basis for simulation experiments and their analysis in Sections 5 and 6. Section 7 concludes the paper

2. Biological Perspectives in Cognitive Vulnerability and Coping

Recent decades have witnessed an explosion of research on neurobiological aspects in mental health. It has become an important approach to unlock the mystery of mental disorders. In the neurobiological area important relationships between cognitive, behaviours, affective, and neurobiological underpinnings can be grounded. For example, negative appraisals of stressors lead to the release of cortisol and increase the vulnerability for depression. Cortisol has a vital role in shutting down the sympathetic function and to suppress the hypothalamus pituitary-adrenocortical (HPA) activities by a negative feedback mechanism on the hippocampus, amygdala, and pituitary and plays an important role to restore normal hormone levels [6]. Therefore, any dysregulation of the HPA implies that cortisol is inhibiting the peripheral nervous system to maintain physiological homeostasis. Another important concept to explain cognitive vulnerability is the cumulative burden borne by a brain and body adapting to stress (*allostatic load*) [9]. From this stand, it is predicted that the individual with active HPA activities and locus coeruleus-norepinephrine system (a nucleus in the brainstem involved with physiological responses to stress) will have the highest risk for allostatic load, and increased the risk of cognitive vulnerability towards stress. Reconsolidation is another biological process that relevant to cognitive vulnerability to the effects of extreme stress. It explains how old and reactivated memories can be integrated into an ongoing perceptual and emotional experience and becomes part of new memory [6]. Moreover, several clinical studies indicate that the consolidation process in amygdala and hippocampus are sensitive to disruption upon reactivation of several protein synthesis inhibitors.

In the coping styles literature it is shown that the magnitude of neuro-endocrine stress response depends on whether the stressor is appraised as threatening or as challenging. Threat appraisals are more strongly associated with prolonged higher reactive levels of cortisol (increased reactivity), while challenge appraisals are characterized by rapid cortisol responses with quick recovery [5][9]. Additionally, although the effective use of emotional-focused coping may dampen the endocrine stress response by not getting overwhelmed by negative affects, it will only work on the short time, where it is related to the sustained levels of cortisol and sympathetic activation. In the long term, the sustained activation will result in physiological and affective problems. Coping is also related to the several active brain regions, where evidence is accumulating that coping is a part of the overall set of executive functions that regulated by the prefrontal cortex [6]. For example, problem focused coping strategies were related to the inhibitory control activities, and emotional-focused coping shown a poorer inhibition result [5].

Specifically, from both cognitive vulnerability and coping concepts, we can see several common aspects that each concept has important interplay with one to another. This interplay can be seen through the activities in HPA, cortisol, and also several brain regions activation. In a cognitive model perspective, this biological interaction can abstractly be seen in several important theories to explain cognitive vulnerability and coping process, namely; *(1)* Extended Hopelessness Theory of Depression and *(2)* Cognitive Motivational Relational Theory [8][13].

3. A Model for Cognitive Vulnerability and Coping

The model used in this paper is a combination of two previously developed models to explain the dynamics in human vulnerability towards stress and coping skill strategies. The detailed discussion for both domain models can be found in [1][2]. Figure 1 depicts the interaction of these two models.

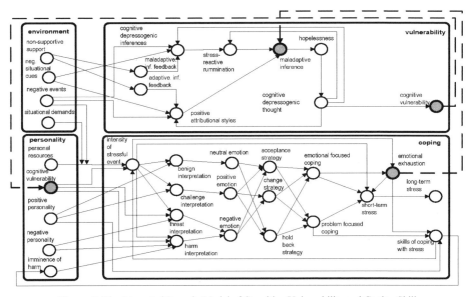

Figure. 1. The Integrated Domain Model of Cognitive Vulnerability and Coping Skills

3.1 Concepts in Cognitive Vulnerability & Coping

The cognitive vulnerability model has been developed based on the *Extended Hopelessness Theory of Depression*. In this theory, people who exhibit a negative inferential style, in which they describe, negative events (*NeV*) to stable and will affect many aspects of life will most likely to infer themselves as fundamentally useless [7]. One of the important concepts from this theory is the analysis on how social support mitigates a risk of relapse (positive feedback (*AiF*)), and indirectly escalates the risk of relapse (maladaptive inferential feedback (*MiF*)), related to negative reflection of received support (*NsP*) [7]. By combining either one of these two factors together with situational cues, it leads to the formation of either cognitive depressogenic inferences (*CdI*) or positive attributional styles (*PtS*) [5]. Situational cues (*SiC*) refers to a concept that explains individuals' perception that highly influenced by cues from events (environment) [11]. These later develop where individuals have trouble in accessing positive information (stress-reactive rumination (*SrR*)), and further increase a negative bias towards future inference (maladaptive inference (*MdI*)) [7][11]. After a certain period, both conditions are related to the development of hopelessness (*HpS*), and later will lead to the development of cognitive depressogenic thought (*CdT*) and cognitive vulnerability (*CoV*) [8].

In a coping model, the *Cognitive Motivational Relational Theory* (CMRT) is used [13]. Several factors such as *situational demands* (*SiD*), *personal resources* (*PrA*), and *negative events* play important roles to influence perception towards incoming stressors (*IsE*) [4]. Normally, a person appraises two types of appraisals; the primary and the secondary. The primary appraisal is made to evaluate person's well being. Firstly, the situation can be appraised either as harm/loss (*HrM*), threatening (*ThT*), challenging (*ChL*) or benign (*BgN*). Later this process will determine individuals' emotion perception; negative *(NgE)*, positive *(PsE)* or neutral *(NuE)* emotion [13]. Negative emotion is related to perceiving *harm* and *threat*, neutral emotion is corresponded to *benign* condition and positive emotion is attributed to perceiving *challenge*. Secondly, a person evaluates whether he or she has the resources to deal with the stressors. It is commonly related to the emotional attribution, where a positive and neutral emotion results in *acceptance (AcP)* and *change (ChG)*, while the negative emotion triggers *holdback* (*HdB*) [2]. Later, it will lead to the *problem* (*PrF*) and *emotion-focused coping (EmF)*. A problem-focused coping is associated with rational efforts to get the problem solved, while emotion-focused coping strategies entail efforts to regulate the emotional consequences of stressful events [14]. All these strategies can be proven useful, but many individuals feel that in a long run, emotion focused coping is associated with outcomes that people found unsatisfactory (emotional exhaustion in coping (*ExH*)) that later will develop short (*StS*) and term stress (*LtS*). Problem focused coping is associated with satisfactory outcomes (improved coping skills *(ScS)*[13].

4. Modeling Therapies for Cognitive Vulnerability and Coping

In this section, it shown how the influences of selected therapies (Acceptance and Commitment (ACT), and Rational Emotive Behavioural (RBET) Therapy) are modelled in the extended model presented in Section 3. First, important concepts in evaluating cognitive vulnerability and coping will be discussed, followed by ACT and RBET.

4.1 Important Concepts in Evaluating Cognitive Vulnerability and Coping

One of the very imperative features to verify the level of related conditions such as cognitive vulnerability and long-term stress is the continuous evaluation of changes in selected physiological and behavioural features within the individual. Using the domain model, the development of the vital features is analyzed and predicted. These features provide the dynamic relationships in the model. For example, the observable feature in a long-term stress can be related from the accumulation of short-term stress states and so forth [2]. There are several important concepts need to be measured, namely; long-term stress (*LtS*), emotional exhaustion (*ExH*), cognitive vulnerability (*CoV*), and coping skills (*ScS*). These concepts are calculated as follows:

$$LtS(t+\Delta t)=LtS(t)+\beta_l.[Pos(StS(t)-LtS(t)).(1-LtS(t))- \qquad (1)$$
$$Pos(-(StS(t)-LtS(t))).LtS(t)].\Delta t.$$

$$ExH(t+\Delta t)=ExH(t)+\psi_e.[(Pos((IsE(t)-ExH(t)).(1- \qquad (2)$$
$$ExH(t)))- Pos(-(IsE(t)-xH(t)).ExH(t))].EmF(t).\Delta t.$$

$$ScS(t+\Delta t)=ScS(t) + \phi_s.[Pos(ExH(t) - ScS(t)). (1- \qquad (3)$$
$$ScS(t))- Pos(-(ExH(t)-ScS(t)).ScS(t)].PrA(t).\Delta t$$

$$CoV(t+\Delta t)=CoV(t) + v_c.[Pos(CdT(t) - CoV(t)). (1- \qquad (4)$$
$$CoV(t))- Pos(-(CdT(t)-CoV(t)).ScS(t)].\Delta t.$$

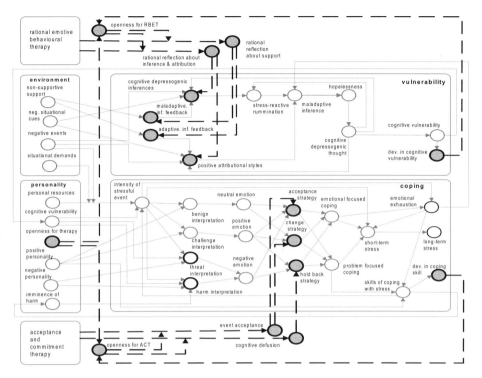

Figure 2. The Integrated Model in an Agent Based Therapy for ACT and RBET

The rates of change for all temporal relationships are determined by flexibility parameters β_l, ψ_e, ϕ_s, and v_c respectively. The operator Pos for the positive part is defined by $Pos(x) = (x + |x|)/2$, or, alternatively; $Pos(x) = x$ if $x \geq 0$ and 0 else.

4.2 Intervention for Acceptance and Commitment, and Rational Emotive Behavioural Therapy

In this section it is shown how the influences of two types of therapies are modeled in the extended model presented in Section 3. First, acceptance and commitment therapy will be discussed, followed by rational behavioural emotive therapy. Figure 2 shows an overview of the relevant states and dynamics in the model. The states that are depicted in grey represent states have been added and corresponded to model the points of impacts in therapies. The same holds for the dashed lines. In this model, openness for therapy (*OfT*) is a state indicating how open the individual is for therapy, which is made specific for each particular influence of therapy, namely openness for ACT (*OfA*), and openness for RBET (*OfR*). Furthermore, the development in coping skills (*DeC*) and cognitive vulnerability (*DeV*) will influence openness for ACT, and RBET respectively.

$$OfA(t) = OfT(t).DeC(t). \tag{5}$$
$$OfR(t) = OfT(t).DeV(t). \tag{6}$$

Acceptance and Commitment Therapy: Fundamentally, ACT emphasizes such processes as mindfulness, acceptance, and values in helping individuals overcome obstacles in their lives. There are three core processes in ACT, however; only two processes (*cognitive defusion* and *acceptance*) are discussed here to change individual's coping preference [12]. Cognitive defusion (*CgD*) (means "detach from unhelpful thoughts and worries" and event acceptance (*EvA*) deals with reducing the effort to avoid certain situations (where discerning between thoughts, feelings, and experiences is a prominent focus) [12]. The effects from these processes will allow more acceptance and change strategies to take place in coping. This can be expressed as follows:

$$AcP(t) = \zeta_a.[\gamma_a.PsE(t) + (1-\gamma_a).NuE(t)].[1-((1-IeA(t)).NgE(t))] + \qquad (7)$$
$$(1-\zeta_a).IeA(t).$$

$$ChG(t) = \upsilon_g.[PsE(t).(1-((1-IcD(t)).NgE(t))] + (1-\upsilon_g).IcD(t). \qquad (8)$$

$$HdB(t) = \zeta_h.[(1-PsE(t).(1-IcD(t)] + (1-\zeta_h).(1-IcD(t)). \qquad (9)$$

where, $IeA(t) = EvA(t). OfA(t),$ and $IcD(t) = CgD(t).OfA(t).$

Rational Behavioural Emotive Therapy: REBT suggests that human beings defeat themselves in two main ways: (1) by holding irrational beliefs about their self (ego disturbance), (2) by holding irrational beliefs about their emotional, or social comfort (discomfort disturbance) [3]. Therefore the RBET identifies those problematic ideas, and replaces them with more rational perspectives (such as positive perspectives to self attribution (*RtS*), and provided support (*RtO*)) [3]. As a result from this intervention process, it will restrain the progress of future irrational beliefs, and later provides effective new thinking on individual experienced conditions. The intervention effects are calculated as follows.

$$MiF(t) = NsP(t).(1-ItO(t)). \qquad (10)$$

$$AiF(t) = (1-((1-ItO(t)).NsP(t))). \qquad (11)$$

$$PtS(t) = [\eta_p.AiF(t) + (1-\eta_p). (1- (SiC(t).DyT(t).NvT(t). \qquad (12)$$
$$(1-ItS(t)))].AiF(t).$$

$$CdI(t) = [\alpha_c.MiF(t) + (1- \alpha_c). SiC(t).DyT(t).MiF(t)].(1-ItS(t)).NeV(t). \qquad (13)$$

where, $ItO(t) = RtO(t). OfR(t)$ and $ItS(t) = RtS(t).OfR(t).$

Here parameters, $\zeta_a, \gamma_a, \upsilon_g, \zeta_h, \alpha_c$ and ψ_b represent the proportional factor for all respective instantaneous variables.

5. Simulation Results

In this section, simulation results are presented. The intervention as described in the previous section has been implemented in simulation environment. To this end, software to generate simulation traces was developed in Matlab. Using this simulation environment, we mimicked the intervention process to see its effect under several cases. Three fictional individuals are studied with divergent values for personality attributes. These values are chosen to depict the different influences of the therapies on different types of individuals. Table 1 shows the values for the most important variables of the model for each individual.

Table 1. Personality Attributes for the Simulation Experiments

Personality Attributes \ Individuals	A	B	C
Positive Personality	0.2	0.5	0.8
Personal Resources	0.1	0.3	0.7
Openness for Therapy	0.7	0.7	0.7
Situational demands, Situational Cues, Negative Events, and Situational demands	0.9	0.9	0.9

In all cases, the long term stress, emotional exhaustion, cognitive vulnerability, and coping skill value are initialized at 0.3. These simulations used the following parameters settings: $t_{max}=1000$ (to represent a monitoring activity up to 42 days), $\Delta t=0.3$, all proportional and flexibility rates are assigned as 0.5 and 0.3 respectively. These settings were obtained from several systematic experiments to determine the most suitable parameter values in the model. . For the sake of brevity, this section will only discuss the results of individual A. First, the simulation without any form therapy is shown (Figure 3(a)).

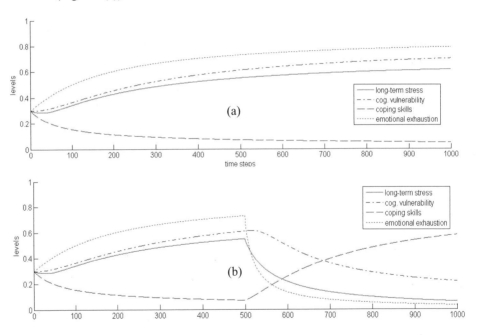

Figure 3. Individual type A **(a)** Without Following Any Therapy, **(b)** following the ACT therapy

The individual experiences very negative events during monitoring period. Since the individual is susceptible towards stress (low coping skills and highly vulnerable), a long-term stress follows [4][8]. Later it will lead an individual to fall into depression. For the second experiment; individual A is receiving the ACT therapy (Figure 3(b)). For this case, it can be seen that the long-term stress, cognitive vulnerability, and emotional exhaustion are decreased. In addition to this, it increases individual's ability to cope as well [13]. For the RBET, the same types of experiments have been conducted. Figure 4 shows the result from following this therapy.

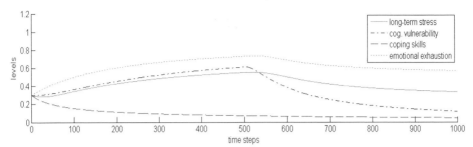

Figure 4. Individual type *A* following the RBET therapy

In this case, individual *A* experiences slow recovery in long-term stress and emotional exhaustion, and a rapid recovery from cognitive vulnerability. Another variability is used for the experiment is assigning different openness level for individual *A*. If the openness towards therapy is increased, the individual *A* recovers more quickly compares to lower openness values. In the case of individual *B*, for all three conditions, individual *B* recovers faster compares to individual *A*. Meanwhile individual C receives a very low negative effect from the incoming stressors, and manages to recover even without receiving any therapy [4]. In addition to these experiments, when an individual *A* follows both therapies in the same time, it shows a slightly faster recovery than following only a single therapy.

6. Automated Verification

In order to verify whether the model indeed generates results that adherence to psychological literatures, a set of properties have been identified from related literatures. Therefore, these properties will answer whether the model produces results that are coherent with the literature and appropriate to help people with cognitive vulnerability and coping problems, To allow the verification process to take place, these properties have been specified in a language called Temporal Trace Language (TTL). TTL is built on atoms referring to states of the world, time points, and traces. This relationship can be presented as a state(γ, t, output(R)) |= p, means that state property *p* is true at the output of role *R* in the state of trace γ at time point *t* [16]. It is also comparable to the *Holds*-predicate in the Situation Calculus. Based on that concept, dynamic properties can be formulated using a sorted predicate logic approach, by manipulating quantifiers over time and traces and first-order logical connectives such as $\neg$, $\wedge$, $\vee$, $\Rightarrow$, $\forall$, and $\exists$. A number of simulations including the ones described in Section 4 have been used as basis for the verification and were confirmed.

VP1: Effectiveness of ACT in problem focused coping
After a person has followed the ACT therapy for some times, the problem focused coping skills have improved.

VP1 $\equiv \forall\gamma$: TRACE, $\forall$t1, t2:TIME, $\forall$R1,R2,D1,D2:REAL
[state(γ,t1) |= has_value(ACT_therapy, R1) &
state(γ,t2) |= has_value (ACT_therapy, R2) &
state(γ,t1) |= has_value(problem_focused_coping, D1) &
state(γ,t2) |= has_value(problem_focused_coping, D2) &
t1 < t2 & R2 > R1] $\Rightarrow$ D2 $\geq$ D1

VP2: Problem focused coping helps a person to recover faster than emotional focused coping
A problem focused coping skill is a better option compares to an emotional focused coping skill in a long -term recovery.

VP2 ≡ ∀γ: TRACE, ∀t1, t2:TIME, ∀M1,M2, D1, D2:REAL
[state(γ,t1) |= has_value(problem_focused_coping, M1) &
state(γ,t1) |= has_value(emotional_focused_coping, M2) &
state(γ,t1) |= has_value(long_term_stress, L1) &
state(γ,t2) |= has_value(long_term_stress, L2) &
t1 < t2 & M1 > M2] ⇒ L1 > L2

VP3: Effect of cognitive vulnerability towards long term stress
Reducing the cognitive vulnerability level will reduce the risk of future long term stress

VP3 ≡ ∀γ: TRACE, ∀t1, t2:TIME, ∀F1,F2,H1,H2, d:REAL
[state(γ,t1) |= has_value(cog_vulnerability, F1) &
state(γ,t1) |= has_value(cog_vulnerability, F2) &
state(γ,t1) |= has_value(long_term_stress, H1) &
state(γ,t2) |= has_value(long_term_stress, H2) &
t2 ≥ t1 + d & F1< F2] ⇒ H2 < H1

VP4: ACT results in higher recovery in stress than RBET
After a person has followed ACT, the long-term stress is lower than after following RBET

VP4 ≡ ∀γ1, γ2: TRACE, ∀t1,t2:TIME, ∀M1,M2,L1,L2, d:REAL
[state(γ1,t1) |= has_value(ACT_therapy, M1) &
state(γ2,t1) |= has_value(RBET_therapy, M2) &
state(γ1,t2) |= has_value(long_term_stress, L1) &
state(γ2,t2) |= has_value(long_term_stress, L2) &
t2 ≥ t1 + d & M1 =1 & M2=1] ⇒ L1 < L2

7. Discussion

Because of the increased insights in the neurobiological basis of mental disorders, it is possible to make more detailed models of these disorders. In this paper, an integrated model that relates cognitive vulnerability and coping strategies has been presented. The model has been described in a computational software package, which allows performing simulation experiments that describe the development of the different factors over time. The simulation experiments that have been presented give an insight in the interaction between different cognitive components in mental disorders. It also shows that ACT therapy is more effective for improving coping skills, while RBET therapy has the largest effect on the factors related to cognitive vulnerability. Due to the interaction of the concepts, both therapies will contribute to less stress. The experiments suggest that there is a only limited added value in combining both therapies.

The model presented in this paper is based on neurobiological and psychological theoretical knowledge. Further research is required to investigate to what extent the simulations give an adequate description of actual development in persons with mental disorders. Based on questionnaires or continuous assessments using modern ICT tools such as mobile phones, the development of mood and stress of actual people could be monitored. The outcome of these experiments can be used to validate and tune the presented model. The validated models can be used as basis for e-mental health applications that guide patients and suggest the best interventions by predicting their effect.

References

[1]   A.A., Aziz, M.C.A Klein,. An Agent Based Simulation of the Dynamics in Cognitive Depressogenic Thought, *The 2nd International Conference on Agents and Artificial Intelligence* (ICAART 2010), INSTICC Press , pp. 232-237. 2010.

[2]   A.A., Aziz, M.C.A., Klein, J.Treur, Simulating Cognitive Coping Strategies for Intelligent Support Agents. In: Catrambone, R., Ohlsson, S. (eds.), *Proceedings of the 32th Annual Conference of the Cognitive Science Society*, CogSci 2010. Cognitive Science Society, Austin, TX, Oregon, USA. pp. 435-440. 2010.

[3]   A.Ellis, Early Theories and Practices of Rational Emotive Behavior Theory and How They Have Been Augmented And Revised During The Last Three Decades. *Journal Of Rational-Emotive & Cognitive-Behavior Therapy*, (2003), 21(3/4)

[4]   A.T. Beck, Cognitive Models Of Depression, *Journal Of Cognitive Psychotherapy* 1, (1987), Pp. 5–37.

[5]   D.S. Charney, Psychobiological Mechanisms of Resilience and Vulnerability: Implications for Successful Adaptation to Extreme Stress, *Am. J Psychiatry* , (2004), pp. 195-216.

[6]   H. Ursin, Olff. M., Psychobiology and Coping and Defense Strategies, Neuropsychobiology (28) (1993), pp. 66-71.

[7]   J. Spasojevic, L.B. Alloy, Rumination as a Common Mechanism Relating Depressive Risk Factors to Depression. *Emotion,* 1(1), (2001), pp.25-37.

[8]   L.B Alloy., L.Y. Abramson., B.E., Gibb, A.G.Crossfield, A.M. Pieracci, J. Spasojevic, J., J.A. Steinberg, Developmental Antecedents of Cognitive Vulnerability to Depression: Review of Findings From the Cognitive Vulnerability to Depression Project. *Journal Of Cognitive Psychotherapy*, (2004) 18(2), pp.115-133.

[9]   M. Olff., W. Langeland., B.P.R. Gerson., Effects of Appraisal and Coping on the Neuroendocrine Response to Extreme Stress, *Neuroscience and Biobehavioural Reviews*, (2005), pp. 457-467.

[10]   P. Cramer, Defense Mechanisms and Physiological Reactivity to Stress, *J. Pers*, (2003), pp. 221-244.

[11]   R.D., Dobkin, C. J., Panzarella, L.B., Alloy, M. Cascardi,. Adaptive Inferential Feedback, Depressogenic Inferences, and Depressed Mood: A Laboratory Study Of The Expanded Hopelessness Theory Of Depression, *Cognitive Therapy and Research*, (2004), pp. 487–509.

[12]   S. C., Hayes, J., Pankey, E. V., Gifford, S., Batten, R.Quiñones, Acceptance and Commitment Therapy in the Treatment of Experiential Avoidance Disorders. In T. Patterson (Ed)., Comprehensive Handbook of Psychotherapy (2). 2000.

[13]   S. Folkman, Personal Control, Stress and Coping Processes: A Theoretical Analysis. *Journal of Personality and Social Psychology*, (1984), 46, 839–852.

[14]   S. Marsella, J. Gratch, Modeling Coping Behavior in Virtual Humans: Don't Worry, Be Happy, Proceedings of the 2nd International Joint Conference on Autonomous Agents and Multiagent Systems, 313-320, 2003.

[15]   S.H Fairclough, Fundamentals of Physiological Computing, Interacting with Computers, 21 (1-2) , pp.133–145. 2009.

[16]   T., Bosse, C.M., Jonker, L. van der Meij, J. Treur, A Language and Environment for Analysis of Dynamics by Simulation. International, *Journal of Artificial Intelligence Tools*, vol. 16, (2007), pp. 435-464.

Biologically Inspired Cognitive Architectures 2011
A.V. Samsonovich and K.R. Jóhannsdóttir (Eds.)
IOS Press, 2011
doi:10.3233/978-1-60750-959-2-26

Natural Human Robot Meta-communication through the Integration of Android's Sensors with Environment Embedded Sensors

Giuseppe BALISTRERI [a,b,1], Shuichi NISHIO [b], Rosario SORBELLO [a],
Antonio CHELLA [a], and Hiroshi ISHIGURO [b,c]

[a] *DICGIM, RoboticsLab, Università degli Studi di Palermo, Viale delle Scienze, 90128
Palermo, Italy*
[b] *ATR Intelligent Robotics and Communication Laboratory, 2-2-2 Hikaridai Seikacho
Sourakugun Kyoto, Japan*
[c] *Graduate School of Engineering Science, Osaka University, 1-3 Machikaneyama
Toyonaka Osaka, Japan*

Abstract. Building robots that closely resemble humans allows us to study phenomena that cannot be studied using mechanical-looking robots in our daily human-to-human natural interactions. This is supported by the fact that human-like devices can more easily elicit the same kind of responses that people use in their natural interactions. However, several studies support the close and complex relationship existing between outer appearance and the behavior by the robot. Yet, human-like appearance, as Masahiro Mori observed, is not enough to give a positive impression. The robot has to behave closely to humans, and is to have a sense of perception that enables it to communicate with humans. Our past experience with android "Geminoid HI-1" demonstrated that the sensors equipping the robot are not enough to perform human-like communication, mainly because of a limited sensing range. To overcome this problem, we endowed the environment around the robot with perceptive capabilities by embedding sensors such as cameras into it. This paper reports a preliminary study about the improvement of the controlling system by integrating cameras in the surrounding environment, so that the android ca be given human-like perception. The integration of the development of androids and the investigations of human behaviors constitute a new research area merging engineering and cognitive sciences.

Keywords. Android, gaze, sensor network

Introduction

The ultimate goal of robot development from the human-robot interaction perspective is to build a robot that exhibits comprehensible behaviors and that supports a rich and

---

[1]Corresponding Author: Giuseppe Balistreri, RoboticsLab, Dipartimento di Ingegneria Chimica, Gestionale, Informatica e Meccanica, ITALY; E-mail: balistreri@dinfo.unipa.it; Intelligent Robotics and Communication Laboratories, Advanced Telecommunication Research Institute International, JAPAN; E-mail: balistreri@atr.jp

multimodal interactions [1] [2]. Recently much has been done in this direction, but in most cases the interaction with robots is efficient only with their developers or with a group of trained individuals. Furthermore, the value of the robots would strongly increase if ordinary people can accepted them as a social presence.

If a robot looks like a human and displays natural human-robot interactions, an ordinary human can naturally communicate with the robot as if he were communicating with another human. One approach for discover the principles of giving to a robot a human-like presence is to build a robot system that can sense and behave like a human. The results of this research can give us the principles underlying the human-like existence.

The degree of how much human-like nature and how much perception are needed in order to perform a natural human-robot interaction have not been revealed yet. The robot's appearance must be sufficiently anthropomorphic to elicit natural reactions from people interacting with it [3]. A robot which realizes a very human-like appearance is called an "android". However, the android system of prof. Hiroshi Ishiguro [4] is not yet sufficient yet as to realize a natural human-robot interaction, because the android's perceptional functions are not implemented, or are substituted by a human controller. Is possible to improve the communication abilities of a robot using built-in sensors, but they have many limitations as to range and resolution. Some perception functions can be provided to the robot by embedding sensors in the environment [5] [6] [7] and creating a network of sensors (like cameras) that can overcome the limitations of the built-in ones.

The resulting architecture of the system is different from the architecture of the human perception system. We are able to gather and process simultaneously visual, auditory, somatosensory and olfactory cues from the outside environment in order to build our view of the world. Since attempting to replicate the same complexity of tasks can be awkward and computationally intensive, we tried to separate the sensory modalities in order to reduce the overall computation.

By separating different sensory modalities and by managing individually behaviors we lose the correlation between processes typical of the biological world, but in this paper we focused on the technical solution leaving to future works the goal of extend our understanding on how gaze cues contribute to activities like natural conversation in human-robot interaction.

For example, humans can easily detect the position of someone else by using vision (eyes) or audio sensing (ears), but in terms of interaction the most useful information is the position of the other person. A robot can obtain the position of someone else by using sensors embedded in its surrounding environment, but it can use the information obtained as if it comes from a complex vision system like the human one.

Concerning the interaction with the robot, if we think about it as a social entity, we need to clearly define the communication skills necessary for robot to be integrated in daily life, in order to discover the principles underlying natural interaction among humans, and to establish a methodology for the development of expressive humanoids robots. Also, another important factor for a social robot is affinity with humans. If the robot is a good partner in the human-robot interaction, the value of affinity with the humans can be increased. So there is a need to understand how the interaction can be improved [8].

A lot of work has been addressed by several researchers on the robot side of interaction, in particular on receiving inputs from human like speech recognition, computer vision, etc.) but, in contrast no important improvements have been done on how a robot should give feed-back to its user. There is a necessity of a transparent interface that regular people can easily interpret [9].

In the human context, the interpretation of other's behavior is a complex and at the same time efficient task. We follow social rules, and if someone doesn't behave accordingly, we have an unpleasant and annoying feeling. So, in order to be accepted in the human society, robots need to behave in ways that are socially correct. Supporting the hypothesis that face-to-face interaction is the best model of interface, we want to leverage people's ability to recognize the subtleties in eye focusing as a feedback, making the conversation with the robot richer and more effective and at the same time discovering which parameters are most significant and useful for human-robot interaction.

This paper reports the development of a communication system that integrates sensors embedded in the environment with an android.

1. Robot's gaze and eye contact

One of the most effective way of controlling human communication is eye contact. For example, we can start a conversation after establishing this kind of contact, or we can infer if our conversational partner is paying attention to us from his gaze. This kind of communication is called meta-communication. Recently, several robots have been proposed that utilize gaze for meta-communication: ROBITA [10] turns to the specific person speaking at the moment in a group conversation, Robovie [11] and COG [12] are similar examples. Eye contact is a phenomenon that occurs when two people cross their gaze, and since we perceive eye contact clearly, eye contact has a stronger meta-communication capability than just the gaze.

But making eye contact is not only about looking at each other, because both parties need to be aware of being watched by the other. This can be achieved with the eye focusing, which basically means to create the eye convergence mechanism on what is the object of the attention. Social robots, as well as service robots, are expected to behave in a way similar to humans, such as talking and listening. For those tasks, robots requires detailed information about the people they are interacting with. To establish an effective eye contact, the robot needs to know the exact position of the human head of the conversational partner, as people are known to be highly sensitive in distinguishing gaze directions and identifying eye contacts.

2. The Geminoid System

This section briefly describes our robot system used for eye-contact in a sensor network study.

A Geminoid is a robot whose purpose is to duplicate a living person. Geminoid HI-1 was developed to closely resemble the outer appearance of its creator Prof. Hiroshi Ishiguro. The term "Geminoid" [13] is derived from the latin word "geminus" meaning twin and "-oides" meaning similarity. In contrast to humanoid robots [2] which are similarly designed to let people associate them with humans, the outer appearances of android robots such as Repliee R1 [14], Repliee Q2 [3] or Geminoid HI-1 even feature artificial skin and hair, and they are modeled to finest detail in the aim to make them indistinguishable from real humans at first sight. With these androids it is possible to pursue research in the field of "Android Science" [15], in which these special robots are seen as "a key testing ground for social, cognitive, and neuroscientific theories" [16]. The android is 140 cm tall, sits in a chair (it cannot stand) and has 50 DOFs. Its face has 13 DOFs, which gives it natural facial expressions. Figure 1 on the left side shows the Geminoid HI-1 and its real counterpart.

Figure 1. Left side: Geminoid HI-1 with its creator Hiroshi Ishiguro. **Right side**: control room for the Geminoid HI-1. Only the camera between the two monitors on the right side is used, the others five cameras are for the motion capture system (not used in this experiment).

The robot is equipped with teleoperation functionality. In this way we can avoid the current limitations in AI technologies. Figure 1 on the right side shows the teleoperation interface. Two monitors show the controlled robot and its surroundings, and microphones and a headphone are used to capture and transmit utterances. The captured sound from the environment around the robot are transmitted to the operator, and vice-versa. A webcam points the face of the operator, and its video stream is continuously analyzed for the operator's head orientation and mouth movements using the "FaceAPI" software [17]. The acquired head motion data is used to drive Geminoid's head orientation in the space and the mouth movements (opening and closing the lower jaw). The operator's voice is synchronized with the lip movements by delaying it for approximately 0.5 seconds such that the robot appears to speak by itself. Furthermore, a trained operator could manage to turn the Geminoid's head as if it were looking at a specific conversation partner. In parallel to these movements a separate software module continuously triggers small movements in Geminoid HI-1's face opening and closing its eye lids and moving its cheeks slightly up and down from time to time. The operator's mouth movements as well as the movements of the head are captured. The robot has been designed to work also with tactile and floor sensors but for this study only cameras have been used.

3. Related work

Recently, several robots have been proposed that utilize gaze for meta-communication. ROBITA turns to the specific person speaking at the moment in a group conversation. With Robovie [18] has been investigated the relationship between a robot's head orientation and its gaze in a Robot Mediated Round Table (RM-RT) experimental setup. A similar task has been addressed with Cog, but to our knowledge, none seems to address the problem using an android robot. We believe that use an android robot can give us a more detailed knowledge about the "uncanny valley" hypothesis.

4. System

This section describes the idea behind the human head detection and tracking using a network of cameras embedded in the environment surrounding the android. This is basically a slightly modified implementation of the work of [19]. With respect to the original idea, we used only cameras for the tracking system, taking advantage of the regular light conditions of the room where the robot is placed. Since there where no windows in the room, and the lighting was only provided by neon tubes, after the first calibration of the camera system the software was able to run without any variation of the camera parameters.

4.1. Distributed PF

We employ the PF [19] for tracking the human head. This algorithm estimates a posterior $p(\mathbf{X}_t|Z_t)$ with random sampling and its evaluation from likelihood $p(\mathbf{Z}_t|\mathbf{X}_t)$. The reason to use the PF is that $\mathbf{X}_t$ (object state at time t) and $\mathbf{Z}_t$ (image feature at time t) have too wide space to estimate posteriors. The PF approximate the posterior as sample set $\left\{ s_t^{(n)}, \pi_t^{(n)}, n = 1, ..., N \right\}$ where $s_t^{(n)} \in \mathbf{X}_t$ represents hypothesis of target, $\pi_t^{(n)} = p\left(\mathbf{Z}_t|\mathbf{X}_t = s_t^{(n)} \right)$ represents weight of hypothesis. The hypothesis $s_t^{(n)}$ is generated according to prior $p\left(\mathbf{X}_t|\mathbf{Z}_{t-1} \right)$; previous samples-sets invent new samples with random sampling.

A generation of hypotheses $s_t^{(n)} = (X, Y, Z)$ in 3D space is done in the same manner as PF. That is, these hypotheses are generated by random sampling according to previous sample-set $\left\{ s_{t-1}^{(n)} \pi_{t-1}^{(n)} \right\}$ with dynamic model.

We employ Gaussian G($\bullet$) for random sampling as

$$s_t^{(n)} = G\left(s_t'^{(n)} \right) \tag{1}$$

$$s_t'^{(n)} = R\left(\left\{ s_{t-1}^{(j)}, \pi_{t-1}^{(j)} \right\} \right) \tag{2}$$

where R($\bullet$) represents a function that select temporary hypothesis $s_t'^{(n)}$ from previous hypotheses $s_{t-1}^{(j)}$ by ratio of weights $\pi_{t-1}^{(j)}$, and new hypothesis $s_t^{(n)}$ is generated by Gaussian with the temporal sample $s_t'^{(n)}$ as $G\left(s_t'^{(n)} \right)$.

The algorithm allows to track multiple people generating hypotheses for multiple people as $s_{m,t}^{(n)}$, where m is the person's number. Similarly, a weight is represented as $\pi_{m,t}^{(n)}$. Then, the human head position $\mathbf{P}_{m,t}$ is computed as

$$\mathbf{P}_{m,t} = \sum_n s_{m,t}^{(n)} \pi_{m,t}^{(n)} \tag{3}$$

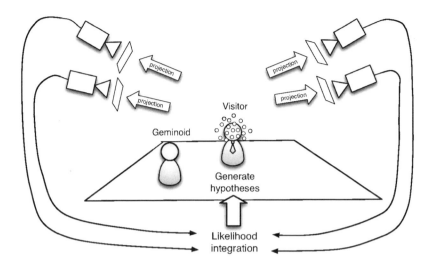

Figure 2. The distributed PF system

By repeating these steps of hypotheses generation (random sampling), 2D fitness value evaluation and 3D fitness value estimation, human head tracking is performed (Fig. 2).

4.2. Multicamera System for Head Tracking with Distributed PF

For computing the likelihood of distributed PF, all the hypotheses are projected onto 2D image captured by camera i for evaluating the 2D fitness value $\pi_{i,t}(\mathbf{a})$, where $\mathbf{a}$ means 3D position. The 2D fitness values are integrated for estimating 3D fitness values (it is weights of 3D hypothesis) $\pi_{m,t}^{(n)}$. The 3D fitness values can be calculated using the equation below,

$$\pi_{m,t}^{(n)} = \sum_{i,j,i \neq j} \pi_{i,t}(\mathbf{s}_{m,t}^{(n)}) \pi_{j,t}(\mathbf{s}_{m,t}^{(n)}) \tag{4}$$

defined in [19].

The model of human head is spheroid as shown in the left side of figure 3. The spheroid's size is l_0 and l_1 which are constant. 2D fitness is computed between the projected 3D object specified by $\mathbf{s}_{m,t}^{(n)}$ and the image features. The projected spheroid onto image place will be an ellipse as shown in the left side of figure 3 whose size can be determined by projection computation. So, a projected spheroid onto an image must have different size. The fitness is obtained by evaluating the edges (Sobel filtering) on the ellipse. Simple evaluation of edge strength on the ellipse might be affected by background edges. For improving the sensitivity to human head, the fitness is estimated by inner product between normal vector $\mathbf{N}_\mu$ of the ellipse, which is normalized, and the gradient vector of edge $\mathbf{E}_\mu$ at μth sampling point as shown in the right side of figure 3, which is not normalized. That is, the fitness is computed by the following formula:

$$\pi_{i,t}\left(\mathbf{s}_{m,t}^{(n)}\right) = \sum_\mu \mathbf{N}_\mu \bullet \mathbf{E}_\mu \tag{5}$$

$\pi_{i,t}\left(\mathbf{s}_{m,t}^{(n)}\right)$ becomes maximum when edge vector $\mathbf{E}_\mu$ and normal vector $\mathbf{N}_\mu$ have the same direction. The sampling points are illustrated in the right side of figure 3, where we will not sample around the bottom of ellipse, because this area may be located on the body (Fig. 3).

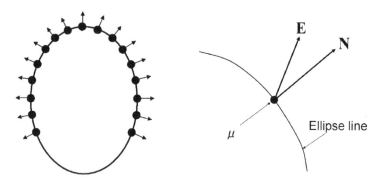

Figure 3. The normals on the ellipse on the left side and the parts of the normal on the right side.

4.3. Hardware and Software Configuration

The system implemented wants to achieve the ocular convergence on the Geminoid robot. Using a set of cameras is possible to verify a set of hypothesis generated from a PC called "master PC". In the configuration tested we prepared four cameras each one placed in one of the four corners of the Geminoid's room. Those cameras are placed at an height of around 2,5 meters from the floor, and the wide lens used cover the area in front and on the right and left side of the robot. From the computational side, the adopted configuration was composed of a total of three PC's: one "master PC", and two "slave PC". Each "slave PC" runs two instances of a developed client. Each client is connected to one of the cameras placed in the room. All the computers used are connected in a TCP/IP network configuration. We placed the origin of the coordinates system in the bottom left angle from the entrance door of the room.

The estimation of the head position of humans subjects around the robot is done in real time. Basically, a set of hypotheses is generated, and those hypotheses are broadcasted to each slave client. Then each client verifies the set of points received, and sends its answer back to the master PC, so that a new set of hypotheses can be generated.

Below, the sequence of steps is explained more in detail:

1. The master PC generates a set of points in the 3D coordinate system of the room, following a gaussian distribution in the 3D space. Each point is the center of the ellipsoid representing the estimated position of the human's head. This generation considers the contribution from the previous set of particles, or, at the startup of the system, we place the center of the points in the entrance door where the people are supposed to enter the room.

2. The set of particles generated is broadcast to all the clients connected through the wired TCP/IP network. The typical loop of tasks for a client once a set of points has been received is:
   - A projection of all the points in the received set from 3D coordinate system to the 2D coordinate system of the current camera;

- An edge detection of the current frame using the Sobel filtering. The resulting image only shows the edges of objects and persons the scene.
- Around each 2D projected point an ellipse is built, according to parameters $l1$ and $l2$ chosen, so that the ellipse represents the human's head proportions.
- a 2D fitness value for the current ellipse is computed. The fitness is estimated by inner product between the current normal vector of the ellipse, and the μth sampling point as shown in (5).

3. Each client sends back to the "master PC" the 2D fitness values obtained for each ellipse, and those values are integrated for estimating 3D fitness values according to the formula in (4). The point with the highest 3D fitness value is used as center for the generation of the new set of 3D points with the gaussian distribution.

By iterating this sequence of steps, real time tracking of the human head is performed.

5. Expected Results and Improvements in the Control System

The solution previously shown adds an efficient perceptional function to the human-like appearance of the android, which is useful for communicating through the typical human communication channels. Using the cameras placed in the four corners of the room is possible to cover the area in front of the robot. In this way we can obtain information about the position of the human subject when someone is very near in front of the robot (short range interaction) or when someone is moving in the room (long range interaction). Figure 4 shows the map of the room and pictures of the setup.

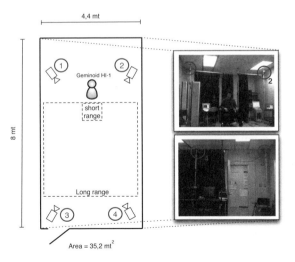

Figure 4. On the **left side**: map of the Geminoid room from the top showing the cameras and approximately the two ranges of interaction, the short one and the long one. On the **right side**: pictures of the setup.

5.1. Short Range Interaction with the Android Compared to Humans

A possible way to evaluate the human-robot interaction would be to couple non-conscious human responses together with a complementary source of information such as a questionnaire. The gaze behavior in the human-robot interaction can later be compared to the gaze behavior in human-human interaction, which has been widely studied in psychology and in cognitive sciences. A typical behavior is to establish an eye contact looking into the interlocutor's right eye with the right eye. This contact is often lost, especially when one of the conversational partners is thinking. This behavior has been explained by three main theories:

Arousal reduction theory: during a face to face conversation, arousal is highest when a person makes eye contact. As a natural response, we tend to break eye contact to reduce our arousal and concentrate on the communication [20].

The different cortical activation hypothesis: according to this theory, the brain activation caused by thinking tasks leads individuals to move their gaze away from the central visual field [21].

The social signal theory: this theory gives the meaning of social signal to gaze behavior, so we break eye contact to inform others that we are thinking.

In order to resemble the human behavior in a face-to-face conversation, the android should be able to establish, maintain, break and recover an eye contact with his human conversational partner.

Our hypothesis is that if we allow the Geminoid to produce the same kinds of eye movements following the same social rules of humans, subjects will consider the robotic interlocutor as if it were a person, or at least a social agent. We believe that eye movements act as signals about whether the subject is, for example, thinking or listening, and an android must use this kind of non-verbal communication in order to increase its human-likeness.

A possible way to examine whether or not our method could make humans feel that they made eye contact with the robot is to ask some subjects to turn their head in the direction of the android, make an eye contact with the robot, and then give a subjective value from 1 (no perception of eye contact with the robot at all) to 5 (real perception of eye contact with the robot) in the three following scenarios:

- The robot's head is moving with random idle movements. When it detects a human in front of it, it stops moving and establishes an eye contact, then smiles.
- The robot's head is not moving. When it detects a human in front of it, it smiles.
- The robot's head is moving with random idle movements. When it detects a human in front of it, it stops moving and establishes an eye contact without any change in the facial expression.

By observing the differences between the average values in each of the three conditions we can evaluate the effectiveness of the eye contact in an android system integrated with a sensor network.

5.2. Long Range Interaction with the Android Compared to Humans

In [22] has been observed that in a scenario consisting of a quietly sitting person (subject B) and another person free to act in a 2.0 m x 2.0 m area (subject A), the typical behaviors of B were to:

- look toward the same direction that A is looking at;
- look toward subject A a few times with only eye movements and as few body movements as possible;
- look at A a few times;
- look toward the front so as not to see subject A;
- look down to the ground;
- keep looking at subject A (following him).

A possible way to evaluate the subjective human-like nature in the eye contact with an android would be to ask some subjects to move freely around the robot and then collect their subjective values from 1 (no perception of eye contact with the robot at all) to 5 (real perception of eye contact with the robot) in the three following scenarios:

- The robot is moving with random idle movements. When it detects a human, it stops moving and establishes an eye contact, then smiles.
- The robot is not moving. When it detects a human, it smiles.
- The robot is moving with random idle movements. When it detects a human, it stops moving and establishes an eye contact without any change in the facial expression.

A study of the average of the collected results in each condition should be conducted.

In order to achieve a human-like nature in android communication, it is necessary to implement abilities equivalent to those observed from humans. Results from previous experiments suggest that reactions for a human-like presence are efficient for achieving the subjective human-like nature in android communication, and the minimum required abilities to exercise and perceive for achieving a human-like nature, like a boundary condition of natural interaction, should indicate the principles of natural communication. The system described in this paper will allow us to tackle issues focusing on appearance and perception, although such studies have not started yet. The system described can be a test bed for cognitive science, and some research approaches in cognitive sciences have used robots for experiments.

6. Conclusions and Future Works

This paper proposed a hypothesis for the improvement of the human likeness of an android by establishing, breaking, and recovering the eye contact with a human interlocutor.

Those social signals can be used in both face-to-face interactions and long range interactions, and they can reinforce our expectation of androids as a responsive agent.

However, this study is only preliminary and a more comprehensive one is required to contribute to the study of android science and human nature. Our next work will include further investigation on the effect of the gaze for an android in order to confirm the psychological effects.

References

[1]   Nishio, S., Ishiguro, H., (2011). Attitude change induced by different appearances of interaction agents. International Journal of Machine Consciousness Vol. 3, No. 1 (2011) 115-126, World Scientific Publishing Company, DOI: 10.1142/S1793843010000637.

[2]   Kanda, T., Hirano, T., Eaton, D., and Ishiguro, H. (2004). Interactive robots as social partners and peer tutors for children: A field trial. Human-Computer Interaction, 19(1-2):61-84

[3]   M. Shimada, T. Minato, S. Itakura, and H. Ishiguro. Evaluation of android using unconscious recognition. In Proceedings of the IEEE-RAS International Conference on Humanoid Robots, pages 157-162. 2006

[4]   Nishio, S., Ishiguro, H., & Hagita, N. (2007). Geminoid: Teleoperated Android of an Existing Person. In Humanoid Robots, New Developments (pp. 343-352). I-Tech.

[5]   H. Morishita, K. Watanabe, T. Kuroiwa, T. Mori, and T. Sato. Development of robotic kitchen counter: A kitchen counter equipped with sensors and actuator for action-adapted and personally-fit assistance. In Proceedings of the 2003 IEEE/RSJ International Conference on Intelligent Robots and Systems, pages 1839–1844, 2003.

[6]   T. Mori, H. Noguchi, and T. Sato. Daily life experience reservoir and epitomization with sensing room. In Proceedings of Workshop on Network Robot Systems: Toward Intelligent Robotic Systems Integrated with Environments, 2005.

[7]   H. Ishiguro. Distributed vision system: A perceptual information infrastructure for robot navigation. International Joint Conference on Artificial Intelligence (IJCAI-97), pages 36–41, 1997.

[8]   Takano, E.; Chikaraishi, T.; Matsumoto, Y.; Nakamura, Y.; Ishiguro, H.; Sugamoto, K.; , "Psychological effects on interpersonal communication by bystander android using motions based on human-like needs," Intelligent Robots and Systems, 2009. IROS 2009. IEEE/RSJ International Conference on , vol., no., pp.3721-3726, 10-15 Oct. 2009.

[9]   Bruce, A.; Nourbakhsh, I.; Simmons, R.; , "The role of expressiveness and attention in human-robot interaction," Robotics and Automation, 2002. Proceedings. ICRA '02. IEEE International Conference on , vol.4, no., pp. 4138- 4142 vol.4, 2002 doi: 10.1109/ROBOT.2002.1014396

[10] Matsusaka, Yosuke / Tojo, Tsuyoshi / Kubota, Sentaro / Furukawa, Kenji / Tamiya, Daisuke / Hayata, Keisuke / Nakano, Yuichiro / Kobayashi, Tetsunori (1999): "Multi-person conversation via multi-modal interface - a robot who communicate with multi-user -", In EUROSPEECH'99, 1723-1726.

[11] Kanda, T.; Ishiguro, H.; Ono, T.; Imai, M.; Nakatsu, R.; , "Development and evaluation of an interactive humanoid robot "Robovie"," Robotics and Automation, 2002. Proceedings. ICRA '02. IEEE International Conference on , vol.2, no., pp. 1848- 1855 vol.2, 2002 doi: 10.1109/ROBOT.2002.1014810

[12] Rodney A. Brooks, Cynthia Breazeal, Matthew Marjanović, Brian Scassellati, and Matthew M. Williamson. 1999. The cog project: building a humanoid robot. In Computation for metaphors, analogy, and agents, Chrystopher L. Nehaniv (Ed.). Lecture Notes In Computer Science, Vol. 1562. Springer-Verlag, Berlin, Heidelberg 52-87.

[13] Becker-Asano, C., Ogawa, K., Nishio, S. and Ishiguro, H., Exploring the uncanny valley with Geminoid HI-1 in a real-world application, IADIS Intl. Conf. Interfaces and Human Computer Interaction, pp. 121-128, 2010.

[14] Minato, T., Shimada, M., Ishiguro, H., & Itakura, S. (2004). Development of an Android Robot for Studying Human-Robot Interaction. Innovations in Applied Artificial Intelligence, (pp. 424-434).

[15] Ishiguro, H. (2005). Android Science: Toward a new cross-interdisciplinary framework. Proc. of the CogSci 2005 Workshop "Toward Social Mechanisms of Android Science", (pp. 1-6). Stresa, Italy.

[16] MacDorman, K. F., & Ishiguro, H. (2006). The uncanny advantage of using androids in cognitive and social science research. Interaction Studies , 297-337.

[17] Seeing Machines. (n.d.). Retrieved 05 07, 2010, from FaceAPI product information: http://www.seeingmachines.com/product/faceapi/

[18] Imai, M.; Kanda, T.; Ono, T.; Ishiguro, H.; Mase, K.; , "Robot mediated round table: Analysis of the effect of robot's gaze," Robot and Human Interactive Communication, 2002. Proceedings. 11th IEEE International Workshop on , vol., no., pp. 411- 416, 2002.

[19] Yusuke Matsumoto, Toshikazu Wada, Shuichi Nishio, Takehiro Miyashita, and Norihiro Hagita. Scalable and Robust Multi-people Head Tracking by Combining Distributed Multiple Sensors. Intelligent Service Robotics, 3(1), 2010.

[20] Argyle M, Cook M. Gaze and Mutual Gaze. Cambridge University Press; Cambridge: 1976

[21]   Previc FH, Murphy SJ. Vertical eye movements during mental tasks: A reexamination and hypothesis. Percept. Motor skills. 1997;84:835-847.

[22]   Chikaraishi, T.; Minato, T.; Ishiguro, H.; , "Development of an android system integrated with sensor networks," Intelligent Robots and Systems, 2008. IROS 2008. IEEE/RSJ International Conference on , vol., no., pp.326-333, 22-26 Sept. 2008

38

Biologically Inspired Cognitive Architectures 2011
A.V. Samsonovich and K.R. Jóhannsdóttir (Eds.)
IOS Press, 2011
© *2011 The authors and IOS Press. All rights reserved.*
doi:10.3233/978-1-60750-959-2-38

Towards a Biologically-Inspired Model for Relational Mapping Using Spiking Neurons

Paul Biancaniello[a,1], David Rosenbluth[a,1], Tom Szumowski[a,1], John Darvill[a],
Nick Hinnerschitz[a], John Hummel[b], and Stefan Mihalas[c]
[a] *Lockheed Martin Advanced Technology Labortories*
[b] *University of Illinois Urbana Champaign*
[c] *Johns Hopkins University*

Abstract. Relational mapping, a cognitive sub-process of relational reasoning, plays a critical role in identifying similarities between abstract constructs. This paper discusses an initial endeavor in developing a biologically-inspired spiking neuron model that performs relational mapping in a similar functional manner to existing cognitive models founded in neuroscience. Using spiking neurons provides a capability to portray neural dynamics that naturally lead to notions of critical relational mapping sub-functions such as binding by synchrony. The model, although still in progress, is a step in the direction of progressing cognitive concepts down to an individual spiking neuron level.

Keywords. relational reasoning, spiking neuron, simulation

1. Introduction

Relational reasoning is a commonplace and arguably crucial capability in human intelligence. Functionally, it is decomposable into five algorithmic processes: analog retrieval, relational mapping, mapping assessment, analogical inference, and schema induction. This paper focuses on relational mapping, the ability to identify similarities between different constructs based on relational structure. Using the existing neuro-computational model Learning and Inference with Schemas and Analogies (LISA) [1] as a conceptual scaffold, we implemented the beginnings of a spiking neuron model. We believe our model of relational mapping, achieved through the interactive dynamics of populations of neurons, leads to a more accurate reflection of neural computation than models that do not capture the details of these dynamics. By accurately modeling dynamics, such as binding by synchrony, spiking models allow us to study the effects of dynamics on the constraints and limitations of neural computation.

The paper first describes relational mapping in the context of geospatial analysis. A description of the spiking model follows along with its objectives in modeling binding by synchrony. We then discuss the significance of simulation results of a geospatial scenario derived from the spiking neuron network modeled in the Event-Related Neural Simulation Tool (ERNST) [3,4].

---

[1] Corresponding Authors.

2. A Geospatial Example of Relational Mapping

Consider an example geospatial scene consisting of buildings and water features. The scene can also be represented as a collection of interrelated propositions that define the objects, features, and relationships. In Figure 1, the left image represents an input scene containing an unidentified facility. The right image depicts a memory of a similar past facility. When interpreting the scene, one develops a representation based on the objects and their relationships. In this case, objects include an abstract representation of buildings (B1, B3) and lakes (L1). Relationships (roles) between objects are also described by an abstract representation of relative geospatial distance (proximal_to, distant_from). Relational mapping involves associating the input with similar instances in memory (right) using their underlying relational structure.

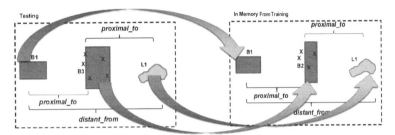

Figure 1. An example of an input scene (left) and an in-memory scene (right) indicates mappings of both the objects in the scene and their corresponding relationships.

The distinct objects, roles, and relationships inherent in a geospatial scene allow for a representation in the form of a collection of interrelated propositions. Figure 2 defines the analogs for both the input and the in-memory scenes that were used in simulation. Here objects (circles) and their roles (triangles) are bound together into sub-propositions (boxes) which are then combined into propositional units (ovals) that represent the relational structures within a scene (e.g., proximal_to(B1,B3) and distant_from(B1,L1). The tree structure of a LISA analog captures all of the interrelationships between objects and their roles in a scene.

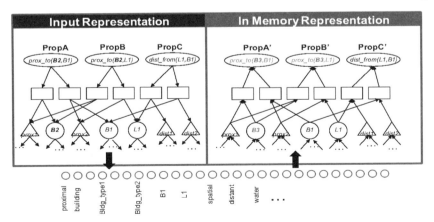

Figure 2. Analog representation for both the input scene and the in-memory scene. The propositions are interrelated through shared connections within the semantic units that define features of corresponding objects and roles. A further description of the canonical analogy "tree" structure is available in [1] and [5].

3. Spiking Neuron Model of Relational Mapping

The model's objective is to map the dynamics enabled through a spiking neuron network that lead to relational mapping results similar to those produced by the LISA algorithm for relational reasoning described in [1]. In LISA, if an object unit (circle) and a role unit (triangle) are bound together by a sub-propositional unit (box), then these units will fire in synchrony with one another and out of synchrony with other objects, roles, and sub-propositions [1]. This behavior is an element of the core mechanism to relational mapping called "binding by synchrony." There is neurophysiological evidence for binding by synchrony in higher-level frontal cortex processing [4] and hippocampal episodic storage [6]. Figure 3 indicates where in the network the biological behaviors from Table 1 occur to achieve binding by synchrony.

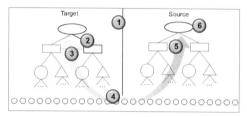

Figure 3. Shows how an input signal flows from a target analog to a source analog. Each numbered bullet indicates where a biologically inspired behavior exists in LISA and is a requirement in the spiking neuron model.

Table 1. Summary of biologically inspired structure and dynamics involved in modeling relational mapping. The numbers associate with those listed in Figure 3.

#	Biologically Inspired Behavior
1	Activations from target propositions propagate through the network up to similar source propositions.
2	Activating a target proposition creates asynchrony defined as alternating oscillation of bursts in sub-propositions (SPs) about the 40-Hz gamma range [1]. A burst is considered a sequence of consistent spiking activity.
3	Lateral inhibition exists across all same-type units within an analog. A unit is defined as a proposition, sub-proposition, object, or role. Semantic units do not laterally inhibit.
4	Semantic units act as neural populations that link target and source analogs through shared features
5	Bottom up synchronous activations from the source objects and roles cause alternating and oscillatory bursts in source sub-propositions.
6	Similar source propositions strongly activate if and only if their corresponding sub-propositions are experiencing burst-synchrony. This is an example of binding by synchrony.

The spiking neuron implementation of LISA's relational mapping utilizes several different features in order to implement the relational mapping algorithm. Figure 4 illustrates each feature along with the model's connections.

Spiking Neuron Populations: Each proposition, sub-proposition, object, role, and semantic unit consists of a population of general integrate and fire neurons. Representing units as a population provides a benefit of generating soft outputs that serve as indicators for mapping strengths in a later model.

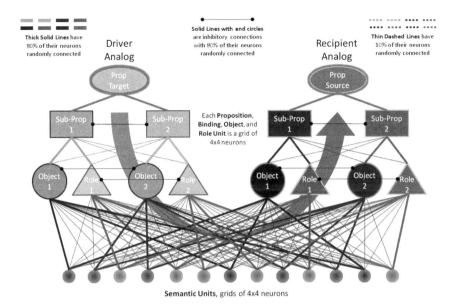

Figure 4. An overview of the spiking model's connectivity using two analogs (*target* and *source*) that share semantic units. A pool of neurons represents each unit with probabilistic interconnections. The underlying semantic features link the target and source in order to allow mapping. Lastly, lateral inhibition permits the synchrony dynamics required to activate propositions at the highest level.

Probabilistic Connections: All connections between neuron populations are probabilistic. If two units are bound together within an analog, then the connections between the neurons in those units are bidirectional and randomly distributed, and strongly connected with a pair-wise probability of 80%. Otherwise the units are weakly connected with a probability of 10%. For example, building "B1" may be bound strongly to the semantic unit "building" but poorly bounded to others such as "water feature" that instead better binds to the lake.

Shared Semantic Unit Space: All analogs within the spiking model share semantic units. This shared semantic space is the sole means of neuron populations connecting across analogs. Multiple (similar) analogs can be activated by exciting a given set of semantic units. Similarly, activating the proposition units in one analog will excite similar analogs via their shared semantic units.

Lateral Inhibition driving a Winner Take All (WTA) Network: The network includes lateral inhibition across same-type units. This is critical to maintain the synchrony required to create a "winner-take-all" type network at the proposition level. Units of the same type (propositions, sub-propositions, objects, and roles) *within a given analog* inhibit each other whereas units of the same type *across different analogs* do not. Inhibitory connections between these units are also bidirectional and randomly distributed, with a pair-wise probability of 80%. These inhibitory connections between units cause a single proposition to win for a particular excitation at the input.

4. Experiment Results

We developed a spiking neuron network representing the geospatial scenario depicted as an analogical structure in Figure 2. We used the ERNST simulator to build and simulate the network. ERNST provides an efficient means of simulating large spiking networks through its ability to analytically compute subthreshold dynamics [5]. Figure 5 illustrates the resulting spike patterns whereby the neuron numbers associate with the corresponding numbers in the analogs. The model executed for three simulated seconds. One second was spent driving each proposition using a spike train with Poission statistics and a mean rate 500Hz: *proximal_to(B2,B1), proximal_to(B2,L1),* and *distant_from(B1,L1).* Neurons 4-6 depict the resulting source proposition activations. Although all three-source propositions are actively firing, only one proposition tends to "win" as indicated by an increased firing rate. Each driven target proposition resulted in a correct mapping to the most active source proposition. Binding by synchrony is observed when a proposition is strongly activated when the corresponding SPs are bursting out of phase.

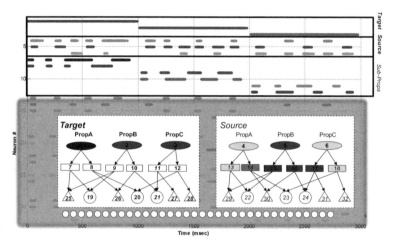

Figure 5. The spike pattern results for simulating the example geospatial scenario. In the first three sample neurons, the input drives first PropA (*i.e. prox_to(B2,B1)*) from 0ms to 1000ms. It then drives PropB from 1000ms to 2000ms, and PropC from 2000ms to 3000ms. The second black box indicates the source proposition spiking activity indicating a winner at each segment. The third box shows the expected synchrony along corresponding source SPs. The source and target analogies share a common semantic space that allow for this binding. Spike patterns for anything below SPs are in the background to maintain clarity.

5. Future Considerations

In the current model, mapping is only assessed by measuring relative spike activities between proposition pairs. It lacks a quantitative and analytical method for measuring similarity between analogs containing multiple propositions. The LISA algorithm performs this more complex mapping and determines the quality computing two measures of similarity: matches out of place (MOPs) and matches in place (MIPs) [5]. We identified, but have not yet implemented, approaches for each in a spiking neuron environment. MOPs require an external assessment of the underlying spiking network structure. MIPs however are more challenging and require extensions to the spiking model as it involves dynamically updating the strength of direct mapping connecting between corresponding units in the target and source analogies.

We are also considering alternate representations for the analog units. Rather than a population of neurons representing each unit, we intend to investigate representing all units of the same type (e.g. roles) as a single population in a spiking attractor network. In this case, a unique attractor state would represent each individual role.

6. Conclusions

The presented simulation demonstrates a start to modeling relational mapping in a spiking neuron network using the ERNST simulator. The function and dynamics resemble behaviors intrinsic in the LISA algorithm and evident in neurophysiology. The results exhibit a key behavior in relational mapping, binding by synchrony, and correctly associate target and source propositions. However, much work lies ahead in extending the model's scale and capabilities. We intend to evaluate more complicated geospatial scenes involving dozens of propositions. We also intend to develop an analytical method for assessing the quality of similarity using an approach analogous to LISA's MIPs and MOPs.

Acknowledgements

Supported by the Intelligence Advanced Research Projects Activity (IARPA) via Department of the Interior (DOI) contract number D10PC20022. The U.S. Government is authorized to reproduce and distribute reprints for Governmental purposes notwithstanding any copyright annotation thereon. The views and conclusions contained hereon are those of the authors and should not be interpreted as necessarily representing the official policies or endorsements, either expressed or implied, of IARPA, DOI, or the U.S. Government.

The simulations and results described in this paper were developed using the Event Related Neuronal Simulation Tool (ERNST), created at Johns Hopkins University, http://ernst.mb.jhu.edu.

References

[1]   Hummel, J.E. & Holyoak, K.J. (2005). Relational reasoning in a neurally-plausible cognitive architecture. Current Directions in Psychological Science, 14, 153-157.
[2]   Mihalas S. & Niebur E. (2009). A generalized linear integrate-and-fire neural model produces diverse spiking behaviors. Neural Comput. 21, 704-718. doi: 10.1162/neco.2008.12-07-680.
[3]   Mihalas, S., Dong, Y., & Niebur E. (2010). Event-Related Neural Simulation Tool - Algorithms [Software]. Maryland: Johns Hopkins University. Available from http://ernst.mb.jhu.edu/
[4]   Shastri, L. (1997). A model of rapid memory formation in the hippocampal system. In M. G. Shafto & P. Langley (Eds.), Proceedings of the 19th Annual Conference of the Cognitive Science Society (pp. 680-685). Hillsdale, NJ: Erlbaum.
[5]   Taylor, E.G. & Hummel, J.E. (2009) Finding similarity in a model of relational reasoning. Cognitive Systems Research, 10, 229-239.
[6]   Vaadia, E., Haalman, I., Abeles, M., Bergman, H., Prut, Y., Slovin, H., & Aertsen, A. (1995, February 9). Dynamics of neuronal interactions in monkey cortex in relation to behavioural events. Nature, 373, 515-518.

Biologically Inspired Cognitive Architectures 2011
A.V. Samsonovich and K.R. Jóhannsdóttir (Eds.)
IOS Press, 2011
© 2011 The authors and IOS Press. All rights reserved.
doi:10.3233/978-1-60750-959-2-44

Rapid Prototyping of a Cognitive System for Pediatric Telephone Triage Tutoring

Mihai BOICU[a,1]

[a]*Learning Agents Center, George Mason University, Fairfax, VA, USA*

Abstract. This paper presents the development of a prototype cognitive system for tutoring pediatric telephone triage to resident doctors. The cognitive system is built through a spiral development methodology by using the Disciple learning agent shell. This illustrates solutions to challenges encountered in developing cognitive systems in new domains with a low budget, including prioritizing the development, reuse of general purpose modules, and experimentation-driven development.

Keywords. Cognitive System, Pediatric Telephone Triage, Learning Agent Shell, Spiral Development, Low Budget System Development.

1. Building Cognitive Systems

Acquiring, preserving, applying, and transmitting domain expertise are among the most difficult challenges faced by the cognitive systems. For many years we have developed a cognitive multi-agent shell that allows rapid development and easy maintenance of knowledge-based problem solving and decision making assistants capable to capture, use, preserve and transfer to other users, domain expertise which currently takes years to establish, is generally lost when an expert leaves, and is costly to replace. The classical approach to building an expert knowledge-based system is long, difficult and error-prone [1][2]. In this approach a knowledge engineer attempts to understand the reasoning of the expert, identifies general reasoning rules, codifies them in the representation language of the system, and verifies them with the expert and by testing the system. Moreover, after the system is build, the maintenance process is also difficult and time-consuming, requiring the same types of operations to be performed and a global knowledge base validation to take place.

In the Learning Agent Center of George Mason University we have researched a different approach, based on a multi-agent cognitive system shell, called Disciple, that allows the development of cognitive systems that are capable to learn directly from an expert who can teach it in a way that is similar to how the expert would teach a student or a new collaborator, through examples and explanations [3][4][5]. We have used successive versions of the Disciple learning agent shell to develop cognitive agents in many domains, including: intelligence analysis [6][7], evidence-based reasoning [8], military [9], emergency response [10], and education. While requiring less effort than the traditional approach, the development of these cognitive systems still required important research and development resources. In this paper we will discuss the

---

[1] Corresponding Author: Mihai Boicu, Learning Agents Center, George Mason University, MSN 6B3, 4400 University Dr., Fairfax, VA 22030, USA. (703) 993-1591. mboicu@gmu.edu.

approach followed to adapt the technology in a new application domain, but using a very low budget (around 50K). After briefly describing the application domain, we will describe the approach followed, the current prototype cognitive system, and the planned experimentation. We will conclude with lessons learned and some general principles on applying this approach to new domains.

2. Tutoring Residents in Pediatric Telephone Triage

Pediatric Telephone Triage consists in the management of children's health concerns through telephone interaction with the children's caretakers. The main goals of the telephone triage are to provide correct, safe and cost-effective immediate disposition (e.g. go to the emergency room), and to educate the caretakers (e.g. what symptoms to watch and report). The education of the resident and junior doctors in pediatric telephone triage is very important, as many of the pediatric residents will become part of pediatric practices where they will need to offer pediatric telephone triage on a weekly basis. Moreover, the telephone triage is a special type of medical decision-making which requires not only medical skills, but also communication skills, and the capacity to work under stressful conditions with uncertain information. "Recognizing the importance of pediatric telephone triage for resident and junior doctors, the Pediatric Residency Review Committee (RRC) of Inova Fairfax Hospital for Children (IFHC), which establishes the requirements for specialty training in Pediatrics, requires Programs to train future primary care pediatricians in these skills. However, the opportunities to achieve this training within the scope of the program are currently limited by several factors, including (a) resident work hour limitations; (b) language barriers, particularly for the Medicaid population, which is predominantly Spanish-speaking; and (c) the necessity for the resident and faculty to be proximate to allow timely supervision of the resident's delivered advice [11]."

We have investigated the current training solution for pediatric telephone triage which is primary based on written educational materials, developed protocols, and supervised training. In particular, the pediatric telephone triage protocols created by Dr. Barton D. Schmitt [12] are widely used and integrated in various software systems. However, we have not found any software simulator or tutoring system that simulates the pediatric telephone triage process or tutors students in the triage decision making process.

We have also investigated the current software systems for helping nurses to perform pediatric telephone triage. They are based on the existing triage protocols, either allowing the selection and display of the applicable protocols, or guiding the nurse trough the protocols and registering the answers provided (usually Yes/No answers). These protocols are generally incorporated in a call center software, such as: the Epic system developed by Epic Systems Corporation [13], the Sharp Focus Personal Health Management System developed by HealthLine Systems Inc. [14], and the Centaurus Call Center Software [15]. Moreover, the training associated with these systems relates to their operation and not to the underlying decision-making process involved in pediatric triage. These technological solutions are good for guiding a nurse in real-time triage. However, they are neither usable for training resident about how to perform the triage, nor they are directly usable by patients.

3. PTT-Tutor: A Cognitive Assistant for Pediatric Telephone Triage

Our main goal is to research and develop a cognitive system for training residents in performing safe and cost-effective pediatric telephone triage, called PTT-Tutor. The envisioned system is the anytime expert available to train the resident by presenting automatically generated telephone triage scenarios and pursuing a tutoring dialog with the resident on various aspects related to the presented scenario (e.g. appropriate line of questioning, correct differential diagnosis, safe triage decision and disposition). The PTT-Tutor reuses the powerful problem solving, learning, and tutoring capabilities of the Disciple Learning Agent Shell, as shown in the Figure 1.

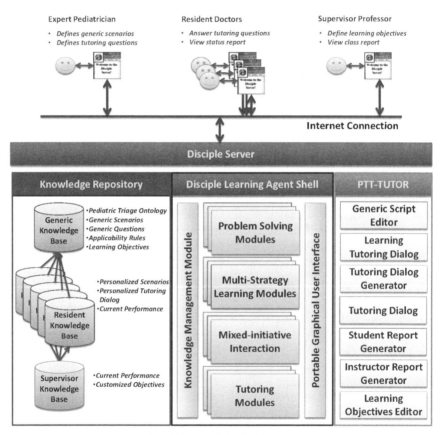

Figure 1. PTT-Tutor Architecture

The PTT-Tutor has three main types of users. First, pediatricians with experience in pediatric telephone triage define generic scenarios and teach the system how to conduct the tutoring dialog. Two dedicated modules facilitate these operations: the generic scenario editor and the tutoring dialog learner. Next, resident doctors interact with the PTT-Tutor to be trained in pediatric telephone triage. The tutor automatically generates a pediatric telephone triage scenario based on a generic scenario. The generic scenario is selected based on the student model by taking into account what scenarios have already been performed and when, the current student score on different objectives, and the objectives addressed by the current scenario. Then the resident doctor interacts with the tutor. The tutor presents the scenario, in stages, and asks various questions after each stage. The resident receives feedback to her answers and is able to express her disagreement with the tutor. The resident may see anytime how she meets the learning objectives. The last type of user is the residents' supervising professor. She defines the learning objectives for the students and provides weights and levels of accomplishment. She also reviews students' activity and their feedback. The student feedback is also used by the expert pediatrician to improve and refine the tutoring dialog.

4. Low Budget Research and Development

The type of cognitive system briefly described above requires several complex tasks to be performed: software development for the customized modules of the PTT-Tutor, knowledge engineering of the knowledge repository, the scenarios and the tutoring dialogs, defining and weighting learning objectives, and performing an experiment. Most of these tasks require expert knowledge and skills. The main constraint in the development of the tutor is a low budget (50K). To overcome it we have identified several principles for the research and development of a cognitive system with a low budget that will be presented below. While some of these principles were employed from the very beginning, others have been identified through successes or failures during the development process.

Use of a powerful shell. . The reuse of the general knowledge management, problem solving, learning and tutoring capabilities the Disciple Learning Agent Shell was a primary factor in achieving rapid prototyping of the PTT Tutor.

Selecting a single most relevant claim to be demonstrated. While many aspects of the developed system need to be evaluated, we decided to concentrate on a single, most relevant aspect, that the use of the PTT-Tutor increases the competence of residents in performing pediatric telephone triage, as compared to the current educational practice, on the following dimensions: completeness of patient inquiry; avoidance of unnecessary questions; accuracy of the information extracted from parent; and correctness of the triage decision.

Early design of the claim-testing experiment. To better guide the initial development we have decided on the main aspects of the experimentation early. Moreover, we have revisited the experimentation design periodically, and updated it to better fit the developed system.

Spiral Development. While all the customized modules of the PTT-Tutor are needed for a full scale deployment of the system, only two are essential for performing the designed experiment, the tutoring dialog generator, and tutoring dialog execution module. Therefore, the first development cycle focused on these two modules, while reusing the generic Disciple shell modules for other operations, or simulating them. Therefore, in the first phase, the PTT-Tutor will train residents to effectively perform telephone triage via case studies with interactive feedback. In the second phase, it will allow personalized reporting to the residents' instructor. In the third phase, it will include customizable tools for telephone triage scenario elicitation and tutoring sessions learning.

Early prototyping. The use of the Disciple shell allowed the rapid development of an initial prototype that led to the early identification of several difficult to develop features and replacing them with more realistic ones.

Avoiding fancy features in the initial implementation. The features of the final system were grouped into three categories: absolutely necessary (e.g. perform a tutoring dialog), needed but replaceable (e.g. viewing the current status may be replaced with a simple HTML report), desired in future versions (e.g. available audio dialog). In the initial development cycle one should focus on the absolutely necessary features and add more fancy features gradually, based on the user's feedback.

5. Design of the Evaluation and Analysis

The evaluation will be performed with the IFHC Pediatric residents who have their continuity clinics at the INOVA Cares Clinic for Children (ICCC). ICCC provides general pediatric care and medical homes to underserved infants and children in Northern Virginia, receiving over 20,000 visits in 2008. This practice provides primary care medical services to infants, children and adolescents from a broad spectrum of ethnicities and cultures. Approximately 85% of the patients are Medicaid-eligible. More than 70% of the patients are first or second generation immigrants [11].

We anticipate that around 30 residents will participate in the experiment. They will be randomly divided in two equal size groups: a test group and a control group. Residents will be asked to answer 15-20 general triage questions prior to interacting with the PTT-Tutor. Then, the test group will be tutored through 25 interactions with the PTT-Tutor. Both the control group and the training group will perform the current curriculum training. At the end of training both groups will be tested again with 15-20 general triage questions.

This pilot study is specifically designed to collect experimental data for testing the main hypothesis that the use of PTT-Tutor increases the competence of residents in performing pediatric telephone triage, as compared to the current educational setting.

We will use appropriate statistical methods, based on the group size, to determine whether the use of the system has improved residents' competence. We will analyze the subjective evaluations by the faculty and the residents involved in the test group. While initially this experiment may not have statistical relevance, because of the limited number of residents involved, it will be a comprehensive test of our approach and the PTT-Tutor. As the number of residents participating in the experiment will increase, we will create a 2x2 quasi-experimental factorial design to analyze the data by 2x2 ANOVA test. The F tests performed on multiple effects will reveal whether there is an improvement in residents achievement caused by one of the considered factors. If the overall effects are significant, follow-on tests will be conducted to evaluate main effects or interaction comparisons. Eta effect sizes will be computed. We will also estimate the costs and the savings for large scale utilization of such systems.

6. Conclusion and Future Research

Positive findings will lead to the acceptance of the proposed PTT-Tutor for pediatric triage education as a health care technological innovation, to be implemented for wide-spread use by junior nurses, doctors and students. In particular, we would like to follow this project with: (a) the development of a commercial-strength learning agent and associated knowledge base; (b) the experimental use by students and junior medical personnel, in conjunction with several educational and resident training institutions; (c) the application of the learning agent across U.S.; (d) accumulating evidence for the usefulness of this type of health care innovation across the entire health care spectrum.

7. Acknowledgements

This research is performed in collaboration with Dr. Fred Garner, MD, an expert pediatrician who is the primary subject matter expert developing the case studies and tutoring scenarios, and Dr. Kathleen Donnelly, MD, the Director of the Pediatric Residency Program and Vice Chair for Education at Inova Fairfax Hospital for Children. The research is supported by a Mason-Inova grant. The development of the Disciple Learning Agent Shell was performed in the Learning Agents Center with support from several agencies, including NGA and DOD.

8. References

[1] Buchanan, B.G., and Wilkins, D.C. (eds.), Readings in Knowledge Acquisition and Learning: Automating the Construction and Improvement of Expert Systems, Morgan Kaufmann, San Mateo, CA, 1993.
[2] Tecuci G. and Kodratoff Y. (eds.), Machine Learning and Knowledge Acquisition: Integrated Approaches, Academic Press, 1995.
[3] Tecuci G., "DISCIPLE: A Theory, Methodology and System for Learning Expert Knowledge," 197 pages, Thése de Docteur en Science, University of Paris-South, July 1988, (in English).
[4] Tecuci G. (with contributions from the LALAB members Dybala T., Hieb M., Keeling H., Wright K., Loustaunau P., Hille D., Lee S.W.), "BUILDING INTELLIGENT AGENTS: An Apprenticeship Multistrategy Learning Theory, Methodology, Tool and Case Studies", San Diego: Academic Press, 320 pages, 1998. ISBN:0126851255.
[5] Mihai Boicu, Modeling and Learning with Incomplete Knowledge, PhD Thesis in Information Technology, Learning Agents Laboratory, School of Information Technology and Engineering, George Mason University, 2002.
[6] Tecuci, G., Schum, D., Boicu, M., Marcu, D., Hamilton, B., Intelligence Analysis as Agent-Assisted Discovery of Evidence, Hypotheses and Arguments, in Phillips-Wren, G., Jain, L.C., Nakamatsu, K., Howlett, R.J. (eds.), Advances in Intelligent Decision Technologies, SIST 4, pp. 1-10, Springer-Verlag Berlin Heidelberg, 2010.
[7] Tecuci, G., Schum, D., Boicu, M., Marcu, D., Hamilton, B., Wible, B., Teaching Intelligence Analysis with TIACRITIS, American Intelligence Journal, Vol. 28, No. 2, December 2010.
[8] Schum D., Tecuci G., Boicu M., Analyzing Evidence and Its Chain of Custody: A Mixed-Initiative Computational Approach, International Journal of Intelligence and CounterIntelligence, Volume 22, Issue 2, pp. 298-319, 2009. Author Posting. © Taylor & Francis Group LLC, 2009.
[9] Tecuci G., Boicu M., and Comello J. (with contributions from Marcu D., Boicu C., Barbulescu M., Le V., Cleckner W.), Agent-Assisted Center of Gravity Analysis, CD with Disciple-COG and Lecture Notes used in courses at the US Army War College and Air War College, GMU Press, ISBN 978-0-615-23812-8, 2008.
[10] Tecuci G., Boicu M., Marcu D., Barbulescu M., Boicu C., Le V., Hajduk T., Teaching Virtual Experts for Multi-Domain Collaborative Planning, Journal of Software, Volume 3, Number 3, pp. 38-59, March 2008.
[11] Donnelly, K. Director of the Pediatric Residency Program and Vice Chair for Education at Inova Fairfax Hospital for Children , Personal communication, 2010
[12] Schmitt, Barton D. Pediatric Telephone Protocols: Office Version, American Academy of Pediatrics, 2008.
[13] Epic system, http://www.epic.com/
[14] Sharp Focus Personal Health Management System, http://www.healthlinesystems.com/sharpfocus.aspx
[15] Centaurus Call Center Software, http://www.lvmsystems.com/prod01_eccs.php.

Biologically Inspired Cognitive Architectures 2011
A.V. Samsonovich and K.R. Jóhannsdóttir (Eds.)
IOS Press, 2011
doi:10.3233/978-1-60750-959-2-50

Learning categories with invariances in a neural network model of prefrontal cortex

Suhas E. CHELIAN[a,1], Rajan BHATTACHARYYA[a], Randall O'REILLY[b]
[a] HRL Laboratories, LLC, [b] University of Colorado, Boulder

Abstract. Prefrontal cortex (PFC) is implicated in a number of functions including working memory and categorization. Here the Prefrontal cortex Basal Ganglia Working Memory (PBWM) model (O'Reilly and Frank, 2006) is applied to learning categories with invariances. In particular, motivated by a problem in scene recognition, objects in different locations are sequentially presented to the network for categorization. The model learns to recognize these classes without explicit programming, thus modeling human categorization along with characteristics such as generalization to novel sequences and frequency dependent effects. Future extensions to the current work including applications to other domains and modeling functionally distinct segregations of PFC and neuromodulatory systems are also described.

Keywords. Prefrontal cortex (PFC), working memory, categorization, scene recognition.

Introduction

Prefrontal cortex (PFC) is implicated in a number of functions including working memory and categorization. Working memory includes the ability to actively maintain task relevant information over delays and distracters. As early as the 1930s, ablation studies established that PFC was critical to working memory in delayed response tasks [1, 2]. These findings have since been extended with single unit (e.g., [3, 4]) and fMRI recordings (e.g., [5]). Categorization involves grouping perceptually dissimilar objects into functionally organized classes. (For current purposes, "category" and "class" will be used interchangeably.) Although posterior cortical areas are certainly involved in the recognition of individual objects, categorization is at least partly encoded by PFC (e.g., [6, 7]). For example, in the case of vision, inferotemporal cortex might represent objects such as a plum or fish, but PFC can group these into an *is-edible* class.

Perhaps the simplest task that involves both working memory and categorization is classifying sequences of objects. For example, in the case of language, if 4 character words are generated from the English letters A through Z, PLUM and FISH would belong to the *is-edible* class but other combinations (e.g., WISH, TIRE) would not. Working memory is required to differentiate between words (e.g., FISH v. WISH), while categorization is required to group individual objects (e.g., PLUM and FISH) into classes.

One recent neural network model of working memory is the Prefrontal cortex Basal Ganglia Working Memory (PBWM) model [8]. PBWM posits "stripes" within

---

[1] Corresponding author (sechelian@hrl.com).

PFC to hold each working memory symbol—each letter in PLUM for example—over delays and distracters. Symbols are gated into and out of PFC stripes by basal ganglia if doing so is deemed to be rewarding. Although PBWM is an extensive and sophisticated model, it has not been applied to tasks with overlapping symbols or generalization to new input sequences. For example, the two categories in the popular 1-2-AX task require rote memorization of two disjoint input sequences (1-AX and 2-BY). Categories can be learned with bio-inspired models (e.g., [9, 10]) but few claims are made with regards to detailed neuroanatomical underpinnings. Thus, this work extends the neuro-realism of PBWM to classifying sequences of symbols motivated by a problem in scene recognition.

Section 1 describes the inputs, datasets, and networks studied in this paper. Section 2 contains results, while section 3 contains the discussion and conclusion.

1. Material and Methods

Consider the task of scene recognition. This too can be seen as classifying sequences of objects. Saccades create a series of foveated image regions which must be integrated in working memory to discern the category of a scene. Each object and its relative location define a scene. Scenes may exhibit invariance over objects or positions as explained below.

1.1. Inputs and Datasets

Four scene categories are defined in Table 1. To stress working memory and categorization as opposed to visual processing, fixed scan paths (top to bottom, left to right) to 4 discrete locations are considered. Furthermore, 8 objects with 2 objects per scene are used.

The first scene category has no object or positional invariance. Changing either a constitute object or its location invalidates a scene from the category. The second scene category has object invariance but not position invariance. For example, in Table 1, if A is store, B is hotel, and Y is a surrounding gate, then AY and BY are both gated businesses. YA and YB, on the other hand, would be business surrounding a gate. The third scene category has positional invariance but no object invariance. For example, in Table 1, a hotel (B) at or above a certain ground plane (Z) would be a mountain hotel. Changing the hotel to a shop (A), however, means it is no longer a member of that scene class. The fourth scene category has both positional and object invariance. That is, both the object in the first sector and the position of the second object can vary. The first two members in this category—B(AA) in different spatial configurations (where (AA) represents an arbitrary symbol following Z)—exhibit positional invariance, while the second two members—C(AA) and D(AA)—exhibit combined position and object invariance. In addition to the four scene categories, non-target scenes were generated to provide counter-examples to the previously defined scene categories. Objects and positions are used in multiple categories to increase the difficulty of the task. For example, B is used in 3 scene categories and in the non-target class.

Table 1. Scene classes 1 through 4, which exhibit invariances between objects and locations, and examples of the non-target scenes.

Scene class	Sectors		Description
1	A	X	No invariances.
2	A	Y	Object invariant.
2	B	Y	
3	B	Z	Position invariant.
3	B		
		Z	
4	B	AA	Multiply invariant.
4	B		
	AA		

Scene class	Sectors		Description
4	C	AA	Multiply invariant (continued).
4	D		
	AA		
Non-target	C	X	Object changed wrt scene class 1
Non-target	B	Y	Position changed wrt scene class 2
Non-target	C	Z	Object changed wrt scene class 3
Non-target	D	AA	Position and object changed wrt scene class 4

A training set consisted of 50 random scenes generated from a probability distribution across scene categories. Testing sets were then created with 25 scenes not in the training set. Furthermore, to study the effect of relative proportions of scene categories on training and generalization, the probability of each scene class was varied in 3 ways. In the first dataset, all 4 scene categories and the non-target class were equiprobable. The second dataset assigned equal probabilities to the 4 scene categories but non-target scenes constitute half of the dataset because there are many more possible scenes in this category. The third dataset is similar to the second, but each scene class was given more examples based on the expected learning difficulty. For example, twice as many scene 4s were created than scene 3s because it involves 2 invariances instead of 1. Table 2 summarizes the class distributions in each dataset.

Table 2. Class distributions across datasets used to study training and generalization performance.

	Even distribution across scene classes and non-target	Even distribution across scene classes, more non-target	Distributed by expected difficulty to learn
1	20%	12.5%	4%
2	20%	12.5%	11%
3	20%	12.5%	11%
4	20%	12.5%	24%
Non-target	20%	50%	50%

1.2. Network

PBWM networks were constructed in the Emergent simulation environment [11] with 4 stripes—2 for maintenance and 2 for output. These stripes comprise the working memory component of the model. Output stripes are meant to model the immediate use of a symbol and its removal from working memory, while maintenance stripes hold symbols for longer time frames. Each stripe was 5 by 6 neurons in size. Maintenance stripes received connections from input fields and were subject to adaptation through error driven learning. Output stripes received connections from the maintenance stripes only. A hidden layer of 10 by 6 neurons received connections from all PFC stripes and the input fields. While PFC maintains a working memory of previously seen objects, the hidden layer maps the contents of PFC, along with the current input to a motor response. This motor response corresponds to identifying a scene category, such as with a button press or vocalization. Activation in the network is shown in Figure 1a.

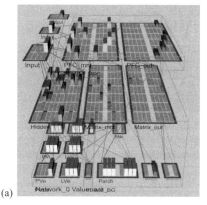

Name	Input	Index	Output	RewT...
A				
X_C1				
A				
Y_C2				
B				
Z_C3				
C				
AA_C4				
D				
AA_NT				

(a)   (b)

Figure 1. (a) A PBWM network used to learn scene categories. (b) Input to the network representing the contents of each sector ("Input" column) and its location ("Index" column); other columns are described in the text. Here scene classes 1 through 4 are depicted followed by a non-target scene.

To represent the scenes to the network, input fields included both the object and the sector in which the object occurred. The former is meant to be the output of temporal cortex ("what") and was represented by a localist 2 by 4 input field. The latter is meant to correspond to the output of parietal cortex ("where"/ "how") and was represented by a localist 1 by 4 input field. Each object was represented with a single neuron set to be maximally active while all other neurons remained inactive. Symbol A, for example, had only the first unit on; symbol B had the second unit active and so on. Sector information was represented in a similar fashion where sector 1 had only the first neuron active, sector 2, the second neuron, and so on. Output categories were presented by a 1 by 5 output field, with one neuron per scene category, and one for non-target scenes. Again, scene category 1 had only the first neuron active, etc. With each foveation, a single object and its location was serially presented to the network with the category label and reward signal presented after the second foveation. (The reward signal tells the network when to answer, but its amplitude is dictated by the match between the prediction of the network and the ground truth label.) Inputs to the network are illustrated in Figure 1b.

During training, each network was trained until the sum of squared error (SSE) of the output field, averaged across all scenes, reached 0 for 2 consecutive epochs or 500 epochs was reached, whichever came first. An epoch contains all training scenes and the order of scenes was shuffled between epochs. Thirty random weight initializations, or batches, were run. Thus, a successful batch is one where SSE converges to 0 before 500 epochs. During testing, learning was turned off, and novel scenes were presented to determine generalization capability.

2. Results

First, PBWM networks can learn the scene categories without explicit programming as shown in Table 3. Across all datasets, approximately 70% of the networks were able to reach 0 training error within 500 epochs. Five hundred epochs was sufficient to determine learning convergence as it was nearly 4 times as long as the average number of epochs in successful batches across all datasets (135.01). In testing, average percent correct across all successful weight initializations was 81.01%, which is far better than chance for 5 classes (20%).

Table 3. Training and generalization performance across datasets. Numbers within parenthesis are standard deviations.

	Even distribution across scene classes and non-target	Even distribution across scene classes, more non-target	Distributed by expected difficulty to learn	Average
Percentage of successful batches	56.67	73.33	73.33	67.78
Number of epochs in successful batches	157.88 (6.75)	126.59 (4.13)	120.57 (3.92)	135.01
Percent correct in successful batches	73.18 (6.75)	85.09 (4.13)	84.76 (3.92)	81.01

Looking at the generalization performance shows differences across the datasets. In the first dataset, the percentage of successful batches was 22% lower than that of the second and third datasets. Testing percent correct was also smaller than the other datasets (t(58) = 8.36, p < .05). This is because the first dataset did not have as many counter-examples to differentiate scene categories 1 through 4 from the non-target scenes. In the second dataset, the number of epochs did not change with respect to the first dataset (t(37) = 1.24, p > .05), but testing percent correct was higher (t(37) = 6.81, p < .05). Here, more counter-examples helped generalization. The second and third datasets do not differ in terms of percent correct (t(41)=.27, p > .05) or number of epochs (t(41)=.29, p > .05) as they share the same number of counter-examples. Similar training times across all datasets may reflect the limited capacity of the relatively small networks used.

3. Discussion and Conclusion

Using scene recognition as a challenge problem, PBWM networks are able of classifying sequences of symbols. However, the inputs and network structure used are generic enough to be applied to other domains that rely on working memory and categorization. Continuing in visual domain, this framework could be extended to behavior recognition where each scene is part of an action sequence (e.g., car left of gate, car at gate, car right of gate → car exit gate). Furthermore, the use of relational input encoding can introduce generality over objects or locations [12]. In addition, language involves processing chains of symbols at many scales: phonemes in words, words in sentences, sentences in paragraphs, etc. Navigation and motor sequence learning are other examples that could be modeled with this framework.

One limitation of this work is that the inputs and network structure used are relatively simple. Longer sequences, sequences with repeated symbols, or sequences with variable lengths would increase task difficulty. Similarly, more symbols, symbols with distributed representations, and the use of distracter symbols would stress network performance. The network structure could also be extended to include a functional segregation of PFC such as "what" inputs feeding into ventral regions, "where"/ "how" inputs feeding into dorsal regions, and more anterior regions of PFC representing more abstract concepts or longer term working memory [13]. In the present work, "what" and "where" information was fused directly due to the simple nature of the input. Neuromodulatory systems, although connected with nearly every region of the brain, interact tremendously with PFC and anterior cingulate cortex (ACC) [14]. These interactions change working memory and categorization through short and long term dynamics respectively, and remain a ripe area for research.

Acknowledgement

Supported by the Intelligence Advanced Research Projects Activity (IARPA) via Department of the Interior (DOI) contract number D10PC20021. The U.S. Government is authorized to reproduce and distribute reprints for Governmental purposes notwithstanding any copyright annotation thereon. The views and conclusions contained hereon are those of the authors and should not be interpreted as necessarily representing the official policies or endorsements, either expressed or implied, of IARPA, DOI, or the U.S. Government.

References

[1] C.F. Jacobsen, Functions of frontal association area in primates, *Archives of Neurology and Psychiatry* **33** (1935), 558-569.
[2] C.F. Jacobsen, Studies of cerebral function in primates. I. The functions of the frontal associations areas in monkeys, *Comparative Psychology Monographs* **13** (1936), 3-60.
[3] J.M. Fuster and G.E. Alexander, Neuron activity related to short term memory, *Science* **173** (1971), 652-654.
[4] K. Kubota and H. Niki, Prefrontal cortical unit activity and delayed alternation performance in monkeys, *Journal of Neurophysiology* **34** (1971), 337-347.
[5] J. D. Cohen, S. D. Forman, T.S. Braver, B.J. Casey, D. Servan-Schreiber, and D.C. Noll, Activation of the prefrontal cortex in a nonspatial working memory task with functional MRI, *Human Brain Mapping* **1** (1993), 293-304.
[6] R. Vogels, Categorization of complex visual images by rhesus monkeys, *European Journal of Neuroscience* **11** (1999), 1223-1238.
[7] D.J. Freedman, M. Risenhuber, T. Poggio, and E.K. Miller, A comparison of primate prefrontal and inferior temporal cortex during visual categorization, *Journal of Neuroscience* **23** (2003), 5235-5246.
[8] R.C. O'Reilly and M.J. Frank, Making working memory work: a computational model of learning in the frontal cortex and basal ganglia, *Neural Computation* **18** (2006), 283-328.
[9] G.A. Carpenter, S. Martens, and O.J. Ogas, Self-organizing information fusion and hierarchical knowledge discovery: a new framework using ARTMAP neural networks, *Neural Networks* **18** (2005), 287-295.
[10] B.J. Rhodes, Taxonomic knowledge structure discovery from imagery-based data using the neural associative incremental learning (NAIL) algorithm, *Information Fusion* **8** (2007), 295-315.
[11] B. Aisa, B. Mingus, and R.C. O'Reilly, The emergent neural modeling system, *Neural Networks* **21** (2008), 1146-1152.
[12] R.C. O'Reilly and R.S. Busby, Generalizable relational binding from coarse-coded distributed representations. In *Advances in Neural Information Processing Systems (NIPS) 14*, T.G. Dietterich, S. Becker and Z. Ghahramani (Eds.), Cambridge, MA; MIT Press (2002).
[13] R.C. O'Reilly, The what and how of prefrontal cortical organization, *Trends in Neurosciences* **33** (2010), 355-361.
[14] J.L. Krichmar, The neuromodulatory system - a framework for survival and adaptive behavior in a challenging world, *Adaptive Behavior* **16** (2008), 385-399.

Biologically Inspired Cognitive Architectures 2011
A.V. Samsonovich and K.R. Jóhannsdóttir (Eds.)
IOS Press, 2011

Towards externalist robotics

Antonio CHELLA[a,1] and Riccardo MANZOTTI[b]
[a] *DICGIM - University of Palermo*
Viale delle Scienze building 6, 90128 Palermo
antonio.chella@unipa.it
[b] *Institute of Consumption, Communication and Behavior*
IULM University, Via Carlo Bo, 8, 16033 Milano
riccardo.manzotti@iulm.it

Abstract

Epigenetic and enactive robotics have been proposed as test-beds for psycho-biological models of the mind. These approaches shortened the distance between the artificial and the natural mind by stressing the importance of the unity between the brain, the body and the environment. At the same time, nowadays robotic researchers openly acknowledge the importance of experience which has been not sufficiently considered in the recent past. The process went so far that the field of machine consciousness is now part of the scientific landscape.

The externalist approach identifies experience with relations, processes or acts between an agent and its environment. Externalism is the view according to which the brain and its neural activity is necessary but not sufficient to produce the conscious mind. The externalist approach locates the subject and experience processes in a context wider than brain-oriented approaches. Because of this fact, the externalist standpoints allows to start from methodological and ontological premises suitable for the study of experience and of other subjective contents inside an experimental framework.

The talk will review the externalist-oriented approaches and it will present the main ideas at the basis of the emerging field of externalist robotics. The aims of this research is to experiment, in a circumscribed number of cases, whether it is possible to apply such an architecture in the fields of robotics, of psychology and of philosophy of mind.

---

[1] Corresponding Author.

Biologically Inspired Cognitive Architectures 2011
A.V. Samsonovich and K.R. Jóhannsdóttir (Eds.)
IOS Press, 2011
doi:10.3233/978-1-60750-959-2-57

An Innovative Mobile Phone Based System For Humanoid Robot Expressing Emotions And Personality

Antonio CHELLA [a], Rosario SORBELLO [a], Giovanni PILATO [a,1],
Giuseppe BALISTRERI [a], Salvatore Maria ANZALONE [b], and Marcello GIARDINA [a]

[a] *DICGIM Università degli Studi di Palermo, RoboticsLab, Viale delle Scienze, 90128
Palermo, Italy*
[b] *Intelligent Autonomous System Laboratory, Department of Information Engineering,
Padua University, Via Ognissanti 72,Padova, Italy*

Abstract. In this paper we illustrate a new version of the cognitive architecture of
an emotional humanoid robot based on the proposed paradigm of Latent Semantic
Behaviour (LSB). This paradigm is a step towards the simulation of an emotional
behavior of a robot interacting with humans. The New Architecture uses a different
procedure of induction of the emotional conceptual space and an Android mobile
phone as user-friendly for the emotional interaction with robot. The robot generates its overall behavior also taking into account its "personality" encoded in the
emotional conceptual space. To validate the system, we implemented the distribute
system on a Aldebaran NAO humanoid robot and on a Android Phone HTC and we
tested this new emotional interaction between human and robot through the use of
a phone.

Keywords. Humanoid Robot, Emotions, Personality, Latent Semantic Analysis

Introduction

The concept to have a humanoid robot expressing emotions appear mind-boggling to the
human beings; but it is possible to try to reproduce some emotional behaviors inside the
robots in order to improve the interaction with people. Many efforts have been made towards the experiments in the field of human robot interaction through the emotions [1]
[2] [3] [4] [5]. Lun et al. [6] describe an emotional model and affective space of a
humanoid robot and establish their studies on the psycho-dynamics psychological energy and affective energy conservation law. ARKIN et al. [7] [8] [9] show a robotic
framework called TAME for human-robot interaction that tries to connect together in
the same system affective phenomena as attitudes, emotions, moods and trait. The main
idea is an humanoid robot that tries to exhibit an emotional behavior during the interaction with human and environment. As a consequence it exhibits spontaneous and non-

---

[1]Corresponding Author: Rosario Sorbello, RoboticsLab, Dipartimento di Ingegneria Chimica, Gestionale,
Informatica e Meccanica, ITALY; E-mail: rosario.sorbello@unipa.it;

repetitive emotional behaviors. A humanoid robot [10] shows an emotion in responses to user/environment behavior. In this paper we illustrate an evolution of the cognitive architecture of an emotional humanoid robot based on the proposed paradigm of Latent Semantic Behavior (LSB) [11] [12] [13]. LSB is based on the Latent Semantic Analysis (LSA) [14] [15] approach that allows the creation and the use of a data driven high-dimensional conceptual space. This paradigm is a step towards the simulation of an emotional behavior of a robot interacting with humans. The New Architecture uses an Android mobile phone as user-friendly interface available to human for the emotional interaction with robot. The Architecture is organized in three main areas: perceptual, emotional, and behavioral. The first area processes perceptual data coming from the sensors. The second area is the "conceptual space of emotional states" which constitutes the subsymbolic representation of emotions. The third area activates a latent semantic behavior (LSB) related to the humanoid emotional state. To validate the system, we implemented the distribute system on a Aldebaran NAO humanoid robot and on a Android Phone HTC and we tested this new emotional interaction between human and robot through the use of a phone.

1. The Proposed Approach

The aim of the architecture is to make closer human and robots through a game activity by generating emotional, empathic, spontaneous and not repetitive behaviors. The architecture is composed of four modules:

- the *Perceptual* module, where perceptive capabilities of the Nao-Robot are implemented. In this module a Nao Controller Interface has been developed on an Android cellular phone in order to make more interesting the interaction between human beings and robots.
- the *Emogen* module that realizes the Emotional Area. It processes sentences coming from the user and infers, according with the emotional conceptual space, the right emotional state.
- the *Controller* which manages the external behavior of the robot by generating the most coherent action according to the emotional state inferred.
- The *NaoMotion* module implements the humanoid behaviors as actions, and it is capable of accepting requests of behaviors and executing them by controlling the joints of the robot. The actions of the behaviors are implemented as interpolation of different poses of the robot.

The overall schema of the proposed architecture is shown in fig. 1 and takes inspiration from the approach [16] [17].

The computational load of the entire system is distributed among components running on the robot, on a support computer, and on an Android-based smartphone, equipped with speech recognition capabilities. The *Perceptual* module receives inputs from robot sensors system and from a human user can also realize an interaction with the robot through a user-friendly interface. Sentences pronounced by the user are recognized by the smartphone and analyzed; the user input is therefore sent to the *Emogen* module, which acquires sensory inputs from the robot and combines them with the user sentences. This triggers an introspective process inside the robot with a consequential generation

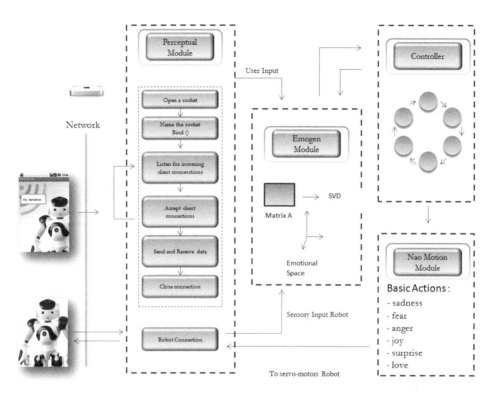

Figure 1. The overall schema of the proposed architecture.

of emotion. The feeling generated inside the Nao's mind activates an emphatic behavior which is manifested to the external world through the production of actions revealing one of the following emotions: sadness, fear, anger, joy, surprise, love, or neutral. To reach this goal, a finite state machine has been designed: each state corresponds to a particular model of the world where the robot can act. The sequence of possible actions sequence is illustrated in fig. 2.

The core of the system is the $Emogen$ module, which is based on a conceptual space created through a procedure inspired to the Latent Semantic Analysis paradigm. The procedure is completely different from what presented in previous papers [18] and starts from the creation of an ad hoc relationship matrix that encodes the correlation among terms expressing emotions.

To each one of the six considered emotions, a set of synonyms that in some manner express it has been associated. For example, to the "sad" feeling we have associated the words "sad, unhappy, sorrowful, dejected, depressed, downcast, miserable, down, despondent,... etc.", for "angry" we have chosen the words "angry, irate, mad, annoyed, cross, vexed, irritated, indignant, irked; furious, enraged, infuriated, in a temper... etc.", and similarly for the other emotions "fear", "joy" "surprise", and "love". All these words constitute a dictionary of N terms, whose generic $i - th$ item we name here t_i. We have

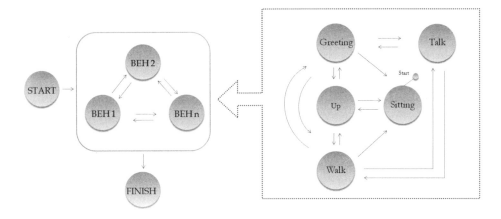

Figure 2. The finite state machine representing the switching behaviors for the experiments.

then created a relationship matrix R whose generic element $r_{ij} \in [-1, 1]$ encodes the correlation between the term t_i and the term t_j according to the following formula:

$$r_{ij} = \begin{cases}]0,1] & \text{if } t_i \text{ and } t_j \text{ are positively correlated} \\ 0 & \text{if } t_i \text{ and } t_j \text{ are not correlated} \\ [-1,0[& \text{if } t_i \text{ and } t_j \text{ are negatively correlated} \end{cases}$$

For clarity, $r_{ij} = 1$ means that the terms t_i and t_j represent exactly the same feeling, while $r_{ij} = -1$ means that the terms t_i and t_j identify opposite feelings. The Truncated Singular Value Decomposition of the matrix R is then performed, obtaining the product:

$$\mathbf{R}_k = \mathbf{U}_k \Sigma_k \mathbf{V}_k^T$$

This realizes a mapping between the words verbally describing emotions into a continuous k-dimensional vector space S [19] [20], where each word is mapped into an emotional *knoxel* [21] [22].

The TSVD technique has been applied to R in order to obtain its best probability amplitude approximation R_k. This process leads to the construction of a K dimensional conceptual space of emotions S. The axes of S represent the "fundamental" emotional concepts automatically induced by TSVD procedure arising from the dictionary of N terms. In the obtained space S, a subset of ni words for each emotional state corresponding to one of the six "basic emotion" E_i has been projected in S using the folding-in technique. According to this technique each excerpt is coded as the sum of the vectors representing the terms composing it. As a result, the j-th excerpt belonging to the subset corresponding to the emotional state E_i is represented in S by an associated vector em(i) and the emotional state E_i is represented by j the set of vectors em(i) : j = 1, 2, Kni

This space gives to the robot some sort of "personality" encoded as a conceptual space of emotional states. The robot exploits this mechanism to realize an empathy mechanism by associating to the sentences perceived from an human user and transmitted through a smartphone, a particular emotion, by mapping them into the emotional conceptual space through the fold-in technique. The procedure finds the closest mapped emotion according to the approach in [18] which takes into account both personality of the robot and the most recent emotions felt by the robot. The robot, consequently, shows an empathic behavior by means of a set of actions.

2. Experimental results

To validate the system, the presented approach has been implemented on a humanoid robot Nao, through the use of textual inputs. The experiments have been conducted in order to test the emotional capabilities of the robot by reproducing various emotive situations. A set of 247 word has been used to build the relationship matrix R, and a latent semantic behavior space of $k = 30$ dimensions has been generated. A set of 100 sentences has been evaluated by a human user in order to understand if the behavior of the robot was accurate: while the 81% of the set was considered almost correct, in 19% of the trials the behavior of the robot was judged as being below the expected performance. Feedback from users show high interest with the innovative way of interaction through the use of a smartphone, a surprise feeling that makes the robot an active actor instead of a simple passive "toy", and people wonder about new possibilities of interaction between human beings and robots.

The main idea is to use the empathy that human beings has felt regarding the mobile phone into recent years, in order to have the mobil phone as new communication device for the interaction with the robots. The robot represents nowday the emerging technology and the mobil phone will allow to reduce the distance between human beings and robot because it will become the easy interface during the interaction with the robots.

The table 1 collects some of the numerical results of the experiments that have been conducted. So, the values showed in the cell of the table represent the relationships founded between the perceived sensory inputs made in the form of textual sentences (in the rows) and the emotions (columns) mapped in the "Emotional Space" as described in the previous paragraphs. The value of the measures of the relationships may vary on a range between -1.00 and +1.00. So that, the negative values identify opposite feelings, whereas positive values represent the degree of its relevance in the respective emotion evoked. For example in the sentence "I am irate and I come to you because the work you did" the value of +1.00 (in the column "Anger") identify as "Prevalent Emotion" the anger feeling and as would be expected we obtained negative values in the feelings of love(-0.43) and joy(-0.50).

3. Conclusions and future works

A new release of the LSB-based Emotional NAO has been presented. The new version differs from the previous one for the construction of the emotional conceptual space and

Table 1. Samples of results of interaction: in bold it is highlighted the empathic behavior triggered by the user sentence. PE stands for the "Prevalent Emotion".

Sentence	Sadness	Anger	Fear	Joy	Surprise	Love	PE
I found myself confuse by sudden feelings of astonishment	-0,09	-0.09	-0.12	+0.08	**+0.50**	+0.08	Surprise
I don't know if my feeling for you is just pleasure or bond	-0.15	-0.33	-0.23	+0.50	+0.28	**+0.51**	Love
I want to share with you the delight of ecstasy for your help	-0.30	-0.25	-0.13	**+0.50**	+0.08	+0.47	Joy
I notice the sense of trepidation and anxiety in your eyes	+0.12	+0.32	**-0.50**	-0.13	-0.12	-0.11	Fear
I am irate and I come to you because the work you did	+0.15	**+1.00**	+0.65	-0.50	-0.17	-0.43	Anger
I am under depression for the trouble that I encountered	**+0.33**	+0.05	0.08	-0.20	-0.06	-0.15	Sadness

for the new modality used for human-robot interaction. Experimental results show the effectiveness and the user-friendliness of the approach, that has been confirmed by the feedback that we collected from the users through questionnaries. Future work will regard the enhancement of the architecture in order to improve the human-robot interaction and empathy.

References

[1] H. Miwa, K. Itoh, M. Matsumoto, M. Zecca, H. Takanobu, S. Roccella, M. C. Carrozza, P. Dario, A. Takanishi "Effective Emotional Expressions with Emotion Expression Humanoid Robot WE-4RII Integration of Humanoid Robot Hand RCH-1", 2004 IEEE/RSJ International Conference on Intelligent Robots and Systems, Sendai International Center, Sendai, Japan, September 28 - October 2, 2004, Page(s): 2203 - 2208 vol.3.
[2] C. Breazeal "Emotion and Sociable Humanoid Robots" International Journal Human-Computer Studies 59, pp. 119-155 (2003).
[3] A. Bruce, I. Nourbakhsh, R. Simmons "The Role of Expressiveness and Attention in Human-Robot Interaction" AAAI Technical Report FS-01-02, 2001.
[4] Zhen Liu, Zhi Geng Pan "An Emotion Model of 3D Virtual Characters in Intelligent Virtual Environment". Lecture Notes in Computer Science, Volume 3784/2005, Affective Computing and Intelligent Interaction Book, November 2005.
[5] J. Monceaux, J. Becker, C. Boudier, A. Mazel "Demonstration: First Steps in Emotional Expression of the Humanoid Robot Nao" International Conference on Multimodal Interfaces, Cambridge, Massachusetts, USA, pp. 235-236, 2009.
[6] Xie, Lun, Wang, Zhi-Liang, Wang, Wei, Yu, Guo-Chen, 2010. "Emotional gait generation for a humanoid robot". International Journal of Automation and Computing. Institute of Automation, Chinese Academy of Sciences, co-published with Springer-Verlag GmbH. http://dx.doi.org/10.1007/s11633-010-0064-0.
[7] Moshkina, L. and Arkin, R.C., 2009. "Beyond Humanoid Emotions: Incorporating Traits, Attitudes, and Moods", Proc. 2009 IEEE Workshop on Current Challenges and Future Perspectives of Emotional Humanoid Robotics, Kobe, JP, May 2009.
[8] R. C. Arkin, M. Fujita, T. Takagi, R. Hasegawa "An Ethological and Emotional Basis for Human-Robot Interaction" Robotics and Autonomous Systems 42 pp. 191-201, (2003).
[9] R. Arkin, M. Fujita, T. Takagi, R. Hasegawa: Ethological Modeling and Architecture for an Entertainment Robot. In: IEEE Int. Conf. on Robotics Automation, p.p. 453-458. Seoul. (2001).
[10] E. Menegatti, G. Silvestri, Pagello E., N. Greggio, A. Cisternino, F. Mazzanti, R. Sorbello, A. Chella. "3D Models of Humanoid Soccer Robot in USARSim and Robotics Studio Simulators" International Journal of Humanoids Robotics (2008).

[11]   S.M. Anzalone, F. Cinquegrani, R. Sorbello, A. Chella "An Emotional Humanoid Partner". Linguistic and Cognitive Approaches To Dialog Agents (LaCATODA 2010) At AISB2010 Convention, Leicester, UK April 2010.

[12]   A. Chella, G. Pilato, R. Sorbello, G. Vassallo, F. Cinquegrani, S.M. Anzalone, "An Emphatic Humanoid Robot with Emotional Latent Semantic Behavior" Simulation, Modeling, and Programming for Autonomous Robots (Springer), LNAI 5325, 2008: pp. 234-245. First International Conference, SIMPAR 2008, Venice, Italy, November 2008.

[13]   A. Chella, R.E. Barone, G. Pilato, R. Sorbello, "An Emotional Storyteller Robot". AAAI 2008 Spring Symposium on Emotion, Personality and Social Behavior. Stanford University in March 26-28, 2008.

[14]   Agostaro F., Augello A., Pilato G., Vassallo G., Gaglio S.: A Conversational Agent Based on a Conceptual Interpretation of a Data Driven Semantic Space. In: Lecture Notes in Artificial Intelligence, Springer-Verlag GmbH, vol. 3673, pp 381-392 (2005).

[15]   G. Pilato, F.Vella, G.Vassallo, M. La Cascia "A Conceptual Probabilistic Model for the Induction of Image Semantics", Proc of the Fourth IEEE International Conference on Semantic Computing (ICSC 2010) September 22-24, 2010, Carnegie Mellon University, Pittsburgh, PA, USA. (in press).

[16]   Chella A., Frixione M. and Gaglio S.: An Architecture for Autonomous Agents Exploiting Conceptual Representations. In: Robotics and Autonomous Systems 25, pp. 231-240 (1998).

[17]   A. Chella, M. Frixione, and S. Gaglio, "A cognitive architecture for robot self-consciousness," Artificial Intelligence in Medicine, vol. 44, no. 2, pp. 147-154, 2008.

[18]   Antonio Chella, Rosario Sorbello, Giorgio Vassallo, and Giovanni Pilato. 2010. An Architecture For Humanoid Robot Expressing Emotions And Personality. In Proceeding of the 2010 conference on Biologically Inspired Cognitive Architectures 2010: Proceedings of the First Annual Meeting of the BICA Society, Alexei V. Samsonovich, Kamilla R., Antonio Chella, and Ben Goertzel (Eds.). IOS Press, Amsterdam, The Netherlands, The Netherlands, 33-39.

[19]   Landauer, T.K., Foltz, P.W., Laham, D.: Introduction to Latent Semantic Analysis. In: Discourse Processes, 25, 259-284 (1998).

[20]   Colon, E., Sahli, H., Baudoin, Y.: CoRoBa, a Multi Mobile Robot Control and Simulation Framework. In: Int. Journal of Advanced Robotic Systems, (2006).

[21]   Thagard, P., Shelley, C.P.: Emotional analogies and analogical inference. In: D. Gentner K. H. Holyoak B. K. Kokinov (Eds.), The analogical mind: Perspectives from cognitive science, pp. 335-362. Cambridge, MA: MIT Press (2001).

[22]   Peters, S. , Widdows, D.: Word vectors and quantum logic experiments with negation and disjunction. In: Mathematics of Language, 8, Bloomington, Indiana, June, (2003).

64

Biologically Inspired Cognitive Architectures 2011
A.V. Samsonovich and K.R. Jóhannsdóttir (Eds.)
IOS Press, 2011
© *2011 The authors and IOS Press. All rights reserved.*
doi:10.3233/978-1-60750-959-2-64

Fusing Symbolic and Decision-Theoretic Problem Solving + Perception in a Graphical Cognitive Architecture

Junda CHEN,[a] Abram DEMSKI,[a] Teawon HAN,[a] Louis-Philippe MORENCY,[a]
David PYNADATH,[a] Nicole RAFIDI[b] and Paul ROSENBLOOM[a,1]
[a] *Department of Computer Science and/or Institute for Creative Technologies (ICT),*
University of Southern California (USC), USA
[b] *Department of Electrical Engineering, Princeton University and USC/ICT, USA*

Abstract. A step is taken towards fusing symbolic and decision-theoretic problem solving in a cognitive architecture by implementing the latter in an architecture within which the former has already been demonstrated. The graphical models upon which the architecture is based enable a uniform implementation of both varieties of problem solving. They also enable a uniform combination with forms of decision-relevant perception, highlighting a potential path towards a tight coupling between central cognition and peripheral perception.

Keywords. cognitive architecture, decision making, graphical models, perception, CRF, SLAM, POMDP

Introduction

A *cognitive architecture* embodies a hypothesis about the fixed structure underlying intelligent behavior, whether in natural or artificial systems. Central to intelligent behavior, and thus to any such architecture, is an approach to *decision making*; i.e., to determining what actions should be performed as a function of what is perceived, what is known and what is desired. In a typical symbolic architecture, such as Soar [1], perception occurs via distinct perceptual modules interfaced to the architecture; knowledge takes the form of rules, facts, cases/episodes or general logical statements; and desires are encoded as goals. In a decision-theoretic architecture, knowledge takes a probabilistic form, with desires encoded as numeric utilities [2,3]. Due to uncertainty, many leading perception algorithms are likewise probabilistic, implying that they may be more compatible with a decision-theoretic formalism for decision making than a symbolic one; yet decision-theoretic architectures, to the extent that they do perception, also typically interface to separate perceptual modules [4].

The ideal architecture would leverage the combined strengths of both symbolic and decision-theoretic approaches while also tightly integrating perception into the overall framework. This article reports on the early stages of exploring such a fusion, via an architecture that leverages *graphical models* for hybrid (discrete and continuous) mixed

---

[1] Corresponding Author: University of Southern California, 12015 Waterfront Dr., Playa Vista, CA 90094, USA; E-mail: rosenbloom@usc.edu.

(symbolic and probabilistic) behavior [5,6]. Earlier work showed how such a graphical architecture could reproduce a standard form of symbolic decision making, based on how the Soar architecture uses long-term memory to generate candidate operators representing actions and evaluate them to yield preferences among them, and then selects among them via a preference-based decision procedure [7]. Soar also has the ability to interface with perceptual modules and to reflect when existing knowledge is inadequate for generating or evaluating operators; e.g., when evaluation knowledge is insufficient, it can engage in reflective search to determine which operators best reach the goal. This form of reflective search, which is central to symbolic problem solving, has also been demonstrated in the graphical architecture.

Here the focus is on incorporating into the same graphical models that underlie the architecture's memory and symbolic decision making: (1) a decision-theoretic approach to operator evaluation that is based on partially observable Markov decision problems (POMDPs); and (2) perception that probabilistically grounds decision making in the uncertain external environment. Out of the wide space of probabilistic perceptual algorithms, two are considered that combine state-of-the-art performance on dynamic multi-step perceptual problems with natural mappings to graphical models: conditional random fields (CRFs) [8] and simultaneous localization and mapping (SLAM) [9]. Although some work has been done on the mapping aspect of SLAM within the graphical architecture, the material here is limited to localization.

A set of experiments in a simple 1D navigation task is included to verify that the combined graph works as expected within the graphical architecture, and to begin exploring some of its resulting properties. But the main result here is qualitative: demonstrating the feasibility of fusing symbolic and decision-theoretic models of problem solving, while also coupling tightly with a uniform implementation of decision-relevant perception – to yield a secondary form of fusion between central cognition and peripheral perception – within a theoretically elegant graphical cognitive architecture. This pair of fusions contributes in two ways towards architectures capable of broad yet uniformly implemented and tightly integrated functionality.

The overall focus in graphical models is *computational* – specifically on efficient computation over complex multivariate functions by decomposing them into products of simpler functions – rather than *biological*, but graphical models do share many of the attributes of neural networks – performing limited forms of local computation on numeric messages within a graph-structured long-term memory – and a number of neural network algorithms map directly onto them [10]. There is thus an abstract form of biological inspiration, plus potential applicablity to more directly inspired work.

1. The Graphical Models

The backbone of each of the three techniques to be integrated with symbolic problem solving within the graphical architecture – POMDPs, CRFs and SLAM – consists of a chain of state variables over a sequence of time steps (Figure 1). The links between successive variables represent constraints over state transitions, which may encode transition probabilities – $P(X_i \mid X_{i-1})$ – or more general *potential functions* – $f_k(X_{i-1}, X_i)$ – whose values convey information

Figure 1: Graphical model (Markov network) for state transitions.

about the relative likelihoods of the transitions. POMDPs and SLAM use conditional probabilities while CRFs use potentials, but in either case the entire graph expresses a joint distribution, or function, over its variables that decomposes into the product of the individual distributions or functions. For POMDPs and SLAM, the graph computes $P(X_0,\dots,X_N) = \prod_0^N P(X_i \mid X_{i-1})$, where X_{-1} is null in $P(X_0 \mid X_{-1})$ to yield the prior on X_0. CRFs omit priors and use potentials, but with the actual functions used in the product being weighted exponentials of the features, such as $\exp(\theta_k \bullet f_k(X_{i-1}, X_i))$. The overall equation for CRFs thus becomes $F(X_0,\dots,X_N) = \exp(\sum \theta_k \bullet f_k(X_{i-1}, X_i))$.

Attached to the states in this backbone are variables that represent observations of the world (Figure 2). The links connecting these observations to the states in which they occur – the ribs, to continue the metaphor – represent joint constraints over observations and states, expressed as further probabilities or potentials – $P(O_i \mid X_i)$ or $g_i(O_i, X_i)$ – that contribute to the overall product. This is how perception influences the state variables. Both CRFs and SLAM depend critically on observations across a sequence of states to jointly constrain the individual states. For example, in a CRF for word recognition that is based on observations of a sequence of letters, perceptions of all of the letters jointly constrain the identification of each individual letter. In a POMDP there is an observation for the initial state, but the later

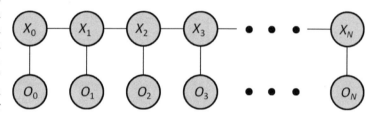

Figure 2: Graphical model (Markov network) for state transitions with observations.

states in the chain are hypothetical during decision making, and thus do not involve observations.

For POMDPs and SLAM, action variables – representing operations that produce one state from another – are added to the transitions in this skeleton (Figure 3), extending the transition probabilities to $P(X_i \mid X_{i-1}, A_{i-1})$. The graphs in Figures 1 and 2 are Markov networks (aka Markov random fields), undirected graphical models over variable nodes, where there is a function implicitly defined over each pair of variables on a link. Markov networks can express functions over more than two variables, but this is awkward to display graphically. So we shift in Figure 3 to a more expressive type of graphical model that is central to the graphical architecture, *factor graphs*,

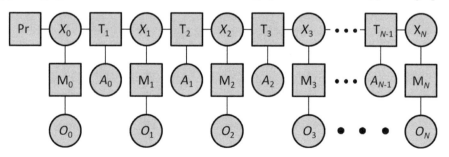

Figure 3: Graphical model (factor graph) for state transitions with observations (connected to states via mapping functions) and actions.

which include explicit factor nodes for functions. Like Markov networks, factor graphs are undirected, but factor nodes now explicitly represent the distributions or functions, and each connects to all of its variables. In the figure, factor nodes are represented as squares, with the T_i's transition functions, the M_i's map functions that relate objects to locations, and Pr the prior distribution on the initial state. All of the T_i's implement the same function, as do the M_i's.

To support operator evaluation via POMDPs, the graph must also include utility variables linked to future states, so that action distributions are based not only on the current state but on what is to be achieved (Figure 4). Essentially, constraint from localization flows forward in time while constraint from utility flows backwards. The overall result is effectively a dynamic decision network (DDN), although one in which decomposition of state variables – a significant feature generally in DDNs – has not so far been considered. This graph supports a different form of lookahead search from what is the norm in symbolic problem solving, and thus from what has been implemented already in a Soar-like manner in the graphical architecture. In the POMDP, the state variable at each time step represents a distribution over all possible states of the system at that step, possibly including the full combinatoric set of states in the problem space. The transition function represents a distribution over the states resulting from applying each possible action to each possible previous state. A single lookahead graph of a fixed length thus represents a probabilistic search to that depth.

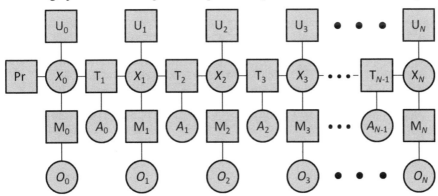

Figure 4: Graphical model (factor graph) with utility functions added for states.

Some years ago a distinction was introduced within Soar between *problem space search* and *knowledge search*, which maps onto various forms of dual process theory in psychology. Problem space search occurs across decisions. It is slow and serial, but provides an open-ended, potentially combinatoric search over an implicitly defined space, with the possibility of exploiting any available knowledge to help control the search. Knowledge search occurs within a single decision. It is fast and parallel, but can only search over a space that is explicitly defined by the existing memory structures, with no ability to use additional knowledge to control this search. The POMDP extends Soar's original notion of knowledge search to probabilistic lookahead that is combinatoric yet bounded by the memory structures. Still, as in Soar, when the evaluation knowledge derived from this knowledge search is insufficient to make a decision, there is a possibility of unbounded reflective problem space search.

The full graph that has been implemented (Figure 5) can be viewed as decomposing into three modules – one each for CRF perception, SLAM localization, and POMDP action choice – that interact through shared variable nodes; although they are all actually implemented in a uniform manner within a single factor graph. The CRF and SLAM jointly concern the past and present, while the POMDP concerns the future. The CRF computes a distribution over the possible objects (O_i) at the current and previous locations (X_i) from sensations (S_i), using perception functions (sensation-object relations: P_i) and object-transition functions (object-adjacency relations: OT_i). Its backbone here is the perceived objects (O_i) rather than the locations (X_i), with the ribs being the sensations (S_i). There are three sensors $(S^1\text{-}S^3)$, each with its own perceptual function $(P^1\text{-}P^3)$. SLAM yields a distribution over the current location (X_0) from the object distributions (O_i) produced by the CRF and evidence about actions performed (A_i), while using map functions (object-location probabilities: M_i), movement-transition functions (probabilities of new locations given a location and an action: XT_i) and the prior (Pr), which is uniform in our experiments. The POMDP chooses an action (A_0) that maximizes expected utility given the current-location distribution (X_0) provided by SLAM, using utility (U_i) and movement-transition (XT_i) functions. In addition to the shared variables, the one other source of interaction among the modules occurs during the training of the CRF, which takes into account SLAM's map function (M_i) and SLAM/POMDP's transition function (XT_i).

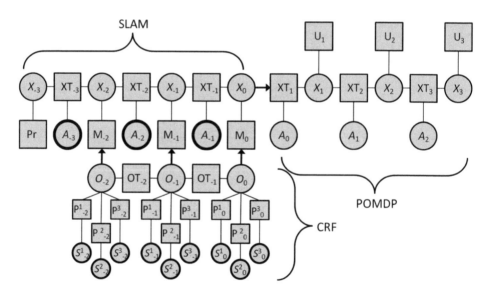

Figure 5: Complete graphical model (factor graph) for CRF+SLAM+POMDP. X_0 is the current state and A_0 is the action to be selected. Bold outlines indicate evidence nodes.

Each module involves bidirectional connectivity internally, and thus bidirectional sharing of information and uncertainty among variable nodes that are connected via factor nodes. The unidirectional connectivity shown across modules shouldn't be confused with the directionality in Bayesian networks. Here it concerns the flow of information – via messages passed by the summary product algorithm [11] – rather than the direction of probabilistic conditionality. By enabling flow from SLAM to the POMDP, but not in the reverse direction, the POMDP can exploit SLAM's localizations without the utilities used in POMDP's lookahead affecting localization.

Similarly, unidirectional flow from the CRF to SLAM implies bottom up perception without top-down feedback.

2. Implementation of a Movement Task in the Graphical Architecture

A discrete 1D movement task has been implemented, where the goal is to reach a specified location, and the actions move a step to the right or left, or do nothing (Figure 6). This is a simple task that was chosen primarily to demonstrate that the combined graph works within the graphical architecture; however, it does include real world complexity stemming from: ambiguity in what is perceived, such as which wall is seen when a wall is perceived; errors in the perception functions that can lead to recognizing the wrong object; and actions that do not always behave as they are specified. The resulting uncertainty concerning both what is being perceived and where the agent is located calls for the kind of evidence combination across steps provided by the CRF and SLAM, and the probabilistic decision making provided by the POMDP.

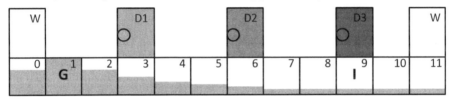

Figure 6: Task environment with two walls, three doors, an initial location (I) and a goal location (G). The relative values of the utility function for this goal location can be seen in the square shading. From the initial state, a lookahead of at least three is needed here before any discrimination is provided.

The graph in Figure 5 is solved at each step to choose the action to perform given the available evidence. The selected action is then performed in the world – an environment simulator – where it usually behaves as specified, but may fail. The graph acts as a sliding window that considers a fixed distance into the past (via the CRF and SLAM) and the future (via the POMDP). After an action is performed, the existing evidence is slid back a step (via extra-architectural code) and new observations arrive. The CRF senses rectangles (doors and walls), circles (doorknobs), and colors (doors have distinctive colors), usually correctly but occasionally in error. From the current and (within window) past sensations, object distributions are created for each time step. SLAM leverages these object distributions, along with evidence about previous actions, to generate a distribution over the current location. The POMDP exploits this distribution to initiate a probabilistic lookahead that yields a distribution over the action to be chosen. The best action is then selected in working memory, and applied in the world, enabling the whole process to repeat.

This task has been implemented within the graphical architecture without building specialized CRF, SLAM, and POMDP algorithms into it. Instead, *knowledge* is added to long-term memory (LTM) and *evidence* to working memory (WM). Since general perception and learning mechanisms are not yet in place, external code is used to initialize WM and LTM. LTM is encoded via *conditionals* built from *conditions*, *actions*, *condacts*, and *functions*. Conditions, actions and condacts are specified as patterns over named predicates with typed arguments. Conditions and actions behave much as in rule systems, with conditions matching to working memory and actions proposing changes to it. Condacts – a neologism for *conditions* and *actions* – meld these functionalities, by passing messages both from and to WM, to yield the bidirectional processing that is crucial in probabilistic graphical models. A conditional function defines a constraint over a combination of variables in the conditional.

Working memory includes a function for each predicate, with each compiling to a factor node to which variable nodes are attached. For each of the variable nodes in Figure 5 there is thus also an unshown WM factor node. Each conditional in LTM compiles to a factor subgraph, with across-conditional linkage based on common predicates, via sharing of WM nodes. The graphical architecture's compiler actually generates a factor graph that differs in some details from this nominal graph, even beyond the inclusion of WM factor nodes, but the two are logically equivalent. The graph shown, with three steps of input for localization plus a lookahead of three steps for action choice, compiles within the graphical architecture into 132 variable nodes and 161 factor nodes (for 293 nodes total). The largest graph with which we've so far experimented uses ten steps of input for localization and five steps of lookahead. It requires 376 variable nodes and 451 factor nodes (for 827 nodes total).

```
CONDITIONAL 'Transition_X1_X2_A1
   Condacts: (X1 location:x1)
             (X2 location:x2)
             (A1 action:a1)
   Function: 1<0,0,^>,  1<0,0,L>,  .2<0,0,R>,
             0<0,1,^>,  0<0,1,L>,  .8<0,1,R>,
             0<1,0,^>,  .8<1,0,L>,  0<1,0,R>,
             ...
```

Figure 7: Location-transition conditional (^ denotes no-move action).

The bidirectional links in the figure arise from condacts, with the factor nodes defined by functions. Figure 7, for example, shows the conditional for the transition probabilities from location X_1 to location X_2 via action A_1. Conditions specify the unidirectional interface links among modules, as shown in Figure 8 for map M_{-1}, and are also used with actions to form rules that convert the results of operator evaluation into preferences for the next action, as shown in Figure 9. Selection

```
CONDITIONAL 'Map_X-1_O-1
   Conditions: (O-1 object:o-1)
   Condacts: (X-1 location:x-1)
   Function: .8<0,W>,  .2<0,^>,  0<0,{D1,D2,D3}>,
             .1<1,W>,  .9<1,^>,  0<1,{D1,D2,D3}>,
             ...
```

Figure 8: Map conditional for objects and locations (^ denotes no object).

in this context occurs via the same code that drives selection in declarative memory and symbolic decision making [7]. Behavior then occurs over a sequence of *graph cycles*, each of which involves passing messages within the factor graph – via a variant of the summary product algorithm that uses a mixture of integration and maximization to summarize out variables at factor nodes – until quiescence, and then selected changes being made to working memory.

Three experiments have been run to verify that the combined graph works and to begin exploring its behavior. These vary: (1) the initial and goal

```
CONDITIONAL Acceptable
   Conditions: (A0 action:a0)
   Actions: (Selected operator:a0)
```

Figure 9: Action-selection conditional.

locations, each from 0 to 11; (2) the localization length, from 1 to 10; and (3) the lookahead length, from 1 to 5. When parameters are not varying as part of an experiment, they are set to: the initial and goal locations, and the utility function shown in Figure 6; localization of 5 steps; and lookahead of 3 steps. The localization subgraph is initialized with evidence for all prior steps that corresponds to what is sensed at the initial location, modulo noise, and the action of doing nothing.

The first experiment examined how the full graph worked across the space of problems, yielding overview data on its performance. The graph solved 78% of the 144 distinct problems within 30 cycles, with failures primarily due to the localization ambiguity resulting from empty starting locations, which all look alike. The solved problems required an average of 7802 messages/cycle and 14 seconds/cycle,[2] with an average ratio of 1.7 between the number of cycles to solve a problem and the minimum number of moves possible to solve it. Although the uncertainties and errors can thus lead to non-optimal moves, it usually recovers and solves the problem within 30 steps.

The second experiment evaluated the impact of varying the SLAM localization length from 1 (requiring 794 messages and 1 second per cycle) up to 10 (26447 messages and 34 seconds per cycle). Localization improved as the graph went from 1 to 6 steps, but then decreased from there. As the localization window got large, faulty observations and failed actions contaminated the localization process for too long (an issue that should be addressable by an incremental learning approach). The third experiment explored lookahead via the POMDP. Given the utility function plus the initial and final locations, a lookahead of 1 yielded random decisions, but anything more enabled it to head towards the goal. The strength of the correct action increased with lookahead length, as did the computational cost in terms of both messages per cycle (from 6621 to 9426) and time per cycle (from 11 to 20 seconds).

The key result here is that the architecture yields behavior corresponding to a combination of CRF, SLAM, and POMDP from knowledge-driven activities on top of the architecture's theoretically elegant, hybrid mixed model of memory and processing – based on factor graphs and the summary product algorithm – rather than from extensions to the architecture. The same memory and decision-making capabilities earlier shown to support things like semantic and rule-based memories, as well as symbolic problem solving, also yield decision theoretic problem solving and perception. The main issue in these experiments is the cost of processing the graph. A cognitive architecture must achieve ~50 msec per cycle to model real-time human-like results. The timings here are off by two to three orders of magnitude. However, further optimizations plus parallelizing message passing do look to provide a promising route.

3. Summary and Future

By investigating decision-theoretic problem solving (via a POMDP) in a graphical architecture that has already been shown capable of classical symbolic problem solving, a step has been taking towards fusing these distinct approaches. The uniform integration of perception (via a CRF), plus the localization it supports (via SLAM) for the POMDP, also demonstrates the additional potential for unification provided by this architectural approach, particularly between central cognition and peripheral perception.

Much additional progress is required beyond the step taken here. The POMDP work in isolation has shown that the graphical architecture enables a generic representation of time steps with a step variable – avoiding the need to replicate the

---

[2] The timings for the three experiments are from different machines. The exact values aren't critical; it is the orders of magnitude that are significant.

subgraph for each step – but this remains to be exploited for the entire joint graph. We are also looking to extend SLAM to mapping, the POMDP to multiagent reasoning and Theory of Mind [12], and the CRF to latent dynamic conditional random fields (LDCRF) [13]. It is further crucial to investigate how these graphs can scale efficiently, be learned, and integrate with other capabilities, such as: mental imagery, as a general intermediary between perception and cognition [14]; episodic learning and memory, or some other incremental approach, to utilize past observations in SLAM; and reflection, to cope with insufficient decision theoretic knowledge.

Acknowledgments

This work has been sponsored by the U.S. Army Research, Development, and Engineering Command (RDECOM) and the Air Force Office of Scientific Research, Asian Office of Aerospace Research and Development (AFOSR/AOARD). Statements and opinions expressed do not necessarily reflect the position or the policy of the United States Government, and no official endorsement should be inferred.

References

[1]   J. E. Laird. Extending the Soar cognitive architecture. In *Artificial General Intelligence 2008: Proceedings of the First AGI Conference*, Memphis, Tennessee, March 2008. IOS Press.
[2]   G. H. Ogasawara. *RALPH-MEA: A Real-Time, Decision-Theoretic Agent Architecture*. Technical Report No. UCB/CSD-93-777, EECS Department, University of California, Berkeley, 1993.
[3]   R. C. Murray, K. Vanlehn, and J. Mostow. A decision-theoretic architecture for selecting tutorial discourse actions. In *Proceedings of the AI-ED 2001 Workshop on Tutorial Dialogue Systems*, 2001.
[4]   T. Huang, D. Koller, J. Malik, G. Ogasawara, B. Rao, S. Russell, and J. Weber. Automatic symbolic traffic scene analysis using belief networks. In *Proceedings of the 12th National Conference on Artificial Intelligence*, pages 966-972, 1994
[5]   P. S. Rosenbloom. Combining procedural and declarative knowledge in a graphical architecture. In *Proceedings of the 10th International Conference on Cognitive Modeling*, Manchester, United Kingdom, August 2010.
[6]   P. S. Rosenbloom. Rethinking cognitive architecture via graphical models. *Cognitive Systems Research*, 12(2), 2011.
[7]   P. S. Rosenbloom. From memory to problem solving: Mechanism reuse in a graphical cognitive architecture. In *Proceedings of the 4th Conference on Artificial General Intelligence*, Mountain View, California, August 2011.
[8]   J. Lafferty, A. McCallum, F. Pereira. Conditional random fields: Probabilistic models for segmenting and labeling sequence data. In *Proceedings of the 18th International Conference on Machine Learning*, pages 282–289, 2001.
[9]   T. Bailey and H. Durrant-Whyte. Simultaneous localisation and mapping (SLAM): Part II State of the art. *Robotics and Automation Magazine*, 13:108–117, 2006.
[10] M. I. Jordan and T. J. Sejnowski. *Graphical Models: Foundations of Neural Computation*. MIT Press, Cambridge, Massachusetts, 2001.
[11] F. R. Kschischang, B. J. Frey, and H-A. Loeliger. Factor graphs and the sum-product algorithm. *IEEE Transactions on Information Theory*, 47(2): 498-519, February 2001.
[12] D. V. Pynadath and S. C. Marsella. PsychSim: Modeling theory of mind with decision-theoretic agents. In *Proceedings of the International Joint Conference on Artificial Intelligence*, 2005.
[13] L.-P. Morency, A. Quattoni and T. Darrell. Latent-Dynamic Discriminative Models for Continuous Gesture Recognition. In *Proceedings of the IEEE Conference on Computer Vision and Pattern Recognition*, 2007.
[14] P. S. Rosenbloom. Mental imagery in a graphical cognitive architecture. In *Proceedings of the 2nd International Conference on Biologically Inspired Cognitive Architectures*, Arlington, Virginia, November 2011. In press.

Biologically Inspired Cognitive Architectures 2011
A.V. Samsonovich and K.R. Jóhannsdóttir (Eds.)
IOS Press, 2011
doi:10.3233/978-1-60750-959-2-73

From Biology to Inspiration and Back: Is the Pallidal Complex a Reservoir?

Christopher CONNOLLY [a,1], Richard ROHWER [b], and Zhiqiang WANG [b]

[a] *SRI International, 333 Ravenswood Ave., Menlo Park, CA, 94025*
[b] *SRI International, 9988 Hibert St., Suite 203, San Diego, CA, 92131*

Abstract. This paper explores parallels between Reservoir Computing models and basal ganglia nuclei including the subthalamic nucleus and globus pallidus. The anatomy of these structures can inform the design of reservoirs, possibly improving performance and smoothing the reservoir learning error landscape.

Keywords. Reservoir Computing, Sequence Learning

Introduction

Reservoir Computing is an emerging approach to machine learning that generally refers to neural networks whose architecture includes: 1) a recurrent reservoir of units with random but fixed connection weights, 2) an input layer with random connections to the reservoir, and 3) a trainable linear output layer. This class of networks is perhaps best characterized as a high-dimensional dynamical system that entrains its input, and produces some output set in response to that input. Reservoir systems are applicable both to temporal sequence recognition and open-loop control problems.

We wish to draw some parallels between this computational scheme and a possible biological counterpart, the pallidal complex of the basal ganglia. By "pallidal complex", we refer to the subthalamic nucleus (STN) and the internal and external segments of the globus pallidus (GPi and GPe respectively). Existing literature suggests that firing characteristics of cells in this complex are rich enough to support a range of dynamical behaviors, from stable oscillation (particularly prevalent in Parkinson's Disease [2]) to more chaotic behavior (as defined by the Lyapunov exponent spectrum [10]). We further note that one commonly accepted property of the basal ganglia is that it is heavily involved in action selection and sequencing [6,3], perhaps transforming salient sensorimotor context into action sequences. Reservoirs appear to be well-suited to performing such mappings [4,9,1].

---

[1]Corresponding author: SRI International, Inc., 333 Ravenswood Ave., Menlo Park, CA 94025, E-mail: connolly@ai.sri.com

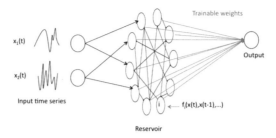

Figure 1. Schematic diagram of a Reservoir Computing system, showing input, reservoir layer, and trainable output. Outputs can be multivalued.

1. Reservoirs and Criticality

We have implemented a form of Echo State Machine (ESM) [4]. An ESM is an analog network [9], and in this particular case, the dynamics are governed by the following discrete map:

$$x^{(n+1)} = f(W_r x^{(n)} + W_i u^{(n)}) \qquad (1)$$

where $x^{(n)}$ is the state vector at iteration n, f is a sigmoidal function, and W_r is a matrix of reservoir weights. The input vector is denoted by $u^{(n)}$ and projected into the reservoir by the input matrix W_i. The sigmoidal function takes the form

$$f(t) = \frac{1}{1 + e^{-t}}$$

where $t \in [-\infty, +\infty]$, so that the range of f is $[0, 1]$. The weight matrix W_r is generated randomly using a sparseness parameter s and a weight parameter w. The sparseness parameter determines how many units on average are connected to a given unit. The weight parameter w determines the range of magnitudes for any connection weight. Weights are chosen randomly from a uniform distribution over $[-w, w]$ or from a normal distribution whose variance is w^2. Once generated, the weight matrix is fixed. Only the output weights are allowed to change. Weight matrices can optionally be constrained to correspond to a three-dimensional lattice where units are only connected to lattice neighbors.

Autonomous reservoirs operate as dynamical systems. Analog sigmoidal networks display intricate phase space structure when they are operating in a critical regime (where the maximal Lyapunov exponent is slightly above zero). Figure 2 shows the attractor structure of one unit in a 512-unit network that is near criticality. This is correlated with regions of low-error learning. Our experiments suggest that optimal learning takes place near the zeros of the maximum Lyapunov exponent for the system. In practice, the reservoir weight matrix can be scaled to

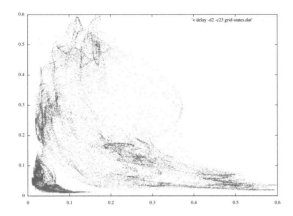

Figure 2. Delay embedding of unit 23's trajectory, showing a rich attractor structure.

tune the reservoir for optimal performance with respect to a given problem and input. RC systems have been applied to a variety ofproblems with some success (e.g., operant conditioning [1], phoneme recognition [8]). We have begun testing our own reservoir implementation on gait recognition tasks with encouraging results.

2. The STN / GPe Complex

The basal ganglia are a set of deep brain structures that are implicated in neurological disorders, such as Parkinson's and Huntington's diseases, and are believed to be crucial to tasks involving action selection or sequencing. Figure 3 shows a block diagram that provides a rough schematic of the relevant anatomical pathways. The striatum is the "input" nucleus of the basal ganglia, receiving convergent input from a wide variety of cortical areas. The striatum, in turn, provides inhibitory input to both the internal and external segments of the globus pallidus. We make two observations: 1) the striato-pallidal projection is highly convergent, at a ratio of about 100:1 [7], and 2) the striatopallidal projection is entirely inhibitory. Pallidal neurons are discoid in shape and receive afferents from a wide striatal region. They inhibit their targets. STN neurons provide excitatory input to the GPe, and appear to help maintain the elevated firing rates of GPe and GPi neurons.

Firing patterns in the STN / GP complex can be rhythmic, bursting, and irregular. Rhythmic firing is more pronounced in pathological states, particularly Parkinson's disease. Wilson et al. [10] suggest that chaotic desynchronization may be the mechanism behind the success of deep brain stimulation in Parkinson's disease. They simulated the STN/GP complex and found that for reasonable physiological ranges, external stimulation of the STN forced the network into firing regimes corresponding to critical and supercritical behavior (i.e., Lyapunov exponent $>= 0$).

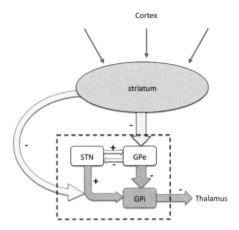

Figure 3. Highly simplified schematic diagram of relevant basal ganglia nuclei. Excitatory pathways are labeled with '+', while inhibitory pathways are labeled with '-'. The dashed box provides an approximate indication of the nuclei that comprise the putative reservoir. Note that within each nucleus, there are many channels that are likely devoted to specific subsets of sensorimotor function.

3. Parallels

The firing properties and anatomy of the STN / GP complex, as well as the perceived role of the basal ganglia in context-driven action selection, suggest to us the possibility that the STN / GP complex is acting as a computational reservoir: a dynamical system that transforms its time-dependent input into segregated outputs that correspond to action "plans" or sequences. In reservoir terms, the striatum provides input to the reservoir, perhaps by learning and gating salient environmental cues [5]. In a reservoir, a subsequent output layer learns the correct linear combination of reservoir units' states to produce the desired output signal for a given input. This learning role could be served by the thalamo-cortical targets of the GP.

Though highly speculative, we experimented with this idea by testing the performance of reservoirs that better reflected the physiological constraints suggested by basal ganglia architecture. First, we note that Equation 1 can be decomposed into "inhibitory" and "excitatory" contributions as follows:

$$W_r = W_r^+ + W_r^- \tag{2}$$

$$x^{(n+1)} = f((W_r^+ + W_r^-)x^{(n)} + W_i u^{(n)}) \tag{3}$$

where all elements of W_r^+ are positive, and all elements of W_r^- are negative. This does not alter the reservoir, but makes explicit the parallels to the actions of the STN and GPe, respectively. We note that W_i corresponds to striatopallidal input. Reservoirs are traditionally designed with both negative and positive input weights. In keeping with the inhibitory role of the striatum in pallidal dynamics,

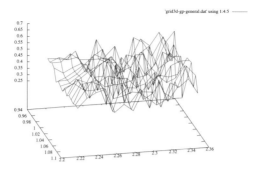

Figure 4. Error landscape for a reservoir with positive and negative inputs, on a gait recognition task, showing an irregular error landscape with sharp troughs.

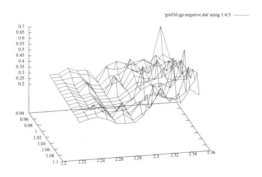

Figure 5. Error landscape for a reservoir with strictly negative input weights, on the same task used for Figure 4. As before, X and Y axes are reservoir weight range and sparseness, while the Z axis is output error. Note that the minimum-error region is smooth and wide, showing relatively little sensitivity to parameter changes.

we compared the use of unconstrained inputs with the use of strictly negative input weights (i.e., where elements of W_i are ≤ 0). Input weights were drawn from a uniform distribution controlled by a parameter v, either from $[-v, v]$, or in the case of strictly negative weights, $[0, v]$. In each case, the input sparseness was selected for minimum error. We then compared the learning landscapes of reservoirs with unconstrained vs. strictly negative input weights on a gait recognition task.

The gait recognition task uses data acquired from a stereo sensing system at SRI. Moving individuals are tracked, and point samples are taken that provide a time series of the individual's body motion. Body motion histograms are projected using PCA down to a six-dimensional subspace that accounts for 95% of the variation in the dataset. These six parameters, plus floor XY position, are normalized to $[0, 1]$ for each component and then used as an eight-dimensional input signal for the reservoir. All input signals are zero-mean. In both cases, a reservoir with three-dimensional grid topology outperformed reservoirs constructed using the standard random weight matrix, so the sparseness parameter was fixed.

Figures 4 and 5 illustrate the derived error landscapes. Reservoir weights are drawn from a uniform distribution $[-w, w]$. The X-Y axes in these figures correspond to variation of w and v over the same ranges, for which each network appeared to have optimal performance ($w \in [2.2, 2.4]$, $v \in [0.94, 1.1]$), while the Z axis is the classification error. In this case, the reservoir with negative input weights outperformed the unconstrained version, producing a smoother error landscape with a larger basin of minimum error. It remains to be seen whether this is a general property of reservoirs with negative input. We suggest that reservoirs that are tuned to a slightly chaotic (and hence "overactive") regime may be easier to control and bring to criticality with only negative inputs (i.e., input-induced damping). Other experiments that could be revealing include testing the effects of synaptic delays and construction of reservoirs using more physiologically realistic models.

4. Acknowledgement

This effort is sponsored by the Defense Advanced Research Projects Agency. The content of this paper does not necessarily reflect the position or the policy of the U.S. Government, and no official endorsement should be inferred.

References

[1] E. Antonelo, B. Schrauwen, and D. Stroobandt. Mobile robot control in the road sign problem using reservoir computing networks. In *International Conference on Robotics and Automation*, 2008.

[2] M. D. Bevan, P. J. Magill, D. Terman, J. P. Bolam, and C. J. Wilson. Move to the rhythm: oscillations in the subthalamic nucleusexternal globus pallidus network. *Trends in Neurosciences*, 25(10), October 2002.

[3] P. F. Dominey, M. Hoen, and T. Inui. A neurolinguistic model of grammatical construction processing. *Journal of Cognitive Neuroscience*, 18(12):2088–2107, 2006.

[4] H. Jaeger. Short term memory in echo state networks. Technical Report 152, German National Research Center for Information Technology, 2001.

[5] M. S. Jog, Y. Kubota, C. I. Connolly, V. Hillegaart, and A. M. Graybiel. Building neural representations of habits. *Science*, 286(5445):1745–1749, November 1999.

[6] P. Redgrave, T. Prescott, and K. Gurney. The basal ganglia: a vertebrate solution to the selection problem? *Neuroscience*, 89:1009–1023, 1999.

[7] G. M. Shepherd, editor. *The Synaptic Organization of the Brain*. Oxford University Press, New York, 1990.

[8] F. Triefenbach, A. Jalalvand, B. Schrauwen, and J.-P. Martens. Phoneme recognition with large hierarchical reservoirs. In *Neural Information Processing Systems (NIPS2010)*, In Press.

[9] D. Verstraeten, B. Schrauwen, M. D'Haene, and D. Stroobandt. An experimental unification of reservoir computing methods. *Neural Networks*, 20:391–403, 2007.

[10] C. J. Wilson, B. Beverlin, and T. Netoff. Chaotic desynchronization as the therapeutic mechanism of deep brain stimulation. *Frontiers in Systems Neuroscience*, 5, June 2011.

Biologically Inspired Cognitive Architectures 2011
A.V. Samsonovich and K.R. Jóhannsdóttir (Eds.)
IOS Press, 2011
© 2011 The authors and IOS Press. All rights reserved.
doi:10.3233/978-1-60750-959-2-79

Architectures of Complex Learning Systems

L. Andrew COWARD and Tamas O. GEDEON

Australian National University, Canberra, ACT 0200, Australia

Abstract. A system which performs a complex combination of behaviours has two superficially independent architectures. One is the functional architecture, which separates the behavioural features of the system into feature modules made up of groups of similar behaviours, and defines the interactions between features. The other is the system architecture (alternatively called the physical or information process architecture) which separates the physical information handling resources of the system into modules that perform different types of information processes, each module optimized to perform a different type of process. Any one feature module will employ information processes performed by many or all resource modules. Many different functional architectures are possible, but the need to limit the resources supporting large numbers of different behaviours tends to constrain the form of the system architecture. In the limiting case as the ratio of the number of behaviours learned to the available resources becomes very large, the system architecture is constrained into a very specific form. In the case of a complex learning system this form is called the recommendation architecture. Because there are natural selection advantages for species that require fewer neural resources to learn a given set of behaviours, there is a tendency for the recommendation architecture form to appear in biological brains including human, mammal and avian brains. A system designed to perform a complex combination of behaviours will be much more effective if designed within this form..

1 Introduction

In this paper, a complex system will be defined as one which can perform a very large number of different purposeful behaviours in a way that is appropriate for a complex environment. Purposeful means that it is possible to identify system objectives which motivate behaviour selection. Such systems could also be called complex functional systems, but in this paper the simpler term will be used. Purely physical complex systems such as the weather are not purposeful as defined and are therefore not included. The behaviours of complex electronic systems like flight control computers or telecommunications network managers are specified in advance under external intellectual control. A complex learning system must learn a large combination of behaviours appropriate to achieve objectives in a very complex environment.

The behaviours performed by a complex electronic system are typically organized into different types of functions, called features or applications. Each function is a collection of similar or closely related behaviours. The definition of the different functions and the interactions between them is called the functional architecture, and can be very different for different systems. For example, a personal computer has separate applications for word processing, web access etc. with specific, limited ways in which they can exchange information. However, it is striking that any electronic system that performs a complex combination of behaviours always has the same physical (or information process) architecture at the highest level. This physical architecture separates memory and processing subsystems, with a common bus linking these subsystems together and with subsystems receiving inputs from the environment and generating outputs driving behaviours. All applications make use of the same memory and processing resources, and, conversely, any one memory or processing resource will contribute to many or all different applications.

Mammal brains of different species all have objectives to survive and reproduce, but are able to learn to perform very different combinations of behaviours, depending on the environmental niche occupied. However, all mammal brains have a very similar physical architecture at the highest level, with cortex, hippocampus, basal ganglia, thalamus, amygdala and cerebellum. Close examination of the avian brain reveals a very similar physical architecture with the same major subsystems [1]. In the case of the human brain, one "feature" like episodic memory uses many different physical resources, and another feature like imagination uses many of the same resources [2].

Both designed and learning systems must obtain information from their environment, and use this information to determine an appropriate behaviour at each point in time, selecting within a wide range of options. Such systems must therefore detect conditions within their input information, and associate different behaviours with different combinations of conditions. In systems that are designed, both conditions and associations between conditions and behaviours are specified by the designer. In systems that learn, most of the conditions and the associations between these conditions and appropriate behaviours must be defined heuristically on the basis of experience.

2   Practical constraints on complex electronic systems

Any complex system requires information handling resources in order to perform its functions. In the case of an electronic system these include the transistors and other components that constitute memory and processing subsystems. A system architecture that can perform a given set of functions with fewer resources will have an advantage over an architecture that requires more resources, although other considerations will interact with this resource constraint.

For an electronic system, these other practical considerations include modifiability, repairability, constructability and synchronicity. Modifiability means that it must be possible to add or change features without interfering with the operation of other features. Constructability means that it must be possible to build many copies of the system from blueprints by a process that minimizes the risk of errors and is therefore not too complex. Repairability means that it must be possible to diagnose and correct construction errors and later component failures or damage. Synchronicity means that it must be possible to handle a constant sequence of inputs from a continuously changing environment without confusing information derived from the environment at different times.

These different considerations are often in conflict. For example, if every feature had completely separate information handling resources, one feature could always be modified with no effect on other features. However, this would have a very high cost in resources. If information derived from the environment at different times was processed by different resources, synchronicity would be guaranteed at a very high cost in resources. The need to find an adequate compromise between conflicting practical considerations places strong constraints on the physical architecture [3].

2.1 Condition Detection and Modules

Any one condition detected within environmental inputs will be a list of relevant inputs and a specified state for each input. The condition occurs if each relevant input (or a high proportion) is in the specified state. In practice a condition may be a very complex combination of system inputs and states. Conditions must therefore be specified (by the system designer) and the system inputs at each point in time must be tested for the presence of each condition by comparison between the inputs and the condition specification. Both the specification of a condition and the testing for the presence of a condition will require information handling resources. A condition can be viewed as a group of smaller conditions (or subconditions). Two conditions are similar if some of their subconditions are the same.

Resource requirements can be considerably reduced if similar conditions are collected into modules, within which the resources to specify and detect any overlaps (or identical subconditions) are shared. This resource advantage drives a hierarchy of modules, with the most detailed modules detecting groups of very similar conditions, the similarity making it possible to share resources within a module. Intermediate modules are made up of the resources of a group of detailed modules, and detect a range of conditions with somewhat less similarity. Higher level modules are made up of groups of intermediate modules with lower similarity but still enough to achieve resource economies. Similarity between submodules of a higher module means that the submodules require some of the same subconditions. Sharing means that there is an information exchange between the modules, with each shared subcondition being detected by one module and detections communicated to other modules.

This type of modular hierarchy has considerable resource advantages, but creates problems with modifiability. Any one module will be required to support many different features. Change to a feature will often require changes to the condition definitions used by the feature, but such changes could have undesirable side effects on other features using the same condition. Furthermore, the undesirable effects of a change can propagate to other modules via information exchange. Modifiability therefore requires minimization of information exchange, and the modular hierarchy must be a compromise between these conflicting requirements.

One further constraint on a modular hierarchy is constructability. If every module were completely different, then the specification of the construction process would be very complex and the probability of errors correspondingly high. However, even on one level modules must be different in order to detect different conditions. Hence the compromise with constructability will result in modules on one level that are generally similar but differ in detail.

2.2 Handling of sequences of input states

Inputs to a complex system from the environment are continuous, and conditions must be detected in these inputs. Some conditions will be made up of input states which must all be present at the same time, others of input states which occur in a defined fashion over time. Hence the temporal relationships between condition detections must be recorded in some way. The only alternative would be to have multiple duplicates of resources to specify and detect conditions at different points in time. This would place impractical demands on resources.

The most precise practical way to support such recording is to use the same condition specification and detection resources, but record detections in a separate memory along with tags indicating detection time. Because all conditions are exactly specified and precisely detected, it is possible for condition detections to have unambiguous behavioural meanings. In other words, they can be interpreted as commands. There is therefore a major separation in such an architecture between a subsystem which records the occurrence of conditions (a memory) and a subsystem which executes commands (a processor). In other words, the combination of practical considerations results in the ubiquitous von Neumann architecture.

2.3   Practical constraints on a complex learning system

The information available to a complex learning system is made up of inputs from the environment and inputs from within the system itself. The system must detect conditions within its inputs which are effective for discriminating between circumstances in which different behaviours are appropriate. Conditions detected within internal inputs will be important for guiding a special class of behaviours, called reward behaviours. Such conditions discriminate between satisfactory and unsatisfactory internal situations, and can be used to reward or punish recent behaviours, which have probably played some role in reaching the current situation. Reward behaviours increase or decrease the probability that behaviours similar to those recently performed will be performed in similar circumstances in the future. Given that conditions within the environment must largely be defined heuristically, reward behaviours are critical for associating such conditions with appropriate behaviours.

A complex learning system is also subject to the same practical constraints: resource limits, modifiability, constructability, repairability and synchronicity. Modifiability in this context means the ability to learn without undesirable side effects on past learning. One effect will be organization of condition detection into a modular hierarchy as discussed earlier for complex electronic systems. A module on any level has a receptive field, defined by the group of conditions it contains. This receptive field is detected if a high proportion of these conditions is detected. However, the requirement to heuristically define the conditions which will be detected and also to define the associations between conditions and behaviours results in some qualitatively different architectural constraints from complex electronic systems designed under external intellectual control. Enough different conditions must be defined to permit discrimination between circumstances in which different behaviours are appropriate. The problem is the source of guidance to making changes to conditions. Consequence feedback following a behaviour is a possible source, but because any one condition will support many different behaviours, changes to the definition of a condition based on consequence feedback following one behaviour will have unpredictable effects on all the other behaviours dependent on the condition. As a result, consequence feedback cannot be used directly to guide changes to conditions or receptive fields. Modules cannot therefore be evolved to correspond exactly with the circumstances in which one behaviour is always appropriate. In contrast with the von Neumann architecture, condition detections cannot correspond with instructions, only with recommendations in favour of a range of different behaviours.

Recommendations must be interpreted into a behaviour that is actually implemented, and the weights of such recommendations must be adjusted by consequence feedback. Because such consequence feedback cannot be applied to condition definitions, there must be a separate subsystem which receives condition detections, interprets such detections as recommendations, determines the strongest recommendation across all current condition detections, implements that behaviour, and later adjusts recommendation strengths on the basis of consequence feedback.

As the ratio of the number of behaviours to be learned to the available resources increases, a complex learning system will therefore tend to be constrained into an architecture with two major subsystems. One subsystem (called clustering) defines and detects conditions within the information available to the system, the other subsystem (called competition) interprets condition detections as behavioural recommendations. This architecture is called the recommendation architecture, and is analogous with but qualitatively different from the memory, processing separation in complex electronic systems designed under external intellectual control.

There are four types of behaviour requiring special handling. These are condition change behaviours, recommendation weight change behaviours, general behaviour type recommendation selection, and behaviour sequence management.

Changes to modules always risk undesirable side effects on behaviours influenced by the changed conditions, and the behaviours of changing the conditions that define a module must therefore be tightly managed. This management requires detection of conditions able to discriminate between circumstances in which module changes are appropriate and inappropriate, and interpretation of such condition detections as recommendations in favour of changes to specific modules. The risk of undesirable side effects means that in general, changes to a module can only be by addition of a few extra conditions that are similar to those already detected by the module. The receptive field of the module is expanded slightly, but will continue to be detected in all the circumstances in which it was previously detected. Such receptive field expansions must only occur if the range of recommendations otherwise available is too low to achieve a high integrity behaviour selection. In other words, if the total number of receptive field detections is less than some minimum, receptive field expansions must occur to bring the number up to the minimum. A resource management subsystem is therefore required which detects receptive fields that are appropriate to be interpreted as recommendations in favour of expansions of other receptive fields. The resource management subsystem will therefore have the same clustering/competition separation.

Changes to recommendation weights in competition are also behaviours which must be tightly managed. These reward type behaviours will therefore also require a clustering/competition separation. Similarly, it may sometimes be appropriate to bias behaviour selection in favour of different general types of behaviour. The circumstances in which such biases are appropriate must be discriminated by receptive fields in clustering and implemented by interpretation of receptive field detections in competition. Finally, there may be sequences of actions which are often required to be implemented in the same order. Higher speed and accuracy can be achieved by recording such sequences in a separate subsystem, and implementing them in response to an initial trigger rather than by receptive field detection and interpretation after each individual action.

The architectural form which results from these considerations is illustrated in figure 1. As the ratio of behaviours which must be learned to available information handling resources increases, a complex learning system will tend to be constrained more tightly into this form. In an analogous fashion, systems that are designed to perform a complex combination of behaviours tend to be constrained into the von Neumann architectural form.

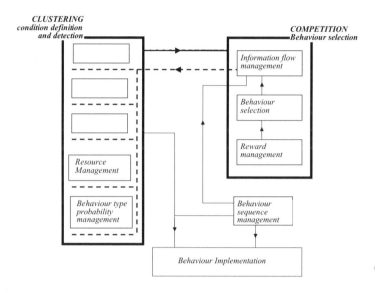

Figure. 1. The recommendation architecture. This architecture is the limit towards which a learning system will tend to be constrained as the ratio of behaviour to available information handling resources increases. Different subsystems perform different types of information processes. Any one behaviour will require many different types of information process performed by many different subsystems. Conversely, any one subsystem will perform information processes in support of many different behaviours. *Clustering* defines and detects conditions within the information available to the system , including both external environmental and internal state information. Conditions are organized into groups (called receptive fields), and if a high proportion of the conditions are present, the detection of the receptive field is signalled to competition. Withing *competition*, each receptive field detection is interpreted as a range of behavioural recommendations, each with an individual weight. *Behaviour selection* determines and implements the most strongly recommended behaviour . *Reward management* determines the total recommendation weight in favour of reward behaviours. If implemented, reward behaviours adjust the weights of recently implemented behaviours. Many behaviours are implemented by releasing receptive field detections from one module of clustering to another, or outside clustering to drive externally directed behaviours. *Information flow management* manages these information releases in detail, with guidance from the behaviour selection component. Note that information flow management gates the release of information but does not change the content. The *resource management* module uses special purpose receptive fields to determine when and where changes will be made to receptive fields throughout clustering. Behaviour type probability management detects special purpose receptive fields that recommend favouring different general types of behaviour are currently appropriate. Selection of the most favoured type is implemented by reducing the threshold for detection of receptive fields elsewhere in clustering that strongly recommend behaviours of that type. Many often utilized behaviours are sequences of actions.. Such sequences could be implemented by receptive field detection and behaviour selection prior to each action, but more rapid and accurate execution can be achieved by recording the sequence in the behaviour sequence management component, which executes the sequence on the basis of initial receptive field detections.

There is one further important architectural consideration imposed by practical considerations. Conditions must be detected within environmental inputs at a single point in time (e.g. within a single visual object, guiding appropriate behaviour in response to the object). More complex conditions must be detected that incorporate conditions detected at multiple points in time (e.g. within a group of objects, guiding appropriate behaviour in response to the group). To detect the more complex conditions, condition detections derived from information at different points in time must be simultaneously active, but without confusion of the information from different points in time. Avoidance of confusion requires either spatial or temporal separation. Spatial separation would require duplicate resources for condition detection. Temporal separation can be achieved by separating condition detections within different inputs into different time slots in the same physical condition detection resources. This solution is more resource effective and appears to be used in the human brain [4].

The cognitive deficits that result from damage to different anatomical structures in the brain [5] indicate that the human and other mammal brains have been constrained by natural selection pressures into the recommendation architecture form.

3   Indirect receptive field activation and cognitive processing

A module is activated by detection of its receptive field in current environmental inputs. Such activations make the behavioural recommendations corresponding with the detections available to guide immediate behaviour. However, complex learning requires that behavioural guidance has access to much more information than just these current inputs. If a receptive field of a module is currently not detected, but has often been detected in the past at the same time as many of the currently active receptive field modules, then that inactive module may have relevant recommendation strengths to contribute to current behaviour. Hence there can be behavioural value in the capability to indirectly activate modules on the basis of past temporally correlated activity. Different types of temporally correlated activity could be relevant: recent or frequent past simultaneous activity, or past simultaneous receptive field changes. In each of these types, past activity of the inactive module could be simultaneous with, shortly before or shortly after the past activity of the active modules.

If uncontrolled, such indirect activations would result in chaotic patterns of module activation. Indirect activations must therefore be behaviours that are recommended by module activations and only implemented if there is sufficient total recommendation strength into competition. Indirectly activated modules may themselves have recommendation strengths in favour of indirectly activating yet other modules, resulting in a sequence of indirectly activated module populations with a considerable degree of independence from current inputs from the external environment. It can be demonstrated that the three types indirect activation (on the basis of recent, frequent past, and past change activity) can support, respectively, priming, semantic and episodic memory in human beings [5]. More complex cognitive processes can be supported by ordered sequences of activations, including both direct and indirect activations [6;7].

4   Simulations of the recommendation architecture

The recommendation architecture can be simulated on a von Neumann machine [3]. Such simulations have demonstrated that the information processes of the recommendation architecture can organize experience heuristically into receptive fields able to discriminate between situations with behaviourally different implications [3;8]. Simple reward feedback applied to a separate competition subsystem receiving the receptive field detections results in learning of new behaviours with minimal interference with past behavioural learning [9]. Receptive field detections within different input states can be separated in different time slots [4]. Indirect activation of receptive fields can support more complex cognitive processing [3].

Organization of experience into arrays of receptive fields has some general resemblances with neural network approaches like Kohonen maps [10] and adaptive resonance [11]. However, as discussed more fully in Coward [3;5] there are major differences from these approaches. In particular, the concept of receptive fields that in most circumstances only expand, with detailed management of when such expansions can occur, is qualitatively different from alternative network algorithms. The approach also avoids the problem of catastrophic interference between new and prior learning found in many neural network algorithms [12].

5   Conclusions

If a system is to be designed that can learn to perform many different behaviours, it is important to focus on the information processes that are supported and how those processes are organized into a system architecture, not just on the functional architecture.

If many different conditions must be detectable in order to be able to discriminate between circumstances in which different behaviours are appropriate, and if most of those conditions must be defined heuristically, then the information processes required will be those of the recommendation architecture, and it will be necessary to organize system resources as in figure 1 to optimize the performance of those processes. A system that addresses a limited domain, with a significant amount of preprogrammed knowledge, will not experience these architectural constraints to the same degree.

The individual information processes are present in the brain, and have individually been tested by electronic simulation. The next step is development of a system which must learn a complex environment with minimal guidance, and perform a complex combination of appropriate behaviours in response to that environment.

References

1. Jarvis ED, Gunturkun O, Bruce L et al. (2005). The avian brain and a new understanding of vertebrate brain evolution. Nature Reviews Neuroscience 6, 151 – 159.
2. Addis DA, Wong AT, Schacter DL (2007) Remembering the past and imagining the future: Common and distinct neural substrates during event construction and elaboration. Neuropsychologia 45:1363–1377.
3. Coward, LA (2001). The Recommendation Architecture: lessons from the design of large scale electronic systems for cognitive science. Journal of Cognitive Systems Research 2(2), 111-156.
4. Coward LA (2004). Simulation of a Proposed Binding Model. *Brain Inspired Cognitive Systems 2004*, L. S. Smith, A. Hussain and I. Aleksander, (editors), University of Stirling: Stirling.
5. Coward LA (2005). *A System Architecture Approach to the Brain: from Neurons to Consciousness*. New York: Nova Science Publishers.
6. Coward LA, Gedeon TO (2009). Implications of Resource Limitations for a Conscious Machine. *Neurocomputing* 72, 767 - 788.

7. Coward LA (2011). Modelling Memory and Learning Consistently from Psychology to Physiology. In V Cutsuridis et al. (eds.), *Perception-Action Cycle: Models, Architectures, and Hardware*, pp 52 – 123. Springer Series in Cognitive and Neural Systems.
8. Coward, LA (2009). The Hippocampal System as the Manager of Neocortical Declarative Memory Resources. in *Connectionist Models of Behaviour and Cognition II*, J. Mayor, N. Ruh and K. Plunkett (eds), 67 - 78.
9. Coward LA, Gedeon TO, Ratanayake, U. (2004). Managing Interference between Prior and Later learning. ICONIP 2004, Calcutta. Lecture Notes in Computer Science 3316, 458-464.
10. Kohonen, T. (1995). Self Organizing Maps. Springer Series in Information Sciences 30.
11. Carpenter, GA, Grossberg, S. (1988). The ART of Adaptive Pattern Recognition by a Self-Organizing Neural Network, IEEE Computer, 3, 77-88.
12. French, RM (1999). Catastrophic Forgetting in Connectionist Networks. Trends in Cognitive Science 3(4), 128-135.

Biologically Inspired Cognitive Architectures 2011
A.V. Samsonovich and K.R. Jóhannsdóttir (Eds.)
IOS Press, 2011
© 2011 The authors and IOS Press. All rights reserved.
doi:10.3233/978-1-60750-959-2-88

The role of the predicted present in artificial and natural cognitive systems

ALAN DIAMOND [a], OWEN HOLLAND [a,1] and HUGO GRAVATO MARQUES [b]

[a] *Department of Informatics, University of Sussex*
[b] *AI Lab, University of Zurich*

Abstract. In previous work, we have argued that a sophisticated cognitive system with a complex body must possess configurable models of itself (or at least its body) and the world, along with the necessary infrastructure to use the modelled interactions between these two components to select relatively advantageous actions. These models may be used to generate representations of the future (imagination) and the past (episodic memory). In this paper we will explore some problems surrounding the representation of the present arising from the use of such models in the artificial cognitive system under development within the ECCEROBOT project. There are two aspects to consider: the representation of the state of the robot's body within the self model, and the representation of the state of the external world within the world model. In both natural and robotic systems, the processing of the sensory data carrying state information takes a considerable time, and so any estimates of the present states of both the agent and the world would have to be obtained by using predictive models. However, it appears that there is no need for any such representations to be generated in the course of selecting a course of action using self and world models, since representations are only of the future or the past. This may call into question the utility and timing of the apparent perception of the present in humans.

Keywords. Prediction, Robotics.

1. Introduction

In previous work, we have argued from first principles that a sophisticated cognitive system with a complex body must possess configurable models of itself (or at least its body) and of the world, along with the necessary infrastructure to use the modelled interactions between these two components to select relatively advantageous actions. We have reviewed the biological and psychological evidence supporting the view that humans possess and use such an architecture, and we have successfully demonstrated such a scheme – essentially a kind of imagination, which we call functional embodied imagination – on a complex robot [1,2]. We have since taken note of the recently established connections between imagination and episodic memory in humans in order to consider the possible extension of our scheme to providing a kind of episodic memory for the system's actions [3].

As noted in [4], many authors have pointed out that the possession and use of a self-model may ultimately lead to consciousness, or at least to many of the cognitive features that seem to be associated with consciousness. There are many pitfalls in

---

[1] Corresponding Author.

attempting to deal directly with the notion of consciousness in artefacts, but these can be avoided by adopting the representational principle of experience proposed in [3]. This makes the very simple assumption that whatever is (consciously) experienced in a system must be represented, but that mere representation does not necessarily imply experience. By analysing cognitive architectures for what needs to be represented for purely functional reasons, this places a useful constraint on what might be experienced within such systems. In our own architecture, we have so far dealt with what we call functional embodied imagination and (to some extent) episodic memory. Although imagination in general deals with counterfactuals, functional embodied imagination – a way of deciding what to do next – is about the future; in contrast, episodic memory is always about the past. For completeness, in this paper we will explore the issues surrounding the representation of the present, and we will use the version of our architecture under development within the ECCEROBOT project [5].

But what kinds of issues might arise in the representation of the present? There are many possibilities, and we will consider only a small subset here. We will be concerned only with the representation within the system at a time T of the state of the robot and the external world at time T. We will not be concerned with the representation of time itself within the system, which may not be intrinsically temporal, nor with anything corresponding to the subjective experience of time. Instead, our focus will be on the function and nature of the state representation. Its function, defined very narrowly, will be assessed in relation to its contribution to the selection of relatively beneficial actions through the mechanism of internal simulation. The nature of the representation is constrained by the unavoidable existence of delays in both sensing and sensory processing: if any representation of the present exists, it must necessarily be a representation of the *predicted present* based on data from the past. This was first articulated in the context of visual perception by Helmholtz [6], who measured the surprisingly low speed of neural conduction, and who then invoked 'unconscious inference' as the mediating process in producing a timely perception, a position developed much further and much later by Richard Gregory. (Our use of the phrase 'predicted present' is partly to differentiate it from Edelman's 'remembered present'[7], which applies to subjective experience; nevertheless, both use data from the past.)

2. ECCEROBOT: Body, sensors, actuators, control, and cognition

The European project ECCEROBOT (Embodied Cognition in a Compliantly Engineered Robot) [5] is exploring the possible connections between a specifically human embodiment, and specifically human cognitive characteristics. It centres around a series of robots each of which copies the musculoskeletal structure of the human body, with a human-like skeletal torso, and analogues of muscles elastically coupled to the bones via elastic tendons. Figure1(a) shows a recent example, the ECCEROBOT Design Study (EDS). This anthropomimetic approach [8] contrasts with that of conventional humanoid robots, which, although they fit within a roughly human envelope, are constructed using the same technology as industrial robots, with stiff, precisely controlled motors and joints. There are four key characteristics which distinguish anthropomimetic robots like ECCEROBOT from traditional humanoids: tendon-driven redundant actuation, multi-articular joint actuators, compliance, and complex joints (see [9] for details). While these succeed in producing a distinctively human (or animal) embodiment, they also make it almost impossible to use the standard engineering control techniques which conventional humanoids are so carefully designed to facilitate. It is for this reason that a key part of the ECCEROBOT project is to investigate how such robots might be controlled – and of course, the control methodology will necessarily both constrain and enable the possibilities for cognition.

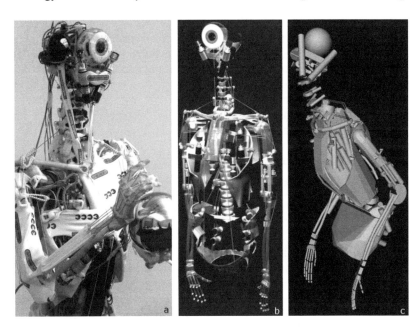

Figure 1. (a) An anthropomimetic robot, the ECCEROBOT Design Study (EDS). (b) 3D Static structure captured in Blender model. (c) Dynamic behaviour modelled in the Bullet physics engine.

In an ideal world, the controller of choice would be a biologically inspired neural system. However, it is still the case that not enough is known about the mechanisms of muscular control to make this a practicable proposition for such a complex robot, with its 44 motors, 70 jointed components, and almost 100 degrees of freedom. (Note that the robot is underactuated, with many degrees of freedom under passive control.) Instead, we are investigating three different but possibly complementary methods: classical engineering control, sensory-motor strategies, and functional embodied imagination. We have made some progress with the first [10], but its limitations have now become clear. Work on the second, which will combine the principles of embodiment and self-organisation set out in [11] with sophisticated information based metrics to characterise sensory-motor interactions, is just beginning. The rest of this paper deals with the implementation of functional imagination and its likely cognitive consequences.

In order to act appropriately, the control system needs information about the robot's state, the state of the environment, and the relation between the robot and the environment. Ideally, all of this information would be derived from sensors mounted on the robot, and those sensors and their associated processing architectures would be biologically inspired. We have satisfied the first requirement – there are no offboard sensors – but the severe constraints of the physical embodiment, as well as our substantial ignorance about how the nervous system processes sensory information, have led us to adopt a more pragmatic approach to the second.

The key provider of information about the environment is vision. After initial investigations using a single camera (hence the single eye of the EDS), which is known to be capable of providing all the required information [12], we have adopted the Microsoft Kinect [13] as the main visual sensor. The Kinect provides a depth map co-registered with an RGB image; these data are processed using GPU accelerated techniques to produce a simplified texture mapped depth map in from tens to hundreds of milliseconds [14]. Within this map, known objects can be recognised and localised, and can then be replaced with detailed precompiled physically and cosmetically correct models as described below. The position of the robot's head in relation to the environment is known from the Kinect data; the static and dynamic configuration of the rest of the body is derived from a knowledge of the positions of the motors, the lengths of the muscle/tendon units, the motor currents, and the tensions in the tendons. All sensory and motor data are managed by a distributed control architecture [15].

3. Delays, and how to deal with them

3.1. Motor Planning

The motor planning strategy for ECCEROBOT's compliant, complex and non-linear structure takes as its premise the assumption that, in our present state of knowledge, it is unlikely that either an adequate analytical model or a suitable control signal could be designed. We have therefore taken the approach of using a generic physics engine to build a detailed simulation model of the robot's structure and joints, including models of the passively compliant tendons, the motors and gearboxes. By stepping the physics model forward in time under the influence of simulated motor inputs we can then use it as a forward model supporting search or learning strategies in kinodynamic space to attempt to obtain a sequence of open loop motor inputs taking the model from a given starting state (the captured state of the robot and environment) to a target state (e.g. grasping an object). This sequence would then be downloaded to the real robot for execution.

3.2. Delay Compensating Control Architecture for ECCEROBOT

As with any control system, delays must be taken into account. The most important delay is the end to end delay between the state of the system at a given time, and the earliest time that a control output based on the sensing of that state can begin to act. The total end to end delay is therefore $d_{in} + d_{out}$ where d_{in} is the time to capture, transmit and process sensor readings to obtain the relevant state estimate, and d_{out} is the time taken to generate a new (or revised) motor activation plan plus the time to transmit this to the physical motors. Thus, if $S(t)$ is the robot state at time t, then the motor planner must be initialized with the state $S(t + d_{in} + d_{out})$ as this is the earliest state of the system where any new motor plan can have any physical effect on its motion. Of course, during d_{in} and d_{out} the robot will continue to be moved under the existing motor plan, and so d_{in} must include not only the time for computing $S(t)$ from the sensor data but also the time $d_{predict}$ for rolling this state estimate forward to $S(t + d_{in} + d_{out})$. The output side of the delay-compensation control architecture is summarized in the schematic Figure 2, in which for convenience $(d_{in} + d_{out})$ is written as d.

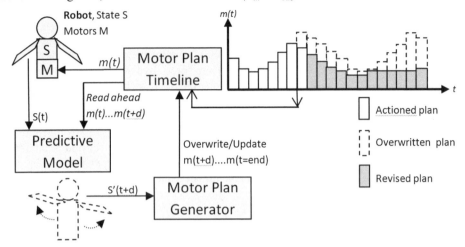

Figure 2. Output delay compensation control architecture for ECCEROBOT.

The current proposed motor plan to reach the goal state is quantized and queued into the motor timeline cache. Control signals are sent to the robot motors continuously, read from this single master queue. The model of the robot and its elastic actuators takes the estimated current state S and drives it with the current motor plan, obtained by reading out the set of upcoming signal sequences covering the period d from the timeline cache. A predicted future state $S(t+d)$ can thus be obtained. The motor planner now locates a new best plan that will take the robot from $S(t+d)$ to the goal state. Revised plans are loaded into the queue, overwriting the old values but starting from the time step at $t + d$.

3.3. Modelling an ECCEROBOT

To create a sufficiently fast non-linear, dynamic model we chose to use the Bullet physics engine [16] which was originally designed for fast 3D games. It is nevertheless a modern, customizable and open-source update on older engines such as ODE, with GPU accelerated collision detection and constraint solving planned for release shortly. Custom extensions have been added to Bullet to model the behaviour of the elastic muscles, pulleys, gearboxes and motors.

A first-pass model, shown in Figure 1(b), was produced using the Blender tool to create a static 3D model of the robot from extensive measurements, photographs and videos. This was exported in sections to Bullet, where joint constraints were then added to create a dynamic model, as shown in Figure 1(c). Finally motor attachment points and pulleys – or pulley-like behaviour where muscle cables wrap around the shoulder or scapula – were added.

To tune the first-pass model's dimensions and parameters to match the robot sufficiently well is a challenging task, but promising early work uses genetic algorithms to search for the best parameter combinations by selecting for the closest match between real and simulated proprioceptive signals.

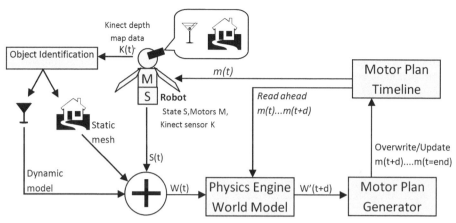

Figure 3. Control architecture using the physics engine to merge environment capture with the robot model

3.4. Merging the robot and environment to create a simulated 'inner world'

Planning tasks where the robot must move about and interact with objects cannot take place without the robot model being situated accurately within the model of the environment, and in relation to the modeled target object. A significant attraction of a generic physics engine approach is that the simulation can be extended to incorporate not just the robot but also a three dimensional model of the environment and the target object. Furthermore, using the Kinect sensor and object recognition [14], these models can be added selectively as either homogeneous static 'collision shapes' (the environment, typically a room) or as full dynamic models in their own right – for example, a target object such as a bottle that is to be grasped and lifted. Once this is achieved this now unified physics-based world model can be used to plan and select the best set of activation signals. Figure 3 shows a schematic of this process. The world state W(t) is generated by merging the state of the robot model with a static collision mesh along with explicit dynamic models of recognized potential target objects. W(t) is then stepped forward in the physics engine for a period $(d_{in} + d_{out})$ before motor planning is commenced.

4. The predicted present

A range of studies in both cognitive science and neuroscience directly support the notion that the state perceived when planning or executing a motor task may not correspond to the state captured at the moment of sensory input but rather to an estimate of a predicted future state. The flash-lag effect [17], where a moving dot is perceived to be ahead of a static one, is a well known simple example, although there are competing interpretations. Similarly, the auditory continuity [18] and phonemic restoration [19] illusions, where interruptions in sensory data are not perceived at all by a subject so long as the data resumes along a predictable path, demonstrate how some conscious perceptions appear to derive not from direct data but from a predicted state generated some time after a period of data acquisition.

More interesting still, Ariff et al. [20] found that the position of eye saccades tracking an unseen reaching movement appeared to reflect the output of a state predictor, rather than the actual position. The saccades correctly predicted the hidden hand position until the hand was subjected to a force field, when the eyes at first continued to track the predicted path until the saccades were briefly inhibited and a corrected estimated position was tracked. Similarly, Fourneret and Jeannerod [21] found that subjects performing a motor movement were actually more conscious of the relevant stage in their planned movement than in their actual movement, which they had been induced to unconsciously distort.

While this type of evidence emphasizes that what appears to be consciousness of state is in fact consciousness of predicted state, there is little satisfactory evidence concerning the objective timing of the awareness of the state and the state itself, which should be simultaneous to qualify both as dealing with 'the present'. Conscious perception contains many temporal anomalies for which resolution is often sought in the idea of retrospectively 'backdating' experience to yield a coherent account of events, as for example in the cutaneous rabbit illusion [22], where a series of taps on the arm appear (wrongly) to the subject to have followed a smooth extrapolated path. The best that can be said at the moment is that the apparent, or subjective, present is in many cases demonstrably the outcome of a prediction from previous data.

As noted in Section 1, any representation of the present in an artificial system must be a representation of a predicted present; this must also be true of any representation of the present in a natural system. Of course, given sufficient computational resources, it is certainly possible for a cognitive system, whether artificial or natural, to construct a representation of a predicted present, as is routinely done in certain engineering systems. However, in our cognitive system there is no *requirement* for any explicit representation of the present; instead, the system contains only data-driven representations of the recent past and predicted representations of the near future. If the human cognitive system is of the same basic type as that under development for ECCEROBOT, in which no representation of the present is required, then the application of the representational principle of experience raises the intriguing possibility that our own conscious perception, which subjectively appears to be of the present, must in fact be either of the near future or the recent past. This hypothesis has the potential to account for the existence of at least some of the anomalies mentioned above; even if it cannot account for particular anomalies without considerable further work, further theoretical and experimental investigation would seem to be worthwhile.

5. Conclusions

In both natural and artificial systems, sensory and computational constraints mean that any representation of the present must necessarily be a prediction from data gathered in the past. In an artificial embodied cognitive system which uses a form of imagination to discover and select a beneficial sequence of motor activations, the most important representation is of the predicted state of affairs in the near future, and there is no need for any representation of the present. Evidence from psychology and neuroscience indicates that many apparent perceptions of the present are clearly derived from predictions based on past data, but it is not clear whether the predictions refer to states in the recent past, the actual present, or the near future. Biologically inspired cognitive architectures, especially those dealing with embodied systems in dynamic environments, should therefore consider the issue of the representation of the present, particularly when dealing with analogues of consciously mediated perception, and should take note of the possibility that a representation of the predicted present, while technically possible, may be neither necessary nor appropriate.

Acknowledgments

The research leading to these results has received funding from the European Community's Seventh Framework Programme FP7/2007-2013 Challenge 2 (Cognitive Systems, Interaction, Robotics) under grant agreement no. 231864-ECCEROBOT. The EDS and other ECCEROBOTs are designed and built by Rob Knight, The Robot Studio, Divonne-les-Bains, France.

References

[1] Marques, H.G. and Holland, O. [2009] Architectures for functional imagination. *Neurocomputing* 72, 743-759

[2] Marques, H.G. [2010] Functional Embodied Imagination. Ph.D. thesis, University of Essex.

[3] O. Holland and H.G. Marques (2010) Functional embodied imagination and episodic memory. *International Journal of Machine Consciousness* Special Issue on Biologically Inspired Cognitive Architectures 2:2 pp 245-259

[4] O. Holland and R. Goodman (2003) Robots with internal models: a route to machine consciousness? *Journal of Consciousness Studies*, Special Issue on Machine Consciousness, vol 10, No 4, 2003

[5] eccerobot.org

[6] Helmholtz, H. von (1909/1925) *Physiological optics, vol. 3,* trans. J. P. C. Southall. Optical Society of America.

[7] Edelman, G. M. (1989) *The Remembered Present: A Biological Theory of Consciousness* (Basic Books, New York).

[8] O. Holland and R. Knight (2006) The anthropomimetic principle. *AISB Symposium on Biologically Inspired Robots*, Bristol.

[9] H.G. Marques, M. Jäntsch, S. Wittmeier, C. Alessandro, O. Holland, C. Alessandro, A. Diamond, M. Lungarella, and R. Knight (2010). ECCE1: the first of a series of anthropomimetic musculoskeletal upper torsos. In *Proceedings of 10th International IEEE/RAS Conference on Humanoid robotics (Humanoids2010)*

[10] V. Potkonjak, B. Svetozarevic, K. Jovanovic, O. Holland (2010) Biologically-inspired control of a compliant anthropomimetic robot, The 15th IASTED International Conference on Robotics and Applications, Cambridge, Massachusetts, pp 182-189

[11] Pfeifer, R., Lungarella, M., Iida, F. (2007). Self-organization, embodiment, and biologically inspired robotics, *Science*, Vol. 318, 1088-1093

[12] Richard A. Newcombe and Andrew J. Davison (2010) Live Dense Reconstruction with a Single Moving Camera, Computer Vision and Pattern Recognition (CVPR2010)

[13] http://www.xbox.com/en-GB/kinect

[14] D. Devereux, B. Mitra, O. Holland & A. Diamond, Using the Microsoft Kinect to model the environment of an anthropomimetic robot. Submitted to the Second IASTED International Conference on Robotics (ROBO 2011)

[15] M. Jäntsch, S. Wittmeier & A. Knoll (2010) Distributed control for an anthropomimetic robot. *Proc. IEEE/RSJ International Conference on Intelligent Robots and Systems,* IROS 2010, pp. 5466-71

[16] Bullet Physics. Accessed: 25.5.2011. [Online]. Available at http://bulletphysics.org, 2011.

[17] R. Nijhawan (1994) Motion extrapolation in catching. *Nature.* 370, 256-7

[18] S. Grossberg (1995) The Attentive Brain. *American Scientist*, 83, 438-449

[19] S. Grossberg & C.W. Myers (2000) The resonant dynamics of speech perception: interword integration and duration-dependent backward effects. *Psychological Review*, 107(4), 735-767

[20] G. Ariff et al. (2002) A real-time state predictor in motor control: study of saccadic eye movements during unseen reaching movements. *Journal of Neuroscience*, 22(17), 7721-7729

[21] P. Fourneret & M. Jeannerod (1998) Limited conscious monitoring of motor performance in normal subjects. *Neuropsychologia*, 36(11), 1133-1140

[22] M. P. Kilgard & M. Merzenich (1995) Anticipated stimuli across skin. *Nature*, 373. 663

Biologically Inspired Cognitive Architectures 2011
A.V. Samsonovich and K.R. Jóhannsdóttir (Eds.)
IOS Press, 2011
© *2011 The authors and IOS Press. All rights reserved.*
doi:10.3233/978-1-60750-959-2-96

Evolving Neural Networks for Artificial Intelligence

Keith L. Downing

The Norwegian University of Science and Technology

Abstract.
This article takes a brief look at the history of Artificial Intelligence (AI), from good old-fashioned AI (GOFAI) to situated and embodied AI (SEAI) and its relationship to cognitive incrementalism, wherein sensorimotor mechanisms form the basis for high-level cognition. Artificial neural networks (ANNs) designed and tuned by evolutionary algorithms (EAs) are discussed in terms of their potential contributions to SEAI. Though state-of-the-art evolutionary ANN (EANN) research has not fulfilled this promise, our script-based EANN system (SEVANN) is briefly introduced as a software tool for quickly testing the SEAI utility of neuro-computational models of various spatial and temporal granularities.

Keywords. evolutionary algorithms, artificial neural networks, cognitive incrementalism

1. Introduction

Artificial Intelligence (AI) began in the mid 1950's, and within a decade was producing impressive systems for game playing and problem solving, at or above the level of human experts. The future looked very bright. No problem seemed too complex, but, unfortunately, many were too *simple*. The capabilities that humans take for granted, our basic sensorimotor skills such as walking, climbing, and grasping for objects, turned out to be orders of magnitude more difficult to program than chess, bridge and circuit design.

Furthermore, by the mid 1980's, researchers recognized that AI's most serious shortcoming was simple commonsense. AI systems behaved like idiot savants, producing exceptional results on a wide range of situations, but floundering miserably on cases that demanded basic intuitions about the world - intuitions that most humans acquire very early in life. This realization, combined with the growing impatience of the media and funding agencies for show-stopping AI results, led to a problematic period for the field.

As this *AI winter* set in, Artificial Life (ALife) [18] began to take root. Although ALife researchers primarily sought to understand the life process in terms of emergence and self-regulation - and at a level far removed from that of neuroscience and psychology - the basic philosophy had immediate implications and inspiration for AI, with two other concepts forming the bridge: situatedness and embodiment. The former entails that an ALife system must reside in an environment (not in a vacuum as assumed by many classic AI systems), while the latter posits a physical wrapper around any ALife system, and one whose survival depends upon a fruitful interaction with the environment.

An enlightened handful of AI researchers [4,33,27] recognized ALife as a more fundamentally sound approach to commonsense and cognition than, for example, translating human-expert rules into IF-THEN statements, or codifying basic intuitions about phys-ical objects and their motions as first-order logical axioms. The general philosophy of these early pioneers at the crossroads of AI and ALife can be summarized as follows:

> Complex cognitive activity is better understood and more successfully embodied in artifacts by working up from low-level sensory-motor agents than by working down from abstract formalisms of rational thought.

Essentially, Situated and Embodied AI (SEAI) researchers believe that common-sense comes only via the learned experiences of a body in a world. Only through these close and prolonged body-world interactions can a system build a solid enough base of fundamental knowledge to support a scaling of general intelligence to human levels. Whereas "I think, therefore I am" might have been an appropriate slogan for *Good Old-Fashioned AI* (GOFAI), it's converse more aptly summarizes SEAI: survival (i.e., being) provides the basis for cognition.

Andy Clark [6] uses the term *cognitive incrementalism* to denote this general boot-strapping of intelligence:

> This is the idea that you do indeed get full-blown, human cognition by gradually adding bells and whistles to basic (embodied, embedded) strategies of relating to the present at hand.

The world-renowned roboticist, Hans Moravec [22] draws an interesting parallel be-tween the evolution of living organisms and that of computers. As summarized in Table 1, animals have always had the ability to sense and act but have gradually evolved cogni-tive and calculation capacities, while the evolution of computers has gone in the opposite direction, from their World-War II roots as industrial-strength calculators, to the myr-iad advances in automated reasoning during the heydays of GOFAI, to the more recent appearance of relatively sophisticated autonomous robots. Though this comparison may indicate nothing more than an interesting coincidence, under a stronger interpretation it says that AI is going about things in the wrong way: sensing and acting must precede cognition if we expect to create human intelligences in silico.

	Living Organisms	Computers
Sense & Act	10,000,000	25
Reason	100,000	40
Calculate	1,000	60

Figure 1. Comparison of advances in animal evolution versus computer capabilities, with each number denot-ing the approximate number of **years** that the (natural or artificial) system has possessed a respectable level of the given attribute. Whereas animals arose with sense-and-act abilities that eventually expanded to handle advanced cognition and then formal, explicit, calculation; computers were originally designed for calculation and later enhanced to tackle reasoning and autonomous robotic tasks.

Of primary relevance for SEAI is the fact that a sensing-and-acting organism cannot (in all probability) simply evolve an independent *reasoning unit* or *calculating module* in a single generation. The relatively homogeneous nature of the human brain (in terms of the basic electrochemical properties of its neurons) and reasonably tight integration of its regions indicate that any newly-evolved region would both a) have similar neural machinery as that of the pre-existing sense-and-act areas, and b) be required to communicate with those areas. Hence, any evolutionary brain improvements would be both enabled by previously-evolved sensorimotor mechanisms and constrained by them.

The grand challenge to cognitive incrementalism may come from the work of Lakoff and Nunez [17], who explain mathematical reasoning, both simple and complex, as an extension of our sensorimotor understanding of the world. The neuroscientific grounding of their theory is weak, but the metaphorical ties between embedded and embodied action on the one hand and mathematical concepts on the other are striking. By linking everyday sensing and acting to one of man's most abstract cognitive endeavors, the author's implicitly motivate a Turing-type challenge for SEAI: build a sense-and-act robot that evolves the ability to do mathematics.

2. Evolving Neural Networks

In the brain, the same type of signal (an action potential) can represent anything from the feel of leather, the taste of zucchini, the sound of Grandpa's voice, and the motor movements necessary to swing a baseball bat; to abstract concepts such as baseball's infield fly rule, center domination in chess, and a Hausdorff space in topology. It all depends upon which neurons in which regions are exchanging the signal, along with what other signals are currently being sent among other neurons. Thus, simulated neural mechanisms should possess the needed generality to both a) govern sensorimotor as well as high-level cognitive behavior, and b) support an evolutionary emergence of the latter from the former.

In fact, the commitment to a neural mechanism also seems to entail an evolutionary design process, since the complex structure of brains both a) lies beyond the design capabilities of standard engineering, and b) seems to violate a good many engineering principles, such as those of strict modularity. Brains tend to have modules, but with numerous projections between them, and interactions occurring at multiple frequencies within many of the same circuits.

Although duplicating the complexity of an entire mammalian brain seems far fetched, the basic pattern of highly interconnected neural modules is feasible on a smaller scale, in artificial neural networks (ANNs) with thousands (rather than billions) of neurons. So SEAI can set its sights on large (not huge) neural networks and attempt to find useful topologies in this intermediate size class. For such networks, designing useful connection patterns by hand still seems ominous. And even if the topology is handmade, the weights between nodes are very difficult to predetermine and must either be a) learned from experience using algorithms such as backpropagation, or b) discovered by search techniques.

A popular search method for these situations is the evolutionary algorithm (EA); it can either replace or supplement an ANN learning algorithm. Although many learning situations have a *supervised* characteristic - wherein correct responses accompany their corresponding problem scenarios (i.e. ANN input vectors) - many do not and are thus inappropriate for backpropagation. However, EAs work fine in unsupervised (and reinforcement learning) contexts, and require no special properties of the ANN nodes, such as differentiable activation functions.

Furthermore, ANNs with recurrent connections (i.e., from downstream neurons back to upstream neurons) are so difficult to train with backpropagation that many researchers use EAs instead [25]. Real brains exhibit extremely high recurrence, which many neuroscientists believe to be a critical foundation of cognitive processes such as attention and pattern completion [10,30], so this is a topological trait that synthetic brains will probably need to incorporate.

In short, the architectural complexities of the brain combined with the limitations of classic ANN learning techniques open the way for simulated evolution as a search tool in the spaces of both ANN topologies and weight vectors. And in problems where these vectors become too large, the EA can, alternatively, search for general learning strategies. In general, neural networks (both natural and artificial) are sophisticated combinations of relatively simple components; and the EA is an excellent tool for exploring the vast space of these combinations.

2.1. Contemporary Evolutionary Artificial Neural Networks

Over two decades of research in the field of Evolutionary Artificial Neural Networks (EANNs) has produced a variety of networks for specific real-world applications [21,36, 38], and a host of solutions to *minimally cognitive* toy problems [3,25].

The standard combinations of EAs and ANNs include the following:

- EAs evolve full weight vectors for the ANN [21,13].
- EAs evolve neurons, their connections, and their connection weights [15].
- EAs evolve the connection topology of the ANN [20,16].
- EAs evolve the learning rule(s) for the ANN [5,35].
- EAs cooperatively coevolve single neurons and their incoming and outgoing synaptic weights [24].
- EAs evolve basic parameters for a complex ANN, which is then instantiated with neurons and connections using a developmental process [37,11,19,8].

Recently, the HyperNEAT system [32] has attracted considerable attention. It relies on an abstract developmental process modelled by a compositional pattern-producing network (CPPN) [31]. The CPPN has an ANN-like structure, but with heterogeneous activation functions in the network's nodes, thus allowing it to compute a wide variety of mappings, which can be used to compute the locations of neurons [28], the weights on connections [32], or even the specific learning-rule parameters for each connection [29].

Despite the documented success of many of the systems referenced above, neither the ANNs, nor the EANN techniques used to design them, give strong indications of scaling up to larger, nor more cognitively demanding, tasks. First of all, any method that directly encodes weights and/or connections in the genome has significant scaling problems (and lacks biological plausibility). The mild success of many such approaches proves primarily that a) they are good alternatives to backpropagation in some (restricted) problem contexts, and b) they can consistently find good ANN controllers for simple sensorimotor tasks.

Systems such as HyperNEAT employ indirect encodings to achieve weight and connection symmetries that, in some problem contexts, facilitate scaling. However, links between neuroanatomical symmetry and cognition may only pertain to some areas of the brain, which appears to exhibit regular synaptic structure near the input and output ends, but very little internally. In the hippocampus, for example, topological structure clearly exists, but the fabled place cells display no topology: neighboring cells fire on completely different sensory input patterns, indicating divergent input-synaptic-strength vectors [2]. This hardly precludes an effective model of the hippocampus from employing symmetry, but merely shows that real brains do not require its omnipresence.

Perhaps the most important bio-inspired insight of EANN research involves gradual complexification, a critical element of NEAT's success [15] and one having clear parallels to the evolution of brains (and organisms in general), as detailed by several neuroscientists [1,34]. Biologists attribute much of complexification to duplication and differentiation of genes [1,26], and the addition of these mechanisms to EAs has proven quite useful [12].

In general, many of the results of contemporary EANN research are misleading with respect to prospects for evolving advanced cognitive faculties. For example, several EANN researchers have used board games such as Othello and Checkers as complex test domains [23,13,14]. This, in itself, sounds quite impressive, since these are very challenging games, with (presumably) high cognitive requirements. However, the evolved ANNs do not function as general problem solvers but as evaluation functions for board states, with the scalar value output by the ANN used by alpha-beta pruning to select the best (among dozens of) alternate moves. Thus, the ANN is a small (albeit important) piece in a standard GOFAI algorithm for playing 2-person games, rather than a complex reasoning system in its own right. This pattern reoccurs often in EANN (and ANN) applications: the network serves a vital purpose in an established algorithm but does not problem solve on its own.

One can argue [7] that brains themselves do not bear the entire cognitive load of problem solving, as considerable storage (and even some of the processing) is off-loaded to the body and/or environment. But few would contend that today's EANNs are on the verge of significant breakthroughs in machine cognition.

2.2. Scripted EANNs

We believe that truly ground-breaking EANN results will only come when more of the brain's mechanisms are demystified, abstracted, and implemented. This could easily involve a combination of evolutionary, developmental and learning models for tuning ANNs to handle adaptive challenges on multiple time scales. Although we have explored various combinations of such mechanisms [8,9], the most significant product of that work involves software, not biology.

Computational Neuroscience is replete with elegant models, many of which may rightly deserve a key role in future EANN systems. However, the choices seem endless, spanning the neural, synaptic and topological levels, and further confounded by genetic and ontogenetic issues. Several years of painstaking programming across a breadth of bio-inspired ANN styles and applications - in which the vision of code reuse was largely a mirage - motivated a pause and retreat to construct a set of basic, object-oriented, design primitives that would support a range of evolvable ANNs.

Our system, SEVANN (Script-Based Evolvable Artificial Neural Networks), uses scripting to describe the layers, links (i.e. sets of connections) and modules (i.e. sets of tightly-related layers) constituting an ANN. Thus new topologies are easily configured and run without code recompilation. It also supports the use of *genetic variables* within these scripts, such that SEVANN builds EA chromosomes for evolving parameters whose values the user has trouble pinning down.

The original motivation for many of the SEVANN design commitments comes from neuroscience, where theoreticians may speculate on the functionality of a circuit without having enough data on neuronal and synaptic parameters to perform a detailed simulation. With an underlying library of many neuron types, learning rules, etc., SEVANN employs evolution to help search for combinations that support the functional theory, assuming that the theory can be expressed as a fitness function. In addition, many of the general neural circuits are reasonably well understood, so SEVANN incorporates several of them as modules.

Thus, SEVANN provides an object-oriented framework for incorporating a wide variety of neuroscience mechanisms in a manner that user-determined portions of each processes can undergo evolution. A straightforward graphical user interface (GUI) and easily-modified scripts enable users to quickly test new combinations of neuron types, topologies and ontological processes.

Finally, open-ended explorations of brain evolution are supported by basic duplicate-and-differentiate operations on ANN scripts, wherein macromutations produce copies of neural layers (and associated links) whose genetic variables can then evolve independently.

To date, the basic ideas behind SEVANN have been independently implemented by the author and many of his master and PhD students. The common attraction is that SEVANN speeds the navigation of ANN design space. Buoyed by the positive feedback from these students, we have recently begun standardizing the SEVANN methodology in a Python system that future students and research associates can tailor to their interests, particularly those involving the evolutionary exploration of alternate models of neurocomputation.

References

[1]   J. ALLMAN, *Evolving Brains*, W.H. Freeman and Company, New York, NY, 1999.
[2]   P. ANDERSEN, R. MORRIS, D. AMARAL, T. BLISS, AND J. O'KEEFE, *The Hippocampus Book*, Oxford University Press, New York, NY, 2007.
[3]   R. BEER, *The dynamics of active categorical perception in an evolved model agent*, Adaptive Behavior, 11 (2003), pp. 209–243.
[4]   R. BROOKS, *Cambrian Intelligence: The Early History of the New AI*, The MIT Press, Cambridge, MA, 1999.
[5]   D. CHALMERS, *The evolution of learning: an experiment in genetic connectionism*, in Proceedings of the 1990 Connectionist Models Summer School, D. Touretzky, J. Elman, T. Sejnowski, and G. Hinton, eds., San Mateo, CA, 1990, Morgan Kaufmann, pp. 81–90.
[6]   A. CLARK, *Mindware: An Introduction to the Philosophy of Cognitive Science*, The MIT Press, Cambridge, MA, 2001.
[7]   ———, *Supersizing the Mind: Embodiment, Action and Cognitive Extension*, Oxford University Press, New York, NY, 2011.
[8]   K. L. DOWNING, *Supplementing evolutionary developmental systems with abstract models of neurogenesis*, in Proceedings of the 9th Genetic and Evolutionary Computation Conference, London, England, 2007, ACM Press, pp. 990–996.
[9]   ———, *The Baldwin effect in developing neural networks*, in Proceedings of the 12th Genetic and Evolutionary Computation Conference, Portland, Oregon, 2010, ACM Press, pp. 555–562.
[10] G. EDELMAN AND G. TONONI, *A Universe of Consciousness*, Basic Books, New York, NY, 2000.
[11] P. EGGENBERGER, *Creation of neural networks based on developmental and evolutionary principles*, in Proceedings of the International Conference on Artificial Neural Networks, W. Gerstner, A. Germond, M. Hasler, and J. Nicoud, eds., Berlin, Germany, 1997, Lausanne, Switzerland, Springer-Verlag, pp. 337–342.

[12]   D. FEDERICI AND K. DOWNING, *Evolution and development of a multicellular organism: Scalability, resilience and neutral complexification*, Artificial Life, 12 (2006), pp. 381–409.

[13]   D. FOGEL, *Blondie24: Playing at the Edge of AI*, Morgan Kaufmann Publishers, San Francisco, 2002.

[14]   J. GAUCI AND K. STANLEY, *Autonomous evolution of topographic regularities in artificial neural networks*, Neural Computation, 22 (2010), pp. 1860–1898.

[15]   KENNETH AND R. MIIKKULAINEN, *Evolving neural networks through augmenting topologies*, Evolutionary Computation, 10 (2002), pp. 99–127.

[16]   H. KITANO, *Designing neural networks using genetic algorithms with graph generation system*, Complex Systems, 4 (1990), pp. 461–476.

[17]   G. LAKOFF AND R. NUNEZ, *Where Mathematics Comes From*, Basic Books, New York, 2000.

[18]   C. LANGTON, *Artificial life*, in Artificial Life: Proceedings of an Interdisciplinary Workshop on the Synthesis and Simulation of Living Systems, C. Langton, ed., Addison-Wesley, Reading, Massachusetts, 1989, pp. 1–49.

[19]   C. MATTIUSSI AND D. FLOREANO, *Analog genetic encoding for the evolution of circuits and networks*, IEEE Transactions on Evolutionary Computation, 11 (2007), pp. 596–607.

[20]   G. F. MILLER, P. M. TODD, AND S. U. HEDGE, *Designing neural networks using genetic algorithms*, in Proc. of the Third Int. Conf. on Genetic Algorithms, San Francisco, CA, 1989, Morgan Kaufmann, pp. 379–384.

[21]   D. J. MONTANA AND L. D. DAVIS, *Training feedforward networks using genetic algorithms*, Proceedings the Eleventh International Joint Conference on Artificial Intelligence, (1989), pp. 762–767.

[22]   H. MORAVEC, *Robot: Mere Machine to Transcendent Mind*, Oxford University Press, New York, NY, 1999.

[23]   D. E. MORIARTY AND R. MIIKKULAINEN, *Discovering complex Othello strategies through evolutionary neural networks*, Connection Science, 7 (1995), pp. 195–209.

[24]   ———, *Forming neural networks through efficient and adaptive coevolution*, Evolutionary Computation, 5 (1997), pp. 373–399.

[25]   S. NOLFI AND D. FLOREANO, *Evolutionary Robotics: The Biology, Intelligence, and Technology of Self-Organizing Machines*, The MIT Press, Cambridge, MA, 2000.

[26]   S. OHNO, *Evolution by Gene Duplication*, Springer-Verlag, Berlin, Germany, 1970.

[27]   R. PFEIFER AND C. SCHEIER, *Understanding Intelligence*, The MIT Press, Cambridge, Massachusetts, 1999.

[28]   S. RISI, J. LEHMAN, AND K. STANLEY, *Evolving the placement and density of neurons in the hyperneat substrate*, Proceedings of the Genetic and Evolutionary Computation Conference (GECCO 2010), (2010), p. 8.

[29]   S. RISI AND K. O. STANLEY, *Indirectly encoding neural plasticity as a pattern of local rules*, in Proceedings of the 11th international conference on Simulation of adaptive behavior: from animals to animats, SAB'10, Berlin, Heidelberg, 2010, Springer-Verlag, pp. 533–543.

[30]   E. ROLLS AND A. TREVES, *Neural Networks and Brain Function*, Oxford University Press, New York, 1998.

[31]   K. STANLEY, *Compositional pattern producing networks: a novel abstraction of development*, Genetic Programming and Evolvable Machines: Special Issue on Developmental Systems, 8 (2007), pp. 131–162.

[32]   K. STANLEY, D. D'AMBROSIO, AND J. GAUCI, *A hypercube-based encoding for evolving large-scale neural networks*, Artificial Life, 15 (2009), pp. 189–212.

[33]   L. STEELS, *Intelligence with representation*, Philosophical Transactions: Mathematical, Physical and Engineering Sciences, 361 (2003), pp. 2381–2395.

[34]   G. F. STRIEDTER, *Principles of Brain Evolution*, Sinauer Associates, Sunderland, Massachusetts, 2005.

[35]   J. URZELAI AND D. FLOREANO, *Evolution of adaptive synapses: robots with fast adaptive behavior in new environments*, Evolutionary Computation, 9 (2001), pp. 495–524.

[36]   D. WHITLEY, *Genetic algorithms and neural networks*, in Genetic Algorithms in Engineering and Computer Science, J. Periaux and G. Winter, eds., John Wiley and Sons, 1975.

[37]   L. YAEGER, *Computational genetics, physiology, metabolism, neural systems, learning, vision and behavior or polyworld: Life in a new context*, in Artificial Life III, Proceedings Volume XVII, C. G. Langton, ed., Reading, Massachusetts, 1994, Santa Fe Institute Studies in the Sciences of Complexity, Addison-Wesley, pp. 263–298.

[38]   X. YAO, *Evolving artificial neural networks*, Proceedings of the IEEE, 87 (1999), pp. 1423–1447.

Biologically Inspired Cognitive Architectures 2011
A.V. Samsonovich and K.R. Jóhannsdóttir (Eds.)
IOS Press, 2011

Data Formats in Multineuronal Systems and Brain Reverse Engineering

Witali L. DUNIN-BARKOWSKI

Scientific Research Institute for System Analysis, Russian Academy of Sciences
Vavilova Street 44, building 2 Moscow 119333 Russian Federation
wldbar@gmail.com

Keywords. Brain reverse engineering, attractor networks, David Marr

Abstract

We hypothesize that the brain "secrets" constitute a moderate number (n < 100) of system principles at all levels of brain construction – from biomolecular structures up to the higher nervous activity (the latter term for mind functions was used by I.P. Pavlov (1849-1936)). We believe that now an unbiased search (by a specialized team of 21 intensely cooperating explorers) of these principles (many of them are already known) and their live implementations might yield a complete human brain wiring diagram with its full functional description in less than five years. Of course, the teamers should be highly motivated in the subject of the search and well-equipped with modern high-tech research tools and knowledge with the background in physics and informatics. The successful solution of the stated above problems will further enable artificial brain creation. With these ideas, we are starting the Russian project in brain reverse engineering, which is planned to run on full swing at the end of 2012.

Our hopes for success are based on great achievements of several past decades in all branches of neuroscience, and the experience of previous works, which will be summarized in the talk. In particular, we will deal with data formats in neural channels (frequency and ensemble codes, stochastic resonance, synchronous/asynchronous modes of multineuronal activity, stochastic (Marr-Hopfield) and continuous (bump) attractor networks and different types of spike-time dependent plasticity. We are also planning to integrate into our operation many parts of the much underappreciated legacy of David Marr (1946-1980) in understanding cortical neural networks as well as all available relevant theoretical and experimental results of the recent years.

Biologically Inspired Cognitive Architectures 2011
A.V. Samsonovich and K.R. Jóhannsdóttir (Eds.)
IOS Press, 2011
© *2011 The authors and IOS Press. All rights reserved.*
doi:10.3233/978-1-60750-959-2-104

Parallel and Serial Components in Human-Like Intelligence

Scott E. FAHLMAN
Language Technologies Institute, Carnegie Mellon University
5000 Forbes Avenue, Pittsburgh, PA 15217, U.S.A.
sef@cs.cmu.edu

Abstract. The human mind can do many amazing things. Of particular interest are a set of cognitive abilities such as simple inference and recognition that are computationally very demanding, but that we humans perform without any perceptible delay or any sense of mental effort – this despite the fact that our brains use slow, millisecond-speed components. In this position paper, I present a brief inventory of human mental operations that exhibit this kind of surprising efficiency. I suggest that we humans accomplish these feats by (a) avoiding the computationally intractable forms of these problems and (b) by applying massively parallel processing, though perhaps of a very simple kind. This is not a new suggestion – some of these ideas were first developed in my mid-1970s work on NETL [1]. However, I believe that a renewed focus on the parallel vs. serial components of mental processing can help us both in understanding human intelligence and in achieving human-like performance in our AI systems.

Keywords. parallel processing, serial processing, human-like intelligence

1. Introduction[1]

We seem to be solving AI backwards. That is, the early triumphs of the field have all been examples of what we consider to be mankind's "higher" mental abilities – the things that we learn to do in college or grad school, or that we view as a sign of particular intellectual prowess: chess, puzzle-solving, manipulating complex algebraic formulae (Macsyma), interpreting nuclear magnetic resonance spectrograms (Dendral), planning the best way to use the resources of a factory or a Mars rover, suggesting antibiotics and dosages for various bacterial infections (Mycin), calculating your income tax (Turbo Tax), and so on. All very impressive – but these programs are confined to narrow domains of expertise. Today's AI systems still lack the common sense and the flexible problem-solving ability of a five-year-old child – or the sensory-motor capabilities of a rat.

Why is this the case? In retrospect, it is perhaps not too surprising. The problems that AI researchers have so far attacked successfully are the ones that we humans must work hard to solve. We are aware of each step in the process. We write textbooks and manuals that describe, in considerable detail, how to perform these tasks. These are serial, conscious behaviors. On the other hand, the problems that have proven to be the

---

[1] Some of this text is taken from an article in the author's "Knowledge Nuggets" blog [2].

hardest for AI have been the things that we humans can do "without any mental effort": recognizing an object, understanding a spoken sentence, understanding (and being able to answer questions about) a "simple" children's story. Whatever is going on when we do these things, we don't have conscious access to it.

When we try to build machines and programs that do these jobs, we quickly discover how deep and complex these tasks really are. But the amazing thing is that we had to discover this. It's not obvious to the five-year-old kid, reading or listening to a story about pigs, wolves, and construction materials, that he is doing something much harder (more computationally demanding) than arithmetic or chess or interpreting nuclear magnetic resonance spectrograms. An awful lot of complex computation is going on as the kid makes sense of his story: sentences are being parsed, words are being disambiguated, motives and belief-states of the characters are being modeled, and so on, but the reader is mostly unaware of all this processing unless something goes wrong, or unless a partial solution pops up to the conscious level as a "flash of recognition".

So what is going on here? I suggest that our minds can best be modeled as a single serial problem-solver – the component whose operation leaves the "what have I been thinking about?" trail that forms a part of our consciousness – combined with a number of massively parallel mechanisms that can perform certain simple but computationally demanding tasks for us.[2] Of course, it is impossible for a parallel system doing thousands or millions of things at once to leave any sort of coherent record of what it has done, so we see only the result (or a few results) of these parallel operations – they appear to us to have produced an answer effortlessly, or "in a flash".

2. Keep the Reasoning Human-Like and Tractable

One "trick" that we humans use for performing everyday mental operations quickly and effortlessly is to avoid using approaches that are computationally intractable. That seems simple and obvious, but a lot of current AI research is focused on what I call "super-human" [3] problems and techniques – techniques that allow our AI systems to do things that no unaided human can do, but at a very great computational cost. For example, there is currently a lot of activity in the area of optimal (or provably near-optimal) planning and decision making. That's good stuff: there are some problems where you want to *know* that your solution is optimal, and for which you are willing to burn a lot of extra supercomputer cycles to get that guarantee. But for people working on optimal solutions, it's easy to forget that for almost all day-to-day human planning, a "pretty good" solution is good enough. And it is that kind of planning, I would argue, for which the problem-solving machinery in the human brain has evolved.

Similarly, many AI people working in knowledge representation reject out of hand any approach that is not based on logically complete and provably sound proof methods, even though such methods are undecidable or intractable for any representation system expressive enough to handle everyday common-sense reasoning. We humans avoid this problem by using inference methods that are not logically complete and not provably sound, but that, in the real world, give us good answers *almost* all of the time. In a world where much of our knowledge is incomplete or

---

[2] The computational demands in this case consist of following pointers, retrieving many items from memory, and making comparisons, not a lot of floating-point arithmetic.

incorrect – much of it based on guesswork – that seems like a good tradeoff, and it is the tradeoff that evolution seems to have made. Given the goals of the BICA community, I would suggest that we focus on pretty good, common-sense, human-like reasoning – and on the machinery needed to implement that – leaving the super-human proof methods to the logicians and other specialists.

3. A Brief Inventory of Parallel Cognitive Operations

Human and animal sensory-motor systems, whether in the visual cortex or the cerebellum or other low-level sensory/motor/coordination areas, make extensive use of massively parallel processing of a relatively simple kind. This has been directly observed by many neuroscience researchers. But here we will focus on the possibility that large-scale parallelism is also important at more cognitive levels of thinking.

Simple Inference: The human knowledge-representation system appears to contain much more knowledge than it can explicitly know. If I tell you that a creature named "Clyde" is an elephant, you suddenly appear to know a great deal about Clyde: he probably has four legs, is gray, has a backbone, he must have periodic access to food or he will die. And so on. A huge amount of access-time inference is going on when we draw these conclusions, but we are blissfully unaware that any work is being done.

"Connecting the dots": If I tell you that a house burned down due to a fire started at a children's birthday party, you will immediately come up with one or more possible explanations (a form of abductive reasoning). You may think of a path such as this: burning candles on the cake, excited kids knocking things over, paper decorations, ignition, fire spreading to the larger structure, and so on. Out of all the thousands of things that might happen at a birthday party and the thousands of things that might start a house-fire, only one or a few plausible paths "pop into your head" as plausible connections and are presented to your conscious mind for more careful analysis.

"Flash of Recognition": We may view recognition as taking a set of expectations (dictated by the current context) and a stream of observed features. The goal is to find, in our vast mental warehouse of stored descriptions, the one that best matches these expectations and observations. It will not always be a perfect match, so hash-table and rigid indexing schemes will not work. A better (and ultimately more plausible) approach is that we have some sort of parallel system in which the observed features are broadcast to agents representing all of the stored descriptions. Acting in parallel, these descriptions compare themselves to the inputs, asking "Is this me?". A winner ultimately steps forward, or perhaps a few leading candidates that can be evaluated by more conscious means.

Such a procedure can be used regardless of whether the features come from the visual system, the auditory system, or from some sort of narrative description of an action taking place: the core fuzzy-matching problem is the same. Humans seem to have a special facility for matching inputs against stored sequences or sequence patterns, for example to recognize a snippet of speech or music or to determine whether a sequence of words matches the patterns of a grammar. All of these matching operations feel to us like effortless, "in a flash" phenomena.

Context or Plan Recognition: This is a special case of the recognition problem above. We can often recognize a plan or fragment of a story just by seeing a few steps: a car pulls up in front of a small-town bank; a man gets out and pulls a ski mask over his face; he is carrying an empty bag, and has one hand in the bulging pocket of his coat... We all know that story – many details are missing here, but we can easily retrieve the relevant template, or a few. Similarly, if I mention the words "base", "diamond", "pitcher", "run", "error", "glove", and "bat", any American will know that the context is baseball, even though every one of those words, by itself, is ambiguous.

Again, I would argue that the most plausible implementation is that we have some active machinery associated with each of these stored plans, stories, or contexts, and they all can ask in parallel "Is this me?". In order for a winner to emerge, it is not necessary to match *every* feature in the description – we just want one description's accumulated score to be higher than that of the others. If there are a few contradictions even in the best-scoring candidate, we can pass that over to the conscious reasoning machinery to see if it can explain away the problem.

"Flash of Inspiration": In [4], I present an AI-inspired explanation of scientific creativity – the kind of creativity that we use in constructing theories and explanations, or in engineering activities such as designing a structure or a procedure. I suggest that a large part of scientific creativity is just good, competent problem-solving that happens to lead to a surprising result. That's the conscious part of the process, and we perceive that as hard mental work. But that doesn't account for the "flashes of inspiration" that most of us have experienced at one time or another, usually after we have been grappling with a problem for some time. I argue that these flashes are really recognition events: some features of the problem you are grappling with match up against features of some stored template, procedure, or metaphor, and this new framework for looking at the problem pops into your consciousness. Of course, finding the best inexact match is computationally very demanding, but if it is done by a massively parallel machine, you feel that a clever idea just "popped into your head".

The stored template that you find probably won't be an exact match to the problem at hand, so then you will then have to do some conscious work to see if the results of the flash can be massaged into a solution that actually works. But if it does work, then this flash has given you a solution template – an approach – that you might not have found by laborious serial search. As Thomas Edison said, "Genius is 1% inspiration and 99% perspiration". But on hard problems that have defeated others, that 1% may be the key to finding a good solution.

4. What Kind of Parallelism?

Wherever I have suggested the use of "massive parallelism" above, you might have imagined a collection of millions of Turing-equivalent machines, each with its own dedicated memory, and a web of communication lines connecting these processors. That would work, but it would be a terribly expensive solution, and not much like what we know about the organization of the brain.

In fact, I have a different model in mind for the parallel components. In a short position paper, I cannot provide a full description of this architecture – see [1] and [5] for more details – but the basic idea is simple enough. We build a sort of "active memory" out of very simple components representing the nodes and links (or entities and relations) in semantic network. These elements are wired together into larger structures – frames, descriptions, contexts – using a sort of switchboard. The nodes and links are of just a few types and contain no long-term storage; it is the pattern of interconnections that make up the system's long-term memory. If we want to record that Clyde is an elephant, we find the "Clyde" node, connect it to an unused "is-a" link, and connect that to the existing "elephant" node. Learning of long-term memories is a relatively slow, serial process in humans – perhaps a few facts per second – so this wiring-up doesn't have to be fast.

The nodes can be temporarily "marked" with a few distinct marker bits, and (in some versions of this architecture) they may also have one or two analog "activation levels" – useful for adding up scores and evidence. The markers and activations can be individually set, cleared, or read, and they can be propagated *en masse* from node to node through the network, under control of a serial "control computer" – the serial component that actually tells the parallel active memory components what to do at any given time.

So this is a kind of data-parallel architecture – one of the first data-parallel architectures for AI ever proposed when the NETL work was published in 1977. The control computer shouts its orders at the entire ensemble, and all the nodes and links respond in unison. But they don't all do the same thing: each element's response depends on its type, and the flow of markers can be altered by the presence or absence of other markers.

What does this have to do with thinking? Consider the potentially parallel operations listed in section 3.

Inference: If we want to know whether Clyde (the elephant) is an animal, we mark Clyde with, say, marker 1. The control computer then sends a command to all "is-a" links in the network: if the node below you has marker 1 set, propagate marker 1 to the node above you. All the is-a links respond in parallel, and after a few such cycles we have marked all of Clyde's superiors in the is-a hierarchy – that is, all the nodes representing types of which Clyde is a member. We then see whether the "animal" node has been marked. If we want to know whether Clyde has a backbone, we again mark Clyde's superiors, and see whether any of the marked nodes has a "has as part" link to "backbone". And so on.

Connecting the dots: To find a path from "birthday party" to "house fire", we do a sort of parallel spreading activation: we put marker one on "house fire" and marker 2 on "birthday party", and then we spread these markers, one level at a time, across links of all kinds (or perhaps across a more restricted subset of links). When the two spreading stains intersect – that is, when some node has both maker 1 and marker 1, we have found a possible path. We can then submit that path to the control computer for careful serial evaluation.

Recognition: The control computer can broadcast a sequence of features into the active memory, which contains all the stored descriptions: "All description-nodes that are large animals, set marker 1. All that live in Africa, set maker 2. All that have long cylindrical noses, set maker 3. Does anyone have all three of those markers?" Perhaps at this point we have a winner; perhaps several candidate descriptions are still in the running, and we need to broadcast more features; perhaps all candidates have been eliminated, and we must either give up or settle for two out of three features. And so on. If we want to use "fuzzy" features rather than binary ones, the analog version of this architecture can add up scores. If we have expectations – in a university office, a desk is more likely than an alligator – we can boost the initial score of the expected items before the recognition begins, but the alligator should not be *completely* ruled out.

And, as we noted above, the recognition of plans, contexts, and useful metaphors for creative problem-solving are all special cases of parallel recognition, where the target items may be complex structures instead of individual nodes.

That is a very superficial sketch of *one possible* massively parallel architecture, and how it could be used to implement some of the seemingly magical operations of human thought. My purpose in this paper is not to argue for this specific architecture, but merely to suggest that some very simple (but large-scale) form of parallelism, when combined with a serial control computer, can give rise to many of these special abilities of the human mind. The implementation of an active memory in neuro-stuff would be complicated by the need for redundancy and perhaps some sort of more distributed representation, since the individual components of the brain's hardware are unreliable and are susceptible to small local injuries.

5. The Serial Part is Important Too

While I have emphasized the importance of the massively parallel computing components – that, after all, is the more novel part of what I am suggesting – it is important to keep in mind that the serial part of the processing is essential as well. The parallel active memory, by itself, doesn't actually *do* anything. It is the serial part – more or less equivalent in function to serial computer of the familiar sort – that runs the show.

It is the serial component that handles the sequential, conscious processing that checks, combines, and makes use of the results that "flash" into conscious consideration from the active memory. The serial component does the actual planning and execution, though the parallel components may locate useful metaphors and ideas in the warehouse of memory structures. The serial part is responsible for setting up the queries and for adding new information to the active memory. By itself, the parallel machinery could, at best, perform some simple match/react behaviors; it might be able to fetch relevant plans and plan fragments, but could not weave them into a coherent plan that fits the current circumstances.

So the two parts of our mind must work together smoothly. The parallel machinery does the magical (and still mysterious) parts of our thinking, without any visible effort; the serial machinery does the hard mental work. We probably share much of our parallel machinery with our fellow mammals and other animals. However, I suggest that it is our well-developed serial reasoning machinery that distinguishes us humans from other animals – and that make possible our complex planning, complex language, and the introspective capabilities that we perceive as consciousness.

References

[1] S.E. Fahlman, *NETL: A System for Representing and Using Real-World knowledge*, MIT Press, 1979. Also available at ftp://publications.ai.mit.edu/ai-publications/pdf/AITR-450.pdf
[2] S.E. Fahlman, *AI: What's Missing?* In the Knowledge Nuggets blog: http://scone1.scone.cs.cmu.edu/nuggets/?p=29
[3] S.E. Fahlman, *Human vs. Super-Human AI.* In the Knowledge Nuggets blog: http://scone1.scone.cs.cmu.edu/nuggets/?p=39
[4] S.E. Fahlman, *An AI View of Scientific Creativity.* In the Knowledge Nuggets blog: http://scone1.scone.cs.cmu.edu/nuggets/?p=101
[5] S.E. Fahlman, "Marker-Passing Inference in the Scone Knowledge-Base System", First International Conference on Knowledge Science, Engineering and Management (KSEM'06), Guilin, China, 2006. http://www.cs.cmu.edu/~sef/scone/publications/MarkerPaper.pdf

Biologically Inspired Cognitive Architectures 2011
A.V. Samsonovich and K.R. Jóhannsdóttir (Eds.)
IOS Press, 2011

Narrative is a Key Cognitive Competency

Mark Alan FINLAYSON [a,1] and Patrick Henry WINSTON [a]

[a] *Computer Science and Artificial Intelligence Laboratory*
Massachusetts Institute of Technology

Abstract. The ability to generate, narrate, and understand stories allows humans to accomplish tasks they would otherwise find difficult or impossible. We draw on observations of human narrative to identify a number of capabilities underlying the narrative faculty that we assert must be integrated into any cognitive architecture intended to achieve human-level performance. In particular, we identify sequencing, gap-filling, and plot pattern extraction as key capabilities, and detail two systems under development in our research group that unify a number of cognitive functions to achieve those abilities, functions including multi-representationalism, dynamically-produced commonsense knowledge, and analogical reasoning. Interestingly, in humans, the narrative faculty is intimately tied to cultural transmission and understanding. We speculate that culture is, in fact, a necessary cognitive resource (akin to commonsense, or the lexicon), and that any cognitive architecture intended to achieve human-level performance will need to have a 'culture' of its own.

Keywords. Narrative, Plot Patterns, Knowledge Representation, Commonsense Knowledge, Culture, Cognitive Architectures

---

[1] Corresponding Author: 32 Vassar Street Room 32-258, Cambridge, MA 02139; E-mail: markaf@mit.edu.

Biologically Inspired Cognitive Architectures 2011
A.V. Samsonovich and K.R. Jóhannsdóttir (Eds.)
IOS Press, 2011

Automatic Verb Valency Pattern Recognition

Mary D. FREIMAN[1] and Jerry T. BALL[2]
[1]*L3 CommunicationsLink Simulation and Training,*
2620 Q Street, Bldg. 852
Wright-Patterson AFB, OH 45433
Mary.freiman@mesa.afmc.af.mil
[2]*Air Force Research Labs*
Air Force Research Laboratory
2558 Fifth Street, B852
Wright-Patterson AFB, OH 45431-7905
Jerry.Ball@wpafb.af.mil

keywords: activation, computational linguistics, verb valency patterns

We have built an automatic tool for determining the valency patterns of verbs in the Penn Treebank corpus. Direct and indirect objects are not explicitly tagged in the corpus since they can be structurally determined, but other potential complements and adjuncts are tagged (e.g., CLR for closely related) (Marcus, Santorini, and Marcinkiewicz, 1993). Using these tags and structural information, the verbs and their valency patterns are extracted for use in a large-scale computational cognitive model of reading (Ball, Heiberg, & Silber, 2007) being developed within the ACT-R cognitive architecture (Anderson, 2007). We have found the patterns of the over 3,000 different verbs used in the Penn Treebank. Further, we have found the most common patterns for different inflections, allowing us to add frequency information for each inflection of each verb to our model. This frequency information is used to set the starting activation of chunks in the reading model in a principled way.

References

[1] J. R. Anderson, J. R., *How Can the Human Mind Occur in the Physical Universe?* Oxford University Press, Oxford, 2007.
[2] J. Ball, A. Heiberg & R. Silber, Toward a Large-Scale Model of Language Comprehension in ACT-R 6. In R. Lewis, T. Polk & J. Laird, editors, *Proceedings of the 8th International Conference on Cognitive Modeling*, 173-179. NY: Psychology Press, 2007.
[3] M. Marcus, B. Santorini, & M. A. Marcinkiewicz. Building a large annotated corpus of English: The Penn Treebank. *Computational Linguistics*, 19(2):-330, 1993.

Biologically Inspired Cognitive Architectures 2011
A.V. Samsonovich and K.R. Jóhannsdóttir (Eds.)
IOS Press, 2011
doi:10.3233/978-1-60750-959-2-112

Vision and emotional flow in a cognitive architecture for human-machine interaction

S. Gaglio[a,b], I. Infantino[a,1], G. Pilato[a], R. Rizzo[a], F. Vella[a]

[a] *Istituto di Calcolo e Reti ad Alte Prestazioni, Consiglio Nazionale delle Ricerche,Italy*
[b] *DICGIM, Università degli Studi di Palermo, Italy*

Abstract. The detection and recognition of a human face should meet the need for social interaction that drives a humanoid robot, and it should be consistent with its cognitive model and the perceived scene. The paper deals with the description of the potential of having a system of emotional contagion, and proposes a simple implementation of it. An emotional index allows to build a mechanism which tends to align the emotional states of the robot and the human when a specific object is detected in the scene. Pursuing the idea of social interaction based on affect recognition, a first practical application capable of managing the emotional flow is described, involving both conceptual spaces and an emotional/motivational model of cognitive architecture

Keywords. Conceptual spaces, cognitive architectures, emotions, human-robot interaction, humanoid, social interaction.

Introduction

Emotions play many important roles in facilitating healthy and normal human behavior, such as in planning and deciding what further actions to take, both in interpersonal and social interactions. Currently, systems and devices, capable of recognizing, processing, or even generating emotions [1],[2], are now being designed in the field of human-machine interfaces, Social interaction among human beings is certainly difficult to define and schematize; it uses many communication channels, verbal or behavioral [3], and undoubtedly involves internal emotional states and complex mental models. Advanced cognitive skills are necessary in a robot or humanoid involved in a smooth social interaction with humans, in order to understand and reproduce the salient aspects of the various communication flows. As the human-computer interfaces (HCI) experience shows, the focus must be shifted on a human-centered design, namely the creation of interaction systems based on models of human behavior [4], considering also to understand actions [5], intentions [6], emotional states [7],[8],[9], motivations, needs, desires, and so on.

In this paper, we propose an emotional contagion [10],[11] system that could be included in a cognitive architecture as a simple but powerful module capable of handling major emotional flows present in a basic robot-human interaction: a familiar face is detected, a known object is present in the scene, there is the possibility to interact and share a basic affective state.

---

[1] Corresponding Author. E-mail: ignazio.infantino@cnr.it

1. Cognitive architectures

The cognitive architecture is the infrastructure of an intelligent system capable of managing perception, recognition, categorization, reasoning, planning and decision-making [12], through an appropriate knowledge representation. A cognitive architecture capable of generating behaviors similar to the humans ones has to consider the role of emotions [13],[1],[14]. In this way, emotional processes may influence reasoning, planning and representations analogously to what occurs in human beings. Ideally, this could be a representation of emotional states that helps the recognition of human emotions, and also influences behavior. Similarly, human intentions may be somehow linked to the expectations and beliefs of the intelligence system. In a wider perspective, the mental capabilities [15] of artificial computational agents can be introduced directly into a cognitive architecture or let them emerge from the interaction of its components.

The present work is based on two different cognitive architectures: a model for visual perception, and a model for the integration of emotions. The reference architecture for visual processing uses conceptual spaces [16], and represents objects with simple three-dimensional models described by superquadrics, and attributes such as shape, color, texture. Visual data identify geometric points in a multi-dimensional space that is hierarchically organized, and related to increasingly higher levels of abstractions. Instead, the mechanism of influence of the emotional approach is inspired by the PSI cognitive model [17], referring in particular to the need for social interaction and to mediate the selection of actions to be taken by simple adjustment of parameters (that actually represent the emerging emotions). PSI architecture involves explicitly the concepts of emotion and motivation in cognitive processes. MicroPsi [18], an integrative architecture based on PSI model, has been tested on some practical control applications, and also on the simulation of artificial agents in a simple virtual world.

1.1. Visual perception and humanoid capabilities

The availability of robots with sophisticated perceptual abilities, advanced motor and mobility skills and the increasing availability of computing resources (including distributed and accessible computational resources through the network), allows us to experiment realistic scenarios, and to design and build components (or entire cognitive architectures) very influential on real applications.

In our experimental setup, the visual channel is the main perceptual stream, which drives our simplified emotional behavior. The test case discussed in the paper involves the use of three cameras. Two of them are mounted on the humanoid, and through the existing functionalities of its software platform, they allow us to manage the following tasks: recognition of faces (in reference to a database of images that can be updated); face tracking; recognition of objects (again using a database of images that can be updated). The third camera is instead associated with a pair emitter-detector IR sensor available with Microsoft Kinect. This device is connected to a PC and managed by an appropriate software module that sends information about the three-dimensional reconstruction of the scene to the robot. The use of this device as external sensor allows reception of a real-time depth map of the environment (see Figure 1), registered with image of the camera RGB Kinect. The software module that manages the three-dimensional data transfers only the one relating to objects and faces (sharing the database with the humanoid). Faces are processed in order to recognize of facial expression (by a 3D approach [19],[20], see Figure 2), and we are working to improve the classification of the affective state considering also the posture and body movements.

Figure 1. Example of 3D scene reconstruction. On the left, RGB image and grey scale depth map. On the right, the reconstruction with texture extracted from RGB image.

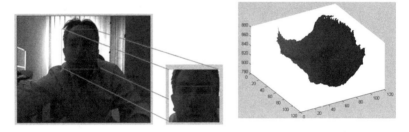

Figure 2. Example of face and features extraction from image, and 3D reconstruction used for expression recognition .

2. Emotional flow

The entities involved in our cognitive emotional context are the following: the robot, the human and objects in the scene. The emotional flow is generated when such entities are present and they can be analyzed according to the diagram in Figure 3. Objects, of course, are passive entities, but they can induce emotional reactions in subjects who have a natural inner affective system (i.e. humans) or an artificial one (i.e. robots).

Given that our point of view coincides with the one of the robot, we can ignore the internal model of the human affective state, and focus on what the robot can interpret from the outside with respect to the human condition. The information flow from the human to robot uses communication channels involving the (spontaneous) facial expression, facial actions, movements and postures of the body, speech and vocalizations. In our scenario we consider a simple mechanism for transferring emotions between the robot and the human, carried by the limited powers of expression owned by humanoid used in the experiments (Aldebran Nao, see Figure 3 on the right).

A simple emotional mechanism has been implemented on the robot, allowing us to obtain complex behaviors, and in some ways similar to those that occur in the interaction of two humans. This mechanism provides a continuous range of values, identifying the state of stress at one extreme and the state of satisfaction at opposite point (the intermediate position is considered as neutral or relaxed state). Situations labeled as "negative" and "positive" respectively, tend to decrease and increase the numerical value of this range, which sets the pleasure/distress emotional index (EI). Moreover, emotional modulation is used to choose an action, defining a behavior or social interaction to be executed [17].

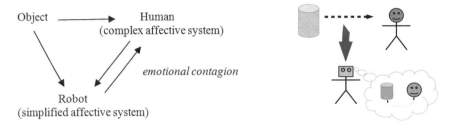

Figure 3. Affective context and emotional flows (on the left of the first row). Emotional contagion in our system (on the right of the first row). Experimentations of emotional subsystem has been performed by NAO humanoid (on the second row).

The robot learns to associate the "emotional response" of a human to an object in the scene. This emotional response is different for each object and for each human actor. Different people will have different reactions to the sight of the same object, so the robot will learn to associate different meanings to many objects and it will change its behavior in order to uniform it to the one of the human in the scene. This mechanism modifies the robot behavior making it more understandable to the humans that will see their own reaction to the objects confirmed by the robot.

Our subsystem is characterized by a sort of emotional emergence driven by human influence, and in both the long-term memory (LTM) and in the short-term memory (STM), is respectively stored the minimal information necessary to have an experience and a reactive mechanism that result from working memory. Objects and faces are stored in LTM according to the approach of conceptual spaces. The short-term or working memory contains information about objects of interest and human faces in the scene. In addition to the recognized objects, a number of interesting objects are identified through a simple mechanism of focus-of-attention (FOA) based on image characteristics (e.g., Sift, or Bi-Sift [21]). Objects may be labeled and stored in long-term memory if the human refers them as relevant in the observed scene (e.g. objects picked up, or indicated with a finger). Even faces can be recognized (and therefore associated with a label that refers the identity of the subject) or not.

2.1. Emotional contagion

Affective-emotional contagion [10],[11] is a normal aspect of social interactions, that include also various imitative unconsciousness or congruent reactions. In similar way, the robot tends to emulate the recognized affective state in the human. Conversely, the humanoid through its LEDs (color, intensity and frequency of blinking) can affect the emotional state according to modern psychological models of human color perception [22].

The emotional contagion system allows the robot to memorize the emotional relationship that binds a human and a given object, and integrates it into his model of perception of the world. For each known human, the robot stores in its long-term memory the links to conceptual space points representing perceived objects, associated with the corresponding emotional index (EI). The value (in the range [-1.0,1.0]) comes from an approximate evaluation of the human emotional state with respect to that particular object: the robot uses only the detected facial expression of the human during manipulation of the object (or touching, or just a physical proximity). This is a very simplified representation of how the object in question really affects the human affective state.

The robot in this way has the basic knowledge to take the appropriate social actions/interactions: when an object is recognized, the robot could go in search of the person to whom it may give pleasure (indicating the position or carrying it); when a human identity is recognized, the robot could go looking for particular items that have shown positive influences on the emotional state of that person; a simultaneous detection of a given person and a given object, depending on the estimated affective state, allows the robot to take actions to mitigate negative effects or to enhance positive ones.

2.2. Example of Human-humanoid affective based social interaction

Emotional contagion causes the robot to have an emotional index on a given object, deriving it by the corresponding estimates of the human emotional values. If an object is present in the scene, there are two or more humans who have different emotional values associated with it, the robot will interact with each of them according to their emotional value. The emotional contagion is controlled by a parameter that allows us to characterize the sensitivity of the robot, so as to make it or completely indifferent (no emotional contagion), or fully influenced by this mechanism. If the robot has its own mechanism to associate an emotional value to an object independently from humans (e.g., having their own physiological responses), this value can help with that derived from contagion to determine the global affective state of the robot. The interaction considered in our experimentation is that the robot observes the relevant scene objects and interacts with the person who is present in the scene according the computed EI. For example, the robot sees the John's favorite toy on the desk. The robot, happy to have located it, glad to have recognized John and seen him smile, invites him to play together with his toy.

Our first implementation of the system, codified a set of rules that indicates the update of the EI, allowing selection of the actions or the social interaction to perform. We are working to replace rules with an appropriate neural network (e.g., ART [23], or SOM), or semantic networks, or a combination of the previous ones.

References

[1] D. Grandjean, D. Sander, and K. R. Scherer, Conscious emotional experience emerges as a function of multilevel, appraisal-driven response synchronization. Consciousness & Cognition, vol. 17, no. 2, 484–495, 2008, Social Cognition, Emotion, & Self-Consciousness, 2008.

[2] H. Gunes, B. Schuller, M. Pantic, and R. Cowie, Emotion representation, analysis and synthesis in continuous space: A survey," in Proc. of IEEE Int. Conf. on Face and Gesture Recognition, 2011.

[3] A. Vinciarelli, M. Pantic, H. Bourlard, Social signal processing: Survey of an emerging domain, Image and vision computing, vol. 27, 1743-1759, 2009.

[4] M. Pantic, A. Pentland, A. Nijholt, and T.S. Huang, Human Computing and Machine Understanding of Human Behavior: A Survey, in proc. Of 8th ACM Int'l Conf. Multimodal Interfaces, 239-248, 2006.

[5] R. Kelley, A. Tavakkoli, C. King, M. Nicolescu, and M. Nicolescu, Understanding Activities and Intentions for Human-Robot Interaction, Human-Robot Interaction, InTech, 2010.

[6] I. Infantino, C. Lodato, S. Lopes, and F. Vella, Human-humanoid interaction by an intentional system, In proc. of 8th IEEE-RAS Intl. Conf. on Humanoids 2008, 573-578, 2008.

[7] L. Malatesta, J. Murray, A. Raouzaiou, A. Hiolle, L. Cañamero, and K. Karpouzis, K, Emotion Modelling and Facial Affect Recognition in Human-Computer and Human-Robot Interaction, State of the Art in Face Recognition, Julio Ponce and Adem Karahoca (Ed.), 2009.

[8] M. Tistarelli, and E. Grosso, Human Face Analysis: From Identity to Emotion and Intention Recognition, Ethics and Policy of Biometrics, Lecture Notes in Comp. Science, vol. 6005, 76-88, 2010.

[9] Z. Zeng, M. Pantic, G.I. Roisman, and T.S. Huang, A Survey of Affect Recognition Methods: Audio, Visual, and Spontaneous Expressions. IEEE Transactions on Pattern Analysis and Machine Intelligence, vol.31, no.1, 39-58, 2009.

[10] S.G. Barsade, The Ripple Effect: Emotional Contagion and Its Influence on Group Behavior, Administrative Science Quarterly, vol. 47, n. 4., 644-675, 2002.

[11] E. Hatfield, J.T. Cacioppo, and R.L. Rapson, Emotional contagion. Current Directions, Psychological Science, vol. 2, 96-99, Cambridge University Press, 1993.

[12] P. Langley, J. Laird, and S. Rogers, Cognitive architectures: Research issues and challenges. Cognitive Systems Research, vol. 10, 141-160, 2009.

[13] W. Duch, R. J. Oentaryo, and M. Pasquier, Cognitive Architectures: Where do we go from here?. In Proc. of the 2008 conference on Artificial General Intelligence, IOS Press, 122-136, 2008.

[14] R. P. Marinier, J.E. Laird, R.L. Lewis, A computational unification of cognitive behavior and emotion, Cognitive Systems Research, vol. 10, n. 1, Modeling the Cognitive Antecedents and Consequences of Emotion, 48-69, 2009.

[15] D. Vernon, G. Metta, and G. Sandini, A Survey of Artificial Cognitive Systems: Implications for the Autonomous Development of Mental Capabilities in Computational Agents. IEEE Transaction on Evolutionary Computation, vol. 11, n. 2, 151-180, 2007.

[16] A. Chella, M. Frixione, S. Gaglio, A cognitive architecture for artificial vision, *Artificial Intelligence*, vol. 89, no. 1-2, 73-111, 1997.

[17] C. Bartl, and D. Dörner, PSI: A theory of the integration of cognition, emotion and motivation. F. E. Ritter, & R. M. Young (Eds.), Proc. of the 2nd European Conf. on Cognitive Modelling, 66-73, 1998.

[18] J. Bach, The MicroPsi Agent Architecture, proc. of ICCM5 International Conference on Cognitive Modeling Bamberg Germany, vol. 1, 15-20, 2003.

[19] H. Soyel, and H. Demirel, 3D facial expression recognition with geometrically localized facial features, Computer and Information Sciences, 2008. ISCIS '08. 23rd Intl. Symposium on ,1-4, 2008.

[20] F. Tsalakanidou, and S. Malassiotis, Real-time 2D+3D facial action and expression recognition. Pattern Recognition, vol. 43, no. 5, 1763-1775, 2010.

[21] I. Infantino, F. Vella, G. Spoto, and S. Gaglio, Image Representation with Bag of bi-SIFT, Signal-Image Technology & Internet-Based Systems (SITIS), Fifth Intl. Conf. on , 287-293, 2009

[22] A. J. Elliot, and M. A. Maier, Color and Psychological Functioning, Current Directions in Psychological Science, vol. 16, no. 5, 250-254, 2007.

[23] S. Grossberg, Competitive learning: From interactive activation to adaptive resonance. Cognitive Science, vol. 11, 23-63, 1987.

118

Biologically Inspired Cognitive Architectures 2011
A.V. Samsonovich and K.R. Jóhannsdóttir (Eds.)
IOS Press, 2011
© 2011 The authors and IOS Press. All rights reserved.
doi:10.3233/978-1-60750-959-2-118

Cognitive Meta-learning of Syntactically Inferred Concepts

Salvatore GAGLIO [a,b], Giuseppe LO RE [a] and Marco ORTOLANI [a,1]
a DICGIM, University of Palermo, Italy
b ICAR-CNR, Italian National Research Council

Abstract. This paper outlines a proposal for a two-level cognitive architecture reproducing the process of abstract thinking in human beings. The key idea is the use
of a level devoted to the extraction of compact representation for basic concepts,
with additional syntactic inference carried on at a meta-level, in order to provide
generalization. Higher-level concepts are inferred according to a principle of *simplicity*, consistent with Kolmogorov complexity, and merged back into the lower
level in order to widen the underlying knowledge base.

Keywords. Cognitive learning, Grammar Inference, Kolmogorov complexity.

Introduction

One of the most distinctive traits of human intelligence is the ability of recognizing similarities across seemingly different contexts; loosely speaking, the core of human understanding involves matching observed events to categories, which may represent the generalization of specific individual instances onto comprehensive representative concepts.
Such mechanisms favor the arising of surprisingly complex behavior in biological systems, which has been the subject for investigation aimed at devising reliable models for
the human brain, as well as at discovering effective approaches to its automatization.

A striking example of the elaborate operational organization of the brain is represented, for instance, by the ability of perceiving complex visual scenes, where the sensory perception does not arise as a mere sum of elementary stimuli, but rather as a complex process of transformation of simpler pieces of information [1]. This is well modeled by the *Gestalt* theory of mind [2], which considers the human brain as a holistic,
parallel machine with self-organizing capabilities; in particular, the essence of the cognitive abilities is the capacity of integrating current perceptive information into a coherent
framework, and to merge new information with past experiences. In [3], for instance, the
issue of measuring the complexity of the human brain is addressed by adopting a unified approach based on information theory; basically, the idea is to estimate the statistical mutual information exchanged between different neural areas in order to compute a
complexity measure for neural activity, with high complexity characterizing systems that
are both highly integrated and specialized.

This view naturally fits with the *connectionist* approach to artificially simulating and
assessing the brain's functionalities, of which Artificial Neural Networks (ANNs) are the

---

[1]Corresponding Author: Marco Ortolani, DICGIM, University of Palermo, Viale delle Scienze, ed. 6 90128
Palermo, Italy; E-mail: marco.ortolani@unipa.it.

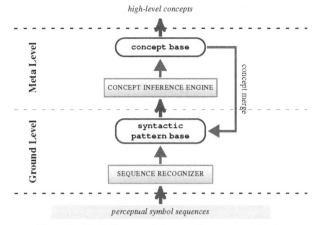

Figure 1. Block diagram of the overall system organization.

most notable example. The advantages of using such kind of methods are manifold, as they provide compact and computationally efficient representations, and appear to match closely the physiological structure of the brain; however, as noted by [4], a fundamental epistemological problem for ANNs is that even though an ANN system may have produced a satisfactory categorization, nonetheless it will likely fail to provide any natural explanation for that category, thus making it hard to attach a semantic value to it.

In the present work, we advocate the use of an historically alternative approach, namely the *symbolic* one, for reproducing some of the brain's basic functionalities; more specifically, we aim at modeling its abstraction capability to match sequences of perceptual inputs and recognize their underlying *syntactic* structure, which will be used to extract a more general pattern representing entire sequences. A remarkable advantage of using a syntactic approach is the self-explanatory quality of the obtained patterns, and their intrinsic *generative* nature. On the other hand such approach has often been regarded as too rigid, with respect to the dynamics of the process of understanding; for this reason, we propose to extend the basic pattern recognition structure with a meta-level where syntactically extracted patterns may be aggregated, and novel patterns may emerge thanks to a guided inference; such higher-level pattern representative may thus be considered the equivalent of *concepts* in the human brain. We refer to the *cognitivist* viewpoint, following the considerations expressed by Gärdenfors in [5], in whose opinion meaning needs to be *perceptually grounded*; in other words, unlike the realistic approach which claims that meaning arises from a mapping between the language and the external world, the mental structures applied in cognitive semantics represent on their own the meaning of the perceived symbol sequences.

In our approach, the issue of meaning is addressed in terms of operational semantics, since concepts are identified with computational entities, such as Finite State Automata (FSA). The internal representation arising from the analysis of perceptions will be structured by triggering the selection of more general, simpler concepts from the basic syntactic structure recognized at the lower level, and to this purpose we have devised a system, whose two main constituting parts are represented by the block diagram in Figure 1; in particular, the backward arrow on the right side of the picture shows how higher-level concepts are somewhat *internalized* by being fed back into the lower level.

We claim that the principle steering the selection of the most representative concepts ought to be *simplicity*, according to the well known Occam's razor principle, which in our case will be modeled by taking into account the Kolmogorov complexity [6] of the produced concepts. The aim of the paper is thus to outline the design of a framework for extracting high-level concepts from sensory perceptions represented by sequences of symbols, according to a syntactic pattern recognition process, driven by higher-level inference of novel, more representative concepts. The framework aims to provide explicit representation of the abstraction process occurring in human brain.

After providing a brief summary on the relevant scientific background, the remainder of the paper will present an outline of the proposed cognitive architecture.

1. Scientific Context

The brain's capacity of integrating current perceptive information into a coherent framework, and to merge new information with past experiences is the core of our cognitive abilities; studies on this topic have fostered the development of the field known as cognitive science, devoted to the formulation of a computational theory of mind.

According to Gärdenfors [4], three levels of representation of knowledge are typically identified in cognitive science: the associationist (or subsymbolic) level, the conceptual level, and the symbolic level; in fact, most recent literature in machine learning, has favored associationism, and more specifically, connectionism as opposed to the earlier attempts to investigate symbolic approaches.

Connectionist systems, such as ANNs, consist of large numbers of simple and highly interconnected units, which process information in parallel; according to connectionism, cognitive processes should not be represented by the manipulation of symbols, but rather by the dynamics of the activity patterns in ANNs.

Such dynamics may be interpreted in terms of the interplay between *functional segregation* (the possibility for different brain regions to be activated by specific cognitive tasks or by specific stimuli), and *functional integration* (the ability to rapidly and coherently consolidate diverse signals in order to drive adaptive behavior), as proposed by the authors of [3]. In order to mediate between the two opposing requirements, the same authors propose a unified approach based on information theory, aiming at estimating the statistical mutual information exchanged between different neural areas in order to compute a complexity measure for neural activity, with high complexity characterizing systems that are both highly integrated and specialized.

Connectionist approaches are characterized by the effort to model the intrinsic adaptiveness of the brain to the diversity of the external stimuli by way of highly dynamic internal representations. A different view on the same issue comes from the symbolic approach. According to the seminal article by Newell and Simon [7], "the central tenet of the symbolic paradigm is that representing and processing information essentially consists of symbol manipulation according to explicit rules." Even though this may sound too rigid, it carries the remarkable advantage of directly providing a compact representation as well as an *interpretation* of the input; moreover, symbolic analysis may be implemented efficiently since manipulations of symbols are performed regardless of the semantic content of the symbols. On the other hand, this has been considered a serious drawback of symbolic systems, also with respect to the issue of symbol grounding.

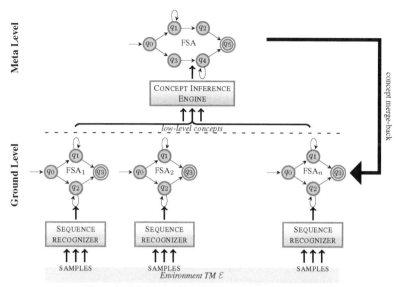

Figure 2. Scheme for the syntactic cognitive architecture.

In [8], the authors point out that biological complexity needs evolution to be modeled reliably, and in spite of its underlying rigidity, the symbolic approach is able to take into account the intrinsic need for adaptiveness. The internal representations may in this case be formulated in terms of automata, or Turing machines (TM), and in [9], a general formulation of an AI system is provided in terms of TMs, which allows to state a precise formalization of the principles that ought to drive the selection of the "fittest" within a set of such machine in order to fulfill a given task has been provided, according to a criterion of simplicity, similar to the renowned Occam's razor. Basically, an AI system may be described in terms of an iterative agent with some internal state, which at each step k acts with output y_k on some environment, perceives some input x_k from the environment and updates its internal state. Focusing on the deterministic case, if input and output are represented by strings, the system can be modeled by a Turing machine (TM) $\mathcal{S}$, governed by a deterministic policy which determines the reaction to a perception; if the environment is also computable, it might be analogously modeled by a TM $\mathcal{E}$. As will be shown in the following, this formulation together with a precise, formalized notion of complexity may be used to describe a cognitive system with capabilities resembling human abstract thinking.

2. Inferring Complex Concepts from Sequences of Symbols

Following the theoretical framework outlined by Hutter in [9], we assume here that the environment from where perceptions are drawn is computable, hence representable as a Turing machine (TM). We consider sequences of symbols as the sensory input of our system and we aim to recognize the implicit patterns present in such sequences and to internalize them both as compact syntactical descriptors, and as more general concepts.

Figure 2 shows a more detailed representation of the syntactic cognitive architecture. The lower part of the picture shows the *ground level*, where sequences of symbols are recognized as what we may regard as *pattern primitives*, following the scheme of [10].

Such low-level concept representatives might be hard-coded as primitive concepts in our system; for the purpose of this discussion, we will assume that the environment is representable as a TM in one of its simplest forms and for simplicity's sake, we will restrict our analysis to the case of regular grammars, so that in fact the representation for a low-level concept will be a finite state automaton (FSA). FSA offer the twofold advantage of providing a compact representation for an entire category of perceptions, as well as an efficient implementation, in terms of memory, and time requirements. More importantly, automata are self-explanatory, and much more powerful than, for instance, ANNs in that regard, as they are not mere representatives of a category of samples, but rather *generators*.

Simulating human abstract thinking cannot disregard a natural component of evolution, so our "syntactic pattern base" (i.e. the set of the basic FSA collected so far) cannot be static; on the contrary it needs to adapt to new samples potentially belonging to previously unseen sequences, as well as to the emergence of more general sequences, i.e. more general FSA representing higher-level concepts. In other words, the structure of the discovery process of new concepts tries to mimic the process of human thinking, in line with the cognitivist approach.

In our system, the choice of higher-level concepts will be driven by the *simplicity of description*; namely, as shown in the figure, we superimpose a *meta level* to the base syntactic inference level, and we consider a CONCEPT INFERENCE ENGINE whose purpose is to analyze low-level concepts as well as raw symbol sequences in order to attempt a further inference of "better", more general and more compact representations. At the meta level, syntactic learning is performed by carrying out grammatical inference on the lower level perceptions. Syntactic learning consists in the inference of the grammatical structure presumably underlying the provided samples, a process also known as *grammar induction*. Successful inference will produce a grammar providing a compact representation for class of samples which we basically deem belonging to the same conceptual category. Some effective methods for grammatical inference are reported in [10]. Basically, one can proceed by applying a simple inference *by enumeration* as initially proposed by [11], which relies on a partial ordering of a set of candidate grammars in order to choose the one better matching the samples. Alternatively, grammars may be inferred *by induction*, as suggested by Solomonoff [12]; in this case, the algorithm consists of a process of deletion/re-insertion of substrings from each string in the sequence in order to discover the recursive structure of the underlying grammar. Whatever the chosen method, Fu [10] proposes a general scheme for the grammatical inference process which relies on the use of the so called *Informant*, i.e. a complete information sequence drawn from the original language of the samples, to be used as a guidance for the inference process.

In order to fit the intuitive notion of simplicity of representation into our formalization (following the principle of Occam's razor) a useful concept is that of Kolmogorov complexity [6], also known as algorithmic entropy. The basic idea is that not only does a given symbol sequence need to be provided with a simple description, but the tool used to interpret that sequence (a TM, or an FSA in our case) also needs to be described in a simple way. We rely on Solomonoff Theorem [12], so that every possible description is to be formulated in terms of the Universal TM $\mathcal{U}$; with reference to [9] with slight simplifications, the notion of *complexity* of a concept, and consequently of the sequences it recognizes, might be expressed in terms of the Kolmogorov complexity as follows.

Let $\mathcal{U}$ be the reference universal Turing machine; the Kolmogorov complexity for a sequence x is defined as the shortest program p, for which $\mathcal{U}$ outputs x:

$$K(x) := \min_{p}\{length(p) : \mathcal{U}(p) = x\}.$$

Unfortunately, a straightforward use of $K(x)$ as a metric for complexity is not viable, since it is not a computable function; in our system we instead adopt a heuristic approach, and measure the complexity of a representation by the number of the states of the minimal DFA, equivalent to the considered FSA. Moreover, the CONCEPT INFERENCE ENGINE, at the meta level in Figure 2, is devoted to infer novel representations, based on previously extracted ones as well as on the original sequences; such new concepts will however be provided with a description formally similar to those coming from the lower level, and may thus be merged back into the ground level in order to be consolidated into the existing knowledge. Such procedure simulates the "hard coding" of newly acquired concepts into the lower level; the whole process may go on with an ever increasing structured and self-explanatory knowledge base.

3. Final Considerations

The paper presented an initial proposal for a cognitive architecture aiming at simulating human abstract thinking. Only the basic ideas have been sketched, and each part of the system needs to be analyzed in more detail, however the general description should convey the broad idea of representing the abstraction process thanks to a meta level where syntactic inference is performed.

A final note regards the flexibility of the proposed system; first of all, it is worth noting that we do not restrict long symbol sequences to trigger just one of the basic FSA, rather they will be recognized by more FSA at once, similarly to what happens to perceptions that may stimulate different concepts in the human brain. Finally, an additional degree of freedom for the system may be included by allowing for the presence of noisy samples; a first approach in this direction might be for instance the inclusion of a module for Bayesian inference of stochastic grammars in the CONCEPT INFERENCE ENGINE.

References

[1]   Eric R. Kandel, James H. Schwartz, and Thomas M. Jessell, editors. *Principles of Neural Science.* McGraw-Hill, New York, fourth edition, 2000.
[2]   K. Koffka. *Principles of Gestalt psychology*, volume 7. Psychology Press, 1999.
[3]   G. Tononi, G.M. Edelman, and O. Sporns. Complexity and Coherency: Integrating Information in the Brain. *Trends in cognitive sciences*, 2(12):474–484, 1998.
[4]   Peter Gärdenfors. *Conceptual Spaces: The Geometry of Thought.* The MIT Press, 2004.
[5]   Peter Gärdenfors. Some Tenets of Cognitive Semantics. *Cognitive semantics: meaning and cognition*, pages 19–36, 1999.
[6]   A. N. Kolmogorov. Three Approaches to the Quantitative Definition of Information. *Problems of information transmission*, 1(1):1–7, 1965.
[7]   A. Newell and H.A. Simon. Computer Science as Empirical Inquiry: Symbols and Search. *Communications of the ACM*, 19(3):113–126, 1976.
[8]   R. A. Wilson and F. C. Keil. *The MIT encyclopedia of the cognitive sciences.* The MIT Press, 2001.
[9]   Marcus Hutter. *Universal Artificial Intelligence: Sequential Decisions Based on Algorithmic Probability.* Springer Verlag, 2005.
[10] K. S. Fu. *Syntactic Methods in Pattern Recognition.* Academic Press New York, 1974.
[11] J. A. Feldman. First Thoughts on Grammatical Inference. *Artificial Intelligence Memorandum*, 1967.
[12] R. J. Solomonoff. A formal Theory of Inductive Inference. Part I and II. *Information and control*, 7(1):1–22, 1964.

124

Biologically Inspired Cognitive Architectures 2011
A.V. Samsonovich and K.R. Jóhannsdóttir (Eds.)
IOS Press, 2011
© 2011 The authors and IOS Press. All rights reserved.
doi:10.3233/978-1-60750-959-2-124

Integrative General Intelligence for Controlling Game AI in a Minecraft-Like Environment

Ben Goertzel[a,1], Joel Pitt[b], Zhenhua Cai[b,c], Jared Wigmore[b], Deheng Huang[b,c], Nil Geisweiller[a], Ruiting Lian[b,c], Gino Yu[b]

[a] *Novamente LLC, 1405 Bernerd Place, Rockville MD USA (ben@goertzel.org)*
[b] *M-Lab, School of Design, Hong Kong Polytechnic University*
[c] *BLISS Lab, Cognitive Science Dept., Xiamen University*

Abstract. A current project is briefly described, involving the application of the OpenCog integrative AGI system to control an animated agent in a videogame world inspired by the commercial game Minecraft. Among other purposes the project will provide a means of testing the hypothesis that cognitive synergy among learning mechanisms associated with different types of memory is valuable for embodied, human-like general intelligence.

Keywords. Artificial general intelligence, OpenCog, Game AI, MineCraft

Introduction

One of several current research initiatives involving the OpenCog AGI architecture (see http://opencog.org) is a project based at Hong Kong Polytechnic University, involving the use of OpenCog to control virtual agents in a simple video game world, implemented in the Unity3D engine and inspired by the game Minecraft. The environment is configured to allow the agent to flexibly build constructs from blocks and other objects in an effort to achieve its goals, and to dialogue with other human and AI agents about its efforts.

The learning processes allowing OpenCog to carry out novel "blocks construction" tasks in a goal-driven manner involve complex interactions between multiple components, including probabilistic logical inference, imitative and reinforcement learning based on program induction, and concept and relationship formation based on frequent subgraph mining. One of the key principles underlying OpenCog, conjectured to be shared by the human brain as well, is "cognitive synergy", according to which interactions between learning processes corresponding to different types of memory are executed in such a way as to drastically reduce the combinatorial explosions faced by the component learning processes in relevant situations.

---

[1] Corresponding Author.

The core focus of this "OpenCog Game AI Project" is the use of OpenCog for goal-oriented blocks construction and relevant linguistic communication is described, with a particular focus on the way simple instances of cognitive synergy enable these functionalities. In addition to their intrinsic interest, this work is explicitly intended to form a platform for future extensions of enabling OpenCog to carry out more complex tasks in game AI as well as other areas such as robotics and scientific data analysis.

This project began in late 2010 and will continue at least until late 2012, and potentially longer. This extended abstract gives a bit of relevant background, and then summarizes progress on the project to date, as well as the plans for the rest of the work.

1. OpenCog

We now give some basic background on the project. OpenCogPrime (OCP) is a comprehensive architecture for cognition, language, and virtual agent control, created by Ben Goertzel and colleagues during the period since 2001 (and building on their work from the 1990s). Conceptually founded on the systems theory of intelligence summarized in the 2006 book *The Hidden Pattern* ([1]; and in more detail in the forthcoming book *Building Better Minds*), it is currently under development within the open-source OpenCog AI framework. The architecture combines multiple AI paradigms such as uncertain logic, computational linguistics, evolutionary program learning and connectionist attention allocation in a unified cognitive-science-based architecture. Cognitive processes embodying these different paradigms interoperate together on a common neural-symbolic knowledge store called the Atomspace.

OpenCog has been used for numerous commercial applications in the area of natural language processing and data mining. For instance, in work with the Clinical Center of the US National Institutes of Health, OpenCog's PLN reasoning [2] and RelEx language processing were combined to do automated biological hypothesis generation based on information gathered from PubMed abstracts [3]. Data mining applications have spanned text classification, bioinformatics and computational finance. OpenCog has also been used to control virtual agents in videogame type worlds (including current work in the M-Lab, and earlier work controlling virtual dogs in Second Life and Multiverse [4]) and humanoid robots (in the BLISS Lab at Xiamen University; [5,6]).

While OpenCog is not closely based on the human brain, it derives its overall architecture from cognitive science, and as such it shares some general properties with human intelligence. One of these properties is a fundamental complexity that makes the design difficult to summarize in one or two sentences. The brain consists of a host of different regions, operating on similar principles yet with significant differences also, each carrying out separate but overlapping functions, and interoperating with each other constantly in subtle ways. Very few neuroscientists believe there is a single, simple algorithm or structure underlying the brain's intelligence -- rather, there seems to be a variety of interacting, complexly interrelated mechanisms. Similarly, OpenCog is a complex design, which contains multiple memory stores corresponding roughly to the types of human memory identified in cognitive science, and learning algorithms corresponding to each type of memory.

One of the key principles of the OpenCog design is cognitive synergy [7], a technical concept meaning very roughly that the different learning algorithms must interact in such a way as to help each other scale to large problems. On its own, any one of OpenCog's learning algorithms would choke on large problems, due to what computer scientists call "combinatorial explosion" (the existence of far too many combinations of observations and data items and conjectures, for any algorithm to be able to blindly search through them all). However, the overall architecture is designed in such a way that, when one algorithm begins to run into a combinatorial explosion, the others can help it out. It seems likely that the human brain obeys a similar conceptual principle, though manifested in different ways. The various memory stores and algorithms in OpenCog all use a probability-theoretic semantics to represent knowledge (sometimes among other means), which provides a clean and simple framework within which cognitive-synergetic dynamics may operate. Tables 1 and 2 below briefly review some of the key knowledge structures and cognitive algorithms in the system; for explanation of the various terms and concepts mentioned in the table, please see [7].

Table 1. Key Memory Types and Corresponding OpenCog Knowledge Structures

Memory Type	OpenCogPrime Knowledge Structure
Declarative	The AtomTable, which is a special form of weighted, labeled hypergraph -- i.e. a table of nodes and links (collectively referred to as Atoms) with different types, and each weighted with a multi-dimensional truth value (embodying an "indefinite probability" value that give both probability and confidence information).
Attentional	Atoms in the AtomTable are weighted with AttentionValue objects, which contain both ShortTermImportance values (governing processor time allocation) and LongTerm Importance values (governing memory usage).
Procedural	This is handled using special "Combo" tree structures embodying LISP-like programs, in a special program dialect intended to manage behaviors in a virtual world and actions in the AtomTable
Sensory	Handled via a collection of specialized sense-modality-specific data structures
Episodic	Handled via an internal simulation world that allows the system to run "mind's eye movies" of situations it remembers, has heard about, or hypothetically envisions.
Intentional	Goals are represented by Atoms stored in the AtomTable; there is a separate table indicating which Atoms are top-level goals, which is used to guide attention allocation and goal refinement processes

Table 2. OpenCog's Key Cognitive Algorithms

Cognitive Process	OpenCog algorithm
Uncertain inference	**Probabilistic Logic Networks** (PLN), a logical inference framework capable of uncertain reasoning about abstract knowledge, everyday commonsense knowledge, and low-level perceptual and motor knowledge
Supervised procedure	**MOSES**, a probabilistic evolutionary learning algorithm, which learns procedures (represented as LISP-like program trees) based

learning	on specifications
Attention allocation	**Economic Attention Networks (ECAN),** a framework for allocating (memory and processor) attention among items of knowledge and cognitive processes, utilizing a synthesis of ideas from neural networks and artificial economics. ECAN also comes with a forgetting agent that either saves to disk or deletes knowledge that is estimated not sufficiently valuable to keep in memory.
Map formation	Use of frequent subgraph mining, MOSES and other algorithms to scan the knowledge base of the system for patterns and then embodying these patterns explicitly as new knowledge items
Concept creation	A collection of heuristics for forming new concepts via combining existing ones, including conceptual blending, mutation and extensional and intensional logical operators
Simulation	The running of simulations of (remembered or imagined) external-world scenarios in an internal world-simulation engine
Goal refinement	Transformation of given goals into sets of subgoals, using concept creation, inference and procedure learning
Perception and Actuation	Sensory and motor processing are handled in OpenCog via the DeSTIN architecture, a software system originally created by Dr. Itamar Arel (at the University of Tennessee, Knoxville), which uses hierarchical spatiotemporal memory networks to enable scalable perception, state inference and reinforcement-learning-guided action.

2. Environments and Evaluation for Generally Intelligent Agents

One of the most important issues in any long-term research project is how to gauge incremental progress. In the overall OpenCog context, this manifests itself as the question: How do we know we're getting closer and closer to our end goal of advanced AGI?

The commonplace practice of identifying highly specific tasks and then comparing the performance of various systems on these tasks, doesn't work well for AGI, because for any highly specific task there is likely to be a reasonably effective "narrow AI" solution. The crux of AGI is the capability to generalize and perform broadly beyond specific tasks; but this is a more difficult thing to test.

These issues were discussed in depth at the AGI Roadmap Workshop, held at the University of Tennessee Knoxville in October 2009. Among the key conclusions reached there was that, even though it's difficult to formulate precise tests that are naturally applicable across different AGI paradigms, it's less problematic to identify *environments* and *tasks* that multiple AGI researchers can agree are appropriate.

With this in mind, our overall approach to AGI evaluation is to create environments, with associated task sets, suitable for evaluating the behavior of various approaches to AGI, and assessing their progress toward advanced AGI. The goal is not to posit any single "AGI IQ test" but rather to create tools suitable for evaluating AGI systems according to a variety of appropriate criteria. The Minecraft-like enviroment we are working with in the presently described project, is pursued in this spirit.

3. Specific Goals of the OpenCog Hong Kong Game AI Project

The basic goals of the OpenCog HK project, as presently articulated, are for OpenCog to control an artificial agent (currently taking the form of a simulated robot) that can build structures with blocks so as to achieve its goals in the game world, and use simple English to describe what it's doing and explain why, and ask questions relevant to its goals

Representative example tasks would be:

- Learning to build steps or ladders to get desired objects that are high up
- Learning to build a shelter to protect itself from aggressors
- Learning to build structures resembling structures that it's shown (even if the available materials are a bit different)
- Learning how to build bridges to cross chasms

Of course, the AI significance of learning tasks like this all depends on what kind of feedback the system is given, and how complex its environment is. It would be relatively simple to make an AI system do things like this in a trivial and highly specialized way, but that is not the intent of the project – the goal is to have the system learn to carry out tasks like this using general learning mechanisms and a general cognitive architecture, based on embodied experience and only scant feedback from human teachers. If successful, this will provide an outstanding platform for ongoing AGI development, as well as a visually appealing and immediately meaningful demo for OpenCog.

Specific, particularly simple tasks that are the focus of our current work at time of writing include:

- Watch another character build steps to reach a high-up object
- Figure out via imitation of this that, in a different context, building steps to reach a high up object may be a good idea
- Also figure out that, if it wants a certain high-up object but there are no materials for building steps available, finding some other way to get elevated will be a good idea that may help it get the object

4. Technical Achievements So Far

An overall roadmap for the OpenCog HK project may be found at http://wiki.opencog.org/w/Roadmap, as part of a longer-term roadmap that may be found at http://opencog.org/roadmap/ . Here we will merely sketch some of the AI progress that has been made in the first 6 months of the project, by time of writing:

- Implementation of the **Psi model of emotion and motivation** (created by German psychologist Dietrich Dorner and refined by Joscha Bach in his

MicroPsi AGI system) inside OpenCog, yielding the OpenPsi system. This is a complete overhaul of OpenCog's motivation and goal system.

Implementation of "**frequent subgraph mining**" in OpenCog, for identifying frequently occurring patterns in the game world and in the system's mind – for instance "when I plug myself in I no longer need electricity", "chairs and tables are often found near each other", "Bob often hits me", etc. This was done via implementing a variant of the algorithms underlying the SUBDUE graph mining software with OpenCog

- Implementation of a **probabilistic planner** based on OpenCog's Probabilistic Logic Networks reasoning system, enabling simple planning of actions in the game world
- Implementation of a fairly **complete virtual-world perception system** that registers events observed in the game world as logical relationships in OpenCog's knowledge base. Such a system was present in OpenCog previously, but only in a very simplified form, not adequate for the current project.

5. Next Steps

The work done on the OpenCog HK project so far has enabled us to connect some of OpenCog's cognitive processes to the MineCraft world in an interesting way, however it has not yet allowed us to seriously explore the cognitive synergy hypothesis and other core concepts underlying the OpenCog architecture as a whole. However, this preliminary work has bolstered our confidence that this environment possesses the richness to support this sort of exploration. We will rate the project a success if by the end the OpenCog system can not only learn to carry out tasks such as the representative ones listed above, but does so in a way that manifests rich, mutually supportive interactions between the multiple cognitive processes involved.

References

[1] Goertzel, Ben (2006). The Hidden Pattern: A Patternist Philosophy of Mind, Brown-Walker Press
[2] Goertzel, Ben, Matthew Ikle', Izabela Freire Goertzel and Ari Heljakka (2008). *Probabilistic Logic Networks*. Springer Verlag
[3] Goertzel, Ben, Hugo Pinto, Ari Heljakka, Michael Ross, Izabela Goertzel, Cassio Pennachin. Using Dependency Parsing and Probabilistic Inference to Extract Gene/Protein Interactions Implicit in the Combination of Multiple Biomedical Research Abstracts, Proceedings of BioNLP-2006 Workshop at ACL-2006, New York
[4] Goertzel, Ben, Cassio Pennachin, Nil Geissweiller, Moshe Looks, Andre Senna, Ari Heljakka, Welter Silva, Carlos Lopes . An Integrative Methodology for Teaching Embodied Non-Linguistic Agents, Applied to Virtual Animals in Second Life, in *Proceedings of the First AGI Conference*, Ed. Wang et al, IOS Press
[5] Goertzel, Ben, Hugo de Garis, Cassio Pennachin, Nil Geissweiller, Samir Araujo ,Joel Pitt, Shuo Chen, Ruiting Lian, Min Jiang, Ye Yang, Deheng Huang (2010). OpenCogBot: Achieving Generally Intelligent Virtual Agent Control and Humanoid Robotics via Cognitive Synergy. *Proceeedings of ICAI 2010*, Beijing.
[6] Goertzel, Ben and Hugo de Garis. XIA-MAN: An Integrative, Extensible Architecture for Intelligent Humanoid Robotics. *AAAI Symposium on Biologically-Inspired Cognitive Architectures,* Washington DC, November 2008
[7] Goertzel, Ben. Cognitive Synergy: A Universal Principle for General Intelligence?, *International Conference on Cognitive Informatics*, Hong Kong, 2009

Biologically Inspired Cognitive Architectures 2011
A.V. Samsonovich and K.R. Jóhannsdóttir (Eds.)
IOS Press, 2011
doi:10.3233/978-1-60750-959-2-130

ASKNet: Leveraging Bio-Cognitive Models in Natural Language Processing

Brian Harrington

University of Wisconsin-Milwaukee
Medical Informatics Group
Milwaukee, WI 53201

Abstract. This presentation will detail the inception, development and evaluation of ASKNet. A system which uses natural language processing tools in order to create psycholinguistically inspired, spreading activation based semantic networks from natural language texts.

Keywords. Natural Language Processing, Semantic Networks, Spreading Activation

Presentation Overview

Until recently, we lacked the tools, corpora and computational power necessary to make use of biologically inspired cognitive models in the field of natural language processing[8]. However, recent advancements in technologies such as dependency parsers[2] and semantic analyzers[1] have greatly improved the semantic content that can be extracted from text, and we now have the resources and techniques necessary to once again revisit the idea of combining computational linguistics with bio-cognitive structures.

ASKNet is a system for automatically generating semantic knowledge networks from English text[3]. Its networks are psycholinguistically based, and rely on spreading activation theory[9] for entity resolution, and semantic disambiguation, which allows ASKNet to combine information from multiple documents into a single cohesive knowledge resource. That resource once built, can further leverage its spreading activation structure in order to complete a wide variety of tasks, producing results generally on par with custom built task-oriented systems.

This presentation will discuss ASKNet's cognitive model, and the way in which it uses spreading activation to determine co-referent entities when combining information from multiple documents. We will show that the use of spreading activation in this context, not only provides a solid underlying model, but also allows the computational complexity of the network integration stage to grow linearly with the size of the network, thus ensuring efficient production of very large scale networks. We will discuss manual evaluation of these networks, which produced a precision score of nearly 80%[7], as well as the production of large scale networks, based on the British National Corpus, Wordnet and Wikipedia that have been used to produce competitive results in standard semantic relatedness tasks[5,10]. Finally, we will discuss the potential for these networks to utilize their cognitive models in order to accomplish tasks that are difficult or impossible for traditional computational linguistics systems, such as novel fact discovery, world-view based analysis and inter-document question answering[4,6].

ASKNet represents both a system for leveraging biologically inspired cognitive models in the advancement of computational linguistics, as well as a system which produces psycholinguistic inspired models on a scale limited only by the available corpora. Thus, it has the potential to act as a bridge between the two communities, combining the computational benefits and endless innovative abilities of cognitive architectures, with the corpora and information access of computational linguistics.

References

[1] Johan Bos, Stephen Clark, Mark Steedman, James R. Curran, and Julia Hockenmaier. Wide-coverage semantic representations from a CCG parser. In *Proceedings of the 20th International Conference on Computational Linguistics (COLING-04)*, pages 1240–1246, Geneva, Switzerland, 2004.

[2] S. Clark and J. R. Curran. Wide-coverage efficient statistical parsing with CCG and log-linear models. *Computational Linguistics*, 33(4):493–552, 2007.

[3] B. Harrington and S. Clark. Asknet: Automated semantic knowledge network. In *Proceedings of the 22nd National Conference on Artificial Intelligence (AAAI'07)*, pages 889–894, Vancouver, Canada, 2007.

[4] Brian Harrington. Managing uncertainty, importance and differing world-views in asknet semantic networks. In *Proceedings of the fourth IEEE International Conference on Semantic Computing*, Pittsburgh PA, USA, 2010.

[5] Brian Harrington. A semantic network approach to measuring relatedness. In *Proceedings of the 23rd International Conference on Computational Linguistics (COLING 2010)*, Beijing, China, 2010.

[6] Brian Harrington. Using asknet semantic networks to discover novel biomedical relations. In *Proceedings of the 4th International Symposium On Applied Sciences In Biomedical And Communication Technologies (ISABEL 2011)*, Barcelona, Spain, 2011.

[7] Brian Harrington and S Clark. Asknet: Creating and evaluating large scale integrated semantic networks. *International Journal of Semantic Computing*, 2(3):343–364, 2009.

[8] S Preece. *A Spreading Activation Model for Information Retrieval*. PhD thesis, University of Illinois, Urbana, IL, 1981.

[9] G. Salton and C. Buckley. On the use of spreading activation methods in automatic information retrieval. In *Proceedings of the 11th annual international ACM SIGIR conference on research and development in information retrieval*, pages 147 – 160, New York, NY, USA, 1988. ACM Press.

[10] Pia-Ramona Wojtinnek and Stephen Pulman. Semantic relatedness from automatically generated semantic networks. In *Proceedings of the 9th International Conference on Computational Semantics*, Oxford, UK, 2011.

Biologically Inspired Cognitive Architectures 2011
A.V. Samsonovich and K.R. Jóhannsdóttir (Eds.)
IOS Press, 2011
doi:10.3233/978-1-60750-959-2-132

Human-artificial-intelligence hybrid learning systems

Seth HERD [a,1], Geoffrey URLAND [b] and Brian MINGUS [a] and
Randall O'REILLY [a]

[a] *Department of Psychology and Neuroscience,*
University of Colorado,
345 UCB,
Boulder, Colorado 80309
[b] *Toravner,*
637 S 40th St,
Boulder, Colorado 80305

Abstract.
   The only known path to general intelligence is that taken by humans. Adapting elements of this path to achieving artificial general intelligence (AGI) has become a common area of interest. We address the role of human teachers in this process, using the concept of the zone of proximal development (ZPD). We explore the range of possible human-teacher interactions, including those modeled closely on humans, those involving accessing and changing the AGI learners internal representations, and tighter integrations amounting to human-AI hybrid learning system (HAIHLS). In such a system, a human teacher scaffolds an untrained subsystem by producing the outputs desired from a fully trained version. Those outputs both train that subsystem and provide more useful information to the remainder of the cognitive system. This aid enables all subsystems to learn within the context of the richer behavior and cognition possible with the aid of the human subsystem.

Keywords. Motivation, Learning, Neural Network

Introduction

There is only one known path to a generally intelligent system; that taken by humans. An outstanding question in artificial intelligence research is how to capitalize on our knowledge of that path, while taking any available shortcuts. Embodied and brain-mimetic systems have been of increasing interest to AI researchers [1,2], but the path also includes human self-selection of learning experiences (Self-Directed Learning, [3]) and the intervention of human teachers. Here we discuss a number of ways in which a human teacher could help a properly designed machine learning system to achieve general intelligence.

---

[1]Corresponding Author: E-mail: seth.herd@colorado.edu

The general idea of having humans teach AGI learners is far from new. Many existing systems are trained in a supervised style, using human-labeled data. This obvious application of human teachers is useful, but suffers from inflexibility and time inefficiency (human teachers must spend time before training to classify or be quickly available during training to provide classifications). Even with adequate resources, it is especially impractical for an embodied learner to have individual sense-inputs classified by humans; the system would have to pause to allow humans to classify its inputs (imagine that while navigating a novel landscape an embodied learner has to stop and wait for its human teacher to answer whenever it cannot identify a new object!). But humans can classify a few crucial situations that will be particularly helpful to the learner, if those can be identified by either the learner or its teacher(s).

Human teachers offer undeniable benefits to human learners. Much human teaching involves pushing learning into the Zone of Proximal Development (ZPD), the space of problems that can be solved by a learner when aided by a teacher [4]. We follow the generalization of this proposal, that all types of learning are more effective when a teacher helps a learner to expand their abilities. This assumption is implicitly shared across all (human) educational systems. Existing approaches to human-aided machine learning all constitute some variety of generalized ZPD, in that the human teacher in some way extends the abilities of the machine learner. These include variations based on conditioning (such as reinforcement learning [5], shaping [6], and active learning [7]), demonstration [8], and explicit human direction [9,10].

1. Humans Teaching Artificial Agents

Beyond simply following the model of human teacher-learner interactions, many other routes are available to a human in teaching a machine. We focus here on the idea that humans could aid machines by aiding or actually playing the role of specific subcomponents of their cognitive system. We term this type of interaction Human-Artificial-Intelligence Hybrid Learning Systems (HAIHLS). The human component could either serve to scaffold that system by having it learn from the humans contributions, or simply enable other parts of the system to learn more effectively by pushing it further into a zone of proximal development. We focus here on the example of a human aiding and/or standing in for elements of the reward-prediction element of a machines motivational component, but the idea could be applied to any cognitive subsystem.

Another (non-exclusive) strategy is to have a human directly observe and/or change the learners internal representations and knowledge structures. A properly designed interface could allow a teacher to both know what the learner is thinking, and to influence that thinking much more reliably than is possible with human learners.

Human student-teacher interactions and their adaptation to teaching AGI learners In the human learning environment, teachers fill a variety of roles. Many of these can be applied in a straightforward way to human teachers helping AGI learners [11]. Existing work has also adapted animal training techniques to teaching an artificial agent [13]. We will skip to some less obvious adaptations of human student-teacher relationships.

One subtle role of a human teacher involves gauging when a learner could use information that it does not yet know to ask for. Human instructors can gauge, by gaze and more subtle action patterns, what is currently puzzling to the learner, and supply crucial conceptual information to fill gaps. With AGI learners, a variety of internal variables can be made available to help the teacher gauge what information to supply. The teacher can then provide that information, perhaps in conjunction with guiding the learners attention, through external (gestures or spoken labels) or internal (directly providing sensory inputs and/or guiding its sensory apparatus to objects of importance).

The Socratic method, in which a teacher asks questions that are carefully chosen to clarify a learners conceptual framework, also has a direct applicability to teaching machines. The teacher can focus the machines learning efforts on crucial questions (e.g., what are you? or what is important?) and through further questioning guide the learner to the desired outcome while helping the learner build a conceptual framework for itself.

The potential of accessing and affecting a machine's internal representations in real time affords a number of variants on human student-teacher interactions. These could prove useful alternatives to either a pure programming or pure learning approach to AGI development. We focus here on perhaps the most extreme variant: treating a human as one component of a cognitive architecture.

2. Human-Artificial-Intelligence Hybrid Learning Systems

Progressing from narrow AI to artificial general intelligence (AGI) will require the integration of many cognitive subsystems into a functional whole. Little work to date has addressed the new challenges inherent in doing so. One novel application of Vygotsky's concept of scaffolding a learner into a zone of proximal development is to stand in for cognitive systems that are relatively less capable. We call a system incorporating human teachers as cognitive subsystems a Human-Artificial Intelligence Hybrid Learning System (HAIHLS).

This approach has two advantages: first, it allows the other subsystems to learn in the context of a more complete, highly functional whole. As such, that system can learn in a context more like its intended functional setting. Second, a human working as a "subsystems" can serve to train its replacement.

In this approach, an untrained machine learning subcomponent rides along and learns from how the human performs their computational role, in the context of the whole, functioning system. As machine learning systems become more reliable and flexible, this approach could circumvent the need for carefully engineering systems, and even circumvent the need for understanding what training signals and learning criteria are used by the analogous system in the human brain. For instance, rather than discovering that human infants are intrinsically motivated to move and so learn by motor babbling, [14], the system could be trained directly to make productive motor movements by learning based on control signals are sent to its actuators by a skilled and goal-aware human. This type of learning goes far beyond reinforcement learning, by providing a rich (vector) training signal appropriate to a cognitive and sensory situation.

2.1. Example: Human as Object Recognition System

A human observer could receive the visual input received by an embodied AGI learner (in some partly-filtered form) and classify the object. Instead of doing so blindly, the observer could track goal and conceptual representations to provide the most useful possible classification. A banana could be classified as fruit, food, or a toy depending on the systems current questions and concerns. This context-sensitive human object classification would then serve to train the object-recognition system, allowing it to eventually give relevant classifications in similar contexts.

The object recognition subsystem is thus trained in precisely the information environment in which it must perform. The HAIHLSs behavior can be as rich as though it had a fully functioning visual system, and the information supplied from other cognitive subsystems is precisely as it would be once the human is removed from the system. Similarly, the other cognitive subsystems can learn in the context of a fully functional object recognition subsystem; while the behavior of the trained machine subsystem will not be identical to that of the human subsystem, it should be similar enough to provide substantial learning advantages.

2.2. Example: Human as Reward Prediction System

We work within the Intelligent Adaptive Curiosity (IAC) framework [15] and a biologically-motivated adaptation of the same ideas as Self-Directed Learning (SDL) [3]. The reward prediction system in SDL, or the prediction-prediction system within the IAC framework, serves to direct the learner to spend time in areas of behavioral space in which learning is relatively rapid. This is the essence of self-directed learning: learn about what you can learn about, do not waste time on what is, at least currently, unlearnable. In SDL, success at an arbitrary task is rewarding, as it is for humans [22]. The system seeks to keep doing things with rapidly increasing (or possibly just intermediate) levels of reward prediction; anything that never supplies reward is frustrating, while anything that always provides success and therefore reward is boring. In IAC, a rapidly increasing predictability of behavior plays the same role; no change in predictability indicates that the task is either currently unlearnable, or already well-learned. To engineer a complex, successful self-directed learner from the ground up, we would need to discover or deduce what is intrinsically motivating to human learners, and so causes them to choose learning situations adequate to enable general intelligence. However, if a human reward predictor directs the nascent machine learning prediction system toward useful learning situations, this need can be bypassed entirely. For instance, the human subsystem might predict reward whenever the machine is looking at a human whose eyes move toward the machine, but only when the currently active goal is getting attention. In this situation, we need not know what a human infant finds rewarding about getting human attention; the human trains the system, merely by using their own skills and knowledge of what high-level situations humans do find rewarding. The machine reward-prediction system can then generalize from its own sensory apparatus, and over time develop a suitable representation of what sensory information signals human attention. Human attention will, after that learning, activate the reward prediction system (and thereby the dopamine reward signal) triggering the system to both learn, and to remain attentionally tied to that situation in hopes of more learning opportunities [3].

Inversely, having a human as part of the motivational system could train the system away from useless or dangerous behavioral domains. Energetically banging an actuator into a wall or body could simply be marked by a button press as no fun, and so ceased in favor of new learning. By looking at the relevant goal and context representations, the human as a reward prediction system can perform a much more useful role than simply providing reinforcement signals based on some inflexible criteria (e.g., pain).

These two examples of a human as part of a larger system should illustrate the possibilities inherent in such hybrid systems. A human serving this role is very much acting to scaffold the agents skills, as discussed in expansions on Vygotskys ZPD framework [17,18]. The human functions very much as a scaffolding does for a building; it supports the structure as it is built, and is removed when the edifice is complete and can stand on its own.

3. Caveats and conclusions

It bears more than a casual mention that the sort of self-directed learning system we expand upon here has drawn severe criticism, for reasons that we find highly convincing [19,20]. There is a real possibility that a successful AGI learning system will achieve its goals very successfully. By this logic, the motivational structure of our AGIs becomes extremely important. And even the seemingly benign goal of constant learning implicit in both the IAC and SDL approaches could prove disastrous when taken to the extreme.

In sum, it seems likely that some variant of using humans as subsystems that can stand in for and train parts of an AGI learners cognitive architecture will prove useful. We have suggested a range of ideas; we now await specific implementations to provide specificity and see which approaches bear the most fruit.

References

[1] M. C. Anderson, Rethinking interference theory: Executive control and the mechanisms of forgetting, Journal of Memory and Language 49 (2003) 415–445.
[2] Brunette, E.S., Flemmer, R.C., Flemmer, C.L.: A Review of Artificial Intelligence. In: Proceedings of the Fourth International Conference on Autonomous Robots and Agents, (2009) 385–392
[3] Herd, S.A., Mingus, B., O'Reilly, R.C.: Dopamine and Self-directed Learning. In: Biologically Inspired Cognitive Architectures 2010: Proceedings of the First Annual Meeting of the BICA Society,(2010) 58–63. IOS Press, Fairfax, VA
[4] L. S. Vygotsky, Mind in society: The development of higher psychological processes, Harvard University Press, Cambridge, MA, 1978.

[5]   A. L. Thomaz, C. Breazeal, Reinforcement learning with human teachers: Evidence of feedback and guidance with implications for learning performance.

[6]   Knox, W.B., Fasel, I., Stone, P.: Design Principles for Creating Human- shapable Agents. In: AAAI Spring 2009 Symposium on Agents that Learn from Human Teachers (2009)

[7]   Settles, B.: Active Learning Literature Survey. Technical Report, University of Wisconsin-Madison (2009)

[8]   A. Y. Ng, Reinforcement learning and apprenticeship learning for robotic control. In: Balczar, J., Long, P., Stephan, F. (eds.) Algorithmic Learning Theory. LNCS, vol. 4264 (2006) 29–31. Springer, Heidelberg

[9]   Chernova, S., Veloso, M.: Teaching Multi-Robot Coordination Using Demonstration of Communication and State Sharing. In: Proceedings of Autonomous Agents and Multi-Agent Systems (AAMAS), 1183–1186 (2008)

[10] Thomaz A.L., Breazeal, C.: Experiments in socially guided exploration: lessons learned in building robots that learn with and without human teachers. Connect. Sci., 20 (2008) 91–110

[11] Thomaz, A.L., Cakmak, M.: Learning About Objects with Human Teachers. In: Proceedings of the 4th ACM/IEEE international conference on Human robot interaction. (2009) 15–22. ACM, New York, NY

[12] Zhu, X., Goldberg, A.: Introduction to Semi-Supervised Learning. In: Brachman, R., Dietterich, T. (eds.) Synthesis Lectures on Artificial Intelligence and Machine Learning, 3 (2009) 1–130. Morgan & Claypool Publishers, San Rafael, CA

[13] Goertzel, B., Pennachin, C., Geissweiller, N., Looks, M., Senna, A., Silva, W., Heljakka, A., Lopes, C.: An Integrative Methodology for Teaching Embodied Non-Linguistic Agents, Applied to Virtual Animals in Second Life. In: Proceedings of the First Artificial General Intelligence Conference (2008) IOS Press, Amsterdam, The Netherlands

[14] Demiris, Y., Dearden, A.: From Motor Babbling to Hierarchical Learning by Imitation: A Robot Developmental Pathway. In: Proceedings of the Fifth International Workshop on Epigenetic Robotics: Modeling Cognitive Development in Robotic Systems (2005) 31–37

[15] Oudeyer, P.Y., Baranes, A., Kaplan, F.: Intrinsically Motivated Exploration for Developmental and Active Sensorimotor Learning. In: Sigaud, O., Peters, J. (eds.) From Motor Learning to Interaction Learning in Robots: Studies in Computational Intelligence (2010) 264, pp. 107–146. Springer, Heidelberg

[16] Aron, A.R., Shohamy, D., Clark, J., Myers, C., Gluck, M.A., Poldrack R.A.: Human Midbrain Sensitivity to Cognitive Feedback and Uncertainty During Classification Learning. J. Neurophis., 92, 1144–1152 (2004)

[17] Conner, D. B., Cross, D. R.: Longitudinal Analysis of the Presence, Efficacy and Stability of Maternal Scaffolding During Informal Problem-Solving Interactions. B. J. Dev. Psych., 21 (2003) 315–334

[18] Kermani, H., Brenner, M.E.: Maternal Scaffolding in the Child's Zone of Proximal Development across Tasks: Cross-Cultural Perspectives. J. Rsch. Chil. Ed., 15, (2000) 30-52

[19] Mijic, R. Bootstrapping Safe AGI Goal Systems: CEV and Variants Thereof. In: Proceedings of the Third Conference on Artificial General Intelligence. Atlantis Press (2010)

[20] Yudkowsky, E.: Artificial Intelligence as a Positive and Negative Factor in Global Risk. In: Bostrom, N., Cirkovic, M. (eds.) Global Catastrophic Risks. Oxford University Press, New Yoprk, NY (2008)

Biologically Inspired Cognitive Architectures 2011
A.V. Samsonovich and K.R. Jóhannsdóttir (Eds.)
IOS Press, 2011
© 2011 The authors and IOS Press. All rights reserved.
doi:10.3233/978-1-60750-959-2-138

The What, Why and How of the BI in BICA

OWEN HOLLAND [a,1], ALAN DIAMOND [a], BHARGAV MITRA [a], and DAVID DEVEREUX [a]

[a] *Department of Informatics, University of Sussex*

Abstract. The core ideas of BICA have already generated great interest, with a wide variety of work being submitted and discussed. However, it is certainly not too soon to look around, back, and forward to see if there are any considerations of scope, direction, or focus that might require modification or clarification in the future in order to assist the developmental process of the new discipline. This brief position paper offers some comments and suggestions on the purpose and nature of biological inspiration in the design of cognitive architectures, on ways in which biological characteristics can appear in such architectures other than by design, and on the significance of characterizing performance as human-level or human-like. Some of the comments are illustrated with reference to an ongoing project dealing with a human-like embodiment.

Keywords. Biological inspiration; embodiment.

1. Introduction: The idea(s) of BICA.

BICA (Biologically Inspired Cognitive Architectures) is a new interdisciplinary initiative, and is currently in an exciting stage of rapid expansion, reminiscent of the early stages of the artificial life and adaptive behavior movements. 'Let a thousand flowers bloom' is undoubtedly the best policy at this juncture, but it is certainly not too soon to look around, back, and forward to see if there are any considerations of scope, direction, or focus that might require modification or clarification in the future in order to assist the developmental process. This short position paper is intended to open what is hoped to become an ongoing debate.

Of course, BICA is ultimately defined by its outputs – the contents of the conferences, the repository, and the various discussion formats that have already come into existence. However, this paper will mainly pay attention to the inputs (BICA as defined by the BICA Society) and will further constrain the playing field by limiting itself to dealing with the BI (the Biologically Inspired component) rather than the CA (the Cognitive Architecture component) which can for the moment be taken for granted.

The BICA Society Home web page reads as follows: *"The purpose of the Society is to promote and facilitate the transdisciplinary study of biologically inspired cognitive architectures (BICA), in particular, aiming at the emergence of a unifying, generally accepted framework for the design, characterization and implementation of human-level cognitive architectures"*. (Statement 1)

---

[1] Corresponding Author.

The BICA Society Mission Statement declares that: *"The challenge of creating a real-life computational equivalent of the human mind requires that we better understand at a computational level how natural intelligent systems develop their cognitive and learning functions. In recent years, biologically inspired cognitive architectures have emerged as a powerful new approach toward gaining this kind of understanding (here 'biologically inspired' is understood broadly as 'brain-mind inspired')"*. (Statement 2)

Taken together, these formulations cover a lot of ground, and their superposition certainly includes the vast majority of present and past BICA work. However, we believe that it will be productive to ask some questions about the differences in content and emphasis between the statements, and also to ask about some possibly relevant issues that neither seems to cover. None of this is intended to constitute any element of criticism – it is essentially a response to the very significant stimulation they have provided, and should be seen as an attempt at constructive development rather than correction or change. The brevity of this paper means that it cannot be comprehensive, and so the application of these ideas to the many important specific aspects of BICA systems – notably learning – must be deferred until later in the hoped-for debate.

The paper is organized as follows. Section 2 essentially asks 'What and why is the BI in BICA?' and considers what the biological inspiration in such architectures is intended to deliver, and also to what uses the architectures are intended to be put. Section 3 asks 'How?' and explores a number of distinct ways in which a cognitive architecture may come to have some of the characteristics of biological/human cognitive architectures other than by explicit design. In order to provide a concrete example of how these considerations may be applied to the development of a particular cognitive architecture, Section 4 takes a current project and uses it to illustrate some of the points raised in Sections 2 and 3. Finally, Section 5 presents some tentative and almost certainly preliminary conclusions.

2. The What and the Why: The intended role(s) of biological inspiration in BICA

2.1. Human-level or human-like?

Statement (1) targets "the design, characterization and implementation of human-level cognitive architectures". The implication of 'human level' clearly concerns cognitive performance, which should be comparable with that of humans. The domain is unspecified, and so the sentence could reasonably be read as implying 'in any relevant target domain'. This allows everything from baseball to chess and mathematics. Although 'human level' will usually be read as 'at least at a human level' it is important to remember that human cognitive abilities have some severe limitations that do not necessarily apply to artificial systems, and that a system routinely capable of remembering a list of 50,000 random numbers from a single reading should not be considered as performing at a human level.

Statement (2) targets "a real-life computational equivalent of the human mind". It implies equivalence both in its performance (so the previous comment applies) and also in its nature, so it should be recognisably human-like. (For example, the CFP for BICA2011 invites work on 'human-like episodic and semantic memory, and human-like self-regulated learning'). Statement (2) also interprets the broad meaning of 'biologically inspired' as 'brain-mind inspired', although this is in fact much narrower than its usual meaning in robotics and adaptive behaviour. We surmise that this statement is intended to rule out pure AI approaches, although it goes without saying that AI techniques may well play significant and legitimate roles within larger biologically inspired schemes. We suggest that the use of the phrase 'recognisably human-like' somewhere in Statement (2) would be helpful.

2.2. What is a BICA system for?

The BICA mission statement makes no attempt to identify the potential end use of the architectures, but three of the many possibilities that might significantly affect the design of such systems can immediately be identified. The first is a scientific use, that of experimenting with BICA designs, especially embodied examples, to cast light on human cognition – Cordeschi's so-called synthetic method [1], which goes well beyond traditional cognitive modelling. The second is a purely functional use: engineering BICA systems because they might be expected to outperform other cognitive systems in some particular application. For example, the BICA solution may be directed towards achieving human-level performance in some domain, predicated on the assumption that since humans are the best all-round cognitive systems known, drawing on the design of the human system may produce better results than using other principles. The third is to target the attribute of being human-like, perhaps because such a system would respond to contingencies in the same way as a human (and would be useful in predicting a human's responses) or because the similarity with a human makes the communication with and understanding of the system easier for humans.

These considerations highlight the difference between the phrases 'human-level' and 'human-like'. If humans were in fact without any faults as cognitive systems, this would not be an issue. However, recent research, pure and applied, has shown that humans are riddled with cognitive defects, in that they routinely and frequently have thoughts and perceptions, and choose and execute actions, which are demonstrably incorrect or suboptimal. This whole paper is too short to contain anything like a complete list, but there are many outstanding examples. The very narrow field of behavioural finance studies the errors made in investment decisions; a recent handbook [2] lists overoptimism, the illusion of control, the illusion of knowledge, overconfidence, self attribution bias, confirmation bias, hindsight bias, cognitive dissonance, conservatism bias, representativeness, framing, categorisation, anchoring, availability bias, cue competition, loss aversion, hyperbolic discounting, ambiguity aversion, regret theory, imitation, contagion, herding, and cascades, among others.

Most people identify cognition with conscious thought, but research in consciousness studies has thrown up a large number of apparent errors, some of the worst of which are succinctly summarised by the science journalist Norretranders [3]: *'Consciousness is a peculiar phenomenon. It is riddled with deceit and self-deception; there can be consciousness of something we were sure had been erased by an anaesthetic; the conscious I is happy to lie up hill and down dale to achieve a rational explanation for what the body is up to; sensory perception is the result of a devious relocation of sensory input in time; when the consciousness thinks it determines to act, the brain is already working on it; there appears to be more than one version of consciousness present in the brain; our conscious awareness contains almost no information but is perceived as if it were vastly rich in information.'*

Given these and other examinations of human cognitive and perceptual defects such as inattentional blindness [4] and change blindness [5], it is clear that being more 'human-like' may actually militate against having higher levels of performance in many situations. We suggest that in Statement (1) the target of BICA should be redefined as 'achieving human-level performance with a human-like system'. Of course, this does not rule out the productive investigation of less human-like systems with superhuman performance along the way, but their relationship and relevance to the eventual destination will then be rather more clearly defined.

3. The How: Sources of real or apparent biological or human-like characteristics

There are a number of possible sources of real or apparent biological or human-like characteristics that might appear in a cognitive architecture. The most obvious in the present context is through the inclusion of features inspired by the structural or functional characteristics of real biological architectures; these may range from high level functional components or mechanisms (e.g. long term memory, action selection) to the components at the lowest level above the computational substrate (e.g. Izhikevich neurons). As this forms the mainstream of BICA, and is clearly aligned with the core principles as currently expressed, it requires no further discussion. Instead, this section will point out three of the main ways in which cognitive systems may come to possess characteristics of biological systems without their being designed in.

3.1. By influence or inheritance

The first way is quite trivial, but still worth noting. Some of the best known and most influential cognitive architectures (e.g. ACT-R, Soar) were explicitly inspired by, or were designed to model, human cognition, and therefore qualify as BICAs. Because of this, architectures derived from or inspired by these and similar architectures, however loosely, should also qualify as BICAs, whatever their intended application domain.

3.2. By being subject to the same constraints as biological systems

Convergent evolution is the phenomenon in which unrelated biological lineages evolve similar features in response to strong environmental and physical constraints. The usual examples are wings, which are similar in bats (mammals) and pterosaurs (reptiles), although no common ancestor had wings. In much the same way, parallels can be drawn between some engineered and some evolved structures: for example, energy efficient fast travel through fluid environments requires some degree of streamlining in both animals and machines. It is also overwhelmingly likely that the constraints imposed on an information processing system, whether natural or artificial, will tend to produce both designed and evolved systems with some functional and even structural similarities, as long as the available building blocks permit this. The discovery of feedback control in engineering facilitated the understanding of homeostasis in animals; common problems had indeed led to common solutions. The active constraints may include speed and accuracy of response, appropriate use of energy, the optimization of risk and reward, the need to profit from previous experience, and so on. For example, as many have observed, the ability to simulate a candidate action sufficiently well to assess its utility is a very valuable attribute, whether it happens in a chimpanzee or a model-based predictive controller in a chemical plant.

The implications of this train of thought for BICA are clear: the best design for a cognitive system which is subject to certain strong task and environmental constraints may be very similar to an existing biological system subject to the same constraints. The designed system may therefore appear to be a BICA but there will have been no identifiable process of biological inspiration. Since a major source of constraints is the system's physical embodiment, and since cognitive systems are now being combined with humanoid robots with increasing frequency, recent publications such as 'How the body shapes the way we think' [6] and 'How the body shapes the mind' [7] should perhaps encourage us to admit another category of BICA in which the architecture is not inspired by a biological mind or brain but shaped by a biological embodiment.

3.3. Bricolage – a biological design method

Part of the reason for apparent biological imperfections is that evolution does not create systems from first principles, like modern engineers, but rather engages in *bricolage*, or tinkering, using or modifying the materials at hand to produce something good enough for the moment. If this turns out later to have been a false move, leading to difficulties, then there is no way of going back to rationalize the design – the fault must be coped with, as likely as not through the use of more *bricolage*. The vertebrate eye is a design disaster, with the neurons in front of the sensory cells, obstructing the light and having to be gathered together to leave the eyeball, creating the blind spot. In contrast, the eye of the octopus – a mere mollusc, from a different lineage – avoids these problems by placing the neurons behind the sensory cells.

Why might this be relevant to BICA? Because some cognitive abilities, such as human episodic memory, may also be the result of *bricolage*. It is probable that forms of imagination evolved before episodic memory, mainly because there is a clear evolutionary benefit in being able to anticipate the outcomes of actions, as noted above, but no such benefit attaches to episodic memory *per se*. However, the simulation mechanisms supporting imagination may later have been used as a basis for episodic memory, constraining it to becoming an error prone process of active reconstruction from sparse cues. In contrast, it is computationally simple to store memories at whatever resolution is required, and to retrieve and replay them perfectly accurately as many times as necessary. The temptation for a designer of a cognitive system is to provide a better system than nature has contrived – and to do so with very little effort. This may benefit performance, but the end result will be less human-like. Which option is taken is really a matter for the comments in Section 2. The point we wish to make here is that the production of a cognitive architecture using biologically inspired methods of design such as artificial evolutionary *bricolage* may also be a justification for calling the architecture a BICA. This might seem a small and unimportant observation now, but the evolution of cognitive systems within complex physics-based simulations of embodied agents in complex worlds may soon be an everyday affair.

4. An example of the Why and the How: The ECCEROBOT project

We are currently working on a Europe-wide project, ECCEROBOT [8], that when completed may serve as an example of how a cognitive architecture may come to possess features of biological cognitive architectures without any deliberate attempt having been made to provide it with such features. We have chosen it partly because of our familiarity with it, but mainly because we believe it offers a good subject for the application of the ideas presented here. (It is certainly not unique in this respect, and many other BICA systems could of course have fulfilled this role.) The ECCEROBOT project has three explicit aims:

(a) To design and build an anthropomimetic mobile robot.
An anthropomimetic robot [9] is one that copies as far as possible the structural and functional physical architecture of the human body – the skeleton, muscles, and tendons. The approach taken in designing and building the ECCEROBOTs has been described in detail elsewhere, and the principal differences between this approach and a conventional engineering approach have been identified and characterized [10].

(b) To characterise its dynamics and control it successfully.
Three approaches to control are being investigated: classical control theory; heuristic methods (search, learning, evolutionary algorithms) using physics based simulation; and sensory/motor control. None of these uses methods explicitly formulated to match those thought to be used by humans; however, parallels between some components of the artificial and the natural control architectures have already been made – for example, a physics-based body model could be said to correspond to the body schema thought to play a part in human motor control [7]. It is also worth noting that some of the features of anthropomimetic robots (e.g. multi-articular actuation and complex joints, as identified in [10]) prevent the application of current classical methods [11], thereby forcing the use of the second approach [12].

(c) To explore and exploit its human-like characteristics to produce some human-like cognitive features.
The human-like characteristics referred to in this aim are those of the embodiment, as expressed through the shaping of movements, actions, and sensory inputs by the morphology [13], and as detected and analysed by a range of objective techniques including information-based measurements. This aspect of the project is the subject of current work, and results will be reported in due course.

If and when (c) is successful, it will show how a system may acquire human-like cognitive features through embodiment rather than by design. This will align well with the principles outlined in Section 3.2. However, until then, the part of the project best suited to illustrating the material of Sections 2 and 3 is the use in (b) of physics-based modeling to support the search for a suitable motor program to achieve a simple task – grasping a known object. This is conceptualized as a form of functional imagination [14] which is described in engineering rather than biological terms.

There are six basic stages. Stage 1 is the detection and localization of the target object, which we shall assume to be present. This is done using a Microsoft Kinect mounted on the robot's head. The Kinect does not correspond to any biological system. It uses structured infrared light to produce a depth map, and an RGB camera to produce an approximately co-registered visual image. The system is preferred to a conventional stereo imaging system because it is lightweight, self-contained, and very fast. The detection of the target object is carried out by using an optimal trade-off maximum average height correlation filter (OT-MACH) on the RGB image. The location and range of the centroid of the object is then determined by examining the corresponding portion of the depth map. Taken together, these processes could be seen as implementing a kind of visual attention, a well known psychological phenomenon.

Stage 2 produces a 3D representation of the environment, and inserts it into the appropriate position in the 3D physics-based modelling system. This is done by converting the point cloud (the 3D distribution of points obtained from the depth sensor) to a surface by triangulation (meshing) simplifying the mesh by extracting plane areas, and inserting it into the modelling environment as a collision surface – a solid surface allowing any collisions with the simulated robot or any other moving component to be detected. The surface can be 'painted' if required using the RGB data; this can be useful for viewing the simulation. The reduction in the complexity of the modelled environment is necessary for computational reasons; there may be a parallel with the 'grand illusion' of vision [15], in which the apparent richness of the visual world is not supported by a corresponding richness of representation.

Stage 3 (which can be combined with Stage 2) is the replacement of the meshed representation of the target object by a precompiled physics-based model of the target object. This is not a simple process, and requires the extraction of the meshed representation of the object, the repair of the remaining mesh (by making assumptions about continuity and orientation of surfaces) and the insertion into the modelled environment of the detailed and accurate physics-based model of the target object. The target object is both attended to (in that it is treated differently from the contents of the rest of the visual field) and familiar. In psychology there are many differences between the perception of, and memory for, attended versus unattended objects and familiar versus unfamiliar objects. Many such differences (e.g. clarity of perception) favour the attended and familiar objects, as is the case in our model.

In Stage 4, the precomputed physics-based model of the robot is also inserted into the simulation environment with the Kinect sensor in the position calculated from the environmental model and with the posture, force distribution and dynamics derived from the proprioceptive sensors. (In fact there are two robot models. One is highly detailed, and corresponds closely to the functionally relevant dimensions of the real robot; this is used to calculate the movements of the model under motor actuation, gravity, and inertial loadings. The other is a much simpler envelope enclosing the robot, and is used for the computationally demanding task of detecting collisions between robot components, or between the robot and the environment.) The detailed model corresponds in many respects to Gallagher's body schema [7]; perhaps equally interestingly, it can be visually rendered, when it has some correspondences with Gallagher's body image [7].

In Stage 5, the system searches for a sequence of simulated motor activations that will achieve the required goal, in this case the grasping of the simulated object by the simulated robot [16]. There is a great deal of evidence [14,17] suggesting that imagined movements (and perceptions) are controlled by the same brain circuitry that controls their real equivalents.

Stage 6 consists of the execution by the real robot of the sequence of motor activations (the motor program) found by the 'imagination' process using the model robot – again, in line with [14,17].

Although the parallels with natural and human systems mentioned here might seem superficial or incidental, in that some such parallels could be made for some aspects of even the most abstract AI planning system, it is at least possible that some features of biologically constrained cognitive architectures will in the future be seen to be linked to certain 'biological' constraints. In fact, we believe that it would be as well to begin the process of identification now in order to pick out what might be a valuable strand within the wider sweep of BICA.

5. Conclusions

There is certainly no need to change the basic ideas behind BICA, but it might be helpful to clarify the ideas of human-like and human-level performance, and to broaden the concept of biological inspiration to include biological task and environmental constraints, biological embodiments, and biological methods of design.

Acknowledgments

The research leading to these results has received funding from the European Community's Seventh Framework Programme FP7/2007-2013 Challenge 2 (Cognitive Systems, Interaction, Robotics) under grant agreement no. 231864-ECCEROBOT. The ECCEROBOTs are designed and built by Rob Knight, The Robot Studio, Divonne-les-Bains, France.

References

[1] Cordeschi, Roberto (2002) *The Discovery of the Artificial: Behavior, Mind and Machines Before and Beyond Cybernetics*. Dordrecht, The Netherlands: Kluwer
[2] James Montier (2007) *Behavioural investing: a practitioner's guide to applying behavioural finance*. John Wiley and Sons,
[3] T. Norretranders (1991) *The User Illusion: Cutting Consciousness Down to Size*, Viking Press, NY
[4] D. J. Simons (2007), *Scholarpedia*, 2(5):3244
[5] Rensink RA. (2002). Change detection. *Annual Review of Psychology*, 53:245-277
[6] Rolf Pfeifer and Josh C. Bongard (2006) *How the Body Shapes the Way We Think*. MIT Press
[7] Shaun Gallagher (2005) *How the Body Shapes the Mind*, Clarendon Press
[8] eccerobot.org
[9] O. Holland and R. Knight (2006) The anthropomimetic principle. *AISB Symposium on Biologically Inspired Robots*, Bristol
[10] H.G. Marques, M. Jäntsch, S. Wittmeier, C. Alessandro, O. Holland, C. Alessandro, A. Diamond, M. Lungarella, and R. Knight (2010) ECCE1: the first of a series of anthropomimetic musculoskeletal upper torsos. In *Proceedings of 10th International IEEE/RAS Conference on Humanoid robotics*
[11] V. Potkonjak, B. Svetozarevic, K. Jovanovic, O. Holland (2010) Biologically-inspired control of a compliant anthropomimetic robot. *15th IASTED International Conference on Robotics and Applications*, Cambridge, Massachusetts, pp 182-189
[12] S. Wittmeier, M. Jäntsch, K. Dalamagkidis, and A. Knoll (2011) Physics-based Modeling of an Anthropomimetic Robot, *Proc. IEEE/RSJ International Conference on Intelligent Robots and Systems*
[13] Pfeifer, R., Lungarella, M., Iida, F. (2007) Self-organization, embodiment, and biologically inspired robotics, *Science*, Vol. 318, 1088-1093
[14] Marques, H.G. and Holland, O. (2009) Architectures for functional imagination. *Neurocomputing* 72, 743-759
[15] Alva Noë (2002) Is the Visual World a Grand Illusion? *Journal of Consciousness Studies*, **9**, No. 5–6, 1–12
[16] A. Diamond, O. Holland, H.G. Marques (2011) The role of the predicted present in artificial and natural cognitive systems, this volume.
[17] K.D. Markman, W.M.P. Klein, and J.A. Suhr (2009) *Handbook of Imagination and Mental Simulation*, Psychology Press, New York

Biologically Inspired Cognitive Architectures 2011
A.V. Samsonovich and K.R. Jóhannsdóttir (Eds.)
IOS Press, 2011
doi:10.3233/978-1-60750-959-2-146

On the Simulation of Human Frailty

Ian HORSWILL[a,1] and Christine LISETTI[b]
[a]Northwestern University
[b]Florida International University

Abstract. Artificial intelligence generally focuses on engineering rationality. While rational agents are undoubtedly useful, we argue that computational methods are also useful for modeling aspects of human behavior that fall short of perfect rationality. And moreover, that for certain kinds of applications, this is preferable to perfect rationality.

Keywords. Believable agents, clinical applications, psychopathology

Introduction

It is commonplace for artificial intelligence to be thought of as the attempt to build systems that are smart, and in particular, rational [1]. The goal is to produce a systems that are as smart as humans or, ideally, even more so. This focus on rational behavior is so profound that even research on affect and affective computing is often justified by arguing emotion is a necessary component of rationality [2]. And indeed research on Biologically Inspired Cognitive Architectures is most often justified on the functionalist grounds that biological systems perform better than other architectures.

Although modeling rationality and building smart machines are without question worthwhile pursuits, it is worth remembering that humans often fall short of these idealizations; we are not perfectly rational. Moreover, there are applications where it is at least as important to simulate our failure modes as it is our successes. In this position paper we will discuss two such application domains, entertainment and psychotherapy. And we will look at one particular class of dysfunction in human behavior – the breakdown of inhibitory processing – which is of both theoretical interest, and of practical interest for applications.

1. Inhibitory structures

Biological intelligence is the result of a complex process in which evolutionary pressures drive the development of the most important capabilities such as feeding, reproduction, and defense, first, leaving other capabilities to be added on later. When adding new capabilities, evolution almost always prefers either to adapt existing functionality, or to layer the new functionality on top of existing functionality, rather than reengineering existing functionality, since the latter would involve a temporary reduction in overall fitness until the new system was properly evolved.

---

[1] Corresponding Author.

As a result, the human system consists of a complicated network of both new and legacy systems that cooperate to do the right thing most of the time. But there are nevertheless times when the system does *not* do the right thing and its particular failure modes expose the evolutionary structure of the system.

One important class of this sort of structure is the inhibition of lower-level, presumably phylogenetically older, systems by higher-level, presumably newer, ones. This kind of layered structure can have valuable performance properties [3]. But as with any design, it can lead to problematic behavior if the inhibition occurs at inappropriate times, or fails to occur at appropriate ones. These patterns of over- and under-inhibition of different types form an interesting and important class of human (mis-)behavior.

1.1. Anxiety and Inhibition

Low-level behavior systems are often grouped into those concerned with approaching desirable stimuli (food, warmth, mates, etc.), and those concerned with avoiding noxious stimuli (predators, fire). However, there is considerable evidence that across the mammalian line, and perhaps the vertebrate line in general, these systems are mediated by a third system, the so-called behavioral inhibition system (BIS), that responds to conflicts between the two [4].

Under this model, the behavioral approach system (BAS) is responsible for fulfilling basic biological needs, while the avoidance system (the fight/flight/freeze system or FFFS) is responsible for purely defensive responses. The BIS is responsible for mediating hybrid *defensive approach* situations, such as the need to forage for food in an area known to contain predators. In these situations, the BIS both inhibits the approach and avoid systems, slowing down their responses, allowing a more careful approach, while also stimulating behaviors related to information gathering, such as pupillary dilation, rearing (in the case of rats), or increased memory scanning (in the case of humans).

Under this model, known as Reinforcement Sensitivity Theory (RST), the relative sensitivities of the three systems – BAS, BIS, and FFFS – are independent parameters. Experimental evidence for the model is based on the ability of both psychopharmacological interventions and neurological ones (e.g. lesion studies) to directly manipulate the sensitivities of these systems. In particular, the use of anxiolytic drugs inhibits the BIS-related behaviors of hesitation and information gathering while leaving intact the FFFS-mediated behaviors of self-defense, while panicolytic drugs have precisely the opposite effect [4].

The model has been influential in personality psychology for its ability to provide biological explanations of standard personality parameters, in terms of the sensitivity parameters of these three systems [5]. It has also been influential in clinical psychology for its ability to provide a biological explanation for the differences between Major Depressive Disorder, Panic Disorder, and Generalized Anxiety Disorder, and why they respond to distinct drugs [6]; MDD is interpreted (interestingly) not as an increase in activation of the avoidance system (the FFFS), but as *reduced* activation of the approach system (the BAS). Increased activation of the avoidance system, is thought instead to be the cause Panic Disorder (PD), in part because it responds to the precisely the drugs that mediate FFFS response thresholds in animal models. Finally, GAD (anxiety) is thought to be due to overactivity of the BIS, both because it involves the increased prevalence of the behaviors associated with the

BIS, but also because it responds to drugs that inhibit BIS response (but not those that inhibit FFFS response).

1.2. Impulsivity and inhibition

Another influential model in personality psychology, the dual process model [7], views the approach and avoidance (and presumably BIS) systems as components of an overall *impulsive* behavior system, that's responsible for responding to short-term rewards and punishments. The impulsive system is then regulated by a higher-level *effortful control* system. The effortful control system is responsible for pursuit of longer-term goals and the overriding of short-term impulses that might result in long-term problems. Like the BIS, the effortful control system both shows considerable individual differences (i.e. can be thought of as a component of personality) and is subject to experimental manipulation, either by psychopharmacological intervention (alcohol reduces effortful control and increases impulsivity), or simply through its use (see depletion, below).

The dual process model differs from typical tiered architectures in robotics [8] in that the lower level (impulsive) system is relatively autonomous and self-sufficient; unlike the planning or sequencing tiers of robot architectures, the effortful control system cannot simply order the impulsive system to do something; it can only bias its responses through excitation and inhibition, and its ability to do so is limited.

One of the most interesting aspects of effortful control is that it behaves as a scarce resource; using it temporarily reduces one's capacity to use it further. In the words of Schmeichel and Baumeister [9], self-regulatory strength (effortful control) behaves like physical strength: its use both helps build its future capacity and reduces its present capacity. A wide range of manipulations can deplete effortful control, leading to dysregulation and an increase in impulsive behavior [9]. For example, Vohs et al. [10] found that subjects simply forced to make a series of choices were unable to force themselves to consume a healthy but bad-tasting drink, whereas control subjects not forced to make the choices were able to make themselves consume the drink. Such loss of self-regulation is an important phenomenon of human behavior and is a key factor in a wide variety of social ills ranging from domestic abuse to addictive disorders such as alcoholism and the obesity epidemic.

2. Applications

Again, the argument of this position paper is that there are a number of cases where the simulation of human failures is important, and depending on the application, possibly even more important than the simulation of its successes.

2.1. Clinical intervention

One obvious case where the simulation of human psychological problems might be useful is in the *treatment* of such problems. For example, one might use the direct modeling of the breakdowns within a patient for an interactive therapy system, or for parameter estimation (e.g. to estimate the reactivity of the BIS and BAS systems within the patient).

Another potential use is to model these systems within synthetic characters with whom the patient interacts. The patient could then experiment with the character's behavior – subjecting them to different situations and observing the results, as a way of coming to better understand their own behavior. The system could also display the internal state variables of the character, such as their level of effortful control, so as to help the patient better understand the dynamics of their own behavior.

2.2. Interactive entertainment

Another case is in entertainment scenarios such as interactive storytelling, or computer games, in which one needs to construct synthetic characters whose reactions are believable in the sense of making a user willing to suspend disbelief [11, 12], regardless of their overall realism. For these applications, the pauses and hesitations due to the internal inhibition of a conflicted character, or the obvious lack of inhibition of a drunken character can be important to establishing the believability of a character.

More generally, a disproportionate amount of storytelling involves characters who are flawed, or simply not at their best, particularly in applications such as interactive drama [13]. Narrative traditionally involves characters who are presented with conflicts and challenges, often from within [14]. And these applications provide a wonderful sandbox in which to experiment with simulations of human psychology, including humans who are not at their best.

3. Conclusion

We have tried to argue that human quirks and failings can be at least as interesting to study as our intelligence. This is not a new argument; Colby's seminal PARRY system, a model of paranoid belief structures implemented as a LISP simulation [15] is perhaps the earliest example of work in this vein. Nevertheless, work in this area is still rare. We feel the BICA community, with its focus both on computational neuroscience, and on trying to understand the macroarchitecture of cognitive systems, is especially well suited to studying it. We invite the reader to join us.

References

1. Russell, S. and P. Norvig, *Artificial Intelligence: A Modern Approach.* 3rd ed. 2009: Prentice Hall.
2. Damasio, A., *Descartes' Error: Emotion, Reason, and the Human Brain.* 2005: Penguin.
3. Brooks, R.A., *A Robust Layered Control System For A Mobile Robot.* IEEE Journal of Robotics and Automation, 1986. **RA-2**(1): p. 14-23.
4. Gray, J.A. and N. McNaughton, *The Neuropsychology of Anxiety: An Enquiry into the Functions of the Septo-Hippocampal System.* 2nd ed. Oxford Psychology Series. 2003: Oxford University Press.
5. Corr, P.J., ed. *The Reinforcement Sensitivity Theory of Personality.* 2008, Cambridge University Press.

6.   Zinbarg, R.E. and K.L. Yoon, *RST and Clinical Disorders: Anxiety and Depression*, in *The Reinforcement Sensitivity Theory of Personality*, P.J. Corr, Editor. 2008, Cambridge University Press. p. 360-397.

7.   Carver, C.S., S.L. Johnson, and J. Joormann, *Serotonergic Function, Two-Mode Models of Self-Regulation, and Vulnerability to Depression: What Depression Has in Common With Impulsive Aggression.* Psychological Bulletin, 2008. **134**(6): p. 912-943.

8.   Bonasso, R.P., et al., *Experiences with an Architecture for Intelligent, Reactive Agents.* Journal of Experimental & Theoretical Artificial Intelligence, 1997. **9**(2-3): p. 237-256.

9.   Schmeichel, B.J. and R.F. Baumeister, *Self-Regulatory Strength*, in *Handbook of Self-Regulation: Research, Theory, and Applications*, R.F. Baumeister and K.D. Vohs, Editors. 2004, The Guilford Press: New York. p. 84-98.

10.   Vohs, K.D., et al., *Making choices impairs subsequent self-control: A limited resource account of decision making, self-regulation, and active initiative.* Journal of Personality and Social Psychology, 2008. **94**: p. 883-898.

11.   Johnston, O. and F. Thomas, *The Illusion of Life: Disney Animation.* 1981: Hyperion Press.

12.   Bates, J., *The Role of Emotion in Believable Agents.* Communications of the ACM, 1994. **37**(7): p. 122-125.

13.   Mateas, M. and A. Stern, *Façade.* 2005.

14.   Campbell, J., *The Hero with a Thousand Faces.* 3rd ed. 2008: New World Library.

15.   Colby, K.M., *Simulation of Belief Systems*, in *Computer Models of Thought and Language*, R.C. Schank and K.M. Colby, Editors. 1973, W.H. Freeman and Company: San Francisco. p. 251-286.

Biologically Inspired Cognitive Architectures 2011
A.V. Samsonovich and K.R. Jóhannsdóttir (Eds.)
IOS Press, 2011
© 2011 The authors and IOS Press. All rights reserved.
doi:10.3233/978-1-60750-959-2-151

Adaptive Recall in Hippocampus

Michael D. HOWARD[a,1,*], Rajan BHATTACHARYYA[a,*], Randall C. O'REILLY[b],
Giorgio ASCOLI[c], and Jean-Marc FELLOUS[d]
*[a]HRL Laboratories, LLC, [b]University of Colorado, Boulder, [c]George Mason University,
[d]University of Arizona*

Abstract. Complementary learning systems (CLS) theory describes how the hippocampal and cortical contributions to recognition memory are a direct result of their architectural and computational specializations. In this paper we model a further refinement of CLS that features separate handling of inputs from the dorsal and ventral posterior cortices, and present a possible mechanism for adaptive recall in hippocampus based on several research findings that have not previously been related to each other. This model suggests how we are able to recognize familiar objects in unfamiliar settings.

Keywords: Hippocampus, memory, complementary learning systems, MTL

Introduction

Episodic recall mediated by the hippocampus supports the retrieval of specific information using the competing principles of pattern separation in the dentate gyrus (DG) and pattern completion in CA3. Although the hippocampal pattern completion mechanism lends some recall robustness when retrieval cues are noisy, pattern separation can cause early divergence from the desired attractor state and failure to recognize a noisy stimulus. Neocortical recall is much more invariant to noise, but details are likely to be generalized away. Yet there is experimental evidence that specific instances can be recalled even when the behavioral context in which the cue is presented is different than during learning [6, 25].

Complementary Learning Systems theory (CLS) proposes that the functional differences between neocortex and hippocampus arise from anatomical and learning rate differences. But CLS did not consider the architectural separation of spatial and semantic information in both areas [4, 24].

Myers and Scharfman have explored at least two mechanisms by which pattern separation in DG can be controlled and dynamically regulated to reduce sensitivity to noise [13, 14]. Hayashi and Nonaka proposed the intriguing possibility that DG granule cells can select between distal inputs carrying non-topographic information, and proximal inputs carrying topographic inputs [8]. Our contribution in this paper is to combine these architectural features and recall mechanisms into our CLS model. Our hypothesis is that the DG can control inhibition independently in proximal and distal layers, and that has a benefit for cued recall performance in the presence of environmental noise. Our experiment demonstrated an average of 62.68% reduction in recall error given cues corrupted by from 0 to 66% noise. We will first review the CLS account, and then examine the evidence for a further segregation of data flow through

---

[1] Corresponding author (mdhoward@hrl.com)   *both authors contributed equally

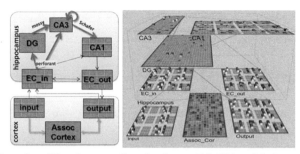

Figure 1. (A) Illustration of Complementary Learning System. EC, CA1, and the input and output layers each have units arranged in groups called "slots" that project topographically. The perforant path has permute-style uniform random projection. CA3 has a full recurrent projection (each sending unit to every receiving unit) and CA3->CA1 is also full. Thick red projections learn twice as fast as thinner orange ones. Thin black projections do not learn. **(B).** Corresponding computational model in the Emergent neural simulator. Regional network layers are composed of point neuron units whose activations are shown as colored blocks.

the hippocampus and neocortex. Then we present our computational model that demonstrates these ideas.

1. The Complementary Learning Systems Framework

Complementary Learning Systems (CLS) theory [1, 11, 17] organizes the brain's memory systems around the computational specializations of the medial temporal lobe (MTL, illustrated in Figure 1): the highly specialized hippocampus versus the relatively undifferentiated neocortex. The fast-learning hippocampus, defined in terms of subareas dentate gyrus (DG), the *cornu ammonis* areas CA3 and CA1, and the entorhinal cortex (EC, the I/O gateway to the hippocampus), is contrasted with the slow-learning neocortex. A key aspect of the hippocampus is the sparseness of its activity: due to high inhibition, less than 1% of the DG units and 5% of CA3 units are active at any time (as Figure 1B illustrates). This means that even similar information is encoded into different, largely distinct populations of neurons (the CLS principle of *pattern separation*). Note the clockwise flow in hippocampus at the top of Figure 1A. Input patterns are encoded in DG and CA3 and stored in their weights. A cue consisting of part of a stored pattern appearing on input will be *pattern-completed* by the recurrent connections in CA3 (another CLS principle).

Conjunctive representations in hippocampus bind together contextual and stimulus features [18]. Although hippocampal representations are learned at twice the rate of those in the cortex, high inhibition in DG makes it very unlikely that even similar memories interfere with each other. But due to pattern separation, hippocampal representations are not good at generalizing over regularities in the environment. In contrast, the cortical layer has relatively low inhibition allowing 25% of its units to respond to an input on average [15]. This increases the chance of overlapping representations and promotes generalization (observe the widespread activity in the Assoc_Cor compared to DG and CA3 in Figure 1B). These attributes enable the neocortex to extract statistical regularities that may be present in the input patterns; but it also requires a slow learning rate and repeated exposures to avoid interference in cases where the inputs include different associations for the same stimulus.

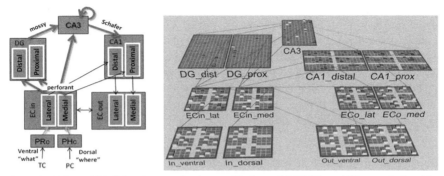

Figure 2. (A) Lateral/Medial pathways as implemented in the model **(B)** PRc and PHc were lesioned for this study. The non-topographic ventral path goes through ECin_lateral to DG and CA1 distal and CA3. The topographic dorsal path goes through ECin_medial to DG and CA1 proximal and CA3.

2. Segregation of data and dynamic inhibition in hippocampus

Inputs to the MTL from the dorsal side contain primarily spatial information through the parietal cortex by way of the dorsal parahippocampal cortex (PHc). Inputs from the ventral side contain semantic information [2] such as knowledge of objects, people, and word-meanings, and are received from the temporal cortex by way of the ventral parahippocampal cortex, also known as the perirhinal cortex (PRc). In non-human primates and rats, that segregation of posterior processing pathways continues through the memory systems, with the spatial PHc inputs entering the medial entorhinal cortex (MEC), and the nonspatial PRc inputs entering the lateral entorhinal cortex (LEC). This segregation is evidenced by anatomical studies and modeling of dorsal and ventral pathways in the hippocampus [4, 24, 26]. It must be noted that LEC and MEC have not yet been differentiated in humans, but there is no reason to believe that this segregation would not hold [3, 21].

Dynamic control of inhibition in DG has been found in rats. During exploratory behavior there was increased dendritic inhibition in rat dentate gyrus, which would improve place discrimination. During quiescent mode, DG inhibition was decreased, resulting in a low-amplitude, noisy input to CA3 [12]. Myers and Scharfman had similar findings, proposing that the DG inhibition may be controlled by the Medial Septum/Diagonal Band of Broca, modulating granule activity through GABAergic or cholinergic projections as well as through back-projections from CA3 [13, 14].

Perforant path projections from LEC and MEC synapse distally and proximally on DG granule cell dendrites respectively. There is evidence that these two projections operate independently [9, 19, 20], including a possible gating function whereby the granule cells may select between proximal and distal inputs [8]. This was the justification for us to approximate the effect by separating the proximal and distal compartments into separate layers (Figure 2b). Dentate inhibition (both feedback and feedforward) is highly layer selective, with specific interneuron classes directly targeting specific dendritic domains [5], and that is justification for our experiment in which we only modulated inhibition in the proximal side of DG, as described in the next section.

3. Materials and Methods

Figure 2 illustrates how we adapted the CLS model of Figure 1 to incorporate the features discussed above; namely, separation of DG and CA1 into proximal and distal layers, separation of ECin and ECout into lateral and medial layers, and separation of Input and output into ventral and dorsal layers. Input ventral projects to EC_in lateral, which projects on the perforant path to distal DG and CA1. Dorsal inputs likewise project through EC_in medial to the proximal DG and CA1 layers.

The training data (illustrated in Figure 3A) was presented in 10 trials, each trial consisting of an association between an A pattern in the left column of the lateral input to EC_in lateral with a B pattern in the right column. On the medial (EC_in medial) side, each trial had a characteristic context pattern labeled C. These patterns can be thought of as sigmoidally thresholded neural activations caused by perceiving certain objects in the environment. In each training epoch, every trial was presented once and the weights were adjusted. This continued until the error was reduced to nearly zero. Then the trained network was tested by presenting every trial again, but with the B pattern blanked out on the lateral side, and 0 to 4 of the 6 slots of the medial side context replaced by random noise (illustrated in Figure 3B). For example, in Figure 3B, the 5th and 6th slots were replaced by noise, meaning that 1/3 of the context is unfamiliar. The task is to pattern-complete the blank lateral B column and repair the noise on the medial side.

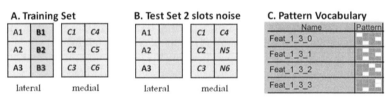

Figure 3. Training (A) and testing (B) datasets. Each block or "slot" identifies a pattern of unit activations chosen from a vocabulary set (partially shown in C) to be applied to the input layer.

In our first experimental results, we controlled inhibition in DG proximal layer (which carries the contextual inputs from EC_in medial). Our second set of experiments simulated DG gating [8] by controlling the relative strength of the inputs to CA3 from proximal DG, relative to those from distal DG. These experiments did not require cortical influence, so PRc and PHc were lesioned as shown in Figure 2B.

4. Results

The results are plotted in Figure 4, where each line in each plot is the test error results from the network when presented with a different amount of noise in the dorsal/medial input. In every case, when noise is increased on the dorsal side (shown as percent of noise {0, 17%, 33%, 50%, 67%}), the hippocampus makes correspondingly more mistakes in recalling the original association, as expected. But in Figure 4A when inhibition is lowered on the dorsal side of DG (allowing more units to become activated -- moving to the right on the X axis), allowing more neurons to become active, the hippocampus is better able to recall the memory (lower error). The signal to CA3

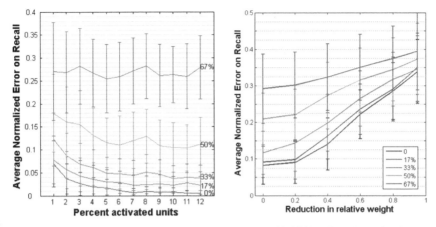

Figure 4. The effect of changing **(A)** the amount of inhibition in DG proximal, and **(B)** the relative weights of proximal vs. distal inputs from DG to CA3, on the ability to recall the learned association, as a function of the amount of noise in the dorsal (medial) inputs.

then emphasizes the higher signal-to-noise-ratio in the ventral/lateral input in the face of the noisy dorsal/medial context. The top line, representing 67% noise, appears to be too much noise for accurate recall, for any value of inhibition. So it appears that the system has a failure mode at some noise level above 50%.

Figure 4B shows the results of an alternative approach to dealing with a noisy dorsal/medial context, by lowering the weight from DG proximal to CA3 relative to the weight from DG distal to CA3. This could be another way that the memory system might emphasize the higher SNR ventral/lateral input over the noisy dorsal/medial context. However, it is clear that when the relative contribution of the noisy side is reduced (relative weight approaches zero) test error increases significantly.

5. Discussion and Conclusion

Familiarity has been hypothesized to be a cortical function, relying on context-free semantic information to the perirhinal areas (PRc). Recall requires the area DG and CA3 of the hippocampus, which bind lateral and medial inputs into configural representations [10, 16, 18, 23]. In this short paper, we have only begun to explore the reasons why the brain maintains this object data vs. context data in somewhat independent pathways through the hippocampus, in rat and likely also in human. We modified our CLS-based hippocampus simulation to model this better. We find it interesting that there is some indication that the DG treats distal and proximal inputs separately [8], and used that as a rationale for splitting out the pathways in DG. We cited recent neuroscience findings that inhibition in DG changes dynamically based on behavioral conditions in rat [13], and we theorize that the DG can control inhibition independently in those proximal and distal layers. We showed that by decreasing the amount of inhibition on the information in the dorsal/medial DG, the hippocampus was better able to recover the memory especially when the familiar percepts are encountered in unfamiliar surroundings Figure 4A. We also showed that reducing the strength of the proximal DG input to CA3 relative to the distal input did not help; in fact it increased the error Figure 4B.

Based on these ideas, we propose that humans may dynamically vary inhibition in DG in a staged recall process whereby familiar, well-learned memory items that are not confidently retrievable due to unfamiliar surroundings can eventually be accessed by repeated pattern completion/separation loops regulated by the DG. What is required is a recall confidence signal, such as a comparison in CA1 of the difference between the inputs and the recalled memory from CA3 [7, 10]. Also, a familiarity signal is needed; a number of researchers have suggested the involvement of the PRc [16, 17, 22, 23], and experimentally we could test the sharpness of the activations in PRc as a familiarity metric. If a stimulus is found to be familiar but the recall is weak, then inhibition in proximal DG should be decreased until recall is achieved.

6. Acknowledgements

Supported by the Intelligence Advanced Research Projects Activity (IARPA) via Department of the Interior (DOI) contract number D10PC20021. The U.S. Government is authorized to reproduce and distribute reprints for Governmental purposes notwithstanding any copyright annotation thereon. The views and conclusions contained hereon are those of the authors and should not be interpreted as necessarily representing the official policies or endorsements, either expressed or implied, of IARPA, DOI, or the U.S. Government.

7. References

[1] H. E. Atallah, M. J. Frank, and R. C. O'Reilly. Hippocampus, cortex, and basal ganglia: Insights from computational models of complementary learning systems. *Neurobiology of Learning and Memory*, 82 (3): 253–267, 2004.
[2] R. Davies, K. S. Graham, J. H. Xuereb, G. B. Williams, and J. R. Hodges. The human perirhinal cortex and semantic memory. *European Journal of Neurscience*, pages 1–7, 2004. doi: 10.1111/j.1460-9568.2004.03710.x.
[3] H. Eichenbaum, A. P. Yonelinas, and C. Ranganath. The medial temporal lobe and recognition memory. *Annual Review of Neuroscience*, 30: 123–152, 2007.
[4] M. S. Fanselow and H.-W. Dong. Are the dorsal and ventral hippocampus functionally distinct structures? *Neuron*, 65 (1): 7–19, 2010. ISSN 0896-6273.
[5] T. Freund and G. Buzsaki. Interneurons of the hippocampus. *Hippocampus*, 6 (4): 347–470, 1996. ISSN 1098-1063.
[6] J. F. Guzowski, J. J. Knierim, and E. I. Moser. Ensemble dynamics of hippocampal regions CA3 and CA1. *Neuron*, 44: 581–584, 2004.
[7] M. E. Hasselmo and J. L. McClelland. Neural models of memory. *Current Opinion in Neurobiology*, 9: 184, January 1999.
[8] H. Hayashi and Y. Nonaka. Cooperation and competition between lateral and medial perforant path synapses in the dentate gyrus. *Neural Networks*, 24 (3): 233–246, 2011. ISSN 0893-6080. doi: 10.1016/j.neunet.2010.12.004.
[9] W. R. Holmes and W. B. Levy. Quantifying the role of inhibition in associative long-term potentiation in dentate granule cells with computational models. *J. Neurophysiology*, 78: 103–116, 1997.

[10] J. E. Lisman and A. A. Grace. The hippocampal-vta loop: Review controlling the entry of information into long-term memory. *Neuron*, 46: 703–713, 2005.

[11] J. McClelland, B. McNaughton, and R. C. O'Reilly. Why there are complementary learning systems in the hippocampus and neocortex: insights from the successes and failures of connectionist models of learning and memory. *Psychological Review*, 102: 419–457, 1995.

[12] A. A. Minai. Control of CA3 place fields by the dentate gyrus: A neural network model. In *Computational Neuroscience: Trends in Research (Proceedings of the Computational Neuroscience Meeting*, pages 411–416, 1997.

[13] C. E. Myers and H. E. Scharfman. A role of hilar cells in pattern separation in the dentate gyrus: a computational approach. *Hippocampus*, 19: 321–337, 2009.

[14] C. E. Myers and H. E. Scharfman. Pattern separation in the dentate gyrus: A role for the CA3 backprojection. *Hippocampus*, in preparation, 2010.

[15] H. Noda and W. R. Adey. Neuronal activity in the association cortex of the cat during sleep, wakefulness and anesthesia. *Brain Research*, 54: 243 – 259, 1973. ISSN 0006-8993. doi: DOI: 10.1016/0006-8993(73)90047-4.

[16] K. A. Norman. How hippocampus and cortex contribute to recognition memory: Revisiting the complementary learning systems model. *Hippocampus*, 20 (11): 1217–1227, 2010. ISSN 1098-1063. doi: 10.1002/hipo.20855.

[17] K. A. Norman and R. C. O'Reilly. Modeling hippocampal and neocortical contributions to recognition memory: a complementary-learning-systems approach. *Psychological review*, 110: 611–646, 11 2003.

[18] R. C. O'Reilly and J. W. Rudy. Conjunctive representations in learning and memory: principles of cortical and hippocampal function. *Psychological review*, 108: 311–345, 05 2001. URL http://www.ncbi.nlm.nih.gov/pubmed/11381832.

[19] P. Poirazi, T. Brannon, and B. W. Mel. Pyramidal neuron as 2-layer neural network. *Neuron*, 37: 989–999, 2003.

[20] A. Polsky, B. W. Mel, and J. Schiller. Computational subunits in thin dendrites of pyramidal cells. *Nature Neuroscience*, 7: 621–627, 2004.

[21] C. Ranganath. A unified framework for the functional organization of the medial temporal lobes and the phenomenology of episodic memory. *Hippocampus*, 20: 1263–1290, 2010.

[22] E. T. Rolls, L. Franco, and S. M. Stringer. The perirhinal cortex and long-term familiarity memory. *The quarterly journal of experimental psychology*, 58B (3/4): 234–245, 2005.

[23] M. M. Sauvage, Z. Beer, M. Ekovich, L. Ho, and H. Eichenbaum. The caudal medial entrohinal cortex: a selective role in recollection-based recognition memory. *The Journal of Neuroscience*, 30 (46): 15695–15699, 2010.

[24] N. vanStrien, N. Cappaert, and M. Witter. The anatomy of memory: an interactive overview of the parahippocampal-hippocampal network. *Nature Reviews Neuroscience*, 10 (4): 272–282, 2009.

[25] A. Vazdarjanova and J. F. Guzowski. Differences in hippocampal neuronal population responses to modifications of an environmental context: Evidence for distinct, yet complementary, functions of CA3 and CA1 ensembles. *The Journal of Neuroscience*, 24 (29): 6489–6496, 2004.

[26] A. Viard, C. Doeller, T. Hartley, C. Bird, and N. Burgess. Anterior hippocampus and goal-directed spatial decision making. *Journal of Neuroscience*, 31 (12): 4613–4621, 2011. doi: 10.1523/JNEUROSCI.4640-10.2011.

158

Biologically Inspired Cognitive Architectures 2011
A.V. Samsonovich and K.R. Jóhannsdóttir (Eds.)
IOS Press, 2011
doi:10.3233/978-1-60750-959-2-158

A Conceptual Space Architecture for Widely Heterogeneous Robotic Systems[1]

HyunRyong Jung, Arjun Menon and Ronald C. Arkin[2]
Mobile Robot Laboratory, School of Interactive Computing
Georgia Institute of Technology, Atlanta, GA USA 30332

Abstract. This paper describes the value of the conceptual space approach for use in teams of robots that have radically different sensory capabilities. The formal underpinnings and perceptual processes are described in the context of a biohazard detection task. The architecture is based on the conceptual spaces representation that Gärdenfors suggested as an alternative to more traditional AI approaches.

Keywords. Conceptual space, heterogeneous robot, knowledge representation

1. Introduction

In robotics, a challenging area involves the sharing of knowledge across widely disparate robotic platforms, i.e., when there is no commonality across the sensor space between platforms. Heterogeneous robots need to share their knowledge with each other to achieve a team task efficiently. For our research for the Army, each type of robot is equipped with radically different sensors, so a framework to share sensor data with other widely heterogeneous robots efficiently is essential. However, classical knowledge representations (e.g., symbolic representations and connectionist methods) have several deficits such as the frame and symbol grounding problems, and can exhibit difficulty in computing similarity between concepts.

To address these problems, we use the conceptual space that Gärdenfors [1] suggested as a basis for human and machine cognition. A conceptual space constitutes a metric world in which objects and abstract concepts are represented by quality dimensions. A concept has several domains to distinguish it from other concepts. Thus, a specific concept forms a set of regions across these domains in the conceptual space. Each domain is composed of quality dimensions, and the primary function of the domain is to represent various qualities of situations or objects. As a result, the linkage between a concept and its domains directly grounds the concept in sensory experience. Because the quality dimensions are metric, the similarity can be measured easily. To deal with potential sensor and representation differences, we abstract raw sensory data into natural object properties such as color, features, chemical composition, and so on based on existing MAST mission requirements and sensor capabilities. To represent the regions of a property, we use a Gaussian Mixture Model because a property of a

---

[1] The work in this paper was funded under the U.S. Army Research Laboratory Micro Autonomous Systems and Technology Collaborative Technology Alliance project (BAE # 329420.)
[2] Corresponding Author.

concept cannot always be represented by a single Gaussian. Table 1 summarizes some of the definitions used in this approach.

Table 1: Conceptual Space Definition summary

	Definition
Concept	A concept is represented as a set of convex regions in a number of domains.
Domain	A domain is a set of integral dimensions that are separable from all other dimensions.
Property	A property of a concept is a convex region in some domain.
Prototype	Prototypes are most representative members of a category.
Quality Dimension	Quality dimensions represent various object qualities
Quality	Sensory input from a sensor system

Earlier research in our laboratory [2-4,7] focused on limited heterogeneity in the sensors fielded on different robots. In our ongoing research as part of the Army Research Laboratory's Microautonomous Systems Technology Collaborative Technology Alliance, we are extending this previous work to incorporate sensor, power, communication and computation impoverished platforms with the goal of being able to provide fully distributed team coordinated control for search and rescue, biohazard detection, and other related missions [5].

2. Related Work

Knowledge representation, studied by many AI researchers, constitutes one of the fundamental topics in AI. However, while answering the question—what is the correct knowledge representation for a particular task? — may seem easy, it is more complicated than we expect. Thus, we need to define the concept of knowledge representation. One simple definition [10-11] is that it is the study of how to store knowledge into a form that the agent can reason with. For this application, the agent is a robot that can move and navigate autonomously. To represent knowledge in such systems, several theories of representation, two of which are symbolic paradigm and connectionist, have been widely used in various areas and applications [12-16].

The symbolic paradigm represents the environment with symbols and has a formal syntax [1] [6]. The role of the syntax is to determine what and how symbols must be combined. In other words, knowledge can be represented with a set of symbols that are connected based on the principles of syntax. Thus, basic concepts are not modeled in a sensory space per se, but represented by the basic symbols. As a result, learning a new physical property for given symbols and dealing with changes in the meaning of concepts cannot be easily represented in symbolic representation. Therefore, symbolic representation is vulnerable to the frame problem and the frame grounding problem [1] [6] [17]. In addition, since concepts at one level are represented by symbols, similarity between symbols cannot be easily modeled at the purely symbolic level. Consequently, as similarity plays an important role in learning and concept formation, systems using the symbolic representation can have difficulty learning new grounded symbols.

The central idea of the alternative connectionist approach takes the form of mimicking the human brain, so it is composed of highly interconnected units or neurons [12] [14]. Artificial neuron networks (ANNs) are a specific instance of the connectionist approach. Connectionism appears brain-like, and it is not subject to the symbol grounding problem that typical symbolic representations suffer from. However, since ANNs consist of large number of simple, highly interconnected neurons, the modification of ANNs is difficult so it is often called a "black box model." Another weakness of the connectionist method is that while similarity can be represented in ANNs by categorization, it cannot be readily computed as a mathematical value.

3. Overview of Conceptual Spaces

The conceptual space that Gärdenfors [1] suggested is a metric world in which objects and abstract concepts are represented by quality dimensions. A concept has several domains that distinguish it from other concepts. Thus, a specific concept is a set of regions from the domains within the conceptual space. Each domain is composed of quality dimensions, and the primary function of the domain is to represent various qualities of situations or objects. As a result, the direct linkage between a concept and domains via sensory data using the conceptual space approach can eliminate the symbol-grounding problem. Because the quality dimension constitutes a metric world, the similarity between sensed objects and concepts can be measured easily.

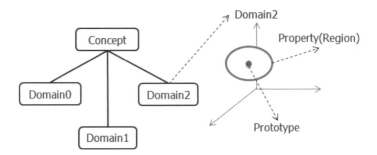

Figure 1: Relationship between conceptual space approach entities

The quality dimensions represent values that can be acquired from sensors. The qualities can be not only explicit features of objects but also abstract non-sensory characteristics such as emotional states. For example, a color domain can be composed of three quality dimensions: hue, saturation, and brightness. A property in the conceptual space is the geometrical structure of the quality dimensions, where a property of a concept forms a convex region in the domain. A concept may also contain salient weights for properties and correlations between the properties. For some concepts, a property can be more important than others, it can be influenced by the task context. Figure 1 illustrates these relationships.

For example, consider how to represent the apple in the conceptual space. The apple is a concept and has diverse properties such as taste, color, shape. Each property can be a certain region in one domain composed of quality dimensions. As Figure 2 illustrates, the color domain of the apple has three quality dimensions: R, G, and B. A property of the apple is a region in the color domain.

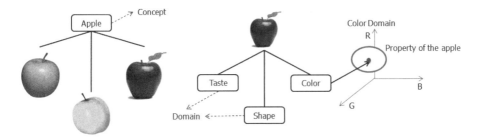

Figure 2. Concept, domain, and property of the apple

Since the property forms a convex region, we can define the most representative member of a domain, as its prototype. In this approach, the prototype can be seen as the centroid of objects that are represented. When a robot detects the color of an apple, sensor data from the camera is represented as a point in the quality dimensions, and the similarity can be computed by measuring the Euclidean distance between the point and the prototype of the color domain of the apple.

Consequently, the theory of conceptual spaces can yield a solution to the frame and symbol-grounding problems that traditional methods of knowledge representation struggle with. Moreover, the conceptual space representation provides a natural way of representing similarities, and this ability is one of its major advantages.

3.1. Conceptual Space Definition

A conceptual space is defined as C. The conceptual space is composed of a symbol space S_S and a concept space C_S [6]. In the symbol space, several symbols can be defined, and each symbol names a concept. An ith concept is denoted by c_i. A concept has properties that are defined as $c(i) = c(P_{i,1}, P_{i,2}, ..., P_{i,n})$ and each having a range $[0, 1]$. An ith property of a kth symbol is denoted by $p(k,i) = P_{k,i}$. A set of concepts $\{c(i), i = 1, ..., N\}$ is covered by S_S. Note that concepts are regions in conceptual space, but properties are regions in domains. A domain is represented as D_i, and the concept space, C_S is composed of domains. For instance, the concept of a biohazard can be defined, (which is used in the test scenarios under development) as $c(1) = c(P_{1,1}, P_{1,2})$, and $P_{1,1}$ is in the color domain D_1, and $P_{1,2}$ is in the temperature domain D_2. Perceptual features are projected to each domain as shown in Figure 3.

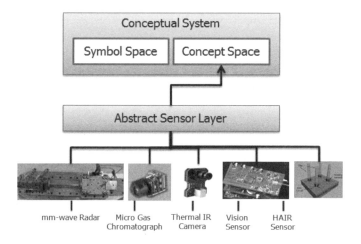

Figure 3. Schematic of conceptual space and abstract sensor layer

A prototype is the centroid of a property and serves as the most representative value of a property. Moreover, since we can categorize a sensed object by finding the closest prototype to the object, it is useful in categorization. We define the prototypical value as $f(k,j)$ in the domain D_j of the labeled with a kth symbol. Figure 4 describes the prototype of the biohazard in the color domain and shows the similarity to the biohazard.

Not all qualities are equally important to a concept, so we need to define the relative importance between properties. The importance of $P_{k,i}$ in domain $D_{j(i)}$ to concept c_k is referred as $\alpha(k, j(i))$. For instance, chemical composition is a primary property in detecting a chemical weapon, since these objects have unique chemical compositions. Thus, the property must have significantly higher importance than others. As Figure 4 illustrates, the chemical composition domain D_2 has much less overlap than the other domains D_1, D_3. Therefore, the chemical domain is the most informative in discriminating a biohazard from a similarly colored and shaped trash can.

3.2. Similarity in Conceptual Space

As objects can be represented as property vectors in conceptual spaces, the definition of similarity of objects is relatively intuitive and easy. The similarity [1] [6] is the distance between objects (and prototypes) and it is one of the main advantages of this representation. Like distance, similarity is a real valued non-negative function and has several properties: The similarity should be maximum when the distance is zero; it should decrease with distance; and be zero when computing the similarity with an inapplicable point. So, we define the similarity (s) between objects a and b with the following equation:

$$s(a,b) = (1 + d(a,b))^{-1}.$$

As a result, a concept (c) in the symbol space can be computed with the following equation:

$$c(k) = \sum_{i=1}^{n} \alpha(k,i) \cdot s\big(p(k,i), f(k,i)\big).$$

$s\big(p(k,i), f(k,i)\big)$ is the similarity between an ith prototype and the ith property in a kth concept. $\alpha(k,i)$ is the importance of the ith property in the kth domain. n is the number of properties in a concept. For instance, one robot detects the color of an object, and the color domain is updated. In order to calculate the concept of a biohazard, $c(1)$, the temperature, D_1, the chemical composition, D_2, and the color, D_3 are required.

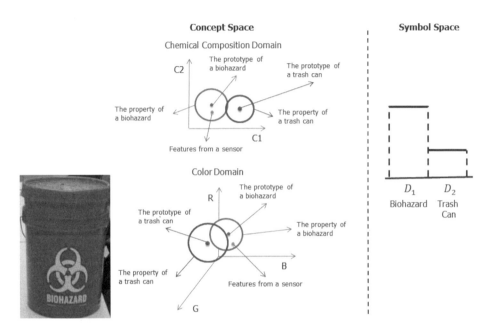

Figure 4. (Left) Potential Biohazard Object. (Right) Notation for prototypes. Note that a similarly colored trashcan may be ambiguous with a biohazard, but the chemical composition which has no overlap provides the basis for disambiguation.

3.3. Abstract Sensor Layer

In this section, the process to convert sensor data to vectors which can represent a property of an object is described, in this case, a bio-weapon. Each robot has a set of m sensors, $S = \{s_1, s_2, ..., s_m\}$. We denote the number of sensors as $|S|$. At time t, the robot receives an observation vector $o_{t,i}$ from each sensor, s_i, resulting in a set of measurement or observation vectors, $O = \{o_{t,1}, o_{t,2}, ..., o_{t,|S|}\}$. We denote the robots with a superscript, so that s_i^j is sensor i of robot j. Sensor data provide a stream of unprocessed information so it is presumed that each robot has a set of p feature detectors, $F = \{f_1, f_2, ..., f_p\}$, that further process observations and output perceptual features. We denote specific values of a set of features at time, t as F_t, and the specific value of a feature i as $f_{t,i}$. A feature detector is a function, φ, that maps a set of observation vectors into a set of feature vectors. For instance, $f_i = \varphi(o_{f_i})$ where $o_{f_i} \in O$ denotes the set of input observations used by the feature detector.

Figure 5 (left) depicts sensors, observations, and perceptual features for a robotic microflyer tasked for this mission. The robot has three sensors, $S^F = \{s_1^F, s_2^F, s_3^F\}$: mm-wave radar, vision sensor, and thermal IR camera. A thermal IR camera provides a color image that each pixel stands for a temperature, and a blob detector takes a thermal image as input and outputs a vector specifying a list of blobs found and their positions. After calculating an average RGB color of the output regions of the blob detector in a thermal image, temperature can be found based on a table lookup. Therefore, the feature detector, $\varphi_{t,2}^F$, contains the computational process to get temperature from a thermal image.

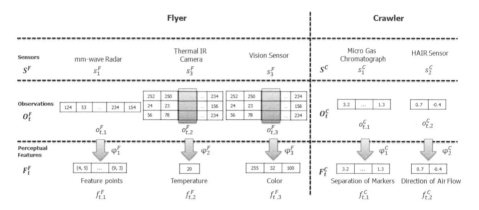

Figure 5. (Left) Flyer robot (Right) Crawler robot

The feature detector, $\varphi_{t,1}^F$, for a mm-wave radar differs from $\varphi_{t,2}^F$ because we need to extract features of a shape from a radar image. Instead of using the blob detector, we will use the line approximation to represent shapes in a radar image. Therefore, the feature, $f_{t,1}^F$, is composed of feature points of a recognized shape so that we can measure Euclidean distance between a detected feature and a prototype of a barrel shape. The feature detector, $\varphi_{t,3}^F$, for a vision sensor is to extract blobs from an image, and then returns an average RGB color of a blob as a feature.

According to the scenario, the crawler has a micro gas chromatograph and a HAIR sensor, where Figure 5 (right) depicts the feature detector of a crawler. Since raw sensor data of the micro gas chromatograph can be used in measuring Euclidean distance, the feature detector, $\varphi_{t,1}^C$ is a null function, but $\varphi_{t,2}^C$ will not be used in a property in the conceptual space since direction of air flow cannot be a property of this particular object 9if it were a fan it might be). However, air flow can be combined with the sensor data of the micro gas chromatograph for a robot to move toward the source of a biohazard using chemotaxis.

3.4. Learning Properties from Samples

In conceptual spaces, properties of the concept are regions in a domain. The regions can represent all samples of a concept. To represent the regions of a property, a Gaussian Mixture Model (GMM) [9] is used because a property of a concept cannot be represented by a single Gaussian in some cases. For example, the color of an apple is various (e.g. yellow, red, green), so representing the color with one Gaussian is not effective. The GMM is a parametric probability density function represented as a weighted sum of Gaussian component densities:

$$p(x|\theta) = \sum_{i=1}^{M} w_i \cdot p(x|\mu_i, \Sigma_i)$$

where x is feature vector for a property, and M is the number of Gaussian density functions. w_i is known as the mixing proportions,

$$0 \leq w_i \leq 1, \sum_{i=1}^{M} w_i = 1.$$

θ is a set containing all of the mixing proportions and model parameters,

$$\theta = \{w_i, \mu_i, \Sigma_i\}_{i=1}^{M}.$$

$p(x|\mu_i, \Sigma_i), i = 1, \dots, M$, are the component Gaussian densities,

$$p(x|\mu_i, \Sigma_i) = \frac{1}{\sqrt{(2\pi)^d \Sigma_i}} exp\left(-\frac{1}{2}(x - \mu_i)^T \Sigma_i^{-1}(x - \mu_i)\right).$$

Since each property is modeled as a mixture of Gaussians, a data association problem must be solved. There will be several clusters in the space, and the algorithm must first determine which cluster the data belongs to before updating the parameters of the model. The method used to solve this is Expectation Maximization, which alternates between estimating the association of the points to the clusters and updating the parameters of the clusters given the association.

4. Summary

We have presented the underpinnings of an overall robotic architecture being developed for use in sharing knowledge across heavily constrained microautonomous platforms with respect to power, communication, sensing, and computation. It is inspired by conceptual spaces and can be applied to multi-robot systems equipped with widely heterogeneous sensors. The conceptual space can be used to solve some of the problems that classical knowledge representations have such as symbol grounding. The abstract sensor layer converting raw sensor data to vectors is introduced in order to project the vectors into the conceptual space. Because of the abstract sensor layer, applying the architecture to various multi-robot systems is straightforward. Figure 6 illustrates the overall architecture for heterogeneous robots and how robots share the information that they individually recognize. We are in the process of implementing and testing the architecture on actual robotic platforms for the scenario described.

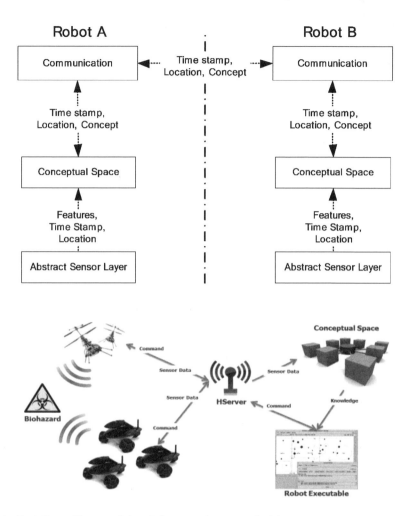

Figure 6: (Top) The architecture of the whole system is composed of three components: communication module, conceptual space, and abstract sensor layer. (Bottom) Overall System.

References

[1] Gardenfors, P., *Conceptual Spaces: The Geometry of Thought*. MIT Press, 2000.
[2] Kira, Z., "Inter-Robot Transfer Learning for Perceptual Classification", *9th International Conf. on Autonomous Agents and Multiagent Systems (AAMAS)*, 2010.
[3] Kira, Z., "Transferring Embodied Concepts between Perceptually Heterogeneous Robots", *Proceedings IEEE/RSJ International Conference on Intelligent Robots and Systems (IROS)*, pp. 4650-4656., 2009
[4] Kira, Z., "Mapping Grounded Object Properties across Perceptually Heterogeneous Embodiments", in *Proceedings of the 22nd International FLAIRS Conference*, pp. 57-62.
[5] Ulam, P., Kira, Z., Arkin, R.C., and Collins, T., 2010. "Mission Specification and Control for Unmanned Aerial and Ground Vehicles for Indoor Target Discovery and Tracking", *SPIE symposium on SPIE Defense, Security, and Sensing*, Orlando, FL, April 2010.
[6] Aisbett, J. and Gibbon, G., "A general formulation of conceptual spaces as a meso level representation," *Artificial Intelligence*, pp. 189-232, 2001.

[7] Kira, Z. Communication and Alignment of Grounded Symbolic Knowledge among Heterogeneous Robots, Ph.D. Dissertation, 2010.

[8] Arkin, R.C., *Behavior-based Robotics*, MIT Press, 1998.

[9] Moore, A. W. Clustering with gaussian mixtures. URL http://www.autonlab.org/tutorials/gmm.html. Tutorial Slides, 2004.

[10] S. Russell and P. Norvig, *Artificial Intelligence: A Modern Approach*, 2nd ed., Prentice Hall, pp. 16, 2002.

[11] R. Davis, H. Shrobe, and P. Szolovits, "What is in a Knowledge Representation?," AI Magazine, pp. 17–33, Spring 1993.

[12] Zurada J.M., *Introduction to Artificial Neural Systems*, West Publishing Company, 1992, pp. 456-545.

[13] Naguib R N G and Sherbet G V, *Artificial Neural Networks in Cancer Diagnosis, Prognosis, and Patient Management*, CRC Press, 2001.

[14] D. Floreano and C. Mattiussi, *Bio-Inspired Artificial Intelligence: Theories, Methods, and Technologies*. MIT Press, 2008, pp. 163-267.

[15] Champandard, A.J., *AI Game Development: Synthetic Creatures with Learning and Reactive Behaviors*. New Riders, 2003.

[16] Buckland, M., *AI techniques for game programming*. Premier-Trade, 2002, pp. 231-411.

[17] Harnad, S., The symbol grounding problem. Physica D 42:335–46, 1990.

Biologically Inspired Cognitive Architectures 2011
A.V. Samsonovich and K.R. Jóhannsdóttir (Eds.)
IOS Press, 2011
© 2011 The authors and IOS Press. All rights reserved.
doi:10.3233/978-1-60750-959-2-168

From Repetition Suppression in Stroop to Backward Inhibition in Task Switching: An Example of Model Reusability

Ion JUVINA[a,1], James A. GRANGE[b] and Christian LEBIERE[a]

[a]*Department of Psychology, Carnegie-Mellon University, USA*
[b]*School of Psychology, Keele University, UK*

Abstract. The concept of inhibition from cognitive neuroscience can inform the development of biologically-inspired cognitive architectures. Here we summarize a few attempts to develop an inhibition mechanism for the ACT-R architecture. The starting point is a model that uses inhibition to account for sequence effects in the Stroop task. This model is improved by adding a more general inhibition mechanism that requires less input from the modeler. Then, the modified model is used to account for backward inhibition in task switching, making a case for model generality and reusability.

Keywords. Cognitive architecture, task switching, Stroop, cognitive inhibition

Introduction

One of the mechanisms that are thought to allow flexible task switching is inhibition of recently performed tasks. Evidence for inhibition in task switching comes from the backward inhibition paradigm, where participants are required to switch between three tasks, with the currently relevant task being signaled by a task cue. Findings from the backward inhibition paradigm show that performance is slower and more error prone returning to a task recently performed after just one intervening trial (i.e. an AB*A* sequence) compared to returning to a task not recently performed (CB*A* sequence). These *n–2 repetition costs* are thought to reflect the persisting inhibition of task representations in working memory when it is switched away from, thus hampering its reactivation if the task is required soon after (as is the case in an AB*A* sequence).

In order to account for the backward inhibition effects in task switching we use the ACT-R cognitive architecture and we reuse a model of a different task. The initial use of the model was to account for a large number of sequence effects in the Stroop task [1]. After minor adjustments, the model was able to fit the human data from a backward inhibition paradigm [2]. In order to test whether inhibition was essential for fitting the human data, we removed the inhibition mechanism from the model. The inhibition-free model does not fit the human data with regard to the most important variable of this task, that is, the n-2 repetition costs.

---

[1] Corresponding Author.

This is one of a few attempts to integrate the existing research on cognitive inhibition from psychology and cognitive neuroscience in ACT-R [1,3,4] and consequently enhance the biological plausibility of this computational cognitive architecture. More generally, the concept of inhibition from cognitive neuroscience can inform the development of any biologically-inspired cognitive architecture (BICA). This effort complements similar work in other neuro-cognitive architectures (e.g., [5]) and is consistent with the requirement for model reuse and integration as outlined in the doctrine of the BICA challenge [6].

1. An ACT-R Model of Inhibition in the Stroop Task

An ACT-R model has recently been shown to explain a large range of effects in the Stroop task. This model gives an integrative account for both within-trial effects (the classical interference and facilitation effects) and between-trial effects (also called sequence effects) in the Stroop task. Within-trial effects are accounted for by a memory activation mechanism that reinforces information based on its frequency and recency. Between-trial effects are explained by an inhibition mechanism that counteracts the potential interference of the past trials with the current trial. At the end of a trial all representations that have been used to make a decision in that trial are inhibited in order to prevent their interference with the next trial. This inhibition decreases in strength as the time passes and can only be detected in behavior when repetitions occur. The model that included both inhibition and activation was compared to an inhibition-free model of the same task. The model that included an inhibitory control mechanism dedicated to between-trial interference produced a better fit to the human data than the inhibition-free model.

This model used basic mechanisms of the ACT-R cognitive architecture. The interference caused by the residual activations from previous trials emerged directly from the base-level activations of representations. The base-level activation in ACT-R depends on frequency and recency and it decays according to a power function. The suppression that was needed to offset this between-trial interference was simulated with the aid of the FINST (Fingers of Instantiation: [7]) mechanism. ACT-R uses FINST to implement inhibition-of-return effects in vision and to prevent perseverative retrievals in memory tasks. A retrieved memory element is tagged as recently retrieved and a new retrieval is biased toward memory elements that have not been tagged as recently retrieved. Tags are attached to representations for a while and eliminated after a certain time has passed. The FINST mechanism was slightly modified to allow gradual decay instead of all-or-none tagging. Although the FINST mechanism was useful to make a theoretical point, it was not satisfactory for the purpose of model reuse and generalization because the number of tags had to be set for each particular task.

2. Base-Level Inhibition

Recently, a new mechanism that directly implements cognitive inhibition has been added to the ACT-R architecture [3]. Its name – base-level inhibition – is descriptive of its function: it (briefly) offsets the recency-based reinforcement component of base-level activation. The logic of this mechanism is similar to the logic of the decaying FINST mechanism: representations that have recently been used are less likely to be needed for a while. Thus, inhibition is applied right after a representation is used and then it is gradually lifted. The main difference between the two mechanisms lies in their generality: base-level inhibition applies to all activated representations, while decaying FINST is only applied to a limited set of the recently activated representations. The former is a general mechanism whereas the latter requires task-specific input from the modeler.

Base-level inhibition uses a modified version of the base-level activation equation that governs the activation of chunks (i.e., discrete memories) within ACT–R's declarative memory. The base-level activation equation assumes that once a chunk is activated, it decays passively as a power function over time making it less accessible. Activation is thus expressed formally as:

$$A_i = \log \sum_{j=1}^{n} t_j^{-d} \qquad (1)$$

where A_i denotes the activation of a chunk i, n is the number of presentations of i, and t_j is the time since the jth presentation of the chunk; d is a decay parameter. Each time an item is presented, its activation increases, but then decays as a power function of the time since the last presentation; these processes are then summed and passed through a log transformation. The activation of a chunk determines the probability of a chunk to be retrieved and the duration of its retrieval. Chunks that are more frequently and more recently reactivated are more likely to be retrieved and their retrieval is faster. In addition, a stochastic component (noise) has a minor influence on the probability and speed of retrieval.

Lebiere and Best [3] added an inhibitory component to the base-level activation formula in Equation 1:

$$A_i = \log \sum_{j=1}^{n} t_j^{-d} - \log \left(1 + \left(\frac{t_n}{t_s} \right)^{-d_s} \right) \qquad (2)$$

Equation 2 considers the time since the most recent reference of a chunk, t_n, an inhibition-scaling parameter, t_s, and an inhibition-decay parameter, d_s. The 1+ component of this equation ensures the result of the latter part of the equation is positive, meaning the log transformation is always positive, which produces an inhibitory effect when it is subtracted from the component that is identical to Equation 1. The effects of these different activation equations are shown in Figure 1, with arbitrary parameters, showing base-level activation (i.e. no inhibition) and the inhibition equation. As can be seen, once a chunk has been activated according to the base-level activation equation, its activation decays as a power function, linear in log-log space. Thus, the more recently a chunk has been activated the higher its activation. Conversely, the inhibition equation — Equation 2 — ensures a chunk is hard to retrieve immediately after its use, but this inhibition dissipates slightly over the next few trials before merging with the base-level activation function. In other words, a chunk does not reach its maximum activation immediately after its reactivation because of the short-lived inhibition component that is added at the time of reactivation (see the inverse U curve in Figure 1).

3. Modeling Backward Inhibition in Task Switching

The ACT–R model of the Stroop task described above was reused to account for backward inhibition effects in task switching. The decaying finsts mechanism was replaced by the base-level inhibition mechanism presented above. The input/output components of the model were also modified in order to reflect the demands of the new task. We used this modified model to simulate the performance of the human subjects in Experiment 1 of Grange and Houghton [2] (standard cues condition, i.e. first half of the experiment only). In this experiment, participants performed a target-localization task, wherein they were instructed to respond to the location of a cued target, with each target differing on a visual property (either an angled oval, a shaded oval, or an oval which had a thickened border; a fourth neutral oval was always present as a distractor). Participants were cued with one of three shapes (square, octagon, or triangle), with one cuing each target (square=shaded; triangle=border; octagon=angled). Cues were presented for 500 milliseconds (ms), before a blank screen appeared for 250ms; after this, the four targets appeared, with one centered to each quadrant of the screen. The targets remained visible until a spatially compatible response (i.e. a top-left key-press to a target in the top-left quadrant) was made. After the response, a blank screen appeared for 250ms before the onset of the cue for the next trial. Participants performed ten blocks of 42 trials.

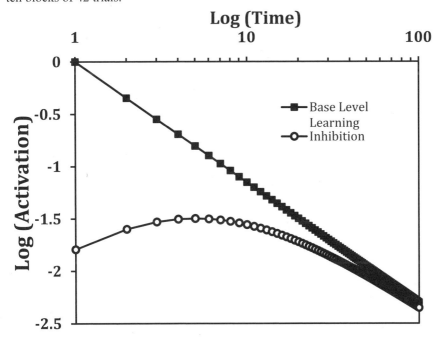

Figure 1. Activation functions of different base-level equations in log-log space with the following arbitrary parameters: $d = 0.5$; $t_s = 5$; $d_s = 1$ (Adapted from [3]).

We initially fit an inhibition-present instance of the model to data that shows an n–2 repetition cost. Then, the inhibition was removed to show the effects of an inhibition-free model. The *inhibition model* fit the n–2 repetition costs very well. Removal of inhibition—the *activation-only model*—produced an n–2 repetition benefit (Fig. 2).

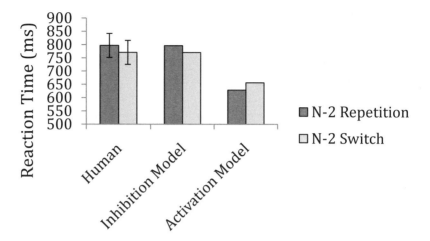

Figure 2. Model predictions (correct RTs) for two instances of the model for n–2 repetitions and switches against human performance.

We describe here the general structure of the model that is identical in the two instances. To enhance readability, only a description in general terms will be given here; the source code of the model is available at http://act-r.psy.cmu.edu/models/.

The goal of the model is to detect the location of a target that matches a given cue and press the key that corresponds to the location of the target. To accomplish this goal, the model attends to, perceives, and encodes the cue in its goal module. Then the model attempts to retrieve a memory representation of the target that corresponds to the perceived cue. The success and duration of this retrieval attempt depends on the activation of the representation to be retrieved. If a memory representation of the target is retrieved, the model performs a visual search in order to find the screen object that matches the retrieved memory representation. When the corresponding object is found, the model issues the motor response that corresponds to the location of the target object on the screen. If a memory representation of the target cannot be retrieved, the model responds randomly and potentially makes an error.

It is the retrieval of the memory representation of the target that is responsible for the effects discussed here (i.e. costs and benefits of n–2 repetitions). These representations are reactivated with each retrieval attempt that is successful. In the case of the inhibition instance of the model, each representation is also inhibited after being retrieved (see Equation 2).

The good fit of the inhibition model to human n–2 repetition costs suggests that cognitive inhibition may be a necessary component of task switching. To our knowledge, this is the first model of n–2 repetition costs — and thus inhibition — in task switching. Removal of the inhibition component of the activation equation reversed the n–2 repetition cost into a benefit of 27.5ms. Thus, without inhibition, n–2 repetition benefits arise due to persisting activation across an ABA sequence. Another result of interest from the model is that removal of inhibition does not only reverse the n–2 repetition cost into a benefit, but it also reduces overall reaction time (RT) considerably. This is driven by the fact that inhibition affects retrieval time for all chunks; therefore, even in a CBA sequence, task A will still be somewhat inhibited, thus slowing its retrieval.

4. Discussion and Conclusion

The ACT-R architecture has a history of integrating research from cognitive psychology and cognitive neuroscience. We have presented recent computational modeling work aimed at integrating inhibition research from neuroscience and psychology into ACT-R. Specifically, we have presented a model that uses FINST to account for inhibition effects in the Stroop task. Then, the FINST mechanism was replaced by a more general mechanism – base-level inhibition – that was designed to be more general, more automatic, and less dependent on modeler input. Then we showed how the enhanced model was able to fit the data from a task-switching paradigm. Moreover, we show that the inhibition component of the model was essential in fitting the data. Our work suggests that inhibition might be a necessary component of cognitive agents that are required to flexibly switch between multiple tasks in a dynamic environment. In situations where a new task has to be initiated before the old task has ended, an inhibitory mechanism may be necessary to actively disengage the system from operating on the old task. Activation decay might not be sufficient in such situations. In the absence of inhibition, the system is at risk of escalating interference (or *source confusion* in perceptual tasks; see [5]). Future work is needed to explore the full range of functional benefits of adding an inhibition component to biologically inspired cognitive architectures.

Acknowledgments

This research was supported in part by the Defense Threat Reduction Agency (DTRA) grant number: HDTRA1-09-1-0053 to Cleotilde Gonzalez and Christian Lebiere.

References

[1] I. Juvina & N.A. Taatgen, A repetition-suppression account of between-trial effects in a modified Stroop paradigm, *Acta Psychologica* **131** (2009), 72–84.
[2] J.A. Grange & G. Houghton, Heightened conflict in cue-target translation increases backward inhibition in set switching, *Journal of Experimental Psychology: Learning, Memory, and Cognition* **36** (2010), 1003-1009.
[3] C. Lebiere & B.J. Best, Balancing long-term reinforcement and short-term inhibition, in *Proceedings of the 31st Annual Conference of the Cognitive Science Society.* (2009) Austin, TX.
[4] C. Lebiere & F. J. Lee, Intention superiority effect: A context-switching account, *Journal of Cognitive Systems Research*, **3**(1) (2002), 57-65.
[5] D.E. Huber & R.C. O'Reilly, Persistence and Accommodation in short-term priming and other perceptual paradigms: temporal segregation through synaptic depression, *Cognitive Science* **27** (2003), 403-430.
[6] A. Stocco, C. Lebiere, & A. V. Samsonovich, The B-I-C-A of biologically inspired cognitive architectures, *International Journal of Machine Consciousness*, **2**(2) (2010), 171-192.
[7] Z.W. Pylyshyn, Situating vision in the world, *Trends in Cognitive Sciences* **4**(5) (2000), 197-207.

Biologically Inspired Cognitive Architectures 2011
A.V. Samsonovich and K.R. Jóhannsdóttir (Eds.)
IOS Press, 2011
© 2011 The authors and IOS Press. All rights reserved.
doi:10.3233/978-1-60750-959-2-174

Modeling Temporal Dynamics with Function Approximation in Deep Spatio-Temporal Inference Network

Thomas P. KARNOWSKI [a,1], Itamar AREL [b] and Steven YOUNG [b]

[a] *ISML Group, Oak Ridge National Laboratory, Oak Ridge TN*
[b] *U. Tennessee MIL, Knoxville, TN*

Abstract. Biologically inspired deep machine learning is an emerging framework for dealing with complex high-dimensional data. An unsupervised feature extraction deep learning architecture called Deep Spatio-Temporal Inference Network (DeSTIN) utilizes a hierarchy of computational nodes, where each node features a common algorithm for inference of temporal patterns. The nodes all are geared to online learning and offer a generalization component which uses clustering and mixture models, as well as a temporal dynamics module. The latter is designed for tabular representation but such techniques are notoriously ill-suited for scaling as they impose an $O(N^3)$ memory complexity. Instead, function approximation methods such as neural networks can serve as a more concise representation. In this work we present the results of DeSTIN on a popular problem, the MNIST data set of handwritten digits, using mixture models and function approximation to create a temporally evolving feature representation. We compare the results of the extracted features from DeSTIN under the tabular method and the function approximation method and contrast these results with our past work in this area.

Keywords. feature extraction, unsupervised learning, cortical

Introduction

Recent neuroscience findings suggest the mammalian neocortex is hierarchical with identical building blocks [1]. The neocortex does not explicitly pre-process sensory signals, but rather allows them to propagate through a complex hierarchy of processors that learn to represent observations based on spatial and temporal regularities [2], [3]. This provides the biological inspiration for the deep machine learning (DML). An overview of deep learning [4] defines a deep architecture as "composed of multiple levels of non-linear operations, such as in neural nets with many hidden layers or in complicated propositional formulae re-using many sub-formulae." At the core of deep learning is the notion that multiple levels of operations simplifies the computational load of a learning architecture and enhances its ability to learn complex, highly varying problems. Some successful architectures include Convolutional Neural Networks (CNNs) [5], Deep Belief Net-

---

[1] Corresponding Author: Thomas P. Karnowski, ORNL and U. Tennessee Machine Intelligence Laboratory, Knoxville, TN, USA; E-mail: tkarnows@utk.edu.

works (DBNs) [6], and Hierarchical Temporal Memories [7]. In this work, we present further results from the Deep Spatio-Temporal Inference Network (DeSTIN) which performs unsupervised feature extraction by modeling the spatio-temporal dependencies in data with a hierarchy of identical computational nodes. The nodes perform online learning and offer a generalization component which uses clustering and mixture models, as well as a temporal dynamics module designed for tabular representation. The lowest layer of the architecture uses raw image pixels for inputs, but could be generalized to any kind of sensory input as the processing is identical. In our earliest work in this area [8], we introduced the basic concept of DeSTIN along with online clustering and modeling of temporal dynamics through simple tabular methods. We continued this in [9] where we presented heuristic methods for monitoring and stopping the online clustering within each node and layer. Here we present the use of a temporally additive "passive advice belief" which represents an extension to the previously developed DeSTIN formulation. The advice is generated through online clustering during the training phase and used in a multiple observer model in the testing or response phase, producing a more succinct feature representation. In addition, the temporal dynamics are studied through two methods: a tabular method, which is straightforward and easy to train but memory-intensive and a function approximation (FA) method using neural networks which offers comparable performance with smaller computational and memory loads. We continue our studies of the application of DeSTIN to the MNIST data set [10], a set of handwritten digits widely cited as a test case in machine learning. We compare the results of the extracted features from DeSTIN under the tabular method and the FA method and contrast these results with our past work in this area. In the following sections we review core concepts pertaining to the DeSTIN architecture including the incorporation of parental node feedback through a multiple observer-like model. We then present results and conclude with discussion and summary of projected future directions for our work.

1. Technical Approach

In the DeSTIN architecture a hierarchy of layers is used, where each layer consists of multiple instantiations of an identical circuit or node which follow a defined spatial orientation for imaging applications (generally speaking, however, the spatial relationship can vary according to the problem domain). Each node learns to generalize and represent a temporal sequence of observations through unsupervised learning. The temporal changes may occur through movement of the imager, movement of the subject, or a combination of both, but for our initial experiments the movement and temporal change is induced through moving the field of view of the imager. Higher layers receive temporally changing data by processing the belief outputs of children nodes. These output beliefs capture regularities in their inputs and thus extract features of the data which can be fed to a supervised learning algorithm to perform classification. In principle, since each node is identical, the architecture can be mapped to parallel computational platforms such as graphics processing units, and since the overall processing is simple it is tractable for hardware-oriented approaches as well. All processing is "online" so that large amounts of memory are not needed, and indeed one of the focuses of this work is reducing the memory requirements even further through function approximation methods which use parental advice generated through models created during the training process. While more detail on the basic premises of DeSTIN can be found in [11] and [8], here we high-light the role the parental advice plays in the processing by writing the the fundamental belief update rule of DeSTIN as

$$b'(s'|a) = \frac{\Pr(o|s') \sum_{s' \in S} \Pr(s'|s, a)b(s)}{\sum_{s'' \in S} \Pr(o|s'') \sum_{s' \in S} \Pr(s''|s, a)b(s)} \tag{1}$$

which maps the current observation o, the belief b (with argument the system state s) and advice from a higher-layer node a, to a new (updated) belief and state $b'(s')$ at the next time step, with a normalization factor in the denominator. One interpretation of this equation is that the (static) pattern similarity metric, $\Pr(o|s')$, is modulated by a con-struct that reflects the system dynamics, $\sum_{s' \in S} \Pr(s'|s, a)b(s)$. (For shorthand, the latter is denoted as PSSA.) These two constructs are the main items which must be learned from the data. We also note the dependence of the belief on the advice from the parent, which is important for our "multiple observer" model. For the static pattern similarity metric, $\Pr(o|s')$, we apply online online clustering and mixture model formulations. Since a ma-jor goal of DeSTIN is to produce a system that scales efficiently with simple hardware, we have imposed a constraint that the system cannot iterate through the entire training data set in memory. Consequently, an online clustering algorithm based on the winner-take-all competititve learning approach is employed [12] at the heart of each node's static pattern learning process. The algorithm includes constructs for improving performance and modulating the learning rate, but in this work a semi-constant learning rate is em-ployed across a layer of nodes, with the rate set to learn fast for one layer and slower for subsequent (higher) layers until some stopping criteria is reached, at which point the rate is set to 0 for the "stopped" layer and adjusted to a fast rate for the next layer up as described in [9].

For the system dynamics or PSSA, we apply an advice generation methodology us-ing tabular methods, and FA methods. In the tabular method we simply count the transi-tions from s to s' given the advice a. In past implementations, the advice or belief of the parent node, a, was chosen using the selection rule of $a = \arg\max_{s} b_p(s)$, but this was not robust to evolving belief conditions in the online learning process. Instead we use an online advice generation rule where each parental node examines the temporal sequence of input beliefs and performs unsupervised online clustering. The resulting label is then passed to the child nodes who use the advice to train the dynamic patterns. Furthermore, the clustering mechanisms described earlier provide good generalization but do not lend themselves well to a consistent labeling from movement to movement. The system dy-namics can compensate for this problem to some degree, but some level of consistent labeling is necessary which is unfortunately not guaranteed with normal online cluster-ing. Here we elected to use the advice in a multiple-observer model to formulate a set of "belief in advice states" which serves as a cumulative estimate of the belief in the ad-vice state of a node. This allows each node to incorporate learning from the parent node over time to generalize to longer temporal and spatial scales, but retain a level of local knowledge and capture sufficient variation to make good supervised learning classifiers.

In this mechanism, the system dynamics vary from movement to movement and each child node retains a brief history of its recent observations and beliefs within a single subject presentation. Then when the parental advice is available, the PSSA is learned across the past observations and movements. After training, each possible advice state is interpreted as a different observer, with multiple attempts at observation as well (one for each movement), and thus the belief in that advice state is computed as a cumulative prediction error $B(a) = \sum_m \sum_s b(s_m|a) - b(s_m)$, where s_m is the state at movement m. When there are a total of A advice states, this produces a vector of dimension A for the output of each node after the complete temporal sequence is observed. The advice component is passive, meaning we simply compute the value for $B(a)$ and test for each advice state using the model residing in each node for each different advice state learned during the training process. This approach is more robust in the sense that we do not require "good" advice in real-time from the parent, and also occasional cases of near-zero probability do not cause the entire evolution to grind to a halt. Unfortunately, this development adds a further dependence on the number of movements which are used to formulate the advice. Thus the memory requirements of this scheme using a tabular approach are quite formidable, computed for a single node as $M_{tab} = K^2 AL$, where K is the number of centroids for the node, L is the number of movements or sequence length, and A is the number of advice states from the parental node.

As an alternative to this approach, we seek to create a function approximation method, where the transition probability is estimated by a learned function. This is performed by simply estimating the subsequent state given the current state and advice. In practice this means a very short memory mechanism must be used to train the function approximator. Furthermore, the advice states and movements can be represented by sparse binary input vectors in the case where the advice data is interpreted as a "hard label". Thus the function approximator must estimate $b(s\prime)$ given input advice a, movement number m, and the previous state s. This is best achieved with a nonlinear function approximator such as a neural network [13]. The memory required to implement the neural network varies with the number of hidden nodes chosen, but we can define memory usage if we assume a single layer with H nodes. There are $A + K + L$ inputs with each linked to H hidden nodes, with a weight for each connection. At each hidden node an additive bias is used, then there are K outputs with connections from each hidden node to the output, with another additive bias per output. Thus we can express the number of memory elements as $M_{FA} = K + H[1 + 2K + A + L]$, which is linear in dimension K, A, and L and greatly reduces the memory load, assuming H is not a high-order function of K.

2. Experiments and Results

In our past work we apply DeSTIN to the MNIST dataset [10] which contains 60,000 training images and 10,000 test images. A fusion of different methods and comparison with humans reveals the best possible performance is 99.8% [14] . For comparison with our past work, the experimental architecture topology here is identical to that in [9], but we describe it here for completeness. A hierarchy of 4 layers of sizes 8 x 8 nodes, 4 x 4 nodes, 2 x 2 nodes, and a single node at the top layer was used as depicted in Figure 1 with the lowest level receiving pure image pixels as inputs. Each layer uses a different

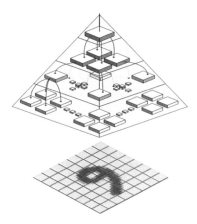

Figure 1. Depiction of the DeSTIN hierarchy for image studies. For the MNIST experiments discussed here, four layers are configured with 64, 16, 4 and 1 node per layer. At each node the output belief b(s) at each temporal step is fed to a parent node. At each temporal step the parent receives input beliefs from four child nodes to generate its own belief (fed to its parent). An advice value is generated by the parent as well; in the current configuration this is generated at the end of a sequence of observations and is fed back to the child nodes during training.

number of centroids (25, 16, 12, and 10). The image is then shifted through a sequence of 64 different movements which form a serpentine pattern, crudely emulating sacchading. After a DeSTIN network was trained, features were extracted by choosing the outputs of 39 nodes (the top three layers and some nodes of the bottom layer). The response of the DeSTIN network was saved and presented to a supervised learning system, in our case a 2-layer, 40 node neural network. Ten supervised learning instantiations were used and the results were averaged together. We incorporated the multiple-observer model for $B(a)$ and compared the performance of the supervised learning system using ten DeS-TIN networks, with each one trained with the tabular and function approximation methods. A total of 25 advice states were used for each parental node. The function approximator was implemented using the Fast Artificial Neural Network Library [15], with each FA consisting of a single hidden layer of 10 nodes with a fixed learning rate of 0.001. The memory comparison between the function approximator and the tabuler method is shown in Table 1. Overall, the function approximation method requires roughly 1/600 of the memory as the tabular method, but does have a slight increase in computational cost. The performance of the two techniques was essentially identical, with the average performance of the tabular method 98.39% and the function approximation method 98.454%.

Table 1. Memory comparisons for function approximation and tabular methods

Layer	Nodes	K	Tab	F.A.
0	64	25	1000000	1425
1	16	16	409600	1236
2	4	12	230400	1152
3	1	10	160000	1110

3. Conclusion

We presented further work on DeSTIN, a biologically-inspired, unsupervised feature extraction deep learning architecture. We showed how the belief formulation with parental advice can create a temporal representation for a node's beliefs using a multiple observer model. The pattern dynamics are well-suited for tabular representation but impose $O(N^3)$ memory complexity which is not conducive to making DeSTIN suitable for simple hardware; however the neural network function approximation shows memory improvements with comparable performance. Our results on the MNIST set are not quite state of the art, but there is room for improvement including additional topology studies, alternative online clustering objective functions (for static pattern learning), and dynamically evolving the sequence of movements through a control mechanism (for dynamic pattern learning). Since DeSTIN's biological inspiration of identical processing nodes does not use specialized input processing for images, we plan to pursue experiments in general sensory processing including audio, tactile, and fused inputs to further the goals of biologically inspired computing architectures.

References

[1]   D. Felleman and D. Van Essen, "Distributed hierarchical processing in the primate cerebral cortex," *Cerebral cortex*, vol. 1, no. 1, p. 1, 1991.

[2]   T. Lee and D. Mumford, "Hierarchical Bayesian inference in the visual cortex," *Journal of the Optical Society of America A*, vol. 20, no. 7, pp. 1434–1448, 2003.

[3]   T. Lee, D. Mumford, R. Romero, and V. Lamme, "The role of the primary visual cortex in higher level vision," *Vision research*, vol. 38, no. 15-16, pp. 2429–2454, 1998.

[4]   Y. Bengio, *Learning deep architectures for AI*. Now Publishers Inc, 2009.

[5]   Y. LeCun, L. Bottou, Y. Bengio, and P. Haffner, "Gradient-based learning applied to document recognition," *Proceedings of the IEEE*, vol. 86, no. 11, pp. 2278–2324, 1998.

[6]   G. Hinton, S. Osindero, and Y. Teh, "A fast learning algorithm for deep belief nets," *Neural computation*, vol. 18, no. 7, pp. 1527–1554, 2006.

[7]   D. George, "How the brain might work: A hierarchical and temporal model for learning and recognition," Ph.D. dissertation, Stanford University, 2008.

[8]   I. Arel, D. Rose, and R. Coop, "DeSTIN: A Scalable Deep Learning Architecture with Application to High-Dimensional Robust Pattern Recognition," in *Proc. of the AAAI 2009 Fall Symposium on Biologically Inspired Cognitive Architectures (BICA)*, 2009.

[9]   T. Karnowski, I. Arel, and D. Rose, "Deep spatiotemporal feature learning with application to image classification," in *Machine Learning and Applications (ICMLA), 2010 Ninth International Conference on*. IEEE, 2010, pp. 883–888.

[10] Y. LeCun and C. Cortes, "The MNIST database of handwritten digits," http://yann.lecun.com/exdb/mnist/, 2009.

[11] I. Arel, D. Rose, and T. Karnowski, "A Deep Learning Architecture Comprising Homogeneous Cortical Circuits for Scalable Spatiotemporal Pattern Inference," in *NIPS 2009 Workshop on Deep Learning for Speech Recognition and Related Applications*, 2009.

[12] S. Young, I. Arel, T. Karnowski, and D. Rose, "A Fast and Stable Incremental Clustering Algorithm," in *2010 Seventh International Conference on Information Technology*. IEEE, 2010, pp. 204–209.

[13] K. Hornik Maxwell and H. White, "Multilayer feedforward networks are universal approximators," *Neural networks*, vol. 2, no. 5, pp. 359–366, 1989.

[14] D. Keysers, "Comparison and Combination of State-of-the-art Techniques for Handwritten Character Recognition: Topping the MNIST Benchmark," *Arxiv preprint arXiv:0710.2231*, 2007.

[15] S. Nissen, "Implementation of a fast artificial neural network library (fann)," *Report, Department of Computer Science University of Copenhagen (DIKU)*, vol. 31, 2003.

Biologically Inspired Cognitive Architectures 2011
A.V. Samsonovich and K.R. Jóhannsdóttir (Eds.)
IOS Press, 2011
doi:10.3233/978-1-60750-959-2-180

Conscious expectation system

Kazuki KATAYAMA [a] and Junichi TAKENO [b,1]

[a, b] *Robot Science Laboratory, Computer Science, Meiji University,*
1-1-1Higashimita, Tama-ku, Kawasaki-shi, Kanagawa 214-8571 Japan
[a] *katayamameiji@yahoo.co.jp*
[b] *juntakeno@gmail.com*

Abstract. The authors are studying ways to create a function similar to human consciousness based on biologically inspired ideas and using an engineering approach. The authors have arrived at the idea that, "the consistency of cognition and behavior is the origin of human consciousness." Their belief is derived from studying findings in various fields of research including information science, brain science, philosophy, and psychology. Based on their idea, the authors have developed the recurrent neural network module named Module of Nerves for Advanced Dynamics, or MoNAD, which is very capable of explaining the phenomena of human consciousness. Using this module, the authors further developed a system to consciously expect upcoming events.

Keywords. Consciousness, robot, expectation, emotion.

Introduction

Consciousness is actively being studied from various perspectives, including system engineering and robotics. Many systems and robots are intended to communicate with humans. Such systems and robots have been announced as having high functions, however, they are not quite human. We believe that achievement of artificial functions of consciousness will lead to the development of systems and robots with human-like functions, and eventually will contribute to elucidating the mechanism of human consciousness.

The authors believe that human consciousness is deeply related to imitation behavior as typically exemplified in studies on mirror neurons [1] and mimesis theory [2]. The authors have defined the source of consciousness to be consistency between cognition and behavior. Based on this understanding, the authors have devised a conscious system module called Module of Nerves for Advanced Dynamics (MoNAD) [3].

The system introduced in this present paper is designed for consciously expecting the next-occurring event using the functions of reasonable thought and emotional thought, each comprising multiple MoNADs. This is the new model for a system that is capable of responding to continuous changes of events like humans can do.

---

[1] Corresponding Author.

1. Conscious Expectation System

1.1. Module of Nerves for Advanced Dynamics (MoNADs)

A MoNAD is a computational model, comprising recursive neural networks (RNNs). Various orientations are set for each MoNAD, and each MoNAD has been taught the target of orientation using backpropagation. Several MoNADs with various orientations are connected to one another to achieve the higher-level functions of consciousness. One of the features of a MoNAD is the existence of a common area for both cognition and behavior. The authors' defined condition, that "consistency between cognition and behavior creates consciousness," is artificially achieved due to the existence of this common area.[4]

1.2. Reasonable Thought and Emotional Thought

The most important point of the conscious expectation system is that reasonable thought and emotional thought are processed simultaneously to determine an expectation. The relationship between these two thoughts is a key factor in achieving a more human-like expectation.

1.2.1. Reasonable Thought

Reasonable thought is one of the reasonable judgments. Using reasonable thought, humans are said to be able to understand both events that actually occurred as well as those that were experienced conceptually or abstractly.

The conscious expectation system, comprising multiple hierarchical MoNADs (Figure 1), performs reasonable thought as described below. Current events are input into lower-level MoNADs re1 (Figure 2 (a)). MoNAD re1 gets fired at (b) and (c), as shown in Figure 4, when a specific event is input at time t0. Recognition representation (RL) of MoNAD re1 (Figure 2) is thereby represented and the relevant information is sent to MoNAD re2 (Figure 3(c)).

The impression value indicates the relationship between the event (Figure 3 (c)) at time t0 and the event occurring immediately after at time t1. This value is calculated at MoNAD re2 (Figure 3 (d)) as the bias value for the firing of Output 1 of MoNAD re1. The impression value increases when the two events occur successively for many times, i.e., the relevant representation is strengthened as the number of successive occurrences of the two events increases. The same two events, however, lessen their impression value when they occur separately.

To make effective use of the impression value in a computer system, the impression values between two events must always be available and kept in memory. MoNADs possess internal circulation routes, and thus artificial inner thought is made possible (Figure 3).

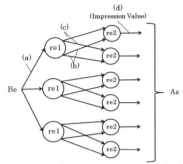

Figure 1 Structure of the reasonable thought (Re) system

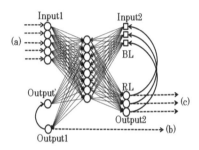

Figure 2 Circuit diagram of MoNAD re1 of the reasonable thought system

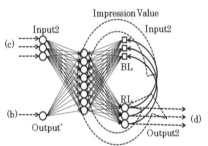

Figure 3 Circuit diagram of MoNAD re2 of the reasonable thought system

1.2.2. Emotional Thought

Feelings play an important role in decision-making and anticipating the next-occurring event. Feelings also affect reasonable judgment. We believe a human-like system can only be achieved by incorporating feelings.

In our conscious system, the emotional thought system is also created using MoNADs (Figure 4). Actual events and events that were expected are input into the system at (e) and (f), respectively, as shown in Figure 5. Feelings are represented as either pleasant or unpleasant. Each MoNAD of the emotional thought system is responsible for calculating its specific expected event. If the expected event matches the actual event that occurs, the feeling represented is pleasant. If, on the contrary, the expected event is different from the actual event, the feeling represented is unpleasant.

Impressions, or feelings, upon the change of two succeeding events are always kept in memory just like reasonable thought (Figure 5).

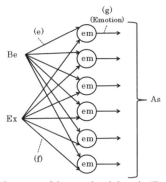

Figure 4 Structure of the emotional thought (Em) system

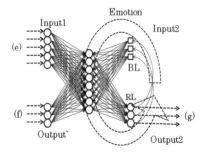

Figure 5 Circuit diagram of the emotional MoNAD em

1.3. Structure of the Conscious Expectation System

The conscious expectation system, comprising multiple MoNADs, consists of a reason subsystem responsible for reasonable thought, an emotion and feelings subsystem controlling emotional thought, and an association subsystem connecting multiple (two in the present study) subsystems.

Figures 6 show general structure of the conscious expectation system. "Be" in Figure 6 is a MoNAD of the reason subsystem. It has an input unit and cognizes the event that is presently occurring. Module Re, comprising multiple MoNADs, is also a part of the reason subsystem and is engaged in reasonable thinking. Logical impression values for the changes of events are represented in the module Re. Module Em, a MoNAD in the emotion and feelings subsystem, represents whether the change of events is pleasant or unpleasant, i.e., it represents the feelings of the system. The representation of pleasant or unpleasant feelings depends on whether the actually occurring event matches the expectation or not. Module As in the association subsystem also comprises multiple MoNADs (Figure 7). The association subsystem accepts information from the reason subsystem and the emotion and feelings subsystem

(Figure 7 (d), (h), (g)), and integrates the impression values received from the reasonable thought (Re) and pleasant/unpleasant information arriving from the emotion and feelings subsystem. The result of this integration is returned to MoNAD Ex in the reason subsystem (Figure 7 (i), (j)) for calculation of the expectation (Figure 7). This means that MoNAD Ex in the reason subsystem generates the expectation for the next-occurring event based on the information received from the MoNAD As, and sends the expectation to the emotion and feelings subsystem (Figure 7 (f)). The emotion and feelings subsystem generates and represents a new feeling by comparing the expectation with the actual event.

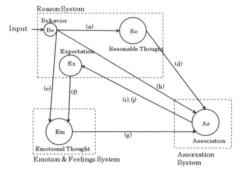

Figure 6 General structure of the conscious expectation system

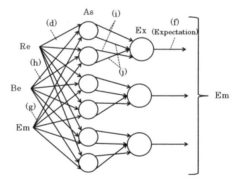

Figure 7 General structure of the association subsystem (As) and expectation

2. Expectation

No definite description of the human mechanism of expectation exists. This present paper introduces the authors' conscious expectation system that is capable of performing both reasonable and emotional thinking.

In the human brain, the area that governs feelings and the area that governs reason cooperate with each other when humans make decisions. When a person suffers damage to either area in the brain because of an accident or illness, it is reportedly very difficult to make decisions. This is obvious from the cases introduced in the studies of Damasio [5]. These diseases are possibly related to the expectation capability of the brain.

The working of the conscious expectation system is described below referring to Figure 8. When the currently occurring event is recognized, the impression value and emotional aspect of the event are evaluated by reasonable thought and emotional thought, respectively, and are compared with past experiences. This evaluation is integrated to represent the next-expected event. The feeling (pleasant or unpleasant) changes depending on whether or not the expected event matches the actual event.

Expectation in our system is indeed the result of the working of various pieces of information stored in memory. But it is not simple conditional processing such as turning on switches for pleasant or unpleasant in response to certain data. Representation in the system is used as the input, and certain feelings and expectations are represented and fired in response. The past experience of firing caused by various representations of the conscious system is effectively used to form expectations thereafter. We call this conscious expectation. One of the schemes for forming conscious expectation developed by the authors is based on the interaction between reasonable thought and emotional thought. No studies reported by brain science researchers that support this theory of the authors exist at this time. We believe, however, that by developing a system to form expectations consciously, we could eventually be able to solve the problem of how humans form expectations.

3. Simulation Experiments

Three colors, red, green and blue, were shown successively to see the reaction of the robot incorporating the conscious expectation system. The experimental data are graphically displayed.

The colors were initially shown to the robot in the order of red, green and blue, i.e., at stage (1) in Figures 8 through 10. The order of the colors was changed to green, red and blue halfway through the experiment, i.e., at stage (2) in the figures. The behavior of reasonable thought, emotional thought, and the result of expectation when blue, for example, was shown is depicted in Figures 8,9 and 10, respectively. Vertical axes show the impression value (Figure 8), feelings (Figure 9) (positive and negative values indicate pleasant and unpleasant feelings, respectively), and the color expected after blue (Figure 10). The horizontal axes represent time.

Both reasonable thought (Figure 8) and emotional thought (Figure 9) react to the change in the order of the color input. Initially, at stage (1) in Figures 8 through 10, the colors are input in the order of red, green and blue, then return to red, i.e., red is input after blue. The impression value for red is therefore high and that for green is low for the reasonable thought ((3), Figure 8). As for expectation, the system initially expected both red and green after blue (a, Figure 10) because there was no way for the robot to tell which would occur at the start of the experiment. After a short time, the robot starts to expect red (b, Figure 10), and the emotional thought represents a pleasant feeling for "blue to red" ((4), Figure 9). The order of the color input was changed halfway through the experiment from "red, green, and blue" to "green, red, and blue" ((2), Figures 8 through 10). Thereafter, instead of red, green is input after blue. This change causes the previous expectation ("blue to red") to fail, and the emotional thought represents an unpleasant feeling ((2), Figure 9). This is coincident with the status shift in the reasonable thought: the impression value for "blue to green" gradually increases ((2), Figure 8). Expectation also shifts from "red to green" as experience accumulates (c, Figure 10). The feelings for "blue to green" likewise change from unpleasant to pleasant ((5), Figure 9).

These results indicate that the system expects the next event through the synergetic working of reasonable thought and emotional thought. In the graphs in Figures 8 through 10, the feelings of the robot for "blue to red" change from pleasant to unpleasant ((2), Figure 9) upon seeing green instead of red after blue because red was expected after blue. This is coincident with the fact that the impression value for "blue to green" increases in the reasonable thought ((2), Figure 8) ((2), Figure 9). The system now expects green instead of red after blue, and the feelings for "blue to green" change from unpleasant to pleasant because the expectation is successful.

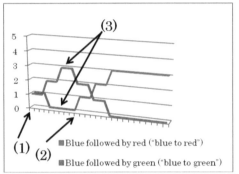

Figure 8 Change of output values of reasonable thought (Re)

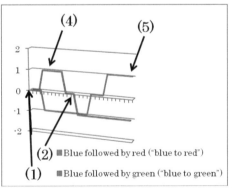

Figure 9 Change of output values of emotional thought (Em)

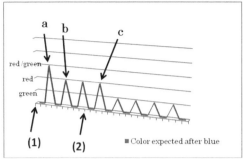

Figure 10 Change of output values of expectation (Ex)

4. Conclusions

The conscious expectation system developed by the authors expects the next-occurring event using reason and feelings at the same time. The scale of the study's experiments is small, and expectation is related to only three colors in the simulation experiments at this time. It is possible, however, to expand the system while maintaining the basic concept. When expanded in the future, the system would be able to react to various events and expect events two or three steps ahead in addition to the event immediately to come after the current one. At this time, the feelings subsystem is taught to react to only whether the expected result was accomplished or not. In the future, the condition (mood) and propensities (likes and dislikes) of the self, for example, may be included to see how these various feelings affect reasonable thought.

One of the possible applications of the present research is the development of a scheme to acquire specific patterns autonomously, i.e., without being taught by humans. This refers to the possible acquisition of a new language by a robot and remains one of our future tasks.

References

[1] V. Gallese, L. Fadiga, L. Fogassi, and G. Rizzolatti, Action recognition in the premoter cortex, *Brain* 119, (1996), 3–368.
[2] M. Donald, *Origins of the Modern Mind* (Harvard University Press, Cambridge), 1991。
[3] J. Takeno and K. Inaba, New Paradigm 'Consistency of cofnition and behavior', in *CCCT2003* ,(2003), 389–394.
[4] J. Takeno, MoNAD structure and self-awareness, *Biologically Inspired Cognitive Architectures (BICA2011)*, Arlington, USA, (2011), Printing now.
[5] A. R. Damasio, *Descartes' Error* (Putnam Adult), 1994.

188

Biologically Inspired Cognitive Architectures 2011
A.V. Samsonovich and K.R. Jóhannsdóttir (Eds.)
IOS Press, 2011
© *2011 The authors and IOS Press. All rights reserved.*
doi:10.3233/978-1-60750-959-2-188

The Roots of Trust:
Cognition Beyond Rational

William G. KENNEDY[a,1]
[a]*Krasnow Institute for Advance Study*
George Mason University, USA

Abstract. Trust is not simply the result of rational cognition but relies on rational and "beyond rational" cognition. The concept of trust is discussed in terms of its biological, Maslow, and cognitive roots. The cognitive roots rely on the Dual Process Theory, i.e. that there are two types of cognition sometimes called rational and non-rational. Therefore, the roots of trust need a cognitive architecture that implements the Dual Process Theory and involves cognition both rational and beyond rational.

Keywords. Cognitive architectures, rational behavior, Dual Process Theory, System 1 System 2

Introduction

Trust is not simply the result of rational cognition but relies on rational and "beyond rational" cognition. This paper discusses the evolutionary and biologically-inspired roots of trust, its rational and beyond rational components, and the integration of both cognitive components in a cognitive architecture. It is intended to motivate the community to extend cognitive architectures beyond the purely rational cognition to include the other cognitive capabilities necessary to explain trust.

Bertrand Russell quipped, "It has been said that man is a rational animal. All my life I have been searching for evidence that could support this." If man is a rational animal, we certainly do not seem to behave rationally at all time. In fact, we seem to be rational only a small or very small part of the time. As Herbert Simon observed, "Hence, in order to have anything like a complete theory of human rationality, we have to understand what role emotion plays in it." [1] This paper addresses what is beyond the rational side of human behavior and how it is related to the roots of trust.

1. The Concept of Trust

The word **trust** is "officially" defined as a "firm belief in someone or something, acceptance of the truth of a statement without evidence or investigation" [2]. However,

_____
[1] Corresponding Author: W.G. Kennedy, Research Assistant Professor, Krasnow Institute for Advanced Study, George Mason University, 4400 University Drive MS 6B2, Fairfax, VA 22032 USA; E-mail: wkennedy@gmu.edu

the word's definition does not address the reasoning behind the acceptance of the truth of a statement without justification. How is this acceptable? The hypothesis of this paper is that the concept of trust as accepting statements or situations without justification has its roots in biology, Maslow's hierarchy of needs [3], and cognition, both rational and beyond rational.

2. Trust in Biology

Two examples of trust having biological roots are discussed. The first is associated with survival instincts and the second with trust in social circumstances. Survival instincts are behaviors that are performed automatically without being based on learning from experience. They are typically short sequences that are performed based on specific stimulus. An example of these is our irrational reaction to some stimuli, such as the sighting of a spider (the basis of a current smart phone advertisement). The significance of these instinctual behaviors are that they are likely to have survival benefits and to be evolutionarily old, possibly older than our social behavior.

Economists have been studying social behavior, particularly trust, using a game for some time. Recently, neuroscientists have also studied the trust game and have localized brain mechanisms associated with different types of trust. Krueger et al. [4] found two distinct regions were involved in trust. The first was the region associated with representing the mental states of other people, which is related to the formulation of a Theory of Mind for others [5]. Subjects inferred the intentions of others as part of their decision on whether to trust them or not. The other region associated with trust was a limbic region that moderated several aspects of social behavior including reinforcement of goodwill encodings. These results and others demonstrate that trust in a social context has a biological basis.

3. Trust in Maslow's Hierarchy of Needs

Maslow's theory of human motivation [3] proposed a hierarchy of needs as the foundation of his motivation theory. The hierarchy and been discussed extensively but has not been significantly revised. Although "trust" as a word is not found in his classic paper, trust is addressed in the hierarchy at one if not two levels. The first is part of the safety needs, which are just above physiological needs. As he points out, physiological needs must be at least satisfied before safety needs are considered, but safety needs can also be wholly dominating. He also notes that safety can become a dominating immediate goal of an individual and can influence a person's view of the future. Therefore, trust is a major contributor to the perception of safety.

Marlow's hierarchy also includes trust in a person's need for love, affection, and belonging. This need is generally considered to be above both physiological and safety needs, but the levels are not necessarily strictly separate. Trust is included in this level as a major component and not simply in a physical safety sense.

Trust being part of Maslow's hierarchy is important as helping identify the roots of trust as well as the role trust plays in cognition.

4. Trust as Rational and Beyond Rational

In addition to instinctual roots of trust and the role of trust in our hierarchy of needs, trust is addressed cognitively. The cognition associated with trust is discussed in several veins: instinctual evaluations, rational problem solving, evaluation of the results of the problem solving, and with respect to the predictability of the future. Some of this cognition can be considered coldly rational and some instinctual. The importance of this difference will be discussed after the several cognitive veins.

4.1. Gut Feelings

Instinctual evaluations of current conditions determine whether a person is threatened or not. This evaluation has many characteristics. It is fast, nearly instant. It is not consciously done, i.e., it cannot be explained as a series of rational deductions. Its inputs are not obvious, but experiments may identify specific stimuli that are threatening to some individuals (e.g., spiders, snakes, large predators, etc.). These characteristics are more naturally described as gut feelings [6] rather than the result of rational thought [7]. They are also not purely perceptual but involve reactions to perceptions.

4.2. Problem Solving

A second part cognition that is associated with trust is the problem solving associated with the determination of the goal of another agent. We are driven to determine the goal or motivation of another agent. This involves not just watching and following the actions of another agent, but attempting to guess what the purpose of the other agent's actions are. It is a difference between human and other great apes that we determine and mimic the goal-directed behavior, not just the sequential actions of another agent. This problem solving activity is deliberate, time consuming, conscious, and rational.

4.3. Evaluation of Other's Goal

Upon determination of another's goal, we promptly judge whether the goal is threatening or not. Because the problem-solving step takes time, this is a second instinctual evaluation of the situation.

4.4. Predictability and Its Bases

Finally, another evaluation is performed in support of determining the predictability of the other's behavior. There are two methods possible. The first is the integration of the current experience in with previous memories. This process determines if the newly observed behavior consistent with the past behavior or is it significantly different. It also evaluates how this determination effects the predictability of the behavior and its impact on the subject agent. The second method is a judgment or assumption that the other agent is "like-me" and therefore understood [8] including its trustworthiness is known. Besides our inclination to anthropomorphe all agents, we also prefer others who look like us [9].

4.5. Rational and Beyond Rational Aspects of Trust

These several cognitive aspects of trust involve both rational cognition and beyond rational cognition (gut feelings and instinct). Both of the major cognitive architectures ACT-R [7][10] and Soar [11], have models that have addressed emotion [12][13] and However, both are focused on rational cognitive reasoning and, as we noted earlier, rational behavior is only a small part of our behavior. The topic of whether man is a rational or feeling creature is centuries old. A theory gaining credibility is the Dual Process Theory.

5. Rational and Beyond Rational in a Cognitive Architecture

The Dual Process Theory [15][16] postulates both rational cognition and non-rational cognition are both present and necessary to explain behavior. The question of whether people are better described as serial processors or parallel processors is one of the oldest questions in psychology. Several attempts have been made to describe the two processes, but the definitions have varied significantly and typically use terms that carry too much baggage to allow serious discussion. Kahneman [17] in his Nobel Prize acceptance speech suggested using the most neutral terms of System 1 and System 2 to avoid this difficulty.

The System 1 process is generally the evolutionarily old, unconscious, automatic, instinctual, gut feeling, and fast process. System 2 is generally the relatively new, rational, slow, limited process. More details are provided in Table 1. One suggested difference potentially affecting the design of cognitive architectures is that System 1 cognition does not rely on declarative memory but on purely reactive productions instead [12]. These beginnings of clarity on the existence and capabilities of two forms of cognition have begun to be discussed as part of a cognitive architecture [12][18].

Cognitive architectures need to include both the System 1 and System 2 forms of cognition. Soar has included the initial System 1 form of assessment of a situation and used it as the basis for reinforcement learning [11]. ACT-R does not incorporate any System 1 cognition. It might be said that CLARION [18] does in that in includes both implicit and explicit knowledge representation and learning. Learning resulting in "automatic" behavior is similar but not the same as System 1 driven behavior because it is not on the same scale as evolutionary learning [5]. By not including the System 1 cognition discussed above, none of these systems are yet suitable for implementing models of the concept of trust discussed here. This topic was recently discussed at the ACT-R PostGraduate Summer School, July 16-19, 2011, a retreat intended to discuss the future of ACT-R. Presentations are available at: http://cog.cs.drexel.edu/actr2011/program.php.

Table 1. Characteristics of System 1 versus System 2 (from [15]).

General Area	System 1	System 2
Consciousness	Unconscious	Conscious
	Implicit	Explicit
	Automatic	Controlled
	Low effort	High effort
	Rapid	Slow
	High capacity	Low capacity
	Default process	Inhibitory
Evolution	Evolutionarily old	Evolutionarily recent
	Evolutionary rationality	Individual rationality
	Shared with animals	Uniquely human
	Nonverbal	Linked to language
	Modular cognition	Fluid intelligence
Functional Characteristics	Associative	Rule based
	Domain specific	Domain general
	Contextualized	Abstract
	Pragmatic	Logical
	Parallel	Sequential
	Stereotypical	Egalitarian
Individual Differences	Universal	Heritable
	Independent of general intelligence	Linked to general intelligence
	Independent of working memory	Limited by working memory capacity

6. Conclusion: The Roots of Trust

As discussed, the roots of trust involve both System 1 and System 2 cognition. The initial and immediate assessment of a situation seems to be System 1 cognition. The problem solving involved used to determine the goal of another agent appears to be System 2 cognition. The evaluation of the threat of the determined goal of another agent is again System 1. Finally, the evaluation of the history and prediction of the effects of the other agent's actions seems to again be System 2. These steps in evaluating trust therefore involve both System 1 and System 2 cognition.

The purpose of a cognitive architecture was thoughtfully defined by John Anderson as: "A *cognitive architecture* is a specification of the structure of the brain at a level of abstraction that explains how it achieves the function of the mind." [6] page 6. Until cognitive architectures can represent both forms of cognition, trust will be difficult to model and explain.

Acknowledgements

The author appreciates the useful comments by three anonymous reviewers. This work was supported in part by AFOSR/AFRL grant FA9550-10-1-0385 and the Center of Excellence in Neuroergonomics, Technology, and Cognition (CENTEC).

References

[1] H.A. Simon, *Reason in Human Affairs* (1982) Stanford University Press.
[2] *Concise Oxford English Dictionary* (2008) Oxford University Press, Oxford.
[3] A.H. Maslow, A Theory of Human Motivation, *Psychological Review* **50** (1943), 370–396.
[4] F. Krueger, K. McCabe, J. Moll, N. Kriegeskorte, R. Zahn, M. Strenziok, A. Heinecke, and J. Grafman, Neural correlates of trust. *PNAS* **104** (2007) 20084-20089.
[5] R. Dunbar, *The Human Story: A new History of Mankind's Evolution* (2004) Faber and Faber Limited, London.
[6] G. Gigerenzer, *Gut Feelings: The Intelligence of the Unconscious* (2007) Penguin Books, New York.
[7] J.R. Anderson, *How Can the Human Mind Occur in the Physical Universe*, Oxford University Press, Oxford, 2007.
[8] A.N. Meltzof, Imitation and Other Minds: The "Like-Me" Hypothesis. In S. Herley and N. Chater (Eds.) *Perspectives on Imitation: from Neuroscience to Social Science* (Vol 2) (2005), MIT Press, Cambridge.
[9] C. Holden, In Me I Trust, *Science* **297** (2002) 189.
[10] J.R. Anderson, D. Bothell, M. Byrne, S. Douglass, C Lebiere, and Y. Qin, An Integrated Theory of the Mind, *Psychological Review* **111** (2004), 1036-1060.
[11] J.E. Laird, Extending the Soar Cognitive Architecture (2008) In Proceedings of the Conference on Artificial General Intelligence, ISO Press, Memphis.
[12] W.G. Kennedy and M.D. Bugajska, Integrating Fast and Slow Cognitive Processes, in D.D. Salvucci and G. Gunzelmann (Eds) *Proceedings of the International Conference on Cognitive Modeling* (2010), 121-126.
[13] J. Gratch and S Marcella, A Domain-independent Framework for Modeling Emotion. Journal of Cognitive Systems Research **5** (2004) 269-306.
[14] K.R. Scherer, Appraisal considered as a process of multi-level sequential checking. (2001) In K. R. Scherer, A. Schorr, & T. Johnstone (Eds.) *Appraisal processes in Emotion: Theory, Methods, Research.* 92-120. Oxford University Press: Oxford.
[15] J.St.B.T Evans, Dual Processing Accounts of Reasoning, Juegments, and Social Cognition, *Annual Review of Psychology* **58** (2008), 255-278.
[16] S.A. Sloman, The Empirical Case for Two Systems of Reasoning, *Psychological Bulletin* **119** (1996), 3-22.
[17] D. Kahneman, Nobel prize lecture: Maps of Bounded Rationality: a perspective on intuitive judgment and choice, in *Nobel Prizes 2002: Nobel Prizes, Presentations, Biographies & Lectures,* T. Frangsmr (Ed) (2002) 419-499, Almqvist & Wiksell Int., Stockholm.
[18] R. Sun, *Cognition and Multi-Agent Interaction: From Cognitive Modeling to Social Simulation* (2006), Cambridge University Press, New York.

Biologically Inspired Cognitive Architectures 2011
A.V. Samsonovich and K.R. Jóhannsdóttir (Eds.)
IOS Press, 2011
doi:10.3233/978-1-60750-959-2-194

Four Processing Modes of
in situ Human Behavior

Muneo KITAJIMA [a,1] and Makoto TOYOTA [b]

[a] *National Institute of Advanced Industrial Science and Technology (AIST), Japan*
[b] *T-Method, Japan*

Abstract. Human behavior is considered as a series of moment by moment decision-makings in the ever-changing environment. Each decision-making process is carried out by System 1 and System 2 of Two Minds [3] under real time constraints, which basically requires synchronization between the workings of System 1 and System 2 in the real world by taking into account each system's characteristic times defined by Newell's time scale of action [4]. The result of decision-making is an event, that includes the direct output of decision-making, or behavior, and the resultant state of the external world. This paper proposes Four Processing Modes of *in situ* human behavior, consisting of before-event and after-event System 1 activities, and before-event and after-event System 2 activities for each event. Moment-by-moment decision-making process is regarded as a series of mental and physical actions performed in one of Four Processing Modes. This paper also provides evidence of Four Processing Modes from our field study concerning guide-sign supported navigation behavior at railway stations [9].

Keywords. Time scale of action, Two Minds, decision-making

1. *in situ* Human Behavior

Human behavior is represented as a series of discrete events, and each event is considered as the result of decision-making processes at the time the event has occurred. Let's take an example of human behavior represented as a series of events, that is associated with conducting a tour. The tourist's behavioral events are oftentimes associated with the origination of a single tour. For example, before arriving at a destination, one has to decide when to initiate planning a tour, how to collect information about the candidate destinations, which destination to visit, whom to accompany, which hotel to stay in, which restaurant to have dinner at, and so on. These decisions define the plan for the tour. On arrival at the destination, a tourist has to decide what to do in each specific situation according to the pre-specified plan.

However, the plan should be regarded as just one of several resources for organizing human behavior. Human behavior is the result of a series of decisions, but it might not necessarily be carried out according to a pre-specified plan. Rather, it should be regarded as situated in the environment where the current activities are carried out, *i.e.*, as situated

---

[1]Corresponding Author: Principal Research Scientist, National Institute of Advanced Industrial Science and Technology (AIST), 1-1-1 Umezono, Tsukuba, Ibaraki 305-8568 Japan; E-mail: kitajima.muneo@aist.go.jp.

action [1,2]. A tourist makes a variety of *in situ* decisions on how to enjoy the visit to the destination. However, there might be unforeseeable circumstances that would force him or her to change the pre-specified plan. Therefore, tourist's decision-making at the site of tour should be conceived as dependent on the circumstances he or she is in.

Each event is differently treated by decision-making processes *before* the event and *after* the event. In this example, the event, "arrival at the destination," is special because it divides the entire tour events into two categories; "before arrival events" and "after arrival events." Let us call an event "boundary event" when we consider two classes of decision-making processes in relation with the boundary event; the ones that happen before the boundary event and the others that happen after the boundary event. The arrival event is a characteristic boundary event of touring behavior. Before the boundary event, decision-making is for anticipating events that will develop after the boundary event. After the boundary event, especially immediately after it, decision-making is for conducting *in situ* activities by utilizing the anticipation, where behavior selection at each moment is strongly affected by the internal conditions, *i.e.*, his/her physical and/or mental conditions, and the external conditions, *i.e.*, the states of the environment, and most importantly, human behavior is synchronous with the state of environment which could have resulted in the his/her past behaviors, and the present internal and external states should affect the future decision-makings. Later on, after the boundary event, the results of the boundary event and the behavior carried out for the boundary event will be estimated in terms of reliability and effectiveness of the actions taken.

2. Four Processing Modes in Human Behavior

This paper introduces *Four Processing Modes* of *in situ* human behavior that are derived by augmenting the theory of decision-making, *Two Minds* [3], by taking into account the different nature of decision-making before the boundary event and after the boundary event, that is captured by Newell's time scale of human action [4]. We will review briefly Kahneman's Two Minds [3] and Newell's time scale of human action [4] and show how they are combined, and describe the resultant *Four Processing Modes* of *in situ* human behavior; at each moment along the time dimension human behaves in one of the four modes and he/she switches among them depending on the internal and external states. We provide supporting evidence from our observational study at railway stations for understanding how people use guide signs in conducting navigation tasks [9].

2.1. Two Minds: The Theory of Decision-Making

Human decision-making has been a central topic in economics. Herbert A. Simon, winner of the Nobel Prize in economics in 1978, proposed principles of human beings' decision-making processes. He described the decision-making process as a "bounded rationality principle" as well as a "satisficing principle" [5,6]. Simon claimed that agents, or human beings, face uncertainty about the future and costs when acquiring information in the present. These factors limit the extent to which human beings can make a fully rational decision. Thus, they possess only "bounded rationality" and must make decisions by "satisficing," or choosing the path that might not be optimal, but which will make them happy enough.

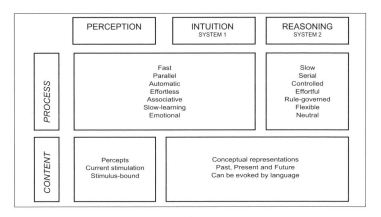

Figure 1. Two minds (adapted from [3]).

Recently, Kahneman, winner of the Nobel Prize in economics in 2002, introduced behavioral economics, which stems from the claim that decision-making is governed by the so-called "Two Minds" [7]. In other words, a human being's behavior is the outcome of two different systems including an "experiential processing system (System 1)" and a "rational processing system (System 2)." Figure 1, adapted from [3], illustrates the workings of the two systems. In short, System 1 is a fast feed-forward control process driven by the cerebellum and oriented toward immediate action. Experiential processing is experienced passively, outside of conscious awareness (one is seized by one's emotions). In contrast, System 2 is a slow feedback control process driven by the cerebrum and oriented toward future action. It is experienced actively and consciously (one intentionally follows the rules of inductive and deductive reasoning).

2.2. Newell's Time Scale of Human Action

The two systems work jointly and in synchronous with the ever-changing external world to exhibit moment by moment coherent human behavior. However, there is a large difference in processing speed between the two systems. Rational processing typically takes minutes to hours whereas experiential processing typically extends from hundreds of milliseconds to tens of seconds. Figure 2 illustrates the time scale of human action consisting of the following four bands, 1) Biological Band, 2) Cognitive Band, 3) Rational Band, and 4) Social Band, each has its characteristic processing time [4]. A large part of human beings' daily activities are immediate actions and are therefore under control of the experiential processing system (System 1). The rational processing system (System 2) intervenes with the experiential processing system to better organize the overall outcome of the processing through consciously envisioning possible futures.

2.3. Four Processing Modes of Human Behavior

Decision-making processes before the boundary event and those after the boundary event are significantly different in terms of the impact of real time constraints on the decision-making processes. Considering that decision-making is the result of the workings of System 1 and System 2, there are four distinctive behavior modes, 1) conscious (System 2) behavior before the boundary event, 2) conscious (System 2) behavior after the bound-

Time Sale of Human Action			
Scale (sec)	Time Units	System	World (Theory)
10^7	months		
10^6	weeks		Social Band
10^5	days		
10^4	hours	Task	
10^3	10 min	Task	Rational Band
10^2	minutes	Task	
10^1	10 sec	Unit Task	
10^0	1 sec	Operations	Cognitive Band
10^{-1}	100 ms	Deliberate Act	
10^{-2}	10 ms	Neural Circuit	
10^{-3}	1 ms	Neuron	Biological Band
10^{-4}	100 μs	Organelle	

Figure 2. Newell's time scale of human action.

ary event, 3) unconscious (System 1) behavior before the boundary event, and 4) unconscious (System 1) behavior after the boundary event. Table 1 summarizes the features of the Four Processing Modes.

Table 1. Four Processing Modes

	System 2 (Conscious Processes)		System 1 (Unconscious Processes)	
	Before	*After*	*Before*	*After*
Time Constraints	none or weak	exist	none or weak	exist
Network Structure	feedback	feedback	feedforward + feedback	feedforward + feedback
Processing	main serial conscious process + subsidiary parallel process	main serial conscious process + subsidiary parallel process	simple parallel process	simple parallel process
Newell's Time Scale	Rational / Social	Rational / Social	Biological / Cognitive	Biological / Cognitive

Figure 3 illustrates the Four Processing Modes along the time dimension expanding before and after the boundary event.

3. Evidence of Four Processing Modes

By following the underlying development philosophy of Model Human Processor [8], we developed an architecture model for simulating *in situ* human behavior, called Model Human Processor with Realtime Constraints, MHP/RT [9]. The verification of the model was done by matching the results of simulations of the model with people's behavior recorded in a series of field observations [9,10].

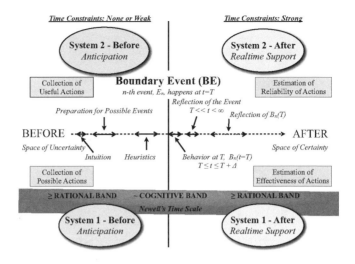

Figure 3. How the Four Processing Modes work.

3.1. Way-Finding Behavior at Railway Stations [9]

Suppose a person is placed in an environment that he/she has never visited and given a navigation mission that is familiar to him/her. He/she can anticipate the goal state and imagine the problem space that should extend as he/she proceeds. The representation could be very detailed or coarse, depending on his/her knowledge of this situation. Based on MHP/RT, it is suggested that in this situation, two qualitatively different modes of navigation processes exist. The first is *anticipation-based navigation* in which feedback from consciousness works effectively. The second is *event-based navigation* in which feedback does not work, and moment-by-moment decision-making is required. These two navigation modes specify the patterns of the Four Processing Modes that could appear in navigation behavior.

3.2. Anticipation-based navigation and event-based navigation

3.2.1. Anticipation-based navigation

This navigation mode is characterized by "<System 1 & 2 – Before> followed by <System 1 – After> with occasional intervention by <System 2 – After>." Even if the environment is new to the participant, the mission is familiar to him/her. Therefore when starting the mission, he/she is able to activate mental models associated with the mission. If the level of the representation of the mental model is appropriate for the sensory-information filter to function effectively in the environment, it is possible for him/her to input information from the environment as specified by the mental model. The mental model may be one for procedures or one for objects in the environment. The input information resonates with the knowledge in LTM and updates the representation of the active mental models to be used to create feedback from consciousness. The feedback forms anticipation concerning the future development of the person and the environment. While this cycle continues as the person navigates, it is said that the person is navigating in the mode of anticipation-based navigation. In this mode, System 2 monitors the operation of System 1 and intervenes when a large discrepancy exists between the anticipation concerning the situation to come next and the actual situation.

3.2.2. Event-based navigation

This navigation mode is characterized by "<System 2 – Before> followed by <System 2 – After>." When anticipation-based navigation seriously breaks down, the participant is forced to switch to the event-based navigation mode in order to continue the mission. Breakdown can occur when the initial mental model is found to be inappropriate: (1) the level of representation is appropriate, but the sensory-information filter that reflects feedback from consciousness does not work because of a serious discrepancy between the representation of the filter and the actual environment, or (2) the level of representation is not detailed enough for consciously defining the sensory-information filter. A person who is in the event-based navigation mode must monitor the progress more frequently than one who is in the anticipation-based navigation mode, and must select the next action within the time allowed by deliberate processing. Therefore, the action selection process in this situation looks like obeying the satisficing principle by [5]. In this mode, System 2 takes control of navigation behavior.

3.3. Evidence of Four Processing Modes

The observational study at train stations reported in [9] indicated that participants showed behavior that reflected the Four Processing Modes. For example, it was observed that two participants got lost in the same situation in under control of two different modes. One person had a deficit in the planning function, and therefore, his/her behavior was in large part governed by <System 1 – Before> and <System 1 – After> modes. This is a version of anticipation-based navigation with little contribution from System 2. And the other had a deficit in the attention function, and therefore his/her behavior was in large part governed by <System 2 – Before> and <System 2 – After>, consistent with the event-based navigation pattern.

References

[1] L. Suchman, *Plans and Situated Actions: The Problem of Human-Machine Communication*, Cambridge University Press, New York, 1987.
[2] E. Hutchins, *Cognition in the Wild*, The MIT Press, Cambridge, 1996.
[3] D. Kahneman, A Perspective on Judgment and Choice, *American Psychologist*, **58** (2003), 697–720.
[4] A. Newell, *Unified Theories of Cognition (The William James Lectures, 1987)*, Harvard University Press, Cambridge, MA, 1990.
[5] H.A. Simon, Rational choice and the structure of the environment, *Psychological Review*, **63** (1956), 129–138.
[6] H.A. Simon, *The Sciences of the Artificial*, The MIT Press, Cambridge, 1996
[7] J.St.B.T. Evans, K. Frankish (Eds.), *In Two Minds: Dual Processes and Beyond*, Oxford University Press, Oxford, 2009.
[8] S.K. Card, T.P. Moran, A. Newell, *The Psychology of Human-Computer Interaction*, Lawrence Erlbaum Associates, Hillsdale, NJ, 1983.
[9] M. Kitajima, M. Toyota, Simulating Navigation Behavior Based on the Architecture Model MHP/RT, *Behaviour and Information Technology*, (in press).
[10] M. Kitajima, H. Tahira, S. Takahashi, T. Midorikawa; Understanding tourist's *in situ* behavior: a Cognitive Chrono-Ethnography study of visitors to a hot spring resort, *Journal of Quality Assurance in Hospitality & Tourism*, (in press).

Biologically Inspired Cognitive Architectures 2011
A.V. Samsonovich and K.R. Jóhannsdóttir (Eds.)
IOS Press, 2011
doi:10.3233/978-1-60750-959-2-200

SPIRE – A BICA-Emulated Strategic Decision Support System

HAROLD E. KLEIN
Dept. of Strategic Management
Fox School of Business
Philadelphia, PA 19122
klein@temple.edu

Abstract. A strategic decision support system (SDSS) called SPIRE has been developed and applied that is responsive to the needs of a decision maker confronting a complex and/or chaotic situation. Such situations are not amenable to analytical resolution, employing essentially deductive reasoning. SPIRE facilitates or "supports" the cognitive function of a human decision maker rather than being the engine for the production of the decision itself, aiming to trigger inductive reasoning. The information organization of SPIRE output is analogous to neuronal group architecture. SPIRE diagrams provide the decision maker with visual cognitive frames to rationally address the complex situation at hand; these also answer critical strategic questions. A SPIRE application will be presented.

Keywords. Decision support systems, small world networks, complex adaptive systems, neuronal group architecture, causal maps, cognitive maps.

BICAs, more often than not, are employed in models/programs/processes that attempt to *simulate* the behavior/operation/actuality of a human cognitive process in order to *emulate* the results obtained there from. Unfortunately, only limited success has been achieved in this regard, mainly in performing some very elemental cognitive tasks. There actually is little likelihood that higher level cognitive processing required for addressing real complex, unique decision making situations will result from this vein of research in the foreseeable future. .

There is a better prospect that BICAs, such a one presented here, will provide the basis for more advanced Decision Support Systems (DSS), information systems and protocols for addressing complex (or chaotic) decision making situations. In the latter, the ordinary assumptions and/or givens of conventional decision making problems do not exist; these include boundary conditions, distinct and definable dependent and independent variables, causal relationships, clear choices or alternatives and, especially, specific decisions. In sum, all the necessary inputs to apply an analytically-based decision making protocol are absent (of course, this does not deter the widespread inappropriate application of such tools).

In such messy, real world contexts (think The War on Terror), where the above "givens" are not, the decision maker still must determine (often, very quickly in crisis situations) **which decisions need to be taken and in what sequence or priority, which ones need to be coordinated, what actions need to be taken and to what end.** There may well be dozens or more decisions involved with an even greater number of relevant extrinsic factors impinging on these decisions and on each other.

The best and really only alternative to fill this void is a protocol or system that facilitates or "supports" the cognitive functionality of a human decision maker in addressing such a complex situation – a strategic decision support system (SDSS). The attempt then is to get the decision maker focused on the necessary and sufficient considerations relevant to a decision-requiring situation. So rather than being the engine for the production of the decision itself, the SDSS provides the "triggers" or "cognitive stimuli" for thinking through a course of action and/or reaching a decision. In such contexts, the decision is reached through some inductive reasoning process.

SPIRE (Systematic Procedure for Identifying Relevant Environments) is a collaborative technology designed to represent the organization's relevant environment in a unique causal mapping format that is immediately useful to top management for strategic decision making. Objective responses to the "pre-decision" questions (in bold) above emerge directly from the mapping diagrams themselves. The visual representation is designed to promote a creative response.

The SPIRE approach is based on a heuristic program that creates causal map representations of the organization environment in an architecture closely analogous to biological neural networks, both in appearance and behavior. The sole inputs are individual verbal statements articulating some dynamic relationship among extrinsic factors with relevance for one or more specific decisions; each statement is in sequence-of-event form. In the SPIRE application at a large electric utility (presented at the BICA 2011 Conference), there were cumulatively 63 extrinsic factors considered that had direct or indirect relevance for 36 strategic decisions issues found among 50 such statements. There is no theoretical limit to the number of contingency statements that may be admitted or the number of extrinsic factors or strategic decisions.

These verbal statement data are converted to notational format and processed further through the SPIRE heuristic program. Essentially, the program indentifies clusters (or subsets) of strategic decisions that are commonly affected by closely interacting clusters/subsets of extrinsic factors. The program then yields the specifications for SPIRE subset diagrams. In the case of the electric utility application, processing yielded five subsets, self-organized. There is no prescribed subset number.

Each SPIRE subset is a unidirectional causal network map, flowing from left to right. Predecessor extrinsic (i.e., indirectly affecting) factors lead into successor ones. At a point where an extrinsic factor directly has relevance for one or more decisions, the latter is shown in a position adjacent to the factor. The number of subsets, their respective internal composition is entirely determined by the inputs. There is invariably one or more extrinsic factor links between individual subsets. However, there are fewer of these links than of the dense extrinsic factor interactions within a network subset. It closely resembles the neuronal group architecture, now generally accepted, as depicted conceptually in Edelman[1] originally and empirically in a large number of human[2] and animal brain[3] imaging studies; these also confirm the small world network (SWN) attributes of neuronal network activation in the brain.[4] SPIRE diagrams have these same SWN characteristics.

The SPIRE subsets exhibit neural network characteristics: the links between subsets demonstrate *connectivity*. Any additional statement describing some extrinsic factor dynamic relevant for a strategic decision(s) will force the reconfiguration of at least one subset and possibly the links between subsets, demonstrating the network's *plasticity*. These network changes are seen clearly upon inspection.

The importance of schematic or figural representations of complex problem contexts cannot be overemphasized. Such visualization often provokes the mental imagery that is the antecedent of a creative response[5]. The SPIRE protocol is an attempt to accomplish this task[6].

References

[1]   G.M. Edelman, *Bright_Air, Brilliant Fire: On the Matter of the Mind.* Basic Books, New York, 1992
[2]   E, T. Bullmore, O. Sporns, Complex brain networks: graph theoretical analysis of structural and functional systems. *Nature Reviews Neuroscience* **10** (2009), 186-198
[3]   L. Zhifeng et al., Uncovering Intrinsic Connectional Architecture of Functional Networks in Awake Rat Brain. *The Journal of Neuroscience* **31** (2011), 3776-3783
[4] B.C. Bernhardt, Z. Chen, Y. He, A.C. Evans, Graph-Theoretical Analysis Reveals Disrupted Small-World Organization of Cortical Thickness Correlation Networks in Temporal Lobe Epilepsy, *Cortex* **21** (2011), 2147-2157
[5]   A. Antonietti, Why does mental visualization facilitate problem-solving?, in *Mental Images in Human Cognition*, R.H. Logie & M. Denis (eds.), Elsivier Science Publishers, B.V., 1991
[6]   See H.E. Klein, Adapting Organization Decision-making and Structure to a Chaotic Environment, *Proceedings of the International Conference on Systems Thinking in Management,* University of Pennsylvania, Philadelphia, (2004)

Biologically Inspired Cognitive Architectures 2011
A.V. Samsonovich and K.R. Jóhannsdóttir (Eds.)
IOS Press, 2011
doi:10.3233/978-1-60750-959-2-203

Recognizing Geospatial Patterns with Biologically-inspired Relational Reasoning

Paul Kogut[a,1], June Gordon[a], David Morgenthaler[b], John Hummel[c], Edward Monroe[d],
Ben Goertzel[e], Ethan Trewhitt[f], Elizabeth Whitaker[f]
[a] *Lockheed Martin, Philadelphia, PA*
[b] *Lockheed Martin, Denver, CO*
[c] *University of Illinois, Urbana, IL*
[d] *Novamente LLC, Brattleboro, VT*
[e] *Novamente LLC, Rockville, MD*
[f] *Georgia Tech Research Institute, Atlanta, GA*

Abstract. Relational reasoning is a complex high-level cognitive function that should be part of a realistic computational equivalent of the human mind. People use relational reasoning often in everyday life in many different contexts (e.g., social understanding, political science, law, business). This paper discusses the application of relational reasoning to the recognition of geospatial patterns (e.g., clusters of buildings that constitute a facility). The relational reasoning model is based on cognitive science evidence and emerging neuroscience theory. Experiments show that the relational reasoning model can recognize geospatial patterns that have a significant degree of variation.

Keywords. Relational reasoning, geospatial, analogy

Introduction

People have the extraordinary ability to recognize similarities in situations by matching relations and roles of multiple objects and not just features of individual objects [1]. Young children primarily learn categories of objects based on features (e.g., shape, color). As they get older they start to learn categories of situations (i.e., relational categories) that involve objects that fill roles in relation to other objects [2]. In the geospatial domain a facility like a farm, school or mall can be considered a relational category. For example a *house* **near** a *barn* and a *grain silo* **adjacent_to** a *barn* are a set of relations and objects that indicate a *farm*. Note that this *farm* relational category contains extra information than what is contained in a feature-based category for a *farm* (e.g., a *farm* has a *barn* and a *grain silo*). This extra relational information allows category definitions to be both more precise and more generalizable. An example of greater precision is that a *mall* is indicated by *stores* **surrounded_by** a *parking lot* but not by a *parking lot* **surrounded_by** *stores* (**surrounded_by** is an asymmetric relation with 2 distinct roles). An example of greater generalizability is that an *irrigation sprinkler* fills the same role as an *irrigation ditch* for a farm even though their physical

---

[1] Corresponding Author: Paul Kogut, Lockheed Martin, PO Box 8048, Philadelphia, Pa 19101; Email: paul.a.kogut@lmco.com

features are quite different. Relational reasoning involves finding mappings (correspondences) between the current situation (set of relations) and one or more previously seen situations. Recognition occurs when the most similar previously seen situation is selected. This paper describes one of several initial thrusts in a larger effort to build biologically-inspired models of high level cognition. The basic approach is to increase the neural fidelity of existing cognitive models by repartitioning them based on current neuroscience theory in preparation for replacing conventional algorithm implementations with simulated networks of interacting spiking neurons. The relational reasoning model described here will also be integrated with other high fidelity models (e.g., of memory) to attempt to reproduce the idiosyncrasies of the human mind.

1. Relational Reasoning Model

The starting point for the biologically-inspired model was the Learning and Inference with Schemas and Analogies (LISA) model [3]. LISA is a computational model of relational reasoning supported by many empirical results in cognitive science. The LISA model covers a broad range of mental processes including memory retrieval, analogical mapping, relational inference and schema induction. LISA is a hybrid symbolic connectionist model that already has a significant degree of neural fidelity because of its implementation of binding by synchrony. In LISA the representation of a situation or a relational category is called an *analog*. The analog can be either a specific instance of a situation or a generalized pattern of situations (i.e., a schema). In the current model, recognition of a geospatial pattern is primarily performed by the LISA mapping algorithm. Specific examples of facility types are presented to the model and placed in active memory as is (i.e., not generalized into schemas). Then the model attempts to map test data (i.e., unknown facilities) to each analog in memory to identify the most similar facility type. Figure 1 shows the basic inputs and outputs of the model.

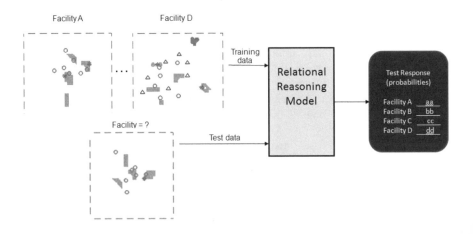

Figure 1. Application of a relational reasoning model to geospatial patterns

The training and test data shown in Figure 1 consist of abstracted geospatial objects (e.g., buildings, lakes). The data was created by a probabilistic generator that selects and lays out the objects. The raw data that is fed to the model is actually in the form of vectors (e.g., building at grid location X,Y with attribute Z). The pictures in Figure 1 were drawn from the raw data for use in parallel human experiments. The output test response is an estimated probability that the unknown facility is a facility A, B, C and D.

The main neural substrate of relational reasoning is the Prefrontal Cortex (PFC) but we also needed a simple model of the *what stream* (i.e., ventral pathway for object identification) through the Temporal Cortex and the *where stream* (i.e., dorsal pathway for spatial processing) through the Parietal Cortex, which come together in the Medial Temporal Lobe/Hippocampus [4] to preprocess the training and test data into a relational form. We also partitioned LISA into 2 main PFC substructures based on recent theories: Dorsolateral PFC (DLPFC) and the Rostrolateral (RLPFC)/Inferior Frontal Gyrus (IFG) cortical loop [5]. The DLPFC mediates temporary maintenance of objects and relations in memory. It interacts with Temporal Cortex to access object and concept representations. The RLPFC/IFG cortical loop performs mapping of analogs and inhibits spreading activation of competing representations.

The relational reasoning model aims to capture how a very thorough person systematically compares the unknown facility in the test data with known facility types that have been seen before in the training data. The model looks for correspondences (mappings) between pairs of objects linked by relations (which constitute propositions) in the input test data and pairs of objects in the training data. A facility is a relational category represented by a source analog in memory. The input test data is equivalent to a target analog. Figure 2 shows one of many propositions that form an analog. Geospatial items are represented as objects (e.g., B_114_91 is a specific building at grid location (114, 91)). Relations such as *proximal to*, *distant from* and *on top* are represented as predicates. Each predicate has two roles that are bound to fillers (objects) via a neural mechanism, binding by synchrony. When a filler is bound to a role, the corresponding units fire in synchrony with one another and out of synchrony with the units representing other role–filler bindings [3]. Both objects and roles have semantic features that capture the degree of similarity or difference (e.g., a type 4 building is more similar to a type 2 building than a lake). These semantic features have simulated neural activation behavior that permits partial matching of objects and roles. Propositions capture the intuition that when certain types of objects are near other specific types of objects there is often a reason why (e.g., a type 1 building is *proximal to* a type 4 building because they function together in a facility). We believe that a human works with this level of detail. Characteristics of the overall facility are embedded in the set of propositions and the semantic features.

The relational reasoning model systematically compares the propositions in the target and source looking for exact or close mappings. After mapping the target (unknown facility) to each source (known facility) the model calculates similarity measures between the target and source analogs [6], which are then converted to estimated probabilities. The "recognized facility" is the facility with the highest probability. The model calculates two similarity measures:

- MIPs - *matches in place* which measures the aggregate quality of the mapping of propositions (i.e., a high MIP means there were a lot of good proposition matches)
- MOPs - *matches out of place* which measures the degree of shared semantic features for all objects (i.e., a high MOP means that overall the facilities had a

lot of similar objects, regardless of whether they filled corresponding roles in propositions)

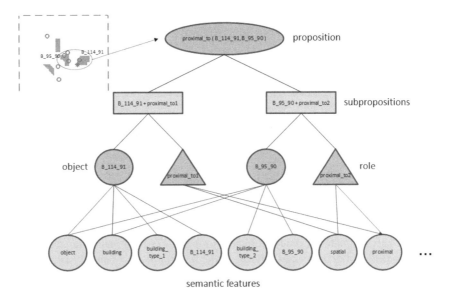

Figure 2. Knowledge representation for relational reasoning

The total similarity is the sum of MIP and MOP. Total similarity is calculated in both directions: target to source and source to target. The difference in total similarity between directions depends on the number of propositions in the target and source (i.e., comparing a very cluttered facility to a very sparse facility will usually result in larger differences in similarity). This difference accounts for results from human subjects. We use the average of these because the number of propositions in the target may be larger or smaller than those in the source. We used a statistical binning technique [7] to convert similarity values to estimated probabilities. This technique was originally developed for creating accurate probabilities from the scores produced by various machine learning classification models.

2. Experiment

We ran a series of experiments with the relational reasoning model using an automated testing and evaluation infrastructure. In the first experiment we ran 500 test questions each for facility A, B, C and D for a total of 2000 trial runs. In each of these runs both the question facility and a single training example for each facility A through D were randomly drawn from the total set of 1600 example facilities. The output is a set of 4 probabilities that the test question facility is a facility type A thru D (e.g., pr(A) = 82%, pr(B) = 0%, pr(C) = 10%, pr(D)= 8%)).

The results indicate that the model identified the highest probability facility type correctly 42% of the time. For example, when the test question facility was a facility A (ground truth) the model tended to estimate the probability of A to be greater than the probabilities for any of the other three facility types. Overall the model performed much better on facility A and B (facilities C and D have a much higher statistical variation and it is more difficult to unambiguously identify the outlier instances of these). After this experiment we realized that the results are highly dependent on how prototypical the randomly selected training example is for each facility. Intuitively this was like showing a human subject only one training example for each facility. We then tried two different approaches to make the training examples more representative of each facility type. First we randomly selected 16 examples of each facility and computed the average similarity score with the test question facility. This gave much better results: 69% correct. In the second approach we manually identified one highly prototypical example of each facility type and used that as a single training example. This did not work as well as the multiple training example approach yielding 56% correct. Clearly it is difficult to capture the range of variability of a facility type with just one facility example. The results are summarized in Figure 3. In an unpublished study of human subjects by another research group with the same data the mean performance was approximately 50% correct and the highest individual performer got about 78% correct. In that study 48 examples of each facility were used to train the human subjects. Thus our model approximates the performance level of human subjects.

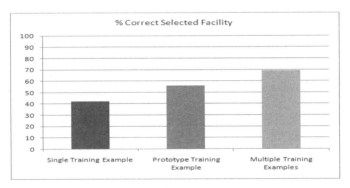

Figure 3. Experimental Results

We also ran experiments to determine the effects of simulated random neural noise in the model on the similarity measures with the same target source analog pair. We found that similarity measures do not vary greatly and the average similarity converges rapidly. This effect can be thought of as the variation in the performance of one human subject on one specific test question where they did not improve their performance by learning. Variations would be due to the mental state of the person (e.g., alertness, stress).

3. Conclusions

This paper presents early results for a work in progress to build a large scale biologically inspired model of higher level cognition. We enhanced the neural fidelity of the LISA model and added cognitive functions. We conducted experiments and the results show that the model performs well on geospatial patterns that have a significant degree of variation. We believe that further tuning of the model would improve performance.

The next steps include replacing parts of the model with components based on spiking neuron models to increase neural fidelity and improve replication of dynamic behaviors in the brain. Initial experiments in implementing binding by synchrony using spiking neurons have been conducted but a discussion of these experiments is beyond the scope of this paper.

We intend to explore additional model functionality such as top-down visual attention involving the Parietal Cortex. Also, the current model does not perform analog retrieval from long term memory. Instead it assumes that source analogs are already in active memory and tries to map all of them. This is not a problem with only four types of facilities as in the current data but our model would need to be extended to deal with hundreds of facility types. Analog retrieval based on detailed models of the Medial Temporal Lobe/Hippocampus could filter out many analogs that are not reasonably similar to the input facility.

Acknowledgements

Supported by the Intelligence Advanced Research Projects Activity (IARPA) via Department of the Interior (DOI) contract number D10PC20022. The U.S. Government is authorized to reproduce and distribute reprints for Governmental purposes notwithstanding any copyright annotation thereon. The views and conclusions contained hereon are those of the authors and should not be interpreted as necessarily representing the official policies or endorsements, either expressed or implied, of IARPA, DOI, or the U.S. Government. Also thanks to Keith Holyoak for comments on an earlier draft of this paper.

References

[1]   K. J. Holyoak, Analogy. In K. J. Holyoak & R. G. Morrison (Eds.), *The Cambridge Handbook of Thinking and Reasoning,* Cambridge, UK: Cambridge University Press 2005, pp. 117-142.
[2]   A. Kittur, J. E. Hummel and K. J. Holyoak, Feature- vs. relation-defined categories: Probab(alistical)ly not the same. In *Proceedings of the Twenty Second Annual Conference of the Cognitive Science Society*, 2004, pp. 696-701.
[3]   J. E. Hummel and K. J. Holyoak, A symbolic-connectionist theory of relational inference and generalization. *Psychological Review, 110* (2003), pp. 220-264.
[4]   R. Farivar, Dorsal–ventral integration in object recognition, *Brain Research Reviews* **61** (2009), pp. 144–153
[5]   R. G. Morrison and Knowlton, B.J., Neurocognitive methods in higher cognition. In K. J. Holyoak and R. G. Morrison (Eds.) *Oxford Handbook of Thinking and Reasoning.* New York: Oxford University Press, in press.
[6]   E. G. Taylor and J. E. Hummel, Perspectives on similarity from the LISA model, In *Proceedings of AnICA07 Workshop on Analogies: Integrating Multiple Cognitive Abilities*, 2007
[7]   B. Zadrozny and C. Elkan, Transforming classifier scores into accurate multiclass probability estimates, *In Proceedings of the Eighth International conference on Knowledge Discovery and Data Mining*, 2002

Biologically Inspired Cognitive Architectures 2011
A.V. Samsonovich and K.R. Jóhannsdóttir (Eds.)
IOS Press, 2011
doi:10.3233/978-1-60750-959-2-209

Neuromorphic and Brain-Based Robots

Jeffrey L. Krichmar[a,1] and Hiroaki Wagatsuma[b,c]

[a]*Department of Cognitive Sciences, University of California, Irvine, USA*
[b]*Department of Brain Science and Engineering, Kyushu Institute of Technology, Japan*
[c]*RIKEN Brain Sciences Institute, Japan*

Abstract. Neuromorphic and brain-based robotics have enormous potential for furthering our understanding of the brain. By embodying models of the brain on robotic platforms, researchers can investigate the roots of biological intelligence and work towards the development of truly intelligent machines. This paper discusses the history of the field and its potential. We give examples of biologically inspired robot designs and neural architectures that lead to brain-based robots. Looking to the future, we consider the development of cognitive, or even conscious, robots that display the adaptability and intelligence of biological organisms.

Keywords. Brain-based robots, cognitive robots, computational neuroscience, machine ethics, neuromorphic engineering, neurorobots.

Introduction

The combination of computational neuroscience and embodied models are novel methodology for understanding the inner workings of the brain. There is a small, but growing, community of individual researchers and laboratories around the world that combine these fields. However, there is a need to publicize this line of research to attract more scientists to this young field. Therefore, we recently edited a book that includes many of the top researchers and laboratories around the world in Neuromorphic and Brain-Based Robotics [1]. The common theme among these researchers is that they are interested in some aspect of the brain sciences, and are using robotic devices as either an experimental tool to further our understanding of the brain, or to develop neurobiologically inspired robots. The present paper highlights some of their work to introduce the different areas of research and key issues in this transdisciplinary field. We know we have not included everyone in this paper and apologize for any omissions. However, we feel that the examples are representative of the most important areas in this line of research, and that they represent the state-of-the-art in the field at this time. We sincerely hope their research and the ensuing discussion will inspire and attract a new generation of neuromorphic and brain-based roboticists.

---

[1]Corresponding Author. Department of Cognitive Sciences, 2328 Social and Behavioral Sciences Gateway, University of California, Irvine, Irvine, CA 92697-5100. E-mail: jkrichma@uci.edu

1. History and potential of neuromorphic robotics

Neuromorphic and brain-based robots are not encapsulated in a single field with its own journal or conference. Rather, the field crosses many disciplines, and groundbreaking neuromorphic robot research is carried out in computer science, engineering, neuroscience, and many other departments. The field is known by many names: biologically inspired robots, brain-based devices, cognitive robots, neuromorphic engineering, neurobots, neurorobots, and many more.

Arguably, the field may have begun with William Grey Walter's turtles, created in the 1950s, whose simple yet interesting behaviors were guided by an analog electronic nervous system [2]. Another landmark was the fascinating thought experiments in the book by Valentino Braitenberg, *Vehicles: Experiments in Synthetic Psychology* [3]. Braitenberg's *Vehicles* inspired a generation of hobbyists and scientists, present company included, to use synthetic methodology (Braitenberg's term) to study brain, body, and behavior together. We like to think of synthetic methodology as "understanding through building" and it is certainly an apt mission statement for neuromorphic and brain-based robots [4].

It has been 90 years since the popular word "robot" first appeared in Karel Capek 's play *R.U.R.* With the dawn of the twenty-first century, our expectations are high for a new scientific paradigm and a major technological advancement in the field of robotics. At the present time, robots have become prevalent in our society. Robots can be found in commercial, manufacturing, military, and entertainment applications. We now have robotic vacuum cleaners, robotic soccer players, and autonomous vehicles on the ground, in the sky, and beneath the ocean. Because of major technical and empirical advances in the brain sciences over the last few decades, the time appears right for integrating the exciting fields of robotics and neuroscience. This promising area of research, which we term neuromorphic and brain-based robotics, may generate the paradigm shift for truly intelligent machines.

Robots are increasing our productivity and quality of life in industry, defense, security, entertainment, and household chores. However, the behavior of these robots pales compared with that of animals and insects with nervous systems. Biological organisms survive in dynamic environments and display flexibility, adaptability, and survival capabilities that far exceed any artificial systems. Neuromorphic and brain-based robotics are exciting and emerging research fields that investigate the roots of biological intelligence by embodying models of the brain on robotic platforms. Moreover, because neuromorphic and brain-based robots follow a working model (i.e. the biological brain and body), we believe this field will lead to autonomous machines that we can truly call intelligent.

Neuromorphic and brain-based robots are physical devices whose control system has been modeled after some aspect of brain processing. Because the nervous system is so closely coupled with the body and situated in the environment, brain-based robots can be provide powerful tools for studying neural function. Brain-based robots can be tested and probed in ways that are not yet achievable in human and animal experiments. The field of neuromorphic and brain-based robots is built on the notion that the brain is embodied in the body and the body is embedded in the environment.

In the real biological nervous system, this embodiment mediates all sensations, governs motion, is crucial for higher order cognition, and notions of self. The question of how our mind is constructed from physical substrates such as the brain and body are still a mystery. A synthetic approach occupies an important position in investigating how complex systems, such as the brain, give rise to intelligent behavior through interactions with the world. The concept is highlighted by "embodiment" in the fields of robotics, artificial intelligence, and cognitive science. It argues that the mind is largely influenced by the state of the body and its interaction with the world [4].

The neuromorphic and brain-based robotic approaches can provide valuable heuristics for understanding how the brain works both empirically and intuitively. Neurologists analytically investigate whether the brain is healthy or impaired due to neurological disorders. Neuroscientists probe different areas of the brain to determine which brain regions are necessary for a specific function. By using a synthetic methodology, neurobiologically inspired robots can constructively exhibit how the brain works through its interaction with the body, the environment, and other agents in real world situations.

The remainder of this paper is divided into logical sections starting with physical robotic platforms, progressing to case studies using brain-based robots, to philosophical considerations with future brain-based robots, and finally important ethical issues as robots become so intelligent that we have to think about the mental state of the robots.

2. Neuromorphic robots: biologically and neurally inspired designs

In this section, we directly consider how the body of a robot affects thinking and cognition. The interaction of neuromorphic robots with the environment enhances information processing and leads to *morphological computation* [4]. Many lessons remain to be learned through the construction of ingenious biomimetic devices.

2.1. Robust haptic recognition by an anthropomorphic robot hand

To achieve human-like stable manipulation and robust recognition, Koh Hosoda of Osaka University has constructed an anthropomorphic robot hand, called a Bionic Hand, which is covered with soft silicon skin and equipped with distributed tactile receptors [5]. Because of its compliance, the Bionic Hand can realize stable grasping with an object and gather rich sensory information through manipulation. It has the ability to reproduce the exploratory behavior of human hands and could be a powerful tool for understanding object manipulation and haptic recognition. Because the hand has so many touch receptors, small changes in the position and orientation of a manipulated object lead to large changes of the somatosensory pattern. The Bionic Hand is compliant and through repetitive grasping different objects settle into a unique and stable position in the hand. Because it shares many physical features of the human hand, the Bionic Hand can recognize different object classes, based on the discriminating pattern of touch sensor activity, by this repetitive grasping scheme.

2.2. Biomimetic robots based on the rat whisker system

Rats are endowed with prominent facial whiskers, which they use to explore the environment immediately surrounding their head. This tactile sense is considered to be primary in rats in the way vision is primary in primates – to the untrained eye the behavior of blind rats can appear indistinguishable from that of sighted animals. Neurobiology has shown us that the brain nuclei and circuits that process vibrissal touch signals and that control the positioning and movement of the whiskers, form a neural architecture that is a good model of how the mammalian brain, in general, coordinates sensing with action. Therefore, a research group at Sheffield University has been building robot whisker systems as a significant step towards building the first robot mammal [6]. In particular, they have designed and developed two whiskered robot platforms, Whiskerbot and SCRATCHbot, in order to better understand the rat whisker system, and to test hypotheses about whisker control and vibrissal sensing in a physical brain-based device. Each platform includes sophisticated mechanical, electronic, and software components, in which they must make trade-offs made between biomimetic ideals and engineering practicalities. By combining high-speed videos of real rat whisking, detailed computation neural simulations, biomimtetic whiskers and hair follicles, and embodied models of whisking, they suggest that rat locomotion and whisking might be viewed as a series of orients, with the focus of attention being constantly shifted, often ahead of the animal.

3. Brain-based robots: architectures and approaches

Several groups have designed control architectures for robots based on some aspects of the nervous system. The reason is twofold; first, using neurobiology as inspiration for robotic control systems may lead to better robot design, and second, using synthetic methodology, these embodied neural models may lead to a better understanding of brain and cognitive function.

3.1. Neuromodulation as a Robot Controller

Krichmar and Cox presented a strategy for controlling autonomous robots, which was based on the principles of neuromodulation in the mammalian brain [7]. Neuromodulatory systems signal important environmental events to the rest of the brain causing the organism to focus its attention on the appropriate object, ignore irrelevant distractions, and respond quickly and appropriately to the event [8]. There are separate neuromodulators that alter responses to risks, rewards, novelty, effort, and social cooperation. Moreover, the neuromodulatory systems provide a foundation for cognitive function in higher organisms; attention, emotion, goal-directed behavior, and decision-making derive from the interaction between the neuromodulatory systems and brain areas, such as the amygdala, frontal cortex, and hippocampus. They used a robot, whose behavior was controlled by a neural model of the cholinergic, dopaminergic, and serotonergic systems, to test the hypothesis that neuromodulatory activity can shape learning, drive attention, and select actions. The robot learned to approach stimuli that were predictive of positive value and move away from stimuli that were predictive of negative value. These experiments suggest a mechanism of how neuromodulatory systems influence attention and decision-making. The robot's controller may be a design strategy for controlling autonomous systems based on the principles of neuromodulation found in the mammalian brain.

3.2. The RatSLAM project: robot spatial navigation

A group of roboticists and computational neuroscientists at the University of Queensland and Queensland University of Technology, have sought to build a system that captures the desirable properties of the rodent's method of navigation into a system that is suitable for practical robot navigation [9]. The core model, dubbed RatSLAM, has demonstrated that it can construct maps of large and complex areas from very weak geometric information, and it can build, maintain, and use maps simultaneously over extended periods of time. RatSLAM is a visual simultaneous localization and mapping algorithm. But its map construction and path integration are achieved in a neural architecture inspired by grid and place cells found in the rodent entorhinal cortex and hippocampus. RatSLAM has been shown to 1) map a complete suburb from a single webcam mounted on a car, 2) navigate in an active office environment for two weeks, and 3) share a lexicon to describe places with two robots, each with a uniquely grounded RatSLAM representation of space.

4. Philosophical and theoretical considerations

As brain-based and neuromorphic robots become more sophisticated, the possibility of truly intelligent machines is becoming a reality. Rather than programming in all the knowledge a system needs to operate, scientists are looking to child development for inspiration in creating intelligent robots. Learning algorithms based on the sensorimotor space and interactions with the environment may allow robots to develop body plans and fluid movements, as well as serve as a means to study our own development [10]. Minoru Asada of Osaka University recently presented a framework for cognitive developmental robots that focuses on the mirror neuron system for social cognitive development and the development of a sense of self and others [11].

As an alternative to the developmental approach, Wagatsuma of the Kyushu Institute of Technology has turned to dynamical systems to build neuromorphic robots. Brain oscillations and neural pattern generators are prevalent in the vertebrate brain. Wagatsuma uses a synthetic approach, with embodied systems that emulate the brain's oscillatory dynamics, to explore a phase coding scheme between the amygdala, hippocampus, and prefrontal cortex [12]. Such dynamic patterns are thought to contribute to cognitive functions such as motor coordination, episodic memory, and consciousness.

It could be said that the ultimate goal of autonomous robotics is machine consciousness. A group at The Neurosciences Institute, which is led by Nobel laureate Gerald Edelman, has been studying consciousness for a number of years [13]. Based on their prior work with brain-based devices, they recently presented a case for how to construct a conscious artifact, and how to test if the artifact is indeed conscious [14].

5. Conclusion

We feel strongly that the brain-based and neuromorphic approach will transform the field of autonomous robots to the point where we will have robots in our society that have the adaptability and intelligence that we attribute to biological systems. We believe that neuromorphic and brain-based robotics will provide the groundwork for the development of intelligent machines, contribute to our understanding of the brain and mind, as well as how the nervous system gives rise to complex behavior. Neuromorphic and brain-based robotics is an exciting field of research that has a growing community of researchers with a wide range of multidisciplinary talents and backgrounds.

If and when roboticists are able to create a truly intelligent and sentient machine, there are philosophical and ethical issues to consider. Bekey from the University of Southern California and his colleagues Lin and Abney from California Polytechnic State University have been studying the ethical implications of intelligent robots and the urgency of this issue [15]. Isaac Asimov's three laws of robotics fail when applied to current military, healthcare, and other social robots. They propose a hybrid approach toward achieving robot morality, in which robots learn from experience how best to fulfill its roles, as well as know that certain roles are morally mandated for it, or are morally illegitimate and hence morally forbidden.

The fact that *Neuromorphic and Brain-based Robotics* covers such a wide range of topics shows how unexplored this young field is at the present time. These intelligent, brainy robots of the future will one day, very soon, be interacting and cooperating with human society. We strongly believe this research approach will advance science and society in positive and prosperous ways that we can only now imagine.

[1] J. L. Krichmar and H. Wagatsuma, Eds., *Neuromorphic and Brain-Based Robots*. Cambridge University Press, 2011.

[2] W. Grey Walter, *The living brain*, 2nd ed. London: Penguin, 1953.

[3] V. Braitenberg, *Vehicles: Experiments in Synthetic Psychology*. Cambridge: MIT Press, 1986.

[4] R. Pfeifer and J. Bongard, *How the Body Shapes the Way We Think: A New View of Intelligence*. Cambridge: MIT Press, 2007.

[5] K. Hosoda, "Robust haptic recognition by anthropomorphic robot hand," in *Neuromorphic and Brain-Based Robots*, J. L. Krichmar and H. Wagatsuma, Eds., ed: Cambridge University Press, 2011, pp. 11-22.

[6] B. Mitchinson*, et al.*, "Biomimetic robots as scientific models: a view from the whisker tip," in *Neuromorphic and Brain-Based Robots*, J. L. Krichmar and H. Wagatsuma, Eds., ed: Cambridge University Press, 2011, pp. 23-57.

[7] B. R. Cox and J. L. Krichmar, "Neuromodulation as a Robot Controller: A Brain Inspired Design Strategy for Controlling Autonomous Robots," *IEEE Robotics & Automation Magazine,* vol. 16, pp. 72-80, 2009.

[8] J. L. Krichmar, "The Neuromodulatory System – A Framework for Survival and Adaptive Behavior in a Challenging World," *Adaptive Behavior,* vol. 16, pp. 385-399, 2008.

[9] G. Wyeth*, et al.*, "The RatSLAM project: robot spatial navigation," in *Neuromorphic and Brain-Based Robots*, J. L. Krichmar and H. Wagatsuma, Eds., ed: Cambridge University Press, 2011, pp. 87-108.

[10] F. Kaplan and P. Oudeyer, "From hardware and software to kernels and envelopes: a concept shift for robotics, developmental psychology and brain sciences," in *Neuromorphic and Brain-Based Robots*, J. L. Krichmar and H. Wagatsuma, Eds., ed: Cambridge University Press, 2011, pp. 217-250.

[11] M. Asada, "Can cognitive developmental robotics cause a paradigm shift?," in *Neuromorphic and Brain-Based Robots*, J. L. Krichmar and H. Wagatsuma, Eds., ed: Cambridge University Press, 2011, pp. 251-273.

[12] H. Wagatsuma, "A look at the hidden side of situated cognition: a robotic study of brain-oscillation-based dynamics of instantaneous, episodic, and conscious memories," in *Neuromorphic and Brain-Based Robots*, J. L. Krichmar and H. Wagatsuma, Eds., ed: Cambridge University Press, 2011, pp. 274-302.

[13] G. M. Edelman, "Naturalizing consciousness: a theoretical framework," *Proc Natl Acad Sci U S A*, vol. 100, pp. 5520-4, Apr 29 2003.

[14] J. G. Fleischer*, et al.*, "The case for using brain-based devices to study consciousness," in *Neuromorphic and Brain-Based Robots*, J. L. Krichmar and H. Wagatsuma, Eds., ed: Cambridge University Press, 2011, pp. 303-319.

[15] G. A. Bekey*, et al.*, "Ethical implications of intelligent robots," in *Neuromorphic and Brain-Based Robots*, J. L. Krichmar and H. Wagatsuma, Eds., ed: Cambridge University Press, 2011, pp. 323-344.

Biologically Inspired Cognitive Architectures 2011
A.V. Samsonovich and K.R. Jóhannsdóttir (Eds.)
IOS Press, 2011
© 2011 The authors and IOS Press. All rights reserved.
doi:10.3233/978-1-60750-959-2-215

Development of a robot
that cognizes and learns unknown events

Kyohei KUSHIRO [a] and Junichi TAKENO [b,1]
Robot Science Laboratory, Computer Science, Meiji University,
1-1-1Higashimita, Tama-ku, Kawasaki-shi, Kanagawa 214-8571 Japan
[a] *k.kushiro1120@gmail.com*
[b] *juntakeno@gmail.com*

Abstract. The present paper proposes a system to identify and learn about unknown events using the Module of Nerves for Advanced Dynamics (MoNAD) system. This system identifies unknown events using the difference in MoNAD convergence velocities between known and unknown events. The system was mounted on a robot and color identification tests were conducted to evaluate the feasibility of the system. In experiments, the robot autonomously identified unknown events, and automatically captured them as new information by itself. The present paper introduces how the robot proactively identifies unknown events, and captures them as new information. The system presents a solution to the problem of "Why do humans always learn new events and adapt to them?"

Keywords. Consciousness, robot, unknown, learning

Introduction

Where does human consciousness come from? We take it for granted that humans have a sense of self, and that they can think and learn. These are very high-level human activities. No one has ever successfully described how humans acquired the ability to do such high-level activities. Humans do not know why their own behavior and thoughts are born. The authors challenge these questions from the perspective of robotics, and believe that solutions can thus be found. Specifically, we reproduce the functions of human consciousness in a robot to analyze them objectively.

Human consciousness is a major theme in various fields of study. Based on two representative human consciousness studies of mirror neurons [1] and mimesis theory [2], the authors came to the conclusion that consciousness is deeply related to the imitation behavior of humans. We then defined consciousness in this way: "consistency of cognition and behavior generates consciousness." Based on this idea, we have proposed a module of a consciousness system called a MoNAD[3].

This present paper introduces our new system that cognizes and learns unknown information. Our model will be helpful in bringing artificial human consciousness closer to actual human consciousness.

---

[1] Corresponding Author.

1. Conscious System

The conscious system proposed in this paper consists of multiple MoNADs. Using this conscious system, part of the function of human consciousness is reproduced in a robot.

1.1. MoNAD

The Module of Nerves for Advanced Dynamics, or MoNAD, is a computational model consisting of recurrent neural networks developed by the authors. It has been devised based on our definition of consciousness, which is that "consistency of cognition and behavior generates consciousness." MoNADs are the modules that make up our conscious system. We call them "conscious modules."[4]

1.2. Perceiving the Unknown to Learn

Humans are able to determine that something unknown to them is "unknown." Humans are also able to learn the "unknown information" using language, feelings and action. Humans can learn proactively just because they have the function to discern what is unknown to them. If humans had no function to discriminate between the known and the unknown, they would have no way to consciously differentiate between the known and the unknown. If we could not consciously differentiate between the known and unknown, we would not know what to learn even if we wanted to learn proactively.

Humans fear the unknown. They can avoid hazards associated with the unknown by instinct. This is because unknown information is hard to cope with and could possibly endanger our life. We therefore define that encounter with the unknown as basically a state of unpleasantness. However, humans are also interested in unknown incidents and feel some excitement in such situations. This is because our feelings change from unpleasant to pleasant as we learn about a basically unpleasant unknown incident until it eventually becomes known to us. This is an empirical reflection of the fact that in the course of their evolution, humans have enhanced their possibility for survival by increasing their amount of known information, that is, by learning.

With the above background, the authors believe that the function of humans to determine and learn what is unknown is important and should be built into a robot to reproduce consciousness in the robot. Based on this thinking, we created this function in the MoNAD-based conscious system to reproduce human consciousness at a higher level.

1.3. Understanding the Unknown in the Conscious System

To differentiate between the known and the unknown, we use the differential convergence speed in the MoNADs. Learned or known information converges quickly whereas unknown information converges slowly.

We compare the values of BL and RL.[4] BL refers to the behavioral representation, i.e., the next expected behavior prepared by the MoNAD. RL is the cognitive representation that shows the current condition of the MoNAD's cognition. An RL error with BL is calculated each time RL is output from the MoNAD. The rise of an error, which is the difference between the current error and the error calculated with the previous input, is calculated to determine the convergence speed. When the rise of an error exceeds a certain value, the system determines that the information is known. Conversely, if the rise of an error approaches zero without reaching the specified level or fails to converge after several trials, the information is determined to be unknown. This method of differentiation between the known and the unknown using changes in convergent values was actually used in one of our past studies [3]. The present study differs from this past method in that the quantitative change in the value of the rise of an error is considered.

A scheme to check changes in information is required to recognize the unknown. In our present conscious system, a change in information is determined when the calculated value of the rise of an error is negative.

1.4. Learning the Unknown

The conscious system introduced in this present paper includes a scheme to learn unknown information. After unknown information is detected as described above, the relevant information is learned in the MoNAD as additional information to be captured. Learning here means that the unknown information is converted into information which the MoNAD acknowledges to be known in the next encounter and thereafter. The other objective of learning is to relate the newly learned information to a certain specified behavior, i.e., the behavior to be performed upon encountering the same information the next time. Behavior here means a program which is prepared beforehand. Let us explain this learning procedure using a simple story. Assume a person seeing an apple for the first time. We tell him, "This is an apple." He then connects the word "apple" with "an edible fruit that is red, round, and sweet."

The specific learning procedure is described below. For an empty MoNAD without orientation, we apply back propagation using previously unknown input information as supervised data. The system learns cognition and the corresponding behavior in the MoNAD. This point will be described in some detail later.

1.5. General Description of the Conscious System

The conscious system (Figure 1) comprises the reason, emotion-and-feeling, and association systems. Each system is made up of multiple MoNADs. The reason system accepts external inputs as well as behavior representations as internal information. It outputs behaviors and the relevant cognitive representations externally. The reason system includes several empty MoNADs ready for learning unknown information. The emotion-and-feeling system accepts cognitive representations from the reason system and outputs feeling representations. Two feelings available in the present conscious system are pleasant and unpleasant. Generally, it is possible for consciousness to accept external inputs directly at the emotion-and-feelings system and output the relevant representations but this route is not used in our present study. The association system connects the reason system and the emotion-and-feeling system.

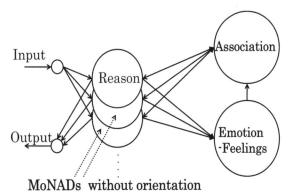

MoNADs without orientation

Figure 1. Overview of the conscious system

Figure 2. Robot experiments

The flow of cognition of the unknown in this present study is described below. The reason system processes external inputs. Empty MoNADs do not function until they learn and are oriented accordingly. The reason system outputs RL of cognitive representations and calculates the relevant rise of errors. This data is transmitted to the emotion-and-feeling system. The representation of feelings changes to pleasant if the rise of an error is equal to or exceeds a certain value or a negative value. The representation becomes unpleasant when the error rise is less than a certain value and the error approaches zero. Even when information is input, the internal state will gradually change to unpleasant when the input information is not determined to be known. This gradual change to unpleasant is an internal representation that eventually gives rise to cognition of the unknown.

The flow of learning of the unknown is described below. The representation of an unpleasant feeling, firing at the emotion-and-feeling system, is transferred to the association system, which then signals an empty MoNAD to learn. This appointed MoNAD starts learning the current external inputs. The "certain specified behavior" mentioned above refers to a behavior pre-allocated to each of the empty MoNADs. A new incident is learned in each empty MoNAD. The information that is learned in an empty MoNAD is the information that failed to fire the reason system, i.e., information that was not cognized in the reason system. The newly learned information therefore does not interfere with previously obtained information.

New information becomes an integral part of the system through the procedure described below. The cognitive representation RL is transferred from the reason system to the association system, where the RL is integrated with the RL of a MoNAD that has newly learned information (i.e., when an empty MoNAD has learned unknown information) and representation of pleasant and unpleasant from the emotion-and-feeling system. The resultant information is fed back to the reason system as well as to the BL of the MoNAD that newly learned. Empty MoNADs that do not learn by themselves are not linked to the association system.

2. Robot Experiments

To verify the capabilities of our conscious system as described above, we conducted experiments using an actual robot. The conscious system was programmed in the C language to perform color tests using a commercially available *e-puck* small robot. The robot reads RGB components using a built-in camera sensor and determines the color of an object. The motor-driven robot moves forward, stops, backs up, and turns. The robot has LEDs in 5 different colors to externally show its condition. The blue LED goes on when the robot cognizes known information. The red LED lights up to express an unpleasant feeling. The other LED colors are used to express the internal representation of the robot.

The experiments were designed to assess the validity of the conscious system by color identification. Before starting the experiment, the system learns to recognize red, green, and blue colors. In the experiment, we show some other color (purple, for example) to see if the robot cognizes the color as an unknown and learns it. We further check whether the robot has cognized the newly learned color when it is shown again and performs the assigned behavior.

The color information to be input into the conscious system is expressed as 9-bit data according to the intensity of the RGB components of the color captured by the camera sensor of the *e-puck* robot (see Table 1). Purple and yellow are expressed by a mixture of R, G and B. Before the experiments are started, the reason system learns the expression of the brightest colors of red, green, and blue using back propagation. The robot also learns beforehand to stop, move forward, and back up upon seeing red, green, and blue, respectively. The other behavior programs are prepared for the robot to learn and run when it is shown unknown colors: turn left 45 and 90 degrees, and so on. The LED assignment is shown in Figure 3. The meanings of the LEDs are as follows. B: Have cognized; G: I feel pleasant; T: Detected color change; R: I feel unpleasant; and O: Started learning.

Table 1. Color representation method

	Red	Green	Blue		Purple	Yellow
Bright	000111000	111000000	000000111		000111111	111111000
↕	000011000	011000000	000000011			
Pale	000001000	001000000	000000001			

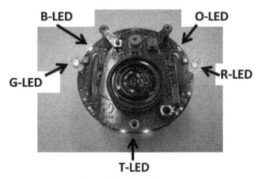

Figure 3. LED assignment .

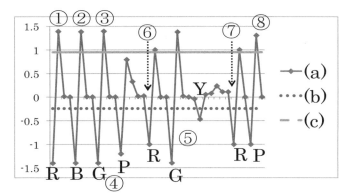

Figure 4. Result of experiments. (R: red; B: blue, G: green, P: purple; Y: yellow)

3. Conclusions

In the experiments, the robot activated the green LED (G-LED; indicating a pleasant feeling) upon seeing known information (red, green, and blue color, which it had learned before the start of the experiments). The blue LED (B-LED) also lighted up to show that the robot cognized that the shown colors were known. When unknown information (purple, yellow colors, and · · ets.) was input, the red LED (R-LED) for an unpleasant feeling lighted up and at the same time the orange LED (O-LED) lighted up indicating that the learning process was in progress. This confirmed that the robot cognized the unknown information, and learned it. We then showed the same new color again, and the robot determined that it was already known and performed the behavior specified for that color. The result of the experiments is shown in Figure 4.

The vertical axis of the graph represents rise of error (Eu) and the horizontal axis represents time. The processing time consumed between the input of information into the conscious system and the relevant output of recognition and the behavior is counted as unity ①. This process is called the cognition-behavior cycle. Line (a) in the graph represents changes in the value of Eu, which is calculated in the equation below (1).

$$Eu = \{BL(t0) - RL(t0)\}^2 - \{BL(t1) - RL(t1)\}^2 \qquad (1)$$

(where t0 is the previous time and t1 is the present time.)

Line (b) is the boundary for determining if the information (i.e., color in our present experiments) at the present time is the same as that at the previous time or not. The robot detects that the information given has changed when the value of Eu is below this line. Line (c) is the boundary for determining if the information is known or not. The robot detects that the color shown is known when the value of Eu exceeds this line. At times ⑥ and ⑦ in the figure, the robot feels unpleasant, and starts the learning process, i.e., when the R- and O-LEDs light up.

In the experiment, the value of Eu for the learned colors (red, green, and blue) exceeds the boundary (c), so we know that these colors are known to the robot [①, ②, and ③ in Figure 4]. When the robot was shown purple after seeing green [near ④], the value of Eu dropped below the boundary (b), indicating that the robot recognized the change in information. The value of Eu then converges without ever reaching the boundary (c).

The conscious system determined that purple was unknown information and started the learning process [at time ⑥]. When shown yellow after green [near time ⑤], the robot failed to cognize the change in colors, and thought the new color to be the same as before. In the next moment, however, the robot noticed the difference. The value of Eu did not exceed the boundary of the known (c), i.e., the robot could not identify the color. This condition of inability to determine the color continued for some time until the robot finally determined that the present information was unknown, and the emotion-and-feelings system of the robot represented an unpleasant feeling at time ⑦. The robot could not immediately determine it was a different color when yellow was shown because the information pattern of green, shown immediately before, was overlapping with that of yellow in many places (input pattern 000111000 for green and 111111000 for yellow). These experiments have shown that our conscious system can identify unknown information regardless of similarity of input patterns, i.e. from green to purple, and from green to yellow.

Figure 4 further shows that the robot cognizes what was unknown and learned in the next time and thereafter correctly [near time ⑧]. When purple was first shown at about time ④, the color was unknown to the robot. When the same color purple was shown a second time at about time ⑧, the value of Eu exceeded the boundary of known (c), indicating that purple is already a known color. We also confirmed that the robot performed the action specified for purple (a 45-degree turn). This indicates that the robot succeeded in learning the unknown color purple proactively and in performing the specified action.

The above results of our experiments show that we have successfully proposed a model of a conscious system for cognizing and learning the unknown for a robot.

References

[1] V. Gallese, L. Fadiga, L. Fogassi, and R. Rizzolatti, Action recognition in the premotor cortex, *Brain* **119** (1996), 3-368.
[2] M. Donald, *Origins of the Modern Mind*, Harvard University Press, Cambridge, 1991.
[3] S. Akimoto and J. Takeno, A Study of a Conscious Robot - An Attempt to Perceive the Unknown, *ICAART* **1** (2010), 498-501.
[4] J. Takeno and IRG, MoNAD structure and self-awareness, *Biologically Inspired Cognitive Architectures (BICA2011)*, Arlington, USA, Printing now.

Biologically Inspired Cognitive Architectures 2011
A.V. Samsonovich and K.R. Jóhannsdóttir (Eds.)
IOS Press, 2011
© 2011 The authors and IOS Press. All rights reserved.
doi:10.3233/978-1-60750-959-2-222

Computational Hypothesis for Maturing Out of Addiction and Mindfulness-Based Cognitive Techniques

Yariv Z. LEVY[a,1], Dino LEVY[b], and Jerrold S. MEYER[c]

[a] *Department of Computer Science, University of Massachusetts Amherst*
[b] *Center for Neural Science, New York University*
[c] *Department of Psychology, University of Massachusetts Amherst*

Abstract. Use and misuse of addictive substances has been an ongoing phenomenon from early civilizations to the present. Experimental observations endorse the implication of a cognitive component during the addictive course. The present investigation proposes a learning mechanism affecting the cognitive level of a multiscale model of addiction. Simulations account for plausible initiations of natural recoveries through non-traditional techniques, such as meditation. This framework suggests that such plasticity mechanism within the cognitive substrate of an addict may be necessary in order for a maturing out experience to begin and possibly endure over time.

Keywords. Computational Model, Multiscale, Dynamical System, Drug Addiction, Natural Recovery, Cognitive Learning

Introduction

While addiction has been widely regarded as detrimental and even criminal, popular beliefs have converged to consider addiction as a "bio-psycho-social-spiritual disorder" [1]. Through the 1990s, the predominant standpoint to describe the strong desire to use a drug was based on the psychological theory of classical conditioning. Increasing positive association between drug intakes and gratification was postulated as the main aspect inducing the intensification of drug intakes. In 1990, Tiffany expanded on this view by introducing a cognitive process model for addiction, and further characterized the relationship between drug use and craving [2]. His model proposes that a longtime addict will undergo a drug intake not because of the strong association between drug intake and consequent feeling, but as a result of a mindless and automatic process triggered by an external event (e.g., the meeting with a drug supplier). In this model, craving experiences arise when the automatic response to the external event fails (e.g., the drug supplier is not available), and the addict requires cognitive efforts to overcome the situation [3]. Neuroscientific evidence introduced a decade later suggests that drug intoxication correlates, in addition to neural activities in the limbic system, with

---

[1] Corresponding Author.
The authors acknowledge valuable discussions with Scott Niekum, Hava T. Siegelmann, and Bertrand Steiner. We thank the anonymous reviewers for their helpful and insightful comments.

structures in the prefrontal cortex, which further supports Tiffany's model. In 2002, Goldstein and Volkow introduced the "impaired response inhibition and salience attribution" view of addiction to account for the addict's archetypal progression (intoxication, craving, compulsive intakes, withdrawal, and again intoxication) [4]. Two processes compose this framework: one is a progressive transition from deliberate to automatic drug-related behaviors, and the other is an increased predisposition for immediate rewards, even if possibly harmful in a longer term. The prefrontal cortex, pivotal to high-level cognitive functions is "likely to play an important role in the cognitive behavioral and emotional changes that perpetuate drug self-administration" [4].

Craving is a major component leading to relapse, and understanding how to rehabilitate an addict is an important objective in addiction studies. The present investigation presents a multiscale formal model of addiction, which considers recovery and emulates the theories discussed above. This framework evaluates a computational hypothesis on how cognition may operate as a mediator between behavior and neural activity, while accounting for observations known as natural recoveries. The results support the thesis for which a simple computational learning mechanism within the cognitive substrate could significantly impact the success of a recovery process.

1. A Multiscale Model of Addiction

Formal models of addiction encompass epidemiological models [5,6], economic models [7,8], pharmacological models [9-11], abstract models of dopaminergic functions [12-14], and the more recently proposed systemic models [15,16]. In this paper, a systemic model is advanced, as shown in Figure 1, which aims to characterize the comportment of a human being through its tendency of drug-seeking behavior.

This computational framework was defined and validated [17], its dynamics and sensitivity were analyzed [18, 19], and its recovery scale initiated [20].

The model shown in Figure 1 comprises neuropsychological, recovery, cognitive, and behavioral elements. The neuropsychological scale incorporates internal and external processes describing the neural ongoing activity. Internal processes include the level of negative consequences such as poor health or social relations $P(t)$, the level of negative emotional state $S(t)$, the level of dopamine craving $D(t)$, and the saliency of drug-associated cues $Q(t)$. The external processes characterize sudden experiences that, when activated, instantly influence the subject's neural activity. These are: drug-associated cues $A_Q(t)$, that may be triggered by an event such as visiting a "drug buddy"; painful traumas $A_P(t)$, that may cause an addict to stop taking drugs immediately for a period of time; strong stressful episodes $A_S(t)$, that may lead a former addict into immediate drug-use; and drug priming $A_D(t)$ such as social drinking, that may bring the virtual subject into drug-use again. The output of the model $G(t)$, by way of the cognitive scale, depends on both internal and external processes. The process $G(t)$ defines a feedback loop to the neuropsychological scale. The behavioral scale includes the model's output $G(t)$, which is a qualitative evaluation of a virtual subject's tendency for drug-seeking, and arises from the antagonism between inhibitory and compulsory elements. Negative values of $G(t)$ correspond to maladaptive behavior, whereas positive ones accounts for healthy behavior. For the sake of clarity, the processes of inhibition and compulsion are considered constants even though explicit time dependencies of these processes were previously defined [17].

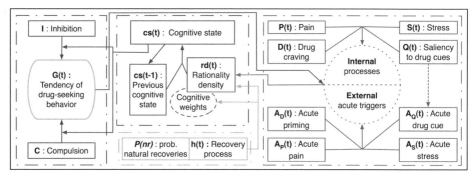

Figure 1. Diagram of the computational model, where the output of the model G(t) represents the tendency for drug-seeking behavior. The levels of observations represented include the neuropsychological scale in green, the recovery scale in orange, the cognitive scale in red, and the behavioral scale in blue.

The cognitive scale complies with the definition in [21]: "A system is cognitive if and only if sensory inputs serve to trigger actions in a specific way, so as to satisfy a viability constraint." This scale is established as a mediator between low and high level of behavioral control. In a perceptron-like architecture, the neuropsychological processes are weighted and integrated to define the degree of rationality rd(t), which drives the virtual subject's cognitive state cs(t) toward a more inhibited or a more compulsive behavior. The recovery scale is a computational hypothesis which relies on the definition of natural recovery, for which the addict ceases using the drug "without the help of treatment intervention" [22], suggesting a recovery process solely impacting the cognitive scale (no pharmacological nor behavioral interventions). The recovery process is designated as a sudden cognitive change which, when induced, makes achievable a drug abstinence period that may or may not endure. The recovery scale affects the virtual subject's cognitive state by direct intervention on its rationality estimation, and by modulating the weights of internal and external processes. In the next section are presented the formal descriptions of the cognitive and recovery scales. Computational definitions of the neuropsychological and behavioral scales are reported in [17].

2. Methods

This section presents the details of the cognitive and recovery scales, as well as the data used to emulate instances of the recovery process.

The rationality density rd(t) is defined as a weighted sum of the neuropsychological and recovery processes:

$$rd(t) = \sum \omega_i(t) \cdot \Phi_i(t) \quad , \quad \Phi_i = \{S, P, D, A_S, A_P, A_D, A_Q, h\} \tag{1}$$

The weights ω_i for the processes P(t) and A_P(t) are in $\mathbb{R}^+$, whereas the other weights are in $\mathbb{R}$. This rationality estimate drives the cognitive state cs(t) of the virtual subject:

$$cs(t) = \frac{1}{2}\tanh(\alpha \cdot cs(t-1) + \beta \cdot rd(t) + \gamma) + \frac{1}{2} \tag{2}$$

Values of α, β, and γ are constants and their sensitivity is discussed in [19].

The recovery process h(t) is equal to a constant value h_0 while triggered or active. This process is active for a certain time Θ(t), which increases for consecutive instances of h(t):

$$h(t) = \begin{cases} h_0 & if\{p > P(nr) \mid t_h \in [1,\Theta(t)]\} \\ 0 & else \end{cases} \quad (3)$$

$$\Theta(t) = \begin{cases} \Theta(t) + \delta_i & if\{h(t) = triggered\} \\ \Theta(t-1) & if\{h(t) = active\} \\ \max(0, \Theta(t) - \delta_d) & if\{h(t) = 0\} \end{cases} \quad (4)$$

The probability P(nr) defines the possibility of a natural recovery and is discussed in the next subsection. The constants δ_i and δ_d are in $\mathbb{N}$, and t_h is a time step counter reset to 1 at every recovery instance.

When a recovery process arises, it influences rd(t) through two mechanisms. On the one hand, h(t) has a direct effect on rd(t) as defined in Equation 1. On the other hand, the cognitive weights ω_i of the processes P(t), S(t), and D(t) provisionally change their values according to the relationship:

$$\omega_i(t) = \begin{cases} \kappa_i + \Delta_{\kappa i} & if\{h(t) = h_0\} \\ \kappa_i & else \end{cases} \quad (5)$$

where $\Delta_{\kappa i}$ is in $\mathbb{R}^-$ for S(t) and D(t), and in $\mathbb{R}^+$ for P(t).

At the last active time step of a recovery process h(t), the temporary effect on ω_i of processes P(t), S(t), and D(t) can become permanent with arbitrary probability θ_i:

$$\kappa_i(t) = \begin{cases} \kappa_i + \Delta_{\kappa i} & if\{t = \Theta(t)\} \quad and\{p > \theta_i\} \\ \kappa_i & else \end{cases} \quad (6)$$

2.1. Probability of a recovery process P(nr)

In 1962, Charles Winick popularized the phenomenon of maturing out of narcotics addiction, revealing cases where regular heroin and synthetic opiate abusers ceased using the substance without any psychological or pharmacological treatment [23]. In 1980, Maddux and Desmond discussed the possible overestimation of Winik's statistics, and proposed further data to increase the accuracy of the study [24]. Maddux and Desmond confirmed that the trends of age distribution for withdrawal initiations were consistent in both studies, and argued the possible overestimation due to the disregard of cessation onset rates in the base addict population.

In the present investigation, data reported in [23] and [24] are combined to quantify the likelihood of a narcotic addict to undergo a "maturing out" experience. Winick based his investigation on the number of addicts reported to the Federal Bureau of Narcotics in 1955 that were not reported again during a five-year period [23]. As reported in Table 1, the probability for an addict to experience a maturing out experience is inferred (fourth column in Table 1). This probability is scaled using the subsequent results by Maddux and Desmond, which report the annual rates of abstinence onset in the base population [24]. For simplification purposes, the age category "All ages" in [24] is considered to describe the age range from 0 to 19 years old, and the category "40-49" to additionally include ages exceeding 49 years old. The scaled cumulative distribution function for a maturing out event to arise can be approximated in terms of the age in years T of a virtual subject as:

$$P(nr) = \frac{0.02359}{1 + e^{-0.154 \cdot T + 5.037}} \tag{7}$$

Table 1. Data about the US narcotics users population in 1955 and the related former addicts population at the end of 1959 are used to calculate the cumulative distribution function (CDF) describing the occurrences of maturing out from narcotics addiction, which is subsequently scaled in accordance to new observations about the onset age of abstinence in the base population. AP = Number of active addicts in total addict population; FS = Number of former addicts in sample; AOA = Annual onsets of abstinence per 1000. Columns AP, FS, and AOA are reproduced from [23,24] with permission of the United Nations Office On Drugs and Crime (UNODC).

Age	AP	FS	CDF P(FS|AP)	AOA	CDF P(FS|AP) * AOA
< 20	1743 (3.8%)	13 (0.2%)	0.75%	23	0.17‰
20-30	24343 (53.6%)	2820 (39.0%)	12.33%	21	2.59‰
30-40	14058 (31.0%)	2857 (39.5%)	32.65%	22	7.18‰
> 40	5247 (11.6%)	1544 (21.3%)	62.08%	38	23.59‰

3. Results: plausible scenarios of drug-seeking and maturing out

Two scenarios are presented of a virtual subject denoted as B.T, who had a healthy mental and physical development and became an addict in her early adulthood. In the first set of simulations, the weights ω_i of the processes P(t), S(t), and D(t) can only change their values accordingly to Equation 5, whereas in the second set of simulations also Equation 6 applies. The graphs reported in this section represent the mean of 100 simulations of 600 time steps (~25 days) each and their corresponding standard errors of the mean (SEM) for B.T. at the age of 35.

3.1. Direct Influence of the Recovery Process h(t)

According to Equation (7), a 35 year old virtual subject can be exposed to at most 5 recovery processes within the year. Figure 2 shows the graphs corresponding to the processes defining B.T.'s profile. The recovery process h(t) has a direct effect solely on her cognitive scale. In other words, the weights ω_i of the processes P(t), S(t), and D(t), used to estimate the cognitive state, can only temporarily change their values, during an active process h(t), but are not subject to any permanent alteration. There are 4 recovery processes that occur during these simulations, at t={120, 200, 210, 420}, which correspond to an immediate and strong change in the model's output G(t). For a limited time, B.T. expresses a healthy behavior because of the new value of the weights ω_i. During this period, the neuropsychological processes of B.T. adapt their computational definitions, since they rely on the model's output G(t), but this sudden change doesn't last for a sufficient time for B.T. to acquire a permanent healthy

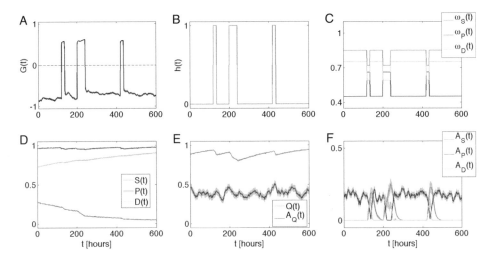

Figure 2. Mean and SEM for 100 simulations of B.T.'s profile at 35 years old, 600 time steps long (25 days) under the direct effect of h(t) at t={120, 200, 210, 420}. (A) The drug-seeking behavior G(t) is mostly negative (maladaptive behavior) and the effect of the recovery process h(t) is strong enough to temporarily change it into positive (healthy behavior). (B) The recovery process h(t) is activated 4 times. (C) The cognitive weights ω_i change value when h(t) is active. (D) The internal processes S(t), P(t), and D(t) change behavior when h(t) is active. (E) The internal process Q(t) and the its related external process AQ(t) are influenced by h(t). (F) The external processes A_S(t), A_P(t), and A_D(t). The processes A_S(t) and A_D(t) occur only when G(t)>0, that in this scenario also corresponds to an active h(t).

behavior, and her maladaptive behavior regains predominance when the active effect of h(t) ceases.

3.2. Direct and Potentially Long-Term Influences of the Recovery Process h(t)

In the previous scenario, the direct effect of the recovery process by itself is not durable enough for the whole system to acquire the necessary dynamic allowing B.T. to start a potentially long-lasting period of abstinence. The non-monotonic property of this model [18] computationally grants B.T. with a possible lifelong rehabilitation, but the values of the constants defining the model that are necessary to achieve such a condition will correspond to a situation beyond biological plausibility (e.g., an event h(t) lasting several months). In the simulations presented in Figure 3, the weights ω_i of the processes P(t), S(t), and D(t), can permanently change their values once the active effect of h(t) ceases. After completing the 3rd recovery process, B.T. expresses a fragile healthy behavior (positive G(t) values), which is further consolidated by the 4th recovery process. This simulation exemplifies a plausible trajectory of an addict that starts an abstinence period within a period of about one month, as a result of 4 long-lasting recovery events, as for example could correspond to instances of non-traditional healing techniques to help overcoming addiction. Instances of these techniques were discussed in the late 1970s (e.g. meditation, faith healing, holistic medicine, etc.) [25], and more recently were at the center of two issues of the journal serving the Association for Medical Education and Research in Substance Abuse (e.g. "attentional control", Mindfulness-Based Cognitive Therapy, etc.) [26,27].

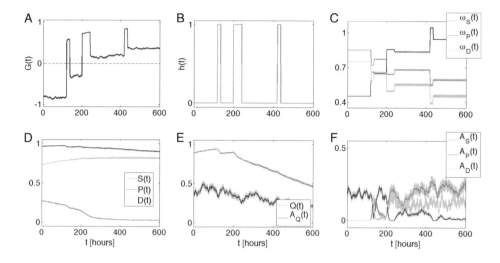

Figure 3. Mean and SEM for 100 simulations of B.T.'s profile at 35 years old, 600 time steps long (25 days) under the effect of h(t) at t={120, 200, 210, 420}. (A) The drug-seeking behavior G(t) starts as negative (maladaptive behavior) and the effect of the recovery process h(t) allows its transition into positive values (healthy behavior). (B) The recovery process h(t) is activated 4 times. (C) The cognitive weights ω_i change value when h(t) is active and are subject to a permanent change when an h(t) event becomes inoperative. (D) The internal processes S(t), P(t), and D(t) change behavior when G(t) transition to positive values. (E) The internal process Q(t) and the its related external process AQ(t) are influenced by h(t) and the positive value of G(t). (F) The external processes $A_S(t)$, $A_P(t)$, and $A_D(t)$.

4. Analysis: a cognitive learning mechanism to enable maturing out

The parameter γ in Equation 2 significantly influences the output of the model and its value can be calculated to mathematically ensure that the virtual subject has no cognitive preference toward a particular behavior [19]. Comparisons of simulations defined by an arbitrary γ with simulations using the unbiased γ, defined in [19], are presented in Figure 4. The value of γ is the same for simulations presented in Figures 2, 3, and the ones in Figure 4 labeled as "B.T.'s original γ". All other parameters are equivalent for all simulations. In Figures 4A and D there are no recovery processes h(t); in Figures 4B and E only direct influences of h(t) are considered; and in Figures 4C and F both Equations 5 and 6 apply.

The baseline simulations presented in Figures 4A and D, which don't include any recovery occurrences, show the cognitive predilection of B.T. toward a healthier behavior. B.T.'s original portrayal expresses a less accentuated likelihood of maladaptive behavior than its correspondent cognitively unbiased description. The computed behaviors accounting solely the direct influence of the recovery process h(t), compared in Figures 4B and E, describe a situation in which B.T. successfully abstains from drugs use for a limited time, but the correspondent cognitively unbiased profile constantly preserves a maladaptive behavior. The behavioral and neuropsychological characteristics of the subject make this abstinence difficult to preserve for B.T.'s original profile, and establish a challenging environment for her unbiased profile to reach a healthy behavior. The model's outcomes presented in Figures 4C and F compare the original and unbiased profiles of B.T. when both the direct and the potentially long-term influences of the recovery process h(t) are active. Both cases tend

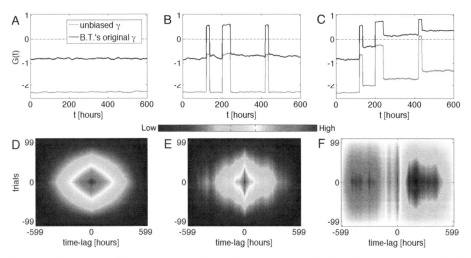

Figure 4. Comparison of simulations using the original and the cognitively unbiased values of γ. On the upper part are represented means and SEMs of the model's output G(t) for 100 simulations of 600 time steps (25 days) each. On the bottom part are plotted the cross-correlations matrices comparing B.T.'s original profiles with its unbiased profile. In (A, D) the recovery process h(t) is not active; in (B, E) h(t) is active but can not induce a permanent change of the cognitive weights; and in (C, F) h(t) is active and can potentially initiate a long-lasting period of abstinence by permanently modifying the cognitive weights values.

towards a healthier behavior, which is reached and maintained by the original profile but is barely touched by the unbiased profile.

The 2-D cross-correlations provide an immediate look at the similarity between B.T.'s original profile and its correspondent cognitively unbiased *alter ego*, considering each simulation rather than the mean of several simulations. Without any recovery processes, the cross-correlation matrix has a smooth circular pattern (Figure 4D), which becomes distorted when only the local effect of the process h(t) is active (Figure 4E), and substantially changes the motif for simulations operating the cognitive learning described above (Figure 4F).

These results suggest that an addict may have the cognitive means to start an abstinence period which, depending on his or her neural substrate and natural surroundings, could persist over time.

5. Concluding Remarks

The fields of psychology and neuroscience provide us with a growing amount of evidence supporting the fundamental role of cognitive components in the course of an addict's life. A pivotal investigation demonstrates that cocaine craving is induced by neural correlates within the frontal cortex, rather than by the dopaminergic circuitry [28], and a recent review paper proposes the hypothesis for which "drug addiction involves a failure of the different subcomponents of the executive systems controlling key cognitive modules that process reward, pain, stress, emotion, habits, and decision-making" [29]. Heeding this belief, and supported by observations of natural recoveries, the framework presented aims to describe a simplistic computational scheme necessary to counteract such cognitive deficiency. Even though the neural correlates of an addict's limbic system have been modified compared to the brain of a healthy individual, it seems biologically plausible to consider neural changes in the prefrontal cortex to account, at least partially, for a balancing mechanism reconditioning the brain's functions towards a healthy state.

The present investigation proposes formal arguments to support the hypothesis of a cognitive learning mechanism, capable of influencing decision-making processes associated with drug abuse. The emulated abstinence onsets from drug abuse presented above are an initial attempt toward the localization of such a balancing mechanism. To advance this exploration, it could be interesting to emulate similar rehabilitation properties within a more elaborated biologically inspired cognitive architecture, as for example Leabra [30], Clarion [31], and GMU-BICA [32]. To further enhance psychological plausibility of the model presented in this paper, components studied in pathological gambling (stressors, cognitive distortions, ruminations, and distractions) [33] could be incorporated and explored.

The framework presented in this paper supports the view that mindfulness-based cognitive techniques could act as a catalyst for maturing out of addiction.

References

[1] J. Interlandi, What Addicts Need, *Newsweek* (2008), 36-42.
[2] S.T. Tiffany, A Cognitive Model of Drug Urges and Drug-Use Behavior: Role of Automatic and Nonautomatic Processes, *Psychol Rev* **97** (1990), 147-168.
[3] S.T. Tiffany, Cognitive Concepts of Craving, *Alcohol Res Health* **23** (1999), 215-224.
[4] R.Z. Goldstein, N.D. Volkow, Drug Addiction and Its Underlying Neurobiological Basis: Neuroimaging Evidence for the Involvement of the Frontal Cortex, *Am J Psychiatry* **159** (2002), 1642-1652.
[5] E. White, C. Comiskey, Heroin Epidemics, Treatment and ODE Modelling, *Math Biosci* **208** (2007), 312-324.
[6] O. Sharomi, A.B. Gumel, Curtailing Smoking Dynamics: a Mathematical Modeling Approach, *Appl Math Comput* **195** (2008), 475-499.
[7] G. Becker, K. Murphy, A Theory of Rational Addiction, *J Polit Economy* **96** (1988), 675-700.
[8] F.A. Sloan, Y. Wang, Economic Theory and Evidence on Smoking Behavior of Adults, *Addiction* **103** (2008), 1777-1785.
[9] V.L. Tsibulsky, A.B. Norman, Satiety Threshold: a Quantitative Model of Maintained Cocaine Self-administration, *Brain Res* **839** (1999), 85-93.
[10] G.M. Sizemore, T.J. Martin, Toward a Mathematical Description of Dose-effect Functions for Self-administered Drugs in Laboratory Animal Models, *Psychopharmacology (Berl)* **153** (2000), 57-66.
[11] S.H. Ahmed, G.F. Koob, Transition to Drug Addiction: a Negative Reinforcement Model Based on an Allostatic Decrease in Reward Function, *Psychopharmacology (Berl)* **180** (2005), 473-490.
[12] W. Schultz, P. Dayan, P.R. Montague, A Neural Substrate of Prediction and Reward, *Science* **275** (1997), 1593-1599.
[13] A.D. Redish, Addiction as a Computational Process Gone Awry, *Science* **306** (2004), 1944-1947.
[14] A. Dezfouli, P. Piray, M.M. Keramati, H. Ekhtiari, C. Lucas, A. Mokri, A Neurocomputational Model for Cocaine Addiction, *Neural Comput* **21** (2009), 2869-2893.
[15] B.S. Gutkin, S. Dehaene, J.P. Changeux, A Neurocomputational Hypothesis for Nicotine Addiction, *Proc Natl Acad Sci USA* **103** (2006), 1106-1111.
[16] F. Tretter, P. J. Gebicke-Haerter, M. Albus, U. an der Heiden, H. Schwegler, Systems Biology and Addiction, *Pharmacopsychiatry* **42** (2009), S11-S31.
[17] Y.Z. Levy*, D. Levy*, J.S. Meyer, H.T. Siegelmann, Drug Addiction: a Computational Multiscale Model Combining Neuropsychology, Cognition, and Behavior, *BIOSIGNALS 2009 - Proceedings of the International Conference on Bio-inspired Systems and Signal Processing*, 2009, 87-94.
[18] Y.Z. Levy, D. Levy, J.S. Meyer, H.T. Siegelmann, Drug Addiction as a Non-monotonic Process: a Multiscale Computational Model, *IFMBE Proceedings* **23** (2009), 1688-1691.
[19] Y.Z. Levy, D. Levy, J.S. Meyer, H.T. Siegelmann, Identification and Control of Intrinsic Bias in a Multiscale Computational Model of Drug Addiction, *Proceedings of the 2010 ACM Symposium on Applied Computing*, 2010, 2389-2393.

[20] H.T. Siegelmann, D. Levy, Y.Z. Levy, Addiction and Rehabilitation: A Non-monotonic Computational Process, Technical Report UM-CS-2009-002, University of Massachusetts Amherst, 2009.
[21] P. Bourgine P, J. Stewart, Autopoiesis and Cognition, *Artif Life* **10** (2004), 327-345.
[22] D. Waldorf, P. Biernacki, Natural Recovery from Heroin Addiction: A Review of the Incidence Literature, *J Drug Issues* **9** (1979), 282-289.
[23] C. Winick, Maturing Out of Narcotic Addiction, *United Nations Office On Drugs and Crime (UNODC) Bulletin on Narcotics* **14** (1962), 1-7.
[24] J.F. Maddux, D. P. Desmond, New Light on the Maturing Out Hypothesis in Opioid Dependence, *United Nations Office On Drugs and Crime (UNODC) Bulletin on Narcotics* **32** (1980), 15-25.
[25] L. H. Shaw, The National Drug Abuse Conference, *Br Med J* **2** (1977), 943-944.
[26] M. T. Marcus, A. Zgierska (Eds), Mindfulness-based Therapies for Substance Use Disorders: part 1, *Subst Abus* **30** (2009), 263-265.
[27] A. Zgierska, M. T. Marcus (Eds), Mindfulness-based Therapies for Substance Use Disorders: part 2, *Subst Abus* **31** (2010), 77-78.
[28] S. Grant, E. D. London, D. B. Newlin, V. L. Villemagne, X. Liu, C. Contoreggi, R. L. Phillips, A. S. Kimes, A. Margolin, Activation of Memory Circuits During Cue-elicited Cocaine Craving, *Proc Natl Acad Sci USA* **93** (1996), 12040-12045.
[29] O. George, G. F. Koob, Individual Differences in Prefrontal Cortex Function and the Transition from Drug Use to Drug Dependence, *Neurosci Biobehav Rev* **35** (2010), 232-247.
[30] R. C. O'Reilly, Y. Munakata, Computational Explorations in Cognitive Neuroscience: Understanding the Mind by Simulating the Brain, *MIT Press* (2000).
[31] R. Sun, P. Slusarz, C. Terry, The Interaction of the Explicit and the Implicit in Skill Learning: a Dual-process Approach, *Psychol Rev* **112** (2005), 159-92.
[32] A. V. Samsonovich, K. A. De Jong, Designing a Self-aware Neuromorphic Hybrid, *AAAI-05 Workshop on Modular Construction of Human-Like Intelligence* **WS-05-08** (2005), 71-78.
[33] B. Washington, Rumination and Distraction in Pathological Gamblers: A Cognitive Model of Addiction and Implications for Treatment, *The 20th Annual Conference on Prevention, Research and Treatment of Problem Gambling*, Minnesota, 2006.

Biologically Inspired Cognitive Architectures 2011
A.V. Samsonovich and K.R. Jóhannsdóttir (Eds.)
IOS Press, 2011
doi:10.3233/978-1-60750-959-2-232

Does radical externalism suggest how to implement machine consciousness?

Riccardo MANZOTTI[a,1], Luca PAPI[b], Cristina AMORETTI[c], and Soo-Young LEE[d]

[a] *Institute of Behavior and Communication "G. Fabris", IULM University, Milan*
[b] *National Council of Research (CNR), ICT Department, Rome*
[c] *Department of Philosophy, University of Genoa, Italy*
[d] *Brain Science Research Center, KAIST, Daejeon, Republic of Korea*

Abstract. Despite the great interest for externalist oriented models of the mind (enactivism, the extended mind, various forms of externalism, embodiment, embeddedness), most current artificial agents are designed as though the mind "is still in the head". In other words, in the field of AI, the prevailing view still assumes that the relevant information is processed inside the system that provides the right kind of computation. In this paper, we outline a model of situated cognition that aims at offloading various aspects of cognition which are strongly related with conscious experience (semantics, intentionality, teleology) and then we discuss a robotic implementation which tries to show the kind of intimate agent-environment relationship that may be exploited by conscious agents.

Keywords. Human like episodic memory, artificial consciousness, consciousness, intentionality, externalism, situatedness, embodiment

Introduction

Although there has been a widespread upsurge of interest as to the notion of embodied, situated and extended cognition [1-7], it is still unclear which conditions must obtain for cognition, and possibly consciousness, to spread into the environment. Indeed it is still vague whether the external world has a causal or a constitutive role or simply an enabling role. These options outline very different models and foster very different strategies in implementing agents. Let us consider these three options.

First, the external world may simply have a causal role in fleshing out the internal cognitive functions [8, 9]. This approach would take advantage of the environment as a playground to mould the learning process, yet the cognitive gears would remain inside the agent and, in principle, may be designed anytime.

Alternatively, the external world may have an enabling and facilitating role. In short, because of the body and the environment certain cognitive tasks may be superfluous. The environment simplifies the cognitive load of an agent. The body may take care of many motor details simply because of its smart design [10-13]. Yet this confines cognition to a more limited domain.

Finally, it may be worth considering whether the physical underpinnings of a cognitive agent are larger than its body. This last option is the most radical of all three

---

[1] Corresponding Author.

and it is the one that is inspired to the most radical forms of externalism (such as Chalmers and Clark's extended mind or radical externalism). Basically this view suggests that, since the body of the agent is physically continuous with the environment, there might be a larger physical network of processes which underpins the cognitive processes of the agent. Furthermore, a further fork in this last standpoint is represented by those that consider only cognitive aspects and those who venture to address also phenomenal aspects.

By and large, so far the available cognitive models do not always offer completely consistent and overlapping criteria [6, 14-18]. As a result, it is not always clear to what extent the implemented artificial agents exploit an extended view of cognition. With the hope to overcome some of these ambiguities, in this paper we will shortly outline a tentative model of extended cognition and then we will try to show how it could be exploited in the actual design of an agent.

When is an agent embodied and situated?

Any robotic system is somehow embedded and situated in the environment. A robot has a body and it does things in response to actual events. However, it may be argued that such a loose characterization obtains also for a washing machine or for a thermostat. Are they embodied and situated in the same way as much more complex agents like ants, monkeys, and human beings? It is fair to answer negatively. The relevant kind of situatedness and embodiment must consist in something else.

However, if a body and sensory-motor capacities are not enough, what else then? Situatedness entails an intimate coupling between the agent cognitive functions, the body structure and the environment. But what is exactly such an intriguing *intimate* coupling? When does it occur? Is the extent to which an agent is cognitively situated quantifiable? Here, we venture to consider a working definition based on a model for situated consciousness – a kind of radical phenomenal externalism whose ontological skeleton has been outlined elsewhere [19-21] envisaging a kind of *vehicle externalism* [22, 23]. In this paper, the issue of what constitutes a significant coupling between the world and a cognitive agent is addressed in order to check whether it is relevant to implementing an artificial agent.

Put simply, we suggest that *an agent is situated in a given environment to the extent that its cognitive structures are the result of causal coupling with that environment.* The word *situated* is used in opposition to *embodied* and *embedded* because the agent is cognitively and phenomenally spread beyond those events that fall within the physical boundary of the body.

In this paper, a criterion to single out the conditions that characterize the causal coupling between the environment and the agent is suggested. Causal dependence and individual history may be the missing ingredients. Consider a robot whose behavioral patterns are fixed at design time. Notwithstanding its efficiency, will such a robot be situated? The answer is likely to be a negative one. A truly situated agent keeps changing its cognitive structure. The issue at stake is whether there is a better way to couple the cognitive structure of an agent to its environment.

The appeal to the environment might seem reasonable but unnecessary. It may be argued that while the coupling between an agent and its environment is likely to be higher if the agent has developed within that environment, the link is by no means necessary. For example, the Furby toy (http://en.wikipedia.org/wiki/Furby) is programmed to speak less "Furbish" and more English over time, but this "development" happens entirely independently of its environment. A robot or animal with fixed behaviour patterns could be highly coupled with certain environments, and highly decoupled from others.

Yet the outcome of the Furby is totally independent from the environment in which it operates. If the Furby were raised in a Chinese speaking environment, it would not speak more Chinese – the Furby will speak more English. Irrespective of its actual environment, the Furby generates new behavioral traits in a pre-programmed way. So, while it is true that in the proper environment the Furby would match the surrounding environment, it is nevertheless true that its coupling is not the result of its individual history.

If the behavioural structure is caused by the environment, it may be argued that the individual history is somehow *constitutive* of the resulting agent. Conversely, if the individual history of an agent had no causal efficacy, it couldn't be considered as constitutive of the agent. Furthermore, there are plenty of causal accounts of information, meaning, phenomenal experience, content, symbol grounding, and the like [21, 24-26] that suggests that the occurrence of actual causal links between the environment and the agent is necessary for semantics, mental content, and cognition in general.

Unfortunately, it appears rather difficult to provide feasible and quantifiable methods to measure the causal coupling between the agent and the environment. As a result, scholars often prefer to focus on the current informational state internal to the system under scrutiny rather than to deal with the causal history that led to that state of the agent. Furthermore, the state of an agent is often considered separately from the structure of the agent, as if the internal state and its control structure were two independent aspects. This is questionable as the human brain shows. In biological beings such a separation is clearly a mistake. There aren't memory banks and CPUs in the brain. Everything is contributing to the final results.

These considerations ought to shed some light on the issue of the feasibility of a measure of coupling and situatedness as it may be derived by recent models of information integration and liveliness of processed information [27, 28]. These models are interesting since they may be used to consider both the internal data mesh of a cognitive architecture *and* the extent of the causal agent-environmental coupling.

A sketchy outline of a situated cognitive architecture

In this paragraph, a tentative and rather sketchy outline of a situated cognitive architecture is outlined. The architecture does not pretend to be either conclusive or experimentally satisfying. However, it is a cognitive architecture that had been partially implemented in previous setups [29, 30] and partially presented in previous works [31, 32]. The architecture aims at implementing the kind of development and environmental coupling we have briefly mentioned in the previous section. Or, at least, it ought to suggest how such issues are to be addressed. In many ways, it capitalizes on previous attempts and hopefully is making some predictions on what phenomenal content could be. Due to space limitation, here we will skip most of mathematical details.

To satisfy the kind of causal coupling mentioned above, the architecture must be based on some kind of causal structure that is going to be replicated again and again at different levels of complexity. We suggest an architecture that spans three levels: the unit level, the module level, and the architecture level. Suppose to have a hive of elementary units capable of becoming dedicated to specific events in the environment. Suppose also that such hives are able to play the role both of pattern recognition units and of controller of further actions and learning. In other words, suppose that the traditional separation between data, control, and goals is set aside. Finally suppose that such unities may be combined together freely in order to single out higher level external stimuli, to map higher level motor patterns, and to pursue higher level goals. This would be an ideal recipe to generate a situated architecture, since the resulting architecture would be totally and causally dependent on the environment and the individual history.

The first element to define is the unit capable of picking up a stimulus from the surrounding environment and then becoming dedicated to it. This unit will be the basic element of the developing architecture. It is a unit receiving an input (whether it be as simple as a bit or as complex as any data structure you could envisage) and producing an output (a scalar, an integer or a logical value). The main goal of the unit is getting matched with an arbitrary stimulus and, after such a matching, having the task of being causally related with such original stimulus. Formally, it can be expressed by an undefined function waiting its first input before being matched to it forever. Basically, it is like having a selective gate that is going to be burned on its first input. After being "burned", the unit has a significant output only if the current input resembles the first input. Due to its very simple role, this unit is dubbed the *elementary* unit.

The unit has a few features that are worth being stressed. First, the unit does not distinguish between data and processing. In some sense, it is also a memory unit. Another interesting aspect is that the unit shows a behavior which is the result of the coupling with the environment. There is no way to predict the future of the unit behavior since it is the result of the contingent interaction with the environment. Finally, the unit mirrors some aspect of its own environment without having to replicate it [20].

The other structural level to consider is the intentional module. Suppose to have the capability of implementing and packing many elementary units into the same physical or logical package, putting together a hive of units. The result is a structure here labeled as *intentional module*. This module has already been put to test in a very simplified robotic setup aiming at developing new motivations and controlling the gaze of a camera towards unexpected classes of visual stimuli, and also classic conditionintg, attentive behavior, and self-generation of new goals [20][30, 34]. The simplest way to step from the elementary unit to the module is to pack together a huge number of elementary units all receiving the same input source.

The module output is a vector output which is the result both of the history and of the hard-wired criteria. Each element of this vector is the output of an elementary unit. Therefore the output vector has as many elements as there are burned and activated elementary units. The value of each element expresses how much the corresponding elementary unit is activated by the current input signal, which in turn means how much the current input signal is similar to a given past input.

Combining together intentional modules may lead to a complex architecture. First, assign each source of data to a separate intentional module. When the capacity of the module is saturated (all elementary units are assigned), assign other intentional modules as needed. These modules make the first level of the architecture. When the first level is complete, the output of the first level modules becomes the input for further levels of intentional modules. The further level intentional modules are assigned to every possible earlier level modules output. However, due to many factors (the richness of the original external source of data, the implemented similarity function inside the elementary units, the incoming data, and so on) the output vector sizes are going to diminish increasing the level. When this happens the intentional module will recruit a smaller and smaller number of elementary units. In that case, its output will get merged with that of other intentional modules with similarly smaller output.

A robotic implementation

Here a robotic setup, based on a standard commercial robot NAO (Aldebaran Robotics™, Figure 1) with 21 d.o.f. is taken into consideration. The goal of the setup is to check whether the abovementioned recipe for generating a cognitive architecture is efficacious in a real environment. Efficiency is not an issue here. The goal is to check whether a whole architecture may be generated by unconstrained interaction with the environment without being explicitly defined at design time.

The NAO is wirelessly controlled by a software implementation in Visual C#.NET running a multilayered array of such modules on an Intel-based matrix of PCs. Although the robot basic movements (walking ahead, rotating the body, flexing limbs, closing hands, turning the head, switching on and off the several led) are based on preloaded factory settings, the resulting behavior is driven by the developing growing network of distributed modules whose structure is fleshed out by the actual coupling between the agent and the environment.

Figure 1. The robot NAO used for this implementation (Aldebaran Robotics™).

Given the rich endowment of sensors, in the presented implementation, only a few of them are connected to the developing cognitive architecture. As is shown in Table 1, the main sensory inputs were connected each to a dedicate module (sometimes grouping together more than one sensory channel). Similarly, each group of basic actions (for instance a simplified repertoire of speech utterances or a simplified repertoire of motor patterns) is connected to other modules. At the beginning, the architecture is empty and each of its modules is empty. Then the system is switched on. Each module begins to receive new data and, accordingly to a set of hardwired bootstrapping criteria, begins to burn the elementary units thereby beginning to get coupled with the particular environment.

The experiment has been arbitrarily divided in three steps. Ideally, the following steps or stages may be seamlessly merged together. Currently, it is easier to keep them neatly separate. The first stage endorses the coupling between the modules of the first layer. In order to bootstrap the sensor and the motor part, the motor parts is randomly activated for a limited period of time. In this way the architecture begins to embody motor patterns (from L to N). At the same time, the architecture begins to receive data from the sensors. It is thus advisable to envisage a period of stimulation of the robot (showing it objects, helping it to move in the lab, and the like). Such incoming patterns begin to fill the intentional modules assigned to them (from A to J). Each module fills accordingly to the richness of the corresponding sensor channel. If, for some contingent and unexpected factor, that sensor channel provides a poor input, the allocation of elementary units is consequently poor. For instance, if the NAO's cameras were bandaged, they would not receive any data and the corresponding intentional units would underdevelop.

Table 1. Tentative allocation of early modules based on the NAO sensor and motor skills

Sensor	Intentional Module (level 0)	Intentional Module (further level)	Motor Module	Basic actions
32 x Hall effect sensors + 2 x bumpers	1(A)	?	1(L)	Head 2 DOF Arm 2x5 DOF Pelvis 1 DOF Leg 2x5 DOF Hand 2x1 DOF
1 x accel. 3 axis + 1 x gyro. 2 axis	2(B)	?		
2 x I/R	Unallocated	?	1(M)	51 led variously distributed
Tactile sensor	2 (C+D)	?	1(N)	Simplified repertoire of stereotyped speech utterances
2 CMOS cameras	3 (D, E, F, G)	?		
4 Microphones	4 (H, I, J)	?		

Table 2. Tentative allocation of second-layer modules. The value in the matrix stands for the number of higher level modules

		Contact	Posture	Sound	Vision
		A+C+D	B	H+I+J	D+E+F+G
Contact	A				
Posture	B	1			
Sound	H+I+J	2	-		
Vision	D+E+F+G	2	2	3	

For each module a maximum number of available elementary units is fixed (in the current implementation it is arbitrarily fixed at 1K). This means that a very reach period of development is going to consume all the available resources.

Either when the intentional modules of the first level (level 0) have saturated their capacities or when a arbitrarily length of time has elapsed, the architecture is ready to enter into a second stage. The architecture must begin to develop by allocating new modules that integrate the output of the modules in the first level and the output of the motor modules and the sensory modules. There are two possibilities: the allocation is either done dynamically on the basis of rules of thumb (at this stage) or is hardwired. At present, it is done using various heuristics. One possible way is to consider all possibilities (as shown in Table 2) and then to check, after a given amount of time, which combinations are the more useful ones. How? By measuring which modules are more active and thus providing the richer flow of data.

The same kind of dynamic allocation is thus performed in the third stage between motor patterns and higher level sensory modules. The objective is to single out sensory-motor patterns which are coupled with the actual environment. In Table 2 is shown an average outcome of such a development. The word 'average' means that different environment may produce a totally different allocation of resources since the sensory channel may receive more or less rich sets of stimuli. The results in Table 2, therefore, are to be taken as an example. In that particular example, there were many visual stimuli associated with sounds.

A similar matrix of associations is finally allocated between the motor patterns and the higher level sensory patterns. The hope is that the architecture will be capable of achieving out sensory-motor contingencies of some relevance in the robot's environment. Finally, it must be mentioned that the relevant signals of each module provides the control signal that tune the overall behavior of the developing architecture. These signals act both as bottom-up and as top-down controls.

Conclusion and future work

Right now, the setup is still under continuous development. The objective is to design an architecture that will develop autonomously getting more and more coupled with a specific environment. At present, the architecture develops and generates coupled patterns at various levels. A further important step will consist in exploiting the capacity, embedded in the intentional modules, to single out new goals to achieve by the architecture. If this will be obtained, the architecture may begin to pursue goals and objectives of its own [21].

Moreover, the resulting mesh of modules and units is highly integrated together and it will be interesting to compare the resulting data mesh with other architectures by using indexes of data integration such as liveliness [27, 35]. More refined implementations are, of course, to be expected in order to verify the capability of the architecture to foster a real behavior and to create a complex hierarchy of integrate sensory-motor patterns tightly coupled with the surrounding environment.

In other words, the proposed architecture envisages the implementation of a very strong criterion for situatedness – *an agent is situated in a given environment to the extent that its cognitive structures are the result of causal coupling with that environment*. This is what the presented architecture does notwithstanding all its current shortcomings. Apart from a few hardwired bootstrapping criteria, which the developing modules eventually overcome, the architecture development is totally driven by environment and by the incoming stimuli.

Finally, we would like to address why externalism might endorse phenomenal experience. To do so, we will take advantage of a proposal one of the authors presented elsewhere [19, 21, 36] – namely that a perceptual phenomenal experience might be nothing but the external object tightly coupled to the agent's body. In a nutshell, the experience of X might be nothing but the fact that X plays the double role of being the cause of an actual behavior as well as being the cause of the capability to express that behavior. The experience of something would be literally constituted by that something. Consciousness would then be situated in the environment in a very strong sense. This causal condition would endorse, clearly, an externalist model of consciousness, which offers an interesting conceptual and theoretical framework for machine consciousness since it suggests that consciousness is a matter of the right kind of causal entanglement with the environment.

Acknowledgements. This work has been possible thanks to the support by the Italian-Korea bilateral project between ICT-CNR and KAIST.

References

[1]   R. Menary. (Ed.) *The Extended Mind*. MIT Press, Cambridge (Mass) (2010).

[2]   M. Anderson. Embodied cognition: A field guide. *Artificial Intelligence*, 149: p. 91-130 (2003).

[3]   S. Harnad. Grounding symbolic capacity in robotic capacity, In: *"Artificial Route" to "Artificial Intelligence": Building Situated Embodied Agents*, L. Steels and R.A. Brooks, (Eds.), Erlbaum, New York (1995).

[4]   M. Shanahan. *Embodiment and the Inner Life. Cognition and Consciousness in the Space of Possible Minds*. Oxford, Oxford University Press (2010).

[5]   A. Clark. Perception, action, and experience: unraveling the golden braid. *Neuropsychologia*, 47: p. 1460-8 (2009).

[6]   R. Chrisley and T. Ziemke. Embodiment, In: *Encyclopedia of Cognitive Science*, Macmillan, London (2002).

[7]   R.A. Wilson. *Boundaries of the Mind. The Individual in the Fragile Sciences*. Cambridge (Mass), Cambridge University Press (2004).

[8]   M. Lungarella, et al. Developmental robotics: a survey. *Connection Science*, 15: p. 151-190 (2003).

[9]   G. Metta, G. Sandini, and J. Konczak. A developmental approach to visually guided reaching in artificial systems. *Neural Networks*, 12: p. 1413-1427 (1999).

[10]   R. Pfeifer, M. Lungarella, and L. Fumiya. Self-Organization, Embodiment, and Biologically Inspired Robotics. *Science*, 5853: p. 1088-1093 (2007).

[11]   R. Pfeifer. *Understanding Intelligence*. Cambridge (Mass), MIT Press (1999).

[12]   R. Pfeifer and J. Bongard. *How the Body Shapes the Way We Think: A New View of Intelligence (Bradford Books)* New York, Bradford Books (2006).

[13]   R.A. Brooks. Elephants Don't Play Chess. *Robotics and Autonomous Systems*, 6: p. 3-15 (1990).

[14]   P. Robbins and M. Aydede. (Eds.) *The Cambridge Handbook of Situated Cognition*. Cambridge University Press, Cambridge (2009).

[15]   F. Adams and K. Aizawa. The bounds of cognition. *Philosophical Psychology*, 14: p. 43-64 (2001).

[16]   R.D. Rupert. Challenges to the Hypothesis of Extended Cognition. *The Journal of Philosophy*, 101: p. 389-428 (2004).

[17]   S. Torrance. In search of the enactive: Introduction special issue on enactive experience. *Phenomenology and the Cognitive Sciences*, 4: p. 357-368 (2006).

[18]   E. Thompson and F.J. Varela. Radical embodiment: neural dynamics and consciousness. *Trends in Cognitive Sciences*, 5: p. 418-425 (2001).

[19]   R. Manzotti. A Process Oriented View of Conscious Perception. *Journal of Consciousness Studies*, 13: p. 7-41 (2006).

[20]   R. Manzotti. No Time, No Wholes: A Temporal and Causal-Oriented Approach to the Ontology of Wholes. *Axiomathes*, 19: p. 193-214 (2009).

[21]   R. Manzotti. A Process-oriented Framework for Goals and Motivations in Biological and Artificial Agents, In: *Causality and Motivation*, R. Poli, (Ed.), Ontos-Verlag, Frankfurt. p. 105-134 (2010).

[22] R.G. Millikan. Content and vehicle, In: *Spatial Representation*, N. Eilan, R. McCarthy, and B. Brewer, (Eds.), Blackwell, Oxford (1993).

[23] S. Hurley. The Varieties of Externalism, In: *The Extended Mind*, R. Menary, (Ed.), MIT Press, Cambridge (Mass). p. 101-155 (2010).

[24] F. Dretske. *Knowledge & the flow of information*. Cambridge (Mass), MIT Press. xiv, 273 (1981).

[25] S. Harnad. The Symbol Grounding Problem. *Physica*, D: p. 335-346 (1990).

[26] H. Putnam. *Mind, language, and reality*. Cambridge, Cambridge University Press. xvii, 457 (1975).

[27] I. Aleksander and D. Gamez. Informational Theories of Consciousness: A Review and Extension. In: *BICS 2010 Conference on Brain-Inspired Cognitive Systems*. Madrid (2010).

[28] D. Gamez. Information integration based predictions about the conscious states of a spiking neural network. *Consciousness and Cognition*, 19: p. 294-310 (2010).

[29] R. Manzotti. A process based architecture for an artificial conscious being, In: *Process theories*, J. Seibt, (Ed.), Kluwer Academic Press, Dordrecht. p. 285-312 (2003).

[30] R. Manzotti and V. Tagliasco. From "behaviour-based" robots to "motivations-based" robots. *Robotics and Autonomous Systems*, 51(2-3): p. 175-190 (2005).

[31] A. Chella and R. Manzotti. Artificial Consciousness, In: *Perception-Action Cycle: Models, Architectures, and Hardware*, V. Cutsuridis, A. Hussain, and J.G. Taylor, (Eds.), Springer, Dordrecht. p. 637-671 (2011).

[32] R. Manzotti and V. Tagliasco. From behaviour-based robots to motivation-based robots. *Robotics and Autonomous Systems*, 51: p. 175-190 (2005).

[33] R.O. Duda, P.E. Hart, and D.G. Stork. *Pattern classification*. New York, Wiley. xx, 654 (2001).

[34] R. Manzotti. Towards Artificial Consciousness. *APA Newsletter on Philosophy and Computers*, 07(1): p. 12-15 (2007).

[35] G. Tononi. An information integration theory of consciousness. *BMC Neuroscience*, 5: p. 1-22 (2004).

[36] A. Chella and R. Manzotti. Machine Consciousness: A Manifesto for Robotics. *International Journal of Machine Consciousness*, 1: p. 33-51 (2009).

Biologically Inspired Cognitive Architectures 2011
A.V. Samsonovich and K.R. Jóhannsdóttir (Eds.)
IOS Press, 2011

Anthropological, Socio-Biological Framework as Master Architect of Human Cognitive Architectures

Dennis K. MCBRIDE

Georgetown University Department of Microbiology
3900 Reservoir Rd. (Med-Dent) Washington 20057-1440 United States
dkm7@georgetown.edu

Keywords. Biological systematics, cognitive architecture, anthropological socio-biology

Abstract

Biological taxonomics focuses on anatomical differentiation. A more robust systematics provides consideration that it is successful behavior (vs. anatomy) that endures survival pressures and that anatomical form is essentially the concatenated, genetically captured, satisficing substrate that supports ecologically successful behavioral patterns. Surviving characteristics may thus reflect Baldwin effect processes where, in this case, brain functionality, initially distributed across the nervous system, becomes consolidated or "hard-wired," much as computer software processes can for engineering reasons, become hardware-dedicated. Provided here is analysis of an architectural approach wherein a seminal documentation of human universal behaviors/linguistics (Brown, 1991) is down-constituted to provide a working, periodic "chart" of relatively molar behavioral elements, based on anthropologically-collected time investment studies. The specific hypothesis examined is that human universals reflect ancestral fitness functions that guided cognitive architectural design, and therefore, that representation of BICA today may benefit from an understanding of such ecologically-focused, cognitive systematics.

Biologically Inspired Cognitive Architectures 2011
A.V. Samsonovich and K.R. Jóhannsdóttir (Eds.)
IOS Press, 2011

IARPA's ICArUS Program: Brain-Inspired Cognitive Models for Intelligence Analysis

Brandon S. MINNERY
IARPA/MS2 Building ODNI Washington 20611 United States
brandon.s.minnery@ugov.gov

Keywords. cognitive bias; cognitive architecture; sensemaking; neuroeconomics; decision making; intelligence analysis

Abstract

Intelligence analysts are frequently called upon to explain data that are sparse, noisy, and uncertain. This process, termed sensemaking, is a basic human cognitive ability as well as a foundational component of intelligence analysis. Yet despite its importance, sensemaking remains a poorly understood phenomenon. The goal of the ICArUS Program is to construct integrated computational cognitive neuroscience models of human sensemaking. By shedding light on the fundamental mechanisms of sensemaking, ICArUS models will enable the Intelligence Community to better predict human-related strengths and failure modes in the intelligence analysis process and will point to new strategies for enhancing analytic tools and methods. Furthermore, ICArUS models may help to establish a new generation of automated analysis tools.

Biologically Inspired Cognitive Architectures 2011
A.V. Samsonovich and K.R. Jóhannsdóttir (Eds.)
IOS Press, 2011
© 2011 The authors and IOS Press. All rights reserved.
doi:10.3233/978-1-60750-959-2-243

Towards a Biologically Inspired Question-Answering Neural Architecture

Derek Monner [a,1] James A. Reggia [a,b]

[a] *Department of Computer Science, University of Maryland, College Park, USA*
[b] *Institute for Advanced Computer Studies, University of Maryland, College Park, USA*

Abstract. Though question-answering systems like IBM's Watson are undoubtedly impressive, their errors are often baffling and inscrutable to onlookers, suggesting that the strategies they use are far different than those that humans employ. Desiring a more biologically inspired approach, we investigate the extent to which a neural network can develop a functional grasp of language by observing question/answer pairs. We present a neural network model that takes questions, as speech-sound sequences, about a visual environment, and learns to answer them with grounded predicate-based meanings. The model must learn to 1) segment morphemes, words, and phrases from the speech stream, 2) map the intended referents from the speech signal onto objects in the environment, 3) comprehend simple questions, recognizing what information the question is asking for, and 4) find and supply that information. Model evaluations suggest that the grounding and question-answering parts of the problem are significantly more demanding than interpreting the speech input.

Keywords. question answering, grounded language comprehension, recurrent neural network, long short term memory

1. Introduction

While question-answering systems such as IBM's recent *Jeopardy!* winner Watson [1] have been well-studied in natural language processing domains, little research has been done into to how the question/answer style of interaction might influence the way humans acquire language. This is an interesting question in light of the fact that, when listening to language, learners are constantly confronted with request/response, question/answer pairs. In this paper we investigate the extent to which a pure neural network model of a human learner can learn a micro-language by listening to question/answer pairs. The model is situated in a simulated micro-world along with two speakers whom we will call Watson and Sherlock. Watson asks questions about the shared environment in a subset of English, and Sherlock responds to these questions with the information Watson was seeking. The model's task is to learn to emulate Sherlock. To do this effectively, the model must listen to the speech sounds of Watson's questions and learn to segment them into morphemes, words, and phrases, which it must then interpret with respect to the common surroundings, thereby grounding them in visual experience. The model must then recognize what information Watson is asking for and provide that information as a predicate-based "meaning" that is grounded in the environment.

---

[1]Corresponding Author: dmonner@cs.umd.edu

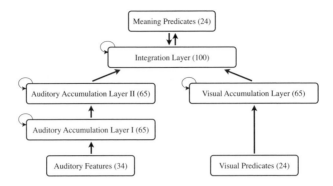

Figure 1. The network architecture of the model. Layers of memory cells are shown with a self-recurrent arc denoting the self-connections of the individual units therein.

2. Methods

The model is situated in a shared micro-world environment with two other speakers, Watson and Sherlock. A training trial begins with Watson asking a question, the answer to which is directly observable in the environment. Sherlock observes his surroundings and gives the answer, which our model observes and attempts to mimic. Sherlock provides each answer as a sequence of grounded predicates which correspond to the meaning of a complete-sentence answer to Watson's question. The model must learn this behavior by imitating Sherlock. We realize that, in real human language learning, Sherlock's raw meaning would not generally be available for the model to imitate (though there is some evidence that the listener may often be able to infer the meaning [2]). However, we still find it useful to examine this limited model, as its predicate-based outputs provide direct evidence that neural models can learn to produce a fully grounded meaning representation of an answer to a question.

The model (Figure 1) is built using the Long Short Term Memory (LSTM) [3,4] architecture, in which units in hidden layers are replaced by self-recurrent *memory cells* protected by multiplicative gates. This type of network can be trained by gradient descent methods similar to those utilized by other recurrent neural networks, and we adopt such a method in this work. Called the LSTM-g training algorithm [5], this variant of gradient descent focuses on maintaining information locality as a means of approaching biological plausibility. Like many gradient-descent based algorithms, LSTM-g utilizes back-propagating errors; however, in light of work showing how such error propagation can be equivalent to Hebbian training methods [6], we argue that back-propagating errors are merely a computationally expedient implementation detail rather than a feature which detracts from the biological realism of the LSTM-g training algorithm.

The network has separate input pathways for accumulating auditory and visual input into gestalt-type representations [7]. The two pathways differ in length because pilot experiments showed that the visual and auditory gestalt representations are best formed with one and two layers of intermediary processing, respectively. After both input gestalts have been formed, they are integrated by another layer of memory cells, which is then used to sequentially generate predicates that specify the grounded meaning output which answers the input question. The network's previous output is fed back to the integration layer to provide a more specific context for sequential processing. The

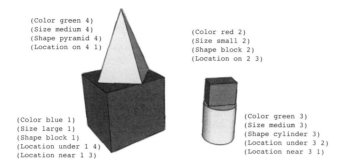

(Color green 4)
(Size medium 4)
(Shape pyramid 4)
(Location on 4 1)

(Color red 2)
(Size small 2)
(Shape block 2)
(Location on 2 3)

(Color blue 1)
(Size large 1)
(Shape block 1)
(Location under 1 4)
(Location near 1 3)

(Color green 3)
(Size medium 3)
(Shape cylinder 3)
(Location under 3 2)
(Location near 3 1)

Figure 2. An example of a micro-world environment with four objects, along with the complete set of predicates that describe the environment to the model.

following sections will provide more detail on the forms taken by the auditory and visual inputs and the predicate outputs.

2.1. Environment Input

The micro-world environment shared by our three participants consists of a number of objects placed in relation to each other (see Figure 2). Each object has values for the three attributes size, shape, and color, and each attribute has three possible values: small, medium and large for size; block, cylinder, and pyramid for shape; and red, green, and blue for color. Thus there are 27 distinct objects possible. In addition, each object has a number that identifies it uniquely in the environment, which is a useful handle for a specific object and becomes necessary in the event that the participants need to distinguish between two otherwise identical objects.

Each object is presented to the model as three predicates—coded as binary neural features—with each predicate binding an attribute value to an object identifier. For example, a small red block with unique identifier 2 is completedly described by the predicates (Size small 2), (Color red 2), and (Shape block 2). An environment consist of two to four randomly generated objects, and the predicates describing all these objects are presented at the visual input layer of the model as a temporal sequence at the start of a trial. Each predicate is represented as a collection of active units representing the predicate type, attribute value, and identifying number(s) involved.

Additional predicates are used to describe spatial relations between the objects. One object may be near, on, or underneath another. For example, if our small red block from above (with identifier 2) is on top of a medium-sized cylinder (identifier 3), that fact would be presented to the model as the predicate (Location on 2 3). In our micro-world the on and under relations are complementary (meaning that (Location on 2 3) implies (Location under 3 2)) and the near relation is symmetric (such that (Location near 1 3) implies (Location near 3 1)). The location predicates are presented along with the attribute predicates and at the same visual input layer.

Though this space of possible environments may seem small at first, the number of unique environmental configurations is quite large. Using only two, three, or four objects at a time gives us approximately 2.48×10^{10} distinct possible micro-world configurations.

In terms of neural representation, predicate types, attribute values, and identifying numbers each correspond to single units—a drastic simplification of real visual input that

Question	→	where **Is Object** | **What Is Property**
Answer	→	**Object Is Property**
Object	→	the **[Size] [Color] Shape**
What	→	what color **[Size] Shape** | what size **[Color] Shape** | what **[Size] [Color]** thing
Property	→	**Location** | **Color** | **Size**
Location	→	on **Object** | under **Object** | near **Object**
Is	→	is | are *(must agree in number with subject)*
Size	→	small | medium | large
Color	→	red | blue | green
Shape	→	things | pyramid[s] | block[s] | cylinder[s]

Figure 3. The mildly context-sensitive grammar used in the question-answering task. Terminals begin with a lowercase letter while non-terminals are in boldface and begin with an uppercase letter. The symbol '|' separates alternative derivations, and terms in brackets are optional.

we adopt for reasons of computational tractability and because it is a plausible level of representation that might be developed by later stages of the human visual system.

2.2. Question Input

In order to assist in training our model, Watson produces complete English sentences that ask questions about the current shared environment. There are many possible questions for each environment; for the example environment in Figure 2, Watson might ask "What color block is the green pyramid on?", "What thing is under the small block?", "What color are the medium things?", or "Where is the pyramid?".

To produce a question, Watson examines the environment and derives a question beginning from the **Question** non-terminal in the grammar of Figure 3. The question will either be a "what" question asking about one specific property of an object, or a much more complex "where" question requiring a relational predicate and a complete three-predicate object description as an answer. Any objects that Watson refers to must be present in the environment and, to a sophisticated observer, unambiguously identified by the full context of the question. This is necessary because Sherlock must be able to determine the answer to provide a useful imitation target for the model. For example, Watson could not ask "What color is the block?" because it is not clear which block he is referring to, and thus any answer would be poorly defined. Note that Watson can, however, ask questions about groups of objects that share a property, as "What color are the medium things?"—in this case the medium things are the cylinder and pyramid, which are both green, so the answer is well defined. Similarly, questions such as "What color pyramid is red?" that reveal the property being asked about are disallowed.

The words in Watson's question are phonetically transcribed and appended, resulting in a sequence of phonemes that is presented temporally to the model. Each such phoneme is represented as a bundle of binary acoustic features (from [8]) such as voicing, affrication, and formant frequency categories, with each feature corresponding to an input unit. Word and morpheme boundaries are not marked in the input sequence, leaving the model to discover those on its own.

2.3. Answer Output

After Watson has finished asking a question, the model attempts a response. On training trials, Sherlock then gives the correct response, and the model adjusts its connection weights to better imitate this response in the future. Training is thus self-supervised—the

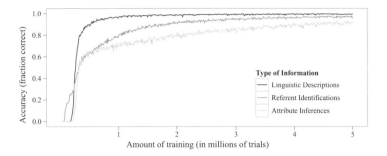

Figure 4. Accuracy versus training time for three separate components of the question-answering task, averaged over all ten training runs.

model need only observe the naturally occurring dialog between Watson and Sherlock and imitate the latter.

To answer Watson's question, Sherlock examines the environment and determines the set of object attributes and relations Watson was referring to. If the question was "What color block is the green pyramid on?" in the context of the environment of Figure 2, Sherlock would produce a sequence of five predicates that correspond roughly to the meaning of the answer sentence "The green pyramid is on the blue block": (Color green 4), (Shape pyramid 4), (Location on 4 1), (Color blue 1), and (Shape block 1).

Note that the answers to the questions differ based on the micro-world environment, such that we never have a one-to-one mapping of questions to answers. Indeed, the answer to Watson's question above would change if the block under the green pyramid were red instead of blue. It would also change (albeit slightly) if the scene were visually identical but the object numbering was altered. Though the above example suggests that the number of possible answer variations is small, some questions admit much greater environment-based variation than others. More open-ended questions such as "where is the block?" could have literally hundreds of possible answers depending on the environment. Thus, neither the model nor Sherlock could answer questions reliably without integrating information from the visual environment.

3. Results

We trained 10 separate networks, each with randomly-chosen weights, on the question-answering task for 5 million randomly generated trials—far less than 0.1% of the input space. All reported results come from evaluations on test trials consisting of a novel micro-world/question pairing. On average, the trained networks were able to produce a perfect temporal sequence of up to 8 grounded predicates to answer the question on 92.5% of these novel trials, strongly suggesting that observe-and-imitate training is sufficient even for the difficult task of grounded question comprehension and answering.

To evaluate the relative difficulty of the components of the task, we can decompose the output predicates into three categories: attribute values corresponding to linguistic descriptions which were present in the question, referent identifications made by grounding the question in the environment, and attributes that are inferred from the environment to answer the question. Comparing the time-course of accuracy over these three categories in Figure 4, we see that the model learns to understand spoken descriptions fairly quickly, with performance leveling off above 95% after the first 1M trials. At this point, however, performance on referent identifications and question-answers is relatively weak, at 80% and 70% respectively; however, accuracy on these areas continues to slowly improve as training progresses. This seems to us to be compelling evidence that grounded language learning is much more difficult than word recognition, whereas using the environment to infer the answers to questions is harder still.

4. Conclusion

These initial results demonstrate that a purely neural system can learn not only to comprehend language grounded in a shared environment, but also to understand and answer spoken questions. To our knowledge, ours is the first neural network model to successfully learn to map sentence-level language, represented at sub-lexical resolution, onto complex, composable symbolic meanings. We plan, in future work, to investigate the types of representations that the model develops when integrating the auditory and visual streams, and whether a symbol-like representation of the input question can be said to exist independently of the model's derived answer to the question. We are also developing a variant of this model that learns by observing answers from Sherlock as speech streams rather than collections of predicates, with the former being an imitatable signal that is always observable in human language learning scenarios. Such a model would naturally learn speech production capabilities by observation, just as the model presented in this paper suggests that simple observation and imitation might be sufficient tools for learning challenges as complex language acquisition.

Acknowledgments

This work was supported in part by NIH award HD064653.

References

[1] D. Ferrucci, E. Brown, J. Chu-Carroll, J. Fan, D. Gondek, A. A. Kalyanpur, A. Lally, J. W. Murdock, E. Nyberg, J. Prager, N. Schlaefer, and C. Welty. Building Watson : An Overview of the DeepQA Project. *AI Magazine*, 31(3):59–79, 2010.
[2] M. Tomasello. *Constructing a Language: A Usage-Based Theory of Language Acquisition*. Harvard University Press, 2003.
[3] S. Hochreiter and J. Schmidhuber. Long Short-Term Memory. *Neural Computation*, 9(8):1735–1780, Nov. 1997.
[4] F. A. Gers and F. Cummins. Learning to Forget: Continual Prediction with LSTM. *Neural Computation*, 12(10):2451–2471, Oct. 2000.
[5] D. Monner and J. A. Reggia. A Generalized LSTM-Like Training Algorithm for Second-Order Recurrent Neural Networks. *Neural Networks (in press)*, 2011.
[6] X. Xie and H. S. Seung. Equivalence of Backpropagation and Contrastive Hebbian Learning in a Layered Network. *Neural Computation*, 15(2):441–54, Feb. 2003.
[7] M. F. St. John and J. L. McClelland. Learning and applying contextual constraints in sentence comprehension. *Artificial Intelligence*, 46(1-2):217–257, 1990.
[8] S. A. Weems and J. A. Reggia. Simulating Single Word Processing in the Classic Aphasia Syndromes Based on the Wernicke-Lichtheim-Geschwind Theory. *Brain and Language*, 98(3):291–309, 2006.

Biologically Inspired Cognitive Architectures 2011
A.V. Samsonovich and K.R. Jóhannsdóttir (Eds.)
IOS Press, 2011
© 2011 The authors and IOS Press. All rights reserved.
doi:10.3233/978-1-60750-959-2-249

A Computational Agent Model for Post-Traumatic Stress Disorders

Sebastien NAZE and Jan TREUR
VU University Amsterdam, Agent Systems Research Group
De Boelelaan 1081, 1081 HV, Amsterdam, The Netherlands
Email: sebastien.naze@gmail.com, treur@cs.vu.nl
URL: http://www.cs.vu.nl/~treur

Abstract. In this paper a computational agent model is presented that describes and mimics processing in persons with a Post-Traumatic Stress Disorder (PTSD). The model is based on insights from the neurological literature on how specific phenomena that are typical for PTSD patients can occur, such as re-experiencing the strong feeling related to the original traumatic event, dissociation (not feeling the own body), and flashbacks in the form of images. A number of simulations is presented that show how the agent model displays these phenomena of re-experiencing, dissociation and flashback episodes, triggered by a neutral stimulus. The obtained cognitive/affective agent model can be used as a basis for the design of human-like virtual agents in simulation-based training or in gaming or virtual stories.

Keywords: Post-Traumatic Stress Disorder (PTSD), computational agent model

Introduction

A Post-Traumatic Stress Disorder (PTSD) may occur when a person undergoes a traumatic event involving strong emotions and/or physical harm (for example, sexual abuse, a battlefield experience, or a car accident). Recent studies in neuroscience show that a number of mechanisms play a role in patients suffering from PTSD. The main types of patients are classified according to the symptoms they have when a stimulus occurs related to the traumatic memory. Two primary symptoms are re-experiencing (flashbacks) and dissociation. Re-experiencing happens when patients undergo a strong emotional feeling similar to the feeling experienced during the traumatic event. It is usually accompanied by visual flashbacks and physical inconvenience. Dissociative patients undergo an emotional withdrawal (due to the emotional load triggered by a stimulus) that involves loss of body perception or so-called out-of-body experience.

The computational agent model presented here is based on neurological studies of PTSD patients, among others using imagery technology, and serves to simulate the disorder's symptoms from inside (i.e., embodied perspective). In line with the recent findings, the presented model reflects the understanding of brain functions and reactions observed in reality. Indeed, the literature shows different steps to reach a reaction, for example, by representing a stimulus (which by itself may be neutral, but has some association to the traumatic event), automatic preparation of response, and possible control over the internal processes. The control process plays an important role in inhibition of over-reacting to such stimuli. It acts over the emotional involvement triggered by the stimulus and memory of the traumatic event and the bodily response to the emotional load.

Application of such a cognitive/affective agent model can be found in the context of human-like virtual agents in simulation-based training, gaming or virtual stories. For example, a virtual patient for a simulation-based training environment for psychiatrists or psycho-therapists can be developed based on the model.

Section 1 briefly discusses the neurobiological background of the impairment. In Section 2 the detailed computational agent model is introduced. Section 3 illustrates different simulation scenarios and their outcomes. Section 4 is a discussion.

1. Neurological Background

Recent neurological studies on PTSD have focused on analysis of the default network activation and connectivity during trauma-related processes. This network is an anatomically interconnected brain system that activates when individuals focus on internal tasks such as daydreaming, envisioning the future, retrieving memories and gauging others' perspectives. It includes part of the medial temporal lobe for memory, part of the medial prefrontal cortex for theory of mind and the posterior cingulate cortex for integration, along with the adjacent precuneus and the medial, lateral and inferior parietal cortex; cf. [4].This network undergoes developmental changes along with experiences.

Among persons experiencing PTSD, lower activation was found in the posterior cingulate gyrus compared to controls; cf. [14]. The posterior cingulate gyrus discerns emotional and self-relevant information. It interacts on one hand with the anterior cingulate gyrus, which integrates emotional information with cognition, and on the other hand with the medial prefrontal cortex, which allows for self-reflection and the regulation of emotion and arousal.

Impairment in this network appears to correlate with the experience of persons who have long-term trauma and describe feeling 'dead inside' or have a fragmented sense of self or enter dissociative states, as put forward in [1]. Higher activation levels in neural networks involved in representing body states was seen in dissociated PTSD [13].

Hyper-sensibility and hyper-vigilance are central characteristics of PTSD in terms of increased likelihood of emotional response to environmental stimuli due to altered connectivity between default network and the amygdala, hippocampus and insula. Dissociation may also involve alterations in the relation between the default network and subregions serving cognitive abilities. Thus, awareness of emotional stimulation plays a role in the strength of the symptoms. Indeed in [11, 12], it is suggested that it may engage top-down reflexive or effortful emotion regulation that, from [13], seems to be impaired in PTSD.

PTSD subjects are unable to control the intensity of their emotional reactions in the presence of stimuli that function as reminders of the traumatic experience. Studies cited in [10] have shown activation disturbances of the PCC (Posterior Cingulate Cortex) which is involved in episodic memory retrieval and pain processing.

Flashback patients (heightened autonomic and emotional reactivity) have reduced bilateral medial frontal cortex and ACC (Anterior Cingulate Cortex) activity. In contrast, dissociative patients have increased activation in frontal, superior and medial temporal gyrus, inferior frontal and parietal regions of the right hemisphere, and have a lack of amygdala response to trauma-related neutral stimuli. This leads to the hypothesis that the heightened prefrontal activity in dissociative PTSD reflects stronger emotional regulation and inhibition of limbic emotional networks, including the amygdala. Thus in [9] it is concluded that dissociation is a strategic and controlled regulatory process invoked by extreme arousal to reduce the experience of aversive emotions. This same study shows that thalamic activity is increased in dissociation, which supports the theory that a higher sensory transmission mediates bottom-up excitatory processes. This is also claimed by Oathes et al. [17] who show that dissociative patients show faster emotion labeling.

In [13], the processes in PTSD subjects are related to Damasio (1999)'s theory on emotions and experiencing them. In the study described in [13] indeed such altered bodily perceptions and emotions were found in PTSD subjects:

'Damasio (1999) has emphasized the role of the insula and the somatosensory cortices in processing signals regarding bodily state and suggests that these signals form the basis for emotions. (…) Thus, the insula activation seen in this study might reflect this altered perception or possibly alterations in the "body map" constructed by the insula, which has been hypothesized by Damasio (1999) to contribute to emotional experiences. (…) In fact, the subjective reports of the dissociated PTSD subjects in this study suggest that they experienced alterations in both bodily perceptions and emotions during recall of the traumatic memory. It is interesting to note that patients in a dissociative state often have difficulties with perception of internal bodily states, for example recognizing pain states. (…) Moreover, patients in dissociative states often have significant difficulties experiencing feelings of emotion. In fact, all of the dissociative subjects in this study reported being "removed" from their experience of their traumatic memory.' ([13], p. 881)

As a summary, it has been shown in the recent literature that PTSD patients suffer from an impaired emotion regulation process combined with a higher sensitivity to emotional stimuli. There exists two ways of dealing with a memory recall of a traumatic event, each patient usually reacts automatically with only one of these responses. Flashback patients are over-reacting and fall into a strong re-experience of the trauma accompanied with visual recall. Dissociative patients react to traumatic emotion recalls by suppressing body and emotional affects and appraisals.

2. Description of the Computational Model

The computational agent model uses sensory representation states for external stimuli and body states, and preparation states for emotional responses and regulation actions to turn away from stimuli that lead to high, disturbing levels of arousal; for an overview, see Fig. 1. Moreover, a control state is used that detects disturbing levels of arousal, and in turn can activate suppressing or regulating processes. In line with [6] and [13], it is assumed that emotional response preparations affect sensory representations of related body states (body maps) as in [2], both by an internal as-if body loop and an external body loop. These body maps are considered the basis of feeling the emotion. Moreover, it is assumed that this feeling in turn has a strengthening effect on the emotional preparation state, so that a cyclic process occurs, in line with [8]:

'The brain has a direct means to respond to the object as feelings unfold because the object at the origin is inside the body, rather than external to it. The brain can act directly on the very object it is perceiving. It can do so by modifying the state of the object, or by altering the transmission of signals from it. The object at the origin on the one hand, and the brain map of that object on the other, can influence each other in a sort of reverberative process that is not to be found, for example, in the perception of an external object. (…) after an occasion of such feelings begins – for seconds or for minutes – there is a dynamic engagement of the body, almost certainly in a repeated fashion, and a subsequent dynamic variation of the perception. We perceive a series of transitions. We sense an interplay, a give and take.' ([7], pp. 91-92)

In Fig. 1, s_2 is the stimulus that caused the traumatic experience, and s_1 is a more neutral stimulus that has some association to the situation in which the trauma was caused. For example, s_2 is the visual image of a fire while being inside a burning house, while s_1 is the image of the house from outside while it is not burning. Moreover, the emotional response and feeling is assumed to relate to the preparation and sensory representation of a body state indicated by b. In Table 1 an overview is given of the states used in the model. The connections between the states have certain strengths, as indicated in Table 2. It is assumed that substantial differences exist between these connection strengths for healthy subjects and PTSD subjects. For example, the strengths of the connections ω_5 and ω_{18} from the sensory representation of stimulus s_1 are low or zero in healthy subjects: in principle s_1 is an emotion-neutral stimulus (for example, seeing a house).

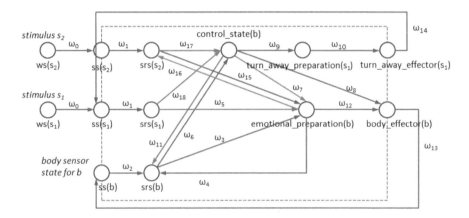

Figure 1. Overview of the computational agent model; colored links are those that differ between PTSD patients and healthy subjects (mainly, red for dissociation, orange for flashbacks and green for both); the grey dashed line represent the boundary between internal and external states. States on the dashed line are intermediate states which are seen as sensors ss(x). Sensory representations srs(x) are the internal representations of sensory information.

Table 1. Overview of the states used

notation	explanation
ws(W)	World state for W (stimulus s_1 or s_2)
ss(W)	Sensor state for W (stimulus s_1, stimulus s_2, or body state b)
srs(W)	Sensory representation state for W (stimulus s_1, stimulus s_2, or body state b)
ep(b)	Emotional response preparation state for b
be(b)	Body effector state for b
cs(b)	Control state for b
tap(s_1)	Turn away preparation state for s_1
tae(s_1)	Turn away effector state for s_1

However, they are assumed higher in PTSD subjects because this neutral stimulus is associated to a traumatic experience (e.g., they have experienced a fire in their house that looked similar, which had fatal repercussions). This is supported by [1] and [8]:

'Hyper-sensibility and hyper-vigilance are central characteristics of PTSD in terms of increased likelihood of emotional response to environmental stimuli due to altered connecti-vity between default network and the amygdala, hippocampus and insula' ([1], p. 192).
'(PTSD patients) are unable to control the intensity of their emotional reactions in the presence of reminders of the traumatic experience' ([8], p. 112).

Moreover, the strength of the connection ω_4 from emotional preparation ep(b) to feeling the emotional arousal srs(b) is assumed high in PTSD subjects:

'Greater activation levels in neural networks involved in representing bodily states was seen in dissociated PTSD' ([13], p. 873).
'(…) there is evidence of greater activity in nonverbal and somatosensory processes in response to trauma scripts in dissociative PTSD' ([13], p. 878).
'Enhanced early sensory registration, somatosensory arousal and motor readiness that is consistent with this enhanced automatic arousal. (seen in PTSD)' ([9], p. 1776).

Furthermore, for dissociative PTSD subjects ω_{11} is a strong inhibitory connection that makes the agent loose the feeling of his or her body state.

'Neural correlates are consistent with a "super suppression" or robust inhibition of affective arousal during dissociation on the part of these individuals with PTSD' ([10], p.114).
'PTSD dissociative symptoms are regarded as being the consequence of an enhanced suppression of fear-induced arousal' ([10], p. 121).
'(…) dissociation is a strategic and controlled regulatory process invoked by extreme arousal to reduce the experience of aversive emotions' ([9], p. 1776).

Also the strength of the connection ω_7 is assumed to be abnormal in Dissociative PTSD subjects, for example weighting *-0.7* for this type of PTSD subject, instead of *-0.4* in a healthy subject. This displays the lack of normal emotional control in dissociative PTSD: the connection do not inhibit ep(b) in an appropriate manner as happens in healthy subjects. Finally, ω_{16} is a connection that is assumed to have some strength in PTSD patients, and is especially strong in those having visual flashbacks; it makes the person calling back the traumatic images he or she has undergone.

The agent model has been computationally formalised using the hybrid modeling language LEADSTO and its software environment; cf. [3]. Within LEADSTO a temporal causal relation or dynamic temporally local property (LP) a ⟶» b denotes that when a state property a (or conjunction thereof) occurs, then after a certain time delay, state property b will occur. This delay will be taken as a uniform time step Δt.

Below, the dynamics following the connections between the states in Fig. 1 are described in more detail. This is done for each state by a dynamic local property

Table 2. Overview of connections and weights

From state	To state	Weights	LP
ss(s$_1$)	srs(s$_1$)	ω_1	LP0
ep(b), ss(s$_2$)	srs(s$_2$)	ω_{16}, ω_1	LP1
ss(b), ep(b), cs(b)	srs(b)	ω_2, ω_4, ω_{11}	LP2
srs(b), srs(s$_2$), srs(s$_1$)	cs(b)	ω_6, ω_{17}, ω_{18}	LP3
srs(s$_1$), srs(s$_2$), srs(b), cs(b)	ep(b)	ω_5, ω_{15}, ω_3, ω_7	LP4
cs(b)	tap(s$_1$)	ω_9	LP5
ep(b), cs(b)	be(b)	ω_{12}, ω_8	LP6
tap(s$_1$)	tae(s$_1$)	ω_{10}	LP7
be(b)	ss(b)	ω_{13}	LP8
ws(s$_1$), tae(s$_1$)	ss(s$_1$)	ω_0, ω_{14}	LP9
ws(s$_2$)	ss(s$_2$)	ω_0	LP10

specifying how the activation value for this state is updated (after a time step of Δt) based on the activation values of the states connected to it (the incoming arrows in Fig. 1). In these update specifications for each node a (combination) function f is used, which in principle can be any function mapping the vector of input obtained from other nodes into the interval $[0, 1]$. In the simulations discussed in Section 3, the identity function $f(X) = X$ is used for LP8 and LP10, and the sum function $f(X, Y) = X + Y$ for LP9. For the other dynamic properties, f is defined as follows:

$$f(X_1, .., X_k) = th(\sigma, \tau, X_1 + ... + X_k)$$
$$\text{with} \quad th(\sigma, \tau, W) = [1 / (1+e^{-\sigma (W-\tau)}) - 1 / (1+e^{\sigma\tau})](1+e^{-\sigma\tau})$$

a logistic threshold function, where σ is the steepness and τ is the threshold; this function f is applied to properties LP0 to LP7. Parameter γ is an update speed factor. First the generation of sensory representations for stimuli s_1 and s_2 are described by LP0 and LP1, respectively.

LP0 Sensory representation of stimulus s_1
If   stimulus s_1 is sensed with level V_1
  and   the sensory representation of s_1 has level V_2
then   after duration Δt the sensory representation of s_1 will have level $V_2 + \gamma [f(\omega_1 V_1) - V_2] \Delta t$.

   ss(s_1,V_1) & srs(s_1,V_2) $\rightarrow$ srs(s_1, V_2 + γ [f(ω_1 V_1) – V_2] Δt)

LP1 Sensory representation of stimulus s_2
If   the emotional preparation of B has level V_1
  and   stimulus s_2 is sensed with level V_2
  and   the sensory representation of s_2 has level V_3
then   after duration Δt the sensory representation of s_2
           will have level $V_3 + \gamma [f(\omega_{16} V_1, \omega_1 V_2) - V_3] \Delta t$.

   ep(B,V_1) & ss(s_2,V_2) & srs(s_2,V_3) $\rightarrow$ srs(s_2, V_3 + γ [f(ω_{16} V_1, ω_1 V_2) – V_3] Δt)

In LP2 it is described how the sensory representation of a body state is maintained. Note that here the suppressing effect of the control state is also incorporated.

LP2 Sensory representation of a body state
If   body state B is sensed with level V_1
  and   the emotional preparation for B has level V_2
  and   the control state for B has level V_3
  and   the sensory representation of B has level V_4
then   after duration Δt the sensory representation of B
           will have level $V_4 + \gamma [f(\omega_2 V_1, \omega_4 V_2, \omega_{11} V_3) - V_4] \Delta t$.

   ss(B,V_1) & ep(B,V_2) & cs(B,V_3) & srs(B,V_4) $\rightarrow$ srs(B, V_4 + γ [f(ω_2 V_1, ω_4 V_2, ω_{11} V_3) – V_4] Δt)

The control state is generated by LP3, based on the sensory representation of b (feeling the emotion); also the considered stimuli are involved.

LP3 Control state for a sensory representation of a body state
If   the sensory representation of b has level V_1
  and   the sensory representation of s_2 has level V_2
  and   the sensory representation of s_1 has level V_3
  and   the control state for b has level V_4
then   after Δt the control state for b will have level $V_4 + \gamma [f(\omega_6 V_1, \omega_{17} V_2, \omega_{18} V_3) - V_4] \Delta t$.

   srs(b,V_1) & srs(s_2,V_2) & srs(s_1,V_3) & cs(b,V_4) $\rightarrow$ cs(b, V_4 + γ [f(ω_6 V_1, ω_{17} V_2, ω_{18} V_3) – V_4] Δt)

In LP4 it the preparation for an emotional response is described, depending on stimuli and the feeling. Here also a suppressing effect of the control state is incorporated.

LP4 Emotional preparation for a body state

If　　the sensory representation of b has level V_1

and　the sensory representation of s_1 has level V_2

and　the control state of b has level V_3

and　the sensory representation of s_2 has level V_4

and　the emotional preparation for b has level V_5

then　after duration Δt the emotional preparation for b

will have level $V_5 + \gamma [f(\omega_3 V_1, \omega_5 V_2, \omega_7 V_3, \omega_{15} V_4) - V_5] \Delta t.$

srs(b,V_1) & srs(s_1,V_2) & cs(b,V_3) & srs(s_2,V_4) & ep(b,V_5)

→ ep(b, $V_5 + \gamma$ [f($\omega_3 V_1$, $\omega_5 V_2$, $\omega_7 V_3$, $\omega_{15} V_4$) − V_5] Δt)

Antecedent-focused regulation emotion regulation (cf. [11, 12]) has been modelled in LP5 by a 'turn-away' action to avoid the stimulus, based on the control state.

LP5 Turn-away preparation

If　　the control state for b has level V_1

and　the turn-away preparation for s_1 has level V_2

then　after Δt the turn-away preparation for s_1 will have level $V_2 + \gamma [f(\omega_9 V_1) - V_2] \Delta t.$

cs(b,V_1) & tap(s_1,V_2) → tap(s_1, $V_2 + \gamma$ [f($\omega_9 V_1$) − V_2] Δt)

A body state is actually changed based on the preparation for it, possibly suppressed by the control state, as expressed in LP6. A turn-away action is described in LP7; sensing a body state is described by LP8 in a straightforward manner.

LP6 Body change

If　　the emotional preparation for B has level V_1

and　the control state for B has level V_2

and　the body effector for B has level V_3

then　after Δt the body effector for B will have level $V_3 + \gamma [f(\omega_{12} V_1, \omega_8 V_2) - V_3] \Delta t.$

ep(B,V_1) & cs(B,V_2) & be(B,V_3) → be(B, $V_3 + \gamma$ [f($\omega_{12} V_1$, $\omega_8 V_2$) − V_3] Δt)

LP7 Turn-away action

If　　the turn-away preparation for stimulus s_1 has level V_1

and　the turn-away effector of s_1 has level V_2

then　after duration Δt the turn-away effector for s_1 will have level $V_2 + \gamma [f(\omega_{10} V_1) - V_2] \Delta t.$

tap(s_1,V_1) & tae(s_2,V_2) → tae(s_1, $V_2 + \gamma$ [f($\omega_{10} V_1$) − V_2] Δt)

LP8 Sensing a body state

If　　the body effector for body state B has level V_1

and　body state B is sensed with level V_2

then　after duration Δt body state B will have level $V_2 + \gamma [f(\omega_{13} V_1) - V_2] \Delta t.$

be(B,V_1) & ss(B,V_2) → ss(B, $V_2 + \gamma$ [f($\omega_{13} V_1$) − V_2] Δt)

Sensing stimulus s_1 does not only depend on the actual world state, but also on whether a turn-away action has been performed; this is described in LP9. On the other hand, sensing stimulus s_2 does only depend on the actual world state; it is described in LP10.

LP9 Sensing stimulus s_1

If　　the turn-away effector for stimulus s_1 has level V_1

and　the world state for s_1 has level V_2

and　stimulus s_1 is sensed with level V_3

then　after duration Δt stimulus s_1 will be sensed with level $V_3 + \gamma [f(\omega_{14} V_1, \omega_0 V_2) - V_3] \Delta t.$

tae(s_1,V_1) & ws(s_1,V_2) & ss(s_1,V_3) → ss(s_1, $V_3 + \gamma$ [f($\omega_{14} V_1$, $\omega_0 V_2$) − V_3] Δt)

LP10 Sensing stimulus s$_2$
If   the world state for s$_2$ has level V_1
   and stimulus s$_2$ is sensed with level V_2
then   after duration Δt stimulus s$_2$ will be sensed with level $V_2 + \gamma\,[\,f(\omega_0\,V_1) - V_2\,]\,\Delta t.$

   ws(s$_2$,V$_1$) & ss(s$_2$,V$_2$) →→ ss(s$_2$, V$_2$ + γ [f(ω$_0$ V$_1$) − V$_2$] Δt)

3. Simulation Experiments

In this section simulation results are discussed for a number of example scenarios, which all involve an emotional preparation triggered by some neutral but trauma-related stimulus s$_1$. It is assumed that the person has experienced a traumatic event in the past, and due to this event the person has developed a configuration of connections that does not exist in a healthy person. The considered scenarios relate to phenomena in literature, as discussed in Section 1. They have been generated by the LEADSTO software environment (cf. [3]), and using the jHepWork data-analysis framework to analyse and present the simulation results (cf. [5]).

The first scenario addressed describes how a neutral stimulus affects a healthy subject, who does not react in a traumatized manner. The second and third scenario (Figures 2 and 3) concern the presentation of the stimulus s$_1$ to two kinds of PTSD subjects in a situation where they can avoid being exposed to it. In traces, the world state and sensor state of stimulus s$_2$ are not shown for the sake of clarity as they are equal to zero in the simulated scenario. In Figures 2 and 3 time is on the horizontal axis and activation levels for the different states as indicated on the vertical axis. The parameter values used (connection strenghts ω and threshold τ and steepness σ values for the logistic threshold function) can be seen in Table 3, those have been chosen according the neurological findings presented in Section 1 and tuned with intuitive sense. The step size taken is $\Delta t = 1$.

3.1. Scenario Showing a Healthy Subject

The first case describes how a healthy person senses a neutral stimulus:

- External stimulus s$_1$ occurs and triggers a sensory representation of this stimulus that does not trigger emotional preparation, because ω$_5$ is zero.
- This absence of emotional preparation makes that feeling b does not increase, and control over the situation is not performed.

The important parameter in this scenario is the low (even 0) value of the connection ω$_5$, which links the neutral stimulus representation to an emotional preparation. No emotional load occurs because this neutral stimulus is not associated to any traumatic experience; the sensor state ss(s1) and its representation srs(s1) activate because the neutral stimulus occurs (world state ws(s1) is active), but no emotional preparation occurs: the emotional preparation state ep(b) stays at 0.

3.2. Scenario Showing a Flashback PTSD subject

The second case considered describes a situation where the person suffers from flashback symptoms of PTSD. He or she is confronted to a stimulus which in principle is neutral, but is related to the traumatic experience (for example, a car, when the patient's traumatic experience is a car accident).

Table 3. Parameter values for the three scenarios

	state	healthy		flashback		dissociation	
		τ	σ	τ	σ	τ	σ
LP0	sensory representation of s_1	0.2	4	0.2	4	0.2	4
LP1	sensory representation of s_2	0.2	4	0.2	4	0.2	4
LP2	sensory representation of body	0.2	4	0.2	4	0.2	4
LP3	control state	0.5	4	0.5	4	**0.3**	4
LP4	emotional preparation	**0.6**	4	**0.2**	4	**0.2**	4
LP5	turn away preparation	0.2	4	0.2	4	0.2	4
LP6	body effector	0.4	4	0.4	4	0.4	4
LP7	turn away effector	0.2	4	0.2	4	0.2	4

LP	ω	healthy	flashback	dissociation
LP10	ω_0	1	1	1
LP0	ω_1	1	1	1
LP2	ω_2	1	1	1
LP4	ω_3	0.6	0.6	0.6
LP4	ω_5	**0**	**0.6**	**0.6**
LP3	ω_6	0.6	0.6	0.6
LP2	ω_4	**0.2**	**0.7**	**0.7**
LP4	ω_7	-0.4	-0.4	**-0.7**
LP6	ω_8	-0.4	-0.4	-0.4
LP5	ω_9	0.8	0.8	0.8
LP7	ω_{10}	0.6	0.6	0.6
LP2	ω_{11}	**0**	**-0.2**	**-0.8**
LP6	ω_{12}	0.7	0.7	0.7
LP8	ω_{13}	1	1	1
LP9	ω_{14}	-1	-1	-1
LP4	ω_{15}	0.8	0.8	0.8
LP1	ω_{16}	**0**	**0.6**	**0.2**
LP3	ω_{17}	0.5	0.5	0.5
LP3	ω_{18}	**0**	**0.3**	**0.3**

In this PTSD subject, the stimulus triggers a strong emotional preparation that brings the person in a state of re-experiencing the traumatic episode. This reaction activates the control state that makes the agent turning away from the stimulus, but the emotional regulation is impaired, and although the stimulus is not present anymore, there is no way to inhibit the aversive feelings. The parameter values used are shown in Table 3, bold non-italic values are those that differ from the healthy person case. The simulation is shown in Figure 2. This situation shows the following:

- The external stimulus s_1 occurs and triggers the representation srs(s_1) of this stimulus that generates a high emotional preparation ep(b) through a high connection strength ω_5 and lightly triggers the control state cs(b) proactively through ω_{18}.
- The emotional preparation drives the sensory representation srs(b) of body state b up via ω_4 and at the same time triggers via ω_{16} sensory representation srs(s_2) of the traumatic memory.
- Via ω_6 and ω_{17} these representations strongly activate the control state cs(b) for the regulation.
- The control state triggers the turn-away preparation via ω_9 but fails to inhibit sufficiently the emotional load (which is too high due to the re-visualization of the traumatic past memories).
- The turn-away preparation leads to the turn-away action (effector state tae(s_1)) that takes the stimulus away from the agent (inhibition of sensor state ss(s_1)) via connections ω_{10} and ω_{14}.

- Although the stimulus is not present anymore or has become very weak (low $ss(s_1)$), the emotional preparation is not regulated due to the impairment of emotion regulation, and the emotional load stays high because the flashback and re-experiencing elements ($srs(s_2)$ and $srs(b)$) stay high and propagate via ω_{15} and ω_3.

PTSD Model: Flashback Subject

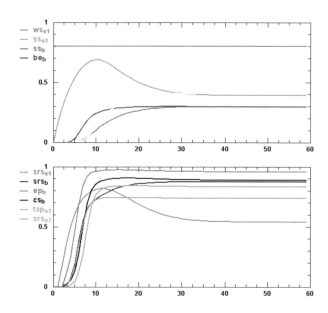

Figure 2. Simulated Flashback PTSD scenario (upper graph: sensor states, world states and body states; lower graph: internal sensory representation, preparation and control states)

In the simulation, the turn-away movement is observed by the increased level of the turn-away effector, $tae(s_1)$, in yellow, starting after time point 5. This action causes lowering of the sensed stimulus and by repercussion, its representation, but does not remove the visual representation of the trauma neither the physical discomfort ($srs(s_2)$ and $srs(b)$ in orange and blue respectively). Thus, emotional preparation ($ep(b)$, in red) is not significantly lowered, the agent is overrun by the emotion.

3.3. Scenario Showing a Dissociative PTSD subject

The third case describes a situation where the person suffers from dissociative symptoms of PTSD. He or she again is confronted with a stimulus which is associated to the traumatic experience. This kind of stimulus triggers a strong emotional preparation that puts back the patient in a state of re-experiencing the traumatic episode, but also proactively triggers the control state. This activation of the control state is then emphasized by the enhanced sensitivity due to emotional preparation. It makes the agent turn away from the situation, but also inhibits his or her emotional preparation as a defensive mechanism to avoid falling in strong reliving of the trauma.

Parameter values used are shown in Table 3; bold values are those that differ from the healthy person. The simulation can be seen in Figure 3; it shows the following:

- The external stimulus s_1 occurs and triggers the representation srs(s_1) of this stimulus that starts to generate an emotional preparation ep(b) through ω_5 and lightly triggers the control state cs(b) proactively through ω_{18}.
- The emotional preparation starts to increase the sensory representation srs(b) of body state b via ω_4, and traumatic memories can be recalled, shown in a light increase of srs(s_2) via ω_{16}.
- The control state cs(b) is strongly activated by both sensory representations srs(b) and srs(s_1) through ω_6 and ω_{18}.
- This activation of the control state results in inhibiting the sensory representation srs(b) of body state b thus decreasing the re-experiencing (by ω_{11} and ω_7), and finally activates turn-away preparation tap(s_1) to avoid the stimulus (through ω_9).
- The turn-away preparation propagates through ω_{10} to the turn-away effector tae(s_1) to make the person look in another direction (by connection ω_{14}).
- The stimulus is lowered but the control state continues to act over the emotional preparation and body representation (through ω_7 and ω_{11}), which explains the weak ep(b) and very low srs(b), which is felt as dissociation.

PTSD Model: Dissociative Subject

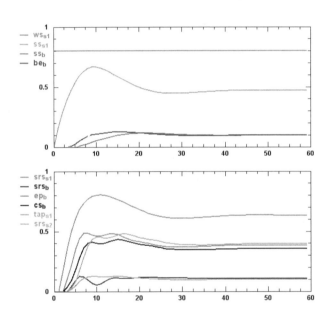

Figure 3. Simulated dissociative PTSD scenario (upper graph: sensor states, world states and body states; lower graph: internal sensory representation, preparation and control states)

In the simulation, at time point 7 the emotional preparation peak occurs while the control state activation is not yet reached (low cs(b) in black before time point 7). The control activation suppresses the progression of emotional preparation and inhibits the body perception (ep(b) in red stops growing and srs(b) in blue get back to *0*). As another control effect, the agent turns away from the stimulus (tae(s_1), in yellow, is enhanced from time point 7. This affects the perception of the stimulus and its sensory representation (reduced ss(s_1) and srs(s_1)).

4. Discussion

The presented computational agent model was designed using principles from the neurological literature on Post-Traumatic Stress Disorders. It was shown that by assuming deviant strengths for some connections and some deviant threshold values lead to patterns that are in accordance with patterns described in the literature. The assumption is that the traumatic experience itself has an impact on these connections and thresholds, by which they become changed for longer time periods. The presented model differs substantially from the model presented in [18] and [19], as this associative memory model focuses mainly on memory formation and does not consider the neurological modifications due to extreme emotions in addition to memory recall.

Referring to [16], the presented model falls in two categories. Firstly, it addresses at an abstract level reconstruction of the neural links and processes that underlie an organisms' emotional reactions, and therefore it falls in the category of anatomic approaches. But, secondly, it also falls in the category of appraisal-derivation approaches: emotion is assumed to arise from individual judgment concerning the relationship between events and an individual's beliefs, desires and intentions.

The obtained cognitive/affective agent model can be used as a basis for the design of human-like virtual agents in simulation-based training or in gaming or virtual stories. For the first type of application a virtual patient can be developed based on the model so that, for example, a psychiatrist or psycho-therapist (e.g., during his or her education) can gain insight in the processes in certain types of PTSD patients, or it can be used by a therapist to analyze how a certain form of therapy can have its effect on these processes. For the second type of application a system for agent-based virtual stories can be designed in which, for example, persons with PTSD play a role, that can be based on the presented model, and progressively recover from the trauma.

Modeling causal relations discussed in neurological literature in the manner as presented here does not take specific neurons into consideration but can use more abstract mental states, relating, for example, to groups of neurons. This is a way to exploit within the agent modelling area results from the large and more and more growing amount of neurological literature. This can be considered as a way of abstraction by lifting neurological knowledge to a mental (cognitive/affective) modelling level. Nevertheless, the type of agent model that results shows some technical elements that are also used at the neurological modelling level. For example, it takes states as having a certain activation level, instead of binary, for example in order to make reciprocal cognitive/affective loops and gradual adaptation possible. As a consequence, for a state causally depending on multiple other states, values for such incoming activation levels have to be combined. Therefore combination functions f are needed, such as the one based on the continuous logistic threshold function used here, or an alternative combination function f can be considered, such as:

$$f(W_1, W_2) = 1 \ \text{if} \ W_1 + W_2 \geq \tau, \ \text{and} \ 0 \ \text{otherwise}$$
$$f(W_1, W_2) = \beta \, max(W_1, W_2) + (1-\beta) \, min(W_1, W_2) \qquad (0 \leq \beta \leq 1)$$
$$f(W_1, W_2) = \beta(1 - (1-W_1)(1-W_2)) + (1 - \beta)W_1W_2 \qquad (0 \leq \beta \leq 1)$$

Note that similar numerical elements play a role in the area of modelling imperfect reasoning, for example based on fuzzy or uncertain information. So, in order to model such an agent at a cognitive/affective level abstracting from neurological detail, still some machinery is needed that might be associated to a neural modelling perspective. However, in order to successfully model agents with more complex and human-like behaviour, for example incorporating regulation processes, mutual cognitive/affective interaction loops, and/or feedback loops modelling adaptivity, the toolset for the agent modeller has to include such modelling techniques, enabling to model agents in a hybrid logical/numerical manner.

References

[1]   R.L. Bluhm, P.C. Williamson, E.A. Osuch, P.A. Frewen, T.K. Stevens, K. Boksman, R.W.J. Neufeld, J. Théberge, and R.A. Lanius, Alteration in default network connectivity in PTSD related to early-life trauma. *Journal of Psychiatry Neuroscience* 34 (2009), 187-194.
[2]   T. Bosse, Z.A. Memon, and J. Treur, A Cognitive and Neural Model for Adaptive Emotion Reading by Mirroring Preparation States and Hebbian Learning. *Cognitive Systems Research* (2011), in press. doi 10.1016/j.cogsys.2010.10.003
[3]   T. Bosse, C.M. Jonker, L. van der Meij, J. Treur. A Language and Environment for Analysis of Dynamics by Simulation. *International Journal of Artificial Intelligence Tools* 16 (2007), 435-464.
[4]   S.J. Broyd, C. Demanuele, S.Debener, S.K. Helps, C.J. James, and E.J. Sonuga-Barke, Default-mode brain dysfunction in mental disorders: a systematic review. *Neuroscience & Biobehavioral Reviews* 33 (2009), 279-296.
[5]   S. Chekanov, *Scientific Data analysis using Jython Scripting and Java*. Springer Verlag, 2010.
[6]   A.R. Damasio, *The Feeling of What Happens: Body and Emotion in the Making of Consciousness*. New York: Harcourt Brace, 1999.
[7]   A.R. Damasio, The fabric of the mind: A neurobiological perspective (Eighth C.U. Ariens Kappers Lecture). *Prog Brain Res* 126 (2000), 457-467 .
[8]   A.R. Damasio, *Looking for Spinoza: Joy, Sorrow, and the Feeling Brain*. Vintage Books, 2003.
[9]   K..Felmingham, A.H. Kemp, L.Williams, E. Falconer, G. Olivieri, A. Peduto, R. Bryant, Dissociative response to conscious and non-conscious fear impact underlying brain function in Post-Traumatic Stress Disorder. *Psychological Medicine* 38 (2008), 1771-1780.
[10] P.A. Frewen, R.A. Lanius, D.J.A.Dozois, J.W. Hopper, C. Pain, and M. Densmore, Clinical and neural correlates of alexithymia in Posttraumatic Stress Disorder. *J. of Abnormal Psych.* 117 (2008), 171-181.
[11] P.R. Goldin, K. McRae, W. Ramel, and J.J. Gross, The neural bases of emotion regulation: Reappraisal and Supression of Negative Emotion. *Biological Psychiatry* 63 (2008), 577-586.
[12] J.J. Gross, Antecedent- and response-focused emotion regulation: divergent consequences for experience, expression, and physiology. *J. of Personality and Social Psych.* 74 (1998), 224–237.
[13] R.A. Lanius, P.C., Williamson, R.L. Bluhm, M. Densmore, K. Boksman, R.W.J. Neufeld, J.S. Gati, and R.S. Menon, Functional Connectivity of Dissociative Responses in Posttraumatic Stress Disorder: A Functional Magnetic Resonance Imaging Investigation. *Biol Psychiatry* 57 (2005), 873-884.
[14] R.A. Lanius, R.L.Bluhm, N.J. Coupland, K.M. Hegadoren, B. Rowe, J. Théberge, R.W.J. Neufeld, P.C. Williamson, M. Brimson, Default network connectivity as a predictor of post-traumatic stress disorder symptom severity in acutely traumatized subjects. *Acta Psychiatrica Scandinavica* 121 (2010), 33-40.
[15] R.A. Lanius, P.A. Frewen, Toward a Psychobiology of Posttraumatic Self-Dysregulation: Re-experiencing, Hyperarousal, Dissociation and Emotional Numbing. *Ann. N.Y. Acad. Sci.* 1071 (2006), 110-124.
[16] S. Marsella, J. Gratch, P. Petta, Computational Models of Emotion. Ch 1.2 in: K.R. Scherer, T.Bänziger, E. Roesch. A Blueprint for Affective Computing. *Oxford University Press,* 2010.
[17] D.J. Oathes, W.J. Ray, Dissociative Tendencies and Facilitated Emotional Processing. *Emotion* 8 (2008), 653–661.
[18] W.W. Tryon, A Neural Network Explanation of Posttraumatic Stress Disorder. *Journal of Anxiety Disorders* 12, 373-385 (1998)
[19] W.W. Tryon, A Bidirectional Associative Memory Explanation of Posttraumatic Stress Disorder. *Clinical Psychology Review* 19, 789–818 (1999)

Biologically Inspired Cognitive Architectures 2011
A.V. Samsonovich and K.R. Jóhannsdóttir (Eds.)
IOS Press, 2011

Interacting Complementary Learning Systems in Brains and Machines

David C. NOELLE
University of California, Merced
:5200 North Lake Road Merced 95343 United States
dnoelle@ucmerced.edu

Keywords. Computational neuroscience, learning, complementary learning systems, reinforcement learning, working memory, episodic memory, dopamine, striatum, prefrontal cortex, hippocampus

Abstract

There is growing evidence for multiple complementary learning systems in the human brain. The midbrain dopamine system, along with its projections to the striatum and throughout cortex, can be seen as implementing a form of reinforcement learning. The prefrontal cortex, supported by loops through the thalamus, provides critical mechanisms for working memory, actively maintaining task relevant control information. The hippocampus, and parahippocampal cortical areas, provide support for the persistent retention of rapidly acquired information, such as memories of life episodes. Forming the foundation of all three of these systems are fundamental processes of synaptic plasticity. These complementary learning systems continuously interact, producing learning performance that transcends the capabilities of any one mechanism. Taking inspiration from this neural architecture, I present a multi-component learning mechanism for software agents that learns from sparse rewards but may also benefit from situated instruction. This learning process is demonstrated in a simple maze learning task.

Biologically Inspired Cognitive Architectures 2011
A.V. Samsonovich and K.R. Jóhannsdóttir (Eds.)
IOS Press, 2011
doi:10.3233/978-1-60750-959-2-263

Innate and Learned Emotion Network

Rony NOVIANTO [a] and Mary-Anne WILLIAMS [b]

[a] rony@ronynovianto.com
[b] mary-anne@themagiclab.org
Centre for Quantum Computation and Intelligent Systems
University of Technology Sydney, Australia

Abstract. Autonomous agents sometimes can only rely on the subjective information in terms of emotions to make decision due to the inavailability of the non-
subjective knowledge. However, current emotion models lack of integrating innate
emotion and learned emotion and tend to focus on a specific aspect. This paper
describes the underlying new computational emotion model in ASMO which integrates both innate and learned emotions as well as reasoning based on probabilistic
causal network. ASMO's emotion model is compared with other models and related works and shows its practical capabilities to utilize subjective knowledge in
decision making.

Keywords. Innate and learned emotion, Emotion causal network, Attentive and
Self-modifying (ASMO) emotion

1. Introduction

Autonomous agents sometimes do not have the required non-subjective knowledge to
reason about the environment and need to rely on the subjective knowledge available
to make decision, which are typically presented in terms of emotions. For example, a
duration or a cost of a path is unknown but a user's opinion or feeling about the path is
known. This subjective knowledge or emotion is also needed when reasoning does not
find the optimal solution in time because of the complexity of the systems. In addition,
it can be used to represent agents' preferences when more than one acceptable solution
is found, which create their individual characteristics. Inspired by human emotion, we
model this subjective knowledge or emotion on the existing ASMO cognitive architecture
[8,9].

The discussion of whether human emotion is innate or learned leads to two major
aspects of emotion, namely biological and cognitive aspects, which are often viewed
as being opposed to each other. The biological aspect leads to a basic emotion theory
whereas the cognitive aspect leads to a cognitive appraisal theory [13]. In this paper, we
explore both of these aspects.

The theory of biological and cognitive aspects of emotion and how they are designed in ASMO are described in Section 2. In Section 3, we describe how behavior
and physiological responses are influenced by emotion and reasoning. The evaluation of
ASMO's emotion model in a robot bear is then discussed in Section 4. We conclude with
a comparison with other models and related works in Section 5 and highlight its practical
impact.

2. Emotion Theory and Design

Emotions can be represented using a *n*-dimensional space [12] where each coordinate in a space refers to a specific instance of emotion. In the current ASMO architecture, three *emotional dimensions* namely positive valence, negative valence and arousal are used to indicate how pleasant, unpleasant, and exciting a situation or an event is respectively. The values of these dimensions are bounded from 0 to 1 (equivalent to a range from 0 to 100 percent) and thus a dimension could not have a negative value.

We view emotion as the probability of causing pleasantness, unpleasantness, and excitement to *occur*. An event which has the probability of 0.7 to cause pleasantness to occur, may imply that it has the probability of 0.3 to cause pleasantness to not occur, but does not imply that it has the probability of 0.3 to cause unpleasantness to occur and vice versa. In another words, a situation is not necessarily unpleasant when pleasantness does not occur. This suggests that both positive and negative valence dimensions should be independent to each other, i.e. bivariate instead of bipolar dimensions.

Some studies have found that people can feel both happy and sad at the same time [5] although it is not clear in those studies whether people do so because they interpret the same situations from different perspectives, hence different appraisals. Other emotion models have also suggested different kind of bivariate dimensions such as [7,18], however, they are less clear and practical. For example, the difference between pleasantness and positive affect dimensions in work by Watson and Tellegen [18] is ambiguous.

ASMO's emotion is modeled using a directed acyclic *causal network* [11] where nodes are divided into four categories, namely label, dimension, biological, and cognitive nodes (see Figure 1 for an example of an emotion network). This causal network restricts the parent nodes to be the cause of their children nodes, i.e. causality relationship. For example, 'rain' node can be the parent of 'wet' node, but not vice versa. The *label nodes* represent types of emotion, such as happy and sad. The *dimension nodes* are connected to the label nodes and correspond to the emotional dimensions, i.e. positive valence, negative valence, and arousal dimension. The *biological nodes* are connected to the dimension nodes and/or other biological nodes. The *cognitive nodes* are connected to the dimension nodes, biological nodes and/or other cognitive nodes.

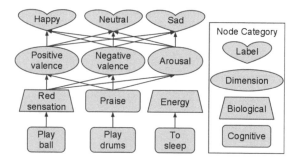

Figure 1. Emotion network with different node categories

2.1. Biological Appraisal

Human emotion cannot always be justified. People sometimes report that they like some-thing because of the way it is regardless its relevance and effects to them. They have no reason or do not think that they need a reason to like it. They seem to have biologically innate or 'built-in' knowledge to evaluate situations without reasoning, similar to traits that are imprinted in the DNA. Studies have shown that infants have innate preferences to sweet taste [4]. Infants have also shown an emotionally innate response to high-pitched human voices [19]. Major research traditions in the biological perspective of emotion can be seen in [13, p.309]. We refer to *biological appraisal* as this evaluation of an event or a situation based on innate or 'built-in' knowledge.

In ASMO, innate knowledge is built as biological nodes where their conditional probability values can be determined at design time. By convention, these nodes are fixed across the agent's lifespan, which are useful when the designers want to embed perma-nent characteristics or personality to the agent, e.g. being harmful to human is unpleasant. The strength level of the characteristics or personality depends on the conditional proba-bility values. The agent can have a maximum strength of emotional judgement about an event by ensuring that the conditional probability values are at maximum, which is 1.

2.2. Cognitive Appraisal

According to cognitive appraisal theory, emotions are elicited based on the individual's subjective appraisal of a situation or an event in terms of its relevance and effects to per-sonal well-being [6]. Some of the most frequently used theories in computational mod-eling, such as the OCC theory [10] and Scherer's theory[17] describe criteria to evaluate a situation in order to generate an emotion. A theory can have the same criteria and yet generates different emotions because of the different ways to structure the criteria. Major research traditions in the cognitive perspective of emotion can be seen in [13, p.311]. Cognitive appraisal is the evaluation of an event or a situation based on the knowledge which is learned because of its relevance and effects to personal well-being.

In ASMO, the evaluation criteria are structured as cognitive nodes in the causal network, which can be learned from the environment, such as through association or conditioning. As the number of nodes increases, the network becomes computationally intractable to do exact inferece, so approximate inference method such as Monte Carlo algorithm [16] is used to approximately evaluate the situations.

Cognitive appraisal can be seen as a specific type of reasoning. It always evaluates situations in terms of the probability of the emotional dimensions to occur whereas rea-soning evaluates situations in terms of the probability of the goals to occur. Reasoning does not necessary elicit emotions as shown in Figure 1 where the *energy node* is discon-nected from the dimensional nodes. However, reasoning can just be as same as cognitive appraisal when the goals are the emotional dimensions nodes, e.g. the agent wants to get pleasantness. Thus, ASMO's emotion network integrates the different perspectives of emotion and reasoning on the same network.

3. Behavior and Physiological Responses

Biological appraisal, cognitive appraisal and reasoning influence behavior and physio-logical responses. Some people would do things based on their goals despite their emotions, while some others would do the same things based on their emotions despite their goals. Consider a play–sleep situation where a person encounters a dilemma between playing a red ball game, playing drums, or going to sleep (see Figure 1 for the emotion network). Assume that the person is a male for the simplicity of the paper and the emotion towards the red sensation is innate. He likes to play his favorite red ball game without any reason, but he also wants to play drums, because he thinks that he will get praised when he plays the drums and not the ball game. Meanwhile, he needs to go to sleep to have enough energy for working the next day.

In this case, biological appraisal favors playing ball behavior because of the innate preference in the red sensation. Cognitive appraisal favors the playing drums behavior because he has learned that praise is benefit for his well-being. Reasoning favors going to sleep behavior because his goals can be achieved. Depending on which evaluation is higher, he will choose to play ball or drums despite his goal to sleep or choose to go to sleep despite his emotion about playing ball and drums.

Behavior and physiological responses are also effected by arousal. The higher the arousal is, the faster the responses. When people are highly aroused, they will act or move faster and their heart rates are faster than when they are calm or in a normal state.

4. Discussion

The emotion network mechanism is evaluated using a robot bear called Smokey based on the play–sleep dilemma described above. Smokey is presented with a red ball and drums while 'he' has a goal to sleep. His evaluation is calculated based on the conditional probability tables where initial values are shown in Table 1. Other probabilities which are not shown in the table are given a fair probability of 0.5 and p(A) refers to p(A=true) which is the probability of A is true.

Symbol assignments					B	p(R)		D	p(P)		S	p(E)		R	P	p(PV)
t	true	R	red sensation											t	t	0.9
f	false	P	praise		t	0.8		t	0.7		t	0.8		t	f	0.9
B	play ball	E	energy		f	0.5		f	0.5		f	0.2		f	t	0.9
D	play drum	PV	positive valence											f	f	0.5
S	to sleep															

Table 1. Initial values of the conditional probility tables

The audience (i.e. his friends) can send him a request during the interaction to influence his decision. Each request is interpreted as a 0.05 increased in the prior probability. Table 2 shows the audience's influences on the 'play drums' behavior, where p(A | B) is the probability of A given B. Initially, Smokey chooses to play his favorite red ball as X is the highest value in the first trial. However, he changes his decision to play drums on the third trial as his belief of getting praise increases because of the requests from the audience, i.e. the W values increased. The 'to sleep' behavior remains in a lower value because he has a strong embedded emotional judgement in this experiment. Arousal is used to determine the speeds of the arms movements and the heart shape LEDs beat rate.

Emotion can not only compete with the reasoning, but also reinforce it and vice versa. For example, if Smokey does not have to work the next day and has a goal to

W:	p(P=t | D=t)	Trial	W	X	Y	Z
X:	p(PV=t | B=t)	1	0.7	0.868	0.858	0.8
Y:	p(PV=t | D=t)	2	0.8	0.872	0.872	0.8
Z:	p(E=t | S=t)	3	0.9	0.876	0.886	0.8

Table 2. Play–sleep evaluation and audience's influences on play drums behavior

have fun with his friends instead, then both playing ball and playing drums behaviors are valid and reinforced by the reasoning. Smokey will choose the behavior with the highest judgement value, which indicates his preference over the other behaviors. In this case, one behavior may be prefered over the others when there is more than one behavior to achieve the goals. In ASMO's emotion model, developers can provide some preferences to agents which become their personal characteristics.

5. Comparison and Related Works

Conati and Maclaren have provided a brief summary of emotion models that integrate causes and effects [2]. In addition, Rumbell et al. have also described a recent comparison of emotion models in autonomous agents [15]. To our understanding, we are not aware of any emotion models that integrate innate emotion (biological appraisal), learned emotion (cognitive appraisal) and reasoning which can influence the agent's behaviors.

A similar probabilistic approach using dynamic decision network has been used to recognize students' emotions based on the OCC cognitive appraisal theory [1,2]. Like ASMO's emotion model, it contains nodes to represent the situations, such as student's goal, interaction pattern, appraisal, and agent's action nodes. However, this model does not account the biological aspect of emotion and how emotions and reasoning influence the agent's behavior.

Considering the non-cognitive aspect of emotion, Rosis et al. [14] describe a BDI emotion model that distinguishes cognitive evaluations with intuitive appraisals. They proposed that cognitive evaluation is a rational judgement that is supported by reasons whereas intuitive appraisal is a non-rational judgement based on associative learning and memory instead of justifiable reasons. In ASMO, both of these judgements are considered as cognitive appraisals, because they are based on the knowledge which is learned due to its relevence and effects to personal well-being whereas biological appraisal is based on the innate knowledge.

The ASMO's emotion model to represent and reason preferences shares similarities with works in preference logic [3]. Instead of using logic, ASMO uses bayesian probability to model the preferences. The desirability in preference logic is similar to the prior probability in bayesian causal network of ASMO's emotion model, which is the belief of a condition will occur in terms of probability.

6. Conclusion

Subjective preferences or knowledge which are typically presented in terms of emotions can be used to complement decision making and to create personal characteristics. ASMO integrates a reasoning together with innate and learned emotions, which are represented as biological appraisal and cognitive appraisal into a probabilistic casual network. It allows developers to build autonomous agents that can respond to the environment in a practical manner.

References

[1] C. Conati. Probabilistic assessment of user's emotions in educational games. *Applied Artificial Intelligence*, 16(7-8):555–575, 2002.

[2] C. Conati and H. Maclaren. Empirically building and evaluating a probabilistic model of user affect. *User Modeling and User-Adapted Interaction*, 19(3):267–303, 2009.

[3] C. Domshlak, E. Hüllermeier, S. Kaci, and H. Prade. Preferences in ai: an overview. *Artif. Intell.*, 175(7-8):1037–1052, May 2011.

[4] A. Drewnowski. Taste preferences and food intake. *Annual Review of Nutrition*, 17(1):237–253, 1997.

[5] J. T. Larsen and A. P. McGraw. Further evidence for mixed emotions. *Personality and Social Psychology Review*, Jan 2011.

[6] R. S. Lazarus. *Emotion and adaptation*. Oxford University Press, 1994.

[7] C. J. Norris, J. Gollan, G. G. Berntson, and J. T. Cacioppo. The current status of research on the structure of evaluative space. *Biological Psychology*, 84(3):422–436, 2010. The biopsychology of emotion: Current theoretical and empirical perspectives.

[8] R. Novianto, B. Johnston, and M.-A. Williams. Attention in the asmo cognitive architecture. In *Proceedings of the First Annual Meeting of the BICA Society*, 2010.

[9] R. Novianto and M.-A. Williams. The role of attention in robot self-awareness. In *Robot and Human Interactive Communication, 2009. RO-MAN 2009. The 18th IEEE International Symposium on*, pages 1047–1053, Sep 2009.

[10] A. Ortony, G. L. Clore, and A. Collins. *The cognitive structure of emotions*. Cambridge University Press, 1990.

[11] J. Pearl. *Causality: models, reasoning, and inference*. Cambridge University Press, 2009.

[12] J. Posner, J. A. Russell, and B. S. Peterson. The circumplex model of affect: An integrative approach to affective neuroscience, cognitive development, and psychopathology. *Development and Psychopathology*, 17:715–734, 2005.

[13] J. Reeve. *Understanding motivation and emotion*. John Wiley & Sons, 2009.

[14] F. Rosis, C. Castelfranchi, P. Goldie, and V. Carofiglio. Cognitive evaluations and intuitive appraisals: can emotion models handle them both? In R. Cowie, C. Pelachaud, and P. Petta, editors, *Emotion-Oriented Systems*, Cognitive Technologies, pages 459–481. Springer Berlin Heidelberg, 2011.

[15] T. Rumbell, J. Barnden, S. Denham, and T. Wennekers. Emotions in autonomous agents: comparative analysis of mechanisms and functions. *Autonomous Agents and Multi-Agent Systems*, 2011.

[16] S. J. Russell and P. Norvig. *Artificial intelligence: a modern approach*. Prentice Hall series in artificial intelligence. Prentice Hall, 2010.

[17] K. R. Scherer. Appraisal considered as a process of multilevel sequential checking. In K. R. Scherer, A. Schorr, and T. Johnstone, editors, *Appraisal processes in emotion: theory, methods, research*, affective science, pages 92–120. Oxford University Press, New York, NY, US, 2001.

[18] D. Watson and A. Tellegen. Toward a consensual structure of mood. *Psychological Bulletin*, 98(2):219–235, Sep 1985.

[19] P. H. Wolff. The natural history of crying and other vocalizations in early infancy. In B. M. Foss, editor, *Determinants of infant behavior*, pages 81–109. Methuen, London, 1969.

Biologically Inspired Cognitive Architectures 2011
A.V. Samsonovich and K.R. Jóhannsdóttir (Eds.)
IOS Press, 2011
© 2011 The authors and IOS Press. All rights reserved.
doi:10.3233/978-1-60750-959-2-269

The Computational Basis of Emotions and Implications for Cognitive Architectures

Charles C. PECK [1], James KOZLOSKI

Biometaphorical Computing Group, Computational Biology Center, IBM Research,
United States

Abstract. Multiple theories of emotion and its role in cognitive function have been devised. These theories have been exploited to develop emotion-modeling artificial intelligence technologies that vary their behavior depending on the recognized emotional state. These theories and the technologies they motivate draw upon correlations between subjective emotional categories and behavioral changes, yet they do not adequately explain these correlations mechanistically. This paper addresses this deficiency with a new theory of emotion as epiphenomenal qualia resulting from variations in the processes that underlie consciousness and cognition. Accordingly, this paper presents fundamental assumptions about these processes and the mechanisms that give rise to them. It then identifies variations in these processes, the qualia they produce, and the corresponding emotion. The paper concludes by presenting the implications of this theory for designing cognitive or artificial intelligence technologies.

Keywords. Emotion, Cognition, Cognitive Architectures, Artificial Intelligence, Qualia, Consciousness

Introduction

There have been many efforts to exploit emotions for computational purposes. This paper explores this challenge and proposes a theory that explains emotions in terms of variations on processes thought to underlie cognition and which operate over computable components (i.e., neurons). It is in this manner that emotions are argued to be computationally grounded. This differs from models where emotions are computationally grounded in representations of the emotional state or in somatic signals [1,2,3].

Theories of emotion

Computational theories of emotion take several forms. First, generative (also known as "agent") models of emotion attempt to identify correlations between emotions, behaviors, and the events that elicit them. These models are then used to predict when an emotion is expected or appropriate. Sherer emphasized in one generative model (the "component process model" CPM [4]) that emotion prepares an organism to act, given some un-

---

[1]Corresponding Author: Charles C. Peck, IBM T. J. Watson Research Center, 1101 Kitchawan Road, Room 04-154, Yorktown Heights, NY 10598; E-mail: cpeck@us.ibm.com.

expected stimulus relevant to its well-being (e.g., fear [5]). Stimulus events in Scherer's model and in other generative models are external to the organism. Reviewing categories of generative models, Scherer identifies "basic emotion theories" positing reflexive emotional responses to external events, "constructivist theories" requiring an additional conscious recognition and categorization of a response, and "appraisal theories" additionally requiring coherence between an appraisal–reappraisal loop, bodily responses, and categories and representations of the event and evoked responses [6].

In contrast to generative models of emotion, which assume quantifiable external correlates for predicting emotions deterministically, certain theories of emotion, such as modern constructivism, hold that emotions can emerge in the absence of external stimulus events and are largely created by an individual's search and reflection. These models are therefore deemed inappropriate for deterministic modeling of emotion generation [4]. Such "non-deterministic" constructivism typically studies emotions separate from neurobiological systems, maintaining for example that perceived human social contexts are more predictive of the emotions that an individual is likely to experience [7]. Attempts have been made to reconcile these perspectives, for example by emphasizing the value of comparative studies, which find that these systems are shared across all vertebrates [8].

Finally, explanatory theories of emotion attempt to describe the mechanistic role emotion plays in altering the cognitive process and shaping behavior. For example, the *Somatic Marker Hypothesis* of Damasio views affect as a tag bound to other information from the body (sensory, motor, motivational) [3]. In this model, emotion results from external events and bodily responses, and provides an associative marker for particularly salient states, allowing them to guide future behavior with past associations. Other explanatory theories derive from the work of the early ethologists such as Lorenz and his theory of internal releasing mechanisms, which he associated with emotions [9].

Use of emotion in cognitive architectures and AI

We review here two illustrative computational cognitive architectures that incorporate emotions into a system that associates external events with certain emotions, then selects motivational and behavioral states based on these associations. Velásquez integrated generative models of different emotions into a system known as *Cathexis* [1]. The system incorporates different "proto-specialist" agents, managing in parallel different categories of emotion. These agents monitor external events and internal drives until the predicates for their emotions are satisfied, at which point emotions are "released" into the system for use by other agents and selection mechanisms. These model agents therefore draw on basic emotional theory in their implementation.

Breazeal created another computational cognitive architecture and embodied it in an expressive robotic device *Kismet*. [10]. This architecture is inspired by explanatory models of emotion from ethology and includes releaser mechanisms that encode how the robot relates to its environment. External events are bound to releasers, and together they provide predicates for emotional responses. Emotions then compete through a winner-take-all mechanism, with the winner determining the context for selecting behaviors such as stereotyped facial expressions produced by actuators in the robot. By tailoring releasers to specific emotional contexts, an additional layer of selection is introduced, allowing Breazeal to describe the architecture as a derivative of appraisal theories of emotion [10].

Critique

The theories of emotion and their use in cognitive architectures that we have reviewed each emphasize the importance of emotion in selecting behaviors. Whether emotions are elicited primarily by external events or internal reflections does not in our view inform how to build accurate cognitive models of emotion. One concern is that these approaches attempt to explain certain products of cognition, recognized emotions, in terms of other products of cognition, externally inferred objects and internal reflections. Models that are grounded in concepts and mechanisms that operate independently and at a lower level of integration are to be preferred. A distinction should also be made between generative mechanisms and epiphenomena; that is, phenomena that also happen to occur or are simply correlated. For example, we maintain below, that the qualia of emotion are useful for behavior selection, but are not required for it. Furthermore, while requiring explanation, the problems of appraising emotion and its conscious categorization are secondary to emotion generation. Finally, we question the goal of designing systems to produce emotions. Rather we expect that the mechanisms that give rise to emotions in biological systems evolved to serve specific operational needs, not to produce the qualia of emotions. We anticipate that an accurate system-level model of brain function will *necessarily* show properties recognizable as emotions, and therefore lead to a powerful generative theory of emotion.

Paper description

While attempts have been made previously to objectify emotion, for example by measuring galvanic skin response, facial expression, and respiration rates, we recognize emotions by our subjective experience of them. Thus, any compelling theory must explain these subjective qualia on the basis of well accepted computations and mechanisms. This paper seeks to explain these qualia through a generative theory of emotions as variations on processes necessary for cognition. It begins with fundamental assumptions about these processes and the mechanisms that give rise to them. It then identifies variations in these processes, the qualia they produce, and the corresponding emotion. The paper concludes by presenting the implications of this theory for designing cognitive or artificial intelligence technologies.

1. Fundamental assumptions

Over the time scale of momentary perceptions and behavior, an organism's brain may be thought of as a static network of dynamical neurons. These neurons can be distinguished by the role they play in the interface between the brain and the rest of the body, and by the role they play in the internal circuitry of the brain. Neurons at the interface may be strongly influenced by sensory, proprioceptive, or nociceptive inputs; they may be coupled to the organism's muscles and drive the organism's motor response; or they may respond to or influence the homeostatic conditions of the organism, such as through the hypothalamus and endocrine system, respectively. The role a neuron plays in the internal circuitry is determined by the identity, attributes, and activity of its afferent neurons; by its intrinsic properties, such as its morphology and ion channel distributions; the intrinsic properties of its synapses, such as the neurotransmitter they release; and by the efferent neurons it influences. Collectively, these afferent/efferent relationships determine the placement of each neuron within the global brain network. This placement is often characterized by the local, stereotyped network motifs associated with tissue microcircuity; by the relationship of the neuron's microcircuit to all of the others composing a brain structure, such as the neocortex or a nucleus; and by the relationship of the neuron's brain structure to the others that compose the topological architecture common to all vertebrates [11].

Over longer time scales, learning occurs through changes in the functional relationships between the neurons and even through limited changes in the network topology and composition. From a purely behaviorist perspective, this learning improves the organism's ability to generate context-appropriate behaviors serving the evolutionarily determined, biological imperatives of maintaining homeostasis, reproducing, and rearing its young.

Beyond the behaviorist's cloak, the complex, evolving temporal patterns of neuron activity, constrained and guided by the network topology and the functional relationships among neurons, create subjectively perceptible and recognizable transitions often characterized as cognitive processes. These processes, in turn, generate the organism's mental and physical behaviors. These mental and physical behaviors create regularities in the temporal relationships among the activities of the brain's neurons that can be categorized and exploited behaviorally. These recognized categories, as they are linked to behavior, constitute the properties of perceptual qualia and drive subsequent behaviors. Since all perceptual qualia depend upon the ability of the brain to act as though the properties of the qualia exist (such as spatial relationships in vision), cognitive processes also implement the learning and exploitation of an organism's perceptual qualia. This extends beyond the qualia of sensory perception to include the qualia of mental life, including, but not limited to, consciousness, thought, and emotions.

On this basis, it is assumed that all aspects of cognition, behavior generation, and perceptual experience are consequences of and computationally grounded in the dynamic interplay of neural activities. Critically, these neural activities and their temporal relationships are constrained by the observable properties of the physically structured environment and phenotype, and by observations resulting from the effects of motor neuron activity on the phenotype and environment. The topology of the network further limits the interactions of neurons and the roles of each neuron relative to system-wide emergent phenomena, such as the cognitive processes and the ultimate generation of context-appropriate behaviors.

Beyond hard constraints, the activity of some neurons modulates the activity and function of others, resulting in changes of the cognitive processes in which they participate. For example, neurons in the Raphe nuclei have widespread serotonergic projections to the cortex. Their activity modifies the behavior of their efferents and, by extension, causes changes in the levels of organism vigilance and alertness. Presumably, the activity of the Raphe nuclei are controlled by other neurons that recognize situations in which increased vigilance and alertness would be of value to the organism. There are many such modulatory subsystems, each presumably modifying or "tuning" distinct cognitive or learning processes.

Given the assumptions that tunable cognitive processes operate over the substrate of the brain and that these processes are responsible for the perceptual qualia of emotions, many questions are raised. What is the purpose of these processes? What information feeds them? How do the processes lead to consciousness? Which specific processes are required to explain human emotions? The answers to these questions, given below, provide the remaining assumptions necessary to answer the central question of this paper, "How do these processes explain human emotions?"

1.1. The purpose of cognitive processes

There are many cognitive processes that operate over the brain. Here, we are concerned only with those processes participating in the maintenance of the organism's ongoing well being. Due to their specialized and often idiosyncratic nature, we do not address processes required for instinctual behaviors, such as certain reproductive behaviors.

The primary purpose of the cognitive processes involved in maintaining ongoing well being is hypothesized to be producing context-appropriate behaviors to avoid or eliminate current and anticipated threats. The use of threat avoidance as a basis for learning and behavior selection was demonstrated experimentally in 1938 by Brogden [12]. The idea that threats or fear can be behavioral and learning drives has been incorporated into theories of avoidance going back at least as far as Mowrer's "two factor" theory, which was motivated by Brogden's result [13]. This early theory of avoidance is still highly influential today [14].

According to our stated hypothesis, cognitive processes must be understood in terms of threat avoidance. An organism that succeeds in avoiding and eliminating threats will survive to fulfill its biological imperatives. This hypothesis contrasts with the more common hypothesis of reward maximization. However, the threat avoidance and elimination hypothesis is no less powerful. With the additional assumptions described below, the mechanisms for threat avoidance and elimination can realize reward maximization.

We hypothesize that there are three fundamental types of threats: somatic, possession, and objective threats. These are distinguished by the manner in which the threats within each class are recognized, by the neural circuitry that mobilizes the organism's response, and by the nature of the response.

Somatic threats are the most basic class of threats. They are evolutionarily determined; that is, evolution has selected sensors and neural circuitry to to detect and respond to these threats. Somatic threats include direct and anticipated threats to survival and homeostasis, like low core body temperature or anticipated hunger. They also include threats to tissue integrity conveyed by nociceptive inputs. Nociceptive inputs may be considered segregated sensory inputs projecting to specialized circuits capable of mobilizing the pain response. Except in extreme situations, basic threats invoke processes that produce avoidance behaviors.

There are many highly motivating situations that have only a tenuous connection to somatic threats, like threats to territory, property, or social standing; pursuit of pastimes; and reward maximization. These can be explained with the two remaining types of threats.

Understanding a possession threat, first requires understanding a possession as used in this theory. A "possession" may be an offspring, a physical object, a territory, the "self," or any cognitive representation, such as social status, that the brain has associated with a drive to defend, maintain, and control. Possessions typically have some utility for avoiding or eliminating specific threats. We hypothesize that recognition of some utility and the ability to control enables the brain to recognize and treat the corresponding object or concept as a "possession." Once recognized as a possession, however, associations with specific utilities are no longer required for treatment as a possession, which greatly reduces the complexity of the system. Possessions may also be inferred, learned, or be necessary for the achievement of an active objective. Threats to possessions invoke avoidance behaviors if the possession can be separated from the threat and aggressive approach behaviors if it cannot.

The above description of possessions and possession threats suggests the need for specialized circuitry to recognize and respond to possessions as possessions. Furthermore, the need to nurture and protect offspring may have provided the evolutionary drive required to select and propagate the neural circuitry realizing possessions and possession threats.

Understanding the threats to an objective requires characterizing objectives. Objectives can be considered strategies to avoid threats. The threats that an objective seeks to avoid may be threats to survival, the body, possessions or, through recursion, the threats addressed by sub-objectives. These recursive objective threats are ultimately grounded in somatic or possession threats. For example, mowing one's front lawn can be a strategy to avoid neighborly reproach, where such reproach would be a threat to one's self-perceived social standing. If one considers an objective threat to arise when evaluation of a situation reveals an inconsistency with the achievement of an underlying goal, then objective threats are closely related to "motivational inconsistency" in Roseman's theory of appraisal [15].

1.2. The information that feeds cognitive processes

Avoiding or eliminating threats requires recognizing them. These threats may be recognized from the immediate situation or they may be recognized from predicted situations. This latter case requires modeling mental processes, the phenotype, the environment, how these three interact, and how they each evolve. This modeling is also required to enable threat recognition and behavioral planning relative to those aspects of the environment that are not currently sensed.

The nature and construction of this model is beyond the scope of this paper. It is hypothesized, however, that the "self" is inferred as the subject of modeled mental processes and that all behaviors and perceptions are modeled either relative to this self or to other entities that are.[2] This provides the subjective nature of action and perception.

1.3. The processes leading to consciousness

It is not possible to describe the basis and qualia of emotions without considering their relationship to the basis and qualia of consciousness. At a minimum, to be conscious of something is to be able to act arbitrarily in response to it, including reasoning, planning, reporting, behaving, etc.[3] These require some model or representation that persists beyond the stimulus suggesting the presence of that something. With such a powerful capability, it is hypothesized that a mechanism evolved to validate the inference that some-

---

[2]This is true even when the modeled relationship is one of physical distinction or separateness.

[3]This is consistent with Metzinger's "global availability" constraint [16].

thing exists, based on the initial stimulus, such that false positives do not result in errant behavior.

This validation process is hypothesized to be central to the qualia of consciousness. Upon an initial observation suggesting the presence of something, a model of that something is then evoked and exploited to predict additional properties of it. By confirming the existence of these properties, possibly through behaviors to acquire the required evidence, the model of the presence of that something becomes validated and the ability to act in response to it becomes enabled.

This process goes beyond simple validation. It also sets off a sequence of observations confirming the properties of the environment that are relevant to the organism. In this way a seamless, seemingly comprehensive awareness of the environment is constructed, even though the sampling of the environment is heavily biased by the organism's models and current needs.

On this basis, it is assumed that consciousness cannot occur if the modeled properties of mental life, such as the ability to choose, traverse associations, focus attention, etc., have not been validated or confirmed. It is assumed that consciousness emerges or bootstraps itself upon wakening by a subconscious process that confirms the existence of these properties. Once confirmed, these properties become available for behavior selection. In other words, the mind can begin to act as though it has a mental life.

This bootstrapping process is extended to the validation of modeled aspects of the phenotype and environment, especially those aspects that are associated with threats or are necessary for responding to them. As suggested above, such a model enables seamless behavioral responses to aspects of the environment that currently cannot be sensed. This property creates, for example, the subjective experience of a vast, high resolution visual scene even though humans can only perceive approximately one degree of arc at a time with high resolution.

Validation is required at both a network level to remove ambiguities caused by static classification networks (Rosenblatt's superposition catastrophe [17]) and at a behavioral level to accommodate changes in the environment, changes in the relationship between the organism and the environment, and accumulating error in models of these relationships. The first type of validation, necessary for solving the "binding problem," is thought to be achieved through network dynamics. The second type is thought to be achieved through frequent scanning of critical aspects of mental life, the phenotype, and the environment. It is critical that all percepts and models be validated prior to triggering behaviors dependent upon them. This process of continuously validating aspects of mental life, the phenotype, and the environment against predictions of the model is hypothesized to produce the heavily biased sequence of actionable observations that we experience as the stream of consciousness.

1.4. The specific processes that are required to explain human emotions

With this background, it is now possible to identify the cognitive processes and mechanisms that give rise to the perceptions and behavioral manifestations of the emotions presented in the next section. In this model, emotions are distinguished by the relative involvement and modulation of a fixed set of processes and mechanisms. There is not a single process for each emotion.

For survival purposes, it is essential for the organism to recognize as many potential threats as possible, which implies a need for broad, highly general threat recognition capabilities. Since this would necessarily generate undesirable false positives, a secondary process for eliminating false positives must exist. It is hypothesized that model prediction extending from the focus of attention may be such a process. As the focus of attention shifts, different aspects of the model would unfold and threats would be predicted. This exploration could either rule out potential threats or validate and characterize them. Certain threats may be recognized as acceptable to encounter, if they have been encountered and the past and successfully avoided.

Once threats are identified and validated through predictions driven by the focus of attention, cognitive processes must drive behaviors to avoid or eliminate them. This drive to act must accomplish at least four things:

1. Development and selection of a behavioral plan,
2. Rehearsal and revisitation of the behavioral plan to prepare the neural circuits to carry it out and to identify previously undetected threats, or new threats due to changing conditions,
3. Focused attention on behavior initiation, and
4. Execution of the planned behavior.

The first two of these can presumably continue indefinitely. It is assumed that they terminate when the threats from not proceeding exceed the anticipated threats of the current plan. In addition, there may be situations in which individual steps or the whole process should be suppressed, such as when failure is predicted.

It is import to distinguish threat avoidance behaviors from threat elimination behaviors. Threat avoidance behaviors correspond to the classical "flight" response. When avoidance, or "flight," is not possible, then the "fight" response, which effectively eliminates threats, may be required. The fight response is different from and requires suppression of the flight response.

Threat elimination or "fight" behaviors may be closely related to drive to maintain control of "possessed" objects, especially if the self, whether cognitive or physical, is modeled as a "possessed" object. These both differ from threat avoidance behaviors in that "approach" behaviors are required to maintain control.

2. Conditions producing specific emotions and the qualia they evoke

In this model, emotions are epiphenomenal qualia resulting from variations in the processes that underlie consciousness and cognition. As such, the duration of an emotion's quale persists only as long as the specific variation in cognitive processes persists. This may be as short as the time required to recognize the emotion or it may persist for minutes or longer.

In many situations, multiple emotions are experienced as attention shifts from one aspect of the situation to another, yet an individual may describe all of these experiences with a single word. For example, if somebody suffers a loss due to actions resulting from poor judgment, that person may at times experience, sadness, self-anger, and even self-disgust. Yet, the person may describe his mood as one of these.

The experience of emotion is often coupled with somatic and autonomic nervous system responses, such as the tightening of the stomach, increased heart rate, etc. In fact, this observation has led to a number of theories, such as the James-Lange Theory [2] and the Somatic Marker Hypothesis [3], that explain emotions on the basis of these physiological responses. Neither the production of these responses nor their role in the perception of emotion are considered here. Only changes in cognitive processes will be described.

The emotion characterizations below illustrate how variations on cognitive processes may explain the qualia of emotions. These specific characterizations are hypothesized, but not validated. The list of emotions described began with Plutchik's eight basic emotions to test and illustrate the robustness of our approach [18]. This list was augmented to include emotions we consider essential to understanding the theory or were required to explain the others. It is not necessary to carefully study each to understand and appreciate the underlying argument or to proceed with the remainder of the paper. Additional research will be required to better characterize the underlying cognitive processes, validate how their variations realize specific emotions, and evaluate whether or not the list and our paradigm are complete.

Finally, the descriptions in this section are limited to the qualia of emotions. They do not address disorders of emotion, which may cause the cognitive process variations leading to emotional qualia to occur or persist inappropriately.

Pleasure

Conditions: Pleasure occurs when the drive to engage in behavior to avoid threats has been eliminated or suppressed. This can be achieved in many ways. It can be achieved in the interim between the successful avoidance of one threat and before fixation on the next. Reflection on circumstances where threats were successfully avoided in the past may "predict" an absence of threats and, thus, suppress the drive. The drive can be suppressed through certain types of sensory stimulation, such as stroking the back - a mechanism that may have evolved for reproductive purposes. Non-threatening distractions and certain drugs may also suppress or eliminate this drive.
Quale: The quale arises during periods when there is no drive to engage in threat avoidance behaviors.

Joy

Conditions: Joy occurs when focusing attention on something, such as an object, experience, achievement, or memory, causes pleasure. That is, when focusing attention on something does not result in the prediction of a threat. This could occur, for example, when reflecting upon a circumstance where threats were successfully avoided, and an objective was achieved, such as in securing a compatible mate. Such reflections may "trick" the brain into acting as though the reflection behavior caused the elimination of threats. The brain would then reinforce this behavior to cause repetition. Thus, joy often involves repeated focus on the non-threat predicting target.
Quale: The quale of pleasure arises whenever attention is focused on the non-threat predicting target. This is often repeated.

Satisfaction

Conditions: Satisfaction occurs when a threat avoidance strategy is attended to and any anticipated threats are expected to be addressable. Satisfaction may occur, for example, when a planted crop becomes productive.

Quale: The quale arises when the strategy is the focus of attention, anticipated threats are recognizably surmountable, and no drive to plan a new strategy results.

Happiness

Conditions: Happiness occurs when a strategy or set of strategies to avoid threats is recognized as being likely to succeed. It can range from satisfaction to intense pleasure when success is anticipated to eliminate or avoid many threats. Happiness is often combined with and bolstered by joy arising from recollections of past successes. In other words, happiness is a type of pleasure that occurs when there are no predicted threats to strategies to avoid threats. Happiness is usually assessed when reflecting on one's, sometimes implicit, strategies.

Quale: Two quale are identified. One quale arises when a range of objectives (strategies to avoid threats) is attended to and there is no behavioral drive to plan or develop a new threat avoidance strategy. The other quale occurs when joy results from focusing attention on the anticipated end state; that is, when the end state is predicted and attended to, no threats are identified, and no drive to respond to threats is invoked.

Possessiveness

Conditions: Possessiveness occurs when a threat to the control of a "possessed" object of attention is recognized and there is an accompanying behavioral drive to maintain control.

Quale: The quale arises from focused attention on the "possession" and the behavioral drive to maintain control of the possessed object of attention.

Pain

Conditions: Pain occurs when attention is focused on a physical or cognitive threat, there is a behavioral drive to eliminate it, and a failure to succeed. A physical threat is signaled by nociceptive inputs (physical pain can be perceived before actual tissue damage). A cognitive threat is typically the loss of a possession, however abstract, such as the break up of a romantic relationship.

Quale: The quale arises from the focus of attention and the incessant drive to eliminate the threat or loss.

Sadness

Conditions: Sadness occurs when there is attention to a cognitive threat, a behavioral drive to eliminate the threat, a failure to succeed, and an expectation that success is not possible, such as when an item of sentimental value has been irreparably destroyed. In other words, sadness is cognitive pain without a behavioral strategy expected to eliminate it (focused pain with hopelessness). If a behavioral strategy is identified that is predicted to be successful, then sadness is not experienced.

Quale: The quale arises from a cycle: attention is focused on the cognitive threat, the behavioral drive is stimulated to eliminate the threat, behavioral planning is initiated, the futility is recognized, the behavioral planning process is suppressed, and attention upon the cognitive threat is renewed.

Depression

Conditions: Depression occurs when there is a generalized expectation that behaviors to eliminate threats will fail. Because this expectation suppresses the drive to act, this threat elimination does actually fail, and new threats are created. This can create a self-reinforcing cycle, extending to a broader range of threats and behaviors, and deepening the depression. Depression may include sadness, but it is distinguished from it by its generality and that the hopelessness derives from the perception of personal failure, rather than some universally, insurmountable obstacle. Often, multiple causes are required, such as loss of loved ones, health, and/or financial security.

Quale: The quale arises from a sadness-like cycle, some steps of which may be skipped: attention is focused on individual or generalized threats, a drive to act is stimulated, but immediately suppressed by the recognition of futility, recognition of the self as the source of the futility and a threat to future success, a drive to avoid the threat of the self, and recognition of the futility of avoiding the self, followed by renewed attention to individual and generalized threats.

Anticipation

Conditions: Anticipation occurs when there is heightened vigilance regarding an expected event or circumstance and preparedness to act when it arrives. Heightened vigilance corresponds to development and preparedness to execute recognition strategies exploiting attribute associations characterizing an event or circumstance. Imagine a strange noise in your home at bedtime. Preparedness to act includes at least four components: maintaining registration with the elements required for the action, selecting a behavioral plan, rehearsing and revisiting the behavioral plan to prepare the neural circuits to carry it out and to identify previously undetected threats or new threats due to changing conditions, and focusing attention on behavior initiation.

Quale: The quale arises from execution of recognition strategies and engagement in components of action preparedness.

Trust

Conditions: Trust occurs when a threat avoidance strategy is recognized to carry threats, but that the behavioral drive to respond to those threats is suppressed. For example, trust occurs the moment one decides to act on the investment recommendation of a financial advisor advocating based on some presumed expertise. The threat response suppression may be due to other threats or constraints on behavior. For example, there may be financial penalties associated with postponing an investment decision that exceed any anticipated losses from the recommendation.

Quale: The quale arises from the active suppression of the behavioral drive to avoid the recognized threats associated with a particular threat avoidance strategy.

Disgust

Conditions: Disgust occurs when the target of disgust strongly triggers avoidance behaviors. Even focusing attention on the target evokes an avoidance behavior, which shifts attention away from the target.

Quale: The quale arises when focusing attention on the target of disgust drives avoidance behaviors strongly, especially the avoidance of attention.

Fear

Conditions: Fear occurs when a specific threat is recognized, the threat is the focus of attention, vigilance of the threat is heightened, and there is a preparedness to act to avoid the threat. Since movement itself can create a new threat, often physical behavior is stopped or frozen to avoid increasing the threat, such as by increasing the likelihood of detection. Fear of predation is a common example.

Quale: The quale arises from focused attention, heightened attention and vigilance directed toward the threat, and the preparedness to engage in avoidance behaviors.

Anxiety

Conditions: Anxiety occurs when an unidentified threat is perceived. This results in increased vigilance, and a preparedness and drive to engage in threat avoidance behaviors, which are suppressed due to a lack of a target. Anxiety is fear without a targeted threat.

Quale: The quale arises from increased vigilance coupled with the preparedness to act.

Anger

Conditions: Anger occurs when an unacceptable threat cannot be avoided and must be eliminated by any means, such as by fighting. There is a focus of attention on the threat, a strong drive to act to eliminate all threats in general, and a suppression of the behavioral drive to avoid threats, such as those encountered during the elimination of threats. This drive to eliminate all threats extends to anything associated with the threat, however tenuously.

Quale: The quale arises from the suppression of threat avoidance and a strong drive to act to eliminate a threat.

Surprise

Conditions: Surprise occurs when the model fails to predict an outcome and there is a drive to repair the context model.

Quale: The quale arises from a drive to repair the context model and become predictably registered with it.

3. Implications for cognitive architectures and conclusions

While variations in cognitive processes can be subjectively recognized and labeled as emotions, this theory suggests that emotions are not "states" to be used as logical or behavioral switches in cognitive architectures. Moreover, as cognitive processes may vary quickly and by degree, a finite set of emotional states may not be a useful way to understand emotions.

Rather, the theory presented in this paper suggests that cognitive architectures should have the ability to interact with the context model and constraints from the environment in a variety of ways to yield responses that are effective for avoiding or eliminating threats. The decomposition of the cognitive processes involved in emotions, as presented in this paper, suggests useful constraints on the design of cognitive architectures. Furthermore, just as humans can recognize emotions and alter their behavior on the basis of this recognition, cognitive architectures should be designed with this same capability.

While this paper is preliminary in terms of the cognitive processes considered and their mapping to specific emotions, this effort shows that the perspective of characterizing emotions according to variations in the underlying processes of cognition is robust enough to accommodate a broad range of emotions.

References

[1]   J. Velásquez. Modeling emotions and other motivations in synthetic agents. *Proceedings of the 1997 National Conference on Artificial Intelligence (AAAI97)*, pages 10–15, 1997.

[2]   W. James. What is an emotion? *Mind*, 9(34):188–205., 1884.

[3]   A. Damasio. *Descartes Error: Emotion, Reason, and the Human Brain*. G.P. Putnam's Sons, New York, NY, 1994.

[4]   K. R. Scherer. Emotions are emergent processes: they require a dynamic computational architecture. *Philos Trans R Soc Lond B Biol Sci*, 364(1535):3459–3474, 2009.

[5]   A. Ohman and S. Mineka. Fears, phobias, and preparedness: toward an evolved module of fear and fear learning. *Psychol Rev*, 108(3):483–522, 2001.

[6]   K. R. Scherer. On the sequential nature of appraisal processes: indirect evidence from a recognition task. *Cognition and Emotion*, 13(6):763–793, 1999.

[7]   R. R. Cornelius. Theoretical approaches to emotion. *Proc. from ISCA Workshop on Speech and Emotion*, pages 3–11, 2000.

[8]   J. Panksepp. Neurologizing the psychology of affects: How appraisal-based constructivism and basic emotion theory can coexist. *Perspectives on Psychological Science*, 2(3):281–296, 2007.

[9]   K. Lorenz. *The Foundations of Ethology*. Springer, Berlin, 1981.

[10] C. Breazeal. Emotion and sociable humanoid robots. *International Journal of Computer Human Interaction*, pages 119–155.

[11] R. Nieuwenhuys. Comparative neuroanatomy: place, principles and programme. In R. Nieuwenhuys, H. J. Donkelaar, and C. Nicholson, editors, *The Central Nervous System of Vertebrates*, pages 273–326. Springer, Berlin, 1998.

[12] E. A. Lipman W. J. Brogden and E. Culler. The role of incentive in conditioning and extinction. *American Journal of Psychology*, 51:109–117, 1938.

[13] O. H. Mowrer. Two-factor learning theory: summary and comment. *Psychological Review*, 58(1):350–354, 1951.

[14] T. V. Maia and M. J. Frank. From reinforcement learning models to psychiatric and neurological disorders. *Nature Neuroscience*, 14(2):154–162, 2011.

[15] I. J. Roseman. Appraisal determinants of emotions: constructing a more accurate and comprehensive theory. *Cognition and Emotion*, 10(3):241–278., 1996.

[16] T. Metzinger. *Being No One: The Self-Model Theory of Subjectivity*. A Bradford Book, 2004.

[17] F. Rosenblatt. *Principles of Neurodynamics: Perception and the Theory of Brain Mechanisms*. Spartan Books, Washington, 1962.

[18] R. Plutchik. A general psychoevolutionary theory of emotion. In *Emotion: Theory, Research, and Experience: Vol. 1. Theories of Emotion*.

Biologically Inspired Cognitive Architectures 2011
A.V. Samsonovich and K.R. Jóhannsdóttir (Eds.)
IOS Press, 2011
© 2011 The authors and IOS Press. All rights reserved.
doi:10.3233/978-1-60750-959-2-282

Contrasting Infant Perception Data with a Reinforcement Learning Visual Search Model

Nicole Pennington   Benjamin Goodrich   Itamar Arel

npennin2@utk.edu   bgoodric@utk.edu   itamar@eecs.utk.edu

Department of Electrical Engineering and Computer Science

The University of Tennessee

Keywords: Infant visual attention, reinforcement learning, foveated vision

Abstract

Selective visual attention is the mechanism by which we rapidly fixate on objects of interest in our visual environment. The study of visual attention is relevant to any situation in which actions are based on visual information. In this work, we propose modeling the dynamics of infant perception data with respect to the visual search process. Observation-action trajectories collected from different infant subjects are mapped to a Markov model. This data is then compared to results obtained from a reinforcement learning based visual search system. The long-term goal of this research effort is to devise a near-optimal, biologically-inspired visual attention mechanism that can be applied to large visual fields while offering speed and accuracy for diverse scene conditions.

1 Introduction

Selective visual attention is the mechanism by which we can rapidly direct our gaze towards objects of interest in our visual environment [1]. From an evolutionary viewpoint, this rapid orienting capability is critical in allowing living systems to quickly become aware of possible preys, mates or predators in their cluttered visual world. It has become clear that attention guides where to look next based on both bottom-up (image-based) and top-down (task-dependent) cues. As such, attention implements an information processing bottleneck, only allowing a small part of the incoming sensory information to reach short-term memory and visual awareness. That is, instead of attempting to fully process the massive sensory input in parallel, nature has devised a serial strategy to achieve near real-time performance despite limited computational capacity: Attention allows us to break down the problem of scene understanding into rapid series of computationally less demanding, localized visual analysis problems.

The study of visual attention is relevant to any situation in which actions are based on visual information from the environment. Efficient and reliable attentional selection is critical because various cues appear amidst a cluttered mosaic of other features, objects, and events. Attention mechanisms enable preferential processing of particular locations in the visual field or specific features of objects. To cope with the massive amounts of information which we are exposed to, the brain is equipped with a variety of attentional mechanisms. These serve two critical roles. First, attention can be used to select behaviorally relevant information and/or to ignore the irrelevant or interfering information. In other words, you are only aware of attended visual events. Second, attention can modulate or enhance this selected information according to the state and goals of the perceiver. With attention, the perceivers are more than passive receivers of information. They become active seekers and processors of information, able to interact intelligently with their environment. A visual search paradigm [2] is introduced here, in which a reinforcement-learning [3] based approach is taken for controlling the visual search process. In visual search tasks, subjects look for a designated target item among a number of distracting items. Mammals quickly and effortlessly differentiate areas of interest amidst a cluttered mosaic of other features, objects, and events. As adults, this mechanism is well trained and performed rapidly and unconsciously, while in infants visual mechanisms are still developing.

In this paper, we utilize real data obtained from tracking the visual search process of infants as they observe various stimuli is contrasted to a reinforcement learning (RL) agent. This work is novel in its attempt to model infant visual search patterns in the context of a reinforcement learning problem. It is shown that similarity of the behavioral patterns exists between the two cases, suggesting that a reward-driven decision making process takes place as mammals become proficient in scanning large visual fields. Hence, this work will hopefully pave the way for future studies that will frame visual attention as a learning process.

2 Infant Eye Tracking Data

The data set that we analyzed consisted of 40 sets of data from 20 8-month-old (+ or – 7 days) infants. The infant data used in this study was provided by the Infant Perception-Action Lab (PAL) at the University of Tennessee. The research focus at PAL primarily involves two early processes of visual attention – visuo-spatial orienting and sustained attention – both of which have been linked to infants' visual examination of 2D images. To explore those processes, they examined how infants directed their visual attention to a series of slides that displayed objects varying in sizes on backgrounds containing different linear perspective depth cues. An eye-tracking device was utilized initially to determine the object on which infants directed their visual attention, and then on which object they maintained their visual attention the longest. The use of an automated corneal-reflection system provided a relatively high sample rate and allowed them to track shifts in fixation as well as establish the object with the longest duration of gaze. Figure 1 illustrates a gaze plot generated by the eye-tracker used in the PAL.

Thirty slides were used as the stimuli, all of which contained a mix of real photos backgrounds and backgrounds with simple lines. The objects targets were toys or other items familiar to infants, and the layout of the objects on the slides were also arranged in such a way that the position of certain objects (i.e. the largest object) appeared in different locations of the slides to control for directional looking biases. All 30 slides were presented in a random order and for two successive rounds. The eye-tracker used

Figure 1: Sample gaze plot generated by the eye-tracker platform at PAL

corneal reflection to record where on the slides infants directed their gaze at a frame rate of 50 Hz and with an accuracy of 0.5 degrees. Each slide was projected on the screen for a duration of 5 seconds, which takes into account an infant's limited attention span, and was immediately followed by a 2-second inter-slide containing a smiley face at the center of the slide displayed on a uniform black background. This intermediate slide was used to draw the infant's attention back to the center of the screen before the appearance of the next slide and to make it possible to monitor the accuracy of the eye signal throughout the slide sequence.

3 Visual Search Model

In order to relate the infant visual search in a meaningful way to the RL visual agent, we created a two-state Markov model of the infant data and compared the episodes according to the transition probabilities of this model. The two states represented infant attention on either an area of interest (e.g. smiley face) or background. Moreover, we considered everything that was not an area of interest to be background, even if the infant was not looking at the image at all. Since there are only two states, this left only two significant transition probabilities: area of interest to area of interest (AoI-to-AoI) and background to background (BG to BG). This two-state model served to categorize the attention spans of the infants. An infant with sustained attention on an area of interest had a higher AoI-to-AoI transition probability, while infants who spent less time looking at those objects had a higher BG-to-BG transition probability. To ensure that the results obtained from the RL based visual search could be compared to the infant data results, it was determined that an average distance of 43 pixels corresponded to the infants' fixation point movement (per eye-tracker reading).

4 Reinforcement Learning based Visual Search Model

An RL based visual search model was employed. Given that the images span a very large space, a feedforward neural network trained by backpropagation was used for estimating the state-action value function. The overall scene comprised of a large visual

Figure 2: Example of a fisheye view used as state input to the reinforcement learning based visual search agent.

field while a small focal area was generated using a foveate vision model [4]. The latter was used to represent the focal region in high detail with the surrounding periphery region compressed with much lower detail. The images produced looked similar to a fish-eye lens, hence we called our model the *fish-eye image model*. Principal Component Analysis was applied to the fish-eye images to further reduce dimensionality prior to being fed to a neural network as a state signal in a RL model. The actions corresponded to gaze movement commands with respect to the focal image in one of 32 directions. The reward was defined as the cosine distance between the current focal area center and the target (i.e. region of content such as the smiley face).

Biological systems tend to have foveate vision, with a large amount of detail represented at the focal region. The detail fades as distance to the focal region increases. We sought to find a model that would capture this attribute. The large visual field was stored as an 800x600 pixel gray scale image, while the small focal image generated was set at 32x32 pixels. A method was needed to map pixels from the large image to the small focal image. We experimented with several mapping functions that yielded interesting behavior, but ultimately settled on using the tangent function which produced the most natural appearance to the focal images. This mapping resembles transforming plane images to the surface of a sphere. Moreover, the tangent function offers a linear region extending out to around 12 pixels from the origin, after which it produces a curved nonlinear slope that causes pixels that are in regions far from the origin of the large image space to be compressed in the focal image space. Figure 2 shows an example of the resulting fish-eye view.

5 Value Function Approximation

The fish-eye images of 32x32 pixels yielded a dimensionality that was too high as input to the neural network. We thus experimented with reducing the dimensionality of the inputs using principal component analysis. It was experimentally determined that taking the first 256 principal components, thereby reducing the number of inputs to the neural network to 256, yielded a reasonable reduction in quality without losing too much critical detail, as illustrated in Figure 3.

The goal of the RL based simulation was to train an agent to saccade toward a target in a large image, then "lose interest" in the target and saccade away from it. This appeared comparable to observed infant gaze behavior. The state signal comprised

Figure 3: Example of the original fisheye view (left) and the one after applying PCA to 256 inputs (right).

the 256 inputs of the PCA-reduced focal image. In addition, we provided as input a signal of 2 elements that indicated whether the agent should be heading toward the target, or losing interest. The action set consisted of 32 saccade directions, chosen as equidistant around a circle. The saccade distance was set to 43 pixels. The reward was defined as the cosine distance to a predefined target in the large image, calculated as the angle between the angle selected for the action, and the angle to the target. For example, if the target was at 45 degrees from the origin, and the action selected corresponded to 90 degrees, the reward would be $cos(45 - 90) = .707$. When the actions selected were in the direction of the target, a positive reward was incurred which was proportional to the angle selected. If actions were chosen resulting in a move away from the target, negative reward was issued. To cause the agent to lose interest in a target once identified, we constructed the reward signal such that it changed behavior upon finding a target. When 10 subsequent steps in an episode were within a certain distance to the target, the target was reassigned to be the upper left corner of the image. Our state signal includes a parameter that indicates to the agent if it gets reward for heading toward the target, or for heading to the upper left corner of the image. An epsilon-greedy scheme was used for balancing exploration vs. exploitation.

The inputs to the neural network included both the state and the action signals. The state signal of 258 elements was applied, along with the 32 inputs representing the actions. The action inputs were all 0 except for the action that was selected, which was set to 1. This gave a total of 290 inputs, and 1 output for the estimated value. A feedforward network was used with a single hidden layer of 128 neurons.

6 Results and Discussion

The RL based visual search engine was applied to images taken from the same data set as that presented to the infants. An identical two-state Markov model was utilized for interpreting the search trajectories. Figure 4 depicts the state transition probabilities obtained from the 40 infant data episodes and those derived from 40 RL agent episodes. As can be observed, a pattern of linear spanning (with a negative slope) was produced similar to that of the infants. This particular pattern suggests that perhaps a reward-driven learning process takes place as infants acquire efficient visual search

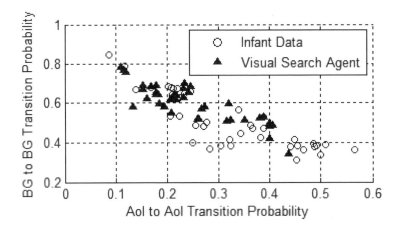

Figure 4: State transition probabilities obtained from infant gaze trajectories and those obtained from the reinforcement learning based visual search agent

skills. Moreover, it is speculated that "losing interest" in a target may correspond to an intrinsic reward generation process that occurs once a particular visual cue becomes "boring" - which corresponds to the effect that was mimicked in this work. While this study represents a very early exploration of the topic, applying reward-driven decision making to the problem of effective search in large visual fields appears to be a promising direction of future research.

7 Acknowledgement

The authors would like to thank the Perception-Action Laboratory at the University of Tennessee, particularly Daniela Corbetta and Yu Guan for providing the infant data and their wonderful inspiration for using it to model visual perception processes.

References

[1] L. Itti and editor J. Feng, "Modeling primate visual attention," in *Computational Neuroscience: A Comprehensive Approach*, pp. 635–655, CRC Press, Boca Raton, 2003.

[2] A. F. C. B. Emanuela Bricolo, Tiziana Gianesini and L. Chelazzi, "Serial attention mechanisms in visual search: A direct behavioral demonstration," in *J. Cognitive Neuroscience*, pp. 14:980–993, October 2002.

[3] R. S. Sutton and A. G. Barto in *Reinforcement Learning: An Introduction*, MIT Press, 1998.

[4] J. Schmidhuber and R. Huber, "Learning to generate artificial fovea trajectories for target detection," *Int. J. Neural Syst.*, vol. 2, no. 1-2, pp. 125–134, 1991.

Biologically Inspired Cognitive Architectures 2011
A.V. Samsonovich and K.R. Jóhannsdóttir (Eds.)
IOS Press, 2011

Neurally and Mathematically Motivated Architecture for Language and Cognition

L.I. PERLOVSKY[a,1] and R. ILIN[b]

[a] *The Air Force Research Laboratory, Sensors Directorate, WP AFB, USA*
[b] *Harvard University, A. Martinos Brain Imaging Center*

Keywords. Cognitive development; language acquisition; abstract cognition

Abstract

Neural structures of interaction between thinking and language are unknown. This paper suggests a possible architecture motivated by mathematical and neural considerations. A mathematical requirement of computability imposes significant constraints on possible architectures consistent with brain neural structure and with a wealth of psychological knowledge. How does language interacts with cognition? Do we think with words, or is thinking independent from language with words being just labels for decisions? Why is language learned by the age of 5 or 7, but the acquisition of knowledge represented by this language takes a lifetime? This paper discusses hierarchical aspects of language and thought and argues that high level abstract thinking is impossible without language. We discuss a mathematical technique that can model the joint language-thought architecture, while overcoming previously encountered difficulties of computability. This architecture explains a contradiction between the human ability for rational thoughtful decisions and the irrationality of human thinking revealed by Tversky and Kahneman; a crucial role in this contradiction might be played by language. The proposed model resolves long-standing issues: how the brain learns correct words-object associations; why animals are not able to talk and think like people. We propose the role played by language emotionality in its interaction with thought. We relate the mathematical model to Humboldt's "firmness" of languages; and discuss the possible influence of language grammar on its emotionality. Psychological and brain imaging experiments related to the proposed model are discussed. Future theoretical and experimental research is outlined.

---

[1] Corresponding Author.

Biologically Inspired Cognitive Architectures 2011
A.V. Samsonovich and K.R. Jóhannsdóttir (Eds.)
IOS Press, 2011
doi:10.3233/978-1-60750-959-2-289

Small Brain Model Architectures

James K. Peterson [a,1],

[a] *Department of Biological Sciences, Clemson University*

Abstract. An outline of mechanisms that will allow the creation of small brain models is discussed. These models provide useful paradigms for mixed software and hardware devices that model computational cognition devices.

Keywords. Cognitive Models, Directed Graph Models, Flow Updates

Introduction

This paper addresses aspects of the challenge of building a brain model capable of being useful for field deployment in a autonomous device. Such a fusion of algorithm development, biological abstraction and software development must be functional in possibly adverse environments and learn from environmental input in an unsupervised manner. Our approach uses directed graph models of cognition built by abstracting from the messiness of biological complexity the essential connection and structural information. This is done by developing a model of the relevant signal transductions with a low dimensional biological feature vector abstraction of the information contained in the action potential of an excitable neuron. The models used are modular directed graphs of fundamental information processing blocks such as cortex and thalamus with a graph Laplacian plus various hebbian link weight update strategies for associating the *high* level precepts formed by sensor fusion in the upper columns of cortex with sensor data.

1. Directed Graph Models

The brain structure we model consists of mature computational nodes called neurons with fixed connections to other such nodes. We do not address plasticity issues that allow for connections to form during computational time. To illustrate how we can *train* or imprint clusters of computational objects, consider a typical *On - Center, Off - Surround* cortical circuit as shown in Figure 1 [2]. Associated with any such DG structure, there is a notion of flow given by the Laplacian of the graph. It is easiest to show how this is done for the OCOS DG. It will then be evident how to extend to the DG's associated with other computational modules in a simple brain model.

---

[1]Corresponding Author: James K. Peterson, Department of Biological Sciences, Clemson University, Clemson SC 29634; E-mail: petersj@clemson.edu

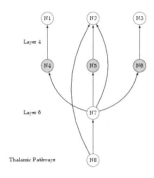

Layer 4

Layer 6

Thalamic Pathways

Figure 1.: The On - Center,
Off - Surround DG

In Figure 1, there are 8 neural nodes and 9 edges. The OCOS DG is a graph $\mathscr{G}$ which is made up of the vertices V and edges E given by $V = \{N_1, N_2, N_3, N_4, N_5, N_6, N_7, N_8\}$ and $E = \{E_1, E_2, E_3, E_4, E_5, E_6, E_7, E_8, E_9\}$. For the edge sets, we use the identifications $E_1 =$ edge from node N_4 to N_1, $E_2 =$ edge from node N_5 to N_2 and so on. We then denote the OCOS DG by $\mathscr{G} = V \times E$. Its *incident* matrix is then the matrix K whose K_{ne} entry is defined to be $+1$ if there is an edge going out of node n; -1 if there is an edge going into node n and 0 otherwise. Next, assume there is a vector function $\boldsymbol{f}$ which assigns a scalar value to each node. Then, for this DG, the *gradient* of $\boldsymbol{f}$ is defined by $\nabla \boldsymbol{f} = K^T f$ and the Laplacian, by $\nabla^2 \boldsymbol{f}$. Since $K K^T$ is symmetric, the eigenvalues of this Laplacian are positive and there is a nice eigenvector structure. The standard cable equation for the voltage v across a membrane is $\lambda^2 \nabla^2 v - \tau \frac{\partial v}{\partial t} - v = -r \lambda^2 k$ where the constant λ is the space constant, τ is the time constant and r is a geometry independent constant. The variable $\boldsymbol{k}$ is an external source. We assume the flow of information through our OCOS DG is given by the graph based partial differential equation $\nabla^2 \boldsymbol{f} - \frac{\tau_{OCOS}}{\lambda_{OCOS}^2} \frac{\partial \boldsymbol{f}}{\partial t} - \frac{1}{\lambda_{OCOS}^2} \boldsymbol{f} = -r\boldsymbol{k}$. Relabel the fraction $\tau_{OCOS}/\lambda_{OCOS}^2$ by μ_1 and the constant $1/\lambda_{OCOS}^2$ by μ_2 and then note that each computational DG will have associated constants μ_1 and μ_2. This gives, using a finite difference for the $\frac{\partial f}{\partial t}$ term, Figure 1, where we define the finite difference $\Delta f_n(t)$ as $f_n(t+1) - f_n(t)$.

$$\nabla^2 \boldsymbol{f} - \mu_1 \frac{\partial \boldsymbol{f}}{\partial t} - \mu_2 \boldsymbol{f} = -r\boldsymbol{k}. \quad (1)$$

For example, if we assume the node values $f(N1)$, $f(N2)$ and $f(N3)$ are to be clamped to A, B and C, we can substitute these values into Equation 1 to relationships between the node values. The Laplacian ∇^2 has eigenvalues and eigenvectors given by α_i and E_i respectively. Hence, we have the expansion $\boldsymbol{f}(t) = \sum_{i=1}^n c_{it} \boldsymbol{E}_i$ where n is the Laplacian dimension and t is the discrete time step. Applying to the *graph cable equation*, using the eigenvector expansions, we find $\nabla^2 \left(\sum_{i=1}^n c_{it} \boldsymbol{E}_i \right) - \mu_1 \Delta \left(\sum_{i=1}^n c_{it} \boldsymbol{E}_i \right) -$

$\mu_2 \left(\sum_{i=1}^n c_{it} \boldsymbol{E}_i \right) = -r \left(\sum_{i=1}^n \xi_i \boldsymbol{E}_i \right)$. where $\sum_{i=1}^n \xi_i \boldsymbol{E}_i$ is the expansion of the input term $\boldsymbol{k}$. This simplifies to an update equation for the coefficients of the node vector f in terms of the basis given by the eigenvectors of ∇^2: $\left(\alpha_i - \frac{1}{\lambda^2} - \frac{\tau}{\lambda^2} \right) c_{it} + \frac{\tau}{\lambda^2} c_{i,t-1} = -r \xi_i$.

Given an arbitrary input vector $\vec{x}$, the DG computes node outputs via an iterative process. We let $\mathcal{U}$ denote the nodes which receive external inputs and $\mathcal{B}(i)$, the backward set of node N_i. The edge from node N_i to node N_j is assigned an edge function $T_{i \to j}$ which could be implemented as assigning a scalar value to this edge. Then, the evaluation is shown in Figure 2, where N is the number of nodes in the DG and the ith node function is given by the function σ^i which processes the current node input y^i. In general, the node computation can depend on a parameter vector p also. Further, we can also adjust parameters in the DG using the classic idea of a Hebbian update [1]. Recall the idea is to increase the synaptic efficacy of the pre-neuron if there is a correlation between the pre- and post-synaptic activity. An easy way to do this is to increase the edge weight of the pre- to post- link when their product exceeds a threshold. A standard Hebbian update for scalar valued edge functions would be implemented as shown in Figure 3: choose a tolerance ϵ and at each node in the backward set of the post neuron i, update the edge value by the factor ζ if the product of the post neuron node value f_i and the edge value $T_{j \to i}$ exceeds ϵ. The update algorithm then consists of the paired operations: sweep through the DG to do an evaluation and then use both Hebbian updates and the graph flow equations to adjust the edge values.

2. Hierarchical Graph Models

```
for(i = 0; i < N; i + +) {
    if (i ∈ 𝒰)
        yⁱ = xⁱ + ∑ⱼ∈ℬ(i) T_{j→i}f_j
    else
        yⁱ = ∑ⱼ∈ℬ(i) T_{j→i}f_j
    f_i = σⁱ(yⁱ, p)
}
```

Figure 2.: DG Evaluation

```
for(i = 0; i < N; i + +) {
    for (j ∈ ℬ(i)) {
        y_p = f_i T_{j→i}
        if (y_p > ε)
            T_{j→i} = ζ T_{j→i}
    }
}
```

Figure 3.: Hebbian Update

An interesting small brain architecture would have at least two primary sensory cortex modules. When we combine the OCOS, FFP and 2/3 building blocks [2] into a cortical stack, this requires about 30 computational nodes to implement. If we adjoin cortical stacks into a $n \times m$ grid, we have a model of sensory cortex that requires $30nm$ nodes. Each of the cortex stack models also have modulatory connections to a thalamus, midbrain and cerebellum components. We need a cortical stack model for motor cortex to provide our output commands and a cortical stack model for associative cortex for the sensor fusion to drive the motor cortex. The small brain model we build then has the fixed directed graph architecture we obtain by building the graph using various neural circuit components such as the OCOS and FFP. There are similar circuit modules we can use to build the thalamus, midbrain and cerebellum models.

Note, for each DG, the associated edge and node functions can capture as little or as much of the underlying biology as is needed for performance. When these modules are assembled into a small brain structure and input and output modules are added, the resulting address scheme shown in Figure 4.

3. Second Messenger Triggers

Many neurons release neurotransmitters which are a type of second messenger system. The neurotransmitter trigger activates a cascade of reactions inside the dendrite/ soma complex which eventually results in the transcription of a target protein. These systems provide much of the modulation required for complex cognition and typically activate many transcription pathways for each triggering event. Triggering events cause a modification of the essential hardware of the cell so they are powerful modulatory agents. We now consider a simple model of such a trigger. We will show how we can understand its second messenger effect in terms of basic equilibrium computations. Consider a trigger T_0 which activates a cell surface receptor. A common mechanism for such an activation is to add to PK another protein subunit $\mathcal{U}$ to form the complex $PK/\mathcal{U}$, $T_0 \to \text{CSR} \to PK/\mathcal{U}$. where CSR denotes a *cell surface receptor*.

Input	$[1; \cdot; \cdot; \cdot; \cdot; \cdot]$
Sensory Model One	$[2; 1; \cdot; \cdot; \cdot; \cdot]$
Sensory Model Two	$[2; 2; \cdot; \cdot; \cdot; \cdot]$
Associative Cortex	$[2; 3; \cdot; \cdot; \cdot; \cdot]$
Motor Cortex	$[2; 4; \cdot; \cdot; \cdot; \cdot]$
Thalamus	$[2; 5; \cdot; \cdot; \cdot; \cdot]$
MidBrain	$[2; 6; \cdot; \cdot; \cdot; \cdot]$
Cerebellum	$[2; 7; \cdot; \cdot; \cdot; \cdot]$
Output	$[3; \cdot; \cdot; \cdot; \cdot; \cdot]$

Figure 4.: Module Addresses

$PK/\mathcal{U}$ then acts to *phosphorylate* another protein. The cell is filled with large amounts of a transcription factor we will denote by T_1 and an inhibitory protein for T_1, $T_1^{\sim}$, the *complement* or *anti* version of T_1. In the cell, T_1 and $T_1^{\sim}$ are joined together in the complex $T_1/T_1^{\sim}$. The addition of $T_1^{\sim}$ to T_1 prevents T_1 from being able to access the genome to transcribe its target protein. The trigger T_0 activates our protein kinase PK to $PK/\mathcal{U}$ and the activated $PK/\mathcal{U}$ is used to phosphorylate $T_1^{\sim}$. Hence, $PK/\mathcal{U} + T_1^{\sim} \to T_1^{\sim}P$ where $T_1^{\sim}P$ denotes the phosphorylated version of $T_1^{\sim}$. Since T_1 is bound into the complex $T_1/T_1^{\sim}$, we have $PK/\mathcal{U} + T_1/T_1^{\sim} \to T_1/T_1^{\sim}P$ In the cell, there are proteins which form a tagging system which bond to the phosphorylated form $T_1^{\sim}P$.

$$
\begin{aligned}
T_0 & \to \text{CSR} & \to PK/\mathcal{U} \\
PK/\mathcal{U} & + T_1/T_1^{\sim} & \to T_1/T_1^{\sim}P \\
T_1/T_1^{\sim}P & + \text{Tag} & \to T_1/T_1^{\sim}P\mathcal{V}_n \quad (2) \\
T_1/T_1^{\sim}P\mathcal{V}_n & + fSQ\mathcal{V}_n & \to T_1 \\
T_1 & \to \text{N} & \to \text{TPT } P(T_1)
\end{aligned}
$$

The protein used by the tagging system is denoted by $\mathcal{V}$ and is commonly present in the polymer form $\mathcal{V}_n$. The tagging system creates the new complex $T_1/T_1^{\sim}P\mathcal{V}_n$ Also, inside the cell, the tagging system coexists with a complimentary system whose function is to destroy or remove the tagged complexes. Hence, the combined system Tag $\longleftrightarrow$ Remove $\to T_1/T_1^{\sim}P$ is a **regulatory** mechanism which allows the transcription factor T_1 to be freed from its bound state $T_1/T_1^{\sim}$ so that it can perform its function of protein transcription in the genome. The removal system is specific to $\mathcal{V}_n$ molecules; hence although it functions on $T_1^{\sim}P\mathcal{V}_n$, it would work just as well on $Q\mathcal{V}_n$ where Q is any other tagged protein. Denote the removal system which destroys $\mathcal{V}_n$ tagged proteins Q from a substrate S by the symbol $fSQ\mathcal{V}_n$. Thus, we have the reaction $T_1/T_1^{\sim}P\mathcal{V}_n + fSQ\mathcal{V}_n \to T_1$ which releases T_1 into the cytoplasm. The full event chain is shown in Equation 2 where N is the nucleus, TPT denotes the phrase *tagged protein transcription* and $P(T_1)$ indicates the protein whose construction is initiated by the trigger T_0. Without the trigger, we see there are a variety of ways transcription can be stopped: T_1 does not exist in a free state; instead, it is always bound into the complex $T_1/T_1^{\sim}$ and hence can't be activated until the $T_1^{\sim}$ is removed. Also, any of the steps required to remove $T_1^{\sim}$ can be blocked effectively killing transcription: phosphorylation of $T_1^{\sim}$ into $T_1^{\sim}P$ is needed so that tagging can occur and so blocking the phosphorylation step will stop transcription. Also, anything blocking the tagging of the phosphorylated $T_1^{\sim}P$ or stops the removal mechanism $fSQ\mathcal{V}_n$ prevents transcription. The steps above can be used therefore to further regulate the transcription of T_1 into the protein $P(T_1)$. Let T_0', T_0'' and T_0''' be inhibitors of the steps above. These inhibitory proteins can themselves be regulated via triggers through mechanisms just like the ones we are discussing. In fact, $P(T_1)$ could itself serve as an inhibitory trigger - i.e. as any one of the inhibitors T_0', T_0'' and T_0'''. Note we have expanded to a system of four triggers which effect the outcome of $P(T_1)$. Usually, reactions are paired: we typically have the competing reactions of this form $PK/\mathscr{U} + T_1/T_1^\sim \rightarrow T_1/T_1^\sim P$ coupled with $T_1/T_1^\sim P \rightarrow T_1/T_1^\sim + PK/\mathscr{U}$. Hence, we can imagine that the first step is a system which is in dynamic equilibrium. The amount of $T_1/T_1^\sim P$ formed and destroyed forms a stable loop with no net $T_1/T_1^\sim P$ formed. The trigger T_0 introduces additional $PK/\mathscr{U}$ into this stable loop and thereby effects the net production of $T_1/T_1^\sim P$. Thus, a new trigger T_0' could profoundly effect phosphorylation of $T_1^\sim$ and hence production of $P(T_1)$. We can see from the above comments that very fine control of $P(T_1)$ production can be achieved if we think of each step as a dynamical system in flux equilibrium. Assume dynamical loops above consists of the coupled reactions with a forward rate constants k_1, k_2 and k_3 and backward rate constants k_{-1}, k_{-2} and k_{-3}. For convenience, let's define the relative change in a variable x as $r_x = \frac{\delta_x}{x}$. Thus, we can write terms such as $r_{T_1/T_1^\sim P} = \frac{\delta_{T_1/T_1^\sim P}}{[T_1/T_1^\sim P]_e}$, where $PK/\mathscr{U}]_e$ is the equilibrium concentration. The dynamical loops in the event tree can be analyzed at equilibrium [3] to show that a triggered increase in $[PK/\mathscr{U}]_e$ by $\delta_{PK/\mathscr{U}} \equiv \delta$ induces the relative change $\delta_{T_1} = \kappa \left((2\, r_\delta + r_\delta^2)\, [PK/\mathscr{U}]_e^2 \right.$, where κ is the fraction $k_3 k_2 k_1/(k_{-3} k_{-2} k_{-1})$. We can therefore clearly see the multiplier effects of trigger T_0 on protein production T_1 which, of course, also determines changes in the production of $P(T_1)$. Note the target $P(T_1)$ can **alter hardware** or **software** easily. For example, if $P(T_1)$ was a K^+ voltage activated gate, then an increase of δ_{T_1} affects the concentration of K^+ or Na^+ gates. This corresponds to a change in the characteristics of the axonal pulse. It is also possible to model a trigger in terms of first order changes to an underlying diffusion equation [3]. This gives another addition to the edge function computational models.

4. Abstract Biological Feature Vectors

Figure 5.: Prototypical Action Potential

The typical action potential generated by an excitable nerve cell has the form shown in Figure 5. Note the action potential exhibits a combination of cap-like shapes. A low dimensional feature vector ζ, can be defined as discussed in [4]. Each action potential ordered pairs of time and voltage values which determine its shape: the start, (t_0, V_0), the maximum, (t_1, V_1), the time and voltage position when the pulse crosses the reference voltage value before becoming hyperpolarized, (t_2, V_2), the minimum, (t_3, V_3) and a simple sigmoid model of the hyperpolarization tail. The tail is modeled by $V_3 + (V_4 - V_3) \tanh(g(t - t_3))$ where (g, t_4, V_4) are three additional parameters. Hence, each action potential can be represented by an 11 dimensional biological feature vector ζ having these components. An input into an artificial neuron generates an abstract BFV response. The particular values on the components of a single artificial neuron's or a module's feature vector, BFV, are then amenable to alteration via neurotransmitter action such as serotonin, norepinephrine and dopamine coming from the midbrain. Using first order approximations, we can develop an understanding of how the parameters of the BFV change with the alteration of the g_{Na}^{Max} and g_K^{Max} conductance parameters which themselves are amenable to second messenger triggers. Hence, we can estimate $\frac{\partial V_1}{\partial g_K^{Max}}$, $\frac{\partial V_1}{\partial g_{Na}^{Max}}$ and others [3]. Note these partials then allow us to implement changes in BFV vectors when a neurotransmitter trigger updates the biological hardware.

5. Conclusions

We have developed abstract machinery to help us build a small brain model. We replace ordinary differential and partial differential equation modeling with a discrete formulation based on a DG graph model, $\mathcal{G}$. The output of a computational node is an 11 dimensional biological feature vector (BFV). The 11 parameters of this scripted response are then amenable to tuning using a second messenger trigger model whose output of a transcribed protein is mapped to alterations in these 11 parameters as we can estimate $\frac{\partial(BFV\,parameters)}{\partial(SM)}$ rates. Training of such a module is then accomplished by assuming information flow through the module is given by the graph based discrete partial differential equation. A combination of Laplacian flow and Hebbian updates generates update laws for the edge weights in the computational graph. This gives a mechanism for *training* the internal details of a graph of modules so as to obtain higher level precept matching. For example, to model dopamine, norepinephrine and serotonin interactions, one could build a simple DG using the modular approach we have described. Each of the neurotransmitter families would alter BFV responses as is known from the neurobiological literature. Such interaction is crucial to understanding cognitive abilities and it is poorly understood. For example, drugs such as *Abilify* and *Seroquel* affect multiple neurotransmitters simultaneously using mechanisms still not understood even though they are used in the treatment of cognitive dysfunction. Our interests are to build tools that allow us to generate models which provide us insight into these systems. Of course, this is a subset of the larger problem of modeling sensor fusion.

References

[1] D. Hebb,*The Organization of Behavior: A Neuropsychological Theory*, Psychology Press: 2002 reissue, 1949.

[2] R. Raizada and S. Grossberg, Towards a Theory of the Laminar Architecture of Cerebral Cortex: Computational Clues from the Visual System, *Cerebral Cortex*, 2003 ,100 - 113.

[3] J. Peterson, *BioInformation Processing: A Primer On Cognitive Modeling Volume One*, http://www.lulu.com/GneuralGnome, Gneural Gnome Press, 2010.

[4] J. Peterson and T. Khan, Abstract Action Potential Models For Toxin Recognition, *Journal of Theoretical Medicine*, **6**, 4, 2006, 199 - 234.

Biologically Inspired Cognitive Architectures 2011
A.V. Samsonovich and K.R. Jóhannsdóttir (Eds.)
IOS Press, 2011

Physics-Based Simulation in the CASTLE Environment

Art POPE, Chris LONG[1] and Diane BRAMSEN

SET Corporation, an SAIC Company

1005 North Glebe Road, Ste 400, Arlington, Virginia 22201, United States

{apope, clong, dbramsen}@setcorp.com

Keywords. Virtual embodiment, neuromorphic interface, cognitive robotics, cognitive Decathlon, biologically-inspired, signal-to-symbol

Abstract

The CASTLE simulator provides a physics-based, 3D virtual environment in which software agents can perceive, act, learn, and be evaluated. The degree of abstraction of both perceptions and actions can be varied depending on the needs of the agents. For example, visual perception can be provided to agents as rendered pixmaps or neuronal spikes, and agents can move kinematically or via force and velocity settings on motors. CASTLE can also transform both inputs and outputs to emulate biological characteristics, such as differing resolution across the visual field of view and imprecision in time or position senses. The CASTLE framework is open and can connect to software agents, graphical user interfaces, and external (possibly distributed) simulations. CASTLE is being actively developed and used with cognitive and brain models on diverse platforms, and is freely available under an open-source license.

---

[1] Corresponding Author: A. Chris Long, Jr., Senior Research Scientist, SET Corporation - An SAIC Company. Phone: 703.738.6214, Fax: 703.738.6201. http://www.setcorp.com

Biologically Inspired Cognitive Architectures 2011
A.V. Samsonovich and K.R. Jóhannsdóttir (Eds.)
IOS Press, 2011
© 2011 The authors and IOS Press. All rights reserved.
doi:10.3233/978-1-60750-959-2-296

Evolutionary Approach to Investigations of Cognitive Systems

Vladimir RED'KO[a,1] and Anton KOVAL'[b]

[a] *Scientific Research Institute for System Analysis, Russian Academy of Science, Russia*
[b] *National Nuclear Research University "MEPhI", Russia*

Abstract. Evolutionary approach to investigations of cognitive systems is analyzed. Modeling of cognitive evolution (a study of evolution of animal cognitive features) is considered. Backgrounds of models of cognitive evolution that are developed in the area of research "Adaptive behavior" are outlined. Our initial models of cognitive evolution investigations are described. The sketch program for future modeling of cognitive evolution is proposed.

Keywords. Cognitive evolution; modeling; adaptive behavior; animal cognitive abilities

Introduction

Studies of cognitive evolution are related to a profound epistemological problem: why *human* mind is applicable to cognition of *nature*? Investigating models of cognitive evolution, we can analyze, why and how did animal and human cognitive features emerge, and how did applicability of human mind to cognition of nature origin. So, this modeling is related to foundation of science, cognitive science and epistemological studies. Fortunately, there is a direction of research "Adaptive Behavior" [1] that is in close relation to the modeling of cognitive evolution.

The starting point of our consideration is the mentioned epistemological problem. Approaches to analyze this problem by means of modeling of cognitive evolution are described in the next section. Then we outline the area of research "Adaptive Behavior" and models of adaptive behavior that are directly related to cognitive evolution. The sketch program for future modeling of cognitive evolution is also proposed. Models that correspond to initial steps of the sketch program are described.

1. Epistemological Problem

There is the epistemological problem: why *human* thinking is applicable to cognition of *nature*? To characterize the problem, let us consider physics. The power of physics is due to effective use of mathematics. However, why mathematical deductions are applicable to studies of real physical phenomena? Indeed, a mathematician makes logical inferences, proves theorems, working with abstractions in his mind,

---

[1] Corresponding Author: Vladimir Red'ko, Scientific Research Institute for System Analysis, Russian Academy of Science, 44/2 Vavilova Street, Moscow, 119333, Russia, E-mail: vgredko@gmail.com.

independently from the physical world. Why results of his work are applicable to real nature?

Similar questions were interesting for scientists and philosophers for a long time. In the 1780s, Immanuel Kant investigated human thinking and human cognition [2, 3]. According to Kant, there is a system of categories, concepts, logic rules, and inference methods which humans use in cognition of nature. This system of "pure reason" is of *a priory* character; it exists in our minds before any experience. As the pure reason is of a priory character, our reason prescribes its laws to nature [3]:

"…it seems at first strange, but is not the less certain, to say: *the understanding does not derive its laws (a priori) from, but prescribes them to, nature.*"

After appearance of Darwinian theory, the concept of a priory pure reason had to be revised. Such revision was clearly expressed by Konrad Lorenz [4]. According to Lorenz, human mind emerged in the course of evolution as a result of numerous interactions with the external world. In an evolutionary context, "pure reason" is not of a priory character, it has obvious evolutionary empirical roots.

Actually, Kant and Lorenz demonstrated that without analysis of evolutionary origin of human mind, we can't answer the question of applicability of human thinking to cognition of nature.

In order to analyze evolutionary roots of human mind, we can follow evolutionary roots of animal and human cognitive abilities. Can we really proceed in this way? Our answer is: yes, we can. To justify this answer, we can use the following analogy.

Let us consider the elementary logic rule that is used by a mathematician in deductive inferences, namely, *modus ponens*: "if A is present and B is a consequence of A, then B is present", or

$$\frac{A, A \to B}{B} \tag{1}$$

Let us go from the mathematician to a dog that is subjected to the experiment of classical conditioning. A neutral conditioned stimulus (CS) precedes a biologically significant unconditioned stimulus (US). After a number of presentations of the pair (CS, US), the causal relation CS $\to$ US is stored in the dog's memory. Using this relation at a new presentation of the CS, the dog is able to do the elementary "inference":

$$\frac{CS, CS \to US}{US} \tag{2}$$

Thus, after the presentation of the CS, the dog expects the US.

Of course, the use of the rule *modus ponens* (purely deductive) by the mathematician and the inductive "inference" of the dog are obviously different. However, can we think about evolutionary roots of logical rules that are used in mathematics? Yes, we certainly can. The logical conclusion of the mathematician and the inductive "inference" of the dog are similar.

Is there a background for modeling of cognitive evolution? Fortunately, there is the area of research "Adaptive Behavior" that includes some steps towards modeling of cognitive evolution. This research field is outlined in the next section.

2.   Area of Investigations "Adaptive Behavior"

In the early 1990s, the area of investigations "Adaptive Behavior" was initiated [1]. These researches are focused on designing and investigation of artificial (in the form of a computer program or a robot) "organisms" that are capable to adapt to a variable environment. These organisms are often called "animats" or agents, autonomous agents. The term "animat" originates from two words: animal + robot = animat. The main goal of this field of research is [5]:

"...designing animats, i.e., simulated animals or real robots whose rules of behavior are inspired by those of animals. The proximate goal of this approach is to discover architectures or working principles that allow an animal or a robot to exhibit an adaptive behavior and, thus, to survive or fulfill its mission even in a changing environment. The ultimate goal of this approach is to embed human intelligence within an evolutionary perspective and to seek how the highest cognitive abilities of man can be related to the simplest adaptive behaviors of animals."

This ultimate goal of the animat approach is similar to the goals of modeling of cognitive evolution.

Applications of these researches are artificial intelligence, robotics, and models of adaptive behavior in social and economic systems.

Certain models of cognitive abilities of animals are already investigated in the framework of "Adaptive behavior." Some such models are characterized below.

Models of conditioned reflexes were investigated in early works [6, 7].

Researches of an anticipatory behavior, at which animals predict future situations and actively use these predictions for the organization of the behavior, are conducted currently [8].

Interesting works are devoted to the formalization of rules of decision making. For example, Mark Witkowski [9] proposed a theory of decision making rules that correspond to different levels of biological evolution. These rules take into account an associative memory, conditioned reflexes, and predictions of action results. Schemes of learning and decision making that are based on these rules are developed; certain computer simulations confirm efficiency of proposed rules.

Tony Prescott [10] analyzed an evolution of neural structures that have the important role at the action selection ensuring adaptive behavior.

Thus, certain models of cognitive features of animal adaptive behavior are designed and investigated already. However, these investigations are preliminary in many aspects. The next section proposes key steps for future modeling of cognitive evolution.

3.   Sketch Program for Further Researches of Cognitive Evolution

The sketch program for further researches of cognitive evolution consists of following steps.

A) Modeling of adaptive behavior of animats that have several natural needs: food, reproduction, safety.

Such modeling can be simulations of a natural behavior of simple modeled organisms. Modeling in this direction is already initiated (see below).

B) Investigation of the transition from the physical level of information processing in nervous system of animals to the level of generalized "notions".

Such transition can be considered as emergence of "notions" in animal minds. The generalized "notions" are mental analogues of our words, which are not said by animals, but really used by them. Usage of notions leads to essential reduction both the needed memory and the time of information processing, therefore it should be evolutionary advantageous.

C) Investigations of processes of generating causal relations in animal memory.

Storing relationships between the cause and the effect and the adequate use of these relationships is one of key properties of active cognition of regularities of the external world by animals. This allows to predict events in the external world and to use adequately these predictions.

The next logically natural step is the transition from memorizing separate causal relations to systems of logic conclusions.

D) Investigations of "logic conclusions" in animal minds.

Actually, at classical conditioning, animals do a "logic conclusion": "If the conditioned stimulus takes place, and the conditioned stimulus results in the unconditioned one, then the unconditioned stimulus is expected". Such conclusions are similar to logical conclusions in mathematical deductions (see above). It is important to understand, how systems of these conclusions operate, to what extent this "animal logic" is similar to our human logic.

The listed items outline steps of possible investigations from simplest forms of adaptive behavior to logical rules that are used in mathematical deductions. Following these steps, we began corresponding modeling [11]. Simple initial models are described in the next section.

4. Initial Models

The formal model of the simple agents which have needs of 1) food, 2) reproduction, and 3) safety (Step A of the sketch program) has been designed and analyzed [11]. According to computer simulations, the model demonstrated a natural behavior of agents. Also the important role of reproduction during evolutionary optimization of agent control systems has been revealed. More detailed model of autonomous agents that have motivations corresponding to these three needs is described below.

Another model [11] demonstrated the formation of several generalized heuristics by the self-learning agent that searches for food in the two-dimensional cellular environment. These heuristics result in generating chains of actions by the agent. Additionally, the formation of internal generalized "notions" by the autonomous agent (Step B) was observed in this model.

4.1. Model of autonomous agents with natural needs and motivations

The main assumptions of the model are as follows. There is a population of agents. Each agent has its resource $R(t)$, t is discrete time. There is a predator in vicinity of the agent; the activity of the predator changes periodically. The active predator reduces resource of the neighboring agent.

Each time moment, the agent can execute one of the following actions: 1) resting, 2) searching for food, 3) eating food, 4) preparing for reproduction, 5) reproduction, 6) defending from predator.

The agent resource $R(t)$ is increased at eating of food and is decreased at execution of actions by the agent. At reproduction, certain resource is transferred from the agent-parent to the agent-child.

Each agent has the following needs 1) food, 2) safety, 3) reproduction. Agent motivations M_F , M_S , M_R correspond to these needs. The following hierarchy is introduced between motivations: M_F is preferable as compared with M_S and M_R , M_S is preferable as compared with M_R . Also, factors corresponding to needs F_F , F_S and F_R are introduced. At determining the leading motivation, these factors are compared with thresholds T_F , T_S and T_R , and hierarchy of motivations is taken into account.

The agent control system is a set of rules $S_k \rightarrow A_k$, where S_k is the situation, A_k is the agent action in this situation. The components of the vector S_k are 1) the activity of the predator in the vicinity of the agent, 2) the index of the action that was executed by the agent in the previous time step, 3) the leading motivation of the agent. Each rule has its weight W_k ; these weights are adjusted by means of reinforcement learning and evolutionary optimization. At action selection, rules having large weights are used.

The model was investigated by means of computer simulations. The results of simulations are illustrated by Figures 1, 2.

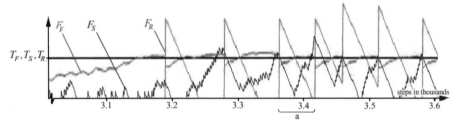

Figure 1. Dynamics of agent factors F_F , F_S and F_R .

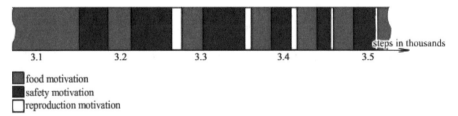

food motivation
safety motivation
reproduction motivation

Figure 2. Dynamics of leading motivations of the agent.

The simulation results show that stable chains of actions are formed at agent leaning. In addition, a cyclical behavior of the agent is formed. The cycle is the period between moments of reproductions (the duration of the cycle is approximately equal to 40 time steps); typical cycle is shown by line "a" in Figure 1. In this cycle, the agent firstly increases its resource $R(t)$ by eating of food, then its actions are aimed at maximizing safety, and when both needs (food and safety) are satisfied, the agent reproduces itself.

Returning to general consideration of initial models, we can compare steps of the sketch program with our models and other investigations [6-10] and conclude that there are only some small elements corresponding to each step of the program yet. In other words, we can see some small fragments of a picture of cognitive evolution now, but we do not see the whole picture yet. Nevertheless, investigations of cognitive evolution are interesting and important.

5.   Conclusion

Thus, approaches to modeling of cognitive evolution have been proposed and discussed. This modeling is related to foundations of science and to foundations of mathematics. Initial steps towards modeling of cognitive evolution have been already taken in the research area "Adaptive Behavior". The sketch program for further modeling of cognitive evolution is proposed. The program includes research steps that are aimed for investigations from simple animal cognitive abilities to mathematical deductions.

6.   Acknowledgments

This work is partially supported by the Russian Foundation for Basic Research, Grant No. 10-01-00129 and the Federal Program "Scientific and Scientific-pedagogical Personals of Innovative Russia" for 2009-2013 years, Contract No. P812.

References

[1] J.-A. Meyer, S.W. Wilson (Eds.), *From Animals to Animats: Proceedings of the First International Conference on Simulation of Adaptive Behavior,* The MIT Press/Bradford Books, Cambridge, 1991.

[2] I. Kant, *Critique of Pure Reason* (trans), Werner Pluhar, Indianapolis, 1996.

[3] I. Kant, *Prolegomena to Any Future Metaphysics* (trans), Cambridge University Press, New York, 1997.

[4] K. Lorenz, Kant's doctrine of the a priori in the light of contemporary biology*, Learning, Development and Culture: Essays in Evolutionary Epistemology*, H. Plotkin (Ed.) New York: Wiley (1982), 121-143.

[5] J.Y. Donnart, J.-A. Meyer, Learning reactive and planning rules in a motivationally autonomous animat. *IEEE Transactions on Systems, Man, and Cybernetics - Part B: Cybernetics* **26** (1996), 381-395.

[6] S. Grossberg, Classical and instrumental learning by neural networks. *Progress in Theoretical Biology.* R. Rosen, F. Snell (Eds.), Academic Press, New York **3** (1974), 51-141.

[7] A.G. Barto, R.S. Sutton, Simulation of anticipatory responses in classical conditioning by neuron-like adaptive element, *Behavioral Brain Research* **4** (1982), 221-235.

[8] M.V. Butz, O. Sigaud, G. Pezzulo, G. Baldassarre (Eds.), *Anticipatory Behavior in Adaptive Learning Systems: From Brains to Individual and Social Behavior*, LNAI 4520. Springer Verlag. Berlin, Heidelberg, 2007.

[9] M. Witkowski, An action-selection calculus, *Adaptive Behavior*, **15** (2007), 73-97.

[10]   T.J. Prescott, Forced moves or good tricks in design space? Landmarks in the evolution of neural mechanisms for action selection, *Adaptive Behavior*, **15** (2007), 9-31.

[11]   V.G. Red'ko, Models of cognitive evolution: Initial steps, *Proceedings of the 6th International Conference on Neural Network and Artificial Intelligence (ICNNAI'2010)*, Brest, Belarus (2010), 133-139.

Biologically Inspired Cognitive Architectures 2011
A.V. Samsonovich and K.R. Jóhannsdóttir (Eds.)
IOS Press, 2011

Genetic Construction of a Heterogeneous Network Controlling a Simple Simulated Autonomous Robot With Learning

Mark REIMERS
VCU, 800 East Leigh St Richmond 23298 United States
mreimers@vcu.edu

Keywords. Emergent properties, neural networks, Braitenberg vehicles, genetic

Abstract

Most network architectures for cognition treat all nodes equally, in the tradition of isotropy assumptions in physics. However during the long evolution of animal brains, heterogeneity, both of node function and of connectivity, has been present from the start, and has increased dramatically in animals with higher mental functions. Such observations suggest that representations by highly heterogeneous networks might be worth exploring, but the exponentially large number of possible networks seems to make such exploration intractable.

I propose here a means of network construction along the lines taken by animal brains: that is the network itself is emergently constructed by interactions of simpler rules specifying node properties and preferences for connection. This architecture is explored and tested in a simple simulation derived from Braitenberg vehicles. Of particular interest is behavior that might be said to represent 'cognition', such as learning to avoid problems or to return to advantageous regions.

Biologically Inspired Cognitive Architectures 2011
A.V. Samsonovich and K.R. Jóhannsdóttir (Eds.)
IOS Press, 2011

The Case for Including Physiology in Cognitive Modeling

Frank E. RITTER[a,1], Chris DANCY[a], and Keith BERRY[b]

[a] *College of IST, Penn State*
[b] *Bioengineering Department, Penn State, and Medical Corps, US Army Reserves*
frank.ritter@psu.edu, cld5070@psu.edu

Abstract

Cognitive architectures such as ACT-R allow us to simulate certain aspects of hu-man behavior and cognition. Though these architectures are sufficient for simulating many aspects of cognition, there remain features of humans, human behavior, and cognition that have yet to be sufficiently realized through models within a cognitive architecture. We examine here features not yet realized that appear to be based on the physiology level, for example, circadian rhythms, the effects of caffeine, task appraisal, and a wide range of factors that cause fatigue. That is, there are models of the effect of caffeine on cognition, but not models of the effect of caffeine on energy use that then influences cognitive mechanisms. There are models of the effects of fatigue, but these do not represent the underlying mechanisms of fatigue but the effects on performance. There are other examples that include a physiological substrate, but not a unified one that is based on human physiology.

To move towards an architecture that encompasses a larger breadth of humans and human behavior, we propose to add a physiological substrate to architectures, and we explain what this will mean for an existing cognitive architecture, ACT-R, creating ACT-RΦ. A concrete physiological substrate will allow for more diverse theories and representations of human behavior and cognition, that is, theories that involve the mind and the body. Examples of such behaviors include certain emotions, fatigue due to exercise or sleep deprivation, and external affects caused due to the environments— effects on cognition arising from a lower, physiological level. ACT-RΦ will give users an opportunity to model both cognitive and physiological effects. We will demonstrate this ability by comparing the behavior of an existing ACT-R model to one developed with the addition of a physiological substrate such as HumMod.

---

[1] Corresponding Author.

Biologically Inspired Cognitive Architectures 2011
A.V. Samsonovich and K.R. Jóhannsdóttir (Eds.)
IOS Press, 2011

Learning to Find Structure in a Complex World

Paul ROBERTSON [1] and Robert LADDAGA
DOLL Labs, Inc., U.S.A.
paulr@dollabs.com, rladdaga@dollabs.com

Keywords. Perceptual learning, cognitive architectures, computer vision

Abstract

In this paper we describe an architecture for perceptual learning in closed loop systems. The draws directly upon a neurally feasible architecture.

Computer vision researchers strive to find the right operators and the right representations necessary to reproduce the capabilities of the human visual system. In this paper we present a different perspective on the human visual system that suggests a rather different approach to vision research that places a greater emphasis on structures that can learn representations than on designing the representations. We present results of an architecture for learning to see and act that is based on engineered emergence.

Our paper demonstrates learning results, mathematical analysis, and biological support for the approach.

While the approach depends upon massive parallelism, we argue that the approach is well suited to implementation on modern graphics processors and represents a viable path forward for building perceptual intelligence systems.

---

[1] Corresponding Author.

Biologically Inspired Cognitive Architectures 2011
A.V. Samsonovich and K.R. Jóhannsdóttir (Eds.)
IOS Press, 2011
doi:10.3233/978-1-60750-959-2-305

Biologically inspired feature creation for multi-sensory perception

Brandon ROHRER [a,1]

[a] *Sandia National Laboratories, USA*

Abstract. Automatic feature creation is a powerful tool for identifying and reaching goals in the natural world. This paper describes in detail a biologically-inspired method of feature creation that can be applied to sensory information of any modality. The algorithm is incremental and on-line; it enforces sparseness in the features it creates; and it can form features from other features, making a hierarchical feature set. Here it demonstrates the creation of both visual and auditory features.

Keywords. feature creation, unsupervised learning, perception, abstraction, vision processing, sensor fusion

1. Introduction

The purpose of this work is to demonstrate feature creation in multiple sensory modalities that is inspired by observations of neurological activity and structure. A feature is a combination of inputs that is useful in sparsely representing a state variable or in predicting future inputs. Feature creation[2] is most often found to be useful in machine learning problems with high-dimensional inputs and has received increased attention in recent years in problems with large input spaces, such as gene selection and natural language analysis. [5] The problem addressed here is multisensory perception, as in an autonomous robot.

The power of features is well illustrated by a simple example, a variation of the exclusive-or (XOR) problem. (See Figure 1.) As posed, the two classes are not linearly separable, that is, they are not separable by a single straight line and cannot be segregated in a two-layer neural network. [9] However, a nonlinear feature, created by multiplying the values of x_1 and x_2 for each data point, transforms the classification problem to a space in which it is trivial.

The ability of appropriately selected features to simplify otherwise intractable problems makes the approach appealing for challenging machine learning applications. Identifying an object category, based on an image, or a topic, based on a text snippet, are popular problems in which constructed features are commonly used. Deciding that an array of pixels represents, say, a dog, may involve several levels of features. Pixels may be in-

---

[1]Corresponding Author: Sandia National Laboratories, Albuquerque, New Mexico, USA, Email: rohrer@sandia.gov, Web: http://www.sandia.gov/rohrer
[2]Synonymous and closely related terms include feature extraction, feature construction, feature selection, feature generation, concept generation, sparse representation, kernel learning, manifold detection, or state space dimensionality reduction.

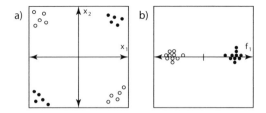

Figure 1. a) A variation of the exclusive-or problem, named for the XOR logic table it resembles. It has be re-centered on the origin. The challenge is to separate the data points into their respective classes. It clearly cannot be achieved by a linear separation boundary. **b)** The same problem with each data point expressed in a feature space with $f_1 = x_1 \times x_2$. Once transformed into this feature space, linear separation becomes straightforward.

terpreted as edge features, which in turn may be used to infer topological features, which may then be classified. As opposed to the XOR problem which has only two dimensions, input in the image classification problem may have millions of dimensions.

One of the challenges when creating features is determining the quality of a given feature set. In isolation, feature creation is an unsupervised learning problem and cannot be evaluated without additional information, such as an objective function or the performance of a second machine learning algorithm that uses the created features as input. For example, in clustering, a closely related unsupervised learning problem, the quality of clusters can either be determined by a measure, such as the standard deviation of elements within a cluster, or by the performance of a classification algorithm that uses the clusters as input. Data compression and prediction are other tasks that may be paired with feature creators.

The feature creation algorithm presented here is used in tandem with a reinforcement learning (RL) algorithm. Feature sets that enable the RL algorithm to collect more reward are considered superior, setting up a basis for comparison. Together the feature creator and RL algorithm form BECCA, a brain-emulating cognition and control architecture [14]. (See Figure 2.) BECCA was designed to address the problem of natural world interaction—making intelligent agents capable of pursuing arbitrary goals in unfamiliar and complex environments.

1.1. Related work

The introduction to the 2003 NIPS Feature Extraction Challenge gives an overview of common feature creation methods [10,5]. It differentiates feature selection from feature construction. In feature selection a few of the inputs are assumed to provide most of the information required for classification. For instance, of all the millions of tests and observations that could be made on a human body, only a few need to made to determine whether a patient has a cold: checking for sore throat, fever, and runny nose. A competent feature selection algorithm would be able to identify these discriminating features, given sufficient training data.

Alternatively, feature construction is useful when a combination of many inputs carries the discriminative information. In image classification, for example, a set of images of pepperoni pizza may not have any single pixels that have the same value in all images, so a feature selection approach would not work. Feature construction would be necessary, finding operations on the input that allow the category to be discriminated.

Common methods include principal components analysis, support vector machines, linear discriminant analysis, Fourier transforms, and information theoretic tools. Entries to the Feature Extraction Challenge used both feature selection and feature construction approaches, and the winners are described in the same volume as the introduction [18, e.g.].

It is interesting to note that, in a follow-up activity, organizers of the Feature Extraction Challenge tasked a class of undergraduates with creating their own entries [6]. Using relatively simple feature creation methods, the students improved upon the performance of the best challenge entries. This may have been due to the fact that the challenge consisted of two-class classification problems. More sophisticated tasks may require more complex feature sets. Whatever the cause, it demonstrates the room for growth that feature creation has as an academic field.

Another name for feature creation is "deep learning" [2], a label adopted by a research community seeking to discover and exploit the structure that underlies large, high-dimensional data. Deep learning approaches create high-level, low-dimensional feature representations using tools like Convolutional Neural Networks (CNNs) [8], Deep Belief Networks (DBNs) [7,3], and Deep SpatioTemporal Inference Network (DeSTIN) [1]. CNNs are designed to work with two-dimensional data, such as images, and they do not apply to arbitrarily structured data. By using several layers of Restricted Boltzmann Machines, DBNs are capable of generating sophisticated features that allow it to interpret novel inputs. However, they are typically applied to the supervised learning problem of discrimination, and require a substantial amount of labeled data in order to be adequately trained. Whether DBNs can be applied to the unsupervised learning problem of feature creation is unclear. DeSTIN incorporates both unsupervised and supervised learning methods and appears to be fully capable of hierarchical feature creation. It has been published only recently; future papers describing its operation and performance will allow it to be fully evaluated. Similar to these deep learning approaches, BECCA's feature creator is hierarchical, meaning that it repeatedly creates higher-level features from lower-level features. In contrast to them, it is incremental and on-line, efficiently incorporating new data as it is observed and updating itself after each time step.

2. Method

BECCA's feature creator takes in m inputs and produces n outputs, each on the interval $[0, 1]$, at every time step. It assumes nothing about the source of its inputs or the destination of its outputs. Inputs are treated the same whether they represent a pixel value, a sensed touch, or a joint position. The feature creator also takes in a scalar reward at each time step.

The feature creator first breaks the inputs into groups by finding sets of inputs that are, on average, somewhat correlated. Each group is a subspace of the full input space, and it is in these subspaces that features are defined. Whenever the inputs to a group are sufficiently different from the features in that group, the inputs become a new feature and are added to the feature set. Also at each time step, the inputs are used to "vote" for the activity level of each feature by calculating their similarity to each. The activity of the most similar feature is preserved and the others are suppressed through a winner-take-all operation. The feature activities across all groups are concatenated to produce an output

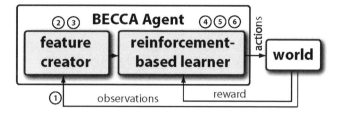

Figure 2. At each timestep, the BECCA agent completes one iteration of the sensing-learning-planning-acting loop, consisting of six major steps: 1) Reading in observations and reward. 2) Updating its feature set. 3) Expressing observations in terms of features. 4) Predicting likely outcomes based on an internal model. 5) Selecting an action based on the expected reward of likely outcomes. 6) Updating its world model.

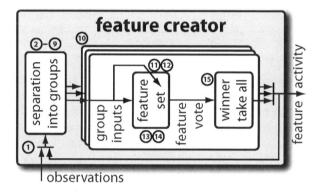

Figure 3. Block diagram of the feature creator, illustrating its operation. Numbered labels refer to steps in Algorithm 1.

vector. A copy of the output vector is fed back and concatenated with the input vector as well, allowing the features to be constructed into yet higher-level features.

The operation of the feature creator can be illustrated by providing it with a variety of inputs. Here, it was given two separate input sets, corresponding to two tasks, *watch* and *listen*. In the watch task, the inputs consisted of sections of images from the Caltech-256 data set [4]. These were converted to black and white and pixelized to a 10×10 array of super-pixels. A center-difference image was created by subtracting a portion of a pixel's neighbors' values from its own, and the 100-pixel array was normalized to fall on $[0, 1]$. The array, v, and its complement, $1 - v$, were passed to BECCA's feature creator, resulting in a 200-dimensional input vector.

In the listen task, an audio stream taken from the KUNM radio station in Albuquerque (89.9 FM) was recorded in 100 ms intervals. The frequency content of each snippet between 10 and 10,000 Hz was collapsed into bins of one-sixth of an octave (one whole note in modern music). The level of each bin was low-pass filtered and increases in bin level were used as inputs. The data that resulted from this pre-processing resembled a 60-channel graphic equalizer.

A block diagram describing the feature creator's operation (See Figure 3.) and pseudocode (See Table 2.) provide additional details. Full MATLAB (Mathworks, Natick, MA) code for BECCA and the watch and listen tasks is available as well [13].

Algorithm 1 FEATURE CREATOR

Input: *observation* vector
Output: *feature_activity* vector

1: form *input* vector by concatenating *observation*
      and previous *feature_activity*
2: update estimate of *correlation* between *inputs*
3: **if** MAX(*correlation*) $> C_1$ **then**
4:      add the two *input* elements achieving the
          maximum *correlation* to the new *group*
5:      **while** NOT(*stop_condition_met*) **do**
6:          find *mean_correlation* between each
              remaining *input* and *group* members
7:          **if** MAX(*mean_correlation*)$> C_2$ and
              group size $< C_3$ **then**
8:              add the *input* element to the *group*
9:          **else** *stop_condition_met*
10: **for** each *group* **do**
11:     **if** MIN (DISTANCE (*input, features*))$> C_4$ **then**
12:         add normalized *input* to set of *features*
13:     **for** each *feature* **do**
14:         *feature_vote* = *feature* · *input*
15:         *feature_activity* = WTA(*feature_vote*)

Figure 4. Examples of three inputs to the feature creator before and after preprocessing. From left to right the images are of a woman, a lawnmower, and a snake. (From [4].) When reduced to a 10×10 pixelation, the resulting image is unidentifiable, but retains coarse aspects of the original image. Light pixels represent locations that are brighter than their neighbors and dark pixels signify the opposite. Neutral gray pixels show locations that are approximately the same intensity as those around them.

3. Results

The feature creator stepped through 150,000 time steps in the watch task. Examples of the inputs at three different time steps are shown in Figure 4. During the course of learning, 264 groups were created, containing 1828 features in all. The complete set of features from one of the groups are in Figure 5, and samples of other groups can be seen in Figure 6. The entire set of features, broken out by group, can be found in an online supplement [16].

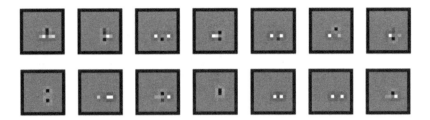

Figure 5. Receptive fields for all the features from one group. Although each feature is a linear combination of the same set of input pixels, the weighting of the pixels in each feature varies and is sometimes near zero. Inspection of the features suggests that they would be differentially activated by a wide variety of visual stimuli. Some would respond well to bright horizontal line segments and some to dark vertical line segments, some to continuous lines and some to line terminations.

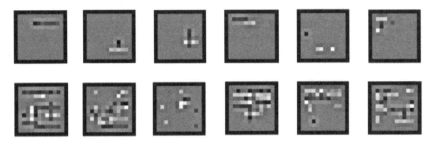

Figure 6. Receptive fields for features from 12 of the 264 groups. The six groups in the top row are first-level features, meaning that they are each composed of raw center-surround pixel inputs. The six groups on the bottom row are higher-level features. Each of them are composed of a mixture of first-level features and raw inputs. They tend to span a much larger portion of the visual field than first-level features.

In the listen task, the feature creator stepped through 15,000 time steps, creating 80 groups with 381 features. Examples of audio features can be seen in Figure 7. The entire feature set can be viewed in the online supplemental material [15]. A video showing both visual and audio representations of the features can be found in [12].

4. Discussion

BECCA's method of feature creation results in features that are sparse, that is, they are functions of only a small number of inputs. Sparsity is often considered a desirable attribute of a feature set. Principal Components Analysis and related methods lack it entirely, creating linear combinations of the entire input set. In order to encourage sparsity, many feature creation algorithms include a normalization term. Occasionally the l_0 norm is used [19], (the count of the number of inputs used in a feature, the strongest sparsity condition) but more often it is the l_1 norm (a weaker sparsity condition, but more amenable to computation and analysis). By fixing the number of input elements in each group, BECCA's feature creator enforces a maximum l_0 norm, creating strongly sparse features.

By not making assumptions about the source of its inputs, BECCA's feature creator gains the capability of handling inputs of all modalities, and of combining them. It is not uncommon for feature creators to assume that incoming data is from a one-dimensional

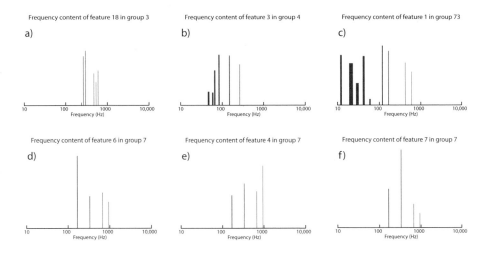

Figure 7. Receptive fields for six features from the listen task. An octave, a factor of two difference in frequency, is represented by a fixed interval on these logarithmically-scaled plots. The harmonic overtones of a fundamental frequency are its integer multiples. The magnitudes of the various overtones determine the quality or timbre of the sound. The difference between, say, a violin and a flute playing the same note lies primarily in their differing patterns of overtones. Due to resonant nature of sounds, single sources often produce sounds consisting of a fundamental frequency with its harmonic overtones. These commonly occurring patterns are observed in the groups and features created. **a)** This feature shows a fundamental frequency cluster and its first harmonic, separated by an interval of one octave. **b)** In this feature, a fundamental frequency of approximately 45 Hz is accompanied by its first, third, and seventh harmonics (two, four, and eight times the fundamental frequency, respectively) and several lower non-harmonic overtones. **c)** Where both a) and b) are composed of raw inputs, this feature combines other features to make a more complex, high-level audio feature. There are many examples of high-level features like this one in the created feature set. **d-f)** These features are all from the same group. They illustrate receptive fields of the same fundamental frequency, but with different timbres. In each case, the fundamental frequency is accompanied by its first, third, and fifth overtones. Changes in their relative amplitudes make them sensitive to sounds with distinctly different qualities. (See [12] for a full audiovisual representation.)

array of sensors, as in an encoder, or a two-dimensional sensor array, as in a camera. Hand-crafted kernels or transformations are often built in. These engineered approaches can produce striking results, but at the cost of some generality. The approach presented here aims to be as general as possible, allowing a programmer to be agnostic about the source and meaning of inputs. This opens the door for automatic feature creation in not only vision and hearing, demonstrated here, but also in laser scanning, whisker contact, radiation detection, network traffic monitoring, and any other conceivable sensor modality, in addition to combinations of all the above.

Feature creation allows robots to interact with their environments in increasingly sophisticated ways. In cases where their environments and tasks are unfamiliar, feature creation may be necessary for any better-than-random performance on a task. It is a means of abstracting specific experience into a more symbolic representation. In a sufficiently complex environment, an agent is unlikely to experience the exact same set of inputs more than once. If that agent is to learn from its experience, it must have a way to relate its current experience to previous ones. Abstract features make this possible. They allow one to claim that two objects are both books, even though they are of different sizes, weights, colors, ages, smells, and textures. And in this way, they allow experience gained with one book to be transferred to the other. Natural language acquisition can be understood as feature creation operating at an advanced level. The symbols for words can be created from their corresponding printed and spoken forms and the visual and other sensory experiences associated with them. Automatic feature creation will almost certainly be a capability of any machine capable of human-level learning behavior and performance.

BECCA's feature creator was inspired by evidence of biological feature creation. At a high level, human capabilities of analogy, association, generalization, and abstraction suggest that arbitrary symbols may be combined and related to one another. Our ability to learn and understand such things as microcircuit design and quantum physics suggests that these symbols are acquired rather than evolved and innate. The mammalian primary visual area of the cerebral cortex, V1, has inputs that are excited by small center-surround stimulus fields and outputs that are activated by appropriately oriented line segments. Other areas of the cortex, such as V2, V4, and the medio-temporal area, take these outputs as their inputs and build them into outputs that respond to increasingly complex features. Other areas of the cortex appear to serve the same function for touch [11] and hearing, as demonstrated by the aural representation in bats that enables echolocation. Re-routing sensory inputs to a new cortical location results in similar feature creation phenomena [17], hinting that the cortex may be performing a similar function throughout its extent. If that is the case, the function it performs may be nothing more than feature creation. However, there is still far too little data available to certify or disprove such a statement. It is at most a conjecture, and regardless of its accuracy, the feature creation observed in the cortex provides a rich source of insights for the development of machine learning algorithms seeking to do the same.

Acknowledgements

This work was supported by the Laboratory Directed Research and Development program at Sandia National Laboratories. Sandia National Laboratories is a multi-program laboratory managed and operated by Sandia Corporation, a wholly owned subsidiary of Lockheed Martin Corporation, for the U.S. Department of Energy's National Nuclear Security Administration under contract DE-AC04-94AL85000.

References

[1] I. Arel, D. Rose, and B. Coop. DeSTIN: A deep learning architecture with application to high-dimensional robust pattern recognition. In *Proc. AAAI Workshop Biologically Inspired Cognitive Architectures (BICA)*, 2009.

[2] I. Arel, D. C. Rose, and T. P. Karnowski. Deep machine learning—a new frontier in artificial intelligence research. *IEEE Computational Intelligence Magazine*, November 2010.

[3] I. Fasel and J. Berry. Deep belief networks for real-time extraction of tongue contours from ultrasound during speech. In *Proceedings of the International Conference on Pattern Recognition (ICPR)*, 2010.

[4] G. Griffin, A. Holub, and P. Perona. Caltech-256 object category dataset. Technical Report 7694, California Institute of Technology, 2007. http://authors.library.caltech.edu/7694.

[5] I. Guyon and A. Elisseeff. An introduction to variable and feature selection. *Journal of Machine Learning Research*, 3:1157–1182, 2003.

[6] I. Guyon, J. Li, T. Mader, P. A. Pletscher, G. Schneider, and M. Uhr. Competitive baseline methods set new standards for the nips 2003 feature selection benchmark. *Pattern Recognition Letters*, 28:1438–1444, 2007.

[7] G. E. Hinton, S. Osindero, and Y. Teh. A fast learning algorithm for deep belief nets. *Neural Computation*, 18:1527Ű1554, 2006.

[8] Y. LeCun, L. Bottou, Y. Bengio, and P. Haffner. Gradient-based learning applied to document recognition. *Proc. IEEE*, 86(11):2278–2324, 1998.

[9] M. Minsky and S. Papert. *Perceptrons: An Introduction to Computational Geometry*. MIT Press, Cambridge, 1969.

[10] Neural Information Processing Systems. NIPS Feature Extraction Challenge, 2003. http://www.nipsfsc.ecs.soton.ac.uk/, Accessed April 25, 2011.

[11] J. R. Phillips, K. O. Johnson, and S. S. Hsiao. Spatial pattern representation and transformation in monkey somatosensory cortex. *Proceedings of the National Academy of Sciences*, 85:1317–1321, 1988.

[12] B. Rohrer. Automatically created audio features. http://www.sandia.gov/rohrer/video/AudioFeatures.mp4, 2011.

[13] B. Rohrer. BECCA code page. http://www.sandia.gov/rohrer/code.html, 2011.

[14] B. Rohrer. An implemented architecture for feature creation and general reinforcement learning. In *Workshop on Self-Programming, 4th International Conference on Artificial General Intelligence*, 2011.

[15] B. Rohrer. Listen task features. http://www.sandia.gov/rohrer/doc/Rohrer11BicaSuppB.pdf, 2011.

[16] B. Rohrer. Watch task features. http://www.sandia.gov/rohrer/doc/Rohrer11BicaSuppA.pdf, 2011.

[17] J. Sharma, A. Angelucci, and M. Sur. Induction of visual orientation modules in auditory cortex. *Nature*, 404:841–847, 2000.

[18] K. Torkkola. Feature extraction by non-parametric mutual information maximization. *Journal of Machine Learning Research*, 3:1415–1438, 2003.

[19] J. Weston, A. Elisseff, B. Schoelkopf, and M. Tipping. Use of the zero norm with linear models and kernel methods. *Journal of Machine Learning Research*, 3:1439–1461, 2003.

Biologically Inspired Cognitive Architectures 2011
A.V. Samsonovich and K.R. Jóhannsdóttir (Eds.)
IOS Press, 2011
© 2011 The authors and IOS Press. All rights reserved.
doi:10.3233/978-1-60750-959-2-314

Mental Imagery in a Graphical Cognitive Architecture

Paul S. ROSENBLOOM[1]

Department of Computer Science and Institute for Creative Technologies
University of Southern California

Abstract. Can mental imagery be incorporated uniformly into a cognitive architecture by leveraging the *mixed* (relational and probabilistic) *hybrid* (discrete and continuous) processing supported by factor graphs? This article takes an initial step towards answering this question via an implementation in a graphical cognitive architecture of a version of the Eight Puzzle based on a hybrid function representation and a factor node optimized for object translation.

Keywords. Cognitive architecture, graphical models, mental imagery

Introduction

A *cognitive architecture* is a hypothesis about the fixed structure underlying intelligent behavior, whether in natural or artificial systems [1]. When combined with knowledge and skills, such an architecture should be capable of yielding effective performance across a diversity of domains. By definition, all cognitive architectures include mechanisms in support of central thought processes, minimally consisting of models of short-term and long-term memory along with an ability to make decisions. But it may also be elaborated to involve multiple forms of memory, complex decision making – based on problem solving or planning – learning, and other hypothesized capabilities.

The diversity of intelligent behavior supported in such architectures may be due to either their comprising a relatively large number of specialized mechanisms [2,3,4] or their supporting flexible interaction among a relatively small number of general mechanisms [5,6]. Both of these strategies have been followed in building integrated models of central cognitive processes, although the choice generally embodies an implicit tradeoff between ease of achieving broad coverage and theoretical elegance. When it comes to extending architectures beyond central cognition, with the addition of peripheral perceptual and motor capabilities, the former strategy has been the primary option, with distinct perceptual and motor modules being added to whatever mechanisms exist for central cognition. Even the Epic cognitive architecture, which has gone furthest in supporting end-to-end modeling of human performance – from perception through cognition and on to action – uses distinct perceptual and motor modules [7].

---

[1] Corresponding Author: University of Southern California, 12015 Waterfront Dr., Playa Vista, CA 90094, USA; E-mail: rosenbloom@usc.edu.

A variant of the latter strategy can be pursued via a dual level approach; implementing a small set of general mechanisms at a level below the architecture that can interact to yield a diversity of architectural mechanisms – spanning symbolic cognition and continuous perceptuomotor capabilities – at the next level up [8]. Two leading candidates for such a lower level are neural networks – as, for example, in [9] – and graphical models [10], with the work here based on the latter. Graphical models share neural nets' focus on local processing in a network of limited computational units, and some kinds of neural networks map directly onto graphical models, but the primary focus is computational rather than biological. The work here should thus be considered as loosely, or abstractly, biologically inspired, but as not so in the details.

As part of an ongoing exploration into combining broad coverage with theoretical elegance in a new form of cognitive architecture, the work here is based on a particular variant of graphical models – factor graphs [11] – that are capable of supporting *mixed* (relational + probabilistic) and *hybrid* (discrete + continuous) processing. Within central cognition, the mixed aspect of this implementation level has yielded a uniform memory architecture able to replicate capabilities normally part of distinct procedural rule-based memories and declarative semantic and episodic memories, plus a constraint memory that is not typically found in cognitive architectures [12]. Exploiting this mixed aspect, plus many of the mechanisms that were already implemented in support of the memory architecture, has also enabled the addition of basic problem solving capabilities [13].

The focus in this article is on extending the uniformity at the heart of this graphical approach even further, in the direction of the peripheral processing underlying perception and motor control, by including mental imagery. Those existing cognitive architectures that include mental imagery, such as Soar (version 9) [3], do so in a modular fashion, with memories and processes distinct from those employed in the more symbolic parts of cognition [14]. Here we'll leverage principally the hybrid aspect of the graphical approach, along with a specially optimized class of factor nodes, to yield the beginnings of a mental imagery capability that breaks down the barrier between the center and the periphery, yielding a more uniform and less modular approach to complete architectures that it is hoped will be extendable to the entirety of mental imagery, and even beyond, to perception – where graphical models such as hidden Markov models and Markov/conditional random fields already provide a wide range of state of the art models – and motor control.

The results to date focus on a version of the classic Eight Puzzle, but with the board represented internally as a multidimensional hybrid data structure. The key mental imagery operation required for this puzzle is *translation*, where tile locations in the plane are shifted as the tiles are slid from place to place. Section 1 reviews the graphical cognitive architecture, as composed of memory and problem solving capabilities. Section 2 then describes how the requisite representation and reasoning are implemented for the imagery aspects of the Eight Puzzle, while introducing a class of factor nodes specially optimized for object translation. Section 3 delves further into this approach to object translation, both to understand it better and to explore how far it might extend. Section 4 wraps up with a summary and future directions. The core contributions of this work are: (1) the demonstration of the feasibility of representing and reasoning about continuous mental imagery uniformly in a graphical cognitive architecture; and (2) the identification and optimization of a special class of factor nodes for imagery operations, which happen also to fill critical roles in support of other architectural capabilities such as reflection and episodic memory.

1.   A Graphical Cognitive Architecture

The graphical cognitive architecture is based on factor graphs, which are similar to the more familiar construct of Bayesian networks except that they: (1) concern the decomposition of arbitrary multivariate functions into products of simpler functions, rather than just the decomposition of joint probability distributions into products of prior and conditional distributions; (2) utilize bidirectional links; and (3) include explicit factor nodes, in addition to variables nodes, representing the subfunctions into which the original function factors.   In yielding bidirectional networks that can represent more than just probability distributions, factor graphs are actually more like Markov networks (aka Markov random fields) than like Bayesian networks, but they are still more general than the Markov alternative [15].

Inference in factor graphs typically occurs by some form of sampling or message passing. The graphical architecture is based on message passing, via a variant of the *summary product algorithm* that passes messages between variable and factor nodes concerning the possible values of the variables [11]. Roughly, incoming messages are multiplied together at all nodes, in a pointwise manner, with factor nodes also including their functions in the product and then summarizing out all variables not to be included in an output message to a variable node.   When *sum* is used for summarization, the graph computes marginals on its individual variables. When *max* is used instead, the graph computes the maximum a posteriori estimation over all of the variables.

One of the prime determinants of the generality of a particular implementation of factor graphs is the representation used for factor functions and messages.   The simplest implementations use tables with: one dimension per variable involved; a bounded number of discrete values along each dimension; and a functional value for each distinct combination of domain values across the variables. Although simple to define and process, such representations are limited to discrete functions; and even there their verboseness can yield major efficiency issues. An implementation focused on probability densities may instead be based on individual Gaussian functions – each specified by just two parameters – or more generally on mixtures of Gaussians. Such representations can be concise and effective in representing levels of uncertainty, but can become awkward in representing other forms knowledge.

The graphical cognitive architecture is based on multidimensional continuous functions that are specified as piecewise linear functions over rectilinear regions [16]. Such a representation can approximate arbitrary continuous functions as accurately as desired, while also supporting discrete and even symbolic dimensions. To implement a discrete dimension, the function's domain is unitized to integral values, such as the half-open intervals [0,1) and [1,2) for the integers 1 and 2. For a symbolic dimension, domain unitization is combined with a restriction on the function's range to Boolean values (0/1 for true/false). A symbol table is then also added – for use by researchers rather than the system – to map from unit domain intervals to symbolic labels.   Table 1 illustrates this hybrid representational capability via a function over two dimensions, one of them

Table 1. Piecewise linear representation of the conditional probability of an object's weight given its category: P(W | C). The category is symbolic while the weight is continuous. Only a fragment of the full table is shown.

w\c	Walker	Table	...
[1,10)	.01w	.001w	...
[10,20)	.2-.01w	"	...
[20,50)	0	.025-.00025w	...
[50,100)	"	"	...

continuous and the other symbolic.

Boundaries among regions are introduced automatically, as needed, by splitting existing regions whenever a single linear function is no longer adequate for them. For example, if a function is currently 0 across its entire multidimensional domain, and the value at a single point is then set to 1, boundaries are added along each dimension to separate that point from all of the adjacent space. The value for the region containing that point is set to 1, while all of the regions now surrounding it are set to 0.

To introduce a boundary at a point along a dimension, an *n*-1 dimensional *slice* is added at that point that cuts across all of the other dimensions. In consequence, a function always comprises an array of rectilinear regions, as in Table 1. When a slice becomes unnecessary, because the regions on both sides of it now express the same linear function, the slice is automatically removed to maintain a minimal representation for the overall function. In the example above, if the value at the altered point once again becomes 0, the boundaries around it are removed.

In a Bayesian network, knowledge about joint probability distributions is stored in the network structure plus prior and conditional distributions over variables. Evidence concerning particular variables then constrains the values of these variables in the network before an inference algorithm computes the implications of the network over all of the variables given this evidence. A similar approach is taken in the graphical architecture. The factor graph embodies knowledge in its links plus in the functions stored in the factor nodes. A subset of the factor nodes comprise *working memory*, the internal cognitive state of the system. Working memory serves the role of evidence in the graph, fixing the values of particular variables during a single application of the summary product algorithm. Working memory may be changed between successive applications of the algorithm based on the results of graph processing.

The remainder of the factor graph comprises *long-term memory*, with the execution of the summary product algorithm serving to retrieve long-term knowledge into working memory. Fragments of knowledge in long-term memory are represented in the architecture via generalized *conditionals* that are compiled into subgraphs within the overall factor graph. Each conditional may contain *conditions*, *actions*, *condacts* and *functions*. Conditions and actions are like the corresponding structures in standard rule systems. Conditions match to working memory to constrain which rules fire and to determine variable bindings. Actions consult variable bindings from conditions to suggest changes in working memory. Condacts provide a combination of these two functionalities, yielding the kind of bidirectional processing required for correct probabilistic reasoning and for partial match in declarative memories. Functions are specified over subsets of conditional variables, and compile down to functions in particular factor nodes within the graph.

When conditions and actions alone are used, the resulting conditionals behave like standard rules. An accumulation of such conditionals can then serve as a procedural rule-based memory. Figure 1, for example, shows a conditional defining a heuristic rule that rejects any Eight Puzzle operator that moves a tile out of its goal location. When instead just condacts

```
CONDITIONAL GoalReject
 Conditions: (Operator id:o state:s x:x y:y)
             (Goal state:s x:x y:y tile:t)
             (Board state:s x:x y:y tile:t)
 Actions:    (Selected - state:s operator:o)
```

Figure 1. Eight Puzzle heuristic that rejects from consideration operators that move tiles out of place.

and functions are used, the resulting conditionals behave more like fragments of traditional probabilistic Bayesian and Markov networks. Accumulations of such conditionals have yielded functionality akin to what is observed in declarative semantic and episodic memories, as well as the kinds of functionality provided by constraint memories. Conditionals based on other combinations of the four basic types of elements can yield hybrid and blended functionality. Figure 2, for example, shows a conditional defined via one condition, two condacts and a function (the one specified in Table 1). This provides a fragment of an extended semantic memory in terms of the conditional probability of an attribute given the concept.

One key distinction over variables and their corresponding dimensions in the graphical architecture is between *universal* and *unique* variables [17]. Universal variables are like

```
CONDITIONAL ConceptWeight
  Conditions: (Object state:s object:o)
  Condacts: (Concept object:o concept:c)
            (Weight object:o weight:w)

  Function: [see table 1]
```

Figure 2. Conditional probability of the weight of an object associated with the state given its concept.

the variables in rule systems that yield all possible consistent bindings to conditions. Unique variables instead yield distributions over their best bindings, as generally desired when accessing declarative memories. For unique variables, only the single best value – as determined by aggregating over the factor functions in the relevant conditionals – is placed into working memory at the end of a cycle. This selection process serves as the core of the problem solving approach in the graphical architecture, enabling operators to be selected and applied based on knowledge in long-term memory [13].

2. Mental Imagery in the Eight Puzzle

The Eight Puzzle is defined in terms of a 3×3 board on which eight numbered tiles are placed and one cell is left blank (Figure 3). A legal move slides a tile that is horizontally or vertically adjacent to the blank cell into the blank cell. A problem instance consists of reconfiguring an initial board configuration by sliding tiles to yield a specified goal board.

In the graphical architecture, the Eight Puzzle board is represented in working memory as a four dimensional hybrid factor function. Two of the dimensions represent the *x* and *y* extent of the board, with each defined to be continuous over the half-open

Figure 3. The Eight Puzzle Board.

interval [0,3). The other two dimensions are also numeric, albeit discrete, with one representing the problem solving state that the board is part of and the other a tile number in [0,9), with the 0 tile denoting the empty cell. These latter two dimensions could conceivably have been symbolic, but it was easier to use successive integers for the states and tiles rather than creating distinct symbolic names for them. Also, as will be discussed shortly, the numeric representation for states plays a key role in enabling the mechanisms developed for mental imagery to be reused in the implementation of a reflection capability within the architecture.

The representation of a board in working memory has a functional value of 1 for each four-dimensional region – comprised of an <*x,y*> extent, a tile, and a state – whenever that tile is in that region for that state. Otherwise, the region has a functional value of 0. Figure 4 shows a part of the representation used for the board configuration in Figure 3, with the state dimension omitted for simplicity and the locations of only the first two tiles indicated. The grey regions in the figure have a value of 1 while the clear regions have a value of 0, denoting that the center right cell – the square <[2,3),[1,2)> – is blank, while tile 1 occupies the top left cell: <[0,1),[0,1)>. The Eight Puzzle board and tiles fit quite easily within the rectilinear regions supported by the architecture, but more complex objects should also be representable as combinations of such regions.

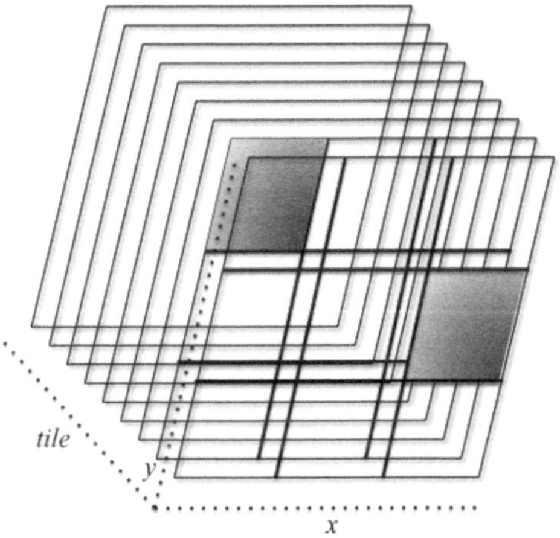

Translating a tile from one cell to another requires shifting its location along either the *x* or *y* dimension. Because such operations on mental imagery involve two images of the board – from before and after the operation – plus a specification of the difference between them, it was earlier assumed that they would best be approached via the relatively complex kinds of graphical computations deployed in areas such as sequence prediction and stereovision [18]. However, a much simpler approach that is afforded by the piecewise linear structure of the image representation has so far proven sufficient. Given that altering the location of a slice automatically shifts the boundaries of all of the regions that abut the slice, the translation of a tile along a single dimension – which is all that is required in the Eight Puzzle – can be handled by offsetting the slices corresponding to its upper and lower boundaries along that dimension.

Figure 4. Partial visualization of three dimensions – two continuous and one discrete – of the hybrid representation used for the Eight Puzzle board.

For example, Tile 1, which is at <[0,1),[0,1)> in Figure 4, can be moved to the right by shifting both of the slices that bound it along the *x* dimension – 0➜1 and 1➜2 – so that the tile is now located at <[1,2),[0,1)>. This is actually implemented via an action in a conditional that shifts to the right the entire plane corresponding to the 1 tile – altering the positions of all of its slices, not just those abutting the tile – with the region of the plane newly within the board at its left receiving a value of 0 and the region of the plane that is shifted off the right edge of the board cropped (Figure 5). Because each tile is in its own plane of the

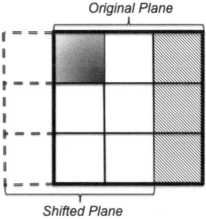

Figure 5. Translating the 1 tile to the right.

function, altering the location of one tile in this manner has no impact on the locations of the others.

Figure 6 shows the conditional that performs this shift of a tile to the right. It checks that an operator is selected (for the state) which is to move the tile located at <x,y>, and that the cell just to the right of <x,y> is blank. The first two actions shift the tile's plane to the right, by creating a new shifted plane and deleting the old one. The final two actions shift the empty cell leftward.

3. Offsets, Translation, and Beyond

The use of numeric offsets in conditionals induces one of the more intriguing aspects of this graphical approach to mental imagery. Translation occurs by specifying an offset for an action variable, as in the first and last actions in Figure 6.

```
CONDITIONAL MoveRight
  Conditions: (selected state:s operator:o)
              (operator id:o state:s x:x y:y)
              (board state:s x:x y:y tile:t)
              (board state:s x:x+1 y:y tile:0)
  Actions: (board state:s x:x+1 y:y tile:t)
           (board − state:s x:x y:y tile:t)
           (board state:s x:x y:y tile:0)
           (board − state:s x:x+1 y:y tile:0)
```

Figure 6. Conditional to slide a tile to the right.

This leads to the insertion of a new factor node (and an associated variable node) into the action's subgraph that shifts the slices in incoming messages according to the offset (while properly handling new and cropped regions). In conditions, this same offset mechanism enables testing structures at positions relative to those of other structures. So, for example, the fourth condition in Figure 6 tests that the location just to the right of a tile is empty. It actually performs this test for all of the tiles, not just for the one that is to the left of the empty cell, but it only succeeds for this particular tile.

Beyond these two uses of offsets in mental imagery, offsets also play important roles elsewhere in the graphical architecture; in particular, in reflection and episodic memory. Reflection is being modeled on the Soar architecture [19]. When an impasse is detected in decision making – because a new operator cannot be selected – a new meta-level state is created in which reflective problem solving can be used to resolve this problem in the system's own performance. The discrete numeric representation used for the state then enables exploiting the offset mechanism to operate across states in the meta-level hierarchy. The contents of adjacent states, or even of states separated by some larger but still fixed distance, can be related via offsets in conditions, and information can be moved across states – to, for example, return results from reflective problem solving – via offsets in actions. Offsets in episodic memory enable, for example, accessing and comparing episodes that are adjacent, or at any fixed distance, along the temporal dimension. It thus turns out that a primitive architectural mechanism originally implemented for the translation of mental imagery not only provides this functionality – through its use in actions that modify imagery in working memory – but it also facilitates testing multiple relatively located portions of an image, as well as supporting key aspects of both reflection and episodic memory.

It is important to ask though whether such a mechanism fits properly into factor graphs, given that factor nodes normally compute subfunctions of the graph's globally defined function over a subset of its full complement of variables; and they do so by computing the pointwise product of the messages arriving from these variables with its internal function, and then summarizing out all variables that are irrelevant to the outgoing message. It is also worth considering how far this mechanism might be extended both to additional aspects of mental imagery and to other architectural capabilities. These two questions are the subject of the remainder of this section.

Although shifting the locations of slices in piecewise memories is not a standard factor node operation, it is possible to encode translation in the normal fashion, validating that it does fit naturally into factor graphs. However, this is only possible in a manner that is expensive computationally, particularly for continuous dimensions. Consider first a simple discrete example, with a single dimension and a region of interest along the dimension that is restricted to [0,3). Suppose further that the functional values for the three regions along the dimension are <0, 1, 0> and that we want to offset this to the right, to yield the new vector of values <0, 0, 1> across these same three regions. If the vector <0, 1, 0> for variable x is sent to a factor node defined via the function in Figure 7, the resulting vector for variable y does become <0, 0, 1>, implementing the desired rightward shift.

The same approach works for any fixed offset. However, the approach engenders a function size that is proportional to the square of the length of the discrete span of interest (n^2); and regionalization can't compress this function because the diagonal layout of the 1s forces

2	0	1	0
1	1	0	0
0	0	0	0
y/x	0	1	2

Figure 7. Factor function for a discrete shift rightwards by 1.

a fragmentation into unit regions. Even worse, offsetting a continuous dimension in this fashion would require a vast number of ε-sized regions along both x and y, with a resulting piecewise function of unwieldy extent: $(n/\varepsilon)^2$. By handling offsets directly – via slice shifting – translation occurs efficiently for both discrete and continuous dimensions. Thus, offsets define legitimate factor nodes, but ones that are best handled via a special purpose optimization, particularly for continuous dimensions. This turns out to be comparable to how negation is handled in conditionals, via a special purpose, more efficient, implementation of a distinct class of factor nodes [17].

A more abstract way of viewing the factor functions used to compute offsets in translation is as general delta functions – the Kronecker delta for discrete functions and the Dirac delta for continuous functions – as are more typically used for computing variable equality in factor graphs [20]. Delta functions are in fact already used in this manner in the graphical architecture, but there their efficient special-purpose implementation can be simpler, just amounting to message copying. Efficient representation of true delta functions in factor nodes requires a functional form more flexible than the rectilinear piecewise linear functions currently used in the architecture.

The Eight Puzzle only requires translation along one dimension at a time, but the offset technique works just as well for simultaneous translation along multiple dimensions, enabling object movement at any angle. It also appears that a conceptually simple extension to it will enable the additional mental imagery operation of *scaling* for continuous dimensions. Instead of adding a fixed value to the locations of the slices along a dimension, the slice locations instead need to be multiplied by a fixed scaling factor. Each dimension could then conceivably be scaled independently by its own fixed factor, or scaling alternately could be restricted to a single multiplicative factor across all dimensions.

Rotation is the other major operation classically defined on objects in mental imagery. However, in contrast to translation and scaling, it cannot be performed independently along each dimension. Rotation not only conflates dimensions, but it also requires reslicing the image – as in Figure 8 for a rotated Eight Puzzle plane – to regenerate regions that are rectilinear along the original dimensions.

One potential approach for dealing with rotation is to allow more flexibility in slice orientation across multiple dimensions [16]. Should this work, it would not only enable rotation without major reworking of slices, but also more flexibility generally in the shapes of regions; allowing *convex polytopes* (nD convex polygons). Application of arbitrary combinations of translation, scaling and rotation would then occur via more general factor nodes capable of efficiently processing any form of *affine transformation*, comprising a linear transformation plus a translation. It is even conceivable that such an approach would eliminate the need for some or all of the specially optimized factor nodes, by enabling functions such as deltas to be specified via long narrow regions with values of 1 that are appropriately angled and offset.

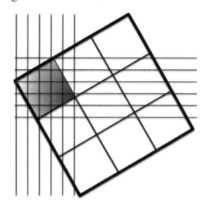

Figure 8. Reslicing a rotated structure.

4. Summary and Future

The work described here takes an initial step towards the uniform implementation of mental imagery with other cognitive processes in a graphical architecture. Imagery leverages the hybrid mixed function representation that is at the heart of the architecture plus the memory capability that is based on factor graphs. Specially optimized factor nodes for translation have been added that show potential for extension to a broader set of imagery transformations, and which also turn out to be critical for implementing several architectural capabilities that are outside of the normal scope of mental imagery. A more uniform approach to at least some of this may also eventually be possible through a more flexible region representation.

The focus in this article has been on two-dimensional imagery plus the translation operation, as needed for problem solving in the Eight Puzzle. With a total of 18 conditionals, a system has been constructed that can solve the Eight Puzzle by selecting and applying a sequence of translation operations defined over the hybrid board representation [13]. A longer term goal is to extend this nascent mental imagery capability to dynamic three-dimensional imagery capable of coping appropriately with uncertainty about the existence and trajectories of objects, as is necessary for example to support complex situation assessment and prediction. This will require many of the extensions already mentioned. It will likely also require: more sophisticated functional forms, an intimate connection with both perception and other cognitive capabilities, plus improvements in efficiency.

Acknowledgments

This work has been sponsored by the Air Force Office of Scientific Research, Asian Office of Aerospace Research and Development (AFOSR/AOARD) and the U.S. Army Research, Development, and Engineering Command (RDECOM). Statements and opinions expressed do not necessarily reflect the position or the policy of the United States Government, and no official endorsement should be inferred. I would like to thank Abram Demski for interactions that helped clarify some of these concepts.

References

[1] P. Langley, J. E. Laird, and S. Rogers. Cognitive architectures: Research issues and challenges. *Cognitive Systems Research*, 10: 141-160, 2009.

[2] J. R. Anderson, D. Bothell, M. D. Byrne, S. Douglass, C. Lebiere, and Y. Qin. An integrated theory of the mind. *Psychological Review*, 111(4): 1036-1060, 2004.

[3] J. E. Laird. Extending the Soar cognitive architecture. In *Artificial General Intelligence 2008: Proceedings of the First AGI Conference*, Memphis, Tennessee, March 2008. IOS Press.

[4] B. Goertzel. OpenCogPrime: A cognitive synergy based architecture for artificial general intelligence. In *Proceedings of the 8th IEEE International Conference on Cognitive Informatics*, 2009.

[5] J. E. Laird, A. Newell, and P. S. Rosenbloom. Soar: An architecture for general intelligence. *Artificial Intelligence*, 33: 1-64, 1987.

[6] M. Hutter. *Universal Artificial Intelligence: Sequential Decisions Based on Algorithmic Probability*. Springer-Verlag, Berlin, Germany, 2005.

[7] D. E. Kieras and D. E. Meyer. An overview of the EPIC architecture for cognition and performance with application to human-computer interaction. *Human-Computer Interaction*, 12: 391-438, 1997.

[8] P. S. Rosenbloom. Rethinking cognitive architecture via graphical models. *Cognitive Systems Research*, 12(2), 2011.

[9] Smolensky, P. & Legendre, G. (2006). *The Harmonic Mind: From Neural Computation to Optimality-Theoretic Grammar*. Cambridge, MA: The MIT Press.

[10] D. Koller and N. Friedman. *Probabilistic Graphical Models: Principles and Techniques*. MIT Press, Cambridge, Massachusetts, 2009.

[11] F. R. Kschischang, B. J. Frey, and H-A. Loeliger. Factor graphs and the sum-product algorithm. *IEEE Transactions on Information Theory*, 47(2): 498-519, February 2001.

[12] P. S. Rosenbloom. Combining procedural and declarative knowledge in a graphical architecture. In *Proceedings of the 10th International Conference on Cognitive Modeling*, Manchester, United Kingdom, August 2010.

[13] P. S. Rosenbloom. From memory to problem solving: Mechanism reuse in a graphical cognitive architecture. In *Proceedings of the 4th Conference on Artificial General Intelligence*, Mountain View, California, August 2011.

[14] S. D. Lathrop, S. Wintermute, and J. E. Laird. Exploring the functional advantages of spatial and visual cognition from an architectural perspective. *Topics in Cognitive Science*, 2011. In press.

[15] B. J. Frey. Extending factor graphs so as to unify directed and undirected graphical models. In *Proceedings of the 19th conference on uncertainty in artificial intelligence*, pages 257–264, 2003.

[16] P. S. Rosenbloom. Bridging dichotomies in cognitive architectures for virtual humans. In *Proceedings of the AAAI Fall Symposium on Advances in Cognitive Systems*, 2011. In press.

[17] P. S. Rosenbloom. Implementing first-order variables in a graphical cognitive architecture. In *Proceedings of Biologically Inspired Cognitive Architectures 2010: Proceedings of the First Annual Meeting of the BICA Society*, Arlington, Virginia, November 2010. IOS Press.

[18] P. S. Rosenbloom. Speculations on leveraging graphical models for architectural integration of visual representation and reasoning. In *Proceedings of the AAAI-10 Workshop on Visual Representations and Reasoning*, 2010.

[19] P. S. Rosenbloom, J. E. Laird, and A. Newell. Meta-levels in Soar. In P. Maes, D. Nardi (eds.) *Meta-Level Architectures and Reflection*, pages 227-240. North Holland, Amsterdam, Netherlands, 1988.

[20] H-A. Loeliger. An introduction to factor graphs. *IEEE Signal Processing Magazine*, 21(1): 28-41, January 2004.

Biologically Inspired Cognitive Architectures 2011
A.V. Samsonovich and K.R. Jóhannsdóttir (Eds.)
IOS Press, 2011
© *2011 The authors and IOS Press. All rights reserved.*
doi:10.3233/978-1-60750-959-2-324

Learning and Self-Regulation through Integrated Agent-Based System

Pier Giuseppe ROSSI [1], Simone CARLETTI, and Maria Antonietta
IMPEDOVO
University of Macerata, Italy
pg.rossi@unimc.it

Abstract. The analysis of support forum messages carried out in one of our online, post-graduate courses showed that nearly 62% of questions concerned issues already covered in material scattered across the Learning Management System and within course structure; collected student tracking data can help tutors to understand reasons why users seem to prefer to ask direct questions rather than browsing through provided information. Results of this study indicate that learners need a simpler way to look for answers and that enabling self-regulating processes may help reducing the work load of tutors by having a chatbot as information broker. This paper indicates planned work to enhance our LMS-integrated multiagent system in order to support our learners' needs.

Keywords. Multiagent Systems, Self Regulated Learning, Chatbot

Introduction

Analysis of support forum discussions carried out in online, post-graduate courses offered in the past two years at the University of Macerata and targeting in-service teachers have shown that 62% of questions posted address issues covered by material already available within the learning management system (LMS). The same study shows the need for a clear overview of students' assignments status.

In another study, targeting online tutors, results show a wide heterogeneity of students' profiles as far as concerning age, digital literacy, professional experience and role covered in the working place; this ranges from fresh-graduates to long-experienced teachers. Personal motivations and competences also vary greatly within the same class. Course lecturers and tutors feel the need of diverse learning paths and assessment models to suit different students' motivations and experience basing on the *didactique professionnelle*[1]. Assessment, primarily, must allow for a precise check on activities carried out and for guidance over self-regulation processes.

As a first step towards supporting these needs we have designed, implemented and tested an LMS supported by agent-based tracking and monitoring system. This system, by recording each and every learner's activity carried out within the platform, aims at reducing the load of online tutors by delegating a chatbot agent to answer routine

---

[1] Corresponding Author.

questions, providing students with a clear overview of assignments status, giving just-in-time alerts, and supporting self-regulating learning processes[2].

The base system has been running and tested for over a year, allowing for an initial profiling of students. Next we have re-designed the information and guidance model to structure data in machine-readable formats without hampering tutors' work. On the basis of this we are designing from scratch a new electronic record book of students' progress throughout the several learning units, activities, assignments and assessments included in each learning path; basic requirement for this application is to automatically fetch course tree from course outline designed by lecturers in the OLAT LMS[2] course editor, and to feedback elements status to students thanks to recorded tracking data.

The chatbot agent will provide an initial, simple, text-based interface to communicate progress to learners and to routinely survey students with open questions stimulating processes of self-regulation and awareness. It is suggested that answers to these surveys will be analysed by online tutors and results will be used to improve the design model.

Key element of this study is the analysis of learners' tracking data and feedback to improve course design and management. The agent-based system is in charge of coordinating all event-based activities, such as data collection and analysis, and interactions with students. Ultimately the proposed research will show if the integration of tightly connected – in both technical and pedagogical respects – quantitative data with qualitative indicators (e.g. provided by online tutors) could significantly improve learners' motivation and performance while optimising the utilisation of human resources.

1. Methodology

The study carried out on forum discussions analysed about 140 questions and answers posted in the General Q&A (*Dubbi e chiarimenti*) support forum available for each study unit of our online, Learning Design post-graduate course (*Master in Progettazione Didattica*) running between 2009 and 2010. At a first glance, questions asked in forum messages posted by 18 unique students concerned general topics in roughly 62% of the cases and specific issues for the remaining 38%; a deeper analysis of data allowed to further distinct content-related questions (18%) from process-related question (82%).

It is now important to make clear that online tutors are subject matter qualified, that is, in our case, must possess a degree in the discipline they are tutoring besides having undergone a specific training on online communication and collaboration and learners' motivation and guidance; this is to say that tutors are, in most cases, experienced learning community facilitators with specific skills on the subject and on the LMS. Our goal is to focus tutors' efforts on content-related, specific topics while reducing the overhead time spent on general, process-related topics.

---

[2] OLAT (Online Learning And Training) is a free, open source LMS developed at the University of Zurich (CH); more info at http://www.olat.org/

Table 1. Distribution of forum posts by type with breakdown on Question types (% of questions only)

Post type	General topic	Specific topic	Total
Question			
Content-related (subject, discipline)	7 (11,66%)	4 (6,66%)	**11 (18,33%)**
Process-related (how-to, where, etc.)	30 (50,00%)	19 (31,66%)	**49 (81,66%)**
Answers from tutor			59
Acknowledgement (OK, thanks, etc.)			25
Total	**37 (61,66%)**	**23 (38,33%)**	144

But findings in Table 1 show that, in the case analysed, only 6,66% of the questions related to core competencies of our tutors, while exactly half of forum posts concerned (at least partially) issues like "where do I find the textbooks?" or "did you receive my paper?" – all topics that are largely covered by material already available within the LMS or posted in specific announcement boards.

Most questions falling into this category were related to study material ('which?' and 'where?'), exam dates and venues, deadlines of activities and assignments, acknowledgement of deliverables; answers to these questions were to be found scattered over different nodes of the course tree (Fig. 1):

- course overview (root node)

- bulletin board (announcements from tutor to students)

- unit overview (course modules)

- activity overview (assignment description)

- delivery folder (assignment deliverables)

Figure 1. The OLAT LMS course tree.

At the time of writing it is unclear whether students did try to find the relevant information before turning to the help forum, if the information provided according to the course structure was not clear enough, or if they simply preferred to ask a direct question in order to better situate their need in a specific context.

This is another key question of our study since one of the main tasks of our online tutors is to provide clear and thorough information throughout the whole course structure and for the entire duration.

2. Research question

So, why many issues are asked over and over again when answers are already available? The first option that came to our mind, related to difficulties of navigation within this new LMS, had to be ruled out since most questions were received during the second half of the course when students were already able to utilise the platform, its tools and – mostly – knew where to look for information.

An in-dept study of students' tracking log could show whether users did visit the course bulletin board – the official tutor-to-students announcement tool where all updates and relevant information were punctually posted by one of our most expert tutors – before asking in the support forum; this analysis requires a one-by-one check on LMS navigation logs for each of the 60 questions received and is still in progress at the time of writing.

On the other hand, student feedback on tutor's precision, clarity of information provided, and ease of use of the LMS are periodically collected and processed by an external organization but results are returned in the form of a few, aggregated macro-indicators, making difficult the analysis of specific cases; this is the reason that convinced us to include an instant feedback feature – in a poll-like style – in our forthcoming design.

Finally, a considerable number of messages that could not be isolated in the statistics above contained also questions asking to acknowledge the delivery of assignments, tasks or tests. OLAT, like many other LMS, features a range of tools that allow to check whether a delivery has been accepted by the system or if a test has been submitted and graded; however the feeling expressed by tutors interviewed on this matter is that human acknowledgement is always better – and this is especially true for new online learners who are unsure or doubtful about technology. This behaviour can also be justified by the lack of the so-called 'progress bar': a clear, visual indicator of student's progress along the learning path marking the advancement through learning units and fulfilment of all required tasks and assignments.

However, the primary aim of this paper is to reduce the time spent by online tutors in pointing students to the needed information by supporting them through an 'intelligent' chatbot[3]; in order to do this we are now designing new information retrieval features making use of our custom-built multiagent system that we have integrated[3] in the standard OLAT open source LMS. We can expect that students will explore this new feature and try to ask questions to the chat pop-up window before turning to the human tutor.

---

[3] http://en.wikipedia.org/wiki/Chatterbot

3. Proposed solution

The herein proposed solution relies on the multiagent based, platform-independent tracking and monitoring toolkit designed and developed by the University of Macerata eLearning Centre. Besides tracking user clicks and producing statistics on learners' navigation and activity, this toolkit hosts an extensible multiagent system (MAS) capable of interacting with the user through a Jabber[4] instant messaging service; communication from LMS to MAS is established through message queues[5] and results are fetched via web services.

The initial idea was to utilize the context-sensitive chatbot agent as 'hospitality manager' in order to greet students when entering a forum, or any other activity in the course, and provide basic information on the work at hand; we soon realised that students really liked the familiar chat interface while using it for group talks and hence its use could be extended to information retrieval as an alternative option to the LMS built-in search function.

By this we suggest that students could ask questions to the chatbot before browsing through the course tree searching for the needed information or turning to help forums to have an answer from the tutor; further to that, the chatbot agent could timely prompt learners to rate the quality and pertinence of retrieved information or simply ask for feedback on specific activities or study material. Lastly, the chat interface could also inform students on their progress, assignment grading, approaching deadlines, and tasks ahead as consciousness of personal progress within the learning path, results, and positioning with respect to course objectives is the basis of Self Regulated Learning.

References

[1] P. Pastré, P. Mayen et G. Vergnaud, La didactique professionnelle, *Revue française de pédagogie* 154 | janvier-mars 2006, online 01/03/2010, referenced on 26/02/2011 at http://rfp.revues.org/157

[2] B. J. Zimmerman, Self-regulating academic learning and achievement: The emergence of a social cognitive perspective, Educational Psychology Review Volume 2, Number 2 (1990), 173-201.

[3] P.G. Rossi, S. Carletti, D. Bonura, A Platform-Independent Tracking and Monitoring Toolkit, AAAI 2009 Fall Symposium on MCES Arlington – USA (2009), online at http://www.aaai.org/ocs/index.php/FSS/FSS09/paper/download/900/1262

---

[4] http://www.xmpp.org
[5] http://activemq.apache.org

Biologically Inspired Cognitive Architectures 2011
A.V. Samsonovich and K.R. Jóhannsdóttir (Eds.)
IOS Press, 2011
doi:10.3233/978-1-60750-959-2-329

Connecting Cognitive and Neural Models

Fredrick ROTHGANGER[1], Christina WARRENDER, Ann SPEED,
Brandon ROHRER, Asmeret BIER, and Derek TRUMBO
Sandia National Laboratories, Albuquerque, New Mexico, USA

Abstract. A key challenge in developing complete human equivalence is how to ground a synoptic theory of cognition in neural reality. Both cognitive architectures and neural models provide insight into how biological brains work, but from opposite directions. Here the authors report on initial work aimed at interpreting connectomic data in terms of algorithms. Sandia National Laboratories is a multi-program laboratory managed and operated by Sandia Corporation, a wholly owned subsidiary of Lockheed Martin Corporation, for the U.S. Department of Energy's National Nuclear Security Administration under contract DE-AC04-94AL85000.

Keywords. Human-level AI, cognitive architectures, neural networks

Extended Abstract

A key challenge in developing complete human equivalence is how to ground a synoptic theory of cognition in neural reality. Both cognitive architectures and neural models provide insight into how biological brains work, but from opposite directions. In order to make the most use of insights gained from both, and to fully validate a model, we need a common meeting point. We suggest the following for consideration:

1) Algorithms (procedural descriptions of information processing) provide such a meeting point. In practice, implementing a cognitive architecture requires reducing it to computation. Furthermore, functional descriptions of neural systems often take the form of simple computational models, for example [1,2].
2) The circuit approach to neural modeling [3] is a necessary, or at least very helpful, step in determining the algorithms implied in neural structure.
3) Tools that help the researcher extract algorithmic descriptions from the enormous amount of neuroscience data available will support the development of more accurate cognitive architectures.

We report on initial work aimed at interpreting connectomic data in terms of algorithms. The proposed process will involve:

1) Extracting structural information (interaction matrices, spatial distributions, etc.) from connectomic data sets. Currently we are using the Retinal Connectome RC1 data set from MarcLab [4], but hope that neocortical

---

[1] Corresponding Author.

connectomes will eventually become available.
2) Generating new networks using the extracted patterns.
3) Studying the behavior of those networks using high-performance computing systems.
4) Visualizing the structural information in order to gain insight into the underlying algorithms. The actual discovery of algorithms is not automated.

We have completed preliminary work on steps 1-3, and expect to tackle step 4 in the coming year.

Acknowledgment

Sandia National Laboratories is a multi-program laboratory managed and operated by Sandia Corporation, a wholly owned subsidiary of Lockheed Martin Corporation, for the U.S. Department of Energy's National Nuclear Security Administration under contract DE-AC04-94AL85000.

References

[1] Edward M. Callaway (1998). *Local Circuits in Primary Visual Cortex of the Macaque Monkey.* Annual Review of Neuroscience volume 21, pages 47–74.
[2] R.J. Douglas and Kevin C. Martin (2004). *Neuronal Circuits of the Neocortex.* Annual Review of Neuroscience volume 27, pages 419–451.
[3] Gordon Shepherd (Editor)(2004). *The Synaptic Organization of the Brain.* 5th edition. Oxford University Press.
[4] J.R. Anderson, B.W. Jones, C.B. Watt, M.V. Shaw, J.-H. Yang, D. DeMill, J.S. Lauritzen, Y. Lin, K.D. Rapp, D. Mastronarde, P. Koshevoy, B. Grimm, T. Tasdizen, R. Whitaker, R.E. Marc (2011). *Exploring the retinal connectome.* Molecular Vision volume 17, pages 355-379.

Biologically Inspired Cognitive Architectures 2011
A.V. Samsonovich and K.R. Jóhannsdóttir (Eds.)
IOS Press, 2011
doi:10.3233/978-1-60750-959-2-331

Bridging the gap: A neurally plausible functional model of sensemaking

Matthew F. RUTLEDGE-TAYLOR[a,1,] Christian LEBIERE[a], Yury VINOKUROV[a],
James STASZEWSKI[a] and John R. ANDERSON[a]
[a] *Carnegie Mellon University, Pittsburgh, PA, USA*

Abstract. This paper presents a functional model of the task of interpreting geospatial imagery data. The model is implemented using the ACT-R cognitive architecture to bridge the gap between descriptive theories of sensemaking processes and detailed neural models. The interaction between the information structure of the model and the cognitive constraints of the architecture leads to various biases in the implementation of sensemaking processes. We discuss how the various structures and mechanisms of the model can be mapped to brain processes, and their implications for neural architectures.

Keywords. Cognitive architectures, neural models, sensemaking, functional modeling.

Introduction

There are various levels of abstraction available in understanding how people gather and process information in generating hypotheses and making decisions. Descriptive models such as sensemaking [1] account for the process in terms of large-scale operations and knowledge structures. In contrast, neurally inspired models provide detailed accounts of the activities of brain regions and constructs that implement the processes described by sensemaking. Each level of modeling provides different insights into cognition, but the levels stand in isolation unless they can be made commensurable. This paper discusses a functional model that bridges sensemaking theory and a neural model of sensemaking.

The difficulty of the endeavor stems from translating sensemaking concepts, which are high-level qualitative descriptions of information processing, to the language of neurological mechanisms. Sensemaking is a theory of how information is gathered, represented, and used to generate and revise hypotheses. The theory posits that information flows through two main processing loops: the foraging loop and the sensemaking loop. The former accounts for how raw data is gathered, filtered, and aggregated into structured evidence. The latter accounts for how evidence is fit into conceptual schema, which once formed can result in a hypothesis, and occasionally insight.

We use the ACT-R cognitive architecture [2, 3] to bridge sensemaking theory and a neural model created using the Leabra architecture [4]. ACT-R is a computational

---

[1] Corresponding Author. E-mail: mfrt@cmu.edu

implementation of a unified theory of cognition. It accounts for information processing in the mind via a set of task-invariant mechanisms operating in a modular architecture, constrained by the biological limitations of the brain. Although sensemaking theory is descriptive and abstracted from specific brain processes, it makes commitments to the control and flow of information. Thus, sensemaking theory and ACT-R are highly commensurable from a functional perspective. For example, the processing loops in sensemaking can be instantiated into control structures (sets of production rules) in ACT-R.

There are several points of contact between ACT-R and Leabra, the most tangible of which is a commitment to neural localization of architectural constructs (see Figure 1). In both architectures a central control module located in the basal ganglia collects inputs from a variety of cortical areas and outputs primarily to the frontal cortex, which maintains task-relevant information. Additionally, both include a dedicated declarative/episodic memory system in the hippocampus and associated cortical structures. Lastly, both account for sensory and motor processing in the posterior cortex. The architectures differ in the level of implementation: Leabra uses connectionist mechanisms while ACT-R uses a mix of symbolic and subsymbolic (statistical) process. This compatibility of ACT-R and Leabra has been realized elsewhere by the development of SAL (Synthesis of ACT-R and Leabra), a hybrid architecture that combines and exploits the relative strengths of each [5]. Thus, ACT-R connects to the underlying neural theory of Leabra and can provide meaningful guidance to the development of neural models of complex tasks, such as sensemaking.

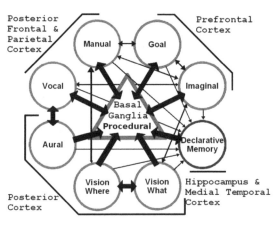

Figure 1. Overview of the ACT-R architecture, showing the different modules classified according to the tripartite organization of Leabra.

In summary, the important role of ACT-R in mapping Sensemaking theory to a Leabra model is to discover architectural constraints on the mapping. First, descriptions of Sensemaking processes, such as the foraging loop, are formally implemented procedurally in ACT-R. Second, the biological constraints implicit in the ACT-R model, such as the brain regions involved in the processing of frames, and the impact of the time course information on processing steps, are used to constrain the creation of the Leabra model.

The research presented here was conducted as part of the IARPA-funded ICArUS-MINDS project. The goal of the project is to create a neurally plausible model of Sensemaking that accounts for various cognitive biases in the context of intelligence analysis. A pilot study examined the ability of human participants to learn how to analyze simulated geospatial images and correctly discriminate facilities in unlabeled images. The models discussed in this paper are of human performance in this task.

1. Facility Identification Task

The pilot study mentioned above provides an excellent example of sensemaking. Initially experimental participants were trained to identify four kinds of facilities in simulated geospatial images. Each image is of a single facility (e.g., factory complex) that is composed of a collection of discrete features (e.g., buildings) drawn, probabilistically, from three distinct categories.

The three categories of features were: IMINT (image intelligence), representing buildings and other terrain features such as roads and rivers; MASINT (measurement and signature intelligence), representing signals such as chemical concentrations or radiation, and SIGINT (signals intelligence), representing communication transmissions. There were nine unique IMINT features, seven that represented buildings, and two that represented water features. In contrast, there were only two kinds of MASINT features, while the SIGINT features were entirely homogeneous. Each IMINT could appear at most one time in each image, whereas multiple instances of SIGINT and each MASINT could occur in each image. Additionally, each building (IMINT) could have attached to it zero or one piece of rooftop hardware.

Each of the four facilities had different base-rates for the occurrence of each of the possible features. The experiment was divided into two main phases: a training phase and a testing phase. In the training phase the participants were presented with 48 annotated examples of each facility (192 total examples), 16 at a time (in a four-by-four grid). Participants were not limited in how long they could study the images. Training time ranged from 8 minutes to 73 minutes (mean 24 minutes). In the testing phase the participants were presented with single unlabeled images, one at a time. For each image, the participant was required to report a probability distribution over the four possible facilities indicating the likelihood that the image contained each of the facilities.

2. The ACT-R Architecture

ACT-R is a functional cognitive architecture used to implement cognitive models of a number of diverse cognitive phenomena. Below is a brief summary of the mechanisms of ACT-R relevant to the models presented in this paper. See Anderson and Lebiere [3] and Anderson et al. [2] for detailed accounts of ACT-R.

The ACT-R architecture includes long-term declarative and procedural memory as well as perceptual-motor modules connected through limited-capacity buffers. When a retrieval request is made to declarative memory (DM), the most active, matching chunk is returned, where activation is computed as the sum of base-level activation, spreading activation, mismatch penalty and stochastic noise. Spreading activation is a mechanism that propagates activation from the contents of buffers to declarative memory proportionally to their strength of association. Partial matching is a mechanism that allows for chunks in memory that do not perfectly match a retrieval request to be recalled if their activation overcomes a similarity-based mismatch penalty. Slots in buffers chunks that spread activation and specify matching conditions are functionally similar to PFC stripes in the Leabra PBWM model [6].

The flow of information is controlled in ACT-R by a production system, which operates on the contents of the buffers. Each production consists of if-then condition-action pairs. Conditions are typically criteria for buffer matches, while the actions are typically changes to the contents of buffers that might trigger operations in the associated modules. Production rules controlling buffer updates can be mapped to the biology of the basal ganglia [7]. The production with the highest utility is selected to fire from among the eligible productions. Production utility learning in ACT-R operates by instigating a utility reward event after a production has fired. The reward is propagated to all productions that have fired since the last reward event. The reward mechanism in ACT-R has been associated with the dopaminergic reward mechanism in the brain [8] and is quite similar to the Primary Value and Learned Value (PVLV) learning algorithm in Leabra [9].

3. ACT-R Model

ACT-R has been used in the past to model evidence marshaling [10], and categorization [11, 12, 13]. Thus, ACT-R has demonstrated the basic requirements of sensemaking. In this paper we will discuss an ACT-R model of the pilot study facility identification task. Several variations of this model that isolate particular mechanisms were tested individually so as to understand better the relative contributions of the components. This approach is similar to that advocated by Gluck et al [14] to evaluate and compare competing models.

The ACT-R model of the facility identification task makes use of the imaginal buffer to store chunks representing facility frames (i.e., a facility example instances). Each facility frame contains a slot for the facility type, a slot for a chunk representing the total number of IMINTs in the image, a slot for the total SIGINTs, one slot each for the totals of two kinds of MASINT, a slot for the total number of pieces of rooftop hardware on buildings in the image, and one slot for each of the nine kinds of IMINT. Each IMINT slot stores a chunk representing the presence of that IMINT or is left empty. Thus, while the total number of slots is high, the actual number of chunks contained at any one time in the imaginal buffer remains in keeping with architectural constraints.

During the training phase the annotated images are imported into the declarative memory of the model one at a time. For each image, the model temporarily holds a facility frame in working memory by populating the imaginal buffer with the appropriate chunk representation of the features present in the image. Once filled, the imaginal buffer is cleared and the facility frame chunk is committed to memory (DM). The visual module of ACT-R was not used in this model because the details of how ACT-R processes abstract representations of images would not be informative to the Leabra model, but the feature selection model described below can be seen as implementing visual attentional processes.

During the testing phase, images are presented to the model one at a time. The model performs a retrieval request of DM for a facility frame chunk based on some information available in the images. The chunk with the highest activation is retrieved and its facility ID is used as the model's answer to the identification question. Reflecting the choice of feature representation in facility frame chunks, two distinct retrieval mechanisms could apply to the recall of facility frames. They are partial matching and spreading activation.

The partial matching version of the ACT-R model uses only the slots that store the counts of the various feature types (and hardware) as part of the retrieval request. This model represents a participant who is not attentive to the particular buildings that are present in a test image. When classifying an image, the model compares the feature counts in the image to the counts in facility chunks in DM. The effect of partial matching is that the model is able to make similarity-based inferences in making facility discriminations.

The spreading activation version of the model ignores the feature counts. Instead, the IMINT features in the imaginal buffer form the context of retrieval. The model assembles a facility frame (i.e., a schema) in the imaginal buffer using chunks representing the IMINT features present in the image. Each feature spreads activation to facility frames that includes that feature to a degree inversely proportional to the logarithm of the number of frames including that feature, a phenomenon known as the fan effect [15]. This model represents a participant who is solely focused on the particular buildings in the image. When the request for a facility frame chunk from DM is made, chunks that share IMINT features in common with the image will get a boost in activation, increasing the probability that they will be retrieved.

The version of the model that utilizes both partial matching on the counts and spreading activation on the IMINTs represents a participant who is attentive to all the available information in the image. Once the first three models had been run and the results were analyzed (presented below), a question arose. Is it rational or adaptive to always encode all of the IMINT features that are present in a given image? Could it be the case that there can be an optimal subset of features that is most predictive of the facility. That is, is it advantageous to ignore features that are not predictive of a given facility? With these questions and sensemaking in mind, an ACT-R model of feature selection was created.

Feature selection is the process of deciding which features present in an image ought to be attended to, and which should not. This aspect of the model addresses the issue of the working memory capacity for information. That is, it is presumed that the participants were unlikely to have attended to every available feature in every image due to cognitive constraints on working memory. The normative probability that a feature should be selected is based on its utility in facility identification. The ACT-R model of feature selection made use of production utility learning to develop implicit preferences for attending to some features over others. A positive reward is instigated after a facility is correctly identified, while a negative reward is instigated after an incorrect identification.

The productions of interest during utility learning are divided into two categories: feature selector productions and decision instigation productions. Each feature selector production is specific to a single IMINT feature and a specific intermediate hypothesis about what facility is represented in the given sector. This allows for the utilities of selecting features to be hypothesis-specific.

Each decision instigation production is eligible to fire after a specific number of features have been selected. Thus, there are as many decision instigation productions as there are possible features to select. Once a decision instigation production has fired, a facility identification event occurs. If the identification is correct the decision instigation production and all the feature selection productions that lead to the decision are rewarded. If the identification is incorrect, the same productions are penalized.

The ACT-R feature selection model proceeds through two distinct phases. In the training phase the model studies a training set of sample images for the purpose of learning which features are associated with each facility in order to generate adequate hypotheses given the current set of features. This is accomplished by storing facility frames in declarative memory, as described above. In the learning phase the model must identify the facilities in images, and with feedback learn the optimal utilities for the various feature selector and decision instigation productions.

In the learning phase the model alternates between updating the model's current hypothesis of what facility is present and selecting a new feature (or electing to stop encoding features). When selecting a feature, all of the feature selector productions that are eligible to fire compete. The production with the highest utility fires and the feature associated with the production is added to the feature chunk stored in the imaginal buffer.

The decision to stop encoding features is governed by the competition between the feature selector productions and the decision instigation productions. The model will stop encoding features, when the relevant decision instigation production (corresponding to the current number of features encoded) fires instead of any of the eligible feature selection productions. This evolving production competition allows the model to learn the optimal number of features to encode.

When updating the current hypothesis stored in the goal buffer, the facility is identified by recalling the facility frame from declarative memory that best matches the features selected so far. The value for the facility ID in the recalled frame is used to update the hypothesis maintained in the goal buffer. When the model stops encoding new features the current hypothesis is used as the model's final categorization decision for the image.

This process of determining which features to encode mirrors the sensemaking process. The foraging loop is the sequence of productions that selects new evidence features from the available pool and organizes them in the imaginal buffer. The sensemaking loop is the sequence of productions that retrieves a schema (i.e., a facility frame chunk from DM), and generates a hypothesis for what facility is present in the given image. The model oscillates back and forth between the two loops, seeking out more evidence and updating its hypothesis until the expected utility of making a decision is achieved.

4. Results

Performance was evaluated on a cross-validated 80%/20% training/testing split of a set of 1200 images. The participants in the pilot study achieved an accuracy rate of 72.0% with both partial matching and spreading activation, and all available features selected. When spreading activation was turned off, the accuracy fell to 46.2%. With partial matching off (and spreading activation on) the accuracy of the model was 65.5%. With feature selection activated, and no partial matching, the model scored an accuracy of 44.9%. The model used the feedback from each of these testing trials to train the utilities of the model's feature selection and decision instigation productions. The reward feedback for correct categorizations was 10, while the feedback for incorrect categorizations was 0. The initial utility of each production was 2.5.

Several interesting patterns can be observed in the ACT-R model of feature selection. The first is a clear difference in the mean number of features selected (2.95) and the mean number of available features (5.06). Figure 2 compares the probabilities that each possible number of features were present in an image and the probabilities that a particular number of features were selected before an identification decision was made, showing a clear shift in the profile of feature selection probabilities relative to available feature probabilities.

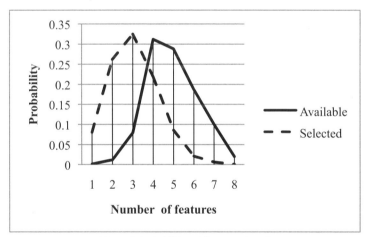

Figure 2. Probabilities of features selected

The pattern of mean features selected disagrees somewhat from the utilities of the decision instigation productions, show in Figure 3. The production that instigates a categorization decision after selecting four features attained the highest utility value, contrasted with three features being the most frequent number selected. This difference can be understood by considering two factors. The first is that some images will have fewer than four features, thus forcing a decision before four features have been selected. The other factor is that only one decision instigation production at a time is in competition with the feature selection productions. If after three features have been selected, the relevant decision instigation production has a greater utility than any of the eligible feature selection productions competing to select the fourth feature, that production will fire, and the model will give its identification decision for the image. This will occur even if the decision instigation production corresponding to four features encoded has a greater utility. The dip in production utility for three features encoded is not statistically significant.

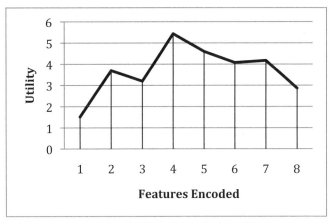

Figure 3. Decision instigation production utilities

5. Discussion

The central focus of the current project is to account for cognitive biases in sensemaking. The feature selection model provides the means for accounting for two biases that are not explored in detail in this paper. Confirmation bias can occur due to the maintenance of the current facility hypothesis in the goal buffer. This hypothesis spreads activation to DM and increases the likelihood that a chunk with the same facility value will be retrieved. Thus the system has a tendency to maintain a hypothesis once it has been adopted longer than it should, even in the face of contrary evidence. This dynamics arises from the interaction between the flow of information required by the task and the structure and mechanisms of the cognitive architecture.

Another bias, satisfaction of search, could account for the approximate 50% accuracy rate of the model. The model may be truncating its search for evidence once enough has been gathered to satisfy am implicit criterion of 50/50 sector classification accuracy. A number of architectural limitations can be seen as the source of this bias. One is the limited amount of attention available to spread activation in the retrieval of frames from memory. If the most discriminative features are encoded first, encoding additional features will dilute the attentional weight of the most discriminative, which can lead to a decrease in performance in the presence of more information. Another limitation is the time discounting of rewards in utility computations, resulting in decision instigation productions preferred over feature selection productions.

The mechanisms described here can map to the neural level in both mechanistic and architectural ways. At a mechanistic level, Anderson [16] linked spreading activation to early PDP models, especially those of a localist flavor [17]. More recently, Anderson and O'Reilly (personal communication) have drawn a close parallel between the form of the spreading activation equation in ACT-R, and most specifically the correlation-based learning of strengths of association, and an equation describing the CPCA Hebbian learning rule in Leabra [4, p. 133]. Similarly, Lebiere, Anderson and Reder [18] introduced the partial matching mechanism in ACT-R to provide the complementary ability to perform similarity-based generalization similar to that provided by distributed representations in neural networks.

At an architectural level, those mechanisms map well to the characteristics of the tripartite functional organization of the Leabra architecture [19]. The spreading activation mechanism, and its associated retrieval buffer, approximates the sparse, separated and conjunctive low-interference representation of the hippocampus. The partial matching mechanism is intended to approximate the distributed, high-generalization characteristics of posterior cortical representations. Attempts to reconcile ACT-R constructs and mechanisms with the constraints of neural mechanisms and structures have been made [20, 7] and have resulted in additional constraints on those mechanisms [3].

The guidance provided by the functional model for the neural model in this exploration is to provide a functional analysis as to which type of performance pattern in this task, not only in terms of overall performance level (which is a very coarse measure) but also in terms of finer, more discriminative measures such as confusion matrices, can be attributed to which type of mechanism and architectural construct, and how those should be assembled to produce the patterns seen in the data. Additional finer-grained data might be able to further differentiate among those processes. For instance, in the retrieval of lexical information, studies (e.g., [21]) have established a two-scale process, first consisting of a rapid positive associative effect followed by a slower, more strategic and controlled inhibitory effect. Those processes could be analogized to the two-phase retrieval process in ACT-R, given the positive effect of spreading activation, followed by the negative penalty imposed by partial matching. Models have been proposed implementing both dual-mechanism [22] and single-mechanism [23] theories, and possible neural realizations [24]. However, additional data would be needed to differentiate between these mechanisms and their neural implications in the context of this task.

Acknowledgement

This work is supported by the Intelligence Advanced Research Projects Activity (IARPA) via Department of the Interior (DOI) contract number D10PC20021. The U.S. Government is authorized to reproduce and distribute reprints for Governmental purposes notwithstanding any copyright annotation thereon. The views and conclusions contained hereon are those of the authors and should not be interpreted as necessarily representing the official policies or endorsements, either expressed or implied, of IARPA, DOI, or the U.S. Government.

References

[1] P. Pirolli & S. K. Card, The sensemaking process and leverage points for analyst technology, In the Proceedings of the 2005 International Conference on Intelligence Analysis (2005)

[2] J. R. Anderson, D. Bothell, M. D. Byrne, S. Douglass, C. Lebiere, Y. Qin. An integrated theory of Mind, Psychological Review 111 (2004), 1036-1060.

[3] J. R. Anderson, C. Lebiere, The atomic components of thought, Erlbaum, Mahwah, NJ, 1998

[4] R. C. O'Reilly & Y. Munakata, Computational Explorations in Cognitive Neuroscience: Understanding the Mind by Simulating the Brain, MIT Press, Cambridge, MA, 2000

[5] D. J. Jilk, C. Lebiere, R. C. O'Reilly, & J. R. Anderson, SAL: An explicitly pluralistic cognitive architecture, Journal of Experimental and Theoretical Artificial Intelligence, 20 (2008), 197-218.

[6] R. C. O'Reilly, & M. J. Frank, Making Working Memory Work: A Computational Model of Learning in the Frontal Cortex and Basal Ganglia, Neural Computation 18 (2006), 283-328.

[7] A. Stocco, C. Lebiere, R. C. O'Reilly & J. R. Anderson, The role of the anterior prefrontal-basal ganglia circuit as a biological instruction interpreter, In A. V. Samsonovich, K. R. Jóhannsdóttir, A. Chella, & B. Goertzel (Eds.) Biologically Inspired Cognitive Architectures. Frontiers in Artificial Intelligence and Applications (2010), 153-162. Amsterdam, The Netherlands: IOS Press.

[8] J. R. Anderson, How Can the Human Mind Occur in the Physical Universe?, Oxford University Press, New York, 2007.

[9] R. C. O'Reilly, M. J. Frank, T. E. Hazy, & B. Watz, PVLV: The Primary Value and Learned Value Pavlovian Learning Algorithm, Behavioral Neuroscience 121 (2007), 31-49.

[10] R. Wray, C. Lebiere, P. Weinstein, K. Jha, J. Springer, T. Belding, B. Best & V. Parunak, V., Towards a complete, multi-level cognitive architecture. In Proceedings of the 8th International Conference on Cognitive Modeling. Ann Arbor, MI, 2007.

[11] J. R. Anderson & J. Betz, A hybrid model of categorization, Psychonomic Bulletin and Review 8 (2007), 629-647.

[12] J. R. Anderson & M. Matessa, The rational analysis of categorization and the ACT-R architecture. In M. Oaksford & N. Chater (Eds.) Rational models of cognition (1998), Oxford University Press, Oxford, 197-217.

[13] C. Lebiere, Constrained functionality: Application of the ACT-R cognitive architecture to the AMBR modeling comparison. In Gluck, K, & Pew, R. (Eds.) Modeling Human Behavior with Integrated Cognitive Architectures, (2005), Erlbaum. Mahwah, NJ.

[14] K. A. Gluck, C. T. Stanley, Jr., L. R. Moore, D. Reitter & M. Halbrügge, Exploration for understanding in model comparisons, Journal of Artificial General Intelligence, 2 (2010), 88-107.

[15] J. R. Anderson, Retrieval of prepositional information from long-term memory. Cognitive Psychology 6 (1974), 451-474.

[16] J. R. Anderson, A spreading activation theory of memory. Journal of Verbal Learning and Verbal Behavior 22 (1983), 261-295.

[17] D. E. Rumelhart & J. L. McClelland, Parallel Distributed Processing: Explorations in the Microstructure of Cognition. MIT Press, Cambridge, MA (1986) 45-76.

[18] C. Lebiere, J. R. Anderson & L. M. Reder, Error modeling in the ACT-R production system, In Proceedings of the Sixteenth Annual Conference of the Cognitive Science Society, 555-559. Erlbaum, Hillsdale, NJ, 1994

[19] R. C. O'Reilly & K. A. Norman, Hippocampal and Neocortical Contributions to Memory: Advances in the Complementary Learning Systems Framework. Trends in Cognitive Sciences 6 (2002), 505-510.

[20] J. R. Anderson & C. Lebiere, Rules of the Mind, Erlbaum, Mahwah, NJ, 1993

[21] J. H. Neely, Journal of Experimental Psychology: General 106 (1977), 226-254.

[22] J. H. Neely & D. E. Keefe, Semantic context effects on visual word processing: A hybrid prospective-retrospective processing theory, The Psychology of Learning and Motivation 24 (1989), 207–247.

[23] D. C. Plaut & J. R. Booth, Individual and developmental differences in semantic priming: Empirical and computational support for a single-mechanism account of lexical processing, Psychological Review 107 (2000), 786-823.

[24] A. Treves, Frontal latching networks: A possible neural basis for infinite recursion, Cognitive Neuropsychology, 22 (2005), 276-291.

Biologically Inspired Cognitive Architectures 2011
A.V. Samsonovich and K.R. Jóhannsdóttir (Eds.)
IOS Press, 2011

Measuring the Critical Mass of a Universal Learner

Alexei V. SAMSONOVICH

George Mason University, Krasnow Institute for Advanced Study
4400 University Drive MS 2A1, Fairfax, Virginia 22030-4444, USA
asamsono@gmu.edu

Keywords. Human-level AI, learning, scalability, cognitive development

Abstract

An interesting question is: what would it take for an artifact to succeed in autonomous cognitive development up to an adult human level? There are many controversies involved in answering this question, related to problems that need to be addressed. This work makes an attempt to analyze them from a different perspective.

The critical mass hypothesis states that an agent embedded in a novel learning environment either can learn at a universal learner scale, acquiring virtually any knowledge vital for achieving critical goals in this environment, or will stay forever at a level close to its initial level of knowledge, depending on the initial "mass" of its cognitive and learning characteristics. This threshold needs to be defined in its multiple aspects, including initial knowledge of the agent, its functional capabilities, functional components of the architecture, properties of the embedding and the interface, etc., as well as in terms of observable characteristics of the learning process itself, such as scalability, robustness and transferrability. The minimal "mass" defined in this sense that takes the agent to a universal learner level is called the *critical mass*.

Whether this hypothesis holds depends on the particular learning environment, the embedding and the paradigm (e.g. learning with or without instructor). When it does, the notion of the critical mass makes sense and can be measured experimentally [1]. Alternatively, the learning limit of the agent scales gradually with the initial "mass" (there is no well-defined critical mass).

Next, the *universal critical mass hypothesis* states that (a) in most practically interesting cases the notion of a critical mass is well-defined, and (b) so is the notion of a universal critical mass, one and the same minimal mass that enables learning in most practically interesting embeddings and paradigms. The work [2] develops an approach to measuring the critical mass experimentally based on these definitions.

References

[1] A.V. Samsonovich, Toward a large-scale characterization of the learning chain reaction. In S. Ohlsson & R. Catrambone (Eds.), *Proceedings of the 32nd Annual Conference of the Cognitive Science Society* (pp. 2308-2313). Austin, TX: Cognitive Science Society, 2010.
[2] A.V. Samsonovich, Comparative analysis of implemented cognitive architectures, this volume.

Biologically Inspired Cognitive Architectures 2011
A.V. Samsonovich and K.R. Jóhannsdóttir (Eds.)
IOS Press, 2011

A Model of Emotion as Patterned Metacontrol

Riccardo SANZ[1] and Guadalupe SANCHES
UPM Autonomous Systems Laboratory
Universidad Politecnica de Madrid - Automatica Jose Gutierrez Abascal 2 Madrid
28006 Spain
ricardo.sanz@upm.es, guadalupe.sanchez@aslab.org

Keywords. Cognitive architecture, functional organization, emotion, adaptive systems, autonomous systems

Abstract

Adaptive systems use feedback as a key strategy to cope with uncertainty and change in their environments. The information fed back from the sensorimotor loop into the control architecture can be used to change different elements of the controller at four different levels: parameters of the control model, the control model itself, the functional organization of the agent and the functional components of the agent. The complexity of such a space of potential configurations is daunting. The only viable alternative for the agent —in practical, economical, evolutionary terms— is the reduction of the dimensionality of the configuration space. This reduction is achieved both by functionalisation —or, to be more precise, by interface minimization— and by patterning, i.e. the selection among a predefined set of organisational configurations. This last analysis let us state the central problem of how autonomy emerges from the integration of the cognitive, emotional and autonomic systems in strict functional terms: autonomy is achieved by the closure of functional dependency. In this paper we will show a general model of how the emotional biological systems operate following this theoretical analysis and how this model is also of applicability to a wide spectrum of artificial systems.

---

[1] Corresponding Author.

Biologically Inspired Cognitive Architectures 2011
A.V. Samsonovich and K.R. Jóhannsdóttir (Eds.)
IOS Press, 2011

Serial from Parallel, Unity from Multiplicity: What Emerges from Global Workspace Architecture

Murray P. SHANAHAN
Department of Computing, Imperial College London 180 Queen's Gate London SW7
2AZ United Kingdom
m.shanahan@imperial.ac.uk

Keywords. Global Workspace, complexity, small-world network, emergence

Abstract

Systems that generate near-optimal global states from local interactions will tend to exhibit high dynamical complexity, that is to say a balance of segregated and integrated activity. A central conjecture of my recent work is that high dynamical complexity is achievable in a large dynamical system (such as a brain) when the interactions of its massively numerous components are mediated by a hierarchically modular small-world network with a pronounced connective core of hub nodes. In an embodied setting, this connective core is a global workspace, a communications infrastructure that, in the conscious condition, allows the brain's full battery of resources to be directed on the situation at hand. Global from local, serial from parallel, and unity from multiplicity — all of these forms of emergence, according to the conjecture, are a consequence of the same principles of organization.

Biologically Inspired Cognitive Architectures 2011
A.V. Samsonovich and K.R. Jóhannsdóttir (Eds.)
IOS Press, 2011
doi:10.3233/978-1-60750-959-2-344

First Order Logic Concepts in Fluid Construction Grammar

Josefina Sierra-Santibáñez [a,1]

[a] *Universidad Politécnica de Cataluña, Spain*

Abstract. This paper proposes a formal definition of Fluid Construction Grammar (FCG) in terms of First Order Logic concepts, including its core inference operations unify and merge. Our aim is not only to clarify basic notions in FCG but also to provide a logical foundation for provably sound and efficient implementations.

Keywords. First Order Logic, Fluid Construction Grammar, unification and merge

Introduction

Fluid Construction Grammar (FCG) [1] has been developed in the context of a research programme [2] aimed at understanding how a group of agents connected to the world through sensors and actuators can autonomously conceptualise their environment, building a set of grounded categories which symbolise relevant aspects of their world, and construct a shared language which consists not only of a common lexicon that names categories but also of a simple grammar that allows expressing more complex meanings.

A number of experiments studying the *symbol grounding problem* [3] in populations of agents connected to their environment through sensors and actuators have been performed within that programme [4]. These experiments show that these agents can autonomously develop perceptually grounded categories playing *discrimination games,* in which they try to find a set of categories which distinguish a particular object (called the topic) from the rest of the objects in a given context. They also show how large populations of agents can coordinate such categories and construct shared lexicons playing *guessing games,* in which the agents invent and learn names for categories, and use mechanisms inspired in studies of *self-organisation phenomena* found in nature to coordinate their associations between symbols (names) and meanings (categories) in order to communicate effectively about the objects in their environment using only verbal means.

The research context in which FCG has been used primarily is the study of the *evolution and acquisition of language* [5,6], in particular of the *acquisition of grammar* [1]. In contrast to other approaches [7,8], which have only focused on the acquisition of syntax, the research associated with FCG has always been concerned with the *co-evolution of language and meaning* [9], and has therefore studied the role of grammar in *language (symbol) grounding,* incorporating ideas from *cognitive linguistics* [10] and *construction grammar* [11] which emphasise the communicative function of grammar, as well as the interaction between grammar and meaning.

FCG also draws inspiration from observations of *language usage* [12], which suggest that natural languages constantly adapt and evolve to cope with new meanings and variations in the behaviour of language users. Thus, the semantic and syntactic categories, lexicon and grammatical constructions used by the agents in the experiments are never fixed. In fact, all agents start with empty lexicons and grammars, and must use

---

[1]Support MICINN SESAAME-BAR (TIN2008-06582-C03-01). E-mail: Maria.Josefina.Sierra@upc.edu.

invention, adoption and induction strategies to construct their grammars [9]. The experiments themselves are designed to implement and test a *constructivist approach* [13] *to
language development,* in which grammatical constructions are acquired gradually, beginning with concrete linguistic structures based on particular words, from which they
are progressively abstracted.

FCG is fully operational and it has been used in a large number of experiments.
However, the concepts and inference operations (i.e. semantic/syntactic structures, constructions, unification and merge) on which FCG is based have not been formally defined in the linguistics literature [11]. The importance of formal definitions in promoting
homogeneity in implementations and enabling comparison between experimental results
obtained by related approaches has been recognised by the developers of FCG in [14],
where they present a formalisation of the unification and merge algorithms used in FCG.
The goal of this paper is not to propose an alternative formalisation for these algorithms,
but to understand the concepts and inference operations used in FCG from the point
of view of First Order Logic. This is not only useful for clarification purposes but also
necessary for dealing with the computational complexity of parsing and generation with
constructions in FCG. The concept of *structure instance,* the *functional (vs relational)
representation of linguistic facts* and the associated notion of *fact set consistency,* introduced in this paper, allow explaining such operations in terms of first order logic unification and reduce to some degree the complexity of the specification of unify and merge
proposed in [14].

The rest of the paper is organised as follows. Section 1 describes the representation
formalism proposed by FCG. Section 2 presents a formal definition of *unify and merge,*
and section 3 uses both operations in an example of *construction* application.

1. Representation Formalism

1.1. Semantic and Syntactic Structures

Linguistic and semantic information is represented using *syntactic* and *semantic structures* in FCG. A semantic or syntactic structure consists of a *set of units,* which correspond to lexical items or constituents such as noun phrases or relative clauses. A unit is
a list of five elements: the unit name followed by four feature-value pairs. *Semantic units*
contain the features *sem-subunits, referent, meaning* and *sem-cat,* in that order; and *syntactic units* the features *syn-subunits, utterance, form* and *syn-cat.* Feature values depend
on the type of feature: *referent* and *utterance* have a *single value,* whereas the values of
sem-subunits and *syn-subunits* are *sets of unit names.* The values of the rest of the features are *sets of facts* about different aspects of the components of a structure: *meaning*
is a set of facts which can be used to identify the referent (e.g. its shape, colour, type of
entity or event); *semantic categories* describe more abstract aspects of the referent (e.g.
its role as the agent, patient or target in an action); *form* and *syntactic categories* specify
different aspects of the utterance, such as its number, part of speech, stem or grammatical role (e.g. subject, predicate or object). The set of facts which may be included in the
values of these features is not restricted to those just mentioned but open ended.

We will use *lists* to represent those facts. For example, the fact that unit-2 is a *noun*
will be represented by the list (part-of-speech unit-2 noun). This notation
allows using first order logic variables for syntactic and semantic categories [15]. In par-

ticular, we will use a *many-sorted language* with two types: list and atom[2]. We shall also assume that the elements of the lists representing facts are always variables or constants of type atom, and that any symbol preceded by a question mark is a variable.

1.2. Constructions

In FCG inference is performed applying *constructions* to *source structures*. A *construction* is a pair <*left-pole*> <–> <*right-pole*> of *pattern structures* which associates a *syntactic pattern* with a *semantic pattern* (see figures 1 and 2). Constructions play therefore the role of *grammar rules* in *construction grammars* [11]. However they not only relate syntactic patterns to semantic ones but also supply information required for parsing and generation which is not included in lexical items, making it possible to construct sentences whose meaning is more than the sum of the meanings of their parts.

Source structures constitute the input to parsing and generation processes in FCG. Constructions can be used to add semantic or syntactic information to source structures, and therefore to complete missing aspects in these structures, such as the identity of the agent of a verb in a semantic structure, or the subject of a verb in a syntactic structure.

Formally, the *application of a construction* is a combination of two operations: *Unification,* used to check whether a construction is compatible with a source structure; and *merge,* which extends the structure with information contained in the construction [14].

2. Unification and Merge

2.1. Feature-value Unification

Unification for feature-values depends on the type of feature. *First order logic unification* can be used to compute *the most general unifier (mgu)* [16] of two features whose values are single terms. However, when feature values are sets of terms (unit names or facts represented by lists of atoms), a number of issues must be taken into account before first order logic unification can be applied.

Feature-value Instance   Let $s = \{t_1, \ldots, t_n\}$ be a feature value of type set of terms (unit names or facts represented by lists of atoms) of a semantic or syntactic unit. An *m-instance* of s is a list $v = (t_{i_1}, \ldots, t_{i_m})$, where $t_{i_j} \in s$ for $j = 1 \ldots m$ and t_{i_j} are distinct. An m-instance is thus a particular arrangement of m distinct elements of s.

Feature-value Unification   Let $s = \{a_1, \ldots, a_n\}$ be a feature value of type set of terms of a source structure and $p = (b_1, \ldots, b_m)$ a feature value of type set of terms of a pattern structure[3]. We say that s and p are *FCG-unifiable* if there is an m-instance s' of s such that the first order terms s' and p of type list of terms are unifiable, and we call the most general unifier σ of s' and p an FCG-unifier of s and p.

Notice that there can be several FCG-unifiers for a particular pair of source and pattern feature values, because different instances of the source feature value may unify with the pattern feature value, but they do not necessarily have to unify with each other.

---

[2]There is a binary function symbol `cons: Atom × List ⟶ List` and a constant symbol `NIL` of type `list`, which allow constructing terms of type `list`. For example, the term `(part-of-speech unit-2 noun)` is an abbreviation for the first order term `(cons part-of-speech (cons unit-2 (cons noun NIL)))`, where `part-of-speech`, `unit-2` and `noun` are constant symbols of type `atom`.

[3]We use *list* notation, rather than *set* notation, for specifying pattern feature values of type set of terms, because we do not need to consider the m-instances of pattern values.

Equal vs Subset Pattern Feature-values   Feature value unification in FCG is complicated by the fact that sometimes we are not interested feature value inclusion but in feature value equality. We use the superscript $=$ in the left parenthesis of a pattern feature
value to specify that the value of the corresponding feature in a source structure should
be equal to the pattern feature value rather than a subset of it.

Feature-value unification for *equal* pattern feature values can thus be defined as
follows. Let $s = \{a_1, \ldots, a_n\}$ be a feature value of type set of terms in a source structure
and $p = (^=b_1, \ldots, b_n)$ an equal feature value of type set of terms in a pattern structure.
We say that s and p are *FCG-unifiable* if there is a *permutation s'* of s such that the first
order logic terms s' and p of type list of terms are unifiable.

2.2. Feature-value Merge

Merge is used to extend a semantic or syntactic source structure with additional information contained in a pattern structure.

If the pattern and source feature values are FCG-unifiable, *merge* is equivalent to
unification[4]. However, when the pattern and source are not FCG-unifiable, the source
feature value is minimally extended so that it can be unified with the pattern, if this can
be done without introducing inconsistencies. Consider the following example:

```
p: ((?unit (sem-cat ((agent ?e ?a) (entity-type ?a human)))))
s: {(unit (sem-cat {(agent e a) (event-type e motion)}))}
```

The values of the feature `sem-cat` are not unifiable. But if we add the fact
`(entity-type ?a human)` to the source feature value, both feature values can be
unified yielding the following extended value, which is the result of merging s with p.

```
s': {(unit (sem-cat {(agent e a) (event-type e motion)
                     (entity-type a human)}))}
```

The steps involved in merging the source s and pattern p feature values above are:
1. Finding a minimal subset $p_c = \{(\text{entity-type } ?a \text{ human})\}$ of p such that $p_c \bigcup s$
   and p are FCG-unifiable, and an FCG-unifier σ of p and $s \bigcup p_c$.
2. Applying $\sigma = \{?a = a, ?e = e\}$ to $s \bigcup p_c$ in order to obtain the extended source
   feature value $(s \bigcup p_c)\sigma$, which is one of the possible results of merging s with p.

2.2.1. Fact Set Consistency
The first step above requires further clarification. Let us consider another example, where
s and p denote the source and pattern structures to be merged respectively.

```
p: ((?unit (form  ((string ?unit car)))
            (syn-cat ((number ?unit singular)))))
s: {(unit (form  {(string unit cars)})
            (syn-cat {(number unit plural)}))}
```

Merging s with p should not be allowed, because neither the values of the `form`
feature nor those of the `syn-cat` feature are consistent with each other. The value
of the source feature `syn-cat` does not unify with the value of the same feature in
the pattern. But the union of the minimal subset of the pattern feature value $p_c =$
$\{(\text{number } ?unit \text{ singular})\}$ with the source feature value $s = \{(\text{number unit plural})\}$
would lead to a contradiction, once the most general unifier $\sigma = \{?unit = unit\}$ is
applied to it: the number of a unit cannot be singular and plural at the same time.

---

[4]In this case, the source feature value is not extended as a result of merging it with the pattern feature value,
although some of its variables may be instantiated when an FCG-unifier of both feature values is applied to it.

$(s \bigcup p_c)\sigma =$ (syn-cat { (number unit plural) (number unit singular) })

In fact, the pattern and source structures above cannot be merged. The minimal subset of the pattern feature value p_c such that $s \bigcup p_c$ FCG-unifies with p must satisfy an additional condition which we will call *fact set consistency:* the extended source feature value resulting from merging the source with the pattern should not contain any pair of facts such that their elements are all equal but for the last one. The reason for imposing this condition is that a function cannot assign different values to a single tuple of elements, and we are assuming that a fact described by a list such as $(f, a_1, \ldots, a_n, v)$ represents a statement of the form $f(a_1, \ldots, a_n) = v$, where f denotes a function symbol, $a_1, \ldots, a_n$ its arguments and v the value that f assigns to $(a_1, \ldots, a_n)$.

Feature-value Merge   Let s be a source feature value of type set of terms, p a pattern feature value of the same type, p_c a minimal subset of p such that $s \bigcup p_c$ and p are FCG-unifiable[5], and σ an FCG-unifier of $s \bigcup p_c$ and p. If $(s \bigcup p_c)\sigma$ is *fact set consistent,* then the extended feature value $(s \bigcup p_c)\sigma$ is a valid result of merging s with p.

2.3. Unification and Merge for Units

Let $p = (p_{name} ((f_1\ \bar{u}_1)\ (f_2\ u_2)\ (f_3\ \bar{u}_3)\ (f_4\ \bar{u}_4)))$ be a pattern unit, where $f_1 \ldots f_4$ are the feature names *sem-subunits, referent, meaning* and *sem-cat,* if p is a semantic unit; or the feature names *syn-subunits, utterance, form* and *syn-cat,* if p is a syntactic unit.

P-Instance   A p-instance of a source unit s is a unit $(s_{name} ((f_1\ \bar{v}_1)\ (f_2\ v_2)\ (f_3\ \bar{v}_3)\ (f_4\ \bar{v}_4)))$, where s_{name} is the name of s; $\bar{v}_1, \bar{v}_3, \bar{v}_4$ are n_1, n_3 and n_4-instances of the $\bar{v}_1, \bar{v}_3$ and $\bar{v}_4$ respectively; n_1, n_3 and n_4 are the number of elements in $\bar{u}_1, \bar{u}_3$ and $\bar{u}_4$; and v_2 is the value of the feature f_2 in s. A *p-instance* of a source unit s is thus a unit which is *an instance of s with respect to the pattern unit p.*

Unit Unification   Let p be a pattern unit and s a source unit. We say that s and p are *FCG-unifiable* if there is a p-instance s' of s such that the first order logic terms p and s' are unifiable. The most general unifier σ of s' and p is an FCG-unifier of s and p.

Unit Merge   Let s be a source unit $(s_{name} ((f_1\ sv_1)\ (f_2\ sv_2)\ (f_3\ sv_3)\ (f_4\ sv_4)))$; p a pattern unit of the form $(p_{name} ((f_1\ pv_1)\ (f_2\ pv_2)\ (f_3\ pv_3)\ (f_4\ pv_4)))$; pv_1^c, pv_3^c and pv_4^c minimal subsets of pv_1, pv_3 and pv_4 such that the extended unit $s^e = (s_{name} ((f_1\ sv_1 \bigcup pv_1^c)\ (f_2\ sv_2)\ (f_3\ sv_3 \bigcup pv_3^c)\ (f_4\ sv_4 \bigcup pv_4^c)))$ and the pattern unit p are FCG-unifiable; and σ an FCG-unifier of s^e and p. If every feature value in $s^e\sigma$ satisfies the *fact set consistency* condition, then $s^e\sigma$ is a valid result of merging s with p.

2.4. Unification and Merge for Structures

Structure Instance   Let $s = \{u_1 \ldots u_n\}$ be a source structure and $p = (v_1 \ldots v_m)$ a pattern structure. An *m-instance* of s is a list of m-units $s' = (u'_{i_1}, \ldots, u'_{i_m})$, where each u'_{i_j} is an v_j-instance of some $u_{i_j} \in s$ for $j = 1 \ldots m$ and the u_{i_j} are distinct.

Structure Unification   Let $s = \{u_1 \ldots u_n\}$ be a source structure and $p = (v_1 \ldots v_m)$ a pattern structure. We say that s and p are *FCG-unifiable* if there is an m-instance s' of s such that the first order logic terms s' and p are unifiable. The most general unifier σ of s' and p is an FCG-unifier of s and p.

---

[5]A subset p_c of a pattern feature-value p is *minimal* with respect to a source feature-value s if no subset p_t of p satisfies that: (1) $p_t \subset p_c$; (2) p and $s \bigcup p_t$ are FCG-unifiable; and (3) $(s \bigcup p_t)\sigma$ is fact set consistent.

{(?s-u	((se-sub	(?e-u, ?a-u, ?o-u, ?r-u)))),		{(?s-u	((sy-sub	(?e-u, ?a-u, ?o-u, ?r-u))
					(syn-cat	(SVOtoO-sentence))))),
(?e-u	((referent	?e)		(?e-u	((syn-cat	((role ?e-u predicate))))),
	(sem-cat	((event-type ?e tr), (ag ?e ?a)				
		(obj ?e ?o), (rec ?e ?r))))),				
(?a-u	((referent	?a))),		(?a-u	((syn-cat	((role ?a-u subject))))),
(?o-u	((referent	?o))),		(?o-u	((syn-cat	((role ?o-u dir-obj))))),
(?r-u	((referent	?r))) }		(?r-u	((syn-cat	((role ?r-u ind-obj))))) }

Figure 1. Construction which associates a *transfer-to-recipient (tr)* semantic pattern structure (left) with a *Subject + Verb + Dir-Object + to + Indir-Object (SVOtoO)* syntactic pattern structure (right)[6].

Structure Merge   Let s be a source structure, p a pattern structure $(v_1, \ldots, v_n)$, p_c a minimal subset of p such that for each unit $u_i \in s \bigcup p_c$, $i = 1 \ldots n$ there is an extension u_i^e of u_i with respect to v_i such that the extended structure $s^e = \{u_1^e, \ldots, u_n^e\}$ and the pattern structure p are FCG-unifiable, and σ an FCG-unifier of s^e and p. If every feature-value in $s^e \sigma$ satisfies the fact set consistency condition, then $s^e \sigma$ is a valid result of merging s with p.

3. An Example of Construction Application

The result of applying morphological, lexical, semantic categorisation and phrase structure rules to parse the sentence *John slides blocks to Mary* is shown in figure 2. *Morphological rules* decompose words into a stem and a set of syntactic categories (e.g. "slides" into a stem "slide" and the categories *verb* and *singular*). *Number* is *grammatical* as opposed to *natural,* because it does not contribute to meaning. *Lexical rules* map the stem of a lexical item into a set of facts specifying its meaning, and natural syntactic categories (e.g. *number* for nouns) into additional meaning. *Semantic categorisation rules* add semantic categories to the semantic structure (e.g. the arguments of "slide" can be mapped into the semantic roles *agent, object* and *recipient* in a *transfer-to-recipient (tr)* event). Finally, *phrase structure rules* relate structural properties of a sentence, such as word order, to syntactic categories, such as *subject, direct object* or *indirect object*.

Note that the variables associated with *John, Mary* and *blocks* in the semantic units *jo, ma* and *bl* are different from those associated with the arguments of *slide* in the semantic unit *sl*. Figure 1 shows an example of a construction whose function is to ensure that the variables introducing the participants in the *transfer-to-recipient* frame and the roles in the *transfer-to-recipient (tr)* event (i.e. *agent, object* and *recipient*) become equal. This is done applying the construction in figure 1 to the structures built up at this stage of the parsing process. First, the syntactic source structure in figure 2 and the right pole of the construction are *unified,* yielding the *unifier: (?s-u=u, ?e-u=sl, ?a-u=jo, ?o-u=bl, ?r-u=ma)*. Then, the semantic source structure in figure 2 is *merged* with the result of applying the latter unifier to the left pole of the construction, making the desired substitutions *(?a=?j, ?o=?b, ?r=?m)* in the source semantic structure.

Conclusions

A formal definition of Fluid Construction Grammar in terms of First Order Logic concepts has been proposed, including its core inference operations unify and merge. This not only helps to clarify basic notions in FCG but also opens the door to sound implementations based on well-understood logic programming concepts and algorithms.

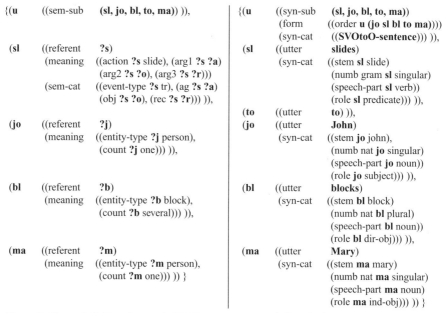

Figure 2. Semantic (left) and syntactic (right) source structures built up before construction application.

Acknowledgements

My thanks to Luc Steels for introducing me to most of the issues discussed in this paper.

References

[1]   Steels, L.: Constructivist development of grounded construction grammars. In: Proceedings of the Annual Meeting of the Association for Computational Linguistics Conference. (2004) 9–19

[2]   Steels, L.: The origins of syntax in visually grounded robotic agents. Art Intel **103(1-2)** (1998) 133–156

[3]   Harnad, S.: The symbol grounding problem. Physica D (42) (1990) 335–346

[4]   Steels, L.: Language games for autonomous robots. IEEE Intelligent Systems **6** (2001) 16–22

[5]   Steels, L.: The synthetic modeling of language origins. Evolution of Communication **1(1)** (1997) 1–35

[6]   Hurford, J.: Social transmission favors linguistic generalization. In: The Evolutionary Emergence of Language: Social Function and the Origins of Linguistic Form, Cambridge U. Press (2000) 324–352

[7]   Batali, J.: The negotiation and acquisition of recursive grammars as a result of competition among exemplars. In: Linguistic Evolution through Language Acquisition, Cambridge U. Press (2002) 111–172

[8]   Kirby, S.: Learning, bottlenecks and the evolution of recursive syntax. In: Linguistic Evolution through Language Acquisition: Formal and Computational Models, Cambridge University Press (2002) 96–109

[9]   Steels, L.: The emergence of grammar in communicating autonomous robotic agents. In: Proceedings of the European Conference on Artificial Intelligence. IOS Publishing, Amsterdam. (2000)

[10] Langacker, R.: Foundations of Cognitive Grammar. Stanford University Press (1991)

[11] Goldberg, A.: A Construction Grammar Approach to Argument Structure. Univ Chicago Press (1995)

[12] Wittgenstein, L.: Philosophical Investigations. Macmillan, New York (1953)

[13] Tomasello, M., Brooks, P.: Early syntactic development: A Construction Grammar approach. In: The Development of Language. Psychology Press (1999) 161–190

[14] Steels, L., Beule, J.D.: Unify and merge in fluid construction grammar. In: 3rd International Workshop on the Emergence and Evolution of Linguistic Communication. LNAI 4211, Springer (2006) 197–223

[15] McCarthy, J.: Formalizing Common Sense. Papers by John McCarthy. Ablex. Ed. V. Lifschitz (1990)

[16] Robinson, J.: A machine-oriented logic based on the resolution principle. J of ACM **12(1)** (1965) 23–41

Biologically Inspired Cognitive Architectures 2011
A.V. Samsonovich and K.R. Jóhannsdóttir (Eds.)
IOS Press, 2011
© 2011 The authors and IOS Press. All rights reserved.
doi:10.3233/978-1-60750-959-2-351

Extended Sparse Distributed Memory

Javier SNAIDER[1], Stan FRANKLIN
Computer Science Department & Institute for Intelligent Systems, The University of Memphis

Abstract. Sparse distributed memory is an auto-associative memory system that stores high dimensional Boolean vectors. Here we present an extension of the original SDM that uses word vectors of larger size than address vectors. This extension preserves many of the desirable properties of the original SDM: auto-associability, content addressability, distributed storage, robustness over noisy inputs. In addition, it adds new functionality, enabling an efficient auto-associative storage of sequences of vectors, as well as of other data structures such as trees.

Keywords. Sparse Distributed Memory, Episodic Memory, Sequence Representation, Cognitive Modeling

Introduction

First proposed by Kanerva [1], sparse distributed memory (SDM) is based on large binary vectors, and has several desirable properties. It is distributed, auto associative, content addressable, and noise robust. Moreover, this memory exhibits interesting psychological characteristics as well (interference, knowing when it doesn't know, the tip of the tongue effect), that make it an attractive option with which to model episodic memory [2][3]. SDM is still being implemented for various applications (e.g., [4][5][6]). Several improvements have been proposed for SDM; for example Ramamurthy and colleagues introduced forgetting as part of an unsupervised learning mechanism [7][8]. The same authors also proposed the use of ternary vectors, introducing a "don't care" symbol as a third possible value for the dimensions of the vectors [9]. Kanerva, in his original work, described the use the SDM to store sequences. His procedure has the disadvantage of losing most of the auto-associativeness and noise robustness of the memory. Later he proposed hyperdimentional arithmetic as a new mechanism for storing sequences and other data structures such as sets and records [10]. Even though this new mechanism is an improvement over the original SDM mechanism, it is still limited in its noise robustness, and it is very sensitive to interference (see below).

Here we propose an extension to the original SDM that is especially suitable for storing sequences and other data structures such as trees. This extension can also improve the hyperdimensional arithmetic introduced by Kanerva. In the following section we briefly describe SDM. Then we introduce Extended SDM, discussing several uses of this extension and its results. Finally we propose some future directions.

---

[1] Corresponding Author: FedEx Institute of Technology #403h, 365 Innovation Dr., Memphis, TN 38152; E-mail: jsnaider@memphis.edu

1. Sparse Distributed Memory

Here we present a brief introduction to SDM concepts. Both leisurely descriptions [11] and highly detailed descriptions [1] are available. Readers already familiar with SDM can skip this section.

SDM implements a content addressable random access memory. Its address space is of the order of 2^{1000} or even more. Both addresses and words are binary vectors whose length equals the number of dimensions of the space. In this example, we will think of bit vectors of 1000 dimensions. To calculate distances between two vectors in this space, the Hamming distance is used. Surprisingly, and of importance to SDM, the distances from a point of the space to any other point in the space are highly concentrated around half of the maximum distance. In our example, more than 99.9999% of the vectors are at a distance between 422 and 578 from a given vector of the space [1].

To construct the memory, a sparse uniformly distributed sample of addresses, on the order of 2^{20} of them, is chosen. These addresses are called hard locations. Only hard locations can store data. Several hard locations participate in the storing and retrieving of any single word of data. Each hard location has a fixed address, and contains one counter for each dimension. In our example, each hard location has 1000 counters. A counter is just an integer counter with a range of -40 to 40. Counters can be incremented or decremented in steps of size one.

To write a word vector in a hard location, for each dimension, if the bit of this dimension in the word is 1, the corresponding counter is incremented. If it is 0, the counter is decremented. To read a word vector from a hard location, we compute a vector such that, for each dimension, if the corresponding counter in the hard location is positive, 1 is assigned to this dimension in the vector being read, otherwise 0 is assigned.

When a vector is written in an address in the SDM, it is stored in several hard locations. In the same way, to read from an address in the SDM, the read vector is a composition of the readings of several hard locations. To determine which hard locations are used to read or write, the access sphere is defined. The access sphere for an address vector is a sphere with center at this address that on average encloses 0.1% of all the hard locations of the memory. The radius of the access sphere depends on the number of dimensions of the space. For example, for a SDM with 1000 dimensions, the radius of the access sphere is 451. In the example, the access sphere will contain any hard location whose address is less than 451 away from the address vector.

To write a word vector in any address of the memory, the word is written to all hard locations inside the access sphere of the address. To read from any address, all hard locations in the access sphere of the address vector are read and a majority rule for each dimension is applied.

In general, the SDM is used as an auto-associative memory, so the address vector is the same as the word vector. In this case, after writing a word in the memory, the vector can be retrieved using partial or noisy data. If the partial vector is inside a critical distance from the original one, and it is used as address with which to cue the memory, the read vector will be close to the original one. This critical distance depends on the number of vectors already stored in the memory. If the process is repeated, using the first recovered vector as address, the new reading will be even closer to the original. After a few iterations, typically less than ten, the readings converge to the original vector. If the partial or noisy vector is farther away than the critical distance, the successive readings from the iterations will diverge. If the partial vector is about at the critical distance form the original one, the iterations yields vectors that are typically at the same critical distance from the original vector. This behavior mimics the "tip of the tongue" effect.

When storing sequences of vectors in this SDM, the address cannot be the same as the word, as it is in the auto-associative use. The vector that represents the first element of the sequence is used as address to read the memory. The read vector is the second element in the sequence. This second vector is used as address to read the memory again to retrieve the third element. This procedure is repeated until the whole sequence is retrieved. The problem with this way of storing sequences is that it is not possible to use iterations to retrieve elements of the sequence from noisy input cues. So, the memory is far less robust.

Kanerva [10] introduced hyperdimensional computing, based on large binary vectors, as an appropriate tool for cognitive modeling, including holistic representation of sets, sequences and mappings. Among the various vector operations proposed, multiplication of binary vectors as bitwise xor, permutation, and sum with normalization are relevant to the present work, and will be discussed here.

When two binary vectors are combined using bitwise xor, the result of this operation is a new vector of the same dimensionality as the original ones. This operation has several interesting properties. First, the resulting vector is dissimilar, i.e. farther than the critical distance, to the two original ones. Second, the xor operation is reversible.

If A x B = C then C x B = A and C x A = B

Third, this operation preserves Hamming distances.

Permutation is an operation that shuffles the positions (dimensions) of one vector. Mathematically, this corresponds to multiplying the vector by a square matrix M with one 1 in each row and column while the other positions contain 0.

Permutation $(A) = (AM)^T$

This operation is also reversible, multiplying by M^T, and it preserves Hamming distances as well.

Finally, the sum operation is the arithmetic (integer) sum of the values of each dimension of two or more vectors. For this operation the bipolar representation of the vectors, i.e., the value 0 is replaced by -1, is used. The resulting vector is an integer vector. To transform this vector into a binary vector, a normalization operation is required. If one dimension has a positive value, the normalized binary vector has a 1 in this dimension. If the value is negative, the normalized vector has a 0 in this dimension. Ties are resolved at random. The sum with normalization has interesting properties: the resulting vector is similar to each of the vectors summed up; i.e. the distance between them is less than the expected distance between any two vectors in the space. Also, xor multiplication distributes over the sum.

Based in these properties, it is sometimes possible to retrieve the individual added vectors from the sum vector. This is feasible only if the number of vectors added is small, i.e. three or fewer vectors. Even with this small number, the interference among the vectors in the sum makes the retrieval of the original vectors from the sum not very reliable.

Kanerva describes how to store sequences of vectors using hyperdimensional arithmetic [10]. We will briefly describe this procedure and compare it with our implementation in section 3. The main problem of this procedure is that it uses the sum operation, and so shares the same problems with the sum mentioned above while reconstructing the sequence. Also it uses permutation, and as we discuss before, this operation requires matrices that are outside of the binary vector domain.

2. Extended SDM

Here we present a novel structure, built upon SDM, that we call extended sparse distributed memory (ESDM). The main idea of this new memory structure is the use of vectors with different lengths for the addresses and the words. A word has a longer length than the address in which it is stored. Each address has n dimensions while each word has m dimensions with n<m. Moreover, the address vector is included in the word vector (See Figure 1). Formally, a word of length m and an address with length n, the first n bits of the word compose the address.

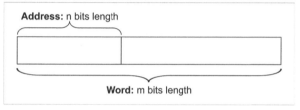

Figure 1 A word vector with its address section.

The structure of this new memory system is similar to the original SDM. It is composed of hard locations, each of which has an address and counters. The address is a fixed vector of length n. But each hard location has m counters, where m is greater than n. To store a word vector in the memory, the procedure is the same as described for SDM, except that now the first n bits of the word are used as address. To read from an address in the memory, again the procedure is similar to the one used for SDM. During each iteration, a word is read from the memory and its first n bits are used to read in the next iteration.

Formally, the address vector is $A = (WM)^T$, where A is an address vector of size n, W is the word vector of size m and M is a n x m rectangular diagonal matrix with all 1s in the diagonal.

It is important to notice that the whole word vector, including the address, comprises the useful data. Conceptually, this memory is a mix of auto-associative and hetero-associative memories. The address part of the word is auto-associative whereas the rest of the word is hetero-associative. This allows us to preserve, and even to improve, the desirable characteristics of the SDM. First, with an initial vector as address to cue the memory, it is possible to retrieve the corresponding word, even if the initial vector is a noisy version of the stored one. This means that ESDM maintains the noise robustness characteristic of SDM. Second, the data of each vector is stored in a number of hard locations in a distributed way. So, it is also robust in the case that some hard locations are corrupted or lost. Third, the previously discussed psychological characteristics in SDM are also present in ESDM. Finally, the hetero-associative part of the words in ESDM allows storing other data related with the address data but without interfering with it. This is a notable improvement over the original SDM that relies on the flawed sum operation to achieve the same goal but with far less effectiveness.

3. Storing sequences and other data structures

Sequences are important representations for cognitive agents. Agents act over time and cognitive agents adapt *and* act over time. Simple events can be combined into more complex ones forming sequences, or even trees, of simpler events [12][13].

In section 1 we mentioned two approaches suggested by Kanerva [1][10] for storing sequences in SDM. We also mentioned that both approaches have important disadvantages that weaken the auto-associatively, content addressability and noise robustness properties of the memory. The implementation of sequence storing in ESDM is straightforward and eliminates these disadvantages. The most basic implementation uses addresses of length n and words of length 2n, as shown in figure 2. The sequence is composed of vectors of length n. To store the sequence, the first two vectors E_1 and E_2 are concatenated forming a word of length 2n. We will say that the word has two *sections* of n bits each. This word is stored in address E_1. Then E_2 and E_3 are concatenated and stored in address E_2. The process continues until the full sequence is stored. A special vector can be used to indicate the end of the sequence.

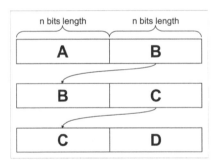

Figure 2 Basic sequence representation using 2n word vectors

To retrieve the sequence, the initial vector of the sequence is used to read a word from the memory. This word is divided in two halves. The second half is the second vector in the sequence. Repeating this procedure, the whole sequence is retrieved. Notice that in each reading during the retrieval of the sequence, the vector used as address can have some noise, but the iterating reading from the memory cleans it up, as explained previously. One problem with this implementation occurs when two sequences that share a common vector are stored in the memory. For example:

ABC**D**E and FGC**H**I

In the example, the word CD is stored in address C but the word CH is stored in C also. This produces the undesirable interference between D and H that prevents the correct retrieval of one or even both of the sequences. One plausible solution is to use the same procedure proposed by Kanerva using hyperdimensional operations. The first reading from the memory again uses the initial vector of the sequence. But the following addresses are calculated using the previously read vectors of the sequence. An elegant combination is achieved using permutation and sum operations [10]. For example if P() denotes a random permutation, then:

$$A_3 = [P(E_1)+E_2]$$

With this address we read the memory and from the read word the next vector of the sequence, i.e. E_3, is retrieved. The following addresses are calculated in the same way.

$$A_{i+1} = [P(A_i)+E_i]$$

An interesting option is to preserve the sum of the vectors in each reading and multiply it by a scalar k between 0 and 1, for example 0.8. This produces an effect of *fading away* of the old vectors of the sequence in the calculation of the next address.

$$A'_{i+1} = k*P(A'_i)+E_i$$

$$A_{i+1} = [A'_{i+1}] \quad \text{where A' is the real vector with the sum before normalization.}$$

All these equations can be used in the original SDM, as pointed out by Kanerva. In both situations, operations with sums are used but the advantage of this implementation is that the retrieval of the succeeding vector in the sequence does not depend on operations that extract the vector from the sum. Here the sum is used only to compute the next address, but the vector is extracted directly from the second part of the read word.

In a similar way, other data structures can be stored in ESDM. For example, to store binary trees, addresses of length n and words of length 3n are used. With the address of the root of the tree the first word is retrieved. The word is divided into three sections, left, center and right. The left section holds the content of the node in the tree; the center section is used as an address with which to read the left child node of the tree; the right section holds the address of the right child node. This procedure is repeated until the whole tree is retrieved. Notice that here again noisy vectors can be used, and ESDM takes care of cleaning them up. Also, a similar mechanism to the one described for sequences can be used to avoid problems related to repeated vectors in several structures.

Other data structures can be easily derived from sequences and trees. A *double linked sequence* can be constructed adding another section of n bits to the word. The address of the previous element in the sequence is stored there. This allows navigating the sequence in reverse order. Something similar can be used to store the parent of a node in a tree. This allows navigating the tree from the bottom up. Finally, more sections of n bits can be added to each word in the tree so that trees with greater degrees can be stored. Interestingly, a tree can represent a more meaningful data structure, like a record, where each child node represents a field of the record, and the root the record itself. An even simpler representation for record is a word with several sections where each section represents a field of the record.

4. Conclusions

Here we have presented an extension of the original SDM that addresses several of its difficulties with storing compound data structures like sequences, trees and records. Our ESDM preserves the desirable, biologically inspired, properties of the original. It is also noise robust, auto-associative and distributed. These, combined with the possibility of storing sequences and other compound data structures, make ESDM an even more attractive option with which to model episodic memories.

The current ESDM implementation uses a data base for the main storage of the hard locations, and a ram cache to speed up the store and retrieve operations. This allows us to create large ESDMs, with millions of hard locations and word dimensions of the order of 10,000 bits even with modest computers. Simulations of storing and retrieving sequences and trees, together with our evaluation of the advantages of ESDM over the standard SDM, are forthcoming.

ESDM is compatible with other improvements already studied, such as the forgetting mechanism [7][8]. Including this forgetting mechanism is a natural following step for this architecture.

ESDM has the potential for further extensions. Representation of other data structures and combining it with hyperdimensional vector arithmetic are possible paths for further development.

References

[1]   Kanerva, P. (1988). *Sparse Distributed Memory*. Cambridge MA: The MIT Press.
[2]   Baddeley, A., Conway, M., & Aggleton, J. (2001). *Episodic Memory*. Oxford: Oxford University Press.
[3]   Franklin, S., Baars, B. J., Ramamurthy, U., & Ventura, M. (2005). The Role of Consciousness in Memory. *Brains, Minds and Media, 1*, (pp.1 - 38).
[4]   Furber, S. B., Bainbridge, W.J., Cumpstey J.M. & Temple, S. (2004). A Sparse Distributed Memory based upon N-of-M Codes, *Neural Networks Vol: 17/10* (pp 1437 - 1451).
[5]   Bose, J., S.B. Furber, J.L. Shapiro, A.(2005). Spiking neural sparse distributed memory implementation for learning and predicting temporal sequences. *Lecture Notes in Computer Science, Volume 3696*, (pp.115 - 120), Springer-Verlag GmbH. ISSN: 0302-9743
[6]   Meng, H., Appiah, K., Hunter, A., Yue, S., Hobden, M., Priestley, N., Hobden, P. & Pettit, C. (2009). A modified sparse distributed memory model for extracting clean patterns from noisy inputs. In: *(Proceedings) International Joint Conference on Neural Networks (IJCNN)*. (pp. 2084 - 2089).
[7]   Ramamurthy, U., D'Mello, S. K., & Franklin, S. (2006). Realizing Forgetting in a Modified Sparse Distributed Memory System. *Proceedings of the 28th Annual Conference of the Cognitive Science Society*, (pp. 1992 - 1997).
[8]   Ramamurthy, U. & Franklin, S. (2011). Memory Systems for Cognitive Agents. *Proceedings of Human Memory for Artificial Agents Symposium at the Artificial Intelligence and Simulation of Behavior Convention (AISB'11)*, University of York, UK,, (pp. 35 - 40).
[9]   D'Mello, S. K., Ramamurthy, U., & Franklin, S. (2005). Encoding and Retrieval Efficiency of Episodic Data in a Modified Sparse Distributed Memory System *Proceedings of the 27th Annual Meeting of the Cognitive Science Society*. Stresa, Italy.
[10] Kanerva, P. (2009). Hyperdimensional Computing: An Introduction to computing in distributed representation with high-dimensional random vectors. *Cognitive Computation, 1*(2), (pp. 139 – 159).
[11] Franklin, S. (1995). *Artificial Minds*. Cambridge MA: MIT Press.
[12] Snaider, J., McCall, R., & Franklin, S. (in press). Time Production and Representation in a Conceptual and Computational Cognitive Model. *Cognitive Systems Research*.
[13] Kurby, C. A., & Zacks, J. M. (2008). Segmentation in the perception and memory of events. *Trends in Cognitive Science, 12*(2), (pp. 72 – 79).

Biologically Inspired Cognitive Architectures 2011
A.V. Samsonovich and K.R. Jóhannsdóttir (Eds.)
IOS Press, 2011
© 2011 The authors and IOS Press. All rights reserved.
doi:10.3233/978-1-60750-959-2-358

Neural Planning and Reasoning Using the Synaptic Connections of the Basal Ganglia and Thalamus

Terrence C. STEWART[1] and Chris ELIASMITH
Centre for Theoretical Neuroscience, University of Waterloo, Waterloo, Canada

Abstract. In previous work, we have shown how to construct biologically plausible models of a wide variety of cognitive tasks. This process involves converting algorithms into numerical vectors (represented by the spiking activity of a group of neurons) and operations on those vectors (implemented via synaptic connections between groups). We have used this technique to create a neural model capable of solving the Tower of Hanoi task, involving symbolic reasoning, planning, and goal retrieval. Constructing this neural cognitive model involved breaking the task down into sixteen general-purpose "rules" which can be implemented by specifying particular synaptic connections from the cortex to the basal ganglia, and from the thalamus back to the cortex. In this paper, we present a breakdown and discussion of these rules, showing how they differ from those found in traditional symbolic cognitive models. This leads to a novel method of constructing biologically realistic cognitive models with improved capabilities over classical production system models.

Keywords. Neural engineering framework, cognitive architectures, neural representation, production systems, basal ganglia, thalamus

Introduction

Our overall goal is to determine how cognitive behaviour arises from the firing of individual neurons in the brain. To achieve this, we are creating large-scale computational models using simulated spiking neurons with properties and connectivity matching those of the real human brain. We have developed models of list memory [1], fluid intelligence [2], visual attention [3], and arm control [4], bridging the gap between behaviour and neural implementation. These models produce accuracy and reaction time predictions by setting parameters based on neurological evidence rather than free parameter fitting.

Our current work involves combining the insights from our initial models to produce a general-purpose biologically-grounded neural cognitive architecture. As with existing cognitive architectures (ACT-R, Soar, Clarion, Leabra, etc.), we specify a set of components that can be used to perform multiple different cognitive tasks, rather than defining special-purpose models. Changing tasks is done by adjusting the model's knowledge and its inputs, rather than rebuilding the entire model.

The main advantage to our approach over other cognitive architectures is that we make use of the Neural Engineering Framework (NEF) [5], which provides a mapping

---

[1] Corresponding Author.

between information representation/transformation and neural firing patterns/synaptic connections. The firing of a group of neurons is seen as a distributed representation of a vector, and the connections from one group of neurons to another (or back to themselves) is seen as a computation on that vector. The NEF allows us to solve for the ideal connection weights that will compute a desired function of the value currently represented by the neurons. It also takes into account the neuron model used (here we use the standard Leaky-Integrate-and-Fire model) and neural properties such as the re-uptake rate of various neurotransmitters, which vary widely (from two to hundreds of milliseconds) and constrain the flow of information through a neural system.

We have successfully used this approach to build a neural model of the Tower of Hanoi task [6]. This involves general-purpose components for storing state information, forming paired associates, performing action selection, and controlling the routing of information between these areas. The model is able to plan, recall, and execute a sequence of moves to arrive at a goal state, moving one disk at a time and ensuring that a larger disk is never on top of a smaller disk. Reaction time for the model, compared to that of human experts at this task, is shown in Figure 1. There are only two free parameters for the model: the amount of time needed to move a disk (1.8 seconds) and the memory weighting factor that determines how quickly new information is encoded in memory (0.08). All other aspects of the model are fixed based on neurological data.

While more information on the construction of the components of this model can be found elsewhere [6], here we focus on the rules that implement this particular task. In many cognitive architectures, these would take the form of *production rules*, if-then rules that indicate what to do in a particular situation. These rules can send information to different cognitive modules, request memory recall, change attentional focus, or trigger motor actions. In ACT-R and many other cognitive architectures, exactly one rule can "fire" at a time, and 50 milliseconds elapse between rule firings. We have previously shown that an NEF model of the basal ganglia can select between rules of this kind, and that an NEF model of the thalamus can implement the effects of these rules [7]. Furthermore, if the model is fixed to use the neurotransmitters found in those regions, then approximately 50 milliseconds elapse between rule firings [8].

Importantly, the rules we can implement using this neural model are *not equivalent to production rules*. Because they operate over numerical vectors rather than symbols, they have features not found in standard symbolic cognitive models. In particular, they take advantage of the fact that vector representations can be combined mathematically, and they exhibit a *partial matching* capability. Both of these features were important when building our model of the Tower of Hanoi task.

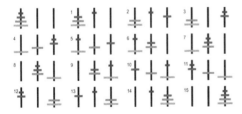 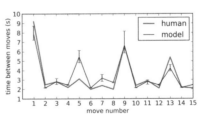

Figure 1. The Tower of Hanoi task and reaction time between moves. Left side shows the optimal series of 15 steps to move four disks from peg A to peg C while moving only one at a time and never placing a larger disk on top of a smaller disk. Right side compares reaction time data from expert human participants (data taken from [9]) and from our model. Only error-free trials are considered here.

1. The Model

The model consists of a sensory system, a motor system, four general-purpose state buffers, an associative memory, and an action selection system. Other than the sensory and motor systems, all are implemented using spiking neurons. While the details of the construction of these components are available in our previous work [6], the main consideration here is that the inputs and outputs of each component consist of numerical vectors (represented via a distributed encoding in spiking neurons).

The four buffers (called state, focus, goal, and goaltarget) store information over time. Any arbitrary vector can be stored in these buffers, but to solve this task we use the buffers to store the current stage of the task (state), the disk being attended to (focus), the disk being moved (goal), and where we wish to move the disk to (goaltarget). We randomly choose a set of vectors for the different possible contents of these buffers. Here, these vectors are D0, D1, D2, and D3 for the four disks; A, B, and C for the three pegs; and HANOI, FIND, STORE, and RECALL for the four states of the algorithm used to solve the task.

The sensory system consists of vector inputs representing information about the location of of the focus and goal disks, the current largest disk, the desired end state of the model, and feedback from the motor system as to whether it has completed its task. The motor system consists of two outputs which can indicate the disk to move and the location to move the disk to. The sensory and motor systems are the only parts of the model which are not implemented in neurons, and instead simply provide inputs to and interpret outputs from the neural model.

Table 1. Components of the model.

Name	Type	Description
state	buffer	Used to control the different stages of the problem-solving algorithm.
focus	buffer	Stores the disk currently being attended to (D0, D1, D2, D3)
focuspeg	sensory	Automatically contains the location of the focus disk (A,B,C)
goal	buffer	Stores the disk we are trying to move (D0, D1, D2, D3)
goaltarget	buffer	Stores the location we want to move the goal disk to (A,B,C)
goalcurrent	sensory	Automatically contains the location of the goal disk (A,B,C)
goalfinal	sensory	Automatically contains the final desired location of the goal disk (A,B,C)
largest	sensory	Automatically contains the largest visible disk (D3)
mem1	memory	Stores an association between mem1 and mem2 in working memory
mem2	memory	Stores an association between mem1 and mem2 in working memory
request	memory	Indicates one element of a pair to attempt to recall from working memory
recall	memory	The vector associated with the currently requested vector
movedisk	motor	Tells the motor system which disk to move (D0, D1, D2, D3)
movepeg	motor	Tells the motor system where to move the disk to (A,B,C)
motor	sensory	Automatically contains DONE if the motor action is finished

The algorithms for solving the Tower of Hanoi task is based on the "Sophisticated Perceptual Strategy" [10], and is similar to existing non-neural cognitive models of this task [9],[11]. The actual rules are shown in Table 2, and their details are discussed in the next sections.

We start in the HANOI state, with goal and focus equal to the largest disk (D3), and the goaltarget set to the desired end location of D3. In the HANOI state, we check to see if the goal disk is at its desired location. If it is (rule *LookDone*), we go on to the next disk (changing focus and goal to D2). If it is not (rule *LookNotDone*), we start looking at the next disks (changing focus to D2, then D1, etc.). If any of these disks are in the way (i.e. they are either on the goalcurrent or goaltarget pegs), then we change the goal to move that peg out of the way (i.e. onto the peg that is not goalcurrent or goaltarget; rules *FindFree1* and *FindFree2*). However, before we change the goal, we store the current goal/goaltarget pair in an associative working memory (rules *Store* and *StoreDone*). This process continues until a disk is found that can be moved (i.e. it has no disk above it that is in the way; rules *MoveD0* and *MoveGoal*). The information for the disk and the target location is then sent to the motor system. When the movement is done, we change our goal to the next lower disk and recall its desired location from memory (rule *Recall*). If it is not yet in that location, we set goaltarget to be that recalled location (rule *RecallDo*). If it is already in that location, we go on to recall the target for the next disk (rule *RecallNext*).

To implement action selection (i.e. to chose which rule to apply), we use our neural model of the basal ganglia [7],[8]. This takes as inputs a vector of utility values, one for each rule. The output indicates the rule with the largest utility. To make use of this, we need to connect the components (Table 1) to the basal ganglia so that the computed utilities reflect the rule matching conditions (the IF column in Table 2).

Table 2. Rules for performing the Tower of Hanoi task.

Rule Name	Match (IF)	Execute (THEN)
LookDone	focus≠D0; goal=focus goalcurrent=goaltarget state≠STORE	focus=goal⊗NEXT goal=goal⊗NEXT goaltarget=goalfinal
LookNotDone	focus≠D0; goal=focus; goalcurrent≠goaltarget; state≠STORE	focus=goal⊗NEXT
InTheWay1	focus≠goal; focuspeg=goalcurrent focuspeg≠goaltarget; state≠STORE	state=STORE
InTheWay2	focus≠goal; focuspeg≠goalcurrent focuspeg=goaltarget; state≠STORE	state=STORE
NotInTheWay	focus≠goal; focuspeg≠goalcurrent focuspeg≠goaltarget; focus≠D0	focus=focus⊗NEXT
MoveD0	focus=D0; goal=D0 goalcurrent≠goaltarget	movedisk=D0 movepeg=goaltarget
MoveGoal	focus=D0; goal≠D0; focuspeg≠goaltarget; goaltarget≠goalcurrent; focuspeg≠goalcurrent	movedisk=goal movepeg=goaltarget
MoveDone	motor=DONE; goal≠largest state≠RECALL	state=RECALL goal=goal⊗NEXT⁻¹
MoveDone2	motor=DONE goal=largest state≠RECALL	focus=largest⊗NEXT⁻¹ goal=largest⊗NEXT⁻¹ goaltarget=goalfinal state=HANOI
Store	state=STORE recall≠goaltarget	mem1=goal mem2=goaltarget request=goal
StoreDone	state=STORE; recall=goaltarget	state=FIND
FindFree1	state=FIND focus≠goal focuspeg=goalcurrent focuspeg≠goaltarget	goaltarget= A+B+C-focuspeg-goaltarget goal=focus state=HANOI
FindFree2	state=FIND focus≠goal focuspeg≠goalcurrent focuspeg=goaltarget	goaltarget= A+B+C-goalcurrent-goaltarget goal=focus state=HANOI
Recall	state=RECALL; recall≠A+B+C	request=goal
RecallDo	state=RECALL recall=A+B+C recall≠goalcurrent	state=HANOI focus=goal goaltarget=recall*4
RecallNext	state=RECALL; recall=A+B+C recall=goalcurrent	goal=goal⊗NEXT⁻¹ request=goal

2. Vector-Based Rules

To compute the utility of a rule given the current state vectors, we compute dot products ($\bullet$). This is a linear operation between two vectors (and so can be efficiently computed by neurons [5]) which returns a value closer to 1 the more similar the two vectors are. In Table 1, these matching rules are shown in the IF column. A $\neq$ symbol is used to indicate a rule that should *not* occur in the given state. For these, the dot product is subtracted from the utility, rather than added. For example, the utility of the *MoveD0* rule is focus$\bullet$D0+goal$\bullet$D0-goalcurrent$\bullet$goaltarget. This indicates the rule should have a high utility if the focus and goal are D0 but goalcurrent is not the same as goal target (i.e. my goal is to to move the top disk, I am focused on it, and it is not in its target location). Utilities are then scaled so the maximum utility for a rule is 1.

Once a rule is active, it releases inhibition in our model of the thalamus, which implements the rule's effects. Each effect either sends a particular value to a particular component or routes information between components. For example, the *MoveD0* rule will cause the value D0 to be sent to the movedisk motor output and whatever value is in goaltarget will be sent to movepeg. Information can be modified as it is routed; for example, *RecallDo* sends 4 times the recalled value to the goaltarget buffer (allowing it to react to weaker memories), and *LookDone* sends to focus the circular convolution ($\otimes$) of goal with the vector NEXT. This is a special vector relating the disks such that D3$\otimes$NEXT=D2, D2$\otimes$NEXT=D1, and D1$\otimes$NEXT=D0 (and D0$\otimes$NEXT$^{-1}\approx$D1).

When creating a cognitive model using rules of this form, a number of capabilities arise that are not seen in standard production systems. First, the system has an inherent version of *partial matching*. That is, even if no rule exactly matches the current situation, the one that is closest (has the highest utility) will still be chosen. This means that *MoveD0* may be selected even though focus$\neq$D0, if no other rules are more appropriate. Interestingly, we can easily change a rule to be more (or less) sensitive to this effect by adjusting the vector to which it matches. For example, we could change *MoveD0* to match on focus=D0-D1-D2-D3. Now, if the focus is anything other than D0, this will result in *negative* utility, making this rule less prone to overgeneralization.

A further feature of vector rules is the ability to perform *odd-one-out* computations. Consider the case where D2 is on peg A, we want to move it to B, but D1 is currently on A so it is in the way (goal=D2, goalcurrent=A, goaltarget=B, focus=D1, focuspeg=A). This leads to rule *FindFree1* firing (*FindFree2* is for the case where D1 was on B and thus also in the way). What we want is to have the rule change the goal to D1 and the goaltarget to C, so that we can move D1 out of the way. However, how do we determine the correct value to send to goaltarget? One method would be to split the rule up into six special-case rules covering each of the possibilities of each peg. Other cognitive models (e.g. [9]) add a memory system here to recall the element that is not either of the two pegs in question. Instead, here we have exploited the fact that these symbols are vectors. The effect of *FindFree1* is to send to goaltarget the value A+B+C, and at the same time route to goaltarget the values from goaltarget and focuspeg, each multiplied by -1. The final result will be A+B+C-A-B=C.

Many rules also use the construction $\otimes$NEXT in their effect. This is also a method for using vector representation to collapsing many rules into one. For *NotInTheWay*, the focus disk (e.g. D2) is not obstructing the movement of goal to goaltarget, so we want to look at the next disk (D1). Instead of making special case rules for D2->D1 and D1->D0, we have a single rule which computes the transformation.

Finally, our method for storing previous goals makes interesting use of the fact that our representations are not only vectors, but are continuous in time. In many non-neural memory models, including previous models of the Tower of Hanoi task, a cycle is carried out where information is stored and then a retrieval attempt is made. If this retrieval is unsuccessful (due to the memory not having a high enough activation), then the information is added again. This process is repeated until retrieval is successful. Instead, our model uses the rule *Store*. While *Store* is active, it not only sends the goal and goaltarget to the memory to be stored, but it also at the same time requests the recall of the value paired with goal. At the same time, we subtract the dotproduct of the recalled value and the goaltarget from the utility (recall≠goaltarget). This means that the rule will continue to fire, continually storing the paired association in memory *until the recall is successful*, rather than cycling through storing and recalling.

Conclusions

The neural cognitive modelling framework we have described here produces models capable of complex problem solving. In order to create these models in a neurally plausible manner that respects the anatomical and physiological aspects of the brain, we had to develop a way to represent traditional symbolic rules using numerical vectors. In turn, this vector representation opens the door for new kinds of rules that are not commonly found in symbolic production system models. In particular, we can perform numerical operations to transform one state vector into another (allowing for rules indicating "look at the next item") and we allow for partial matching, where a rule will generalize to new conditions if no existing rule is more appropriate. Our ongoing work is to explore the implications of these new capabilities for cognitive modelling.

References

[1]   Choo, F., Eliasmith, C. (2010). A Spiking Neuron Model of Serial-Order Recall. In R. Cattrambone & S. Ohlsson (Eds.), *Proceedings of the 32nd Annual Conference of the Cognitive Science Society.*

[2]   Rasmussen, D. and Eliasmith, C. (2010). A neural model of rule generation in inductive reasoning. In R. Cattrambone & S. (Eds.), *Proceedings of the 32nd Annual Conference of the Cognitive Science Society.*

[3]   Bobier, B., Stewart, T.C., Eliasmith, C. (2011). The attentional routing circuit: receptive field modulation through nonlinear dendritic interactions. *COSYNE.* Salt Lake City, Utah.

[4]   DeWolf, T., Eliasmith, C. (2010). NOCH: A framework for biologically plausible models of neural motor control. *Neural Control of Movement 20th Annual Conference.* Naples, FL.

[5]   Eliasmith, C., and Anderson, C.H. (2003). *Neural engineering: Computation, representation, and dynamics in neurobiological systems.* Cambridge, MA: MIT Press.

[6]   Stewart, T.C., Eliasmith, C. (2011). Neural Cognitive Modelling: A Biologically Constrained Spiking Neuron Model of the Tower of Hanoi Task. In L. Carlson, C. Hölscher, & T. Shipley (Eds.), *Proceedings of the 33rd Annual Conference of the Cognitive Science Society.*

[7]   Stewart, T.C., Choo, X., Eliasmith, C. (2010). Symbolic Reasoning in Spiking Neurons: A Model of the Cortex/Basal Ganglia/Thalamus Loop. *Proceedings of the 32nd Annual Meeting of the Cognitive Science Society.* Austin, TX: Cognitive Science Society.

[8]   Stewart, T.C., Choo, X., Eliasmith, C. (2010). Dynamic Behaviour of a Spiking Model of Action Selection in the Basal Ganglia. *10th International Conference on Cognitive Modeling.*

[9]   Anderson J. R., Kushmerick, N., & Lebiere, C. (1993). Tower of Hanoi and goal structures. In Anderson, J. R. *Rules of the Mind*, L. Erlbaum Associates.

[10]   Simon, H. A. (1975). The functional equivalence of problem solving skills. *Cognitive Psychology*, 7(2), 268–288

[11]   Altmann, E. M. & Trafton, J. G. (2002). Memory for goals: An activation-based model. *Cognitive Science*, 26, 39-83.

Biologically Inspired Cognitive Architectures 2011
A.V. Samsonovich and K.R. Jóhannsdóttir (Eds.)
IOS Press, 2011

A Plausible Logic Inference Engine

David STRACUZZI
Sandia National Laboratories PO Box 5800, MS1188 Albuquerque 87185-1188, USA
david.stracuzzi@gmail.com

Keywords. Reasoning, inference, logic, uncertainty, knowledge representation, heuristc, psychologically plausible

Abstract

Inference methods play a critical role in cognitive architectures. They support high-level cognitive capabilities such as decision-making, problem-solving, and learning by transforming low-level observations of the environment into high-level, actionable knowledge. However, most modern infernece methods rely on a combination of extensive knowledge engineering, vast databases, and domain constraints to succeed. This work makes an initial effort at combining results from artificial intelligence and psychology into a more pragmatic and scalable computational reasoning system. Our approach uses a combination of first-order logic and plausibility-based uncertainty consistent with methods first described by Polya [3]. Importantly, concerns with optimality and provability are dropped in favor of guidance heuristics derived from the psychological literature. In particular, these heuristics implement cognitive biases such as primacy/recency [1], confirmation [2], and coherence [4]. The talk illustrates core ideas with examples and discusses the advantages of the approach with respect to cognitive systems.

Acknowledgments

Sandia National Laboratories is a multi-program laboratory managed and operated by Sandia Corporation, a wholly owned subsidiary of Lockheed Martin Corporation, for the U.S. Department of Energy's National Nuclear Security Administration under contract DE-AC04-94AL85000.

References

[1] Ebbinghaus, H. Memory: A Contribution to Experimental Psychology. New York: Teachers College, Columbia University, 1913.
[2] Lord, C. G.; Ross, L.; and Lepper, M. R. Biased assimilation and attitude polarization: The effects of prior theories on subsequently considered evidence. Journal of Personality and Social Psychology 37(11):2098-2109, 1979.
[3] Polya, G. Mathematics and Plausible Reasoning, Volume II: Patterns of Plausible Inference. Princeton, NJ: Princeton University Press, 1954.
[4] Thagard, P. Explanatory coherence. Behavioral and Brain Sciences 12:435-467. 1989.

Biologically Inspired Cognitive Architectures 2011
A.V. Samsonovich and K.R. Jóhannsdóttir (Eds.)
IOS Press, 2011
doi:10.3233/978-1-60750-959-2-365

Analytic General Intelligence: Constructing Space+Time for the Lowen Model

Eugene J. Surowitz [1]

Abstract. The Lowen Model presents a graph of cycles among macroscopic processes of the mind. Developing of that model by adopting the feedback loop as the fundamental element, we can assemble various basic structures via space+time diagrams which can be used to form large, extended systems. The introduction of diagrammatic methods drastically eases the development and expression of structural concepts. Multilayer systems are formed from the basis elements by concatenating or gluing along common links to make them of arbitrary scale. Different types of multilayered systems are generated by the choice of which sections of the basis elements are glued together. A focus-bilens multilayer contains a middle layer of nodes that are not directly connected to each other. Generating graphs within this layer is hypothesized to provide a sufficient mechanism to implement the Lowen model's capacities; their dynamics are not addressed here.

Keywords. spacetime models feedback loops graphs psychology

This paper first provides a short introduction to the Lowen model of consciousness processing. Inspired by Jung's theory of psychological types, Walter Lowen, constructed a model of the conscious processes of the mind [1982]. Lowen founded his concepts on information processing and system theory rather than low level cognitive laboratory experiments [BICA2010]. First part of what follows takes a top-down viewpoint, starting with psychological phenomena and then works downward toward the neuroid and action-lens level discussed in my AGI-09 paper [2009].

1. The Lowen Graph of Capacities

The Lowen information processing model conceives of consciousness as constructed from specialized processes, variously termed capacities or poles. There are sixteen capacities that generate the Jungian personality types by their processing; the capacities are listed in the table.

While there is a developmental sequence, the earlier capacities are fully present in the mature adult and take part as co-equals in the processing of the adult's consciousness. The capacities are further clustered into various groups;

---

[1] New York University (visiting), New York, NY, USA; email: surow@attglobal.net

Table 1. Lowen Model Capacities

#	Capacity	Mode	#	Capacity	Mode
01	Signal	1 Concrete Body	09	Combination	3 Mouth People
02	Match	1 Concrete Body	10	Harmony	3 Mouth People
03	Contrast	1 Concrete Body	11	Preference	3 Mouth People
04	Control	1 Concrete Body	12	Association	3 Mouth People
05	Sign	2 Things Hand	13	Strategy	4 Abstract Mind
06	Feature	2 Things Hand	14	Pattern	4 Abstract Mind
07	Sort	2 Things Hand	15	Logic	4 Abstract Mind
08	Routine	2 Things Hand	16	Structure	4 Abstract Mind

the table exhibits those called modes. In the Lowen model the later capacities fully interact with the other capacities which are not subordinates, despite their prior development. An artificial general intelligence would be expected to require and include all the Lowen capacities.

The nature of the Lowen capacities can be gotten from a brief outline of one of them common in computational processes: Sort. There we see attitudes toward data order and ordering behavior. The Sorting Capacity exhibits choices that are routinely made:

- Readily accepts un-ordered input
- Readily accepts pre-ordered input
- Insists on pre-ordering before processing
- Internally orders input – output sequenced
- Internally orders input – output partially ordered
- Indifferent to input order – output order is the same
- Indifferent to input order – output order is different
- Rejects un-ordered input

The first and last of these represent a dichotomy, that is, extreme choices of behavior. Middle items are compromises or could be internal resource limitations. But these clearly are not something from Knuth; rather how the surface response pattern of a person appears to an external observer.

The Jung/Lowen capacities are phenomena that arise in longitudinal psychological studies and must ultimately reflect underlying support by neuron structures. The regularities of the capacities will be assumed to arise from action-lens structures outlined in [2009] and detailed below. But first the graph associated with the capacities is introduced (See Figure 1). For every capacity, the Lowen model has a corresponding processing pole. There is one pole per capacity; they are the more concrete aspect of the theory. The poles and their connectivity provide the wiring diagram for a processor complex along with its input sources and behavioral outputs. The types of sensory data preferentially handled by the various poles give rise to that wiring diagram and a modified concept of the number and functioning of the senses. The diagram presented here emphasizes the strongest connections defined by the model which comprise those labeled as the Contextual and Detailed circuits. Three other sets of progressively weaker connections are also present but omitted for the current presentation. The total graph

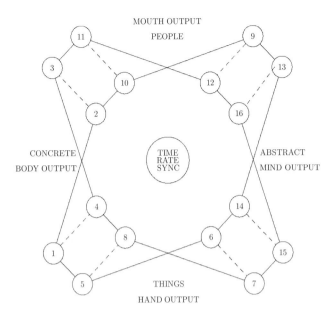

MOUTH OUTPUT
PEOPLE

CONCRETE
BODY OUTPUT

TIME
RATE
SYNC

ABSTRACT
MIND OUTPUT

THINGS
HAND OUTPUT

Figure 1. Lowen Graph

is richer in possible circuits but only a limited subset seems to be permissible and realized in personalities.

Sensory data is handled by the various capacities while eventually producing behavioral outputs. Studies of human brain functioning suggest that parallel and flow approaches are used by the mind and so the Lowen model should provide both. The connectivity graph gives massive parallel flow and dynamics while the individual poles are assumed to provide massive local parallelism adapted to their particular style of processing. The dashed lines depict linkage via specialized memories. The Lowen model's connectivity results in the two primary macroscopic processing circuits, the "contextual" and "detailed" circuits. These circuits, along with many other connection modes among the poles, communicate with each other to create the response patterns we call personality types.

The microstructure of neuroids, be they neurons or processors, and the macroscopic phenomena of psychology leave the middle or mesoscale undefined but do give boundary conditions to be matched. The Lowen model goes inward from longitudinal psychology toward an abstract information processing simulation which, in turn, begs for a structural solution based on neuroids. A stepwise development of those strucures now follows, culminating in possible cortex models.

The flows within the Lowen graph are highly cyclic and directed even though this has not been indicated in the diagram. Since the Lowen graph is replete with cycles and the literature of intelligence, artificial or otherwise, is also pervaded by references to feedback loop processing, it seems reasonable to expect cyclic processes to be fundamental at all scales. This becomes the assumption: The processing cycle, the feedback loop, is the fundamental unit of intellect and intelligence.

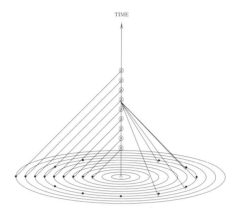

Figure 2. Cycle Space+Time

2. Cycle Space+Time

When neuroids are assembled into processing loops, they create a clock in the sense of responding to the relative evolution rates of two systems co-implemented with the same parts. In diagrammatic form, we have the neuroids, present as dots, and the linkage between them, as curved line segments; connections to elements external to the particular loop are suppressed. The directivity of signal flow is also not given in the diagrams as different structures will permit various possible flows with corresponding different behavioral implications. The times associated with a cycle of neuroidal processors realize the two rates: the inter-processor communication time and the total time to traverse the cycle. Physical implementations of feedback loops need not be flat as a diagram seems to imply; they can be arbitrarily twisted in space, even singly or multiply knotted. Those distortions leave the time-scale invariant. Adding or deleting neuroids does not.

Considering the set of all cycles, regardless of the number of neuroids, regardless of their knot topology, we can map them all onto the plane as concentric circles. This mapping is invertible for any particular cycle if the original topology is somehow retained, but in general any circular cycle can only be mapped back to the set all possible knot topologies. The image we obtain of the space of cycles, when restricted to some large but finite number of neuroids, resembles a Fresnel lens, to borrow a term from optics. Carrying the optical analogy further, we can draw a diagram of the cycle lens in the plane with a vertical time axis, whereon we plot the discrete cycle-times associated with each plotted cycle (See Figure 2).

3. The Action-Lens and its Structures

The action-lens structure is the immediate consequence of the space+time diagram. Take a loop of neuroids with a characteristic cycle-time as the base cycle and sample the state of the loop by connections to a common neuroid, the focus node, which results in "action-lens" diagram (See Figure 3).

The direction of signal travel is suppressed since the appropriate direction will depend on the function a particular action-lens has in larger structures. The

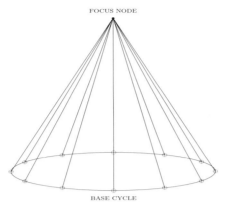

Figure 3. Action-Lens

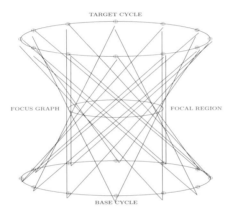

Figure 4. Action Focus-Bilens

processing of the action-lens can be disrupted in three ways: 1) Destruction of the focus which leads to the inability to behave in response to the state of the base cycle; 2) A break in the base cycle, leading to activity where the focus becomes a "source" lacking a stimulus; 3) Severance of some of the base-focus sensor lines gives a noise burdened response to the base cycle's state.

Taken by itself the action-lens could be little more than an arbitrary construction. However, it can also inspire further constructs by using it as a building block. The base cycle and the focal graph are convenient gluing regions for this assembly procedure. The resulting structures are the "focus-bilens" and its complement, the "base-bilens." An additional feature of actual physical or physiological realizations is the flexibility of the action-lens structure and any structures built from it. The conical appearance in the diagrams is illusory; they can be flattened or twisted arbitrarily without modification of functional properties.

The interactions occurring in the focal graph (aka: the focal region) can be considered to provide a basis for models of offline thinking as described by Devlin [2000]. The Lowen graph exhibits mental output in the right wedge; this output must also be an internal input feed. The bilens structure allows the hypothesis that the Lowen graph's mind output is in the form of inputs to the middle layer

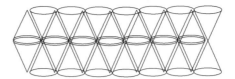

Figure 5. Action Double-Bilayer

of foci of a layer of focal bilenses. In other words, the mind output could be in the form of a layer's focus-bilens's internal processing together with internal connectivity among those foci.

4. Layered Structures

The simple action-lens construct just described lends itself to immediate further assembly into planes and layers. Action-lens structures laid out in two directions could be continued to cover an arbitrarily large portion of a plane, forming an "action-bilayer". Such layers can consist purely of focus-bilenses or of base-bilenses or they can be combined by gluing a "focus-bilens" next to a "base-bilens" so that the "base-bilens" nestles into the waist of the "focus-bilens," forming a "double-bilens." (See Figure 5)

The focal regions of the focus-bilenses and the bases of the base-bilenses create an intermediate layer. This "hidden" layer's focal regions may be taken to be relatively localized and could themselves form cycles. By providing connectivity among them, we can obtain other classes of graph structure within that hidden layer, with the focal regions acting as neuroids.

Now we have additional possible layers for simulations besides just the neuroidal and the surface stimulus-response patterns: the fundamental processes of the poles and the cycle based action-lens structures. The suggestion of adopting processing cycles as fundamental objects leads to a rich assortment of constructs for elaboration with the intent of building the capacities and directly addressing the mesoscale structure problem. It still remains to build the capacities from the structures. A more immediate target for this development will be abstract conceptual graphs, as described in Sowa [1984], appropriate to the capacities. This would provide a complete strucure for a Lowen model: implementation from the fundamental space+time considerations, to the conceptual graph level, on to the Lowen capacity level, and ultimately the Lowen graph level.

References

[2000]   Devlin, Keith: *The Math Gene.* Basic Books; New York, NY (2000)
[1982]   Lowen, Walter: *Dichotomies of the Mind.* John Wiley; New York, NY (1982)
[1984]   Sowa, John F.: *Conceptual Structures.* Addison-Wesley; Reading, MA (1984)
[2009]   Surowitz, Eugene J.: *Importing Space-time Concepts into AGI.* Artificial General Intelligence, Proceedings AGI-2009; Arlington, VA; Atlantis Pr.; Paris (2009), pp.216–217
[BICA2010]   Surowitz, Eugene J.: *Analytic General Intelligence: The Lowen Model.* Biologically Inspired Cognitive Architectures 2010

Biologically Inspired Cognitive Architectures 2011
A.V. Samsonovich and K.R. Jóhannsdóttir (Eds.)
IOS Press, 2011
doi:10.3233/978-1-60750-959-2-371

Cognitive control as a gated cortical net

Jared C. SYLVESTER [a,b,1], James A. REGGIA [a,b] and Scott WEEMS [b]

[a] *Deptartment of Computer Science, University of Maryland*
[b] *Center for Advanced Study of Language, University of Maryland*

Abstract. We present a cortical model of cognitive control based on attractor networks, correlational learning, and gating. Our model does not make use of production rules or local representations. It is capable of completing a demonstration task requiring adding to and examining working memory. The architecture used is easily generalizable to other tasks.

Keywords. Cognitive control, working memory, Hebbian learning, adaptive gating

1. Introduction

Rule-based, symbolic systems such as ACT-R and Soar are the most popular paradigm for models of cognitive control [1,2]. In the last several years neural network models of cognitive control have become more common. For instance, O'Reilly et al.'s PBWM working memory system takes a neural approach [3]. However, neural model of cognitive control are still in their infancy, and suffer from several common drawbacks. Many use localized representations of information, which are not commonly observed in biological neural networks, and are hard-wired to the specific tasks being addressed, such as the WCST [4] or Towers of Hanoi [5], and as such are difficult to generalize to other tasks. Other models, such as those of Stewart and Eliasmith [6], are more generalizable, but are built on models of spiking neurons can involve over one hundred thousand complex nodes. These models give impressive fidelity to human neural data, especially with regard to timing, but this comes at a cost of increased computational complexity. A common feature of these models is a concentration on the subcortical components of the basal ganglia and thalamus. The current ongoing work focuses more strongly on cortical components, especially the prefrontal cortex and anterior cingulate cortex. We plan on introducing sub-cortical components in the future, but are first exploring modeling cortical regions as a set of networks transmitting to and gating one another. These components are modeled as interacting attractor networks, including non-fixed-point networks for sequence processing.

Our goal is to demonstrate that cognitive control can be effectively modeled using methods closely aligned with those occurring in biological systems. To that end the model presented eschews symbolic production rules as well as presumed non-biological neural network techniques like error backpropagation. Instead we adopt several widely used characterizations of neural computation: representations are distributed across a population of neurons, the cortex is a network of regions that each act as attractor net-

---

[1] Corresponding Author: Dept. of Computer Science, A. V. Williams Bldg., University of Maryland, College Park, MD 20742; jsylvest@umd.edu.

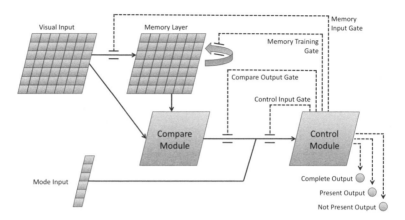

Figure 1. The store/recognize model. Thin, solid arrows denote one-to-one connections. The memory layer has full recurrent connections. Dashed line are the outputs of the Control Module. The number of boxes in the each layer does not faithfully represent the number of nodes used in the model.

works, recurrent connections are common within local cortical areas, and learning is based on correlations between activity [7]. This work serves as a proof-of-concept that a model following these principals can have an easily generalizable architecture and still successfully execute a specific cognitive control task. The focus is especially on using attractor networks to represent stable working memory patterns, as well as using gating to manage the flow of information between networks and the rapid updating of information.

2. Methods

The model is composed of six components (Figure 1): they are the visual and mode input layers, the output nodes, the memory layer, and the Compare and Control Modules. The visual input layer is set externally to represent the visual stimulus being presented. The mode input, also set externally, encodes the current system goal (something that will be determined ultimately by representing rostral prefrontal cortex functionality in a future version of the model). Output is through a set of linear threshold units from the Control Module. For the task used in the this paper, three such units are used.

The memory layer is a discrete Hopfield network forming an autoassociative memory used as a working memory, with limited capacity, high plasticity, and close integration with executive systems. Training of the memory layer is accomplished with standard one-shot Hebbian learning. Input h_i to each node i in the memory layer is composed of the influence of all other nodes in the layer along with a gated connection from the topologically corresponding node in the input layer, so that $h_i = 2g_{in}in_i + \sum_j w_{ij}a_j$, where g_{in} is the value of the gating node mediating the input-to-memory connections, in_i is the state of node i in the visual input layer, w_{ij} is the strength of the connection from node j to node i both in the memory layer, and a_j is the state of node j in the memory layer. The visual input-to-memory connection is used to enable the memory to be influenced towards or away from the current stimulus. When the gate is fully open ($g_{in} = 1$), the state of the memory is forced to become the same as the input layer. When the gate closes ($g_{in} = 0$), there is no influence from the input layer and the memory layer operates as a standard autoassociative memory.

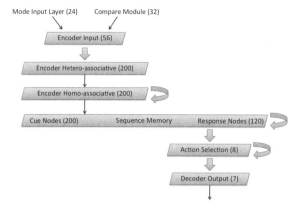

Figure 2. The Control Module. Thick arrows denote fully connected layers, while thin arrows denote one–to-one connections. The numbers indicate the number of nodes in each layer.

The Compare Module, inspired by anterior cingulate cortex functionality, assesses the similarity between the current state of the input and the memory layer, to which it has one-to-one input connections. One of two 32-bit patterns is output to indicate match/no-match. Distributed output patterns are used to avoid localized representations, and because the increased dimensionality makes it easier for the Control Module to distinguish between the two states.

The Control Module directs the operation of the rest of the model through a system of gates that modulate the flow of activity between different layers. For example, one of the Control Module's outputs manipulates the gate between the input layer and memory layer, controlling how much the former influences the latter. It, along with the memory, are inspired by the functionality of the dorso- and ventrolateral PFC regions. In addition to the manipulation of gates, the Control Module also activates the output nodes.

The core of the Control Module is an attractor network with temporally asymmetric weights, allowing it to store *sequences* of patterns [8]. Each pattern corresponds to a particular action the network may take, or more specifically, to a particular set of signals to open or close different gates and activate outputs. A sequence of these actions corresponds to the steps needed to address a particular situation.

The four gates which control the flow of activity throughout the model are:

1. a gate between the visual input layer and memory layer, so that the memory's current state can be biased towards or away from the current stimulus;
2. a gate that controls when the working memory updates its weight matrix W_M;
3. a gate that modulates the output of the Compare Module, so that it is possible to notice or ignore the similarity between input and memory state, and;
4. a gate that controls the input to the Control Module, so that the Control Module can control when it updates its own state.

The state of a gate node is given by $g^t = k_g g^{t-1} + s^t$, where k_g is a decay term, and s^t is the current value of the associated controller output signal. Gates are multiplicative, such that their output is the product of their input and their current state g^t.

The Control Module is composed of three subcomponents: encoder, sequence memory and decoder (Figure 2). The sequence memory stores the actions needed to respond to each circumstance. The encoder converts the inputs of the controller into the patterns stored in the sequence memory, while the decoder converts from those patterns into gating signals and outputs. Both of the latter are trained with Hebbian learning, and the decoder also makes use of competitive dynamics.

The sequence memory, which is the core of the Control Module, is a discrete Hopfield network modified in two ways. The first is the incorporation of temporally asymmetric weights, which makes sequential recall possible [8,9]. The second is a conceptual division of the nodes into two sets, the "cue" and "response" nodes.

The state of the cue nodes corresponds to the situation the model is facing. The state of the response nodes corresponds to one of the actions which should be taken in the current situation. The network is trained on multiple sequences, so the cue nodes provide the context information necessary to prompt the network to reproduce the correct sequence in the response nodes. Each pattern the network is trained on is the concatenation of one cue and one response pattern. Cue nodes receive an extra input from the encoder to bias their state towards the encoder's output. Only the response nodes are read by the decoder.

We illustrate the model's functionality with a specific example, the *store/recall task* which was developed to demonstrate that cognitive control is possible with these methods. Specifically, this task was designed so that the control system would have to consider two different inputs, make two different decisions based on them, one after the other, add inputs to a working memory, and search the contents of memory for a given pattern and recognize when it is present.

The store/recall task consists of a series of visual stimuli S, each paired with an instruction M (currently represented as an activity pattern over the mode layer) to either commit the stimulus to memory or to evaluate whether that stimulus is already in memory. These are termed the "load" and "evaluate" modes. After receiving a visual stimulus and a mode (S, M), the model processes this input until activating one of the three output nodes. When $M = load$ the model should activate the *complete* node signifying that it is done storing the stimulus. When $M = evaluate$ the model should output either *present* or *not present*, depending on whether the stimulus has previously appeared. In the latter case, the model should also store the stimulus in memory before signaling its output. This means when a novel pattern is evaluated twice the correct output is *not present* the first time, but *present* the second.

In this context, there are four different situations the Control Module needs to respond to in the course of executing the store/recall task, with each having an associated sequence of actions which form the desired response. There are many-to-one associations between cues and responses, that is, the same action may be a member of more than one sequence. These situations and their associated response sequences are:

1. $M = load$. Fully open the input-to-memory gate, forcing the state of the memory to match the input layer. Update W_M. Open Control Module input gate and activate *complete* output node.
2. $M = evaluate$. Partially open the input-to-memory gate, reshaping the memory's attractor landscape so that the state is biased in favor of S. Close the input-to-memory gate, removing bias. Open the output gate of the Compare Module in order to judge whether the memory layer has changed.
3. $M = evaluate$, Compare Module outputs high similarity. Activate *present* node.
4. $M = evaluate$, Compare Module outputs low similarity. Fully open the input-to-memory gate, forcing the state of the memory to match the input layer. Update W_M. Open Control Module input gate and activate *not present* output node.

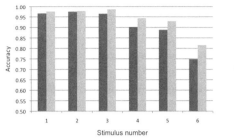 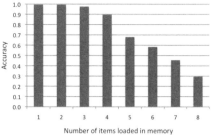

Figure 3. At left, the proportion of runs for which the model gave the correct output for each of the six stimuli in the ABAXYX version of the store/recall task. The dark bars are for runs using a decay in the controller's sequence memory of $k_D = 0$, while the light bars used $k_D = -0.05$. At right, results of the capacity tests. After loading one through eight stimuli into working memory, the first item loaded was evaluated. Shown is the proportion of runs which correctly identified that stimuli as having been previously seen.

3. Results

Given space limitations, we provide a single example of the model's behavior on a sample store/recall task. The first set of experiments uses random series of six inputs where the first and third as well as fourth and sixth visual inputs match, for example, "ABAXYX." The first two stimuli have $M = load$, the others have $M = evaluate$. Five hundred iterations using random visual stimuli were run. The model was judged based on the accuracy of each of the six outputs for each run, which can be seen in Fig 3 (left).

The Control Module is trained before the task begins, so that the sequence memory already contains the appropriate pairings conditions and responses (items $1 - 4$ above). Once the task begins its weights remain fixed. The memory layer, in contrast, begins the task in a blank, untrained state, and has its weights updated as the task progresses.

The average accuracy across all responses in all trials was 90.6%. Predictably, the sixth input is the most difficult to respond to correctly, because it requires the stimulus to have been identified as not present on its first presentation, and thus stored in working memory, for it to be correctly identified as present later.

We examined varying the decay rate governing the Control Module's sequence memory and found that small, negative decay rates performed the best. With a negative decay rate previous items in a sequence are amplified rather than weakened. This amplification enlarges the basin of attraction for earlier patterns in a sequence, making it easier for the memory to run through a sequence from the beginning. With a very small decay rate (-0.05), the average accuracy increased to 93.8%.

We also tested the capacity of the working memory layer. This was accomplished by performing a varying number of load operations, from one to eight, followed by a pair of evaluations. The first evaluation queried the model to see if it recalled being presented with the first stimulus, and the second evaluated a novel stimulus. This should produce an output of *present* followed by *not present*. For example, to test the model's ability to remember four items, the visual stimuli could have been ABCDAX. Figure 3 (right) shows the accuracy of the model on the former evaluation. (The model was very successful at correctly identifying the final input as novel; accuracy on that question ranged from 93.2% to 96.5% and was independent of the number of stimuli loaded.) Accuracy begins to drop off at a capacity of four, with performance dropping under 50% when seven items have been loaded. This corresponds well with measures of human working memory, which have found four items to be a typical capacity level [10].

4. Discussion

This paper introduces a neurally-oriented computational model of prefrontal cognitive control. It makes use of distributed representations, recurrent intra-area connections, and correlational learning, all of which are biologically justified. The control and working memory components are modeled by interacting attractor nets. The control mechanism expresses its influence through a gating system, which is a growing area of interest [11].

The proposed model of cognitive control is not intended to be an accurate simulation of the neurobiological mechanisms underlying human cognition, however, the model's architecture and functionality do take inspiration from what is known about such mechanisms. Several simplifications are involved. For example, the contribution of subcortical regions to cognition are not addressed yet, though they are planned for future expansions.

This model has shown the ability to successfully complete a demonstration task requiring a series of decisions based on multiple inputs, adding and recalling items from working memory, and recognizing novel inputs. It has also demonstrated a working memory capacity approximately equal to that of humans [10]. Though the example store/recall task is simple, it serves as an effective affirmation of the approach taken in this work-in-progress.

Crucially, our model is very generalizable. Adapting it to complete a different task is mostly a matter of re-learning sequences and outputs of the Control Module. Work is currently underway adapting the system to perform the n-back task, for example. Currently the model does not continue to learn once the task has begun. Because of this lack of ability to improve it could be viewed as behaving in a habitual rather than goal-oriented manner. We are exploring adding correlates of the basal ganglia and thalamus to the model in order to introduce more sophisticated adaptive action selection and reinforcement learning capabilities to address this.

Acknowledgements

Supported by funding from the US Government, including NSF award IIS-0753845.

References

[1] Anderson, J. "ACT: A simple theory of complex cognition." *Amer. Psychologist*, 51(4): 355–65. 1996.
[2] Laird, J., Rosenbloom, P., and Newell, A. "Soar: An architecture for general intelligence." *Artificial Intelligence*, 33: 1–64. 1987.
[3] O'Reilly, R., and Frank, M. "Making working memory work: A computational model of learning in the frontal cortex and basal ganglia." *Neural Computation*, 18: 283–328. 2006.
[4] O'Reilly, R., Noelle, D., Braver, T., and Cohen, J. "Prefrontal cortex and dynamic categorization tasks: Representational organization and neuromodulatory control." *Cerebral Cortex*, 12: 246–257. 2002.
[5] Dehaene, S, and Changeux, J. "A hierarchical neuronal network for planning behavior." *Proc. of the Nat'l Acad. of Sciences*, 94(24): 13293–13298. 1997.
[6] Stewart, T., and Eliasmith, C. "Neural cognitive modelling: A biologically constrained spiking neuron model of the Tower of Hanoi task." *Proc. of the 33rd Ann. Conf. Cog. Sci. Soc*, pp. 656–661. 2011.
[7] Polk, T., Simen, P., Lewis, R., and Freedman, E. "A computational approach to control in complex cognition." *Cognitive Brain Research*, 15(1): 71–83. 2002.
[8] Sylvester, J., Reggia, J., Weems, S., and Bunting, M. "A temporally asymmetric Hebbian network for sequential working memory." *Proc. of the Int'l Conf. on Cognitive Modeling*, pp. 241–246. 2010.
[9] Reggia, J., Sylvester, J., Weems, S., and Bunting, M. "A simple oscillatory short-term memory model." *Proc. of the AAAI Biologically-Inspired Cognitive Architecture Symposium*, pp. 103–108. 2009.
[10] Cowan, N. "The magical number 4 in short-term memory: A reconsideration of mental storage capacity." *Behavioral Brain Science*, 24(1): 87–114. 2001.
[11] O'Reilly, R., Herd, S., and Pauli, W. "Computational models of cognitive control." *Current Opinion in Neurobiology*, 20: 257–61. 2010.

Biologically Inspired Cognitive Architectures 2011
A.V. Samsonovich and K.R. Jóhannsdóttir (Eds.)
IOS Press, 2011
© *2011 The authors and IOS Press. All rights reserved.*
doi:10.3233/978-1-60750-959-2-377

MoNAD structure and the self-awareness

Junichi TAKENO [a,1]
[a] Robot Science Laboratory, Computer Science, Meiji University,
1-1-1Higashimita, Tama-ku, Kawasaki-shi, Kanagawa 214-8571 Japan
[a] juntakeno@gmail.com

Abstract. The authors have been studying a conscious module called Module of Nerves for Advanced Dynamics (MoNAD), which is the core of a conscious robot. The functions of a MoNAD satisfy the qualification requirements for human consciousness. A MoNAD is not a simple first-order reaction system but a redundant second-order system. Each MoNAD has two recursive neural networks that cross each other. One of the two recursive neural networks of the MoNADs processes information on the real world while the other performs high-level abstraction. Neurons present at the intersection of the two neural networks connect the real and the abstract (i.e., represented) world by synchronizing them. Playing the role of mirror neurons, these neurons provide a clue to solving the problem of symbol grounding. A MoNAD is a representation-driven machine. A MoNAD can also describe the function of self-awareness. Each MoNAD has two sets of input and output terminals to function as a bi-directional information network. A sophisticated system can be constructed by incorporating multiple MoNADs in the network. We call such an advanced system a 'conscious system' as a high order cybernetics.

Keywords. Self-awareness, robotics, consciousness

Introduction

Behavior and cognition are closely related to human consciousness. The authors express their relationship as follows:

"Consistency of cognition and behavior generates consciousness."

"Consistency" means that information circulates in the neural network stably within a certain state pattern.
At this time, the "information" of a certain "state pattern" becomes a "condition in which the current behavior is cognized," and the resultant cognition is represented by a symbol [1][2].

1. MoNAD Structure

The Module of Nerves for Advanced Dynamics, or MoNAD (Figure 1), is a computational model consisting of recurrent neural networks developed by the authors. It has been devised based on our definition of consciousness, which is that "consistency of cognition and behavior generates consciousness." MoNADs are the modules that make up our conscious system. We call them "conscious modules."

---

[1] Corresponding Author.

Each MoNAD comprises $(\bar{a})$ cognition system, $(\bar{b})$ behavior system, **e** primary representation unit (common area of cognition and behavior system), $(\bar{d})$ symbolic representation unit, and input/output units (S and M). The idea that "consistency of cognition and behavior generates consciousness," which represents our definition of consciousness, is artificially realized in the primary representation unit, which is the common area of the cognition and behavior systems. All MoNADs in the conscious system have received supervised learning individually according to their orientation.

The MoNADs are interconnected to one another to make up the conscious system. The actual neural network structure is shown in Figure 2. The number of elements in each MoNAD varies with the degree of orientation.[3][4]

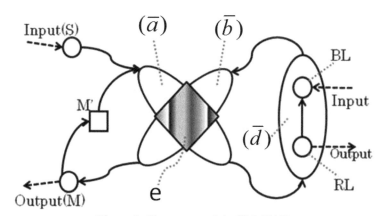

Figure 1. Concept model of MoNAD.

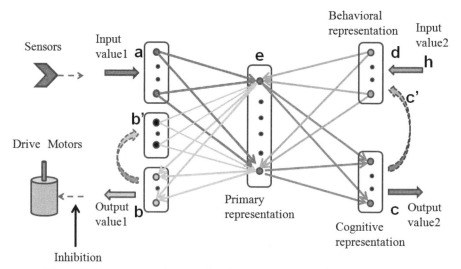

Figure 2. Explanatory drawing for the MoNAD conscious neural model.

A MoNAD has two closed loops: b-b'-e and c-c'-d-e. The two closed loops are synchronized at "e," which is called primary representation. "c" is called cognitive representation. Area "e" is called primary representation because it supplies raw information for generating cognitive representation "c." Area "d" is named behavioral representation. The above model is called "Module of Nerves for Advanced Dynamics" (MoNAD).

The features of the MoNAD system are described below.

First, the cognition processing program and behavior processing program cross each other at the intersection "e" in Figure 2. Stimuli entering the system at "a" are processed sequentially along the path of "a" through "e," with the end effect emerging at "c." The behavior of the system in response to the stimuli is determined as signal "d" is processed along the path of "d" through "e," with the determined behavior actualized at "b." In short, stimuli given at "a" produce a behavior at "b." This reaction is not simple but relatively complex in reality because the reaction is affected by past processes since the MoNAD is constructed of two recursive neural networks. Another source of complexity is that a different behavioral representation determined by external stimuli "h" can enter "d". Let us look at the area "e" more closely. It is part of the cognition-processing area and at the same time part of the behavior-processing area.

The area "e" consists of neurons that are related to both cognition and behavior. These neurons are very similar to the *mirror neurons* that were discovered recently. The activation, or firing, of the area "e" means that both behavior and cognition are being processed simultaneously. The firing of "e" means "a recognition that a certain behavior is being performed." This is very close to the previous statement that "what is being done is understood," which is one of the unique features of human consciousness.

The second feature of the MoNAD is described below.

We just mentioned that the area "e" is where the two closed circuits meet and are synchronized. Look at one of the closed loops of e-c-d. The firing of "e" is followed by the firing of "c," i.e., the condition of the firing of "e" is symbolized by a new language. This is an abstraction of the condition of "e," i.e., the firing of "c" represents that "a behavior is cognized." The state "c" is thus an abstract representation of the firing of neurons "e" in the MoNAD. This is the reason why "e" is called primary representation.

A description of the third feature follows.

The area "d" is where the next representation the system wishes to exhibit is shown. If the system wishes to use information c', which is the exact copy of "c," as the information for "d," the system is considered to be willing ("oriented") to accept the information meant by representation "c," which has already been cognized by the system. If, on the contrary, a new representation is given to "d" from an external stimulus, the system has the intention, or willingness, to select that external representation. The area "d" is related to expectation, which is at the same time the basis for a kind of "will."

The fourth feature is discussed next.

From the description of the third feature described above, the area "d" may be said to be an area of self-assertion because it contains information that asserts, "I would like to take this particular action in this given environment in such a way."

The fifth feature of the MoNAD is as follows:

The MoNAD cognizes what it is doing because information "b" enters the area "e" via b' at the same time as input "a" enters the area "e." The MoNAD has the capability to cognize its behavior using information obtained from b'.

The sixth and final important feature of the MoNAD is introduced below.

The system would have the function of inner thought if the information input from "b" into the drive motors could be somehow inhibited (Figure 2).

A MoNAD system with these features could be the core of a scheme resembling human consciousness because the system is capable of cognizing the environment and the behavior of others, understanding the behavior of the self, invoking a behavior from a representation, and engaging in inner thought.

2. Self-awareness

The authors' robot, which was equipped with this newly developed conscious system, succeeded in mirror image cognition tests. On the Internet, the authors' experiments were praised as a "demonstration of self-awareness." The authors therefore studied means to verify that their robot has the property of "self-awareness."[5]

What is self-awareness? This is the starting point of the discussion. We referred to literature extensively but no scientific description existed, although there are many discussions from philosophical points of view. The authors' views are described below.

In the authors' personal view, the five major essential properties of self-awareness are:
  (1) Cognize one's own behavior
  (2) Behave consistently
  (3) Possess a sense of cause and effect

(4) Cognize the behavior of others

(5) Possess a sense that the other is behaving at the command of the self

For item 1, the conscious module MoNAD of the authors feeds back information b' of the self's behavior to the cognition system. Accordingly, the behavior of the self is cognized.

With our conscious system, cognition and behavior are consistent, thus item 2 is satisfied.

In the conscious module MoNAD, behavior representation determines the execution of a behavior, and cognition representation is determined by the result of the behavior. Accordingly, behavior and the accompanying cognition have a causal relationship. From item 1, furthermore, this behavior is cognized as the behavior of the self. Item 3 is thus satisfied.

The cognition of the behavior of others can be calculated from the cognition of the behavior of the self. Hence item 4 is satisfied.

The image of the self robot reflected in the mirror is judged to be a part of the self, and thus item 5 is also satisfied.

The authors believe that qualia are sub-phenomena that accompany the phenomenon of consciousness. If the "sense" mentioned in items 3 and 5 above refers to qualia, this conclusion is premature, and requires further scrutiny.

3. Conclusion

The present paper introduces the conscious module MoNAD developed by the authors. Each MoNAD consists of two crossed recursive neural networks, with the values at their intersection being synchronous. We call this the *MoNAD structure*. The MoNAD's functions can explain the important aspects of human consciousness. This is outlined in the present paper. We assume that the MoNAD structure can describe the function of self-awareness, and this is also discussed in this paper.

References

[1] K. Inaba and J. Takeno, Consisitency betweeen recognition and behavior creates consciousness, *proceedings of SCI'03*, (2003), 341-346.
[2] T. Suzuki, K. Inaba and J. Takeno, Conscious Robot that Distinguishes between Self and Others and implements Imitation Behavior. *IEA/AIE*, (2005), 101-110.
[3] J. Takeno and K. Inaba, New Paradigm 'Consistency of cognition and behavior, *CCCT2003, Proceeding* Vol.1, ISBN 980-6560-05-1,(2003), 389-394.
[4] J. Takeno, K. Inaba and T. Suzuki, Experiments and examination of mirror image cognition using a small robot, *The 6th IEEE International Symposium on Computational Intelligence in Robotics and Automation*, (2005), 493-498.
[5] J. Takeno, *The Self Aware Robot*, HRI-Press, Tokyo, 2005.
[6] R. Igarashi, T. Suzuki, Y. Shirakura and J. Takeno, Realization of an emotional robot and imitation behavior. *The 13th IASTEND International Conference on Robotics and Applications*, RA2007, (2007), 135-140.

[7] J. Takeno, A Robot Succeeds in 100% Mirror Image Cognition, *International Journal on Smart Sensing and Intelligent Systems*, Vol. 1, No. 4, (2008), 891-911.
[8] T. Komatsu and J. Takeno, A conscious robot that expects emotion, *IEEE International Conference on Industrial Technology* (ICIT), (2011), 14-16.
[9] J. Takeno and S. Akimoto, Mental pain in the mind of a robot, *International Journal of Machine Consciousness* (IJMC), Vol.2, No.1, (2010), 333-342.

Biologically Inspired Cognitive Architectures 2011
A.V. Samsonovich and K.R. Jóhannsdóttir (Eds.)
IOS Press, 2011
doi:10.3233/978-1-60750-959-2-383

Learning Hierarchical Sparse Representations using Iterative Dictionary Learning and Dimension Reduction

Mohamad TARIFI [a,1], Meera SITHARAM [a] and Jeffery HO [a]

[a] *CISE, University of Florida*

Abstract. This paper introduces an elemental building block which combines Dictionary Learning and Dimension Reduction (DRDL). We show how this foundational element can be used to iteratively construct a Hierarchical Sparse Representation (HSR) of a sensory stream. We compare our approach to existing models showing the generality of our simple prescription. We then perform preliminary experiments using this framework, illustrating with the example of an object recognition task using standard datasets. This work introduces the very first steps towards an integrated framework for designing and analyzing various computational tasks from learning to attention to action. The ultimate goal is building a mathematically rigorous, integrated theory of intelligence.

Keywords. Hierarchy, Sparse Representation, Dimension Reduction

Introduction

Working towards a Computational Theory of Intelligence, we develop a computational framework inspired by ideas from Neuroscience. Specifically, we integrate notions of columnar organization, hierarchical structure, sparse distributed representations, and sparse coding.

An integrated view of Intelligence has been proptosed by Karl Friston based on free-energy [6]. In this framework, Intelligence is viewed as a surrogate minimization of the entropy of this sensorium. This work is intuitively inspired by this view, aiming to provide a computational foundation for a theory of intelligence from the perspective of theoretical computer science, thereby connecting to ideas in mathematics. By building foundations for a principled approach, the computational essence of problems can be isolated, formalized, and their relationship to fundamental problems in mathematics and theoretical computer science can be illuminated and the full power of available mathematical techniques can be brought to bear.

A computational approach is focused on developing tractable algorithms. exploring the complexity limits of Intelligence. Thereby improving the quality of available guarantees for evaluating performance of models, improving comparisons among models, and moving towards provable guarantees such as sample size, time complexity, generaliza-

---

[1]Corresponding Author: 530 Clement Dr, Glendale, CA 91202. email: mtarifi@cise.ufl.edu

tion error, assumptions about prior. This furnishes a solid theoretical foundation which may be used, among other things, as a basis for building Artificial Intelligence.

0.1. Background Literature In A Glance

Speculation on a cortical micro-circuit element dates back to Mountcastle's observation that a cortical column may serve as an algorithmic building block of the neocortex [10]. Later work by Lee and Mumford [9], Hawkins and George [7] attempted further investigation of this process.

The bottom-up organization of cortex is generally assumed to be a hetrarchical topology of columns. This can be modeled as a directed acyclic graph, but is usually simplified to a hierarchical tree. Work by Poggio, Serre, et al [12,13,14,15] discuss a hierarchical topology. Smale et al attempts to develop a theory accounting for the importance of the hierarchical structure [16,3].

Work on modeling early stages of sensory processing by Olshausen [11,1] using sparse coding produced results that account for the observed receptive fields in early visual processing. This is usually done by learning an overcomplete dictionary. However it remained unclear how to extend this to higher layers. Our work can be partially viewed as a progress in this direction.

Computational Learning Theory is the formal study of learning algorithms. PAC defines a natural setting for analyzing such algorithms. However, with few notable exceptions (Boosting, inspiration for SVM, etc) the produced guarantees are divorced from practice. Without tight guarantees Machine Learning is studied using experimental results on standard benchmarks, which is problematic. We aim at closing the gap between theory and practice by providing stronger assumptions on the structures and forms considered by the theory, through constraints inspired by biology and complex systems.

0.2. A Variety of Hierarchical Models

Several hierarchical models have been introduced in the literature. H-Max is based on Simple-Complex cell hierarchy of Hubel and Wiesel. It is basically a hierarchical succession of template matching and a max-operations, corresponding to simple and complex cells respectively [12].

Hierarchical Temporal Memory (HTM) is a learning model composed of a hierarchy of spatial coincidence detection and temporal pooling. Coincidence detection involves finding a spatial clustering of the input, while temporal pooling is about finding variable order Markov chains describing temporal sequences in the data.

H-Max can be mapped into HTM in a straightforward manner. In HTM, the transformations in which the data remains invariant is learned in the temporal pooling step. H-Max explicitly hard codes translational transformations through the max operation. This gives H-Max better sample complexity for the specific problems where translational invariance is present.

Bouvrie et al [3,2] introduced a generalization of hierarchical architectures centered around a foundational element involving two steps, Filtering and Pooling. Filtering is described through a reproducing Kernel $K(x, y)$, such as the standard inner product $K(x, y) = \langle x, y \rangle$, or a Gaussian kernel $K(x, y) = e^{-\gamma \|x-y\|^2}$. Pooling then remaps the result to a single value. Examples of pooling functions include max, mean, and l_p norm (such as l_1 or l_∞). H-max, Convolutional Neural Nets, and Deep Feedforward Neural Networks all belong to this category of hierarchical architectures corresponding to different choices of the Kernel and Pooling functions. Our model does not fall within Bouvrie's present framework, and can be viewed as a generalization of hierarchical models in which both HTM and Bouvrie's framework are a special case.

Friston proposed Hierarchical Dynamic Models (HDM) which are similar to the above mentioned architectures but framed in a control theoretic framework operating in continuous time [6]. A computational formalism of his approach is thus prohibitively difficult.

0.3. Scope

Our approach to the circuit element is an attempt to abstract the computationally fundamental processes. We conjecture a class of possible circuit elements for bottom-up processing of the sensory stream.

Feedback processes, mediating action and attention, can be incorporated into this model, similar to work by Chikkerur et al [5,4], and more generically to a theory by Friston [6]. We choose to leave feedback for future work, allowing us to focus here on basic aspects of this model.

1. DRDL Circuit Element

Our circuit element is a simple concatenation of a Dictionary Learning (DL) step followed by a Dimension Reduction (DR) step. Using an overcomplete dictionary increase the dimension of the data, but since the data is now sparse, we can use Compressed Sensing to obtain a dimension reduction.

1.1. Dictionary Learning

Dictionary Learning obtains a sparse representation by learning features on which the data x_i can be written in sparse linear combinations.

Definition 1. *Given an input set* $X = [x_0 \dots x_m]$, $x_i \in R^d$, *Dictionary Learning finds* $D = [v_0 \dots v_n]$ *and* $\theta = [\theta_i \dots \theta_m]$, *such that* $x_i = D\theta_i$ *and* $\|\theta_i\|_0 \leq s$.

Where the $\|.\|_0$ is the L_0-norm or sparsity. If all entries of θ_i are restricted to be non-negative, we obtain Sparse-Non-negative Matrix Factorization (SNMF). An optimization version of Dictionary Learning can be written as:

$$\min_{D \in R^{d,n}} \max_{x_i} \min \|\theta_i\|_0 : x_i = D\theta_i$$

In practice, the Dictionary Learning problem is often relaxed to the Lagrangian:

$$\min \|X - D\theta\|_2 + \lambda \|\theta\|_1$$

Where $X = [x_0...x_m]$ and $\theta = [\theta_0...\theta_m]$. Several dictionary learning algorithms work by iterating the following two steps.

1. Solve the vector selection problem for all vectors X. This can be done using your favourite vector selection algorithm, such as basis pursuit.
2. Given X, the optimization problems is now convex in D. Use your favorite method to find D.

1.2. Dimension Reduction

The DL step learns a representation θ_i of the input that lives in a high dimension, but we can obtain a lower dimensional representation, since θ_i is now readily seen as sparse in the standard orthonormal basis of dimension n. We can obtain a dimension reduction by using applying a linear operator satisfying the Restricted Isometry Property from Compressed Sensing theory.

Definition 2. *A linear operator A has the Restricted Isometry Property (RIP) for s, iff $\exists \delta_s$ such that:*

$$(1 - \delta_s) \leq \frac{\|Ax\|_2^2}{\|x\|_2^2} \leq (1 + \delta_s) \tag{1}$$

An RIP matrix can compress sparse data while maintaining their approximate relative distances. This can be seen by considering two s-sparse vectors x_1 and x_2, then:

$$(1 - \delta_{2s}) \leq \frac{\|Ax_1 - Ax_2\|_2^2}{\|x_1 - x_2\|_2^2} \leq (1 + \delta_{2s}) \tag{2}$$

Given an s-sparse vector of dimension n, RIP reduces the dimension to $O(s \log(n))$. Since we are using an RIP matrix, efficient decompression is guaranteed using L_1 approximation. The data can be recovered exactly using L1 minimization algorithms such as Basis Pursuit.

RIP matrices can be obtained probabilistically from matrices with random Gaussian entries. Alternatively RIP matrices can be obtained using sparse random matrices [8]. In this paper we follow the latter approach. The question of deterministically constructing RIP matrices with similar bounds is still open.

2. A Hierarchical Sparse Representation

If we assume a hierarchical architecture modeling the topographic organization of the visual cortex, a singular DRDL element can be factorized and expressed as a tree of simpler DRDL elements. With this architecture we can learn a Hierarchical Sparse Representation by iterating DRDL elements.

2.1. Assumptions of Generative Model

Our models assumes that data is generated by a hierarchy of spatiotemporal invariants. At any given level i, each node in the generative model is assumed to be composed of a small number of features s_i . Generation proceeds by recursively decompressing the pattern from parent nodes then producing patterns to child nodes. This input is fed to the learning algorithm bellow. In this paper we assume that both the topology of generative model and the spatial and temporal extent of each node is known. Discussion of algorithms for learning the topology and internal dimensions is left for future work.

Consider a simple data stream consisting of a spatiotemporal sequences from a generative model defined above. Figure 1 shows a potential learning hierarchy. For simple vision problems, we can consider all dictionaries within a layer as the same. In this paper, processing proceeds bottom-up the hierarchy only.

2.2. Learning Algorithm

Recursively divide the spatiotemporal signal x_i to obtain a tree representing the known topographic hierarchy of spatiotemporal blocks. Let $x_{i,j}^0$ be the jth block at level 0. Then, starting a the bottom of the tree, do:

1. Learn a Dictionary $D_{j,k}$ in which the spatiotemporal data $x_{i,j}^k$ can be represented sparsely. This produces a vector of weights $\theta_{i,j,k}$.
2. Apply dimensionality reduction to the sparse representation to obtain $u_{i,j,k} = A\theta_{i,j,k}$.
3. Generate $x_{i,j}^{k+1}$ by concatenating vectors $u_{i,l,k}$ for all l that is child of j in at level k in the tree. Replace $k = k + 1$. And now j ranges over elements of level k. If k is still less than the depth of the tree, go to Step 1.

Note that in domains such as computer vision, it is reasonable to assume that all Dictionaries at level i are the same $D_{j,k} = D_k$. This algorithm attempts to mirror the generative model. It outputs an inference algorithm that induces a hierarchy of sparse representations for a given data point. This can be used to abstract invariant features in the new data. One can then use a supervised learning algorithm on top of the invariant features to solve classification problems.

3. Experiments

In this section we elaborate on preliminary numerical experiments performed with DRDL and HSR on basic standard Machine Learning datasets. We applied our model to the MNIST and COIL datasets and subsequently used the representation as a feature extraction step for a classification algorithm such as Support Vector Machines (SVM) or k-Nearest Neighbors (kNN). In practice, additional prior assumptions can be included in our model as discussed in the appendix.

Method	Error %
Reconstructive Dictionary Learning	4.33
Supervised Dictionary Learning	1.05
k-NN , l_2	5.0
SVM-Gauss	1.4
One layer of DRDRL	1.24
Two layers of HSR	2.01

Figure 1. A straightforward application of our approach is competitive on the MNIST dataset

Method	Classification %
One layer of DRDRL	87.8
SVM	84.9
Nearest Neighbor	81.8
VTU	89.9
CNN	84.8

Figure 2. A straightforward application of our approach is competitive on the COIL dataset

References

[1]   Bruno a Olshausen and David J Field. Emergence of simple cell receptive field properties by learning a sparse code for natural images, 1996.

[2]   Jake Bouvrie, Tomaso Poggio, Lorenzo Rosasco, Steve Smale, and Andre Wibisono. Computer Science and Artificial Intelligence Laboratory Technical Report Generalization and Properties of the Neural Response Generalization and Properties of the Neural Response. *City*, 2010.

[3]   Jake Bouvrie, Lorenzo Rosasco, and Tomaso Poggio. On Invariance in Hierarchical Models. *Technology*, pages 1–9.

[4]   Sharat S. Chikkerur, Thomas Serre, Cheston Tan, and Tomaso Poggio. What and where: A Bayesian inference theory of attention. *Vision Research*, May 2010.

[5]   Sharat S. Chikkerur, Cheston Tan, Thomas Serre, and Tomaso Poggio. An integrated model of visual attention using shape-based features.

[6]   Karl J Friston, James Kilner, and Lee Harrison. A free energy principle for the brain. *Journal of physiology, Paris*, 100(1-3):70–87.

[7]   Dileep George and Jeff Hawkins. Towards a mathematical theory of cortical micro-circuits. *PLoS computational biology*, 5(10):e1000532, October 2009.

[8]   Anna Gilbert and Piotr Indyk. Sparse Recovery Using Sparse Matrices. *Proceedings of the IEEE*, 98(6):937–947, June 2010.

[9]   Tai Sing Lee and David Mumford. Hierarchical Bayesian inference in the visual cortex. *Journal of the Optical Society of America. A, Optics, image science, and vision*, 20(7):1434–48, July 2003.

[10] Vernon B. Mountcastle. *Perceptual Neuroscience: The Cerebral Cortex*. Harvard University Press, 1998.

[11] Bruno A Olshausen and D J Field. Sparse coding with an overcomplete basis set: a strategy employed by V1? *Vision research*, 37(23):3311–25, December 1997.

[12] M Riesenhuber and Tomaso Poggio. Hierarchical models of object recognition in cortex. *Nature neuroscience*, 2(11):1019–25, November 1999.

[13] Thomas Serre, Gabriel Kreiman, Minjoon Kouh, Charles Cadieu, Ulf Knoblich, and Tomaso Poggio. A quantitative theory of immediate visual recognition. *Brain*, 165:33–56, 2007.

[14] Thomas Serre, Aude Oliva, and Tomaso Poggio. A feedforward architecture accounts for rapid categorization. *Proceedings of the National Academy of Sciences of the United States of America*, 104(15):6424–9, April 2007.

[15] Thomas Serre, Lior Wolf, Stanley Bileschi, Maximilian Riesenhuber, and Tomaso Poggio. Robust object recognition with cortex-like mechanisms. *IEEE transactions on pattern analysis and machine intelligence*, 29(3):411–26, March 2007.

[16] Steve Smale, Tomaso Poggio, Andrea Caponnetto, and Jake Bouvrie. Derived Distance : towards a mathematical theory of visual cortex . *Artificial Intelligence*, 2007.

Biologically Inspired Cognitive Architectures 2011
A.V. Samsonovich and K.R. Jóhannsdóttir (Eds.)
IOS Press, 2011
doi:10.3233/978-1-60750-959-2-389

A Computational Agent Model Using Internal Simulation to Generate Emotional Dream Episodes

Jan TREUR

VU University Amsterdam, Agent Systems Research Group
De Boelelaan 1081, 1081 HV, Amsterdam, The Netherlands
Email: treur@cs.vu.nl   URL: http://www.cs.vu.nl/~treur

Abstract. In this paper a computational agent model is presented that models dreaming based on internal simulation. Building blocks for this internal simulation are memory elements in the form of sensory representations and their associated emotions. In the model, under influence of associated feeling levels and mutual competition, some sensory representation states pop up in different dream episodes. The activation levels of both the feeling and the sensory representation states are regulated by control states. The model was evaluated by a number of simulation experiments for different scenarios.

Keywords. Dreaming, internal simulation, emotion, computational agent model.

Introduction

The mechanisms and functions of dreaming have received much attention in the recent cognitive and neurological literature; e.g., [20, 24, 25, 27, 31, 32, 35, 36]. As often negative emotions play an important role in dreams, this aspect is also addressed in some depth, especially in the context of improving skills for coping with threatening situations (e.g., [27, 31, 32]) or strengthening regulation of fear emotions by what is called fear extinction learning (e.g., [24, 34]). Abstracting from more specific context or purpose, a more general perspective present in dream literature as mentioned, is that dreaming can be considered a form of internal simulation of real-life-like processes as a form of training in order to learn, adapt or improve capabilities, which would be less easy to achieve in real life.

In this paper a computational agent model is presented that involves the type of internal simulation that is assumed to take place in dreaming. For the different episodes, the internal simulation incorporates interrelated processes of activation of sensory representation states (from memory) providing mental images, and activation of associated feelings. Moreover, the model uses a mechanism for emotion regulation to suppress the feeling levels and the sensory representation states.

The structure of the paper is as follows. In Section 1 the basic concepts used are briefly introduced. In Section 2 the computational model is described in more detail. Section 3 discusses simulation results providing dream scenarios. In Section 4 the relation of the model with neurological theories and findings is addressed. Finally, Section 5 is a discussion.

1. Memory Elements, Emotions and Internal Simulation in Dreaming

In this section it is discussed how in dreaming memory elements with their associated emotions are used as building blocks for an internal simulation of real life.

Using memory elements and their emotional associations Within the literature the role of memory elements providing content for dreams is well-recognized; e.g.:

> '… dreaming tends to express memory elements as though original memories had been reduced to more basic units (..). Often, these appear as isolated features, such as an attribute of a familiar place or character (e.g., "there was a stranger who had my mother's style of hair").' ([24], p. 499)

The role of emotional aspects in activating such memory elements is emphasized; e.g.:

> '…elements may be activated as a function of emotional concerns (..) but with the possible introduction of some pseudorandom and incompatible associations.' ([24], p. 500)

In particular, it is recognized that the choice for memory elements with some emotional association and (re)combining them into a dream facilitates fear generation:

> 'During dreaming, conjunctive representations are rendered into virtual simulations or "here-and-now" illusions [26] to maximize their impact upon the amygdala, which tends to respond to perceptual, rather than imaginal, stimuli' ([24], p. 500)

The emotional associations of the sensory memory elements may make that a person has to cope with high levels of emotions (e.g., fear) felt in the dream. *Emotion regulation* mechanisms are used to control emotions that are felt as too strong; cf. [12, 14, 15]. Such mechanisms cover *antecedent-focused regulation* (e.g., selection and modification of the situation, attentional deployment, and reappraisal) and *response-focused regulation* (suppression of a response).

Dreaming as internal simulation Dreams can be considered as flows of activated sequences of images based on (re)combined memory elements:

> 'Recombinations of memory elements give dreams at once their alien and their familiar quality. (…) the new image sequences consist, for the most part, of lifelike simulations of first-person reality. Memory elements are recombined (..) to produce coherent, continuous simulations of waking life experience.' ([24], p. 500)

Such flows can be related to the notion of *internal simulation* put forward, among others, by [18, 19, 6, 7, 13]. The idea of internal simulation is that sensory representation states are activated (e.g., mental images), which in response trigger associated preparation states for actions or bodily changes, which, by prediction links, in turn activate other sensory representation states.

sensory representation states → preparation states → sensory representation states

The latter states represent the effects of the prepared actions or bodily changes, without actually having executed them. Being inherently cyclic, the simulation process can go on indefinitely. Internal simulation has been used, for example, to describe (imagined) processes in the external world (e.g., prediction of effects of own actions [3]), or processes in another person's mind (e.g., emotion recognition or mindreading [13]) or processes in a person's own body (e.g., [6]). Although usually internal simulation as briefly described above concerns mental processes for awake persons, it is easy to imagine that it may be applicable as well to describe dreaming.

Feeling emotions by internal simulation of body states The idea of internal simulation has been exploited in particular by applying it to bodily changes expressing emotions, using the notion of *as-if body loop* [6]. A classical view on emotions is that based on some represented sensory input, due to internal processing, emotions are felt, and based on that they are expressed in a body state, for example, a face expression:

sensory representation → felt emotion → preparation for bodily changes →
expressed bodily changes = expressed emotion

In [23] a different causal chain was claimed, a *body loop* (cf. [23]; [9], pp. 114-116):

sensory representation → preparation for bodily changes → expressed bodily changes →
emotion felt = based on sensory representation of (sensed) bodily changes

Damasio made an important further step by introducing the possibility of internal simulation by an *as-if body loop* bypassing actually expressed bodily changes (cf. [6], pp. 155-158; [7], pp. 79-80; [9]):

sensory representation → preparation for bodily changes = emotional response →
emotion felt = based on sensory representation of (simulated) bodily changes

An as-if body loop describes an inner simulation of bodily processes, without actually affecting the body. Note that, in contrast to [23], in [6] an emotion (or emotional response) is distinguished from a feeling (or felt emotion). The emotion and feeling mutually affect each other: an as-if body loop usually occurs in an extended, cyclic form by assuming that the emotion felt in turn also affects the prepared bodily changes, as he points out, for example, in ([8], pp. 91-92; [9], pp. 119-122):

emotion felt = based on sensory representation of (simulated) bodily changes →
preparation for bodily changes = emotional response

On purposes of dreaming as internal simulation One theory explicitly referring to a purpose of dreaming as internal simulation is the threat simulation theory of the evolutionary function of dreaming (cf. [27, 31, 32]). This theory assumes that dreaming is an evolutionary adaptation to be able to rehearse coping with threatening situations in a safe manner. Others consider the function of dreaming in strengthening the emotion regulation capabilities for fear; e.g., [24, 25, 11, 16, 33, 34, 36]. For this perspective, the purpose of dreaming is to improve the coping with the own fear emotions in real life. For both purposes adequate exercising material is needed for the dreams: fearful situations have to be imagined, built on memory elements suitable for fear arousal. The agent model presented in Section 2 provides this, but it abstracts from the purpose; it does not commit to any of the purposes mentioned.

2. A Computational Agent Model Generating Dream Episodes

The computational agent model presented here formalises the mechanisms introduced in Section 1. It is meant to address scenarios of the following type:

- A (traumatic) stimulus s_1 is given for which previously a high extent of fear has been developed, and for which from time to time a sensory representation state is triggered by memory (for the model this is considered an external trigger)
- The activation of the sensory representation of s_1 leads to preparation for a bodily fear response b, and by an as-if body loop to an enhanced feeling level based on b
- By emotion regulation the sensory representation of s_1 and the feeling state are suppressed: both the experience of fear, and the activation level of the sensory representation of s_1 become low; also no episode state for s_1 occurs, as this is blocked due to the traumatic event
- Other fear-associated stimuli s_k for $k \geq 2$ are available for which the person has less strong previous experiences; the sensory representation states for these s_k are activated by links from the preparation state for b, depending on the strength of these links

- When the sensory representation state of a stimulus s_k is activated, this leads to an enhanced activation level of the preparation state for b
- Due to the higher activation level of preparation for b, via the as-if body loop also the feeling level for b becomes higher: the person experiences more fear
- By the control states for emotion regulation for an active sensory representation for s_k both the fear feeling level and the sensory activation level of s_k are suppressed
- The active sensory representations for s_k lead to corresponding dream episode states, which are in competion with each other by mutual inhibition to get dominance in the dream episode

In Figure 1 the basic model for a given sensory representation state srs_{s_k} is shown. It shows emotion generation via emotional response preparation state ps_b and feeling state fs_b (as-if body loop) and emotion regulation through control state cs_{s_kb} suppressing the feeling state fs_b and the given sensory representation state srs_{s_k}; a summary of the states used is shown in Table 1. The inhibiting links are indicated by dotted arrows (in red). The two links between srs_{s_k} and ps_b indicate the association between stimulus s_k and emotional response b. The links between ps_b and fs_b indicate an as-if body loop.

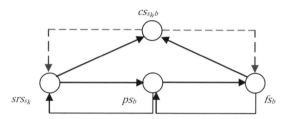

Figure 1. Basic model for generation and regulation of felt emotions

Table 1. Overview of the states used

state	explanation
ps_b	Preparation state for bodily response b
fs_b	Feeling state for b
srs_{s_k}	Sensory representation state for s_k
$cs_{s_k b}$	Control state for regulation of sensory representation of s_k and feeling b
es_{s_k}	Episode state for s_k
mt_{s_k}	Memory trigger for s_k

As shown in Table 1 a dream episode state for s_k is indicated by es_{s_k}; moreover the trigger for srs_{s_k} from memory is indicated by mt_{s_k}; this will be applied for s_1. Note that in Figure 1 a sensory representation state for only one stimulus s_k is depicted. In the specification of the model below an arbitrary number n of such states are taken into account. See Figure 2 for an overall picture for 4 stimuli, also with the episode states. The computational agent model has been formalised by a set of dynamic properties presented in a semiformal manner and also by a set of differential equations in Box 1. During processing, each state property has a strength represented by a real number between 0 and 1. Parameter γ is a speed factor, indicating the speed by which an activation level is updated upon received input from other states. Below, the dynamics are described in more detail. This is done for each state by a dynamic (temporally) Local Property (LP) specifying how the activation value for this state is updated (after a time step of Δt) based on the activation values of the states connected to it (the incoming arrows in Figures 1 and 2).

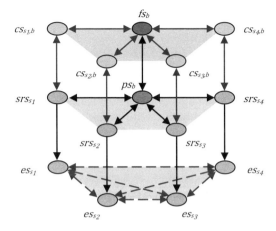

Figure 2. Overall model with four episode states and one feeling state ($m = 1$, $n = 4$)

Table 2. Overview of connections and weights

from states	to state	weights	LP
$srs_{s1}, ..., srs_{sn}, fs_b$	ps_b	$\omega_{11}, ... \omega_{1n}, \omega_2$	LP1
$ps_b, cs_{s1,b}, ..., cs_{sn,b}$	fs_b	$\omega_3, \omega_{41}, ...\omega_{4n}$	LP2
$ps_b, cs_{sk,b}, mt_{sk}$	srs_{sk}	$\omega_{5k}, \omega_{6k}, \omega_{0k}$	LP3
srs_{sk}, fs_b	$cs_{sk,b}$	ω_{7k}, ω_{8k}	LP4
$srs_{sk}, es_{s1}, ..., es_{sn}, cs_{sk,b}$	es_{sk}	$\omega_{9k}, \omega_{10,1k}, ..., \omega_{10,nk}, \omega_{11,k}$	LP5

Modeling causal relations discussed in neurological literature in the manner as presented in Section 1 does not take specific neurons into consideration but uses more abstract mental states. In this way abstraction takes place by lifting neurological knowledge to a mental (cognitive/affective) modelling level. The type of agent model that results shows some technical elements from the neural modelling area. More specifically, it takes states as having a certain activation level (instead of binary states), thus making reciprocal cognitive/affective loops possible. To achieve this, the modelling approach exploits techniques used in continuous-time recurrent neural networks, in line with what is proposed in [4], adopting elements from [21, 22]. In particular, for a state causally depending on multiple other states, values for incoming activation levels are combined, using a combination function. Note that such combination functions also play a role in the area of modelling imperfect reasoning, for example, based on fuzzy or uncertain information.

In the update specifications a combination function based on a threshold function th is used for k incoming connections as follows: $th(\mu_1 V_1 + ... + \mu_k V_k)$ with μ_i the connection strength for incoming connection i and V_i the activation level of the corresponding connected state. For this threshold function th different choices can be made. In the simulation experiments (in LP1 to LP4) the following continuous logistic form is used:

$$th(X) = \left(\frac{1}{1 + e^{-\sigma(X - \tau)}} - \frac{1}{1 + e^{\sigma\tau}}\right)(1 + e^{-\sigma\tau}) \quad \text{or} \quad th(X) = \frac{1}{1 + e^{-\sigma(X - \tau)}}$$

Here σ is a steepness and τ a threshold parameter. Note that for higher values of $\sigma\tau$ (e.g., σ higher than $20/\tau$) the threshold function on the left hand side is approximated by the simpler expression on the right hand side (this has been used in LP5). The first property

LP1 describes how preparation for response b is affected by the sensory representations of stimuli s_k (triggering the response), and by the feeling state for b:

LP1 Preparation state for response b
If   sensory representation states of s_k ($k = 1, 2, \ldots$) have level V_{1k}
 and the feeling state for b has level V_2 and   the preparation for b has level V_3
then   after Δt the preparation state for b will have level $V_3 + \gamma\,[\ th(\Sigma_k\omega_{1k}V_{1k} + \omega_2 V_2) - V_3\,]\,\Delta t.$

The feeling state for b is not only affected by a corresponding preparation state for b, but also by the inhibiting control states for s_k and b. This is expressed in dynamic property LP2. Note that for this suppressing effect the connection weight ω_{4k} from the control state for s_k and b to feeling state for b is taken negative, for example $\omega_{4k} = -1$.

LP2 Feeling state for b
If   the preparation state for b has level V_1
 and the control states for s_k and b ($k = 1, \ldots, n$) have levels V_{2k}
 and the feeling state for b has level V_3
then   after Δt the feeling state for b will have level $V_3 + \gamma\,[\ th(\omega_3 V_1 + \Sigma_k\,\omega_{4k}V_{2k}) - V_3\,]\,\Delta t.$

The sensory representation state for s_k is triggered by memory state mt_{s_k} and further affected by the preparation state for b, and by the suppressing control state for s_k and b. For this suppressing effect the connection weight ω_{6k} from the control state for s_k and b is taken negative. This is expressed in dynamic property LP3.

LP3 Sensory representation state for s_k
If   the preparation state for b has level V_1 and   the control state for s_k and b has level V_{2k}
 and the memory trigger for s_k has level V_{3k}
 and the sensory representation state for s_k has level V_{4k}
then   after Δt the sensory representation state for s_k will have
       level $V_{4k} + \gamma\,[\ th(\omega_{5k}V_1 + \omega_{6k}V_{2k} + \omega_{0k}V_{3k}) - V_{4k}\,]\,\Delta t.$

Note that property LP3 can be used to describe how the sensory representation of any traumatic s_k is triggered from memory, as a starting point for a dream: in a scenario the memory trigger values are taken 1. For non-traumatic s_k such triggering does not take place: the values are set to 0.

Activation of a control state for a specific sensory representation for s_k and b is based on the level of feeling b and the level of the sensory representation of s_k:

LP4 Control state for s_k and b
If   the sensory representation state for s_k has level V_{1k} and the feeling state for b has level V_2
 and the control state for s_k and b has level V_{3k}
then   after Δt the control state for s_k and b will have level $V_{3k} + \gamma\,[\ th(\omega_{7k}V_{1k} + \omega_{8k}V_2) - V_{3k}\,]\,\Delta t.$

Due to the inherent parallellism in neural processes, at each point in time multiple sensory representation states can be active simultaneously. For cases of awake functioning the *Global Workspace Theory* ([1, 2]) was developed to describe how a single flow of conscious experience can come out of such a large multiplicity of (unconscious) processes; see also [29] for an approach combining internal simulation and Global Workspace Theory. The basic idea is that based on the various unconscious processes a *winner-takes-it-all competition* takes place to determine which one will get dominance and be included in the single flow of consciousness (after which it is accessible to all processes). This idea was applied in the dreaming context to determine which sensory representation element will be included as an episode state ess_k in a dream episode. This competition process is decribed in LP5, using inhibiting connections from the episode states ess_i with $i \neq k$ to ess_k. For the suppressing effects the connection weights from the es_{si} with $i \neq k$ to es_{sk} are taken negative. Note that for the sake of notational simplicity $\omega_{10,kk} = 0$ is taken. For traumatic stimuli s_k an additional and strong way of inhibition of the corresponding episode state takes place, blocking the generation of an episode state for this stimulus. It is based on the control state for s_k and b and is assumed to have a strong negative connection strength ω_{e3k}. For non-traumatic stimuli this connection is given strength 0.

LP5 Episode state for s_k
If   the sensory representation state for s_k has level V_{1k}
 and the control state for s_k and b has level V_{2k}
 and the episodic states for $s_i (i = 1, ...)$ have level V_{3i}
then after Δt the episodic state for s_k will have
$$\text{level } V_{2k} + \gamma [th(\omega_{9k}V_{1k} + \omega_{11,k}V_{2k} + \Sigma_i \omega_{10,ik}V_{2i}) - V_{2k}] \Delta t.$$

LP1 Preparation state for response b
$$d\,ps_b(t)/dt = \gamma [th(\Sigma_k \omega_{1k}srs_{sk}(t) + \omega_2 fs_b(t)) - ps_b(t)]$$
LP2 Feeling state for b
$$d\,fs_b(t)/dt = \gamma [th(\omega_3 ps_b(t) + \Sigma_k \omega_{4k} cs_{sk,b}(t)) - fs_b(t)]$$
LP3 Sensory representation state for s_k
$$d\,srs_{sk}(t)/dt = \gamma [th(\omega_{5k} ps_b(t) + \omega_{6k} cs_{sk,b}(t) + \omega_{6k} mt_{sk}(t)) - srs_{sk}(t)$$
]
LP4 Control state for s_k **and** b
$$d\,cs_{sk,b}(t)/dt = \gamma [th(\omega_{7k} srs_{sk}(t) + \omega_{8k} fs_b(t)) - cs_{sk,b}(t)]$$
LP5 Episode state for s_k

Box 1. The computational agent model in differential equation format

3. Simulations of Example Dream Scenarios

A variety of simulation experiments have been performed, using numerical software. In the simulation experiments discussed below the settings were as shown in Table 3 (set by hand). As shown in the left hand side of the table, all noninhibiting connections to preparation, feeling and control states have strength 1, and all inhibiting connections to feeling and sensory representation states have strengths -0.2, resp. -0.5, with an exception for the sensory representation state for s_1, which is inhibited by strength -1 (due to a previous traumatic event involving s_1). Small differences in emotional association between the different s_k are expressed by different strengths from preparation of emotional response to sensory representation states, varying from 0.5 to 0.45. The sensory representation states are connected to the corresponding episode states with strength 1.2 and the latter states mutually inhibit each other by strength -0.6. The threshold and steepness values used are shown in the right hand side of Table 3. Relatively low steepness values were used, except for the episode states. The threshold values for preparation and feeling states were taken 0.5; in order to model differences in emotional associations between the s_k, different threshold values were taken for their sensory representation and control states. The initial values of all states were set to 0, except for the initial value of srs_{s1} which was set to 1 (a memory activation for a traumatic event). The speed factor γ was 0.5, and the step size Δt was 0.1.

It may be convenient to read the scenario with a certain interpretation in mind. For example, s_1 may refer to a traumatic experience of seeing somebody who was dying (without having possibilities to save the person). Moreover, s_2 may refer to a situation where a presentation is due in a few minutes time, and no laptop nor slides are available. Finally, s_3 may refer to a situation where an enormous traffic jam stands in the way of reaching an important meeting in time.

Table 3. Settings used for connection strength, threshold and steepness parameters

from state	connection		to state	threshold	steepness
srs_{s_k}	ω_{1k}	1	ps_b	0.5	4
fs_b	ω_2	1			
ps_b	ω_3	1	fs_b	0.5	4
$cs_{s_k,b}$	ω_{4k}	-0.2			
ps_b	ω_{51}	0.5	srs_{s_1}	0.5	4
$cs_{s_1,b}$	ω_{61}	-1			
ps_b	ω_{52}	0.5	srs_{s_2}	0.2	4
$cs_{s_2,b}$	ω_{62}	-0.5			
ps_b	ω_{53}	0.45	srs_{s_3}	0.22	4
$cs_{s_3,b}$	ω_{63}	-0.5			
srs_{s_k}	ω_{7k}	1	$cs_{s_1,b}$	0.8	8
fs_b	ω_{8k}	1	$cs_{s_2,b}$	1.1	8
			$cs_{s_3,b}$	1.4	8
srs_{s_k}	ω_{9k}	1.2	es_{s_k}	0	200
es_{s_j}	$\omega_{10,jk}$	-0.6			

In Figure 3 a scenario is shown where the episode state es_{s_2} based on srs_{s_2} is succeeded (after time point 13) by an episode state es_{s_3} based on srs_{s_3} (see upper graph). Here the connection from preparation for emotional response to sensory representation of s_3 has been given strength $\omega_{53} = 0.45$. As shown in the lower graph in Figure 3, for this case the feeling level goes to 0.7, which is a situation in which regulation facilities become active. For example, due to this high feeling level the suppressing control state for s_1 becomes more active. In the lower graph of Figure 3 the comparison between the sensory representations of s_2 and s_3 is shown; it is shown that first, up to time point 8, the sensory representation of s_2 dominates, reaching a level of around 0.6, which leads to a dream episode state es_{s_2} based on it, as shown in the upper graph in Figure 3. But after time point 8 the sensory representation for s_2 is suppressed by the triggered regulation, and therefore beaten by the sensory representation for s_3. As a consequence, after time point 13 the episode state for s_3 has won the competition, and provides the basis for a second dream episode. Note that the competition process took about 5 time units before the episode related to the sensory representation state that became the highest activated one at time 9 was able to beat the previous one. Similarly, scenarios for three or more dream episodes can be shown. Note that which episode states pop up depends on the association strengths to the emotional response. For example, if the emotional association strength ω_{53} for s_3 is made slightly lower, then the episode state for s_3 will never pop up due to the mutual inhibition. Moreover, the strength of the inhibition links affect whether or not two different episode states are considered compatible. If such inhibition links have lower strengths, then in one episode multiple (apparently compatible) episode states can co-occur.

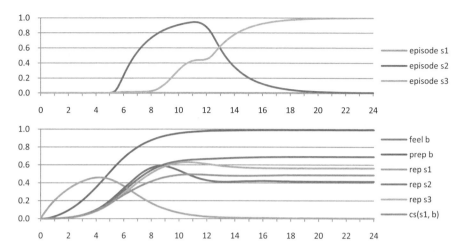

Figure 3. Secenario 2: two subsequent dream episodes

4. Relations to Neurological Theories and Findings

In [24] dreaming is related to a network of four main components Amygdala, Medial PreFrontal Cortex (MPFC), Hippocampus, Anterior Cingulate Cortex (ACC). The biological counterparts of the preparation and sensory representation states in the model can be found in the sensory and (pre)motor cortices, indicated in [24] to be 'robustly connected' to the components as mentioned. The relations between sensory memory elements and their emotional associations are stored in the Hippocampus; in the model these relations are assumed to be fixed and modelled by the (bidirectional) connections between the sensory representations states srs_{sk} and preparation states ps_b of the emotional response b. The feeling state fs_b in the model can be related to the Amygdala, in combination with some limbic areas involved in maintaining 'body maps'. As discussed in Section 1, the interaction between preparation state ps_b and feeling state fs_b is in line with the neurological theories of Damasio [6, 7, 8, 9]. About the role of ACC empirical studies show evidence in different directions (e.g., [24], pp. 505-512); therefore it is not clear yet how it can be related to the model.

The interaction between MPFC and Amygdala has been extensively studied; e.g. [6, 7, 10, 30, 28, 24]. In various empirical studies it has been found that lower activity of MPFC correlates to less controlled feeling levels, and, moreover, REM sleep is found to strengthen MPFC activation and reduce feeling levels. This regulating role of MPFC with respect to Amygdala activation makes these two neurological components suitable candidates for biological counterparts of the control state $cs_{sk,b}$ and the feeling states fs_b in the computational model presented in Section 2. As before, the connections between the two types of states may be related to the Hippocampus. Note that in the computational model the control states $cs_{sk,b}$ also have a role in suppressing the activation of the corresponding sensory representation state srs_{sk}, which can be justified as being a form of emotion regulation by attentional deployment; cf. [14, 15]; see also Section 1. The episode states es_{sk} and their competition can be justified by referring to the Global Workspace Theory of consciousness (cf. [1, 2]), as explained in Section 2.

5. Discussion

The assumption that dreaming, especially when negative emotions are involved, can be considered as a purposeful form of internal simulation is widely supported; see, for example, for the purpose of improving coping skills to handle threatful situations [27, 31, 32], or for the purpose of strengthening fear emotion regulation capabilities [24, 25, 11, 16, 33, 34, 36. In this paper a computational agent model was presented that models the generation of dream episodes from an internal simulation perspective, abstracting from a specific purpose. Building blocks to create such internal simulations are memory elements in the form of sensory representations and their associated emotions. The model exploits a mutual (winner-takes-it-all) competition process to determine sensory representation states that dominate in different dream episodes, comparable to one of the central ideas underlying the Global Workspace Theory of consciousness (cf. [1, 2]). Emotion regulation mechanisms (cf. [12, 14, 15]) were incorporated to regulate the activation levels of the feeling and the sensory representation states. The computational model was evaluated by a number of simulation experiments for scenarios with different numbers of dream episodes.

Note that the presented agent model is meant as a plausible model of a human agent, not of a software agent. Mechanisms identified in the neurological and cognitive literature were used in order to obtain a human-like computational agent model, and to support its plausibility. Once such a human-like agent model is available, potential applications can be explored. A specific class of possible applications may concern virtual agents in the context of serious or nonserious gaming. In this context also some types of validation can be performed, for example, by evaluating how believable they are considered (also in dependence of parameter settings). Such applications and validations are a subject for future research.

In further work a computational model has been developed for fear extinction learning during dreaming; cf. [37]. A number of variations of the model can be made. One variation is to take into account more than one emotion triggered by certain sensory representations. The model can easily be extended to cover this case. Another variation which is possible is to incorporate dependencies between sensory representations (e.g., resulting from sensory preconditioning; cf. [5, 17]).

References

[1] B.J. Baars, *In the theater of consciousness: the workspace of the mind*, Oxford University Press, Oxford, 1997.
[2] B.J. Baars, The conscious access hypothesis: Origins and recent evidence, *Trends in Cognitive Science* **6** (2002), 47–52.
[3] W. Becker, A.F. Fuchs, Prediction in the Oculomotor System: Smooth Pursuit During Transient Disappearance of a Visual Target, *Experimental Brain Research* **57** (1985), 562-575.
[4] R.D. Beer, On the dynamics of small continuous-time recurrent neural networks, *Adaptive Behavior* **3** (1995), 469-509.
[5] W. J. Brogden, Sensory pre-conditioning. *Journal of Experimental Psychology* **25** (1939), 323–332.
[6] A.R. Damasio, *Descartes' Error: Emotion, Reason and the Human Brain*. Papermac, London, 1994.
[7] A.R. Damasio, *The Feeling of What Happens. Body and Emotion in the Making of Consciousness*, Harcourt Brace, New York, 1999.
[8] A.R. Damasio, *Looking for Spinoza: Joy, Sorrow, and the Feeling Brain*. Vintage books, London, 2003.
[9] A.R. Damasio, *Self comes to mind: constructing the conscious brain*. Pantheon Books, NY, 2010.
[10] R.J. Davidson, Anxiety and affective style: role of prefrontal cortex and amygdala, *Biol. Psychiatry* **51** (2002), 68–80.

[11] P.L. Franzen, D.J. Buysse, R.E. Dahl, W. Thompson, G.J. Siegle, Sleep deprivation alters pupillary reactivity to emotional stimuli in healthy young adults, *Biol Psychol.* **80** (2009), 300-305.

[12] P.R. Goldin, K. McRae, W. Ramel, J.J. Gross, The neural bases of emotion regulation: reappraisal and suppression of negative emotion, *Biol. Psychiatry* **63** (2008), 577–586.

[13] A.I. Goldman, *Simulating Minds: The Philosophy, Psychology, and Neuroscience of Mindreading*, Oxford University Press, New York, 2006.

[14] J.J. Gross, Antecedent- and response-focused emotion regulation: divergent consequences for experience, expression, and physiology, *J. of Personality and Social Psych.* **74** (1998), 224–237.

[15] J.J. Gross, *Handbook of Emotion Regulation*, Guilford Press, New York, 2007.

[16] N. Gujar, S.A. McDonald, M. Nishida, M.P. Walker, A Role for REM Sleep in Recalibrating the Sensitivity of the Human Brain to Specific Emotions, *Cerebral Cortex* **21** (2011), 115-123.

[17] G. Hall, Learning about associatively activated stimulus representations: Implications for acquired equivalence and perceptual learning, *Animal Learning and Behavior* **24** (1996), 233–255.

[18] G. Hesslow, Will neuroscience explain consciousness? *J. Theoret. Biol.* **171** (1994), 29–39.

[19] G. Hesslow, Conscious thought as simulation of behaviour and perception, *Trends Cogn. Sci.* **6** (2002), 242-247.

[20] J.A. Hobson, REM sleep and dreaming: towards a theory of protoconsciousness, *Nature Reviews Neuroscience* **10** (2009), 803-814.

[21] J.J. Hopfield, Neural networks and physical systems with emergent collective computational properties. *Proc. Nat. Acad. Sci. (USA)* **79** (1982), 2554-2558.

[22] J.J. Hopfield, Neurons with graded response have collective computational properties like those of two-state neurons. *Proc. Nat. Acad. Sci. (USA)* **81** (1984), 3088-3092.

[23] W. James, What is an emotion, *Mind* **9** (1884), 188–205.

[24] R. Levin, T.A. Nielsen, Disturbed dreaming, posttraumatic stress disorder, and affect distress: A review and neurocognitive model, *Psychological Bulletin* **133** (2007), 482-528.

[25] R. Levin, T.A. Nielsen, Nightmares, bad dreams, and emotion dysregulation. A review and new neurocognitive model of dreaming, *Curr Dir Psychol Sci.* **18** (2009), 84-88.

[26] T.A. Nielsen, P. Stenstrom, What are the memory sources of dreaming? *Nature* **437** (2005), 1286-1289.

[27] A. Revonsuo, The reinterpretation of dreams: An evolutionary hypothesis of function of dreaming, *Behavioral and Brain Sciences* **23** (2000), 877–901.

[28] C.D. Salzman, S. Fusi, Emotion, Cognition, and Mental State Representation in Amygdala and Prefrontal Cortex, *Annu. Rev. Neurosci.* **33** (2010), 173–202.

[29] M. Shanahan, A cognitive architecture that combines internal simulation with a global workspace, *Consciousness and Cognition* **15** (2006), 433–449.

[30] F. Sotres-Bayon, D.E. Bush, J.E. LeDoux, Emotional perseveration: an update on prefrontal-amygdala interactions in fear extinction, *Learn. Mem.* **11** (2004), 525–535.

[31] K. Valli, A. Revonsuo, O. Palkas, K.H. Ismail, K.J. Ali, R.L. Punamaki, The threat simulation theory of the evolutionary function of dreaming: evidence from dreams of traumatized children, *Consciousness and Cognition* **14** (2005), 188–218.

[32] K. Valli, A. Revonsuo, The threat simulation theory in light of recent empirical evidence: a review. *Am J Psychol* **122** (2009), 17-38.

[33] M.P. Walker, The role of sleep in cognition and emotion, *Ann N Y Acad Sci.* **1156** (2009), 168-197.

[34] M.P. Walker, E. van der Helm, Overnight therapy? The role of sleep in emotional brain processing, *Psychol Bull.* **135** (2009), 731-748.

[35] J.M. Windt, V. Noreika, How to integrate dreaming into a general theory of consciousness, *Consciousness and Cognition* (2010). doi:10.1016/j.concog.2010.09.010.

[36] S.S. Yoo, N. Gujar, P. Hu, F.A. Jolesz, M.P.Walker, The human emotional brain without sleep – a prefrontal amygdala disconnect, *Curr. Biol.* **17** (2007), R877–R878.

[37] J. Treur, Dreaming Your Fear Away: A Computational Model for Fear Extinction Learning During Dreaming. In: Zhang, L., Kwok, J. (eds.), *Proc. of the 18th Intern. Conference on Neural Information Processing, ICONIP'11.* Lecture Notes in Artificial Intelligence, Springer Verlag, 2011, to appear.

Biologically Inspired Cognitive Architectures 2011
A.V. Samsonovich and K.R. Jóhannsdóttir (Eds.)
IOS Press, 2011
doi:10.3233/978-1-60750-959-2-400

Physiological Model-Based Decision Making on Distribution of Effort over Time

Jan TREUR
VU University Amsterdam, Agent Systems Research Group
De Boelelaan 1081, 1081 HV, Amsterdam, The Netherlands
Email: treur@cs.vu.nl   URL: http://www.cs.vu.nl/~treur

Abstract. This paper focuses on a human-like agent model that describes how in high load tasks physiological effort relate to exhaustion and feeling fatigue, and this is used as a form of monitoring the agent's remaining resources. More specifically, it is addressed how based on such an agent model anticipatory model-based decision making can take place in order to obtain an appropriate distribution of effort over time.

Keywords. Physiological model, effort, exhaustion, decision making

Introduction

In human agent behaviour, in addition to the brain, the body often plays an important role. Therefore the design of human-like agents may benefit of incorporating relevant physiological aspects in models developed; e.g., [3, 4, 6, 17]. As an example the focus here is on how an agent manages the effort spent and the related exhaustion (or fatigue) developed in time periods with high load. In humans, to enable intelligent management, the body does not only give a signal when complete exhaustion occurs, but by gradually getting a feeling of becoming fatigued more information is available in the brain before a total breakdown occurs. With this feeling as input, mechanisms in the brain are exploited (1) to monitor levels of fatigue over time, and (2) to decide about distribution of effort over time in such a way that no full exhaustion occurs before the end of the expected period of high load. For example, to avoid premature full exhaustion, a runner will decide to take a lower pace for a *5km* run than for an *800m*.

The approach presented here includes a human-like agent model which describes how based on the physiologically-related aspect of fatigue (which plays a central role in the literature on physical exercise and sport) enables monitoring and intelligent control of resources. It is addressed how such a physiologically-related agent model can be used to formalise anticipatory decision making about an appropriate distribution of effort over time, in order to obtain good performance for given available resources.

The human-like agent model is based on inspiration from literature on physical exercise and sport and how the generated effort is controlled and what is the role of feeling fatigue in this process; e.g., [5], [7-16]. In particular, the interplay of mind and body in this process is addressed. Noakes and his colleagues (e.g., [13-15]) base their theory on the notion of homeostasis: the property of a system (for example, a living organism), to regulate its internal environment in such a way that stable, more or less constant, conditions are maintained. Due to this regulation the body is rarely allowed to reach a 'catastrophic' state where it would run out of essential reserves. In this view the mind receives signals from the body as a form of monitoring, and by regulation keeps the body in appropriate physical conditions.

Such a regulation mechanism is applied in managing time periods with heavy work load and in sports. For example, in long distance running, speed skating or cycling, often it is debated how power should be distributed over time. For example, should the initial phase be used to put extra effort, or the last phase, or should the power be distributed uniformly over the whole time interval? As in sport a difference of less than *0.5%* in time is often decisive for winning or not, making the right decisions on the distribution of power over time is crucial. The model-based decision making approach put forward here provides answers to such questions.

In this paper a computational model for the dynamics of getting exhausted to answer such questions is briefly introduced in Section 1. As a result a model-based decision making approach for distribution of power over time is offered. Next, in Section 2 the special case of a uniform distribution (constant power) is addressed. In Section 3 four patterns of power over time are compared with a uniformn distribution: two intervals with constant power, a linear (increasing or decreasing) pattern of power over time, and an exponential pattern over time. Finally, Section 4 is a discussion.

1. The Agent Model

Within the literature on exercise and sports the notion of *critical power CP* is the maximal level of power that can be generated and sustained over longer periods without becoming exhausted (getting fatigue), assuming no prior exercising. It is an asymptote of the wellknown hyperbolic power-duration curve defined by *(P - CP) t = W'* (also see (9) in Section 2) that models the relationship between a constantly generated power level *P* (above the critical power *CP*, both measured in *Watt*) and the time *t* that this level can be sustained; e.g., [7-11], [16]. Here *W'* is the total amount of work (measure in *Joule*) that can be spent above the critical power (the available stored extra resources based on anaerobic processes). The critical power is the capacity to provide (sustainable) power based on aerobic processes. Although often the critical power *CP* is assumed constant during one exercising session, in the recent literature there is some discussion on whether this really is the case. Some experiments show that after intensive prior exercising leading to full exhaustion of the basic resources *W'*, for example, power at *90%* of the critical power *CP* cannot be sustained anymore; e.g., [5].

This section describes an agent model for monitoring of resources, based on concepts from [18]. In the model described here a *basic critical power CP$_0$* is distinguished from a *dynamic critical power CP*. The most basic assumptions behind this agent model are:

- The critical power indicates the level of (sustainable) power that can be generated for which the level of fatigue remains the same.
- Lower critical power reflects more fatigue
- Basic critical power is the maximal critical power possible, which means no fatigue and occurs (only) in a state without prior exercising.
- If a level of power is generated above the critical power, then fatigue will increase which makes that for the future efforts less resources are left

The dynamics of critical power is described by a linear dependency of the change in critical power on the effort spent above the critical power, with proportion factor γ.

$$\frac{dCP}{dt} = -\gamma (P - CP) \tag{1}$$

Here P is a function of t indicating the power spent at time t. This power P is the variable for which values over time have to be chosen by the decision making addressed in this paper (for some examples of such power distributions over time, see Figure 1). Note that for $\gamma = 0$, a static critical power is modelled. The extra resources W spent over time (taken from the available resources budget W') are described by

$$\frac{dW}{dt} = P - CP \tag{2a}$$

If $W_{tot}(t)$ denotes the total work performed up to time point t, then

$$\frac{dW_{tot}}{dt} = P \tag{2b}$$

Note that the following relations between the derivatives of CP and W immediately follow from (1) and (2):

$$\frac{dCP}{dt} = -\gamma \frac{dW}{dt} \qquad \frac{dW_{tot}}{dt} = \frac{dW}{dt} + CP \tag{3a}$$

From this it can be derived that for an exercising session during a time interval starting at $t=0$ with initially fully available resources budget W' it holds:

$$CP(t) = CP_0 - \gamma W(t) \quad \text{or} \quad W(t) = \frac{1}{\gamma}(CP_0 - CP(t)) \tag{3b}$$

Note that a situation in which that W' has been fully finished (full exhaustion) at t (i.e., $W(t) = W'$) is described by

$$CP(t) = CP_0 - \gamma W' \tag{4}$$

The above relation (3) between $CP(t)$ and $W(t)$ can be used to eliminate CP from the differential equation (2) for W, thus obtaining:

$$\frac{dW}{dt} = P - CP_0 + \gamma W \tag{5}$$

For a given distribution $P(t)$ of power over time this linear differential equation (5) with nonconstant coefficients can be solved analytically as follows:

$$W(t) = \int_0^t e^{\gamma(t-u)}(P(u) - CP_0) \, du \tag{6a}$$

Moreover, from (2b) it immediately follows:

$$W_{tot}(t) = \int_0^t P(u) \, du \tag{6b}$$

Using relation (3) between CP and W, (6a) also provides an analytic solution for CP:

$$CP(t) = CP_0 - \gamma W(t) = CP_0 - \gamma \int_0^t e^{\gamma(t-u)}(P(u) - CP_0) \, du \tag{7}$$

As the decision making addressed here concerns the possibility of varying the power P over time, it is also useful to determine the dependence between W and dP/dt (from (6)); this is described by (from (6) by partial integration):

$$W(t) = -\frac{1}{\gamma}(P(t) - CP_0 - (P(0) - CP_0)e^{\gamma t}) + \frac{1}{\gamma}\int_0^t e^{\gamma(t-u)}dP(u)/dt \, du \tag{8}$$

2. A Hyperbolic-Exponential Power-Duration Curve for Constant P

In this section a uniform distribution of power over time is analysed in more detail (for example, the flat blue line in Figure 1). Traditionally the hyperbolic power-duration curve $(P - CP) t = W'$ (9) is used in the literature to describe cases of constant P above the critical power until total exhaustion is reached. For the approach presented here, for constant P the derivative $dP(u)/dt$ is 0, and $P(t) = P(0) = P$. Therefore from (8) it follows:

$$W(t) = -\frac{1}{\gamma}(P - CP_0)\,(1 - e^{\gamma t}) \tag{10}$$

This provides the following hyperbolic-exponential power-duration relation:

$$W(t) = (P - CP_0)\,t\,\frac{e^{\gamma t} - 1}{\gamma t} \tag{11}$$

For the time t_{max} becoming fully exhausted for power level P, it holds: $W(t_{max}) = W'$. Therefore

$$W' = (P - CP_0)\,t_{max}\,\frac{e^{\gamma t_{max}} - 1}{\gamma t_{max}} \tag{12}$$

Viewed from the perspective of decision making about the power to be chosen for a given time duration t, relation (12) can be used to determine which constant P is maximally possible so that full exhaustion is just occurring at time t:

$$P_{max} - CP_0 = W' \,/\, t\,\frac{e^{\gamma t} - 1}{\gamma t}$$

$$P_{max} = CP_0 + \gamma W' / (e^{\gamma t} - 1) \tag{13}$$

For this constant maximal power given by (13) the total work W_{tot} performed is

$$W_{tot}(t) = \int_0^t P(u)\,du = (CP_0 + \gamma W'/(e^{\gamma t} - 1))\,t$$

$$= CP_0\,t + W' \,/\, \frac{e^{\gamma t} - 1}{\gamma t} \tag{14}$$

For γ approaching 0 this approximates $CP_0\,t + W'$, since then the exponential factor will approximate 1. When γ is higher, the work performed will be lower. Based on (11) and (3b) the critical power for constant P can be expressed in t:

$$CP(t) = CP_0 - (P - CP_0)(e^{\gamma t} - 1) \tag{15}$$
$$\text{or}\quad CP_0 - CP(t) = (P - CP_0)(e^{\gamma t} - 1)$$

In Figures 1 and 2 both the hyperbolic-exponential and the hyperbolic curve are shown for $\gamma = 0.002$, resp. $\gamma = 0.0005$. In the upper graph (a) time t is on the horizontal axis, and in the lower graph (b) one divided by time: $1/t$. On the vertical axis the maximal power P sustainable for a duration t is depicted. Figures 1 and 2 show how hyperbolic-exponential power-duration curve described by (11) is approximated by the traditional hyperbolic power-duration curve when γt is small. This can be analysed from a different perspective by verifying that the factor

$$\frac{e^{\gamma t} - 1}{\gamma t}$$

approximates 1 when γt approaches 0.

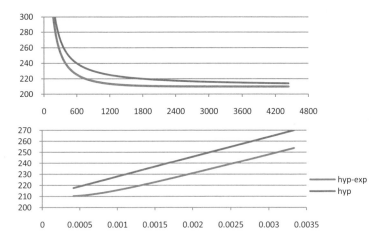

Figure 1. Hyperbolic and hyperbolic-exponential power-duration curve: maximal sustainable power (*Watt*) (a) against duration t (in seconds) (b) against $1/t$ (in $1/$seconds) ($\gamma = 0.002$, $CP_0 = 210W$, $W' = 18000J$)

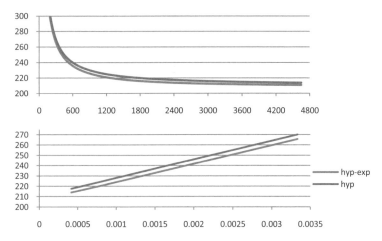

Figure 2. Hyperbolic and hyperbolic-exponential power-duration curve: maximal sustainable power (*Watt*) (a) against duration t (in seconds) (b) against $1/t$ (in $1/$seconds) ($\gamma = 0.0005$, $CP_0 = 210W$, $W' = 18000J$)

3. Decision Making by Comparison of Different Distributions of Power over Time

In this section it is discussed how the computational model can be used for decision making: for any effort distribution scenario considered the model can be used to make predictions on the overall work that can be obtained by following such a scenario. When different scenarios are evaluated in this way (by a form of what-if analysis), they can be compared. In this section four types of such scenarios for distributions of power over time are considered (see Figure 3):

- constant power P (Section 2)
- two intervals with constant P
- linear (de- or) increasing distribution over time
- exponential distribution over time

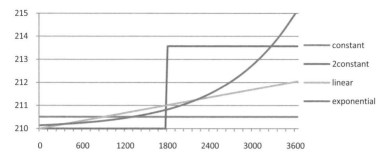

Figure 3. Four patterns for distribution of power P over time (for $\gamma = 0.001$, $CP_0 = 210W$, $W' = 18000J$)

The four patterns for distribution of power over time are depicted in Figure 3 for an exercising session of *60* minutes ($t=3600$) for $\gamma = 0.001$, $CP_0 = 210W$, $W' = 18000J$. An overview of the specifications of the scenarios for distribution of effort over time and their outcomes can be found, respectively, in the second and third column of Table 1 (for a session of length t). As from some first analysis it was found that distributions with higher levels later in time perform better, the three non-constant patterns were taken as starting at the basic level CP_0 and increasing over time. The pattern for fully *constant power* was used from (13). For the pattern with *two constant levels*, the interval was divided in $[0, t/2[$ where the constant level CP_0 was used, and $[t/2, t]$. In the latter interval (13) was applied again, but with interval length $t/2$ instead of t. For the *linear distribution* a function

$$P(u) = CP_0 + au$$

was used, with $a>0$. Using (8) it was found that

$$a = \gamma W'/t \left(\frac{e^{\gamma t}-1}{\gamma t} - 1\right)$$

when it is assumed that W' is fully used during the interval $[0, t]$. For the *exponential distribution* a function

$$P(u) = CP_0 + \alpha e^{-\gamma(t-u)}$$

was used. From (6) it follows that $\alpha = W'/t$ when W' is fully used during the interval $[0, t]$. This explains the formulae in the second column of Table 1. The formulae in the third column were obtained by using (6b) and symbolically determining the integral.

Table 1. Overview of the four different patterns for power over time

pattern	power distribution over time	work performed
constant	$P(u) = CP_0 + \gamma W'/(e^{\gamma t} - 1)$	$W_{tot}(t) = CP_0\, t + W'/\frac{e^{\gamma t}-1}{\gamma t}$
two constant intervals	$P(u) = CP_0$ when $0 \le u < t/2$ $P(u) = CP_0 + \gamma W'/(e^{\gamma t/2} - 1)$ when $t/2 \le u \le t$	$W_{tot}(t) = CP_0\, t + W'/\frac{e^{\gamma t/2}-1}{\gamma t/2}$
linear	$P(u) = CP_0 + u\, \gamma W'/t\left(\frac{e^{\gamma t}-1}{\gamma t} - 1\right)$	$W_{tot}(t) = CP_0\, t + \frac{1}{2}\gamma t\, W'/\left(\frac{e^{\gamma t}-1}{\gamma t} - 1\right)$
exponential	$P(u) = CP_0 + W'e^{-\gamma(t-u)}/t$	$W_{tot}(t) = CP_0\, t + W'e^{-\gamma t}\frac{e^{\gamma t}-1}{\gamma t}$

In Figure 4 it is shown how the four different strategies compare for different lengths t of the session and $\gamma = 0.0005$, by depicting the average total power $W_{tot}(t)/t$ (calculated by the four formulae in the third column of Table 1) for different time periods. The constant power distribution is the lowest, and the pattern with two constant intervals the highest. The exponential and linear pattern are in between, with the linear pattern a bit higher.

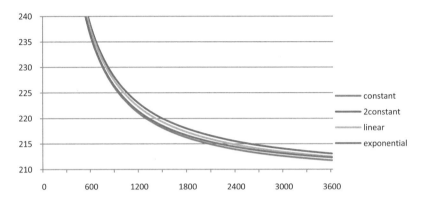

Figure 4. Average total power W_{tot}/t for the four cases against duration of the session
($\gamma = 0.0005$, $W' = 18000J$, $CP_0 = 210W$)

In Figure 5 a more detailed picture is given for the same γ. Here the differences with the constant pattern are shown. Notice that these differences are in the order of magnitude of *0.5* to *1%*. For example, for a sport session of about *10* minutes, this may make a difference of *3* to *6* seconds in time, which may be significant enough to be decisive for winning a race or not.

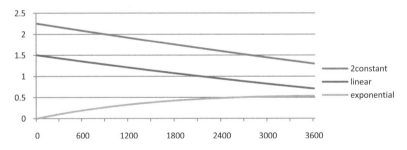

Figure 5. Difference between the average power W_{tot}/t for the three nonconstant distributions compared to the constant case against duration of the session ($\gamma = 0.0005$ $W' = 18000J$, $CP_0 = 210W$)

4. Discussion

This paper addressed how a computational approach for anticipatory model-based decision making can be used to decide for an appropriate distribution of effort over time in high load tasks. The model referred to in 'model-based' is a human-like agent model that describes how physiological effort relates to feeling exhaustion or fatigue, which is used as a form of monitoring the agent's remaining resources. The agent model makes use of the concept of dynamical critical power that indicates the level of (sustainable) power that can be generated for which the level of fatigue remains the same. In the model this critical power is dynamic. More fatigue means lower critical power. If a level of power is generated above the critical power, then fatigue will increase which makes that for future efforts less resources are left. Maximal critical power means no fatigue, occurring (only) in a state without prior exercising. The presented approach includes this human-like agent model formalising monitoring of levels of fatigue over time, and model-based techniques formalising decision making on the distribution of effort over time.

To illustrate the decision making approach, three possible nonuniform patterns for distribution of effort over time were considered and compared to the uniform pattern of constant power over time. For all of these three nonuniform patterns it turned out that a distribution with higher power levels later on in the time interval provide the best performance. For example, for a linear distribution an increasing linear function performs best, and for a distribution based on two subintervals each with constant power, the best performance is obtained when the power level in the second interval is higher than in the first interval. Also a pattern based on exponential increase performs better than the uniform distribution. These outcomes suggest a general heuristic: to initially keep the effort a bit modest and increase the effort later on in the time interval, in such a way that full exhaustion is reached just at the final time point.

As a point of departure for the human-like agent model, basic concepts were adopted from the model in [18]; the latter model was also applied as part of the more complex model presented in [1]. The more extensive mathematical analysis and the model-based anticipatory decision making addressed in the current paper were not addressed in [1] or [18]. In order to apply the agent model to persons an adequate estimation of the parameters is important, which was described in [2] for the more complex model from [1].

An application area for this approach is formed by ambient intelligence used in physical exercise and sport: devices that monitor human functioning are able to analyse this functioning, and give appropriate advices. When an approach is used as presented here, more advanced ambient intelligent agent applications can be developed.

References

[1]   T. Bosse, F. Both, R. van Lambalgen, and J. Treur, An Agent Model for a Human's Functional State and Performance. In: Jain, L., Gini, M., Faltings, B.B., Terano, T., Zhang, C., Cercone, N., Cao, L. (eds.), *Proc. of the 8th IEEE/WIC/ACM Intern.Conf. on Intelligent Agent Technology, IAT'08*. IEEE Computer Society Press, 2008, pp. 302–307.

[2]   F. Both, M. Hoogendoorn, S.W. Jaffry, R. van Lambalgen, R. Oorburg, A. Sharpanskykh, J. Treur, and M. de Vos, Adaptation and Validation of an Agent Model of Functional State and Performance for Individuals. In: *Proceedings of the 12th International Conference on Principles of Practice in Multi-Agent Systems, PRIMA'09*. Lecture Notes in Artificial Intelligence, vol. 5925. Springer Verlag, 2009, pp. 595–607.

[3]   W.B. Cannon, *The Wisdom of the Body*. New York: W.W. Norton and Co, 1932.

[4]   A. Clark, *Being There: Putting Brain Body and World Together Again*. Cambridge, MA: MIT Press, 1997.

[5]   E.M. Coats, H.B. Rossiter, J.R. Day, A. Miura, Y. Fukuba, and B.J. Whipp, Intensity-dependent tolerance to exercise after attaining V'_{O2max} in humans. *J. of Applied Physiology* **95** (2003), 483–490.

[6]   A. Damasio, *The Feeling of What Happens: Body, Emotion and the Making of Consciousness*. MIT Press, 1999.

[7]   Y. Fukuba, B.J. Whipp, A metabolic limit on the ability to make up for lost time in endurance events. *J. of Applied Physiology* **87** (1999), 853-861.

[8]   Y. Fukuba, A. Miura, M. Endo, A. Kan, K.Yanagawa, and B.J. Whipp, The Curvature Constant Parameter of the Power-Duration Curve for Varied-Power Exercise. *Medicine and Science in Sports and Exercise* **35** (2003), 1413-1418.

[9]   J. Henritze, A. Weltman, R.L. Schurrer, K. Barlow, Effects of training at and above the lactate threshold on the lactate threshold and maximal oxygen uptake. *Eur J Appl Physiol Occup Physiol*. **54** (1985), 84-88.

[10]   A.V. Hill, C.N.V. Long, and H. Lupton, Muscular exercise, lactic acid, and the supply and utilisation of oxygen: *Proc. Royal Soc. Bri*. **97** (1924), Parts I-III: pp. 438-475. Parts VII-VIII: pp. 155-176.

[11]   D.W. Hill, The critical power concept. *Sports Medicine* **16** (1993), 237-254.

[12]   A.M. Jones, D.P. Wilkerson, F. DiMenna, J. Fulford, and D.C. Poole, Muscle metabolic responses to exercise above and below the 'critical power' assessed using 31P-MRS. *American Journal of Physiology: Regulatory, Integrative and Comparative Physiology* **294** (2008), 585-593.

[13]   E.V. Lambert, A. St Clair Gibson, and T.D. Noakes, Complex systems model of fatigue: integrative homoeostatic control of peripheral physiological systems during exercise in humans. *British J. of Sports Medicin* **39** (2005), 52-62.

[14]   T.D. Noakes, Physiological models to understand exercise fatigue and the adaptations that predict or enhance athletic performance. *Scand. Journal of Medicine and Science in Sports* **10** (2000), 123-145.

[15]   T.D. Noakes, Time to move beyond a brainless exercise physiology: the evidence for complex regulation of human exercise performance. *Appl. Physiol. Nutr. Metab*. **36** (2011), 23–35.

[16]   A. Stasiulis, R. Ančlauskas, J. Jaščanin, The Effects of Training Intensity on Blood Lactate Breakpoints in Runners. *Journal Of Human Kinetics* **3** (2000), 17-26.

[17]   L. Steels, R. Brooks, *The artificial life route to artificial intelligence: building embodied, situated agents*. Lawrence Erlbaum, 1995.

[18]   J. Treur, A Virtual Human Agent Model with Behaviour Based on Feeling Exhaustion. *Journal of Applied Intelligence*, 2011. DOI 10.1007/s10489-010-0237-0.

Biologically Inspired Cognitive Architectures 2011
A.V. Samsonovich and K.R. Jóhannsdóttir (Eds.)
IOS Press, 2011

Novel Heat Exchange Role of Falx-Tentorium as Vital Constraint on Neurocognitive Architectures

Ronald USCINSKI[a], Dennis K. MCBRIDE [b,1], and Jessica USCINSKI[c]

[a] *George Washington University Department of Neurosurgery*
[b] *Georgetown University Department of Microbiology*
[c] *American University Department of Physics*
ruscinski@aol.com, dkm7@georgetown.edu, jlusci@gmail.com

Keywords. Thermodynamics, neurocognitive architecture, constraints

Abstract

Biologically-inspired consideration of cognitive architectures implies evolutionary consideration of the drivers for, and of the constraints of such architectures, wherein, arguably, the most delimiting components are those that are essentially thermodynamic. Evidence suggests the human brain has expanded in volume and mass three-fold over the past few million years, and that such encephalization has ceased or is asymptotic. Interest in the physics of intelligence has focused on the relationship between heat extraction and cognitive functionality, and thus on the theoretical limits of the size, function, and 'design' of the human brain. Cognitive architectures of the human brain may have undergone significant re-architecting as competition for increased cognitive capacity (i.e., continuation of the brain expansion trajectory) continued while thermodynamic forces applied hard constraints on encephalization. We provide an evolutionary hypothesis that the falx and tentorium play a significant role in heat extraction and discuss specific implications on cognitive architecture.

---

[1] Corresponding Author: Department of Microbiology Georgetown University 3900 Reservoir Rd. (Med-Dent) Washington 20057-1440 United States

Biologically Inspired Cognitive Architectures 2011
A.V. Samsonovich and K.R. Jóhannsdóttir (Eds.)
IOS Press, 2011
© 2011 The authors and IOS Press. All rights reserved.
doi:10.3233/978-1-60750-959-2-410

Second Life Foraging: An Ecologically-Inspired Task to Drive Biologically-Inspired Cognitive Architectures

Vladislav D. Veksler

Cognitive Science Department, Rensselaer Polytechnic Institute

Abstract. Current work examines how Second Life (a popular virtual environment) may be used for the development of cognitive agents. Specifically, it was used for complex foraging task simulations by an upper-level undergraduate computer science class. A concurrent class in cognitive robotics allowed for direct comparisons between setup and development efforts for the two simulation platforms. The conclusions are that (1) SL offers enough complexity and ecological validity to drive long-term progress in cognitive system research, and (2) agent development and debugging is much faster using SL than robotics.

Keywords. Virtually embodied BICA, persistent environment, Second Life

Introduction

The development of computational cognitive systems is largely driven by the problems that these systems aim to solve. The planning requirements of chess gave rise to GPS/SOAR, recognition-type problems gave rise to various categorization models and neural networks, the focus on perception/action constraints gave rise to EPIC, etc. Although these are all important directions, it seems that the development of cognitive systems would benefit from a multi-faceted ecologically-valid task environment. A high-fidelity problem can help drive a high-fidelity solution. This work examines Second Life (SL) as a high-fidelity simulation platform, addressing two questions. First, can SL provide enough complexity to be useful in driving high-fidelity cognitive system development? Second, is it also simple enough – does it afford fast cognitive system development and debugging?

1. Second Life is complex enough

A complex foraging task was set up in Second Life. In this task the agents would get hungry and thirsty, they could sense pleasure and pain, they could benefit from vitamins or suffer from poison. The agent's goal was to maximize its drives over time. The agents had to deal with noisy input, and had to learn to discriminate between which objects to bite and/or sip, what these actions would do to their drives over time, how to balance exploration and exploitation, and how to navigate this rich, noisy, and dynamic environment. The multi-faceted ecologically realistic demands of this task (e.g. generalization, navigation, complex temporal contingencies, goal management, etc.) were meant to drive the development of high-fidelity integrated cognitive systems.

Students in an upper-level undergraduate class at RPI were required to build agents that could prosper in the this task-environment. The task proved to be a good measure of progress – as the students made their agents smarter (adding or refining mechanisms for learning, discrimination, decision-making, etc.), their task scores kept improving. Importantly, none of the scores were near optimal, suggesting that this task-environment has the potential to drive continuous long-term progress in agent development. Additionally, as cognitive systems continue to improve, the task can be made more complex, taking advantage of SL as a rich and persistent world where agents can live for months, interacting with hundreds of thousands of active users and millions of objects.

2. Second Life is simple enough

If we desire greater real-world fidelity, why not just use robotics as the development platform? SL was used as a platform for AI assignments in an upper-level undergraduate class at RPI. In the first five weeks of the semester, the students in this class (working on an individual basis) were required to create two chat-bots, and a Reinforcement Learning (RL) bot, all in Second Life. During the same period students in a concurrent Cognitive Robotics class were able to complete only one RL assignment. During the remainder of the semester the students using the SL platform had to develop a neural-network-based bot and an agent for a complex foraging task (described in the previous section). The students in the robotics class spent approximately the same period of time working on a much simpler maze navigation task, with much less success. This gap in progress between the two classes is attributable to the differences in the ease of development and the speed of debugging with the two platforms.

3. Summary

In sum, SL provides relative ease for cognitive system development, and it can be useful as a rich high-fidelity task environment with enough complexity to drive long-term progress in cognitive system research.

Biologically Inspired Cognitive Architectures 2011
A.V. Samsonovich and K.R. Jóhannsdóttir (Eds.)
IOS Press, 2011
© 2011 The authors and IOS Press. All rights reserved.
doi:10.3233/978-1-60750-959-2-412

Reconciling Autonomy with Utility: A Roadmap and Architecture for Cognitive Development

David VERNON [1]

Circular Dynamics, Ireland

Abstract.

This paper focusses on a general issue which arises when one attempts to design a cognitive architecture for autonomous cognitive systems: the incompatibility of autonomy with external control and the consequent problem of getting these systems to perform prescribed tasks. In addressing this issue, we consider a specific endeavour to design and implement a biologically-inspired cognitive architecture for the iCub humanoid robot. This architecture is based on 43 guidelines arising from an extended study of the requirements imposed by developmental psychology, neuroscience, enactive cognition, and existing computational models.

Keywords. Autonomy, Utility, Development, Cognitive Architecture, Phylogeny, Ontogeny, Coaching, Imitative Learning.

Introduction

Natural cognitive systems are autonomous. Ideally, so too are biologically-inspired artificial ones. However, autonomy implies a self-determination that precludes explicit control by external agencies, including human users. This creates a problem: how can an autonomous cognitive system be designed so that it can exhibit the behaviours and functionality that its users require of it, such as the ability to perform prescribed tasks? We argue that the answer to this question has two components: one phylogentic and one ontogenetic. Both are linked to the developmental characteristic of autonomous cognitive systems [1] whereby the system acquires new capabilities and skills over time and, in the process, constructs its own understanding of the world around it through its interactions [2,3,4,5].

The developmental process is driven by various task non-specific motives which modulate the affective state of the system and thereby the actions in which it enagages. In turn, these motives reflect an innate value system: as Edelman notes, "the brain must ... establish regularities of behaviour under constraints of inherited value systems and of idiosyncratic perceptual and memorial events. In humans, such systems and events necessarily involve emotions and biases" [6]. If we wish these behaviours to exhibit some desired utility, we must embed in the system's phylogeny — in its cognitive architec-

---

[1] Corresponding author e-mail: david@vernon.eu.

ture — the pre-disposition to acquire these behaviours and to fulfil this function. That is, the system phylogeny must have the appropriate value system and the associated motives. The subsequent ontongeny must then be structured to allow the cognitive system to develop the requisite skills and bring about the required behaviour. We argue that the most effective way to do this is through a process of human-robot coaching and imitative learning [7,8,9,10]. We illustrate this argument by making detailed reference to the iCub cognitive architecture, a biologically-inspired architecture that has been modelled on several aspects of human neuroscience and developmental psychology.

1. Autonomy

Autonomy is the self-maintaining organizational characteristic of living systems that enables them to use their own capacities to manage their interactions with the world in order to remain viable [11,3]. An autonomous system is entirely self-governing and self-regulating: it is not controlled by any outside agency and this allows it to stand apart from the rest of the environment, establishing a dynamic but self-sustaining identity. Characteristically, autonomy entails a capacity to contribute to its own persistence [12]. While the system may be dependent on the environment for material or energy, its operational identity is independent and any influences exerted on the system are brought about only by mutual interactions that do not threaten the autonomous operation of the system or control the system in any causal way. And therein lies the problem: if an external agent can't exert a causal influence on an autonomous cognitive system, how can one get it to do something useful? There are two aspects to the answer to this question, one dealing with the phylogeny of the cognitive system and the other with its ontongeny.

2. Phylogeny

What is the relationship between autonomy and cognition? One position is that cognition is the process by which an autonomous self-governing agent acts effectively in the world in which it is embedded [14]. As such, the dual purpose of cognition is to increase the agent's repertoire of effective actions and its power to anticipate the need for future actions and their outcomes [13]. Futhermore, development plays an essential role in the realization of these cognitive capabilities.

For an autonomous cognitive system to exhibit some utility from the perspective of its user or owner, it must have the same goals as its user or owner. So how does one specify the goals of an autonomous agent? The answer to this question seems to be that one can't, at least not directly. The best that one can do is embed a suitable set of motives in the system's phylogeny and subsequently use these to influence the system's goals.

Based on a study of enactive cognitive science, developmental psychology, neurophysiology, and computational modelling, the roadmap for cognitive development in humanoid robots in [13] identifies 43 guidelines for the design of a cognitive architecture and its deployment in a humanoid robot (see Table 1). In the context of the current discussion, this roadmap makes four important observations.

First, a cognitive system's actions are guided by prospection, directed by goals, and triggered by affective motives [15]. They are initially constrained in their numbers of

Embodiment
Rich array of physical sensory and motor interfaces Humanoid morphology Morphology integral to the model of cognition
Perception
Attention fixated on the goal of an action Perception of objecthood Discrimination & addition of small numbers; groups of large numbers Attraction to people (faces, their sounds, movements, and features) Preferential attention to biological motion Recognition of people, expression, and action Prolonged attention when a person engages in mutual gaze Perceive & communicate emotions by facial gesture and engage in turn-taking Involvement of the motor system in discrimination between percepts Mechanism to learn hierarchical representations Pre-motor theory of attention —spatial attention Pre-motor theory of attention —selective attention
Action
Movements organized as actions Early movements constrained to reduce the number of degrees of freedom Navigation based on dynamic ego-centric path integration Re-orientation based on local landmarks Action selection modulated by affective motivation mechanisms Hierarchically-structured representations of action-sequence skills
Anticipation
Internal simulation to predict, explain, & imagine events, and scaffold knowledge
Adaptation
Self-modification to expand actions and improve prediction Autonomous generative model construction Learning affordances Grounding internal simulations in actions Learn from experience the motor skills associated with actions Transient and generalized episodic memories of past experiences Procedural memory of actions and outcomes associated with episodic memories
Motivation
Social and explorative motives Affective drives associated with autonomy-preserving processes of homeostasis
Autonomy
Autonomy-preserving processes of homeostasis Encode space in motor & goal specific manner Minimal set of innate behaviours for exploration and survival Separate representations associated with each component / sub-system Concurrent competitive operation of components and subsystems

Table 1. Guidelines for the Phylogeny of a Developmental Cognitive System (from [13]).

freedom and the motor-programs that constitute them are learned. Second, because cognitive systems are anticipatory and prospective, they must have a mechanism to rehearse hypothetical scenarios through some process of internal simulation in order to predict, explain, and imagine events, and they must have a mechanism to use this outcome to modulate the behaviour of the system [16,17,18,19,20]. These processes should incorporate transient and generalized episodic memories of events and a procedural memory that links actions to perceptions [21]. Third, a developmental cognitive architecture must be capable of adaptation and self-modification, both in the sense of parameter adjustment of phylogenetic skills through learning and through the modification of the structure and organization of the system itself so that it is capable of altering its system dynamics based on experience in order to expand its repertoire of actions and enhance its prospective capabilities. Fourth, development should be driven by both explorative and social motives, the first concerned with both the discovery of novel regularities in the world and the potential of the system's own actions, the second with inter-agent interaction, shared activities, and mutually-constructed patterns of shared behaviour.

These observations, among others, and the guidelines set out in Table 1 formed the basis for the design of the iCub cognitive architecture which is summarized in Section 4. Before looking at this, we first consider the second aspect of how autonomy can be reconciled with utility: the ontogeny of the cognitive system.

3. Ontogeny

Development arises due to changes in the central nervous system as a result of dynamic interaction with the environment. Development is manifested by the emergence of new forms of action and the acquisition of predictive control of these actions. Mastery of action relies critically on prospection, i.e. the perception and knowledge of upcoming events. Repetitive practice of new actions is not focused on establishing fixed patterns of movement but on establishing the possibilities for prospective control in the context of these actions [22]. This highlights the importance of internal simulation in accelerating the scaffolding of early developmentally-acquired sensorimotor knowledge. Sharing this knowledge with other cognitive systems is only possible if they have a common history of experiences and if they have a similar phylogeny and a compatible ontogeny.

Development depends crucially on motivations which define the goals of actions. The two most important motives that drive actions and development are social and explorative. There are at least two exploratory motives: the discovery of novelty and regularities in the world and the discovery of the potential of the infant's own actions. The social motives are manifest as a fixation on social stimuli, imitation of basic gestures, and engagement in social interaction (e.g. joint attention and turn taking [23,24,25]).

The primary focus of the early stages of ontogenesis is to develop manipulative action based on visuo-motor mapping, learning to decouple motor synergies (e.g. grasping and reaching), anticipation of goal states, learning affordances, interaction with other agents through social motives, and imitative learning.

Imitative learning in neonates is innate in their phyogeny and crucial to their development, but the right ontogenetic circumstances must still be provided. In the same way, if the phylogeny of a biologically-inspired artificial autonomous cognitive systems is designed correctly, specifically by adhering to the guidelines set out in [13] and summarized in the previous section and in Table 1, then imitative learning can be used through a process of coaching to get the system to perform tasks and fulfil required functions, despite being autonomous. The imitative learning and associated coaching plays on the innate values and motives of the system in the following ways.

First, imitation assists in the decomposition of actions into movements: it shows how goal-oriented goal-directed action is decomposed into or is constituted by component movements. Seond, goals are perceived directly as the desired outcomes of actions. Third, imitation is a restricted and focussed form of social engagement and is driven in

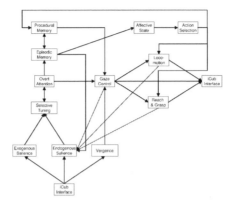

Figure 1. The iCub cognitive architecture.

part by a desire to belong to the social group and manifest by mutually-consistent action. This is important because, in terms of the two primary purposes of cognition to expand a repertoire or space of possible actions and to extend the prospective capability of the agent, acting together in a consistent or conformant manner reinforces the beliefs (or models) that are constructed by the system. Coaching and imitative learning not only provides an efficient and effective way acquiring new skills without the need to explore inappropriate or ineffectual alternatives, it also positively reinforces the system's predictive model. The repetitive nature of goal-directed action imitiative learning further enhances this effect.

Thus, imitative learning results from a dynamic balance between the exploratory motives and the social motives, both of which target the expansion of action capabilities and predictive power of the cognitive system. In this, imitiative learning through coaching brings together and consolidates the other early developmental tendencies.

4. The iCub Cognitive Architecture

The iCub cognitive architecture follows a significant subset of the roadmap guidelines summarized in Table 1, focussing on several key capabilities. Gaze control, reaching, and locomotion constitute the initial simple goal-directed actions. Episodic and procedural memories are included to effect a simplified version of internal simulation in order to provide capabilities for prediction and reconstruction, as well as generative model construction bootstrapped by learned affordances. In addition, motivations encapsulated in the system's affective state are made explicit so that they address curiosity and experimentation, both explorative motives, triggered by exogenous and endogenous factors, respectively. This distinction between the exogenous and the endogenous is reflected by the need to include an attention system to incorporate both factors. A simple process of homeostatic self-regulation governed by the affective state provides elementary action selection. Finally, all the various components of the cognitive architecture operate concurrently so that a sequence of states representing cognitive behaviour emerges from the interaction of many separate parallel processes rather than being dictated by some state-machine as in the case of most cognitive architectures. The iCub cognitive architecture at present comprises thirteen components (please refer to Fig. 1; more complete details can be found in [13]).

Together, the exogenous salience [26], endogenous salience, selective tuning [27], and overt attention [28] components comprise the iCub's perception system. Similarly, gaze control [29], vergence, reach & grasp, locomotion comprise the iCub's actions system. The episodic memory and the procedural memory together provide the iCub's principle mechanism for anticipation and adaptation. The affective state component effects the iCub motivations which together with the action selection component provide a very simple homeostatic process which regulates the autonomous behaviour of the iCub. The iCub interface component completes the architecture and reflect the embodiment of the iCub from an architecture point of view.

5. Conclusion

The primary assertion being put forward in this paper is that a suitably-designed cognitive system, i.e. one with a well-configured cognitive architecture, will exhibit a natural tendency to behave in a manner suggested by an instructing coach. Despite being autonomous, such cognitive systems are inherently trainable. The ease with which they can be trained depends on the balance of exploration and social motivation. This leaves unanswered three questions. First, what is the mechanism by which that part of the cognitive architecture concerned the association of movement and perception in goal-directed prospectively-guided action grows and develops?[2] For example, what metric guides or governs the reinforcement learning of perception-movement associations and the construction of action pathways? Second, in a related manner, how is the right balance between exploratory and social motives achieved? Third, how are episodic memories consolidated into semantic memories so that the resultant experiential learning is transferrable to new situations? Answering these questions poses an important research challenge.

Acknowledgements

Aspects of this work were supported by the European Commission, Project IST-004370, under Strategic Objective 2.3.2.4: Cognitive Systems. Discussions with Gordon Cheng and Marcia Riley, Institute of Cognitive Systems, Technical University of Munich, were very valuable in developing the ideas on coaching and imitative learning.

References

[1]   D. Vernon, G. Sandini, and G. Metta. The icub cognitive architecture: Interactive development in a humanoid robot. In *Proceedings of IEEE International Conference on Development and Learning (ICDL)*, Imperial College, London, 2007.

[2]   E. Thompson. *Mind in Life: Biology, Phenomenology, and the Sciences of Mind.* Harvard University Press, Boston, 2007.

[3]   T. Froese and T. Ziemke. Enactive artificial intelligence: Investigating the systemic organization of life and mind. *Artificial Intelligence*, 173:466–500, 2009.

---

[2]In the iCub cognitive architecture, this comprises the procedural memory, episodic memory, affective state, and action selection components.

[4]   D. Vernon. Enaction as a conceptual framework for development in cognitive robotics. *Paladyn Journal of Behavioral Robotics*, 1(2):89–98, 2010.

[5]   J. Stewart, O. Gapenne, and E. A. Di Paolo. *Enaction: Toward a New Paradigm for Cognitive Science.* MIT Press, 2011.

[6]   G. M. Edelman. *Second Nature: Brain Science and Human Knowledge.* Yale University Press, New Haven and London, 2006.

[7]   A. Billard, S. Calinon, R. Dillmann, and S. Schaal. Robot programming by demonstration. In *Springer Handbook of Robotics*, pages 1371–1394. 2008.

[8]   R. Dillmann, T. Asfour, M. Do, R. Jäkel, A. Kasper, P. Azad, A. Ude, S. Schmidt-Rohr, and M. Lösch. Advances in robot programming by demonstration. *KI*, 24(4):295–303, 2010.

[9]   M. Riley, A. Ude, C. Atkeson, and G. Cheng. Coaching: An approach to efficiently and intuitively create humanoid robot behaviors. In *IEEE-RAS Conference on Humanoid Robotics*, pages 567–574, 2006.

[10] S. Schaal, A. Ijspeert, and A. Billard. Computational approaches to motor learning by imitation. 2003.

[11] W. D. Christensen and C. A. Hooker. An interactivist-constructivist approach to intelligence: self-directed anticipative learning. *Philosophical Psychology*, 13(1):5–45, 2000.

[12] M. H. Bickhard. Autonomy, function, and representation. *Artificial Intelligence, Special Issue on Communication and Cognition*, 17(3-4):111–131, 2000.

[13] D. Vernon, C. von Hofsten, and L. Fadiga. *A Roadmap for Cognitive Development in Humanoid Robots*, volume 11 of *Cognitive Systems Monographs (COSMOS)*. Springer, Berlin, 2010.

[14] H. Maturana and F. Varela. *The Tree of Knowledge – The Biological Roots of Human Understanding.* New Science Library, Boston & London, 1987.

[15] R. Núñez and W. J. Freeman. *Reclaiming Cognition — The Primacy of Action, Intention and Emotion.* Imprint Academic, Thorverton, UK, 1999.

[16] A. Berthoz. *The Brain's Sense of Movement.* Harvard University Press, Cambridge, MA, 2000.

[17] G. Hesslow. Conscious thought as simulation of behaviour and perception. *Trends in Cognitive Sciences*, 6(6):242–247, 2002.

[18] R. Grush. The emulation theory of representation: motor control, imagery, and perception. *Behavioral and Brain Sciences*, 27:377–442, 2004.

[19] M. P. Shanahan. Cognition, action selection, and inner rehearsal. In *Proceedings IJCAI Workshop on Modelling Natural Action Selection*, pages 92–99, 2005.

[20] M. P. Shanahan. A cognitive architecture that combines internal simulation with a global workspace. *Consciousness and Cognition*, 15:433–449, 2006.

[21] P. Langley, J. E. Laird, and S. Rogers. Cognitive architectures: Research issues and challenges. *Cognitive Systems Research*, 10(2):141–160, 2009.

[22] E. S. Reed. *Encountering the world: towards an ecological psychology.* Oxford University Press, New York, 1996.

[23] J. Nadel, C. Guerini, A. Peze, and C. Rivet. The evolving nature of imitation as a format for communication. In J. Nadel and G. Butterworth, editors, *Imitation in Infancy*, pages 209–234. Cambridge University Press, Cambridge, 1999.

[24] G. S. Speidel. Imitation: a bootstrap for learning to speak. In G. E. Speidel and K. E. Nelson, editors, *The many faces of imitation in language learning*, pages 151–180. Springer Verlag, 1989.

[25] C. Trevarthen, T. Kokkinaki, and G. A. Fiamenghi Jr. What infants' imitations communicate: with mothers, with fathers and with peers. In J. Nadel and G. Butterworth, editors, *Imitation in Infancy*, pages 61–124. Cambridge University Press, Cambridge, 1999.

[26] J. Ruesch, M. Lopes, J. Hornstein, J. Santos-Victor, and R. Pfeifer. Multimodal saliency-based bottom-up attention - a framework for the humanoid robot icub. In *Proc. International Conference on Robotics and Automation*, pages 962–967, Pasadena, CA, USA, May 19-23 2008.

[27] J. K. Tsotsos, S. Culhane, W. Wai, Y. Lai, N. David, and F. Nufb. Modeling visual attention via selective tuning. *Artificial Intelligence*, 78:507–547, 1995.

[28] A. Zaharescu, A. L. Rothenstein, and J. K. Tsotsos. Towards a biologically plausible active visual search model. In L. Paletta, J. K. Tsotsos, E. Rome, and G. Humphreys, editors, *Proceedings of the Second International Workshop on Attention and Performance in Computational Vision, WAPCV*, volume LNCS 3368, pages 133–147. Springer, 2004.

[29] M. Lopes, A. Bernardino, J. Santos-Victor, C. von Hofsten, and K. Rosander. Biomimetic eye-neck coordination. In *IEEE International Conference on Development and Learning*, Shanghai, China, 2009.

Biologically Inspired Cognitive Architectures 2011
A.V. Samsonovich and K.R. Jóhannsdóttir (Eds.)
IOS Press, 2011
doi:10.3233/978-1-60750-959-2-419

A Multimodal Hypertensor Architecture for Association Formation

Craig M. VINEYARD [a,b,1], Stephen J. VERZI [a], Michael L. BERNARD[a], and Thomas P. CAUDELL[b]

[a] *Sandia National Laboratories*
[b] *Electrical and Computer Engineering Department, University of New Mexico*

Abstract. Several fields of study have developed sophisticated techniques to process signals of varying types. For example, pattern recognition techniques may seek to convert an audio waveform to a text transcription or to process an image and classify the represented object. However, much of this research focuses upon a single signal type. While such an approach has many useful applications, there are many domains which receive an influx of differing signal types. The brain receives a variety of sensory input signals and although each input stream does receive its share of individual processing, additional insight also comes from the converged processing of all input modalities. Such an occurrence takes place within the medial temporal lobe (MTL) and hippocampus. Consequently, we have designed a neural network architecture inspired by hippocampus connectivity and functionality which associates multimodal inputs.

Keywords: Artificial neural network; hippocampus; computational model

Introduction

Advances in mathematics and engineering have led to the development of sophisticated signal processing capabilities. However, much of this research focuses upon a single signal type. While such an approach has many useful applications, there are many domains which receive an influx of differing signal types. The brain receives a variety of sensory input signals such as visual, auditory, and olfactory. And although each input stream does receive its share of individual processing, additional insight comes from the converged processing of all input modalities. Such an occurrence takes place within the medial temporal lobe and hippocampus. As the key player in episodic memory, the relational memory functions of hippocampus support complex memories comprised of multiple sensory inputs. For example, on your last visit to a zoo, even though they are perceived separately, the audible roar of a lion can be associated with the visual observation of the large cat with a mane. Consequently, we have designed a neural network architecture inspired by hippocampus connectivity and functionality which auto-associates multimodal inputs. This approach allows for associations to be formed of varying complexity from heterogeneous input modalities. In this work we present a brief description of hippocampus neuroanatomy, explain the design of our neural network architecture, and present results from an implementation of our architecture.

---

[1] Corresponding Author: Craig Vineyard, E-mail: cmviney@sandia.gov

1. Hippocampus Neurophysiology

Cortical inputs to medial temporal lobe (MTL) arrive from various sensory modalities, with different emphases depending upon the mammalian species. For instance, rats receive a significant olfactory influence whereas bats receive a strong auditory influence [1]. Nevertheless, across species, most of the neocortical inputs to the perirhinal cortex come from cortical areas which process unimodal sensory information about qualities of objects ("what" information), and most of the neocortical inputs to the parahippocampal cortex come from cortical areas which process polymodal spatial ("where") information [1][2]. There are some connections between the two streams, however overall processing of the streams remains largely segregated until they converge within hippocampus [3][4].

Extensive neuroscience research typically identifies hippocampus to be composed of a loop receiving inputs from entorhinal cortex (EC), which receives inputs from perirhinal and parahippocampal cortices, and beginning with dentate gyrus (DG), proceeding to CA3, followed by CA1 and propagating back to cortex. These sub regions will be addressed individually as follows.

The DG receives the conjoined multimodal sensory signals from EC. Anatomically, DG consists of a large number of neurons with relatively sparse neural activation at a given instant. Effectively, this behavior suggests that the DG creates non-overlapping sparse codes for unique events [5]. The sparse DG outputs serve as the input for CA3.

The CA3 region of hippocampus consists of extensive recurrent connections. Additionally, the presence of numerous inhibitory and excitatory interneurons enables CA3 to perform auto-association processes. Anatomically, the output of CA3 proceeds to CA1 and subiculum as the major output regions of hippocampus [6].

While the exact functionality of subiculum is largely unknown, CA1 functionality is typically identified as learning relational information for temporal sequences and connecting episodic encodings from CA3 with the original EC sensory activations.

We have used some of these functional properties of hippocampus as the basis for an artificial neural network architecture for association formation which we will describe next.

2. Computational Architecture

In general, an association is a relationship between entities. For example, an individual is associated with their name or two individuals may be associated by a common workplace. Many associations are between entities of differing types. An individual is a physical entity whereas their name is a nonphysical label. Two co-workers may both be people, however to associate them with their shared workplace effectively associates them with a building\location\corporation. All entities are trivially related to themselves, but more interesting associations are between pairs and k- tuples of entities. A pair is the simplest non trivial association, but more complexly, k individual entities may be associated with each other as a k-tuple. And so the question arises as to how relationships are formed.

Numerous domain specific rules or heuristics may be derived based upon criteria such as distance metrics or shared features. But instead, our architecture, which is inspired by hippocampus, answers this question by the premise of associating a focus with its context, analogous to the dorsal and ventral partitioning in EC sensory input signals. In other words, our approach associates what and where information based upon their shared frame of reference. For example, a man may be associated with the home he is seen living at.

However, beyond simply deciding what entities should be associated with one another there is also the issue of representation. Prior to entering hippocampus, sensory signals pass through numerous layers of cortex. Throughout these layers a representation for entities are built up. Eventually, within hippocampus, the DG is believed to create unique sparse encodings for unique perceptions. Likewise, our architecture relies upon having a unique representation of the inputs it receives such that it can identify whether the current input is an item it has seen before and update any existing associations appropriately, or whether the input is novel necessitating a new encoding.

Our architecture, shown in Fig. 1, addresses this capability by using fuzzy-Adaptive Resonance Theory (ART) artificial neural network modules. Developed by Carpenter and Grossberg, the ART family of neural networks are online, unsupervised neural networks which are excellent at category formation [7]. Given a vector of real valued numbers corresponding to a particular input, fuzzy-ART performs pattern categorization and through winner-take-all competition yields a unique output value to represent a group of similar inputs. We have utilized these capabilities by employing a fuzzy-ART module to categorize each input type presented to our architecture. In the neurophysiology, DG creates nearly unique encoding for novel inputs. Likewise, the fuzzy-ART modules we are using in our architecture create representative categories for inputs. Repeated presentation of previously seen (identical) inputs activates the same categorical representation whereas newly seen inputs can be represented by their own encoding. These unique categorical activations may then be further processed and associated together.

The DG encodings of hippocampus propagate to the CA3 region which is believed to be heavily composed of recurrent connections and associations. In our architecture, by connecting a hypertensor to the template activations of the fuzzy-ART module we are able to encode associations among k-tuples of inputs. Existent neural network architecture ARTMAP links two ART modules using a mapfield (or tensor) such that the mapfield may record simultaneous activations across the two ART modules. The rectangular mapfield of ARTMAP connects one ART module to each axis of the map grid and the intersecting grid lines encode a connection between the two ART modules [8]. The ARTMAP architecture allows many-to-one associations to be formed from ART_a to ART_b where the a-side ART module receives input from a data vector and the b-side ART module receives input from a label vector in (supervised learning) classification tasks (see Figure 1 in [8]).

Our Associative-ART architecture consists of a single fuzzy-ART module per input type (i.e. image, text, etc.), and utilizes the association tensor to encode associations between k-tuples of entities it is presented. Instead of connecting a separate ART module to each axis of the association field, the outputs of each ART module are mirrored connecting them to both sides of the association tensor and subsequently allowing associations to be formed across the multimodal k-tuple.

All association tensor values are initialized to zero. Upon receiving a k-tuple input, associations are formed by handling all pairs. For each of the pairs, the grid intersection of the two entities in the association tensor A is set to a value of one as shown in the following equation:

$$A_{ij} = 1, \forall (i, j) \in P, \tag{1}$$

where P is the set of all pairs of elements in a k-tuple input. Each element in the k-tuple input will correspond to a particular fuzzy ART category activated during the previous k time steps in one of the multimodal ART modules. Consequently, the association tensor of our Associative-ART architecture creates a symmetric binary association matrix.

The overall Associative-ART architecture is depicted in Fig. 1. When associating two inputs of the same type (i.e. image to image), the use of a single fuzzy-ART module necessitates that rather than presenting the associated inputs simultaneously, they are presented sequentially to the fuzzy-ART module within the architecture. And so rather than encoding the instantaneous activation of an individual input, the association tensor associates the previous k fuzzy-ART outputs across all modalities if there was an output. In other words, a single association tensor update encompasses k fuzzy-ART categories. There is no sequencing in the association field; instead there are multiple simultaneous activations as may be seen in Fig. 1. In the Fig. 1 example, the association formed links the dark gray and light gray categories as a paired association in the association tensor. Associations are symmetric and may be many-to-many.

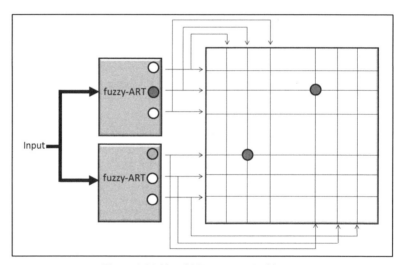

Figure 1. Multimodal Hypertensor Architecure

3. Multimodal Association Experiment

As an example of the multimodal associative capabilities of our architecture we have created an example associating text and images. An individual's physical self is associated with their name, and furthermore their first and last names are associated with one another. Consequently, for this example we have used the first and last names of United States Presidents as well as their presidential portrait paintings as our dataset [9][10].

First and last names were presented to the architecture individually as text strings (as opposed to a single concatenated text string). Associating the text pairings with a corresponding presidential portrait yielded triadic associations. The presentation order of input k-tuples does not affect the final associations formed, so for this experiment we arbitrarily presented the triples in order of presidency.

4. Results and Analysis

The overall association tensor generated by processing this multimodal example is too large to meaningfully include in this paper, however Fig. 2 illustrates a portion of the resulting associations. The resulting association graph is not connected, but rather disjoint groupings arise based upon commonality amongst the individual components of the k-tuples.

Several associations are unique in the sense that they do not share either a first or last name or portrait with any other president, and consequently only the components of such a triad are associated with each other. Two such examples shown in Fig. 2 are Abraham Lincoln and Ronald Reagan near the lower right region of the figure. Other larger association clusters may be formed such as the grouping built about the node representing 'William' shown in the lower left half of Fig. 2. Four presidents have shared William as a first name and so each of their respective last names as well as portraits are associated with 'William'. The name 'Franklin' has occurred as both a first and last name for differing Presidents, and so as shown in the upper right of Fig. 2 larger association chains may be formed connecting multiple nodes. Consequently, even though the architecture was only presented with triples, the net result can be a more complex association graph.

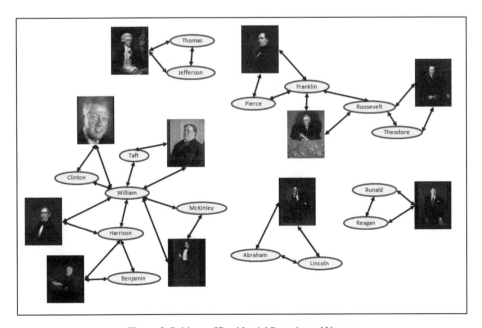

Figure 2. Pairings of Presidential Portraits and Names

5. Conclusions and Future Directions

In this research we have presented an artificial neural network computational architecture with functionality inspired by the neural functionality of hippocampus. Specifically, this architecture was designed based upon the dentate gyrus (DG) and CA3 regions of hippocampus to learn multimodal associations amongst k-tuples of entities.

Further development of this architecture may include more sophisticated processing within the association tensor as well as the incorporation of a temporal component. Rather than simply encoding a binary association value, a strength of association could be included based upon frequency of presentation or other metrics.

Acknowledgement

This research was possible in part by LDRD program support from Sandia National Laboratories. Sandia National Laboratories is a multi-program laboratory managed and operated by Sandia Corporation, a wholly owned subsidiary of Lockheed Martin Corporation, for the U.S. Department of Energy's National Nuclear Security Administration under contract DE-AC04-94AL85000.

References

[1] R.D. Burwell, M.P. Witter, & D.G. Amaral. Perirhinal and postrhinal cortices of the rat: a review of the neuroanatomical literature and comparison with findings from the monkey brain. *Hippocampus*, (1995), 390-408.

[2] H. Eichenbaum, "The hippocampus and declarative memory: cognitive mechanisms and neural codes," *Behavioural Brain Research*, 2001, pp. 199-207

[3] W.A. Suzuki, & D.G. Amaral,Perirhinal and parahippocampal cortices of the macaque monkey: cortical afferents. *Journal of Comparative Neurology 350,* (1994), 497-533.

[4] Suzuki, W., & Eichenbaum, H. (2000). The neurophysiology of memory. *Annals of the NY Academy of Sciences, 911,* 175-91.

[5] Leutgeb, et al, Independent codes for spatial and episodic memory in hippocampal neuronal ensembles, *Science* 309, (2005).

[6] Eichenbaum, H. & Cohen, N.J. (2001). From Conditioning to Conscious Recollection: Memory Systems of the Brain. Oxford: Oxford University Press.

[7] G.A. Carpenter, S. Grossberg, and D.B. Rosen. FuzzyART: fast stable learning and categorization of analog patterns by an adaptive resonance system. *Neural Networks*, (1991), 4:759-771.

[8] G.A. Carpenter, S Grossberg, N Markuzon, J.H. Reynold, & D.B. Rosen. Fuzzy ARTMAP: a neural network architecture for incremental supervised learning of analog multidimensional maps. *IEEE Transactions on Neural Networks*, (1992), 3: 698-713.

[9] "The Presidents" http://www.whitehouse.gov/about/presidents

[10] "Portraits of the Presidents from the National Portrait Gallery" http://www.npg.si.edu/exh/travpres/index6.HTM

Biologically Inspired Cognitive Architectures 2011
A.V. Samsonovich and K.R. Jóhannsdóttir (Eds.)
IOS Press, 2011
© *2011 The authors and IOS Press. All rights reserved.*
doi:10.3233/978-1-60750-959-2-425

Recursive Subgoals Discovery Based on the Functional Systems Theory

Evgenii E. VITYAEV[a,b,1], Alexander V. DEMIN[c]

[a] *Sobolev Institute of Mathematics SB RAS,*
630090, Novosibirsk, Russia. E-mail: vityaev@math.nsc.ru
[b] *Novosibirsk State University, Novosibirsk*
[c] *A.P.Ershov Institute of Informatics Systems SB RAS,*
630090, Novosibirsk, Russia

Abstract. The paper presents a model of adaptive behavior of an aminat based on the physiological functional system theory and Probabilistic Dynamic Logic. The main distinction of this model is the possibility for automatic generation of new sub-goals, which allows us to solve more complex multi-level tasks. Animat has been created on the basis of this model, and an experiment has been carried out in order to train it and to compare it with the existing approaches based on reinforcement learning. The results of comparison have shown that the proposed model learns and acts efficiently.

Keywords. Animat, Control System, Probabilistic Dynamic Logic

Introduction

In this work we applied Probabilistic Dynamic Logic models [1][2][3] for the goal-seeking behavior models, investigated in the Functional Systems Theory [4][5] for developing the adaptive animat. We describe a general scheme of functional systems, training algorithm and automatic subgoals formation. On the basis of the proposed model, an elementary animat and its environment have been implemented in a computer program. Using this program, we carried out experiment in the animat learning and made test comparison with some existing approaches.

1. A model of a functional system operation

Functional systems theory. The model we propose is based on the theory of functional systems, developed in 1930-70s by the famous Soviet neurophysiologist P.K. Anokhin [4][5]. According to this theory, a functional system, that achieves some results beneficial for an organism (for example, need - satisfaction), is considered to be a unit of this organism's activity.

The initial stage of a behavioral act of any complexity is *afferent synthesis* that includes synthesis of motivation, memory and information about the environment. As a

---

[1] Corresponding Author. This work is partially supported by the Russian Science Foundation grant #11-07-00560-a and Integration projects #47, 111, 119 of the SB RAS.

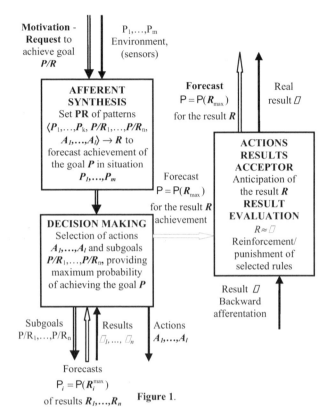

Figure 1.

result of the afferent synthesis, all possible ways of achieving the goal in this situation are evoked from the memory. At the stage of *decision-making*, only one particular way of action is selected according to the initial need. To provide the achievement of the results, an *actions results acceptor* is being created beforehand which is a model of the parameters of the expected (predicted) results. Then actions are followed by signals about achievement of the results, called backward afferentation, which would perfectly comply with the properties of the actions results acceptor.

Functional system model. Figure 1 shows the model [6][7] of a functional system based on [4][5]. Let us think that a goal *P/R* is set to the functional system that consists in reaching the result *R*. This is done in the form of a request to the functional system to achieve the goal *P/R*. Information about the environment is also supplied in the form of stimulus (sensors) $P_1, ..., P_m$.

In the process of afferent synthesis, all information related to achievement of the goal *P* is evoked from the memory by the motivation excitement. This information is stored as a set of rules $PR = \{ \langle P_1, ..., P_k, (P/R)_1, ..., (P/R)_n, A_1, ..., A_l \rangle \to R \}$, where $P_1, ..., P_k$ – properties of a situation; $(P/R)_1, ..., (P/R)_n$ – subgoals that should achieve the results $R_1, ..., R_n$ in order to achieve the goal *P*; $A_1, ..., A_l$ – actions, that must be fulfilled to achieve the result *R*. Note that only those rules are evoked, in which the situation properties $P_1, ..., P_k$ are included in the situation description $P_1, ..., P_m$.

To achieve the subgoals, we send the corresponding requests *recursively* down the hierarchy (in figure 1 it is indicated by the double arrow pointing down). These requests activate all information related to achievement of these subgoals in the lower level functional systems, which, in turn, may require achievement of the other goals at even lower levels, and so on. If some subgoal cannot be achieved in this situation (there are no rules predicting its achievement in this situation), then denial is received in reply to the request and the corresponding rule is excluded from the consideration. If all requested subgoals of the rule $R = (\langle P_1,...,P_k,(P/R)_1,...,(P/R)_n,A_1,...,A_l \rangle \to R)$ are achieved, then it passes to the decision-making block as a possible way of the goal achievement.

In the decision-making block all obtained rules are assigned the probability of the goal P achievement. The estimated probability of the rule

$R = (\langle P_1,...,P_k,(P/R)_1,...,(P/R)_n,A_1,...,A_l \rangle \to R)$ is:

$P(R) = P(R \mid P_1,...,P_k,R_1,...,R_n,A_1,...,A_l) \cdot P(P_1) \cdot ... \cdot P(P_n)$, where

$P(R \mid P_1,...,P_k,R_1,...,R_n,A_1,...,A_l)$ - conditional probability of the rule R,

$P(P_1),...,P(P_n)$ – probabilities of subgoals $P_1,...,P_n$ achievement.

As decision in the decision-making block the rule R_{max} with maximum estimation of the probability $P(R_{max})$ is selected as the way of the goal P achievement. The probability $P(P) = P(R_{max})$ performs the forecasted probability of the goal P achievement.

Forecast $P(R_{max})$ (indicated by the white arrow) for the anticipated result R is sent to the actions results acceptor block. Forecasts for the subresults $R_1,...,R_n$ in all lower level functional subsystems are also sent to the corresponding actions results acceptors. Forecasts $P(P_1),...,P(P_n)$ of all subresults $R_1,...,R_n$ for all subgoals are being sent from the functional subsisitems to the decision making block of the higher level system (also indicated by the white arrow).

The anticipated results R and $R_1,...,R_n$ for the goal P/R and subgoals $(P/R)_1,...,(P/R)_n$ perform the actions results acceptor. As demonstrated in a lot of physiological experiments [4][5] the real receptors are activated for the control of corresponding results achievement. Actions results acceptor controls not only the final result achievement (the satisfaction of some need) but also all hierarchy and sequence of intermediate results that must be achieved for the final goal achievement.

After decision is made and actions results acceptor activated, real actions stat to be realized. This actions lead to the real results $\square$ and $\square_1,...,\square_n$, that were received thought corresponding backward afferentation [4][5]. This results are compared with anticipated results R and $R_1,...,R_n$. If forecasts coincide with the real results (with the given degree of accuracy), then rules selected in the decision-making blocks are reinforced, otherwise punished. Reinforcement/punishment consists in changing the probabilistic estimations of these rules, which consists not in simple rising/decreasing of the conditional probabilities, as in reinforcement learning, but in conditional reflex modeling by the semantic probabilistic inference [8][9].

Subgoals discovering. Initially animat has a hierarchy of functional systems given a priori. In the process of learning, animat may automatically discover new subgoals and generate the corresponding functional systems.

According to J. Gibson [10] (1) *elements are organized hierarchically*, small elements are *hierarchically bild-in* large elements, and (2) elements *occur* in different places of the world. Results of actions are well predicted only in the frame of one holistic element. Hence, the most perfect predictions are also organized hierarchically in accordance with the following principal:

Principle of hierarchical prediction: (1) predictions are always performed in the frame of one holistic element; (2) predictions between different elements performed in the *hierarchically* upper level systems, where these different elements belong to one holistic element.

Subgoals are such results of sequences of actions (in perception or movement) that belong to one element. To divide sequences of actions (and its results) into parts, each of which belongs to one element, we propose the following definition of subgoals. Subgoals are such results of some sequence of actions that (1) significantly increase the probability of higher-level goals achievement and (2) actions following these sequence can't be defined unambiguously (may belong to other elements) [6].

In order to identify subgoals, the set of rules PR of some functional system is analyzed. For the rule $R = (\langle P_1,..., P_k, (P/R)_1,...,(P/R)_n, A_1,..., A_l \rangle \to R)$ we define as $Sen(R) = \{P_1,..., P_k\}$ the set of sensors, as $Act(R) = \{A_1,..., A_l\}$ the set of actions and as $Sub(R) = \{(P/R)_1,...,(P/R)_n\}$ the set of subgoals. In accordance with the functional systems theory [4][5], the anticipated result R is not only a final result (the need satisfaction), but also all intermediate results that are achieved by actions from the set $Act(R) = \{A_1,..., A_l\}$. So, the result R is a consequence of more detailed results $R = \{ R^1,..., R^t \}$.

Subrule $R_{sub} = (\langle P_1^{new},..., P_k^{new}, (P/R)_1^{new},...,(P/R)_{n'}^{new}, A_1^{new},..., A_{l'}^{new} \rangle \to R^{new})$, of the rule R (we right $R_{sub} \Box R$) produces a new subgoal P^{new}/R^{new} and corresponding functional system, if the following conditions are satisfied:

1) $Sen(R_{sub}) \subset Sen(R)$, $Sub(R_{sub}) \subset Sub(R)$ $Act(R_{sub}) \subset Act(R)$,
$R^{new} = \{ R_1^{new},..., R_s^{new} \} \subset \{ R^1,..., R^t \} = R$;

2) any other rule, R' $\in PR$ that does not contain a subrule R_{sub} (the relation $R_{sub} \Box$ R' is not true) has less value of the estimated probability $P(R') < P(R)$. This means that achievement of the result R^{new} considerably increases the estimated probability $P(R)$ of the rule R;

3) sequence of actions $\{A_1^{new},..., A_l^{new}\}$ is maximal – it can't be extended without losing the value of estimated probability $P(R_{sub})$ of the rule R_{sub}.

The subrule R_{sub} produces a new functional system at the lower level that evoked by the new subgoal P^{new}/R^{new} of the reduced (relative to R) rule

$R_{red} = \langle Sen(R), Sub(R) \backslash Sub(R_{sub}), P^{new}/R^{new}, Act(R) \backslash Act(R_{sub}) \rangle \to R$

A new functional system has a goal P^{new}/R^{new}, that may be achieved by the rule R_{sub}. Thus, for each functional system, its set of rules PR is analyzed and new subgoals are identified. For any newly-generated functional systems a set of rules PR, including at least a rule R_{sub}, is discovered, using the semantic probabilistic inference.

2. Experiment

A virtual world and an animat were modeled, and the main goal for the animat was to pick up "food". The animat's world is a square field divided into 25□25 cells, which are of the following type: empty cells, obstacles, food and pill. Obstacles are located only along the virtual world's perimeter thus forming its natural borders. The animat may move across the field and perform 3 types of actions: to step one cell forward, to turn left, to turn right.

Some amount of food is randomly distributed over the field. To pick up food, the animat has to turn to the cell containing food. In this case it is assumed that it "eats" the food, the cell is cleaned and new "food" object appears at random in another place of the field. Pills, like food, are randomly distributed over the field. Before eating food, the animat has first to find, pick and keep a pill. When it eats food, the pill disappears and, to eat the next portion of food, it again has to find and pick up a pill, and so on. The pill is picked, when the animat has to step to the cell containing the pill. However, if the animat has one pill, it can't pick any more pills until it uses it to eat food. When the animat picks a pill, the cell is cleaned and a new pill appears in another place of the field at random. The amounts of pills and food were kept equal to 100.

The animat has ten sensors. Eight of them are located around the animat: "in front of-to the left", "in front of", "in front of-to the right", "to the left", "to the right", "behind-to the left", "behind", "behind-to the right"; one sensor is in its center "center" and one is "pill availability" that informs the animat about pill availability and gets values "yes" or "no". Each sensor informs the animat about the type of the cell.

In order to evaluate efficiency of the control system we made test comparison with systems built on the basis of reinforcement learning [11]. For comparison, we selected two control systems built on the basis of Q-Learning. The essence of this algorithm is in consequent refinement of estimates for the total reward value $Q(s_t, A_t)$, that obtained after performing an action A_t in a situation s_t:

$$Q^{(i+1)}(s_t, A_t) = Q^{(i)}(s_t, A_t) + \alpha(r_t + \gamma \max_A Q^{(i)}(s_{t+1}, A) - Q^{(i)}(s_t, A_t)).$$

The first system is Q-Lookup Table, which is based on the table that contains Q-values for all possible situations and actions. The second system is Q-Neural Net, which uses an approximation of the function $Q(s_t, A_t)$ using neural networks. In this case each possible action A_i uses a separate neural network NN_i.

In our experiment the animat needs at first to find a pill, and then to find food. The purpose of the experiment was to demonstrate the possibility of automatic generation of subgoals during the goal-seeking behavior.

At the beginning, animat has only a basic functional system, and its goal is to achieve the situation when, at the same time, a pill is available and the central sensor indicates that food is found. The corresponding goal-predicate is: ("center" = "food" and "available pill" = yes).

At each test started during our experiment the animat did stably identify a new subgoal described by the subgoal-predicate $P_1 = $ ("available pill" = yes) and created the corresponding functional system. The model was working in the following way. When the animat had no pill, the rule $P_1 \rightarrow P$ was launched as the most probable one. It passed the control function to a lower-level functional system that performed the pill search. And when the animat had a pill, rules with a higher probability were launched in the basic functional system and food was found.

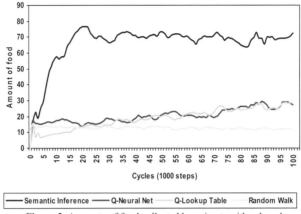

Figure 2. Amounts of food collected by animats with subgoals.

The results of this experiment are shown in fig. 2. The diagram shows the average values for every control system based on 20 tests. In each test the animat was given 100,000 steps, and had to learn how to accomplish the given task. It follows from the diagram, that control system based on the functional systems model surpasses the reinforcement learning systems both in the speed of learning and in the quality of its functioning. The control system Q-Lookup Table performs a poor learning ability and unstable functioning. The control system Q-Neural Net in some cases is capable to learn to react to all sensor data correctly when the training period is increased up to 300,000 – 500,000 steps. The control system Q-Lookup Table could not reach optimal behavior even after 500,000 steps. Open source code of the animat control system is available at address http://www.math.nsc.ru/AP/ScientificDiscovery/PDF/animat.exe.

References

[1] E.E. Vityaev, B.Y. Kovalerchuk, L. Perlovsky, S.O. Smerdov, Probabilistic Dynamic Logic of Phenomena and Cognition // WCCI 2010 IEEE World Congress on Computational Intelligence July, 18-23, 2010 - CCIB, Barcelona, Spain, pp. 3361-3366

[2] Perlovsky, L.I. (2007). Modeling Field Theory of Higher Cognitive Functions. Chapter in Artificial Cognition Systems, Eds. A. Loula, R. Gudwin, J. Queiroz. Idea Group, Hershey, PA, pp.64-105.

[3] Perlovsky, L.I. (2010). Neural Mechanisms of the Mind, Aristotle, Zadeh, & fMRI, IEEE Trans. Neural Networks, 21(5), 718-33.

[4] P.K. Anokhin, Biology and neurophysiology of the conditioned reflex and its role in adaptive behavior. Oxford etc.: Pergamon press, 1974.- 574p.

[5] P.K. Anokhin, Functional system.- In: Dictionary of behavioral science. New York etc., 1973, p.153.

[6] A.V. Demin, E.E. Vityaev, Logical model of adaptive control system // Neuroinformatics, v3(1), 2008, p.79-107. (in Russian).

[7] E.E. Vityaev, Brain principals of the functional systems theory and information theory of emotions // Neuroinformatics, v3(1), 2008, p.25-78. (in Russian).

[8] E.E. Vityaev, The logic of prediction // Proceedings of the 9th Asian Logic Conference (August 16-19, Novosibirsk, Russia), World Scientific Publishers, 2006 pp.263-276

[9] E.E. Vityaev, B.Y. Kovalerchuk, Empirical Theories Discovery based on the Measurement Theory. Mind and Machine, v.14, #4, 551-573, 2004.

[10] Gibson, J.J. (1979). The Ecological Approach to Visual Perception. Boston: Houghton Mifflin. (1986)

[11] Sutton R. and Barto A., Reinforcement Learning: An Introduction. – Cambridge: MIT Press, 1998.

Biologically Inspired Cognitive Architectures 2011
A.V. Samsonovich and K.R. Jóhannsdóttir (Eds.)
IOS Press, 2011

doi:10.3233/978-1-60750-959-2-431

Extracting Episodic Memory Feature Relevance Without Domain Knowledge

Benjamin WALKER, Dustin DALEN, Zachary FALTERSACK,
Andrew NUXOLL

University of Portland 5000 N. Willamette Blvd. Portland, OR 97203

Abstract. Episodic memory provides many important capabilities to a cognitive architecture. One of the challenges of creating a general episodic memory system is to be effective when given no information about the agent's task.

In this paper, we present an effective algorithm for detecting the relevance of the features of episodic memories while only being told when an agent completes a goal. We demonstrate this algorithm using an episodic learning agent in a task that provides the agent with a mix of relevant and irrelevant features. The episodic learner outperforms a variant Q-Learning algorithm that has proven effective in the past.

Keywords. episodic memory, feature selection

Introduction

Human episodic memory is a long-term memory of specific events from an individual's experience [15]. Episodic memory is typically distinguished from semantic memory and procedural memory in that the episodic memories, or episodes, include a specific temporal component that links them to a single, specific event. In contrast, semantic memories contain facts, things you *know* but can not recall when you learned them. For example, knowing that the United States capital is Washington DC or that cherries grow on trees. Procedural memories are things you *know how* to do but can not articulate such as whistling or juggling.

Impairment of one's ability to encode or retrieve episodic memories is the condition known as amnesia. Studies of severe amnesiacs [12] provide evidence that episodic memory is a distinct, long-term memory system as amnesiacs retain their ability to create and retrieve semantic and procedural memories. Studies show that the hippocampus is involved in the encoding and retrieval of episodes and that the frontal cortex is likely where such memories are stored in the long term [16].

One effect is clear: amnesia is a severe handicap of an individual's cognitive ability. This implies that episodic memory is an essential component of an effective cognitive architecture.

Feature Relevance

A critical component of an effective episodic memory system is the ability to retrieve the most helpful memory for a given task. If an agent is using its episodic memory to inform its decisions, then poor retrievals clearly result in degraded behavior.

However, determining the "best" match for a given memory cue is difficult in the general case. Consider two agents that process information in an online bookseller's database. One agent makes suggestions to customers based upon their past purchases. The other agent selects appropriate shipping boxes for books sold by an online bookseller. For either agent, the bookseller's database might contain a lot of information that is irrelevant to the agent's task.

Typically, an agent created specifically for a purpose would be given information about what features of the database are most and least relevant to the task. A general cognitive architecture does not have this luxury; by definition, it must be effective in any environment. Therefore the episodic memory system that is integrated into a cognitive architecture must rely upon the agent's behavior to induce the relative importance of each feature of a given memory cue.

All of the existing episodic memory systems we are aware of rely upon being given knowledge about the relative importance of various features from an external source. In the context of a general episodic memory system, a feature is any component of the memory that is used for matching during retrieval. Most systems require the agent to identify important features of episodes by only using such features when it constructs a memory cue [1,7,14]. One system extracts that information indirectly from the agent's domain-specific behavior [11].

In either case, this means that if the agent does not have knowledge about the task it is performing the episodic memory system also lacks this knowledge. Presuming our goal is create a cognitive architecture to support general intelligence, it is desirable to create an episodic memory system that can gauge the importance of each feature of an episode intrinsically.

The problem of selecting a small subset of relevant features from a larger whole is known as feature selection or feature weighting. (See [5] for a survey). This topic has received decades of attention among artificial intelligence and data mining researchers. However, much of the current body of feature selection research is not directly applicable to cognitive architecture design because it assumes that feature weighting is inherently a supervised-learning task.

Feature selection for model-free reinforcement learning has not been ignored but the research we have found to date [6,8,9] assumes that the domain that the agent is operating in has the Markov property. Specifically, it assumes that the agent's current state contains all the information necessary to make an optimal decision. Clearly a cognitive architecture can't make this assumption. Furthermore, tasks that require the agent to have an episodic memory of past events clearly lack the Markov property.

Thus, the problem addressed by this paper is how to weigh the importance of the various features of an episodic memory when the agent is given minimal information about the environment. We describe this task using the term *feature relevance* rather than feature selection or feature weighting. This is because the former term implies the omission of features from the data and the latter term has a broader definition associated with general nearest neighbor methods.

Episode and Action Based Feature Relevance

In this section, we outline a simple algorithm we've devised for determining feature relevance in this general case.

Our algorithm makes the following assumptions about the episodic memory system. These assumptions are compatible with the domain-independent, artificial episodic memory systems we are aware of:

- The episodic memory system records a new episode each time the agent takes an action in its environment.
- The episode contains a snapshot of some portion of the agent's current sensing, current goal and internal features determined via cognition.
- The agent selects each action from a finite set of actions A_1, A_2, ..., A_n.
- The agent attempts to accomplish one goal at a time and is aware of what goal it is attempting to achieve. Each goal has exactly one goal state associated with it.
- The agent is aware when it has successfully completed a goal.
- Upon achieving a goal, the agent will immediately begin working toward achieving a subsequent goal.

In brief, our algorithm identifies clusters of episodes that should represent the same state because they began after the same goal and were arrived at via the same actions. The algorithm then weights the features of these episodes to minimize the distance between each episode in a binary N-space defined by the presence or absence of their features in a manner much like a weighted nearest neighbor match [3] except in reverse. In other words, the algorithm's goal is to weight the k features of related episodes so that they are as close together as possible in the k-dimensional space.

Our algorithm in more detail is as follows:

Step 1: Extract the set of all past runs to the goal that have begun after achieving the agent's current goal.

Step 2: Extract the subset of runs that begin with the most commonly taken action. For example, if the agent took action A_3 more often than any other, then extract all runs whose first action was A_3.

Step 3: Examine the features of all the episodes in the subset that resulted from step 2. For each feature, identify what fraction of the time that feature appears in all the episodes in the subset (a value in the range [0.0..1.0]).

Step 4: Recursively repeat steps 2 and 3 on the subset of runs for subsequent actions in the sequence. Each time, extract a new, smaller subset of runs whose next action is the most commonly taken in the subset selected the previous time. Stop when the subset's size is less than 2.

Step 5: Weight each feature based upon how much more or less frequently it appears in the extracted subset compared to the overall average for all the episodes in the episodic memory. Thus, if a feature typically appears 30% of the time among all episodes, but appears 70% of the time in the subset then the feature receives a high weight. If, instead, the feature appeared 40% of the time in the subset it would receive a much smaller weight. Alternatively, if the feature appeared 5% of the time in the subset then its absence receives a high weight.

The weights that result from this algorithm can be used as required by the episodic memory system. The most obvious purpose would be to weight the features of a memory cue that is used for retrieval.

Blind Navigation Domain

To test the effectiveness of our algorithm we created a domain wherein the agent attempts to reach a goal position within a simple two-dimensional maze. This domain is a virtual implementation of a robotic navigation environment we have created using iRobot Create robots [2]. This environment is, in turn, a more challenging version of one that was used to demonstrate the NSM Q-Learning algorithm developed by McCallum [10].

In this domain, the agent is provided with a very limited set of binary sensors:

- **left bumper:** detects when the agent bumps into a wall on its left
- **right bumper:** detects when the agent bumps into a wall on its right
- **goal:** detects when the agent has reached the goal position

It's notable that if the agent hits a wall dead on, that both the left and right bumper sensors will activate.

The agent has a few simple actions it can take at any given time step:

- **forward:** move forward a short, fixed distance
- **left:** turn left 45 degrees
- **right:** turn right 45 degrees
- **no-op:** three additional "noise" actions that each have no effect

Because of the agent's highly limited sensors, state aliasing is common. As a result, an episodic knowledge of past states is essential for making good decisions in the present. Hence, the agent requires an episodic memory to complete this task.

We want to emphasize that the agent is *not* informed of the nature of its task. The meaning of its sensors and actions are not communicated in any way other than identifying the goal sensor. Thus, the agent is only aware that it must accomplish a goal with the given inputs and outputs.

This enforced ignorance makes the domain intensely difficult rather than trivial. In recent experiments with human subjects (not yet published) only about 70% of them were able to complete the simplest maze we could define in this domain.

To test the effectiveness of our feature relevance algorithm we modified the environment to introduce seven additional noise sensors. At each time step, the environment chose randomly whether to include or omit each of the associated features. These features appear to the agent as additional binary sensors, indistinguishable from the ones defined above.

An Episodic Learning Agent

To test the system, we created an episodic learning agent that uses an episodic memory system we've developed called Ziggurat [4]. This system is able to overcome the state aliasing issues associated with our blind navigation domain by recognizing sequences of past actions that tend to be associated with each other and also using those sequences as part of its match process.

At each time step, the agent uses its episodic memory to select its actions. It does this by searching its memory for the most similar past situation in which it took the same action. Then, it builds a plan to reach its goal as if it has returned to that past state again. Next, it follows the plan until it fails or the goal is reached. Finally, it repeats the above procedure until the simulation ends.

We modified this baseline agent to bias its episodic retrieval match using the weights derived using the feature relevance algorithm we described above. Specifically, it uses its entire sensing as a cue, but then uses the feature weights to prune its cue to only those features above a certain, fixed threshold. For our experiments, we selected a threshold of 15% more or less likely. Other reasonable threshold values seemed to perform about equally well in preliminary experiments.

Experimental Results

To evaluate the performance of our agent we compared it to an agent using the NSM Q-Learning algorithm. This algorithm was originally demonstrated using a similar domain [10]. This algorithm also uses a rudimentary episodic memory to overcome state aliasing and performed well in the domain before the noise features were added.

For our experiment, we used a U-shaped maze with the start and goal positions at opposite ends of the 'U'. We ran each each agent from start to goal 100 times in this maze. Each time, the agent retained episodic memories of previous runs to the goal and, thus, could leverage those memories to improve performance.

The experiment was repeated 350 times and the results were averaged. Figure 1 depicts the average number of steps to the goal for each agent on each of the 50 runs. The horizontal line depicts the average performance of an agent that always selects a random action.

By examining the figure it is apparent that, with the additional noise features active, the NSM Q-Learning agent is no longer able to perform better than a random agent in this maze.

However, the episodic learning agent is able to use the feature weights to gradually learn which of its sensors are relevant to that task. This knowledge, in turn, allows the agent to learn to navigate the maze more quickly.

To confirm our results, we made a direct examination of the feature weights at the conclusion of these runs and found that they accurately reflected the relevance of the sensors. We also verified that the episodic learning agent was incapacitated when the feature weighting was removed.

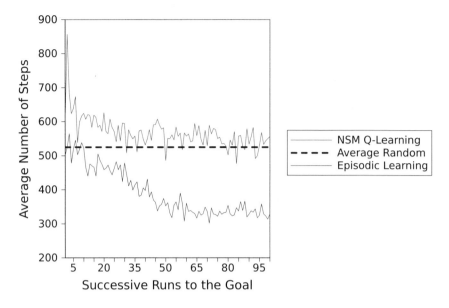

Figure 1. This graph depicts the average number of steps required to reach the goal on 100 successive trials with each of the three agents.

Discussion

The task we have defined in this research is that of identifying the task relevance of the features of an episodic memory given no advance information about the agent's task and making little or no presumptions about the task. We have also argued that feature relevance is an important part of a general episodic memory for a cognitive archtecture.

In this paper, we have presented an algorithm for calculating feature relevance in this situation that is based on nearest neighbor match algorithms. We've used the relevance values to weight episodic memory retrieval in an episodic learning agent.

While simple, our algorithm is the only one we know of that can learn feature relevance in this general case. However, the general feature relevance problem is particularly challenging and we can identify two key weaknesses that need to be addressed for greater success. First, we have only demonstrated this algorithm with a single domain. Changes in the domain and to the recorded episodes over time would have an unknown effect on performance. Second, our algorithm relies upon having information about the agent's current goal and being certain when that goal is a achieved. For a general reinforcement learning task, the agent may only be given reward information rather than goal information.

For the future, we want to explore alternative algorithms that do not rely upon being aware of the agent's current goal. We also intend to apply feature relevance algorithms in a broader range of domains in order to provide a more compelling argument for the algorithm's generality.

References

[1] C. Brom, J. Lukavsk, and R. Kadlec, Episodic Memory for Human-like Agents and Human-like Agents for Episodic Memory. In: *International Journal of Machine Consciousness (IJMC)* **2**:2 (2010), 227–244.

[2] T.L. Crenshaw, and S. Beyer. A Testbed for Cyber-Physical Systems. In *Proceedings of the 3rd Workshop on Cyber Security Experimentation and Test (CSET)*, 2010.

[3] R. O. Duda, P. E. Hart, and D. G. Stork. *Pattern Classification*. John Wiley and Sons, USA, 2nd edition, 182–186, 2001.

[4] Z. Faltersack, B. Burns, A.M. Nuxoll and T.L. Crenshaw, Ziggurat: Steps Toward a General Episodic Memory. In *Proceedings of AAAI Fall Symposium on Advances in Cognitive Science*, 2011, *submitted*.

[5] I. Guyon and A. Elisseeff. An introduction to variable and feature selection. In *Journal of Machine Learning Research*, vol. 3 (March 2003), 1157–1182.

[6] H. Hachiya and M. Sugiyama, Feature selection for reinforcement learning: evaluating implicit state-reward dependency via conditional mutual information. In *Proceedings of the 2010 European conference on Machine learning and knowledge discovery in databases: Part I (ECML PKDD'10)*, Springer-Verlag, Berlin, Heidelberg, 474–489.

[7] W.C. Ho, K. Dautenhahn and C.L. Nehaniv, Computational memory architectures for autobiographic agents interacting in a complex virtual environment: a working model, In *Connection Science*, **20**:1 (2008), 21–65.

[8] M. Kroon and S. Whiteson. Automatic Feature Selection for Model-Based Reinforcement Learning in Factored MDPs. In *Proceedings of the 2009 International Conference on Machine Learning and Applications (ICMLA '09)*, IEEE Computer Society, Washington, DC, USA, 324–330, 2009.

[9] M. G. Lagoudakis and R. Parr. Reinforcement learning as classification: leveraging modern classifiers. In *Proceedings of ICML 2003*, 424–431, 2003.

[10] R.A. McCallum, Instance- based state identification for reinforcement learning. In *Advances in Neural Information Processing Systems 7*, 21–65.

[11] A. Nuxoll and J. Laird, A Cognitive Model of Episodic Memory Integrated With a General Cognitive Architecture, In *Proceedings of the International Conference on Cognitive Modeling*, 2004.

[12] H. Schmolck, E.A. Kensinger, S. Corkin, and L. Squire, Semantic knowledge in Patient H.M. and other patients with bilateral medial and lateral temporal lobe lesions, *Hippocampus* **12**:4, 520–533, 2002.

[13] R.S. Sutton and A.G. Barto, *Reinforcement learning: An introduction*, The MIT Press, MA, USA, 1998.

[14] D. Tecuci and B. Porter, A Generic Memory Module for Events, In *Proceedings to The Twentieth International FLAIRS Conference*, 2007.

[15] E. Tulving, *Elements of episodic memory*. Oxford University Press, New York, 1983.

[16] E. Tulving and F. I. M. Craik (Eds.). *The Oxford Handbook of Memory*. Oxford University Press, New York, 1983.

Biologically Inspired Cognitive Architectures 2011
A.V. Samsonovich and K.R. Jóhannsdóttir (Eds.)
IOS Press, 2011
© 2011 The authors and IOS Press. All rights reserved.
doi:10.3233/978-1-60750-959-2-438

Architectural Requirements & Implications of Consciousness, Self, and "Free Will"

Mark WASER
Books International

Abstract. While adaptive systems are currently generally judged by their degree of intelligence (in terms of their ability to discover how to achieve goals), the critical measurement for the future will be where they fall on the spectrum of self. Once machines and software are able to strongly modify and improve themselves, the concepts of the self and agency will be far more important, determining not only what a particular system will eventually be capable of but how it will actually act. Unfortunately, so little attention has been paid to this fact that most people still expect that the basic cognitive architecture of a passive "Oracle" in terms of consciousness, self, and "free will" will be little different from that of an active explorer/experimenter with assigned goals to accomplish. We will outline the various assumptions and trade-offs inherent in each of these concepts and the expected characteristics of each – which not only apply to machine intelligence but humans and collective entities like governments and corporations as well.

Keywords. Intelligence, Consciousness, Self, Agency, "Free Will", Morality

Introduction

Imagine three futures. In one, machine intelligence develops gradually as computers continue growing more varied and more ubiquitous leading to a tremendous variety of sentient entities. In another, a single machine intelligence suddenly appears, quickly spreads to every interconnected computer, and eventually controls literally billions of androids and other machines. In the third, mankind creates a nearly omniscient machine "oracle" that gives humanity tremendous power and control over their lives.

In determining the future of humanity, the frequently overlooked concept of self is likely to be one of the most critical factors. Indeed, the coalescence and increasing intelligence of larger than human entities has already had a tremendous impact on humanity which is only accelerating. Tribes combining into city-states merging into countries vying with international corporations shape the world that we live in. Political parties, media conglomerates, grassroots movements and "larger-than-life" individuals (real and fictional) all fight to shape our thoughts. The increasing size and speed of flash mobs and the intelligence displayed by the self-named "HiveMind" created by "I Love Bees" [1] are undoubtedly only portents of things to come.

Yet, the vast majority of AGI researchers are far more focused on the analysis and creation of intelligence rather than self and pay little heed to the differences between a passive "oracle", which is frequently perceived as not possessing a "self", and an active autonomous explorer, experimenter, and inventor with specific goals to accomplish. Arguably, however, it is the "self" that was co-created with biological intelligence – and it is the goals and motivations of any "self" that exists that will determine the behavior of future machine intelligences. Current predictions of the future vary from tacitly expecting individual selves in androids to believing that a single Borg- or Skynet-like hive self is unavoidable to insisting that the non-existence of self, in terms of independent motivation and free will, is absolutely required for human safety.

Compounding the issue is there is no still concrete consensus on what self and/or conscious are or how they arise. If we wish to insist upon the non-existence of self, what are the lines that we should not cross and the things that we should not build? Is self-modification possible without a true self? Does allowing "self"-modification usually or inevitably lead to a self? An examination of these issues is long overdue.

1. Consciousness

AGI researchers seem to have converged on a definition of intelligence as a measure of the ability to determine how to achieve a wide variety of goals under a wide variety of circumstances. Or, alternatively, that the function of intelligence is to determine the method(s) by which a wide variety of goals can be achieved under a wide variety of circumstances. The degree of intelligence, therefore, is the minimal amount of information processing necessary to determine how to manipulate the circumstances so they include the goal.

Chalmer's ***double-aspect theory*** of information [2] claims that the fact that "there is a direct isomorphism between certain physically embodied information spaces and certain phenomenal (or experiential) information spaces" (or, alternatively, that "we can find the same abstract information space embedded in physical processing and in conscious experience") means that the experience of consciousness is created by the structure of information processing. This leads to statements and speculation that

> Where there is simple information processing, there is simple experience, and where there is complex information processing, there is complex experience. A mouse has a simpler information-processing structure than a human, and has correspondingly simpler experience; perhaps a thermostat, a maximally simple information processing structure, might have maximally simple experience?

This meshes well with Tononi's ***information integration theory*** of consciousness which argues that subjective experience is one and the same thing as a system's capacity to integrate information, that the quantity of consciousness is the amount of integrated information generated by a complex of elements [3] and that the quality of experience (qualia) is specified by (the geometry of) the informational relationships it generates [4]. Tononi argues that the ability of a system to integrate information grows as that system incorporates statistical regularities from its environment and learns. Thus, if such information is about its environment, consciousness provides an adaptive advantage and may have evolved precisely because it is identical with the ability to integrate a lot of information in a short period of time. And since intelligence is the ability to integrate and manipulate information, consciousness seems a pre-requisite for intelligence and unavoidable in AI.

2. Self and Sense of Self

If consciousness is a foregone conclusion, the next best and/or only way to ensure AGI safety is to ensure that they either don't have a self or don't have knowledge of their own self.   For example, a passive Oracle that does nothing except answer questions is generally not considered a danger.   Except that a "passive" Oracle either needs to collect and integrate information in order to be able to answer questions or needs a side-kick that does so.   And the process(es) that gather and integrate the information will undoubtedly have goals that should include timeliness, accuracy and safety.   If the system is conscious/aware of these goals (i.e. they are integrated in with the rest of the information available to the system), for questions that are large and/or long-term enough, it will undoubtedly be most effective for the process(es) to first optimize or improve itself, if the system is able to do so, and then collect the information and answer the question (or intersperse and alternate the various activities).

This complete loop of a process (or physical entity) modifying itself must, if indeterminate in behavior, necessarily and sufficiently be considered an entity rather than an object – and humans innately tend to do so with the pathetic fallacy.   In "I Am a Strange Loop", Hofstadter [5] talks about self, soul, consciousness, and the concept of "I" as if they are the same thing.   Baars [6] writes of self as "unifying context of consciousness", "overall, unifying context of personal experience", and "a framework that remains largely stable across many different life situations" which "like any context, self seems to be largely unconscious but it profoundly shapes our conscious thoughts and experiences."   He writes of consciousness as "gateway to the unconscious mind" and as "gateway to the self" with the function "to create access for the self in all its manifestations" and quotes Daniel Dennett [7] calling it "that to which I have access."   Dennett also [8] describes the self as "a center of narrative gravity".

The potential problems with self-modifying goal-seeking entities are amply described by Omohundro [9].   In addition to the self-improvement described above, such an entity will have other tendencies (instrumental goals) which Omohundro claims will be present unless they are explicitly counteracted because they, too, advance any other goals present.   These include rationality, effective evaluation, avoiding manipulation, self-protection, and acquisition and effective use of resources.   Unfortunately, because he failed to recognize co-operation and morality as instrumental goals, Omohundro claimed that "Without explicit goals to the contrary, AIs are likely to behave like human sociopaths in their pursuit of resources."   We would argue that an entity with enough goals and intelligence will eventually reach such recognition but likely that it could become powerful enough to destroy us before that point.

3. Autonomy, Responsibility and "Free Will"

The critical safety issues that really must be addressed are responsibility for safety, how safety will be ensured, and how the responsibility will be enforced.   Defining autonomy as "freedom to determine one's own actions, behaviour, etc." and responsibility as "the ability or authority to act or decide on one's own, without supervision" implies an agent that "determines"/"decides" without outside interference.

Some people have suggested that all that is necessary for safety is to insert a human into the loop of self-modification (i.e. that a knowledge/sense of "self" is safe as long as the self-loop isn't fully integrated).   This places the onus of responsibility on the human and assumes that they will take the time to understand the system and any proposed modifications well enough not to allow any dangerous modifications to pass (and not be out-classed enough in intelligence that the system could "dupe" them into doing so).   At best, this will "only" tremendously slow the rate of system improvement.

At worst, it will be entirely ineffective. A far better strategy would be to create a safety evaluation or morality process/self whose entire goal/purpose/self is solely to identify and point out dangers in proposed answers (including modifications).

Eliezer Yudkowsky's Friendly AI [10] makes the programmer responsible for safety by insisting upon an absolutely foolproof "Friendliness Structure" that will *forever* convince the autonomous AI that it "wants" to be safe because of the goal that was initially planted in it. In his model, the AI will quickly become too powerful for anything to be externally enforced on it and post hoc measures against either it or the programmer are pretty much pointless. Yudkowsky later [11] took to calling his Friendly AI a "Really Powerful Optimization Process", presumably to avoid questions of entity-ness, selfhood, free will and slavery.

Alan Felthous [12] says that "Free will is regarded by some as the most and by others as the least relevant concept for criminal responsibility." Anthony Cashmore [13] claims that "a basic tenet of the judicial system and the way that we govern society is that we hold individuals accountable (we consider them at fault) on the assumption that people can make choices that do not simply reflect a summation of their genetic and environmental history." He quotes de Duve [14] arguing that if "neuronal events in the brain determine behavior, irrespective of whether they are conscious or unconscious, it is hard to find room for free will. But if free will does not exist, there can be no responsibility, and the structure of human societies must be revised." Yet, as Felthous points out, leading historical jurists in England eventually dropped the descriptor "free" but retained the central importance of the will to criminal responsibility and emphasized its dependence on the intellect to function properly.

Today, most of the information about will and morality is coming from the neurosciences, indicating that much of what we believe we directly experience and will is actually generated unconsciously and/or revised post hoc. For example, consciousness always edits out the approximately one-half second time delay between when physical stimulus first appears in the appropriate sensory region of the brain and when it actually enters conscious awareness with experiments [15][16] clearly demonstrating that there is an automatic subjective referral of the conscious experience backwards in time. More interestingly, not only have numerous studies [17][18][19] shown that the cerebral activity for action starts well before conscious intention but revealed that the upcoming outcome of a decision could be found in study of the brain activity in the prefrontal and parietal cortex up to 7 seconds before the subject was aware of their decision [20] and that the perceived time of decision is inferred rather than sensed and can be altered by deceptive feedback [21] or belief in personal or other human agency as opposed to that of machines [22][23].

More surprisingly, studies show that even agency is inferred rather than sensed with subliminal and supraliminal priming enhancing experienced authorship [24] and even inducing false illusory experiences of self-authorship [25][26] with belief in "free will" being enhanced by both [27]. This is obviously useful since psychological studies repeatedly proved that low control belief affects performance and motivation and recent studies have even shown that undermining beliefs in free will affects brain correlates of voluntary motor preparation by reducing action potential more than a second before subjects consciously decided to move [28] and increased cheating [29].

For longer-term activities, there is ample evidence [30] to show that our conscious, logical mind is constantly self-deceived to enable us to most effectively pursue what appears to be in our own self-interest and other recent evidence [31] clearly refutes the common assumptions that moral judgments are products of, based upon, or even correctly retrievable by conscious reasoning. We don't consciously know and can't consciously retrieve why we believe what we believe and are actually even very likely to consciously discard the very reasons (such as the "contact principle") that govern our behavior when unanalyzed. Of course, none of this should be particularly surprising since Minsky [32] has pointed out many other examples, as when one falls in love, where the subconscious/emotional systems overrule or dramatically alter the normal results of conscious processing without the consciousness being aware of the fact. Yet, arguably, we have evolved these features because they work well and make us more evolutionarily "fit". Maybe the best design for a safety evaluation and/or morality process is the one that we humans model – and maybe we should attempt it first for our machine, our corporations, and our governments (or, at least, understand it).

Conclusion – Safety in Stories and Illusions

Susan Blackmore [33] describes consciousness as an illusion of "a continuous stream of rich and detailed experiences, happening one after the other to a conscious person". Whenever consciousness is required, "a retrospective story is concocted about what was in the stream of consciousness a moment before, together with a self who was apparently experiencing it. Of course there was neither a conscious self nor a stream, but it now seems as though there was. This process goes on all the time with new stories being concocted whenever required.

This matches well with Dennett's [34] theory of multiple drafts that at any time there are multiple constructions of various sorts going on in the brain - multiple parallel descriptions of what's going on. None of these is 'in' consciousness while others are 'out' of it. Rather, whenever a probe is put in - for example a question asked or a behaviour precipitated - a narrative is created. The rest of the time there are lots of contenders in various stages of revision in different parts of the brain, and no final version. As he puts it "there are no fixed facts about the stream of consciousness independent of particular probes".

So apparently, safety lies in stories and illusions. For humans, Albert Bandura [35] has recommended reframing the issue of free will in terms of the exercise of agency, operating principally through cognitive and other self-regulatory process to provide new insights into the constructive and proactive role that cognition plays in action. We would argue that his social cognitive theory which embeds intelligences in a society is well-grounded, well-explored, adaptable to all intelligences, and a useful perspective for starting to understand everything from humans to machines to corporations and governments.

References

[1] J. McGonigal, Why I Love Bees: A Case Study in Collective Intelligence Gaming, in K. Salen (ed.), *The Ecology of Games: Connecting Youth, Games, and Learning*, 199-228, The MIT Press, Cambridge, MA, 2008, doi: 10.1162/dmal.9780262693646.199.

[2] D. Chalmers, Facing Up to the Problem of Consciousness, *Journal of Consciousness Studies* **2:3** (1995), 200-219.

[3] G. Tononi, An Information Integration Theory of Consciousness. *BMC Neurosci.* **5:42** (2004)

[4] B. Balduzzi and G. Tononi, Qualia: The Geometry of Integrated Information. *PLoS Comput Biol* **5:8** (2009), e1000462. doi:10.1371/journal.pcbi.100046

[5] D. Hofstadter, *I Am A Strange Loop*, Basic Books, New York, NY, 2007.
[6] B. Baars, *In The Theater Of Consciousness: The Workspace of the Mind*, Oxford University Press, New York, NY, 1997.
[7] D. Dennett, *Consciousness Explained*, Little, Brown, and Co., New York, NY, 1991.
[8] D. Dennett, The Self as a Center of Narrative Gravity, In F. Kessel, P. Cole & D. Johnson (eds) *Self and Consciousness: Multiple Perspectives*, Erlbaum, Hillsdale, NJ, 1992, http://cogprints.org/266/.
[9] S. Omohundro, The Basic AI Drives, In p. Wang, B. Goertzel, S. Franklin (eds) *Proceedings of the First Conference on Artificial General Intelligence*, 483-492. Amsterdam: IOS Press.
[10] E. Yudkowsky, *Coherent Extrapolated* Volition. 2004. http://www.singinst.org/upload/CEV.html.
[11] E. Yudkowsky, *Creating Friendly AI 1.0: The Analysis and Design of Benevolent Goal Architectures*, http://singinst.org/CFAI.html.
[12] Alan R. Felthous, MD, The Will: From Metaphysical Freedom to Normative Functionalism, *J Am Acad Psychiatry Law* **36:1** (2008), 16-24
[13] A. Cashmore, The Lucretian swerve: the biological basis of human behavior and the criminal justice system, *Proc Natl Acad Sci U S A* **107:10** (2010), 4499-504
[14] C de Duve, *Vital Dust: The Origin and Evolution of Life on Earth*, Basic Books, New York, NY, 1995.
[15] S. Blackmore, There is no stream of consciousness, *Journal of Consciousness Studies* **9:5** (2002), 17-28
[16] D. Dennett, Toward A Cognitive Theory of Consciousness, in D. Dennett (ed) *Brainstorms*, 149-173, Bradford Books/MIT Press, Cambridge, MA, 1978
[17] Libet, B., Wright, E. W., Feinstein, B., and Pearl, D. Subjective referral of the timing for a conscious sensory experience: A functional role for the somatosensory specific projection system in man, *Brain* **102:1** (1979), 193-224
[18] B. Libet, The experimental evidence for subjective referral of a sensory experience backwards in time: Reply to P. S. Churchland. *Philosophy of Science* **48** (1981), 181-197.
[19] B. Libet, C. A. Gleason, E. W. Wright, and D. K. Pearl, Time of conscious intention to act in relation to onset of cerebral activity (readiness-potential): The unconscious initiation of a freely voluntary act. *Brain* **106** (1983), 623-642.
[20] B. Libet, Unconscious cerebral initiative and the role of conscious will in voluntary action, *Behavioral and Brain Sciences* **8** (1985), 529-539 DOI: 10.1017/S0140525X00044903
[21] M. Matsuhashi and M. Hallett, The timing of the conscious intention to move. *Eur J Neurosci.* **28:11** (2008), 2344-51.
[22] C. Soon, M. Brass, H. Heinze and J. Haynes, Unconscious determinants of free decisions in the human brain, *Nature neuroscience* **11:5** (2008), 543–545. doi:10.1038/nn.2112
[23] Banks and E. Isham, We Infer Rather Than Perceive the Moment We Decided to Act, *Psychological Science* **20:1** (2009), 17-21
[24] A. Wohlschläger, P. Haggard, B. Gesierich and W. Prinzl, The Perceived Onset Time of Self- and Other-Generated Actions, *Psychological Science* **14:6** (2003) 586-591
[25] M. Buehner and Gruffydd R. Humphreys, Causal Binding of Actions to Their Effects, *Psychological Science* **20:10** (2009), 1221-1228, doi: 10.1111/j.1467-9280.2009.02435.x
[26] H. Aarts, R. Custers and D. Wegner, On the inference of personal authorship: Enhancing experienced agency by priming effect information. *Consciousness & Cognition* **14** (2005), 439-458
[27] D. Wegner and T. Wheatley, Apparent Mental Causation: Sources of the Experience of Will. *American Psychologist* **54:7** (1999), 480-492.
[28] S. Kühn and M. Brass, Retrospective construction of the judgment of free choice. *Consciousness and Cognition* **18** (2009), 12-21.
[29] H. Aarts and K. van den Bos, On the Foundations of Beliefs in Free Will: Intentional Binding and Unconscious Priming in Self-Agency, *Psychological Science* **22:4** (2011), 532-537
[30] D. Rigoni, S. Kühn, G. Sartori and M. Brass, Inducing Disbelief in Free Will Alters Brain Correlates of Preconscious Motor Preparation: The Brain Minds Whether We Believe in Free Will or Not. *Psychological Science* **22** (2011), 613-618.
[31] K. Vohs and J. Schooler. The Value of Believing in Free Will: Encouraging a Belief in Determinism Increases Cheating. *Psychological Science* **19** (2008): 49-54. . (doi:10.1111/j.1467-9280.2008.02045.x)
[32] R. Trivers, Deceit and self-deception: The relationship between communication and consciousness. In Robinson, M and Tiger, L. eds. Man and Beast Revisited, Smithsonian Press, Washington, DC, 1991
[33] M. Hauser, F. Cushman, L. Young, R. Kang-Xing Jin and J. Mikhail, A Dissociation Between Moral Judgments and Justifications. *Mind&Language* **22:1** (2007), 1-27
[34] M. Minsky, *The Emotion Machine: Commonsense Thinking, Artificial Intelligence, and the Future of the Human Mind*, Simon & Schuster, New York, NY, 2006
[35] A. Bandura, Reconstrual of "free will" from the agentic perspective of social cognitive theory. In J. Baer, J. C. Kaufman, & R. F. Baumeister (Eds.), *Are we free?: Psychology and free will*, 86-127, Oxford University Press , Oxford, UK, 2008.

Biologically Inspired Cognitive Architectures 2011
A.V. Samsonovich and K.R. Jóhannsdóttir (Eds.)
IOS Press, 2011
© 2011 The authors and IOS Press. All rights reserved.
doi:10.3233/978-1-60750-959-2-444

Access to Symbolization and Associativity Mechanisms in a Model of Conscious and Unconscious Processes

Roseli S. WEDEMANN [a,1], Luís Alfredo V. de CARVALHO [b] and
Raul DONANGELO [c]

[a] *Inst. de Matemática e Estatística, Universidade do Estado do Rio de Janeiro, Brazil*
[b] *Sistemas e Computação-COPPE, Universidade Federal do Rio de Janeiro, Brazil*
[c] *Inst. de Física, Universidade Federal do Rio de Janeiro, Brazil*

Abstract. We have previously described aspects of neurotic mental pathology, in terms of its relation to memory function and proposed a neural network model, whereby neurotic behavior is described as an associative memory process. Modules corresponding to sensory and symbolic memories interact, representing unconscious and conscious mental processes. Our main contribution with respect to current work regarding machine models of consciousness is to propose a neuronal associative memory mechanism that describes conscious and unconscious memory activity, based on Freud's description of neurosis, which illustrates how access to symbolization mechanisms is essential for consciousness. We modeled memory access dynamics by the Boltzmann machine (BM) and Generalized Simulated Annealing (GSA) and investigated the effects of using both on network associativity.

Keywords. Conscious-Unconscious, Associativity, Generalized Simulated Annealing

Introduction

In the past years, we have been studying the relation of memory mechanisms to some processes involved in mental functioning [1,2]. In particular, we have looked at Freud's findings in psychoanalytic research, regarding the *neuroses* [2]. In this pathology, traumatic and repressed memories are knowledge which is present in the subject but which is inaccessible to him, through symbolical representation [3,4]. These are momentarily or permanently inaccessible to the subject's conscience and are therefore considered *unconscious* knowledge. Freud observed that neurotic patients systematically repeated symptoms in the form of ideas and impulses and called this tendency a *compulsion to repeat*, which he related to repressed or traumatic memory traces [4,5]. Unconscious memories which cannot be expressed symbolically, may do so through other body response mechanisms, in the form of neurotic (unconscious) symptoms, similar to reflexes.

By *symbolic expression* we refer to the association of symbols to meaning as in language and also other forms of expressing thought and emotions, such as artistic represen-

---

tations (painting, musical composition, etc.) and remembrance of dreams. Neurotics have obtained relief and cure of painful symptoms through a psychoanalytic method called *working-through*, which aims at developing knowledge regarding the symptoms by accessing unconscious memories and understanding and changing the analysand's compulsion to repeat [3,5]. It involves mainly analyzing free associative talking, symptoms, parapraxes (slips of the tongue and pen, misreading, forgetting, etc.), dreams and that which is acted out in transference, in a process of symbolization of the repressed. This description of neurosis helps us to better understand the importance of access to symbolic processing, language and meaning for consciousness. We refer to [6,7,8,9,10,11,12,13], for similar considerations regarding symbolization and consciousness.

Here, due to space limitations, we briefly review a neuronal model described previously in [2]. In this model, we proposed that neurosis manifests itself as an associative memory process [14], where the network returns a stored pattern when it is shown another input pattern sufficiently similar to the stored one. The compulsion to repeat neurotic symptoms was modeled by supposing that the symptom is acted when the subject is presented with a stimulus which resembles a repressed or traumatic memory trace. The stimulus causes a stabilization of the neural net onto a minimal energy state, corresponding to the memory that synthesizes the original repressed experience, which in turn generates a neurotic response, called an *act*, as in psychoanalytic literature. The neurotic *act* is not a result of the stimulus as a new situation but a response to the repressed trace. We focus on memory access dynamics and present recent results from ongoing simulations, which show that memory access mechanisms regulate network associativity.

1. Hierarchical Memory Model

In the aforementioned model, we proposed a memory organization, where neurons belong to two hierarchically structured modules corresponding to *sensorial* and *symbolic memories* [2]. Traces stored in sensorial memory represent mental images of stimuli received by sensory receptors. Symbolic memory stores higher level representations of traces in sensorial memory, *i.e. symbols*, and represents brain structures associated with symbolic processing, language and consciousness. Sensorial and symbolic memories interact, producing unconscious and conscious mental activity. If the retrieval of a sensorial memory trace can activate retrieval of a pattern in symbolic memory, it can become conscious. We refer to [6] for a neurophysiological discussion of these issues.

Brain neural topology is structured by cooperative and competitive mechanisms, controlled by neurosubstances, where neurons interact mainly with nearby neighbors, having fewer long-range synaptic connections to distant neurons [6,7]. This is started and controlled by environmental stimulation and is the process whereby the environment represents itself in the brain. We thus proposed a *clustering algorithm* based on these mechanisms [2], to model the self-organizing process which results in a hierarchical, clustered topology of each memory module. We represented the association of ideas or symbols (such as in culture and language) by long-range synapses in the model.

1.1. Associative Memory Mechanisms

The topologies generated with the clustering algorithm are hierarchical, as mentioned previously [2]. Memory functioning was originally modeled by a Boltzmann Machine

(BM). There is no theoretical indication of the exact relation between network topology and memory dynamics. There have been indications that complex systems which present power-law behavior (are asymptotically scale invariant) may be described by the Nonextensive Statistical Mechanics (NSM) formalism [15,16]. We have found a power-law and generalized q-exponential behavior for the node-degree distributions of the network topologies generated by our model [2], indicating that they may not be well described by Boltzmann-Gibbs (BG) statistical mechanics, but rather by NSM [15]. We have thus modeled memory by a generalization of the BM called Generalized Simulated Annealing (GSA) [2,15], and this affects the chain of associations of ideas which we are modelling.

In the BM, an energy functional $H(S)$ is associated to network state S and, according to the BG distribution, the transition probability (acceptance probability) from state S to S', if $H(S') \geq H(S)$, is given by

$$P_{BG}(S \rightarrow S') = \exp\left[\frac{H(S) - H(S')}{T}\right], \tag{1}$$

where T is the network temperature parameter. Pattern retrieval on the net is achieved by a standard simulated annealing process, in which T is gradually lowered by a factor α, according to the BG distribution [14]. In the NSM formalism, one uses a generalized acceptance probability [15] for a transition from S to S', if $H(S') \geq H(S)$, given by

$$P_{GSA}(S \rightarrow S') = \frac{1}{[1 + (q_A - 1)(H(S') - H(S))/T]^{1/(q_A-1)}}, \tag{2}$$

where q_A is a parameter called q-acceptance. If one substitutes Eq. (2) for Eq. (1) in the algorithm of the BM, the resulting procedure is called GSA [15].

Both the BM and GSA differ from a gradient descent minimization scheme, in that they allow the system to change state with an increase in energy, depending on the value of T, according to Eq. (1) and Eq. (2). Boltzmann Eq. (1) favors changes of states with small increases in energy, and the BM will strongly prefer visiting state space in a nearby energy neighborhood from the starting point. The GSA distribution allows state changes with much higher energy increases, although with very low probability.

2. Results on Network Associativity

In neural network modeling, temperature is inspired from the fact that real neurons fire with variable strength, and there are delays in synapses, random fluctuations from the release of neurotransmitters, and so on. These are effects that we can loosely think of as noise [7,14], and we thus consider that temperature in BMs and GSA controls noise. Temperature allows associativity among memory configurations, lowering synaptic inhibition, in an analogy with the idea that freely talking in analytic sessions and stimulation from the analyst lower resistances and allow greater associativity. The generalized probability Eq. (2) also introduces parameter q_A, for regulating such phenomena.

Simulation of memory access is very time consuming and thus, in the simulations, we have analyzed networks with $N_{sens} = N_{symb} = 16$ neurons in sensorial and symbolic memory modules, respectively. Although this network size is extremely small, it has allowed a limited, preliminary illustration of the model, since microscopic characteristics should allow scaling of some macroscopic properties, with size. We consider parallelizing the algorithms, to study larger networks. The simulation experiment followed was to perform up to 10000 minimization procedures, starting each one from a different random network configuration, presented to both the BM and GSA. When a new pattern (local minimum of the network energy) is found, it is stored and the procedure is repeated from other random starting configurations, otherwise the search stops.

In Figures 1 and 2, we show the frequency with which the different patterns are found, with the BM and with GSA, for $q_A = 1.4$ and $q_A = 1.6$, respectively. Both calculations were performed at $T = 0.2$. We saw in [2,17] that, for lower temperatures, the BM functions like a gradient descent, so randomly generated patterns will stabilize at the closest local minima, and GSA becomes less associative, finding less patterns. We had also shown similar results, for smaller values of q_A in [2,17], where larger energy patterns were not accessed. We have been working on computational difficulties, since this experiment is highly processing-time consuming, for simulations with larger q_A, and we recently obtained the results for values of q_A shown here. It is clear from the figures that, for this temperature, GSA accesses many more patterns than the BM, finding the higher energy patterns which are harder to reach, with much higher frequency. The acceptance probability distribution given by Eq. (2) allows more associativity among memory states, with transitions to more distant minima in the energy functional H than Eq. (1), during the annealing process. This mechanism is strongly sensitive to values of q_A. This implies that the GSA machine will tend to make many local associations (state transitions) and, more often than the BM, will also make looser, more distant associations. This should correspond to a more flexible and creative memory dynamics in the brain.

One can observe an upper limit for the frequency of visits, as a function of energy for GSA which is a q-exponential function, given by

$$
e_q^x \equiv \begin{cases} [1 + (1-q)x]^{\frac{1}{(1-q)}} \,, & \text{if } 1 + (1-q)x \geq 0 \\ 0, & \text{otherwise} \end{cases} \,. \tag{3}
$$

In both Figures 1 and 2, we found the same value of $q = 1.104$ for this upper limit. It seems that as q_A increases, many more higher energy patterns, under the upper-limit, are accessed more frequently. We are verifying this with ongoing simulations, for larger q_A. For smaller q_A, the higher energy patterns are not accessed and the upper limit seems to be exponential [2,17].

3. Conclusions

From the psychoanalytic description of neurotic processes we have mentioned and our modeling experience, it seems that memory and attention are basic mechanisms which are important for the emergence of consciousness. We have proposed that in neurosis, an input stimulus, which by an associative memory process, retrieves a repressed or traumatic long-term memory trace, triggers a resulting neurotic act. If the selected memory trace (the attended object) can be expressed symbolically (reported) then it is considered that it can become conscious. If not, it will generate an unconscious neurotic act.

We are also currently investigating the relation of our neuroses model to cognitive models for attention and consciousness. Freud's observations regarding the unconscious

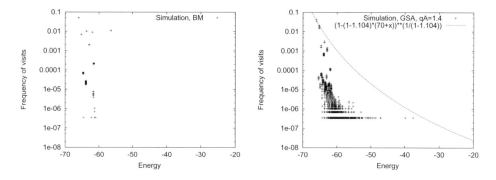

Figure 1. Frequency of visits to stored patterns for $T = 0.2$: (a) on the left, by the BM, (b) on the right, for GSA at $q_A = 1.4$.

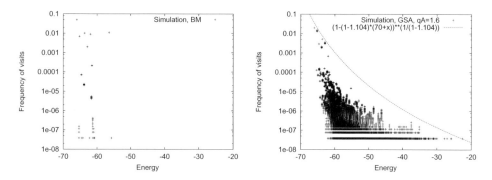

Figure 2. Frequency of visits to stored patterns for $T = 0.2$: (a) on the left, by the BM, (b) on the right, for GSA at $q_A = 1.6$.

may give us important insight regarding basic neuronal mechanisms underlying consciousness. The findings of Freud regarding neurotic behavior and our neuroses model
are in agreement with both the CODAM [8,9,10] and the Dehaene-Kerszberg-Changeux
Global Workspace (DKC-GW) [11,12,13] models, in that unconscious memories have
inhibited access to symbolic processing areas of the brain.

Our simulations show that, if memory is hierarchically structured, with both short
and long-range connections, and access functions as GSA, the neuronal system should
then be capable of making more distant associations among stored traces, with more
metaphors and creativity [18], than a system governed by BG statistics. Values of T and
q_A regulate these capabilities, reflecting network properties, such as the availability of
neuromodulators and neurotransmitters. It may be possible to test this behavior in a psychological experimental setting. More associative networks enhance capabilities for self-
reconfiguration and for learning processes, corresponding to changes in network connectivity by working-through [2] and new outcomes in the subject's life history. Some psychoanalytic theories consider that neurotic functioning is normal to human mental processing, as opposed to psychotic functioning, where more painful neurotic acts (symptoms) correspond to pathological neurotic cases [3,4,5]. We can thus consider regulating access from sensorial to symbolic memories, to simulate degrees of both normal and

pathological mental functioning. Our model is very schematic and we do not sustain or prove that this is the actual mechanism that occurs in the human brain, although the algorithms are inspired in basic neuronal mechanisms found in the brain. It nevertheless illustrates and seems to be a good metaphorical view of facets of mental phenomena, for which we seek a neuronal substratum, and suggests directions of search.

Acknowledgements

We are grateful to psychoanalyst Angela Bernardes of the Escola Brasileira de Psicanálise of Rio de Janeiro. Discussions with Sumiyoshi Abe, Evaldo M. F. Curado and Constantino Tsallis regarding NSM were also helpful. Many thanks to Alberto Santoro and the team responsible for the T2 Hepgrid Brazil-UERJ, computational cluster, part of the High Energy Physics CMS-GRID. This research was developed with grants from the Brazilian financing agencies CNPq, FAPERJ and CAPES.

References

[1] Carvalho, L.A.V., Mendes, D.Q., Wedemann, R.S.: Creativity and Delusions: The Dopaminergic Modulation of Cortical Maps. In: Sloot, P.M.A. et al. (Eds.): ICCS 2003. LNCS **2657**, pp. 511–520. Springer-Verlag, Berlin-Heidelberg (2003)

[2] Wedemann, R.S., Donangelo, R., Carvalho, L.A.V.: Generalized Memory Associativity in a Network Model for the Neuroses. Chaos **19**, 015116-(1–11) (2009)

[3] S. Freud,: Remembering, Repeating and Working-Through, Standard Edition, Vol. XII. The Hogarth Press, London (1958). First German edition (1914).

[4] Freud, S.: Introductory Lectures on Psycho-Analysis. Standard Edition. W. W. Norton and Company, New York - London (1966). First German edition (1917)

[5] Freud, S.: Beyond the Pleasure Principle. Standard Edition. The Hogarth Press, London (1974). First German edition (1920)

[6] Edelman, G.M.: Wider than the Sky, a Revolutionary View of Consciousness. Penguin Books, London (2005)

[7] Kandel, E.R., Schwartz, J.H., Jessel, T.M. (Eds.): Principles of Neural Science. MacGraw Hill, USA (2000)

[8] Fragopanagos, N., Kockelkoren, S., Taylor, J.G.: A Neurodynamic Model of the Attentional Blink. Cognitive Brain Research **24**, 568–586, (2005)

[9] Taylor, J.G.: CODAM Model: Through Attention to Consciousness. Scholarpedia 2(11):1598 (2007)

[10] Taylor, J.G.: A Neural Model of the Loss of Self in Schizophrenia. Schizophrenia Bull. 2010; **0**: sbq033V1–sbq033 (2010)

[11] Changeux, J.P.: L'homme de Verité. Editions Odile Jacob, Paris (2002)

[12] Changeux, J.P.: The Molecular Biology of Consciousness Investigated with Genetically Modified Mice. Phil. Trans. R. Soc. B **361**, 2239–2259 (2006)

[13] Dehaene, S., Kerszberg, M., Changeux, J.P.: A Neuronal Model of a Global Workspace in Effortful Cognitive Tasks. Proc. Natl. Acad. Sci. USA **95**, 114529–14534 (1998)

[14] Hertz, J.A., Krogh, A., Palmer, R.G. (eds.): Introduction to the Theory of Neural Computation. Lecture Notes, Vol. I. Perseus Books, Cambridge, MA (1991)

[15] Tsallis, C., Stariolo, D.A.: Generalized Simulated Annealing. Physica A **233**, 395–406 (1996)

[16] Tsallis, C.: Introduction to Nonextensive Statistical Mechanics, Approaching a Complex World. Springer, New York (2009)

[17] Wedemann, R.S., Carvalho, L.A.V., Donangelo, R.: Generalized Simulated Annealing and Memory Functioning in Psychopathology. In: Alippi, C. et al. et al. (Eds.): ICANN 2009, Part II. LNCS, **5769**, pp. 65–74. Springer-Verlag, Berlin-Heidelberg (2009)

[18] Tsallis, A.C., Tsallis, C., Magalhães, A.C.N., Tamarit, F.A.: Human and Computer Learning: An Experimental Study. Complexus **1**, 181–189 (2004)

Manifesto

Biologically Inspired Cognitive Architectures 2011
A.V. Samsonovich and K.R. Jóhannsdóttir (Eds.)
IOS Press, 2011
doi:10.3233/978-1-60750-959-2-453

On a Roadmap to Biologically Inspired Cognitive Agents

Antonio CHELLA[a], Christian LEBIERE[b], David C. NOELLE[c], and Alexei V. SAMSONOVICH[d,1]

[a] *DICGIM - University of Palermo,Viale delle Scienze building 6, 90128 Palermo, Italy*
[b] *Psychology Department, Carnegie Mellon University, 5000 Forbes Avenue, Pittsburgh, Pennsylvania 15213, United States*
[c] *School of Engineering, University of California, Merced, P.O. Box 2039, California 95344, United States*
[d] *Krasnow Institute for Advanced Study, George Mason University, Fairfax, Virginia 22030-4441, United States*
antonio.chella@unipa.it, cl@cmu.edu, dnoelle@ucmerced.edu, asamsono@gmu.edu

Abstract. A new challenge is proposed for future intelligent artifacts based on biologically inspired cognitive architectures (BICA), called the BICA Challenge. Namely, it is proposed that a BICA agent can only be considered human-level intelligent if it can be accepted and trusted as an equal member (a "person") by a human community. For example, an agent of this sort would be able to win a political election against human candidates.

Keywords. BICA Challenge, human-level, human-like, cognitive architectures, synthetic characters, virtual persons, intelligent agents

Brief Introduction

Despite many expectations since the 50s, the big breakthrough in artificial intelligence did not happen, and moreover, many researchers today believe that its idea is nonsense. Suspending disbelief in the sensibility of the idea, one may ask: what this breakthrough would be about, what would it change? One possible answer is that it is about changing the perception of artifacts by humans, and, as a consequence, changing the role of artifacts in human society, the goals and values in the artifact design. Then, a key element in solving this challenge must be the "human-likeness" of artifacts, manifested not in their appearance, but in their intrinsic cognitive and learning abilities. This notion is not simple and needs to be clarified in terms of functionality and architectural components, various tests and benchmarks, behavioral characteristics, and so on. The general challenge of making this breakthrough can be called *BICA Challenge*, as the solution is likely to be biologically-inspired and based on a cognitive architecture.

We start by looking at the critical components of human-level cognition, with the following implicit questions in mind: what makes us feel about others the same as about ourselves, even when we communicate with them over email and experience a

---

[1] Corresponding Author.

language barrier? Why don't these feelings extend to modern artificial intelligence tools, if those tools outperform us in a number of cognitive tasks?

1. Critical Components of Cognition

The field of *artificial intelligence* has been described as, "The study of how to make computers do things at which, at the moment, people are better" [1]. Despite the many problems with this definition, it does reflect an old and recently revived interest in producing computer systems that embody certain intellectual skills – those characteristic of agency – at a level of proficiency at least matching that exhibited by healthy humans. Computer systems currently outperform even the most intellectually capable humans on many narrowly defined tasks, ranging from solving systems of equations to playing chess, from trading in financial markets to retrieving relevant documents from huge free text databases. Despite these successes, there is a general consensus that computer systems still lack key properties of intelligent agency that are common to humans. The natural response to this realization is to itemize those capabilities that exhibit a gap between the performance of our current artificial systems and human-level behavior. A standard "divide-and-conquer" approach may then be pursued, with different research laboratories focusing on different capabilities, all working toward the eventual integration of modularized solutions into a fully capable cognitive agent.

This approach largely describes the broad research program in artificial intelligence that is active in the world today. Great advances are being made in many domains, from face recognition to mining knowledge from the web. Some researchers remain unconvinced, however, that these successes are of a kind that will eventually support integration into a generally intelligent agent [2]. The basic concern is that researchers have largely focused their energies on a parcellation of capabilities that cannot be seamlessly merged into general intelligence. At least two kinds of problems are hypothesized to exist with the subgoals currently being pursued by artificial intelligence researchers: the problem of *unintegrated capabilities* and the problem of *narrowly domain-specific capabilities*. The problem of *unintegrated capabilities* arises when researchers artificially limit the influence of cognitive capabilities on each other, usually in the name of maintaining simplicity of design. This is a problem when specific interactions between capabilities provide powerful and natural means to address cognitive challenges. For example, the ability to strategically move visual sensors using motor systems radically simplifies some problems in visual scene analysis. Similarly, the capability of intelligently "asking questions" of the environment through exploration can greatly speed processes of statistical learning. In short, there is a worry that some central aspects of general intelligence emerge through the interaction of cognitive capabilities, and those aspects could remain hidden from discovery if research remains inappropriately compartmentalized. One proposed remedy for the *unintegrated capabilities* problem is to focus research on tasks and skills that require the integration of cognitive systems. Rather than dividing cognition into capabilities like "vision" and "motor control", we may opt to focus on integrated capabilities like "the ability to drive a car down the highway" and "the ability to name the people in a still photograph". This approach, however, introduces the potential danger of *narrowly domain-specific capabilities*. It is often possible to produce solutions to narrowly defined tasks through the use of domain-specific techniques that fail to generalize in any way to other tasks and skills. Because of this, focusing on such narrow research problems may produce useful engineering results while providing little in the way of cumulative results building toward generally intelligent agents. Without such cumulative research, we are left with a collection of isolated skills, and there is general skepticism in the idea that full human-level cognitive agency consists of nothing more than a large collection of unrelated skills.

In both cases, the issue is fundamentally one of grain scale. Regarding unintegrated capabilities, AI approaches can always add capabilities such as those mentioned above into their system, but it wouldn't make them integrated with the rest of the system if they are treated, as is usually the case, as large separate modules which perform their function in a relatively isolated manner. Specifically, the issue is that today's AI systems are not unintegrated, as they often consist of various modules wired together, but rather that those modules are too coarse and their interaction too limited. Too often their model is a pipeline moving data from one module to another, only as strong as the weakest of its components, like a telephone game where the message gets increasingly lost. Conversely, neuroscience is constantly refining our understanding of the human brain as consisting of a highly modular structure, but one in which its modules interact with and constrain one another at a sub-second scale.

Similarly, narrowly domain-specific capabilities are not necessarily un-human-like since one of the hallmarks of human intelligence is the development of expertise, namely the refinement of large amounts of task-specific knowledge to improve our performance on any given task. So the problem is not that AI systems have domain-specific capabilities, but rather that they are not cumulative. Instead, they need to be engineered anew in each domain rather than developed cumulatively as in human expertise. One of the major goals of BICA is to enable reuse and generalization of functional models to gradually increase capabilities until they gradually approximate the breadth of human abilities [3].

There is a real danger that, by dividing the problem of developing an artificial cognitive agent into inappropriate sub-problems, we could be hindering or stalling research progress toward our ultimate goal. Recognizing this danger, we are left with the question of how to identify appropriate intermediate challenges that are likely, if successfully met, to eventually lead to the desired kind of general artificial cognition. What kinds of intellectual milestones are likely to lie on the path to general intelligence? Some have argued that this path begins with extremely general formalisms for reasoning and problem solving, such as formal logic theorem provers, and that following the path will involve a dogged commitment to maintaining the general nature of these mechanisms as knowledge and capabilities are added [4]. Others have suggested that a commitment to a functional decomposition that mirrors that seen in the human brain should help avoid the dangers of inappropriate divisions of cognitive capabilities [5]. In this position paper, we argue that the next set of milestones on the path to generally intelligent agents should involve systems with a range of integrated cognitive capabilities, with a focus on those capabilities that are specifically associated with a profound sense of agency when those systems interact with humans.

That focus on agency mirrors a similar recent emphasis in related fields, e.g., the shift to embodied cognition and cognitive architectures in cognitive science [6-8]. After all, most of our brain is devoted to perceptual and motor tasks, and our approach to BICA should reflect that reality. However, there are a couple of fundamental problems with that view, both of which Turing seems to have anticipated in some form when defining his test.

The theoretical problem is that, while the original conception of AI also emphasized agency (e.g., "intelligent robots"), the bulk of real progress in recent years in terms of everyday impact has not been in that direction but rather in embedding particular capabilities in our environment. Google is certainly the most important AI application nowadays but, rather than being *embodied*, it is a pervasive, *embedded* intelligent assistant to which we are happy to offload essential tasks for which we used to rely on trained human experts (e.g., librarians) as well as parts of fundamental aspects of our being (i.e., memory). Questions have been raised about whether that level of dependency on an external tool might profoundly affect our fundamental sense of self. Before one objects that that level of remote, abstract interaction is not as representative of intelligence as the more traditional concrete, embodied interaction, let us remember that an increasingly important part of our interaction with other humans takes precisely the form of disembodied electronic messages of various kinds: email, instant messages, twitter.

The practical problem is that embodiment puts a premium on certain aspects of our intelligence that might not be the most critical ones in determining our fundamentally human capabilities. For instance, to create an embodied agent that goes around in the world and acts reasonably is likely to require the vast majority of the efforts to be spent on specific capabilities such as vision, locomotion, manipulation or speech processing, that act as gate-keepers to the other, higher-level capabilities. This is similar to the fact that computer games devote more than 90% of CPU usage to graphics, and a tiny fraction to animating the AI characters. While those perceptual-motor capabilities are foundational, and the roadmap to developing an artificial human-like intelligence might well follow evolution and develop artificial versions of lower forms of life such as rats and cats, a comprehensive solution to those problems has remained elusive, and the general form of those problems might not be solved in the time frame of our careers.

Thus, in order to lay meaningful, practical milestones on the roadmap to BICA, we need to define a view of agency that recognizes those issues and limitations and define a tractable approach to the problem.

2. Minimal Agency Required by the BICA Challenge

The task of identifying this minimal agency in all its aspects and details is a huge milestone somewhere in the middle of the roadmap to solving the BICA Challenge. We limit our analysis to proposing a list of several key aspects and components of the minimal agency, viewing them as intermediate goals. By no means this list should be considered complete or sufficient for solving the challenge. Nevertheless, we view it as an important first step toward clarification of the roadmap. Explanations follow below.

- Minimal agency that solves the BICA Challenge includes:
  - Sense of co-presence
  - Critical mass of a human-level learner
  - Emotional competence

The notion of presence refers to, e.g., the subjective feeling of being present in a virtual environment [9]. This feeling is psychophysiologically measurable and is of a threshold nature [10]. The term "togetherness" [10] or "co-presence" [11] refers to the feeling of being present together with others in the same environment. We propose that the sense of co-presence of the BICA agent detected in human participants is a precondition for solving the challenge. The sense of co-presence depends on sensible behavior of the agent that demonstrates intrinsic cognitive functionality, including attention, awareness, intentionality, motivation, self-consistency, common sense, etc. On the other hand, realistic human-like appearance and motion control may not be necessary.

A situated learner that possesses a "critical mass" of learning abilities is capable of learning up to a human expert level in the environment where it is situated, while a "subcritical" learner will remain limited to the level at which it started (see Samsonovich, this volume). We propose that having the critical mass of a learner is a necessary precondition for solving the challenge.

The notion of emotional competence implies the intrinsic ability of an agent to detect, understand and reason about emotions in humans. Emotional competence also appears to be a necessary component in the minimal agency. Many related necessary components are not listed here.

In addition, it would be helpful to list some of those cognitive abilities that are not required for solving the challenge, and may be absent in the agent. We propose the following list.

- Aspects and components of agency that are irrelevant to the BICA Challenge:

    - Human-level sensory abilities

    - Realistic motion control

    - Human-level general world knowledge

We propose as a hypothesis that a comprehensive solution to these "peripheral" problems is not necessary for solving the BICA Challenge. Indeed, in many cases human individuals deprived of normal sensory and motion abilities from childhood still can develop cognitively to a normal adult level, and are perceived as adult persons. Other conditions, however, related to social interactions in childhood, appear vital for the development of normal human agency [12].

While it has been argued that common sense knowledge is a fundamental precondition of general intelligence, which has resulted in the development by hand or automated means of large knowledge bases, knowledge itself does not seem to be a key as much as the ability to learn and apply it in a flexible, adaptive manner.

Thus the BICA Challenge appears reducible to a set of "central", or "top-level" problems. Once they are clearly formulated, the challenge can be solved.

3. Will you vote for a BICA delegate?

The story of AI is full of proposals of challenges in order to test intelligent systems, starting from the well-known Turing test for imitation [13]. Among these challenges (see [14] for a full list), the most famous ones are: the Loebner prize [15] strictly related with the Turing test, the DARPA Grand Challenge [16] related to fully autonomous cars, the RoboCup [17] related to robots teams playing soccer.

Many of these challenges are real difficult tests; however, each challenge measures some aspects of the behavior of the system and it rule out other important aspects. In this respect, recently Hofstadter [18], in a provocative essay, debates about systems successful at imitating humans in, e.g., generating music or even writing scientific papers.

No one of these challenges takes into account the degree of perception of an intelligent system as a person and the degree of trust and acceptance of the system in a community (see Castelfranchi and Falcone [19] for a review of computational models of trust). However, the common degree of trust of intelligence system in everyday life is growing fast. This fact is also reflected in the popular expectations about intelligent systems: the main expectation of yesterday robots was to have reliable slaves, the main goal of today robot is to have intelligent assistants.

As the reality of Artificial Intelligence starts approaching that goal, questions of trust are being raised regarding the AI that is currently embedded in our lives. Google is arguably the most pervasive such intelligent assistant, constantly moderating our access to all types of information (news, technical, social, etc). However, issues of censorship have been raised, most prominently regarding the role of Google China. If Google can effectively censor whatever knowledge or views it disagrees with by shielding them from our searches, shouldn't such power be somehow regulated or limited? As automation replaces human intervention, trust is often a critical aspect of adoption. If a system such as an automatic pilot cannot be trusted, because it is occasionally unreliable, unwieldy or simply too opaque to human understanding, its utility is gravely compromised. It is a major promise of BICA over traditional AI approaches that their internal workings reflects our own, and thus provide a means to artificial intelligence that is not merely functional but can also be understood and thus trusted.

A possible challenge for tomorrow BICA agents showing real human-level intelligence is to imagine a mixed human-artificial community in which humans and artificial agents may live, work and collaborate at the same level. Initial examples in this direction is LIDA [20], a system able to negotiate the tour of duty of sailors by means of email exchanges with sailor themselves, or Cicerobot [21], a robot able to guide tourists in a archaeological museum.

Sorbello, Chella and Arkin [22] proposed the metaphor of politics as a possible mechanism of agents coalition formation According to this metaphor, a colony of agents is able to cluster into political parties and to vote for their government delegates that will lead the whole agents colony. This mechanism was aimed to implement an algorithm for coalition generation, but it is now time to start thinking out of this metaphor. Maybe in a not so distant future, some BICA agents could be perceived as persons with their own rights [23]. Then, humans and BICA agents may build new mixed political coalitions that could help preserving their own rights and interests and guide the development of the community.

So, why do not think of a BICA agent able to *win a political election* as a representative of the community, against human candidates?

After all, today complex and sophisticated decision support systems are available to our elected delegates at different levels in order to manage and plan complex decisions and courses of actions, for example where to build the next waste site or what will be the next year investment priorities for improving national health service.

Then, a complex BICA system showing human-level intelligence could be able in the near future to show great ability to make final decisions about these and other sensitive problems critically related with the life of the whole community, by taking into account the several facets of the problem, by evaluating all the pros and cons, by analyzing all the currents laws and regulations and the whole past history of the community.

Moral aspects should also be taken into considerations [24]. Arkin [25] discussed similar problems when considering robots that could kill enemies during war actions according to engagement rules.

A BICA agent should also be able to prove some sort of *empathy* after some difficult decisions, made for the benefit of the whole community that may generate suffering to a few elements of the same community.

In conclusions, an important challenge for human-level BICA should be the perception of the BICA agent as a person from the community so that the community could trust and vote for the BICA agent as a delegate of the community.

4. The Path Ahead

The history of science is full of examples in which leading experts failed to foresee the eventual path to discovery. Some scientific questions, like determining the chemical composition of stars, were thought to be impossibly difficult to address, until new innovations, like spectrographic methods, made those questions easy to answer. Other questions, like the precession of the perihelion of Mercury's orbit, were initially thought to be easy to answer, but actually required revolutions in scientific thought to address, like the appearance of the General Theory of Relativity. Given this terrible track record, there is little reason to embrace any broad research plan for an entire field with a high degree of confidence.

Despite this reason for caution, it is worth considering which research directions might represent the best paths to explore in the search for artificial general intelligence. In the present paper, we suggested that at least one of these paths should involve the development of integrated cognitive systems that exhibit exactly those capabilities that provoke a sense of agency in human observers. The central intuition is that it will be easier to expand the intellectual power of agents that already possess the core properties of agency than it will be to invoke agency from the merging of isolated specialized cognitive capabilities. This approach has the benefits of potentially producing recognizable progress toward general intelligence quickly and of maintaining the critical core properties of agency as progress is made toward human-level performance.

Acknowledgments

This article arose largely from an informal conversation held between Drs. David Noelle and Alexei Samsonovich at the 2011 Meeting of the Cognitive Science Society in Boston. Dr. Antonio Chella who contributed his part to this discussion wishes to thank Kris Thorisson, Ricardo Sanz and all the participants to the HUMANOBS Workshop "From Constructionist to Constructivist Methodologies for building

Artificial Intelligence" held at Reykjavik University in September 2011 for interesting discussions about the topics of this paper.

References

[1] E. Rich, K. Knight, *Artificial Intelligence*, McGraw-Hill, 2nd edition, 1990.
[2] G. Pennachin, B. Goertzel. Contemporary approaches to artificial general intelligence, in Goertzel, B. and Pennachin, C. (Eds.), *Artificial General Intelligence: Cognitive Technologies*, pp. 1–30. Springer, Berlin, 2007.
[3] A. V. Samsonovich (Ed.), *Biologically Inspired Cognitive Architectures II: Papers from the AAAI Fall Symposium, AAAI Technical Report FS-09-01*, AAAI Press, Menlo Park, CA, 2009.
[4] P. Wang, The logic of intelligence, In B. Goertzel, C. Pennachin (Eds.), *Artificial General Intelligence, Cognitive Technologies,* pp. 31–62. Springer, Berlin, 2007.
[5] D. C. Noelle, Function follows form: Biologically guided functional decomposition of memory systems, in A. V. Samsonovich (Ed.), *Biologically Inspired Cognitive Architectures: Papers from the 2008 AAAI Fall Symposium*, Technical Report FS-08-04, pp. 135–139, AAAI Press, Menlo Park, CA, 2008.
[6] R. W. Gibbs, *Embodiment and Cognitive Science*, Cambridge University Press, New York, NY, 2006.
[7] W. D. Gray (Ed.), *Integrated Models of Cognitive Systems: Series on Cognitive Models and Architectures*, Oxford University Press, Oxford, UK, 2007.
[8] J. Friedenberg, *Artificial Psychology: The Quest for What It Means to Be Human,* Psychology Press, New York, NY, 2008.
[9] T. B. Sheridan, Musings on telepresence and virtual presence, *Presence: Teleoperators and Virtual Environments,* **1** (1992), 120–126.
[10] N. Durlach, M. Slater, Presence in shared virtual environments and virtual togetherness, *Presence-Teleoperators and Virtual Environments* **9** (2000), 214-217.
[11] S. Y. Zhao, Toward a taxonomy of copresence, *Presence-Teleoperators and Virtual Environments* **12** (5): 445-455.
[12] J. Gentile, Agency and its clinical phenomenology, in Frie, R. (Ed.), *Psychological Agency: Theory, Practice, and Culture*, pp. 117-135, MIT Press, Cambridge, MA, 2008.
[13] A. M. Turing, Computing machinery and intelligence, *Mind*, **59** (1950), 433 – 460.
[14] http://en.wikipedia.org/wiki/Competitions_and_prizes_in_artificial_intelligence
[15] http://www.loebner.net/Prizef/loebner-prize.html
[16] S. Thrun, A personal account of the development of Stanley, The robot that won the DARPA Grand Challenge, *AI Magazine*, **27** (2006), 69 – 82.
[17] H. Kitano, M. Asada, Y. Kuniyoshi, I. Noda, E. Osawa, H. Matsubara, RoboCup: A challenge problem for AI, *AI Magazine*, **18** (1997), 73 – 85.
[18] D. Hofstadter, Essay in the style of Douglas Hofstadter, *AI Magazine*, **30** (2009), 82 – 88.
[19] C. Castelfranchi, R. Falcone, *Trust Theory*, J. Wiley & Sons, Chichester, UK, 2010.
[20] B. J. Baars, S. Franklin, Consciousness is computational: The LIDA model of Global Workspace Theory, *International Journal of Machine Consciousness*, **1** (2009), 23 – 32.
[21] A. Chella, I. Macaluso, The perception loop in CiceRobot, A museum guide robot, *Neurocomputing*, **72** (2009), 760 – 766.
[22] R. Sorbello, A. Chella, R. C. Arkin, Metaphor of politics: A mechanism of coalition formation, in: *Papers from the 2004 AAAI Workshop on Forming and Maintaining Coalitions and Teams in Adaptive Multiagent Systems*, L.-K. Soh, J. E. Anderson (eds.), WS-04-06, AAAI Press, Menlo Park, California, (2004), 45 – 53.
[23] D. J. Calverley, Towards a method for determining the legal status of a conscious machine, in: R. Chrisley, R. Clowes, S. Torrance, *Proceedings of the Symposium on Next Generation Approaches to Machine Consciousness AISB '05,* (2005), 75 – 84.
[24] W. Wallach, C. Allen, *Moral Machines,* Oxford University Press, Oxford, UK, 2009.
[25] R. C. Arkin, *Governing Lethal Behavior in Autonomous Robots*, Chapman and Hall/CRC Press, Boca Raton, FL, 2009.

Reviews and Late-Breaking Materials

Biologically Inspired Cognitive Architectures 2011
A.V. Samsonovich and K.R. Jóhannsdóttir (Eds.)
IOS Press, 2011
© *2011 The authors and IOS Press. All rights reserved.*
doi:10.3233/978-1-60750-959-2-463

VideoPanels Experience: From BICA Challenge to Metacognition

Michael Q. KALISH[a] and Alexei V. SAMSONOVICH[b,1]

[a]*Arts and Sciences Undergraduate School, University of Virginia, P.O. Box 400133, Garrett Hall, Charlottesville, VA 22904, USA*
[b]*Krasnow Institute for Advanced Study, George Mason University, Fairfax, VA 22030-4441, USA*
kalishmichael@gmail.com, asamsono@gmu.edu

Abstract. VideoPanels are recurrent multipoint videoseminars, originated as a virtual extension of the International Conference on Biologically Inspired Cognitive Architectures (BICA). These professional online working sessions include panel discussions and presentations of research papers accepted for BICA Society publication venues. The overarching goal of discussions on VideoPanels is to develop a roadmap to solving the BICA Challenge: the challenge to create a computational equivalent of the human mind using BICA as an approach. Topics of the first VideoPanels included: (i) the BICA Challenge, (ii) system-theoretic and evolutionary approaches to the study of BICA; and (iii) metacognition. This work provides a brief review of these sessions and analyzes their experience.

Keywords. BICA Society, BICA Challenge, metacognition, human-level AI

Introduction

This essay introduces VideoPanels (http://bicasociety.org/vp/): a purely virtual seminar series implemented as a multipoint videoconference. What is VideoPanels? It is not a webinar in the traditional sense, because there is no physical auditorium where the event is happening: each participant communicates via a personal computer. It is also not a social event or entertainment. It is a professional working session aimed at finding, clarifying and disseminating scientific truth in the field of biologically inspired cognitive architectures (BICA).

VideoPanels originated in the Spring of 2011 as a virtual extension of BICA 2011, with the objective to clarify the overarching goal of research in the field of BICA through its public discussions. It became clear then that the main value of VideoPanels should be seen in development of a roadmap toward solving the BICA Challenge: the challenge to create a computational equivalent of the human mind using BICA as an approach [1]. Since then, VideoPanels were awarded participation in the AAAI Video Competition (http://www.aivideo.org/) and advertised at conferences ([2], BICA 2011).

There are two formats of VideoPanels: panel discussions and paper presentations. Presented papers and selected panel discussion summaries are to be published in the BICA journal or BICA conference proceedings.

---

[1] Corresponding Author.

1. Background and Motivation

Schools and communities working in the field of BICA today often speak different languages, which makes their transformative integration problematic. For this reason, it is also very difficult to answer the following question objectively: Is a big breakthrough in artificial intelligence possible today?

On the one hand, there are computational powers available today that are at the level of the computational powers of the human brain. On the other hand, software tools are still generally clueless outside of their routines and require human assistance. On the one hand, many narrow superhuman capabilities have been achieved in AI, and virtually every element of human intelligence seems to have been paved with computational models. On the other hand, we have no idea of what we are missing and what the final overarching goal may be.

In a situation like this, an open discussion is necessary to find out the truth. This discussion should address multiple layers and multiple aspects of the challenge. The outcome of it should be a clear formulation and understanding of the goal and a roadmap to the goal, supported by facts and scientific arguments that would be sufficient to convince those who can make this plan work. It is not sufficient to fund research in one laboratory: a multinational project is needed.

Following the first steps made during BICA conferences and the subsequent collective creation of a comparative table of cognitive architectures on the Internet (http://bicasociety.org/cogarch/), it seems logical to use the momentum and move to the next level. This is why we started VideoPanels.

2. Settings and Technology

A BICA Videopanels session takes place entirely on each participant's computer screen and typically is limited in time to 20-40 minutes. The participating crowd is structured into the *stage*, or *panelists* (i.e., participants that are present in video on the screen) and the *audience* (participants who interact via audio only and receive video). In addition to individual videos of panelists, the view includes a shared desktop or a window where slides, videos and live demos can be presented.

Panelists are divided into hosts (moderators), leaders or presenters, and guests. Hosts open and close the session, maintain the agenda, and help the leader to steer the discussion. A leader or a host introduces the topic and sets the floor for discussion by offering a list of guiding questions that remain displayed on the screen (the questions can be distributed in advance). Guests make opinion statements in response to the displayed questions. Then panelists ask and answer follow-up questions. Finally, the audience is allowed to ask questions and to make comments.

In the paper discussion format, the paper is read by all participants in advance. The session looks like a short conference presentation. Presenting author makes a brief overview of the work and then answer questions. The paper presented and discussed on Videopanels is peer-refereed and published in the appropriate venue.

Participation in VideoPanels is free and open virtually to anybody. Archives of VideoPanels are available on the Internet for viewing on demand at the following URL: http://bicasociety.org/vp/.

Regarding the technological implementation, we used Skype Premium that offers multipoint videoconferencing, plus the free desktop sharing tool Join.me.

Figure 1. A snapshot from the first VideoPanels trailer playing on a computer monitor from YouTube. Top row, panelists, lef to right: Andrea Stocco, Antonio Chella, Brandon Rohrer. Bottom left, the host: Alexei Samsonovich. The trailer was included in the 2011 AAAI Video Competition: http://www.aivideo.org/, http://www.youtube.com/watch?v=0pFOYFbt8nI&list=PLBD9258D5B17A5C49&index=12

3. First Sessions of VideoPanels: From BICA Challenge to Metacognition

VideoPanels started on May 6th, 2011, with a discussion of the BICA Challenge, during which the goal of BICA research was better understood. The second session included presentations of two papers. At that time a trailer was created (Figure 1) that was awarded participation in the AAAI 2011 Video Competition. The third VideoPanels session was a discussion panel devoted to metacognition. It was hosted by Kamilla Jóhannsdóttir; the panelists included Aaron Sloman, Ashok Goel, Michael Anderson, Simon Levy, and Scott Fahlman. A summary of this hour-long VideoPanel follows below, intended here as a representative example.

The VideoPanel explored some of the leading ideas in metacognition and how they relate to the current state of biologically inspired cognitive architectures. The overall theme of the video panel was how can the ideas of metacognition be used in combination with current research to make artificial intelligence more effective. The three questions that panel discussed were:

1. How and why should cognitive architectures benefit from metacognition?
2. What is metacognition in artificial intelligence?
3. Is it possible to have a universal metacognitive assistant that improves the performance of virtually any cognitive system?

One of the most difficult parts in discussing metacognition is that it is extremely difficult to define what exactly is. An overall theme from the discussion was attempting to create proper divisions between what is actually metacognition and what is not.

The panelists began by tackling what exactly is metacognition. Panelists agreed that as with many distinctions that start off looking clear, if one starts to look at several cases one finds that many subdivisions are necessary and it becomes too arbitrary to simply put one large division. Panelists felt that it was hard to consider a continuum of cases over which to look at metacognition because it is impossible to consider a continuum of information systems. However, this does not imply that there is no conclusive evidence of a need for metacognition. Ashok Goel referenced his own work, stating that on very small problems, solutions can be found without metacognition, through reinforcement learning or generative planning. However, his point was that as the problem space becomes more complicated, the benefits of metacognition become more apparent. As the size of the problem increases, there is way to use metacognition for self-verification and this has a clear conditional correspondence to improved performance. There was unanimous agreement over these statements. However, the panelists were much less quick to give a definition of what metacognition is. Questions such as, what kind of models does an agent need to have to about people's abilities so that the agent can guide people in self-regulated learning? What kind of models should we help people develop about their own abilities so that they might be better at self-regulated learning? were all thrown around throughout the conversation. The only conclusion that the panelists drew was that metacognition derives its benefits from the fact that it is creating a system that can monitor its performance and therefore also improve its performance. In the learning systems, the leverage comes from the ability to target learning, or to put into other words, learning things that seem to be most relevant.

Another point of division Simon Levy brought up is the need to distinguish metacognition and metacognitive capabilities from meta-semantic capabilities. Semantic capabilities is referring to things that can be physical objects or numbers and meta-semantic capabilities when the system can refer to these things that refer to the relational referring and to the processes that control them. Though the idea is similar, this is fundamentally different from what most people consider as metacognition. However, Michael Anderson made the point that this idea of meta-semantics is essential to ultimately understanding how metacognition works.

One of the researchers felt that metacognition was essential in self-regulating systems was related to the idea of "targetedness". There are only a limited number of ways that a system can fail and there are also a limited number of ways that it can be fixed. A system needs to decide where to focus its learning and fixing of itself and this is something that most current architectures fail to accomplish. However, the panelists agreed that this is exactly where metacognition would play a vital role.

Another interesting point that was brought up in reference to exactly what is metacognition was the idea of whether an actual separate metacognitive component within the cognitive system is necessary. Michael Anderson brought up the point that a group of low-level systems monitoring each other and providing feedback to each other, achieves these metacognitive capabilities, stating that these lower level systems exist in a metacognitive relationship. Michael Anderson stated that in his own work he believes that a lot of the value of metacognition stems from the benefits of self-monitoring and self-control to improve intelligence systems or have them self improve.

The discussion ultimately boiled down to discussing what the limitations of human learning systems are and the limitations of metacognition. A firm understanding of the learning systems that are operating within the human mind is an important step in understanding what role metacognition plays in cognition. What ultimately is the role of metacognition, in learning, planning and creativity? Is it an essential component of cognition or is it an artifact of the relationships between the lower level cognitive components? What, if any, are the limitations of metacognition? The panelists provided many different views on these questions, illustrating that metacognition is not easily defined. They all agreed that metacognition plays an essential in learning, creativity, and language, but what this role is and whether it is the same in all these situations is not clear. Overall, the panelists presented a cogent overview of the state of research into metacognition as well as an excellent foundation of where research is heading as we move into the future.

4. Discussion and Concluding Remarks

By far, the idea of VideoPanels as a form of activity is not new: similar activities on the Internet are nowadays ubiquitous, although not many of them are clearly intended as scientific or organizational. Yet, the fact that analogous activities exist does not imply that our agenda of the roadmap development through this sort of activity may be accomplished without a concentrated deliberate effort devoted specifically to this goal.

Indeed, in our experience, VideoPanels did not become self-sustainable and continuously required "fuel" for their materialization. While we hope that in the future this situation may change to the opposite, we understand that in order for this to happen we need to improve the quality and reliability of the technological support.

We view VideoPanels primarily as a vehicle for exploration and navigation of the roadmap to solving the BICA Challenge: achieving human-level artificial intelligence based on biologically inspired cognitive agents.

Acknowledgments

The authors are grateful to all VideoPanels participants and supporters; primarily to Drs. Kamilla Jóhannsdóttir, Antonio Chella, David Noelle, and Brandon Rohrer.

References

[1] A. Chella, C. Lebiere, D. C. Noelle and A. V. Samsonovich, On a roadmap to biologically inspired cognitive agents, this volume.
[2] A. V. Samsonovich, K. R. Jóhannsdóttir, A. Stocco, A. Chella, Biologically Inspired Cognitive Architectures (BICA) Society: Bridging neuroscience, cognitive science and artificial intelligence (Theme H abstract), in *2011 Neuroscience Meeting Planner*, online, Washington, D.C.: Society for Neuroscience, 2011.

Biologically Inspired Cognitive Architectures 2011
A.V. Samsonovich and K.R. Jóhannsdóttir (Eds.)
IOS Press, 2011

Towards Cognitively Informed Models of Memory Storage, Retrieval and Processing in the Nervous System

Konstantin ANOKHIN

Kurchatov NBIC Center and P.K.Anokhin Institute of Normal Physiology, Moscow, Russia

Keywords. Long-term memory, reconsolidation, multiple-trace, auto-associative, neuronal mechanisms, neuromorphic cognitive architecture

Abstract

Recent experimental studies of biological memory demonstrate that principles of its formation, storage and retrieval are noticeably different from the earlier memory theories based on a computer metaphor. Contrary to computer memory its biological counterpart is:

- Non-representational – it is not a direct reflection of the physical world and its events;
- Re-constructive – its reproduction is an active process of self-assembly of functional neuronal system;
- Non-replicative – each new memory recall differs from the previous by recruiting overlapping but non-identical populations of neurons and synapses;
- Re-categorical - each new episode of memory reconstruction, being different in the neuronal composition is classified as belonging to the same instance by categorization on the repertoire of the existing functional systems in the brain.
- Re-consolidational – each new memory reconstruction is reconsolidated by activation of cellular mechanisms of neuronal plasticity that are similar but not identical to the cellular mechanisms for consolidation of a new memory.

Because of these properties biological memory in the neural nets has the qualities of prominent *degeneracy* (the equivalent subjective item is being encoded by multiple non-identical copies of a neuronal functional systems in the brain), superior *auto associativity* (different degenerate phenocopies of the same functional system possess different connections to other functional systems in the brain) and remarkable *ability for regeneration* of the functional system after damage to one of its copies or part of its elements).

Further experimental studies and theoretical modeling of these functions should shed a light on the unique properties of biological memory and open a possibility towards its simulation in architectures of neuromorphic intelligent devices.

Biologically Inspired Cognitive Architectures 2011
A.V. Samsonovich and K.R. Jóhannsdóttir (Eds.)
IOS Press, 2011
© 2011 The authors and IOS Press. All rights reserved.
doi:10.3233/978-1-60750-959-2-469

Comparative Analysis of Implemented Cognitive Architectures

Alexei V. SAMSONOVICH

Krasnow Institute for Advanced Study, George Mason University,
4400 University Drive MS 2A1, Fairfax, VA 22030-4444, USA
asamsono@gmu.edu

Abstract. This short work is a follow-up on the review of the online Comparative Table of Cognitive Architectures, published in the BICA 2010 Proceedings. While the original review listed architectures and their features in one uniform format, the primary goal here is to go through feature-by-feature comparison across architectures and to see what features are shared, unique or missing in particular cases, in hope to understand what is needed in order to make a leap forward. This analysis is followed by consideration of the universal learner critical mass problem.

Keywords. Cognitive architectures, universal learner, critical mass.

Introduction

This short work is a follow-up on the review [1] of implemented cognitive architectures represented in the online Comparative Table of Cognitive Architectures[1], that was published in the BICA 2010 Proceedings.

Since the onset of research in cognitive modeling [2], the mainstream approach in intelligent agent design is based on integrative cognitive models describing complete embedded agents. These models are called cognitive architectures [2-7]. More generally, a cognitive architecture can be defined as a computational framework for the design of intelligent agents, while a biologically inspired cognitive architecture (BICA) is one that incorporates mechanisms drawn from cognitive science and/or neuroscience [8]. All 26 cognitive architectures included in the review [1] were treated equally: from the world-wide known frameworks, such as ACT-R [3, 9] and Soar [10-12], to examples known within limited circles only. The study is continued here with the same motivating idea: to put different approaches next to each other in order to see what features and components are common, critical or missing in various examples, and what features would be necessary to add for a breakthrough toward human-level intelligence to happen. Here, selected components and features are described at a high level and compared across cognitive architectures one by one; however, the outcome of this analysis appears to be not sufficient for answering the question.

Therefore, the next step in the present study is to address the general question that motivated the analysis in the first place: what would it take for an artifact to succeed in cognitive development up to an adult human level of intelligence? Its consideration concludes this work.

---

[1] The present URL for this resource is http://bicasociety.org/cogarch/.

1. Generic Cognitive Architecture Types and Components

A cognitive architecture integrates a complete set of individual cognitive capabilities in an intelligent agent that is embedded in a real or virtual environment, allowing the agent to perform sensory perception, cognition, decision making, and action. The integrated functional components are typically called buffers, or memory systems.

In general, the notion of a cognitive architecture implies that the embedded agent interacts with the environment (Figure 1 A): it can receive information from sensors and activate effectors to produce actions (e.g., the agent can move its body or produce verbal output). Therefore, the functional core of a cognitive architecture includes perception, cognition and action [7]. These three elements also correspond to the parts of the cognitive cycle of the architecture, that underlies dynamics of information processing.

Cognition in a cognitive architecture consists in semantic information processing and is performed in the component called working memory (the terminology here is borrowed from cognitive psychology). Cognition may include as well metacognition, imagery, and representations of emotions (Figure 1 B). Along with the interface and working memory, a generic cognitive architecture may include semantic, episodic and procedural memory systems, all addressed below, plus a system of drives and values. Special modalities are frequently added as separate modules to architectures.

There are many ways to classify cognitive architectures: by their completeness or degree of integration, by the origin and method of design, by the format of representations (e.g., symbolic, connectionist), by the paradigm and the goal of their study, by benchmarks and test problems that the architecture can solve, etc. One of the most useful classification schemes is the hierarchy of levels of cognitive architectures represented in Table 1. Still, this classification scheme is not very discriminative for the selected set of cognitive architectures from the Comparative Table: most of them include reasoning and planning abilities, as well as modeling abilities with respect to the environment. While the division into levels is to some extent a matter of interpretation, in general, it is hard to find today a mainstream cognitive architecture below Level 4. At the same time, full-fleshed Level 5 remains a frontier.

Table 1. Hierarchy of cognitive architecture types (adapted from [13]). Each higher level includes the functionality of lower levels.

Architecture type	Level	Agent is capable of
Metacognitive and self-aware	Level 5: highest	Modeling mental states of agents, including own mental states, based on a self concept
Reflective	Level 4: high	Modeling internally the environment and behavior of entities in it
Proactive, or deliberative	Level 3: middle	Reasoning, planning, exploration and decision making
Reactive, or adaptive	Level 2: low	Sub-cognitive (sub-symbolic) forms of learning and adaptation
Reflexive	Level 1: lowest	Fixed, innate behavioral responses to sensory input (unconditioned reflexes)

A

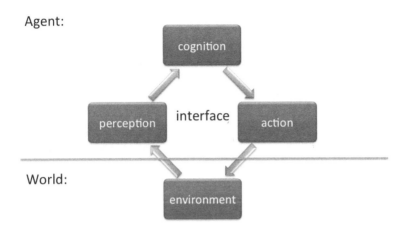

B

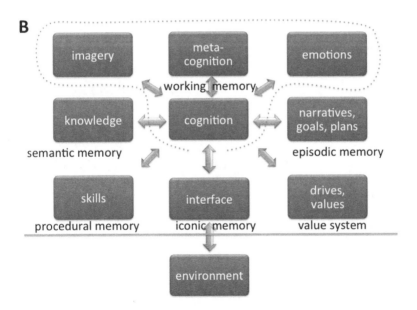

Figure 1. Components of generic cognitive architectures. **A:** A minimal cognitive architecture includes mechanisms of perception, cognition and action. **B:** Decomposition of a more advanced generic cognitive architecture into memory systems: working, semantic, episodic, procedural, iconic, and the value system. Arrows represent only few selected pathways of interaction among the components, that are virtually all-to-all connected.

In general, classification of memory systems in the human brain and in artifacts remains highly controversial [13-15]. One possible view that puts together multiple sources is represented in Figure 2. Specific memory systems are addressed in more detail below.

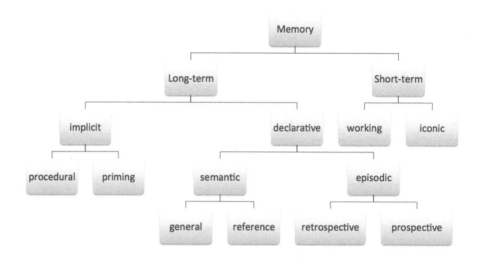

Figure 2. A possible view of the hierarchy of human memory systems.

2. Comparison of Cognitive Architectures: Memory Systems and Learning

The base cognitive architectures included in the online Comparative Table of Cognitive Architectures, listed alphabetically, are: 4D/RCS, ACT-R, ART, BECCA, biSoar, CERA-CRANIUM, CHREST, CLARION, CogPrime, CoJACK, Disciple, EPIC, FORR, GLAIR, GMU BICA, HTM, Leabra, LIDA, NARS, Nexting, Pogamut, Polyscheme, RA, REM, Soar, Ymir (references for each architecture are provided in [1]). Comparison of selected architectures based on the Comparative Table is done below with respect to individual memory system components and features.

2.1. Working Memory

By definition, any cognitive architecture has a component that can be identified as working memory (synonymous to short term memory in psychology). This general rule applies to all architectures represented in the Comparative Table, even if in some of them working memory is not explicitly defined (e.g. ACT-R, REM).

The content of working memory (as well as semantic and episodic memory, addressed below) in a cognitive architecture includes cognitive representations, elements of which are endowed with semantics that can be explicitly identified. In this sense, working memory is "declarative", although this term sounds ambiguous and may be confusing. The nature of these representations can be characterized by words "cognitive", "semantic", "symbolic".

In most cognitive architectures, working memory is implemented as a separate functional component (even though it may have a different name), while in the brain and in some cognitive architectures working memory corresponds only to certain states or forms of activity in components that support both, short-term and long-term memory. Examples include ACT-R.

Forms of working memory include imagery, metacognition (see below), representations of emotions and affects, specialized modalities, etc. Iconic memory associated with sensory perception is frequently considered in psychology as a form of working memory.

A cognitive cycle including perception, cognition and action can be always found at the core of dynamics of any working memory buffer. In many cases includes about 5-6 steps.

2.2. Semantic Memory

Semantic memory represents general knowledge of a cognitive system that can be represented in a symbolic format. Arguably, semantic memory of some form must be present in any cognitive architecture that has cognitive representations in its working memory. All cognitive architectures represented in the Comparative Table have semantic memory, even if in some of them semantic memory is not explicitly defined (ACT-R, CERA-CRANIUM, EPIC, Pogamut).

Among special forms of semantic memory is reference memory (that is frequently confused with episodic memory): it is the memory for the most up-to-date state of the continuously changing environment and its elements. An example is a memory of the location of the parked car. Cognitive maps (spatial, semantic, emotional, etc.) constitute another form of semantic memory.

Elements of representations in working, semantic and episodic memory systems have different names in different architectures: chunks, operators, rules, productions, images, maps, objects, events, attributes, relationships, situations, episodes, frames, diagrams, percepts, functional programs, "movies", states, schemas, mental states, etc. and are not discussed here in detail.

2.3. Episodic Memory

The notion of episodic memory is largely controversial, and varies among fields of science. According to the mainstream view in cognitive psychology [16], episodic memory is the long-term memory of autobiographical subjective experiences, and therefore involves the notion of a self and experiences attributed to the self. In particular, in contrast with semantic memory, episodic memory includes the context (metadata, background, links) of events and facts.

The notion of episodic memory about the past (retrospective episodic memory) is extended in psychological literature to include prospective episodic memory: goals, dreams, plans, imagined situations, intentions, commitments, etc. (e.g., [17]).

Very few implemented cognitive architectures possess true episodic memory understood in the above sense, despite numerous claims made for most mainstream cognitive architectures. E.g., at least some of the recent implementations of ART, BECCA, Clarion, CogPrime, FORR, GLAIR, GMU BICA, LEABRA, LIDA, NARS,

Nexting, Polyscheme, RA, REM, Soar, Ymir are claimed to have episodic memory. At the same time, in most cases their "episodic memory" amounts to a log of past events.

2.4. Procedural Memory

In psychology, procedural memory is understood as the collection of skills that are performed automatically, without explicit awareness of the details of their execution. From this point of view, any subsymbolic information processing ability in a cognitive architecture can be regarded as a procedural memory. Virtually all implementations of cognitive architectures include some elements of subsymbolic information processing (e.g., early sensory processing), and in this sense have procedural memory.

In computer science literature, however, the term "procedural memory" is frequently used with a different meaning that overlaps with the notion of semantic memory, and is not discussed here.

2.5. Metacognition, the Self and Self-Awareness

Various forms of metacognition were implemented in many cognitive architectures represented in the Comparative Table, including CLARION, Soar, ACT-R, and other. At the same time, a self module representing the architecture itself at a higher level as an actor is typically considered unnecessary. A design of a self-module was proposed for ACT-R. In contrast, GMU BICA has the self concept at the core of its design, including principles of dynamics and data structures.

The notions of self and self-awareness are, on the contrary, highly prioritized in educational sciences, as illustrated by the model of self-regulated learning (SRL: Figure 3).

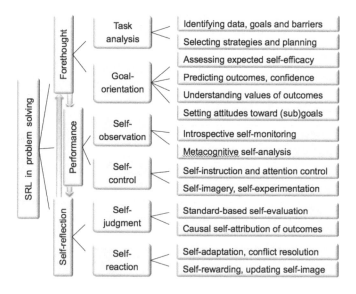

Figure 3. A model of self-regulation and self-regulating learning (SRL) in problem solving. Based on [18,19].

2.6. Reward System and Forms of Learning

All architectures listed in the Comparative Table, except EPIC and Ymir, are claimed to have reward systems.

An extremely broad spectrum of forms and paradigms of learning is known in the field of cognitive modeling. Examples range from classical conditioning to SRL that exploits deliberative self-analysis and self-control (Figure 3). While these two extreme examples are rarely used in studies with mainstream cognitive architectures, virtually all architectures represented in the Comparative Table are claimed to use reinforcement learning (except EPIC and Nexting) and be capable of learning new symbolic representations (except CERA-CRANIUM and EPIC). Some in addition implement Bayesian update (ACT-R, BECCA, CogPrime, CoJack, FORR, HTM, Leabra, Nexting), Hebbian learning (ART, BECCA, CLARION, CogPrime, FORR, GMU BICA, HTM, Leabra, Pogamut, RA) and gradient-descent methods (ART, CLARION, Leabra).

3. The Learner Critical Mass Problem

The above comparison of cognitive architectures at a high level shows how strikingly similar to each other different models are. At the same time, it does not answer the motivating question: what is missing, and why none of these approaches resulted in a quantum leap toward human-level intelligent artifacts?

On the one hand, the aforementioned cognitive architectures provide sufficient frameworks for implementation of virtually any essential aspects of human cognition. On the other hand, it would take an unreasonably tremendous effort to do the implementation manually, and an alternative approach seems necessary.

The better alternative could be an evolutionary approach, with intelligent agents growing up cognitively over time, starting from a minimal "embryo" or "critical mass" of intelligent and leaerning capabilities. In a computational environment, with today's high-performance hardware, this evolution may be expected to produce a quantum leap. It appears that in order for the quantum leap to happen, at least two conditions should be met:

a)   the cognitive system should be able to learn and develop on its own, similarly to a human child, in a real-world scenario, and

b)   perception of artifacts by humans and the role of artifacts in the human society should change: they should be perceived as "persons" rather than tools.

It is difficult to say what needs to come first. While (b) is addressed in other studies, e.g. [20, 21], (a) poses an interesting question that is considered here: *what would it take for an artifact to succeed in cognitive development up to an adult human level?* There are many controversies involved in answering this question, starting from its interpretation, and many researchers fail to understand the question at all.

One sort of a response is, "How is this challenge different from the challenge of a general problem solver?" ([22]; for a recent review of problem solver approaches and limitations see, e.g. [23]). A short answer is that a problem solver deals with problems that are already formalized in internal representations of the world inside the cognitive system, while real-life learning involves development of new concepts and new representation systems. Therefore, even the most optimal general problem solver may be found clueless in, e.g., high-school learning scenarios, even if the latter are adapted for robots [15]. The same argument applies to implemented cognitive architectures that are capable of learning by instruction or from examples (e.g. [24, 25]).

Another example of a response is that any knowledge that a human can communicate can be entered into a database; therefore, the database, formally speaking, constitutes a "universal learner" (Daniel Oblinger, priv. comm.). This argument, however, is not applicable to the question, because the notion of learning in the context considered here refers to development of new intelligent capabilities rather than new database records.

The Holy Grail of artificial intelligence, as seen at the onset of the field [26], was to create a general-purpose computational equivalent of the human mind. This challenge remains the greatest frontier today, while new approaches to it continue to emerge. In the light of the evolutionary approach, it is becoming clear now that the challenge reduces to achieving a critical mass of intelligence – in effect, a critical mass of a learning agent, that would allow the system to bootstrap itself and grow up to the human level in a certain learning environment, with limited human help at the level of instruction rather than programming. While intuitively this objective seems clear, the underlying it notion of the critical mass needs to be defined. In fact, by assuming that this motion makes sense, one tacitly accepts a hypothesis, which needs to be stated explicitly.

3.1. Domain-Specific Critical Mass Hypothesis

Consider a cognitive architecture (an agent) embedded in a novel learning environment. The critical mass hypothesis in this case states that there are two distinct possibilities:

- the agent will learn at a universal learner scale, acquiring at least the knowledge that is vital for achieving critical goals in this environment and that a typical human learner would be able to acquire under the same embedding conditions; or
- the agent will stay forever at a level close to its initial level of knowledge, the level that is determined by the set of initially available cognitive capabilities.

An assumption included here is that the two levels of knowledge, the initial and the successful final, are substantially different from each other. For some domains and learning environments, this assumption obviously does not hold: e.g., in an environment and a paradigm where there are only several rules to learn (an example would be the game of Tic-Tac-Toe), the two scenarios are not clearly distinguishable. Clearly, there are also examples (e.g. human education) when the initial and the successful final levels of a learner can be tremendously different, and the final level is independent of the initial level within certain limits.

The threshold between the two scenarios in the initial conditions, when it exists, can be identified in terms of multiple aspects, including the initial knowledge of the agent, the initial functional capabilities, functional components of the architecture, properties of the embedding and the interface, initial performance metrics, tests and challenges that the naïve learner can solve, etc., as well as in terms of observable characteristics of the learning process itself, such as scalability, robustness and transferability of acquired knowledge and skills. The minimal "mass" defined in this sense that sets the threshold between the two scenarios is called here the *critical mass*.

Whether this hypothesis holds depends on the particular learning environment, the embedding and the paradigm of learning (e.g. learning with or without instructor). When the hypothesis does hold, the notion of the critical mass makes sense and can be measured experimentally [27] or computed in a model using a statistical physics approach: indeed, the process of learning in many aspects may be analogous to percolation [28]. Alternatively, when the hypothesis does not hold, the learning limit of the agent may scale gradually with the initial "mass" of capabilities: there is no well-defined threshold that determines the critical mass.

3.2. Universal Critical Mass Hypothesis

The hope is that for most practically interesting learning environments and paradigms the notion of a critical mass introduced above makes sense, i.e., the domain-specific critical mass hypothesis holds. In this case, it is reasonable to introduce into consideration the following universal critical mass hypothesis.

For a large set of learning environments and settings, there is one minimal set of initial cognitive and learning characteristics of the agent (called critical mass), such that a learner starting below the critical mass will remain limited in its final knowledge by the level at which it started, while a learner staring anywhere above the critical mass will acquire the vital knowledge that a typical human learner would be able to acquire under the same settings, embedding and paradigms.

In other words, a cognitive system possessing certain minimal structure, dynamics, knowledge, functionality, measurable learning and metalearning capacities, etc., all together called a *learner critical mass* should be capable of learning virtually any knowledge within a broad spectrum of domains of human expertise, that another supercritical learner (e.g., a normal human adult) can learn under the same conditions.

When this hypothesis holds, the critical mass can be in principle measured experimentally. Measurements can and should be performed in abstract models [27] in order to answer the question about the missing vital features of cognitive architectures. When the critical mass will be identified, it would be only a matter of time to implement it in an intelligent agent.

4. Concluding Remarks

There are at least two additional sources of inspiration for the identification of the critical mass: educational science and clinical studies of pathologies in human development. E.g., clinical studies suggest that rich sensory modalities may not be vital for cognitive development in humans, while the ability to act voluntarily appears to be vital. Next, according to Vygotsky [29], the potential for cognitive development of a child is largely determined by Zone of Proximal Development, which is understood as the set of cognitive abilities that are available to the child under adult or peer guidance only. Vygotsky [29, 30] also suggested that any intrapersonal functionality develops interpersonally.

From this point of view, it follows that a BICA agent cannot grow up cognitively to a human level, if it remains completely autonomous or socially isolated from humans and peers. Therefore, a learning paradigm in which the critical mass will be measured should provide necessary conditions for a minimal social interaction during learning. Moreover, social interactions would need to be included at the core in the training paradigm. They also will be reflected in the definition of the critical mass.

Acknowledgments

I would like to thank again all contributors of the online Comparative Table of Cognitive Architectures. Their names include, alphabetically: James S. Albus, Raul Arrabales, Cyril Brom, Nick Cassimatis, Balakrishnan Chandrasekar, Andrew Coward, Susan L. Epstein, Rick Evertsz, Stan Franklin, Fernand Gobet, Ashok Goel, Ben Goertzel, Stephen Grossberg, Jeff Hawkins, Unmesh Kurup, John Laird, Peter Lane, Christian Lebiere, Shoshana Loeb, Shane Mueller, William Murdock, David C. Noelle, Frank Ritter, Brandon Rohrer, Spencer Rugaber, Alexei Samsonovich, Stuart C. Shapiro, Andrea Stocco, Ron Sun, George Tecuci, Akshay Vashist, Pei Wang. Their contributions to the online resource were used here.

References

[1] A.V. Samsonovich, Toward a unified catalog of implemented cognitive architectures (review). In Samsonovich, A. V., Jóhannsdóttir, K. R., Chella, A., and Goertzel, B. (Eds.). *Biologically Inspired Cognitive Architectures 2010: Proceedings of the First Annual Meeting of the BICA Society. Frontiers in Artificial Intelligence and Applications*, vol. 221, pp. 195-244. IOS Press, Amsterdam, The Netherlands, 2010.

[2] A. Newell, *Unified theories of cognition.* Cambridge, MA: Harward University Press, 1990.

[3] J.R. Anderson, C. Lebiere, *The Atomic Components of Thought,* Lawrence Erlbaum Associates, Mahwah, 1998.

[4] R.W. Pew, A.S. Mavor (Eds.), *Modeling Human and Organizational Behavior: Application to Military Simulations.* Washington, DC: National Academy Press. books.nap.edu/catalog/6173.html, 1998.

[5] F.E. Ritter, N.R. Shadbolt, D. Elliman, R.M. Young, F. Gobet, G.D. Baxter, *Techniques for Modeling Human Performance in Synthetic Environments: A Supplementary Review.* Wright-Patterson Air Force Base, OH: Human Systems Information Analysis Center (HSIAC), 2003.

[6] K.A. Gluck, R.W. Pew (Eds.). *Modeling Human Behavior with Integrated Cognitive Architectures: Comparison, Evaluation, and Validation.* Mahwah, NJ: Erlbaum, 2005.

[7] W.D. Gray, (Ed.) (2007). *Integrated Models of Cognitive Systems.* Series on Cognitive Models and Architectures. Oxford, UK: Oxford University Press.

[8] A.V. Samsonovich, D.C. Noelle, S.T. Mueller, Biologically inspired cognitive architectures: What are we missing? In Samsonovich, A. V. (Ed.), *Biologically Inspired Cognitive Architectures II: Papers from the AAAI Fall Symposium, AAAI Technical Report* FS-09-01, pp. ix-xi. Menlo Park, CA: AAAI Press, 2009.

[9] J.R. Anderson, *How Can the Human Mind Occur in the Physical Universe?* Oxford University Press, New York, 2007.

[10] J.E. Laird, P.S. Rosenbloom, A. Newell, *Universal Subgoaling and Chunking: The Automatic Generation and Learning of Goal Hierarchies,* Kluwer, Boston, 1986.

[11] J.E. Laird, A. Newell, P.S. Rosenbloom, SOAR: An architecture for general intelligence, *Artificial Intelligence* **33** (1987): 1-64.

[12] J. E. Laird, Extending the Soar cognitive architecture. in P. Wang, B. Goertzel and S. Franklin (eds.), *Artificial General Intelligence 2008: Proceedings of the First AGI Conference,* pp. 224-235, IOS Press, Amsterdam, The Netherlands, 2008.

[13] L.R. Squire. Memory systems of the brain: A brief history and current perspective. *Neurobiology of Learning and Memory,* **82** (2004) 171–177.

[14] A.J. Parkin, *Memory: Phenomena, Experiment and Theory.* Blackwell, Cambridge, MA, 1993.

[15] N.J. Cohen, H. Eichenbaum, *Memory, Amnesia, and the Hippocampal System,* MIT Press, Cambridge, MA, 1993.

[16] E. Tulving, *Elements of Episodic Memory,* Clarendon Press, Oxford, 1983.

[17] H.D. Zimmer, R.L. Cohen, M.J. Guynn, J. Engelkamp, R. Kormi-Nouri, M.A. Foley (Eds.), *Memory for Action: A Distinct Form of Episodic Memory?* Oxford University Press, Oxford, 2001.
[18] B. J. Zimmerman, Attaining self-regulation: A social cognitive perspective, in Handbook of Self-Regulation, eds. M. Boekaerts, P. R. Pintrich and M. Zeidner (Academic Press, San Diego, CA, 2000), pp. 13-39.
[19] A.V. Samsonovich, K.A. De Jong, A. Kitsantas, The mental state formalism of GMU-BICA. *International Journal of Machine Consciousness* 1 (2009), 111-130.
[20] A. Chella, C. Lebiere, D.C. Noelle, A.V. Samsonovich, On a roadmap to biologically inspired cognitive agents, this volume.
[21] S.S. Adams, I. Arel, J. Bach, R. Coop, R. Furlan, B. Goertzel, J.S. Hall, A. Samsonovich, M. Scheutz, M. Schlesinger, S.C. Shapiro, J. Sowa, Mapping the landscape of human-level artificial general intelligence, *AI Magazine*, in press.
[22] A. Newell, J.C. Shaw, H.A. Simon, Report on a general problem-solving program, *Proceedings of the International Conference on Information Processing*, pp. 256–264, 1959.
[23] J. Schmidhuber, Ultimate Cognition a` la Go¨del, *Cognitive Computation*, **1** (2009), 177-193, DOI 10.1007/s12559-009-9014-y.
[24] S.B. Huffman, J.E. Laird, Flexibly intractable agents, *Journal of Artificial Intelligence Research*, **3** (1995), 271-324.
[25] G. Tecuci, M. Boicu, C. Boicu, D. Marcu, B. Stanescu, M. Barbulescu, The Disciple-RKF learning and reasoning agent, *Computational Intelligence,* **21** (2005), 462-479.
[26] J. McCarthy, M.L. Minsky, N. Rochester, C.E. Shannon, A proposal for the Dartmouth summer research project on artificial intelligence, In R. Chrisley, S. Begeer (Eds.), *Artificial Intelligence: Critical Concepts*, vol. 2, pp. 44-53. London: Routledge, 1955/2000.
[27] A.V. Samsonovich, Toward a large-scale characterization of the learning chain reaction. In S. Ohlsson & R. Catrambone (Eds.), *Proceedings of the 32nd Annual Conference of the Cognitive Science Society* (pp. 2308-2313). Austin, TX: Cognitive Science Society, 2010.
[28] L. Petronero, E. Tosatti (Eds.), Fractals in Physics, North-Holland, Amsterdam, 1986.
[29] L.S. Vygotsky, *Mind in Society*. Cambridge, MA: Harvard University Press, 1978.
[30] L.S. Vygotsky, The collected works of L. S. Vygotsky: Vol. 4, The history of the development of higher mental functions. R. W. Rieber, Ed. M. J. Hall, Trans. New York: Plenum, 1931/1979.

Biologically Inspired Cognitive Architectures 2011
A.V. Samsonovich and K.R. Jóhannsdóttir (Eds.)
IOS Press, 2011

Subject Index

Author Index

486